www.wadsworth.com

wadsworth.com is the World Wide Web site for Wadsworth and is your direct source to dozens of online resources.

At *wadsworth.com* you can find out about supplements, demonstration software, and student resources. You can also send email to many of our authors and preview new publications and exciting new technologies.

wadsworth.com
Changing the way the world learns®

ADULT DEVELOPMENT AND AGING

JOHN C. CAVANAUGH
University of North Carolina at Wilmington

FREDDA BLANCHARD-FIELDS
Georgia Institute of Technology

FOURTH EDITION

WADSWORTH

THOMSON LEARNING ™

Australia • Canada • Mexico • Singapore • Spain • United Kingdom • United States

WADSWORTH

THOMSON LEARNING™

Psychology Publisher: EDITH BEARD BRADY
Development Editor: SHERRY SYMINGTON
Assistant Editor: JULIE DILLEMUTH
Editorial Assistant: MARITESS A. TSE
Marketing Manager: MARC LINSENMAN
Marketing Assistant: MEGAN E. HANSEN
Technology Project Manager: LESLIE KRONGOLD
Project Manager, Editorial Production: LISA WEBER
Print/Media Buyer: MARY NOEL
Permissions Editor: STEPHANIE KEOUGH-HEDGES
Production Service: GRAPHIC WORLD

Text Designer: JOHN WALKER DESIGN
Photo Researcher: SUE C. HOWARD
Illustrators: SUSAN BRIETBARD, LORI HECKELMAN, AND
  GRAPHIC WORLD ILLUSTRATION STUDIO
Cover Designer: LAURIE ANDERSON
Cover Image: BRICOLAGE, MEG SHIELDS, OIL ON LINEN
  © MEG SHIELDS; COURTESY FISCHBACH GALLERY, NEW YORK
Cover Printer: R. R. DONNELLEY & SONS, CRAWFORDSVILLE
Compositor: GRAPHIC WORLD, INC.
Printer: R. R. DONNELLEY & SONS, CRAWFORDSVILLE

Library of Congress Cataloging-in-Publication Data
Cavanaugh, John C.
  Adult development and aging / John C. Cavanaugh, Fredda
  Blanchard-Fields —4th ed.
    p. cm
  Includes bibliographical references and indexes.
  ISBN 0-534-50761-1
  1. Adulthood—Psychological aspects. 2. Aging—psycho-
  logical aspects. 3. Adulthood—Physiological aspects.
  4. Aging—Physiological aspects. 5. Aging—Social
  aspects. I. Blanchard-Fields, Fredda. II. Title.
BF724.5.C38 2001
155.6—dc21   2001026223

Wadsworth/Thomson Learning
10 Davis Drive
Belmont, CA 94002-3098
USA

For more information about our products, contact us:
Thomson Learning Academic Resource Center
1-800-423-0563
http://www.wadsworth.com

International Headquarters
Thomson Learning
International Division
290 Harbor Drive, 2nd Floor
Stamford, CT 06902-7477
USA

UK/Europe/Middle East/South Africa
Thomson Learning
Berkshire House
168-173 High Holborn
London WC1V 7AA
United Kingdom

Asia
Thomson Learning
60 Albert Street, #15-01
Albert Complex
Singapore 189969

Canada
Nelson Thomson Learning
1120 Birchmount Road
Toronto, Ontario M1K 5G4
Canada

To Patrice and Dorothy

BRIEF CONTENTS

CONTENTS

PREFACE

The late 20th and early 21st centuries demonstrated that having a solid grounding in research and theory about adult development and aging is essential even for understanding the evening news. The U.S. Presidential election in 2000 saw two of the most central issues having direct relevance: Social Security and Medicare. Other stories about genetic breakthroughs, interventions for cognitive decline, and the latest advice on lifestyle factors affecting longevity were reported quite frequently To understand why these issues were so critical, of course, one must understand aging in a broader context. That is why *Adult Development and Aging* is now in its fourth edition.

The first few decades of this century will witness a fundamental change in the face of the population—literally. Along with many countries in the industrialized world, the United States will experience an explosive growth in the older adult population due to the aging of the Baby Boom generation. Additionally, the proportion of older adults who are African American, Hispanic American, Asian American, and Native American will increase rapidly. To deal with these changes, new approaches will need to be created through the combined efforts of people in many occupations—academics, gerontologists, social workers, health care professionals, financial experts, marketing professionals, teachers, factory workers, technologists, government workers, human service providers, and nutritionists, to mention just a few. Every reader of this book, regardless of his or her area of expertise, will need to understand older adults in order to master the art of living.

This fourth edition of *Adult Development and Aging* continues to provide in-depth coverage of the major issues in the psychology of adult development and aging. The fourth edition adds numerous topics and provides expanded coverage of many of the ones discussed in earlier editions.

MAJOR NEW FEATURES

The most exciting addition to the fourth edition is Fredda Blanchard-Fields as a new co-author. Fredda is a world-renowned expert in social cognition, and she brings 20 years of research and teaching experience to the project. In addition to the new chapter on Social Cognition, Fredda also handled the extensive revisions of the cognition chapters, personality, and the chapter on work, leisure, and retirement.

The fourth edition represents a thorough revision and, in some areas, a reordering of the chapters from the third edition. The most obvious content changes include a new, separate chapter on social cognition, placing the mental health material after the physical health chapter, recasting the material on nursing homes, person–environment interactions, and prevention into a thoroughly revised chapter, chapter opening vignettes describing real people as a way of introducing key concepts, embedding the material on diversity throughout the text rather than in a separate chapter, eliminating the material on neighborhoods and housing, and eliminating the material about looking into the future. These changes reflect shifts in the field, especially regarding the rapid growth of the social cognition literature.

The strong pedagogical helps introduced in the third edition have been improved. The goal of embedding a study guide within the text is achieved even better by including several Web sites at the end of each chapter that will allow students to find additional information about topics emphasized in the text. Terminology has been updated and considerable recent research has been added (while retaining classic studies).

Each chapter received a thorough revision; among the most important changes in each chapter are:

- Chapter 1 now includes a discussion of the demographics of aging, a separate discussion of ethics in conducting research, and boxes concerning culture and ethnicity and concerning the degree to which personality in young adulthood determines personality in old age.
- Chapter 2 reorders topics from the most visible to the most microscopic, provides expanded coverage on genetic theories of aging and research on Tai Chi as a means for improving mobility, and restructures the discussion of brain changes into central and autonomic nervous systems.
- Chapter 3 represents a major reorganization of health topics and provides a discussion of the meanings of health and illness and more thorough presentations of chronic conditions and pharmacology and medication adherence.
- Chapter 4 provides a new section on developmental issues in assessment and therapy, discussion of genetics research on Alzheimer's disease, and coverage on substance abuse.
- Chapter 5 includes a more thorough treatment of how older adults respond to patronizing speech, a new discussion of decision-making capacity and individual choices in nursing home residents, and a new section on optimal aging.
- Chapter 6 eliminates the section on psychomotor speed and replaces it with a more up-to-date section on speed of processing, highlights the current controversy on speed of processing as general slowing or process-specific slowing, and includes a new section on attentional resources and eliminates the section on feature integration theory.
- Chapter 7 reviews hot topics in memory research including false memory, automatic retrieval, source memory, how memory functioning relates to vulnerabilities in older adults' everyday information processing, and recent developments in situation models and the influence of social context on memory.
- Chapter 8 provides an updated definition of intelligence that includes mechanics and pragmatics, a discussion of the controversy of whether lifestyle affects intelligence, and research including decision making and more recent work on wisdom.
- Chapter 9 (a new chapter on social cognition) interweaves what we know about basic cognitive abilities and how they influence reasoning in a social context, questions the role processing capacity plays in social cognition (it plays a major role in mainstream cognitive aging), and includes the topics social knowledge and social beliefs, stereotypes, collaborative cognition, motivation and social processing goals, and the social context of memory.
- Chapter 10 illuminates the hot controversy pitting intraindividual change with stability of personality traits, and provides more thorough coverage of intraindividual variability, personality change, and well-being.
- Chapter 11 provides a new box on the topic of elder abuse, and reorganized presentations on the family life cycle and intergenerational relationships.
- Chapter 12 includes more detailed discussions of research on the degree to which older adults can be retrained when their jobs become obsolete and research on planning for retirement.
- Chapter 13 includes a new section on end-of-life issues and creating a final scenario and more thorough discussions of physician-assisted suicide and hospices.

WRITING STYLE

Although *Adult Development and Aging* covers complex issues and difficult topics, we use clear, concise, and understandable language. We revised all of the chapters to achieve this goal, and many were completely rewritten. We examined all terms to ensure that their use was essential; otherwise, they were eliminated.

The text is aimed at upper-division undergraduate students. Although it will be helpful if students have completed an introductory psychology or life span human development course, the text does not assume this background.

INSTRUCTIONAL AIDS

The many pedagogical aids introduced in the third edition have been retained in the fourth edition.

Learning Aids in the Chapter Text

Each chapter begins with a chapter outline. At the start of each new section, learning objectives are presented. These objectives are keyed to each primary subsection that follows, and they direct the students' attention to the main points to be discussed. At the conclusion of each major section are concept checks, one for each primary subsection, which help students spot-check their learning. Key terms are defined in context; the term itself is printed in *bold italic,* with the sentence containing the term's definition in **boldface**.

End-of-Chapter Learning Aids

At the end of each chapter are summaries, organized by major sections and primary subsection heads. This approach helps students match the chapter outline with the summary. Numerous review questions, also organized around major sections and primary subsections, are provided to assist students in identifying major points. Integrative questions are included as a way for students to link concepts across sections within and across chapters. Key terms with definitions are listed. Suggestions for additional readings from both the scientific and popular literatures are provided, with estimates of difficulty level based on undergraduates' evaluations. Key Web sites are included with brief descriptions of the content of the site. Additionally, students may access InfoTrac® College Edition to find additional readings and Web sites.

Boxes

The fourth edition includes four types of boxes. Those entitled *How Do We Know?* draw attention to specific research studies that were discussed briefly in the main body of the text. Details about the study's design, participants, and outcomes are presented as a way for students to connect the information about these issues in Chapter 1 with specific research throughout the text.

Current Controversies boxes raise controversial and provocative issues about topics discussed in the chapter. These boxes get students to think about the implications of research or policy issues and may be used effectively as points of departure for class discussions. Additional information on the topic can be obtained through InfoTrac College Edition by using the suggested search terms provided.

Discovering Development boxes give students a way to see developmental principles and concepts in the "real world" as well as some suggestions as to how to find others. These boxes provide a starting point for applied projects in either individual or group settings.

New to the fourth edition are *Forces in Action* boxes that describe how the four fundamental developmental forces (biological, psychological, sociocultural, and life cycle) can be seen in specific developmental phenomena. These boxes help students understand how development is shaped by the interaction of these four forces.

INSTRUCTOR'S MANUAL

The fourth edition of *Adult Development and Aging* is accompanied by an instructor's manual. Each chapter begins with a lecture outline that highlights the main points of the chapter. Additionally, supplemental information is included, as are suggested activities and discussion topics. A list of suggested videos is also provided. Included in the manual are numerous test items, which are also available in electronic format.

ACKNOWLEDGMENTS

As usual, it takes many people to produce a textbook; such is the case with the fourth edition. The editorial group at Wadsworth is excellent. Publisher Edith Beard Brady shepherded the new edition through the editorial process. We also appreciate the assistance of Senior Development Editor Sherry Symington, Senior Project Editor Lisa Weber, Editorial Assistant Maritess Tse, and Marketing Manager Marc Linsenman. We also want to thank Carol O'Connell of Graphic World and Photo Researcher Sue Howard.

We also want to thank the reviewers of the third edition, who provided extremely helpful and insightful commentary that improved the book: Yiwei Chen, Bowling Green State University; Kim L. Sondergard, Alaska Pacific University; Brad Caskey, University of Wisconsin, River Falls; R. Kevin Rowell, University of Central Florida; Joseph M. White, South Dakota State University; Susan Hillier, Sonoma State University; Jeff Penick, Central Washington University; Heather Unger-Robertson; University of North Alabama; Victor G. Cicrelli, Purdue University; Julie Hicks Patrick, West Virginia University; David N. Carpenter, Southwest Texas State University; and Norman Abeles, Michigan State University. A special thanks to Katherine Fowler for her helpful suggestions and help on the literature search.

We also want to thank the special supports in our lives, without whom this book would not have been possible. Patrice, John's wife, put up with long hours at night and on weekends and piles of papers, journals, and books with nothing but patience and support. She was always there with words of encouragement.

Finally, to a group too often overlooked—the sales representatives. Without you none of this would have any payoff. You are an extension of us and the whole Wadsworth editorial and production team. What a great group of hard working folks you are!

Thanks to you all. Live long and prosper!

John C. Cavanaugh
Fredda Blanchard-Fields

About the Authors

JOHN C. CAVANAUGH is Provost and Vice Chancellor for Academic Affairs at the University of North Carolina at Wilmington. A researcher and teacher of adult development and aging for more than two decades, he has published nearly 70 articles and chapters and 9 books. He is a Past President of Division 20 (Adult Development and Aging) of the American Psychological Association (APA) and is a Fellow of APA, the American Psychological Society, and the Gerontological Society of America. John is a devoted fan of Star Trek and a serious chocoholic.

FREDDA BLANCHARD-FIELDS, PH.D., is Professor and Associate Chair of the School of Psychology at Georgia Institute of Technology. She received her undergraduate degree from University of California, Los Angeles, and her Ph.D. in developmental psychology from Wayne State University in 1983. Blanchard-Fields is a Fellow of the American Psychological Association and the Gerontological Society of America. She has served on the executive committee of Division 20 (adult development and aging) of the APA since 1990 in the capacity of continuing education chair, member at large, co-editor of the Division 20 newsletter, and APA Fellowship chair. She serves on the editorial board of *Psychology and Aging, Journal of Gerontology: Psychological Sciences,* and the *Journal of Adult Development.* Blanchard-Field's program of research examines adaptive developmental changes in adulthood in various areas of social cognition. She has numerous publications in the general area of social cognition and aging including causal attributional processing, everyday problem solving, coping, and perceived controllability from adolescence through older adulthood. She has co-edited two books, including *Perspectives on Cognitive Change in Adulthood and Aging* and *Social Cognition and Aging.* Her research on causal attributional processing and aging as well as everyday problem solving and aging have been and are currently funded by grants from the National Institute on Aging.

STUDYING ADULT DEVELOPMENT AND AGING

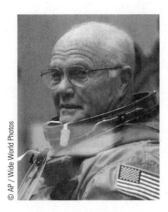

© AP / Wide World Photos

On October 29, 1998,
John Glenn became the
oldest human to travel
into space. Glenn spent 9
days in the space shuttle
Discovery conducting experiments focused on
understanding the con-
nections between aging
and space flight. Glenn's
1998 flight was his sec-
ond history-making trip;
he also was the first U.S.
astronaut to orbit the earth on February 20, 1962. Between his space trips, Glenn served 24 years as a senator
from Ohio, distinguishing himself as a staunch supporter of older adults and a lay expert in the biology
of aging.

By his own admission, Glenn is in better health than
many other people his age. Still, the fact that the National Aeronautics and Space Administration was willing to allow him to return to space is an admission that
chronological age alone is a very poor index of people's
capabilities. John Glenn is a great example of how older
adults are being looked at differently. Glenn showed
that older adults are capable of feats thought unimagin-
able just a few years ago. He also illustrates how the
normal changes people experience as they age vary
across people and why we need to rethink common
stereotypes about older adults.

In this chapter, we examine several fundamental issues
relating to adult development and aging, such as who
older people are, the forces that shape us, and several developmental controversies. We also consider the ways in
which gerontologists study adult development and aging.

Perspectives on Adult Development and Aging

Learning Objectives

- What is gerontology? How does ageism relate to stereotypes of aging?
- What is the life-span perspective?
- What are the characteristics of the older adult population?
- How are they likely to change?

*R*oberto's grandmother Maria is an 89-year-old Chicana woman who worked hard all of her life. Maria tells Roberto that when she was a young girl in El Paso there were very few older women from any Hispanic group. Roberto knows that there are many older women in his own neighborhood but wonders whether this is representative of other neighborhoods around the United States.

Before you read any more, do the following exercise. Write down all the adjectives you can think of that describe aging and older adults, as well as the "facts" about aging that you know.

Look over your list carefully. Are your descriptors more positive or negative? Do you have lots of "facts" or only a few? Most people's lists contain at least some words and facts that are influenced by media stereotypes that are only loosely based on reality.

What is it like to be an older adult like Maria? Do you want your own late life to be described by the descriptors you used? Do you look forward to becoming old, or are you afraid about what may lie ahead? Most of us want to enjoy a long life like Maria's but don't think much about growing old until we are confronted with it.

You already enjoy a major advantage compared with Maria and others her age. Until the last few decades, very little information was available about old age, which was thought to be characterized only by decline. Over the past 50 years, though, the science of *gerontology*, which is the study of aging from maturity through old age, has flourished. As you can imagine from reading the vignette about John Glenn, and as you will see throughout this book, aging in-

volves both growth and decline. Still, many myths about old people survive. *These myths of aging lead to negative stereotypes of older people, which may result in* **ageism,** *a form of discrimination against older adults based on their age.* Ageism occurs in many ways (Edelstein & Kalish, 1999). It may be as blatant as believing that all old people are senile and are incapable of making decisions about their lives. It may occur when people are impatient with older adults in a grocery store checkout line. Or it may be as subtle as dismissing an older person's physical complaints with the statement, "What do you expect for someone your age?" As you will learn by doing the activities in the Discovering Development feature, such stereotypes surround us.

This book rebuts these erroneous ideas, but it does not replace myths with idealized views of adulthood and old age. Rather, it strives to paint an accurate picture of what it means to grow old today, recognizing that development across adulthood brings growth and opportunities as well as loss and decline. To begin, we consider the life-span perspective, which helps place adult development and aging into the context of the whole human experience. Afterward, we consider the fundamental developmental forces, controversies, and models that form the foundation for studying adult development and aging. In particular, we examine the biological, psychological, sociocultural, and life-cycle forces; the nature–nurture and continuity–discontinuity controversies; and the mechanistic, organismic, and contextual models. We consider some basic definitions of age and will see that it can be viewed in many different ways. Finally, by examining various research methods, we will see how the information presented in this book was obtained.

The Life-Span Perspective

Imagine trying to understand what your best friend is like without knowing anything about his or her life. We cannot understand adults' experiences without appreciating what came before in childhood and adolescence. Placing adulthood in this broader context is

We are surrounded by misconceptions of older adults. We have all seen cartoons making jokes about older adults whose memories are poor or whose physical abilities have declined. Most damaging are the ideas portrayed in the media that older adults are incapable of leading productive lives and making a difference. As a way to discover something about development, try to find several examples of myths or stereotypes about aging. Look at advertisements and articles in popular magazines, television, and music. Gather as many as you can, and then check them against the research on the topic discussed in this text. See how many myths and stereotypes you can show to be wrong by the end of the course.

what the life-span perspective is all about. *The* **life-span perspective** *divides human development into two phases: an early phase (childhood and adolescence) and a later phase (young adulthood, middle age, and old age).* The early phase is characterized by rapid age-related increases in people's size and abilities. During the later phase, changes in size are slow, but abilities continue to develop as people continue adapting to the environment (Baltes et al., 1998).

Viewed from the life-span perspective, adult development and aging are complex phenomena that cannot be understood within the scope of a single disciplinary approach. Understanding how adults change requires input from a wide variety of perspectives. Moreover, aging is a lifelong process, meaning that human development never stops.

One of the most important perspectives on life-span development is that of Paul Baltes (1987; Baltes et al., 1998), who identified four key features of the life-span perspective:

Multidirectionality: Development involves both growth and decline; as people grow in one area they may lose in another and at different rates. For example, people's vocabulary ability tends to increase throughout life, but reaction time tends to slow down.

Plasticity: One's capacity is not predetermined or set in concrete. Many skills can be trained or improved with practice, even in late life. There are limits to the degree of potential improvement, however, as described in later chapters.

Historical context: Each of us develops within a particular set of circumstances determined by the historical time in which we are born and the culture in which we grow up. Maria's experiences were shaped by living in the 20th century in a Chicano neighborhood in southwest Texas.

Multiple causation: How we develop results from a wide variety of forces, which we consider later in this chapter. We will see that development is shaped by biological, psychological, sociocultural, and life-cycle forces.

The life-span perspective emphasizes that human development takes a lifetime to complete. It sets the stage for understanding the many influences we experience and points out that no one part of life is any more or less important than another.

Based on these principles, Baltes et al. (1998) argue that life-span development consists of the dynamic interaction between growth, maintenance, and loss regulation. This interaction is shown in Figure 1.1. In their view, four factors are critical:

There is an age-related reduction in the amount and quality of biologically based resources as people grow older.

There is an age-related increase in the amount and quality of culture needed to generate

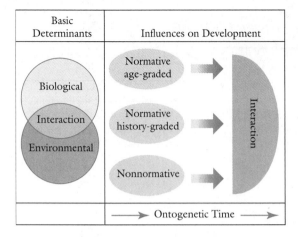

Basic Determinants	Influences on Development
Biological / Interaction / Environmental	Normative age-graded → / Normative history-graded → / Nonnormative →	Interaction
	⟶ Ontogenetic Time ⟶

FIGURE 1.1 **Representation of how three major influences operate in life-span development.**

Source: Baltes, P. B., Lindenberger, U., & Staudinger, U. M. (1998). Life-span theory in developmental psychology. In R. M. Lerner (Ed.), *Handbook of child psychology: Vol. 1. Theoretical models of human development.* Copyright © 1998. Reprinted by permission of John Wiley & Sons, Inc.

continuously higher growth. Usually, this results in a net slowing of growth as people age.

- There is an age-related decline in the efficiency with which cultural resources are used.

- There is a lack of cultural, "old-age friendly" support structures.

Taken together, these four factors create the need to shift more and more resources to maintain function and deal with biologically related losses as we grow old, leaving fewer resources to be devoted to continued growth. As we see throughout this book, this shift in resources has profound implications for experiencing aging and for pointing out ways to age successfully.

The Demographics of Aging

Did you ever stop to think about how many older adults you see every day? Maria doesn't remember seeing very many when she was a young girl, but how much has the world changed? One thing is certain: There have never been as many older adults in industrialized countries as there are now. The numbers in-

creased dramatically during the 20th century because of better health care and the lowering of women's mortality during childbirth.

Age distributions in the U.S. population for 1900, 1950, and 1980 and projections for 2030 are dramatically different. In 1900, there were many more young people than older adults; the age distribution graph resembles a pyramid. Projections for 2030 (when the last of the baby boomers reach age 65) show that the distribution will be nearly turned upside down.

This dramatic change in the number of older adults has already brought profound changes to everyone's lives. Through the first few decades of the 21st century, older adults will be a major economic and political force. They will strain the Social Security and other pension systems, health care (especially long-term care), and other human services. The costs will be borne by a smaller group of taxpayers in younger generations.

The strain on services will be exacerbated because the most rapidly growing segment of the U.S. population is people over age 85. In fact, the number of such people is projected to increase 400% between 1995 and 2050 (Administration on Aging, 1999). As we discuss in Chapter 3, people over age 85 generally need more assistance with daily living than do people under age 85.

The population trends in the United States are mirrored in many other industrialized countries. Other economically powerful countries, such as Japan, are trying to cope with rapid increases in the number of older adults. In fact, the rate of growth of older adults in Japan is the highest in the industrialized world; by 2025 there will be twice as many adults over age 65 as there will be children (WuDunn, 1997). The economic impact will be profound; the much higher pension and health care costs will have to be borne by far fewer workers (WuDunn, 1997). In other countries, the older adult population has yet to surpass the childhood population. Why is this so? In large part, it is determined by the overall quality of health care available to the general population, birth rate, and diseases.

Although the financial impact of an aging population is predictable, we have done surprisingly little to

It's impossible to tell much about these people simply by knowing how old they are. We must know more about what developmental phase they are in.

© Kathy Sloane / Jeroboam

prepare. For example, few data exist on older workers (even though mandatory retirement in nearly every job in the United States was eliminated many years ago), on differences between the young old (ages 65–80) and the old old (over age 80), or on specific health needs of older adults with regard to chronic illness. As of 2000, the U.S. Congress had not adopted long-term plans for funding Social Security and Medicare, even though the first baby boomers will turn 60 in 2006. These issues must be addressed in the very near future so that the appropriate policies can be implemented (Binstock, 1999).

THE DIVERSITY OF OLDER ADULTS. Just like people your age, older adults are not all alike. Older women outnumber older men in all ethnic groups in the United States and in most other countries around the world, for reasons we explore later. One thing is clear: Men and women experience aging differently. In most cases, this is because men and women play different roles throughout their lives. Whether men or women have it better in late life depends on the particular society being considered (Keith, 1990).

The number of older adults among U.S. ethnic groups is increasing faster than among European Americans. This trend is projected to continue, as can be seen in Figure 1.2 (U.S. Bureau of the Census, 1999). Note the very large increases in the numbers of Asian, Native, and Hispanic American older adults compared with those of African and European American older adults.

Older adults' educational levels continue to improve. At present, only about half the people over age 65 have a high school diploma, and 10% have 4 or more years of college. By 2030, estimates are that 85% will have a high school diploma and 75% will have a college degree (U.S. Bureau of the Census, 1999). Such dramatic changes are caused by better educational opportunities for more people and the greater need for formal schooling, especially college, to obtain a good job. Better-educated people also tend to live longer, mostly because they have higher incomes, which give them access to better health care and a chance to live more healthful lifestyles.

CONCEPT CHECKS

1. What is ageism?

2. What are the four characteristics of Baltes's life-span perspective?

3. What are the primary implications of a rapid increase in the number of older adults?

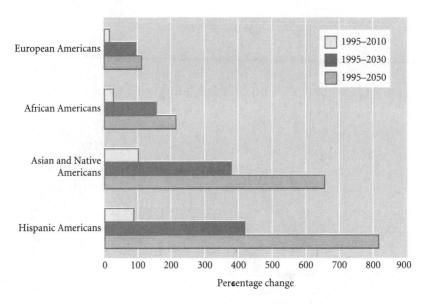

FIGURE 1.2 Projected growth of minority populations of older adults in the United States, 1995–2050.

Source: Data from the U.S. Census Bureau.

ISSUES IN STUDYING ADULT DEVELOPMENT AND AGING

LEARNING OBJECTIVES

- What three main forces shape development? What are normative age-graded influences, normative history-graded influences, and nonnormative influences?
- What are the nature–nurture, stability–change, continuity–discontinuity, and universal versus context-specific development controversies?
- What is the meaning of *age?*

Levar Johnson smiled broadly as he held his new-born granddaughter for the first time. So many thoughts rushed into his mind. What would Devonna experience growing up? Would the poor neighborhood they lived in prevent her from realizing her potential? Would the family genes for good health be passed on? How would Devonna's life growing up as an African American in the United States be different from Levar's experiences?

Like many grandparents, Levar wonders what the future holds for his granddaughter. The questions he asks are interesting in their own right, but they are important for another reason: They get to the heart of general issues of human development that have intrigued philosophers and scientists for centuries. You have probably wondered about many similar issues. How do some people manage to remain thin whereas other people seemingly gain weight merely looking at food? Why do some people remain very active mentally well into later life? How does growing up in a Spanish-speaking culture affect one's views of family caregiving? Answering these questions requires us to consider the various forces that shape us as we mature. Developmentalists place special emphasis on four forces: biological, psychological, sociocultural, and life-cycle. These forces direct our development much as an artist's hands direct the course of a painting or sculpture.

Following from the forces that shape development are questions such as: What is the relative importance of genetics and environment on people's behavior? Do people change gradually, or do they change more abruptly? Do all people change in the same way? These questions reflect four core controversies that historically underlie the study of human development (Lerner, 1986): the nature–nurture controversy, the change–stability controversy, the continuity–discontinuity controversy, and the universal versus context-specific development controversy.

Having a firm grasp on the forces and controversies of development is important because it provides a context for understanding why researchers and theorists believe certain things about aging or why some topics have been researched a great deal and others have been hardly studied at all. For example, one who believes that a decline in intellectual ability is an innate and inevitable part of aging is unlikely to search for intervention techniques to raise performance. Similarly, one who believes that personality characteristics change across adulthood would be likely to search for life transitions.

The Forces of Development

Why do some people develop gray hair in young adulthood? Why do some adults continue to remember everything well whereas others do not? Why are some older adults very active whereas others withdraw? Why might a 26-year-old woman's reactions to an unplanned pregnancy be different from those of a 46-year-old woman? These questions require us to understand the basic forces that shape us. Developmentalists typically consider four interactive forces:

Biological forces *include all genetic and health-related factors that affect development.* Examples of biological forces include menopause, facial wrinkling, and changes in the major organ systems.

The developmental forces that shaped this grandparent have some similarities and some differences with those that will shape this child.

Psychological forces *include all internal perceptual, cognitive, emotional, and personality factors that affect development.* Collectively, psychological forces provide the characteristics we notice about people that make them individuals.

Sociocultural forces *include interpersonal, societal, cultural, and ethnic factors that affect development.* Sociocultural forces provide the overall contexts in which we develop.

Life-cycle forces *reflect differences in how the same event or combination of biological, psychological, and sociocultural forces affects people at different points in their lives.* Life-cycle forces provide the context for the developmental differences of interest in adult development and aging.

As depicted in Figure 1.3, each of us is a product of a unique combination of these forces. Even identical twins growing up in the same family eventually have their own unique friends, partners, occupations,

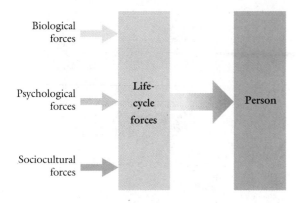

FIGURE 1.3 Each person is the product of the interaction of biological, psychological, sociocultural, and life-cycle forces.

and so on. To see why all these forces are important, imagine that we want to know how people feel about forgetting. We would need to consider several biological factors, such as whether the forgetting was caused by an underlying disease. We would want to know about such psychological factors as what the person's memory ability has been throughout his or her life and about his or her beliefs about what happens to memory with increasing age. We would need to know about sociocultural factors, such as the influence of social stereotypes about forgetting. Finally, we would need to know about the age of the person when a forgetting experience occurs. Focusing on only one (or even two or three) of the forces would provide an incomplete view of how the person feels. How the forces interact is explored further in the Forces in Action feature.

INTERRELATIONS BETWEEN THE FORCES: DEVELOPMENTAL INFLUENCES. All the forces we have discussed combine to create people's developmental experiences. One way to consider these combinations is to consider the degree to which they are common or unique. Based on this approach, Baltes (1979; Baltes et al., 1998) identifies three sets of influences that interact to produce developmental change over the life span: normative age-graded influences, normative history-graded influences, and nonnormative influences.

Normative age-graded influences *are experiences caused by biological, psychological, and sociocultural forces that are highly correlated with chronological age.* Some of these, such as puberty, menarche, and menopause, are biological. These normative biological events usually indicate a major change in a person's life; for example, menopause is an indicator that a woman can no longer bear children without medical intervention. Normative psychological events include focusing on certain concerns at different points in adulthood, such as a middle-aged person's concern with socializing the younger generation. Other normative age-graded influences involve sociocultural forces, such as the time when first marriage occurs and the age at which one retires. Normative age-graded influences typically correspond to major time-marker events, which are often ritualized. For example, many younger adults formally celebrate turning 21 as the official transition to adulthood, getting married typically is surrounded with much celebration, and retirement often begins with a party celebrating the end of one's employment. These events provide the most convenient way to judge where we are on our social clock.

Normative history-graded influences *are events that most people in a specific culture experience at the same time.* These events may be biological (such as epidemics), psychological (such as particular stereotypes), or sociocultural (such as changing attitudes toward sexuality). Normative history-graded influences often give a generation its unique identity, such as the baby-boom generation (people born roughly between 1946 and 1960) or generation X (people born after roughly 1965). These influences can have a profound effect. For example, the emergence of acquired immune deficiency syndrome (AIDS) during the 1980s fundamentally changed the attitudes toward dating and casual sexual relationships that had developed during the preceding decades.

Nonnormative influences *are random or rare events that may be important for a specific individual but are not experienced by most people.* These may be favorable events, such as winning the lottery or an election, or unfavorable ones, such as an accident or layoff. It's the unpredictability of these events that

Culture and ethnicity jointly provide status, social settings, living conditions, and personal experiences for people of all ages, and it influences and is influenced by biological, psychological, and life-cycle developmental forces. Culture can be defined as shared basic value orientations, norms, and beliefs and customary habits and ways of living. Culture provides the basic worldview of a society in that it gives it the basic explanations about the meanings and goals of everyday life (Luborsky & McMullen, 1999). Culture is such a powerful influence because it connects to biological forces through family lineage, which is sometimes the way in which members of a particular culture are defined. Psychologically, culture shapes people's core beliefs; in some cases this can result in ethnocentrism, or the belief that one's own culture is superior to others. Being socialized as

a child within a culture usually has a more profound effect on a person than when one adopts a culture later in life, resulting in significant life-cycle timing effects. Culture is extremely important in gerontology because how people define basic concepts such as *person, age,* and *life course* vary a great deal across cultures.

Equally important is the concept of ethnicity, which is an individual and collective sense of identity based on historical and cultural group membership and related behaviors and beliefs (Luborsky & McMullen, 1999). Compared with culture, ethnic group identities have both solid and fluid properties, reflecting the fact that there are both unchanging and situation-specific aspects to ethnic identity (Luborsky & Rubinstein, 1997). An example of these properties is that the terms referring to an ethnic group can change over time; for

example, the terms *colored people, Negroes, black Americans,* and *African Americans* have all been used to describe Americans of African ancestry. Ethnic identity is first influenced by biology through one's parents. However, how one incorporates ethnic identity depends on numerous psychological factors as well as age.

Both culture and ethnicity are key dimensions along which adults vary. However, we know very little about how culture or ethnicity affect how people experience old age. Throughout the rest of this book, we explore areas in which culture and ethnicity have been studied systematically. Unfortunately, most research focuses only on European Americans. Given the demographic trends discussed earlier, this focus must change so we can understand the experience of growing older in the United States in the next few decades.

makes them unique. Such events can turn one's life upside down overnight.

Life-cycle forces are especially key in understanding the importance of normative age-graded, normative history-graded, and nonnormative influences. For example, history-graded influences may produce generational differences and conflict; parents' experiences as young adults in the 1960s may have little to do with the complex issues faced by today's young adults. In turn, these interactions have important implications for understanding differences that appear to be age related. That is, differences may be explained in terms of different life experiences (normative history-graded influences) rather than as an integral part of aging itself (normative age-graded influences). We return to this issue when we discuss

age, cohort, and time-of-measurement effects in research on adult development and aging.

Controversies in Development

Is it your genes or experiences that determine how intelligent you are? If a young adult woman is outgoing, does this mean that she will be outgoing in late life? If people change, is it more gradual or sporadic? Is aging the same around the world? These and similar questions have occupied some of the greatest Western philosophers in history: Plato, Aristotle, René Descartes, John Locke, and Ludwig Wittgenstein, among many others. Four main issues occupy most of the discussion: nature versus nurture, stability versus change, continuity versus discontinuity, and universal versus context-specific development. Because each of these issues cuts across the topics we discuss in this book, let's consider each briefly.

THE NATURE–NURTURE CONTROVERSY. Think for a minute about one of your personal characteristics, such as intelligence, good looks, or a great personality. How do you think you got this trait? From your parents through genetic inheritance or through the experiences you had growing up?

The extent to which inborn, hereditary characteristics (nature) and experiential, or environmental, influences (nurture) determine who we are makes up the **nature–nurture controversy.** Until the 1980s, most theorists viewed adult development and aging from a predominantly nature position: Certain changes occur inevitably as people grow older, and one can do little to alter their course. This approach to aging can be seen in the works of such divergent writers as Shakespeare, who describes old age in *As You Like It* as a second childhood, and David Wechsler, who believed that intellectual development in adulthood meant an inevitable loss of skills and that there was little that could be done about it. More recently, the pendulum has shifted toward a recognition that nature and nurture interact. For example, whether one gets Alzheimer's disease, which in some cases has a genetic component, and possibly even the course of the disease itself, may be influenced by the environment. Specifically, an environmental trigger may be needed for the disease to occur. Moreover, some evidence indicates that providing a supportive environment for people with Alzheimer's disease improves their performance on cognitive tasks, at least for a while (Camp et al., 1997).

To answer Levar's questions in the vignette, to understand Devonna's future, we must simultaneously consider her inborn, hereditary characteristics (good health runs in her family) and her environment (she lives in a poor section of the city). Each of us is genetically unique and has unique interactions with a given environment. Both factors must be considered together to yield an adequate account of why we behave the way we do. To explain a person's behavior and discover where to focus intervention, we must look at the unique interaction for that person between nature and nurture.

THE STABILITY–CHANGE CONTROVERSY. Ask yourself the following question: Are you pretty much the same as you were 10 years ago, or are you different? How so? Depending on what aspects of yourself you considered, you may have concluded that you are pretty much the same (perhaps in terms of learning style) or that you are different (perhaps in some physical feature such as weight). *The* **stability–change controversy** *concerns the degree to which people remain the same over time.* Stability at some basic level is essential for us (and others) to recognize that we are the same individual as time goes on. But we also like to believe that our characteristics are not set in concrete, that we can change ourselves if we so desire. (Imagine not being able to do anything to rid yourself of some character defect.)

Although there is little controversy about whether children change in some ways from birth through age 18, there is much controversy about whether adults do as well. For example, whether adults' personalities change over time is the focus of heated debates, as we will see in Chapter 10, and the issue is summarized in the Current Controversies feature. Much of the controversy over stability and change across adulthood stems from how specific characteristics are defined and measured. For example, a personality trait is defined as an unchanging characteristic. Thus, to discover that traits remain stable over time should not be all that surprising. By the same token, if aspects of the self are defined as changing in a predictable way, then finding out that they do may not be surprising either. How much we remain the same and how much we change, then, turns out to be a difficult issue to resolve in an objective way. For many gerontologists, whether stability or change is the rule depends on what personal aspect is being considered and what theoretical perspective one is adopting.

THE CONTINUITY–DISCONTINUITY CONTROVERSY. The third major issue in developmental psychology is a derivative of the stability–change controversy. *The* **continuity–**

Lest you think that the controversies underlying adult development and aging do not reflect ongoing debate, consider the case of personality in adulthood. Perhaps no other topic in gerontology has resulted in such heated debates as whether people's basic personality remains the same throughout adulthood or undergoes fundamental change. As we explore in detail in Chapter 10, numerous theories have been developed just to account for the data on this one topic.

Consider yourself and other adults you know. Is the person labeled "class clown" in high school likely to be as much of a fun-loving person 10, 20, or 30 years later? Will the shy person who would never ask anyone to dance be as withdrawn? Or will they be hardly recognizable at the various class reunions? It's likely that in your experience you've encountered both outcomes; that is, some people seem to remain the same year after year, whereas some people seem to undergo tremendous change. Why is that?

For one thing, it depends on how specific you get in looking at aspects of a person's personality. In the case of a very specific trait, such as shyness, it is probable that you will see overall stability across adulthood. But if you look at a more global aspect such as the degree to which a person is concerned with the next generation, then you are more likely to find change.

What does this mean? Certainly, it means that you have to be very careful in making general statements about stability or change. It also means that you have to be quite specific about what you are interested in measuring and at what level of complexity. We will encounter many more examples of both stability and change throughout the book that reflect both of these needs.

Search Online with InfoTrac College Edition

For more information on these controversies, explore InfoTrac College Edition, your online library. Go to http://www.infotrac-college.com/wadsworth and use the passcode that came on the card with your book. Try these search terms: personality, traits, aging.

---

discontinuity controversy *concerns whether a particular developmental phenomenon represents a smooth progression over time (continuity) or a series of abrupt shifts (discontinuity).* Continuity approaches usually focus on the amount of a characteristic a person has, whereas discontinuity approaches usually focus on the kinds of characteristics a person has.

An example of continuity is discussed in Chapter 6: reaction time. As people grow older, the speed with which they can respond slows down. But in Chapter 8 you will read about an example of discontinuity: How people approach problems, especially ones with complex and ambiguous features, undergoes fundamental shifts from young adulthood through middle age.

THE UNIVERSAL VERSUS CONTEXT-SPECIFIC DEVELOPMENT CONTROVERSY. *The* **universal versus context-specific development controversy** *concerns whether there is just one path of development or several.* Consider the !Kung tribe, who live in the Kalahari Desert of Botswana in southwest Africa (Brown, 1990). If you were to ask an older !Kung "How old are you?" you would quickly learn that the question has no meaning. !Kung also do not keep track of the number of years they have been alive, the number of children they have, or how often they move. !Kung mothers can describe in detail each of their children's births, but they leave it to others to figure out how many children this adds up to. To the !Kung, age per se is unimportant; when asked to describe people who are "younger" or "older," they give the names of specific people. Social roles among the !Kung also do not differ by age; for example, women in their 20s and 60s all tend gardens, draw water from wells, and take care of children.

Life among !Kung adults contrasts sharply with life among adults in the United States, where age matters a great deal and social roles differ accordingly. Can one theory explain development in both

© Peter Johnson / CORBIS

This member of the !Kung tribe experiences development in ways very different from the ways most Americans do.

groups? Maybe. Some theorists argue that such differences are more apparent than real and that development worldwide reflects one basic process for everyone. According to this view, differences in development are simply variations on a fundamental developmental process, much as Hershey, Nestlé, Schmidt, and Godiva chocolates are all products of the same basic manufacturing process.

The opposing view is that differences between people may not be just variations on a theme. Advocates of this view argue that adult development and aging are inextricably intertwined with the context in which they occur. A person's development is a product of complex interactions with the environment, and these interactions are not fundamentally the

same in all environments. Each environment has its own set of unique procedures that shape development, just as the "recipes" for chocolates, computers, and pens have little in common.

The view adopted in this book is that adult development and aging must be understood within the contexts in which they occur. In some cases, this means that contexts are sufficiently similar that general trends can be identified. In others, such as the !Kung and U.S. societies, these differences prevent many general statements. In Levar's case with his granddaughter, it may be a blend of the two.

The Meaning of Age

When you are asked the question "How old are you?" what crosses your mind? Is it the number of years since the day of your birth? Is it how old you feel at that time? Is it defined more in terms of where you are biologically, psychologically, or socially than in terms of calendar time? You may not have thought about it, but age is not a simple construct (and in the case of people such as the !Kung, it has no meaning at all).

Likewise, aging is not a single process. Rather, it consists of at least three distinct processes: primary, secondary, and tertiary aging (Birren & Cunningham, 1985). **Primary aging** *is normal, disease-free development during adulthood.* Changes in biological, psychological, sociocultural, or life-cycle processes in primary aging are an inevitable part of the developmental process; examples include menopause, decline in reaction time, and the loss of family and friends. Most of the information in this book represents primary aging. **Secondary aging** *is developmental changes that are related to disease, lifestyle, and other environmentally induced changes that are not inevitable (e.g., pollution).* The progressive loss of intellectual abilities in Alzheimer's disease and related forms of dementia are examples of secondary aging. *Finally,* **tertiary aging** *is the rapid losses that occur shortly before death.* An example of tertiary aging is a phenomenon known as terminal drop, in which intellectual abilities show a marked decline in the last few years before death.

Increasingly, researchers are emphasizing that everyone does not grow old in the same way. Whereas most people tend to show usual patterns of aging that reflect the typical, or normative, changes with age, other people show highly successful aging in which few signs of change occur. For example, although most people tend to get chronic diseases as they get older, some people never do. What makes people who age successfully different? At this point, we do not know for sure. It may be a unique combination of genetics, optimal environment, flexibility in dealing with life situations, a strong sense of personal control, and maybe a bit of luck. For our present discussion, the main point to keep in mind is that everyone's experience of growing old is somewhat different. Although many people develop arthritis, how each person learns to cope is unique.

When most of us think about age, we usually think of how long we have been around since our birth; this way of defining age is known as chronological age. *Chronological age* is a shorthand way to index time and organize events and data by using a commonly understood standard: calendar time. Chronological age is not the only shorthand index variable used in adult development and aging. Gender, ethnicity, and socioeconomic status are others. No index variable itself actually causes behavior. In the case of gender, for example, it is not whether a person is male or female per se that determines how long he or she will live on average but rather the underlying forces, such as hormonal effects, that are the true causes. This point is often forgotten when age is the index variable, perhaps because it is so familiar to us and so widely used. However, age (or time) does not directly cause things to happen, either. Iron left out in the rain will rust, but rust is not caused simply by time. Rather, rust is a time-dependent process involving oxidation in which time is a measure of the rate at which rust is created. Similarly, human behavior is affected by experiences that occur with the passage of time, not by time itself. What we study in adult development and aging is the result of time- or age-dependent processes, not the result of age itself.

There are several other definitions of age in addition to chronological age. *Perceived age* refers to the age you think of yourself as. The saying "you're only as old as you feel" captures perceived age. Where people are relative to the maximum number of years they could possibly live is their *biological age*. Biological age is assessed by measuring the functioning of the various vital, or life-limiting, organ systems, such as the cardiovascular system.

Psychological age refers to the functional level of the psychological abilities people use to adapt to changing environmental demands. These abilities include memory, intelligence, feelings, motivation, and other skills that foster and maintain self-esteem and personal control.

Finally, *sociocultural age* refers to the specific set of roles individuals adopt in relation to other members of the society and culture to which they belong. Sociocultural age is judged on the basis of many behaviors and habits, such as style of dress, customs, language, and interpersonal style. Sociocultural age is especially important in understanding many of the family and work roles we adopt. When to get married, have children, make career moves, retire, and so on often are influenced by what we think our sociocultural age is. Such decisions also play a role in determining our self-esteem and other aspects of personality. Many of the most damaging stereotypes about aging (e.g., that older people should not have sex) are based on faulty assumptions about sociocultural age.

In sum, a person's age turns out to be quite complex. Think about yourself. You probably have days when even though the calendar says you're a certain age, your exploits the day before resulted in your feeling much younger at the time and much older the next morning. How "old" anyone is can change from one moment to the next.

Concept Checks

1. What are some examples of the biological, psychological, sociocultural, and life-cycle forces of development?
2. What are the major issues in each of the controversies underlying adult development and aging?
3. What are the three distinct processes of aging?

RESEARCH METHODS

LEARNING OBJECTIVES

- What approaches do scientists use to measure behavior in adult development and aging research?
- What are the general designs for doing research?
- What specific designs are unique to adult development and aging research?
- What ethical procedures must researchers follow?

*L*eah and Sarah are both 75 years old and are in fairly good health. They believe that their memory is not as good as it once was, so they both use various memory aids: Leah tries to think of images in her mind to remember her grocery list, whereas Sarah writes them down. Leah and Sarah got into a discussion recently about which technique works better.

Suppose that Leah and Sarah know that you're taking a course in adult development and aging, so they ask you to settle the matter. You know that research could show whose approach is better under what circumstances, but how? Gerontologists must make several key decisions as they prepare to study any topic. They need to decide how to measure the topic of interest, they must design the study, they must choose a way to study development, and they must respect the rights of the people who will participate in the study.

What makes the study of adult development and aging different from other areas of social science is the need to consider multiple influences on behavior. Explanations of development entail consideration of all of the forces we considered earlier. This makes research on adult development and aging more difficult, if for no other reason than it involves examining more variables.

Measurement in Adult Development and Aging Research

Researchers typically begin by deciding how to measure the topic of interest. For example, the first step toward resolving Leah and Sarah's discussion about remembering grocery items would be to decide how to measure remembering. Gerontologists usually use one of three approaches: observing systematically,

using tasks to sample behavior, and asking people for self-reports. Additionally, researchers need to be concerned with how representative the participants in the study are of the larger group of people in question.

Regardless of the kind of method chosen, researchers must show that it is both reliable and valid. *The **reliability** of a measure is the extent to which it provides a consistent index of the behavior or topic of interest.* A measure of memory is reliable to the extent that it gives a consistent estimate of performance each time you administer it. All measures used in gerontological research must be shown to be reliable, or they cannot be used. *The **validity** of a measure is the extent to which it measures what researchers think it measures.* For example, a measure of memory is valid only if it can be shown to actually measure memory (and not vocabulary ability, for example). Validity often is established by showing that the measure in question is closely related to another measure known to be valid. Because it is possible to have a measure that is reliable but not valid (a ruler is a reliable measure of length but not a valid measure of memory), researchers must ensure that measures are both reliable and valid.

SYSTEMATIC OBSERVATION. *As the name implies, **systematic observation** involves watching people and carefully recording what they say or do.* Two forms of systematic observation are common. In *naturalistic observation,* people are observed as they behave spontaneously in some real-life situation. For example, Leah and Sarah could be observed in the grocery store purchasing their items as a way to test how well they remember.

Structured observations differ from naturalistic observations in that the researcher creates a setting that is particularly likely to elicit the behavior of interest. Structured observations are especially useful for studying behaviors that are difficult to observe naturally. For example, how people react to emergencies is hard to study naturally because emergencies generally are rare and unpredictable events. A researcher could stage an emergency and watch how people react. However, whether the behaviors observed in staged situations are the same as would happen naturally often is hard to determine, making it difficult to generalize from staged settings to the real world.

SAMPLING BEHAVIOR WITH TASKS. When investigators can't observe a behavior directly, another popular alternative is to create tasks that are thought to sample the behavior of interest. For example, one way to test older adults' memory is to give them a list of items, perhaps a simulated grocery list, to learn and remember. This approach is popular with gerontological researchers because it is so convenient. The main problem with this approach is its validity: Does the task provide a realistic sample of the behavior of interest? For example, asking people to learn simulated grocery lists may underestimate what they do in the real world when the list is the actual items they need to purchase.

SELF-REPORTS. The last approach, self-reports, is a special case of using tasks to sample people's behavior. **Self-reports** *are simply people's answers to questions about the topic of interest.* When questions are posed in written form, the verbal report is a questionnaire; when they are posed verbally, it is an interview. Either way, questions are created that probe different aspects of the topic of interest. For example, if you think imagery and lists are common ways people use to remember grocery items, you could devise a questionnaire and survey several people to find out.

Although self-reports are very convenient and provide information on the topic of interest, they are not always good measures of people's behavior because they are inaccurate. Why? People may not remember accurately what they did in the past, or they may report what they think the researcher wants to hear.

REPRESENTATIVE SAMPLING. Researchers usually are interested in broad groups of people called *populations*. Examples of populations are all students taking a course on adult development and aging or all Asian American widows. Almost all studies include only a *sample* of people, which is a subset of the population. Researchers must be careful to ensure that their sample is truly representative of the population of inter-

est. An unrepresentative sample can result in invalid research. For example, what would you think of a study of middle-aged parents if you learned that the sample consisted entirely of two-parent households? You would, quite correctly, decide that this sample is not representative of all middle-aged parents and question whether its results apply to single middle-aged parents.

As you read on, you'll soon discover that most of the research we consider in this text has been conducted on middle-class, well-educated European Americans. Are these samples representative of all people in the United States? In the world? Sometimes, but not always. Be careful not to assume that findings from this group apply to people of other groups. Additionally, some developmental issues have not been studied in all ethnic groups and cultures. For example, the U.S. government does not always report statistics for all ethnic groups. To change this, some U.S. government agencies, such as the National Institutes of Health, now require samples to be representative. Thus, in the future we may gain a broader understanding of aging.

General Designs for Research

Having selected the way we want to measure the topic of interest, researchers must embed this measure in a research design that yields useful, relevant results. Gerontologists rely on primary designs in planning their work: experimental studies, correlational studies, and case studies. The specific design we choose for our research depends in large part on the questions we are trying to address.

EXPERIMENTAL DESIGN. To find out whether Leah's or Sarah's approach to remembering works better, we could gather groups of older adults and try the following. We could randomly assign the participants into three groups: those who are taught to use imagery, those who are taught to use lists, and those who are not taught to use anything. After giving all the groups time to learn the new technique (where appropriate), we could test each group on a new grocery list to see who does better.

What we have done is an example of an **experiment,** *which involves manipulating a key factor that the researcher believes is responsible for a particular behavior and randomly assigning participants to the experimental and control groups.* In our case, the key variable being manipulated is the instructions for how to study. More generally, in an experiment the researcher is most interested in identifying differences between groups of people. One group, the experimental group, receives the manipulation; another group, the control group, does not. This sets up a situation in which the level of the key variable of interest differs across groups. Additionally, the investigator exerts precise control over all important aspects of the study, including the variable of interest, the setting, and the participants. Because the key variable is systematically manipulated in an experiment, researchers can infer cause-and-effect relations about that variable. In our example, we can conclude that type of instruction (how people study) causes better or worse performance on a memory test. Discovering such cause-and-effect relations is important if we are to understand the underlying processes of adult development and aging.

An important distinction is made between **independent variables,** *which are the variables manipulated by the experimenter, and* **dependent variables,** *which are the behaviors or outcomes that are measured.* In our example, the instructions we give people would be the independent variable and the number of groceries people remember would be the dependent variable.

The results of experiments can come out in various ways. If everyone reacts the same way to the manipulation regardless of age, then we can conclude that the phenomenon under study may work in parallel ways in the age range examined. If older adults improve their memory performance to equivalent degrees by using imagery and lists, then we could argue that both strategies have the same benefit. If one group reacts very differently than the other to the manipulated variable, we obtain an age-by-condition interaction. Suppose the one group of older adults benefited a great deal from using lists and the other group of older adults did not benefit from imagery at all. This group-by-condition interaction could mean that imagery instructions are ineffective for older adults. By mapping out the conditions under which interactions are and are not present, we get a better picture of which psychological processes differ with age and which ones do not.

Finally, we must note that age cannot be an independent variable because we cannot manipulate it. Consequently, we cannot conduct true experiments to examine the effects of age on a particular person's behavior. At best, we can find age-related effects of an independent variable on dependent variables.

CORRELATIONAL DESIGN. In a correlational study, investigators examine relations between variables as they exist naturally in the world. *In the simplest* **correlational study,** *a researcher measures two variables, then sees how they are related.* Suppose we wanted to know whether the amount of time spent studying a grocery list like Sarah might create was related to how many items people remember at the store. To find out, the researcher would measure two things for each person in the study: the length of study time and the number of items purchased correctly.

The results of a correlational study usually are measured by computing a correlation coefficient, abbreviated r. Correlations can range from -1.0 to 1.0, reflecting three different types of relations between study time and number of groceries remembered.

When $r = 0$, the two variables are unrelated: Study time has no relation to remembering groceries.

When $r > 0$, the variables are positively related: As study time increases (or decreases), the number of grocery items remembered also increases (or decreases).

When $r < 0$, the variables are inversely related: When study time increases (or decreases), the number of groceries remembered decreases (or increases).

Correlational studies do not give definitive information about cause-and-effect relations; for example, the correlation between study time and the number of groceries remembered does not mean that one variable caused the other regardless of how large the relation was. However, correlational studies do provide important information about the strength of the relation between variables, which is reflected in the absolute value of the correlation coefficient. Moreover, because developmental researchers are interested in how variables are related to factors that are very difficult, if not impossible, to manipulate, correlational techniques are used a great deal. In fact, most developmental research is correlational at some level because age cannot be manipulated within an individual. What this means is that we can describe a great many developmental phenomena, but we cannot explain very many of them.

CASE STUDIES. Sometimes researchers cannot obtain measures directly from people and are able only to watch them carefully. *In certain situations, researchers may be able to study a single individual in great detail in a* **case study.** This technique is especially useful when researchers want to investigate very rare phenomena, such as uncommon diseases or people with extremely high ability. Identifying new diseases, for example, begins with a case study of one individual who has a pattern of symptoms that is different from any known syndrome. Case studies are also very valuable for opening new areas of study, which can be followed by larger studies using other methods (e.g., experiments). However, their primary limitation is figuring out whether the information gleaned from one individual holds for others as well.

Designs for Studying Development

Once the general design is chosen, most gerontologists must decide how to measure possible changes or age differences that emerge as people develop. For example, if we want to know how people continue (or fail) to use imagery or lists in remembering grocery items as they get older, we will want to use a design that is particularly sensitive to developmental differences. Such designs are based on three key variables: age, cohort, and time of measurement. Once we have considered these, we will examine the specific designs for studying development.

AGE, COHORT, AND TIME OF MEASUREMENT. Every study of adult development and aging is built on the combination of three building blocks: age, cohort, and time of measurement (Cavanaugh & Whitbourne, 1999). **Age effects** *reflect differences caused by underlying processes, such as biological, psychological, or sociocultural changes.* Although usually represented in research by chronological age, age effects are inherent changes within the person and are not caused by the passage of time per se.

Cohort effects *are differences caused by experiences and circumstances unique to the generation to which one belongs.* In general, cohort effects correspond to the normative history-graded influences discussed earlier. However, defining a cohort may not be easy. Cohorts can be specific, as in all people born in one particular year, or general, such as the baby-boom cohort. As described earlier, each generation is exposed to different sets of historical and personal events (such as World War II, home computers, or opportunities to attend college). Later in this section we consider evidence of how profound cohort effects can be.

Time-of-measurement effects *reflect differences stemming from sociocultural, environmental, historical, or other events at the time the data are obtained from the participants.* For example, data about wage increases given in a particular year may be influenced by the economic conditions of that year. If the economy is in a serious recession, pay increases probably would be small. In contrast, if the economy is booming, pay increases could be large. Clearly, whether a study is conducted during a recession or a boom affects what is learned about pay changes. In short, the point in time in which a researcher decides to do research could lead him or her to different conclusions about the phenomenon being studied.

The three building-block variables (age, cohort, and time of measurement) can be represented in a single chart, such as the one shown in Table 1.1. *Cohort* is represented by the years in the first column, *time of measurement* is represented by the years across the top, and *age* is represented by the numbers in the individual cells. Note that age is computed by subtracting the cohort year from the time of measurement.

TABLE 1.1	Three Basic Building Blocks of Developmental Research			
	Time of Measurement			
Cohort	**2000**	**2010**	**2020**	**2030**
1950	50	60	70	80
1960	40	50	60	70
1970	30	40	50	60
1980	20	30	40	50

Cohort is represented by the years in the first column, *time of measurement* by the years across the top, and *age* by the values in the cells.

In conducting adult development and aging research, investigators have attempted to identify and separate the three effects. This has not been easy because all three influences are interrelated. If one is interested in studying 40-year-olds, one must necessarily select the cohort that was born 40 years ago. In this case age and cohort are *confounded* because one cannot know whether the behaviors observed occur because the participants are 40 years old or because of the specific life experiences they have had as a result of being born in a particular historical period. *In general,* **confounding** *is any situation in which one cannot determine which of two or more effects is responsible for the behaviors being observed.* Confounding of the three effects we are considering here is the most serious problem in adult development and aging research.

What distinguishes developmental researchers from their colleagues in other areas of psychology is a fundamental interest in understanding how people change. Developmental researchers must look at the ways in which people differ across time. Doing so necessarily requires that they understand the distinction between age change and age difference. An *age change* occurs in an individual's behavior over time. Leah's or Sarah's memory at age 75 may not be as good as it was at age 40. To discover an age change one must examine the same person (in this case, Leah or Sarah) at more than one point in time. An *age difference* is obtained when at least two different people of different ages are compared. Leah and Sarah may

not remember as many grocery items as another person of age 40. Even though we may be able to document substantial age differences, we cannot assume that they imply age change. We do not know whether Leah or Sarah has changed since she was 40, and of course we do not know whether the 40-year-old will be any different at age 75. In some cases age differences reflect age changes, and in some cases they do not.

If what we really want to understand in developmental research is age change (what happens as people grow older), we should design our research with this goal in mind. Moreover, different research questions necessitate different research designs. We will consider the most common ways in which researchers gather data about age differences and age changes: cross-sectional, longitudinal, time lag, and sequential.

CROSS-SECTIONAL DESIGNS. *In a* **cross-sectional study,** *developmental differences are identified by testing people of different ages at the same time.* Any single column in Table 1.2 represents a cross-sectional design. Cross-sectional designs allow researchers to examine age differences but not age change.

Cross-sectional research has several weaknesses. Because people are tested at only one point in their development, we learn nothing about the continuity of development. Consequently, we cannot tell whether someone who remembers grocery items well at age 50 (in 2000) is still able to do so at age 80 (in 2030) because the person would be tested at age 50 or 80, but not both. Cross-sectional studies also are affected by cohort effects, meaning that differences between age groups (cohorts) may result as easily from environmental events as from developmental processes. Why? Cross-sectional studies assume that when the older participants were younger, they resembled the people in the younger age groups in the study. This isn't always true, of course, which makes it difficult to know why age differences are found in a cross-sectional study. In short, age and cohort effects are confounded in cross-sectional research.

Despite the confounding of age and cohort and the limitation of being able to identify only age dif-

TABLE 1.2	Cross-Sectional Design			
	Time of Measurement			
Cohort	2000	2010	2020	2030
1950	**50**	60	70	80
1960	**40**	50	60	70
1970	**30**	40	50	60
1980	**20**	30	40	50

TABLE 1.3	Longitudinal Design			
	Time of Measurement			
Cohort	2000	2010	2020	2030
1950	50	60	70	80
1960	**40**	**50**	**60**	**70**
1970	30	40	50	60
1980	20	30	40	50

ferences, cross-sectional designs dominate the research literature in gerontology. Why? The reason is a pragmatic one: Because all of the measurements are obtained at one time, cross-sectional research can be conducted more quickly and inexpensively than research using other designs. As long as their limits are recognized, cross-sectional studies can provide a snapshot of age differences that may reveal issues that can be followed up with other designs that are sensitive to age change.

LONGITUDINAL DESIGNS. *In a* **longitudinal study,** *the same individuals are observed or tested repeatedly at different points in their lives.* As the name implies, a longitudinal study involves a lengthwise account of development and is the most direct way to watch growth occur. A longitudinal design is represented by any horizontal row in Table 1.3. A major advantage of longitudinal designs is that age changes are identified because we are studying the same people over time. But if age changes are found, can we say why they occurred?

Because only one cohort is studied, cohort effects are eliminated as an explanation of change. However, the other two potential explanations, age and time of measurement, are confounded. For example, suppose that we wanted to follow the 1980 cohort over time. If we wanted to test these individuals when they were 20 years old, we would have to do so in 2000. Consequently, any changes we identify could result from changes in underlying processes or factors that are related to the time we choose to conduct our measurement. For instance, if we conducted a longitudinal study of salary growth, the amount of salary change

in any comparison could stem from real change in the skills and worth of the person to the company or from the economic conditions of the times. In a longitudinal study we cannot tell which of these factors is more important.

Longitudinal studies have three additional potential problems. First, if the research measure requires some type of performance by the participants, we may have the problem of practice effects. Practice effects result from the fact that performance may improve over time simply because people are tested over and over again with the same measures. Repeatedly using the same measure on the same people may have significant effects on their behavior, may make the measure invalid, and may have a negative impact on the participants' perceptions of the research (Baltes et al., 1977).

Second, we may have a problem with participant dropout because it is difficult to keep a group of research participants intact over the course of a longitudinal study. Participants may move, lose interest, or die. Suppose we want to examine the relation between intelligence and health. Participant dropout can result in two different outcomes. We can end up with positive selective survival if the participants at the end of the study tend to be the ones who were initially higher on some variable (for example, the surviving participants are the ones who were the most healthy at the beginning of the study). In contrast, we could have negative selective survival if the participants at the conclusion of the study were initially lower on an important variable (for example, the surviving participants may have been those who initially weighed the least). The extent to which the characteristics of the group change over time determines the degree of the problem. We may not know exactly what differences there are between those who return for every session and those who do not. What we do know is that, in general, the people who always return are more outgoing, are healthier, have higher self-esteem, and are more likely to be married than those who drop out (Schaie & Hertzog, 1985). In any case, the result may be an overly optimistic picture of aging.

The third problem with longitudinal designs is that our ability to apply the results to other groups is limited. The difficulty is that only one cohort is followed. Whether the pattern of results that is observed in one cohort can be generalized to another cohort is questionable. Thus, researchers using longitudinal designs run the risk of uncovering a developmental process that is unique to that cohort.

Because longitudinal designs necessarily take more time and usually are expensive, they have not been used very often. However, researchers now recognize that following individuals over time is badly needed to further our understanding of the aging process. Thus, longitudinal studies are becoming more common in the literature.

TIME LAG DESIGNS. *A **time lag study** involves measuring people of the same age at different points in time.* Time lag designs are represented in Table 1.4 by any top-left to bottom-right diagonal. Because only a single age is studied, there are no age-related differences. Because each cohort is associated with a unique time of measurement, however, these two effects are confounded. Time lag designs are used to describe characteristics of people at a particular age, such as first-year college students, at various points in time. But because they provide no information on age differences or age change, time lag designs are not used often.

SEQUENTIAL DESIGNS. Thus far, we have considered three developmental designs, each of which has problems involving the confounding of two effects. These effects are age and cohort in cross-sectional designs, age and time of measurement in longitudinal designs, and cohort and time of measurement

TABLE 1.4	Time Lag Design			
	Time of Measurement			
Cohort	**2000**	**2010**	**2020**	**2030**
1950	**50**	60	70	80
1960	40	**50**	60	70
1970	30	40	**50**	60
1980	20	30	40	**50**

in time lag designs. These confounds create difficulties in interpreting behavioral differences between and within individuals, as illustrated in the How Do We Know? feature. Some of these interpretive dilemmas can be alleviated by using more complex designs called sequential designs, which are shown in Table 1.5. Keep in mind, though, that sequential designs do not cure the confounding problems in the three basic designs.

Sequential designs *represent different combinations of cross-sectional or longitudinal studies.* In the table, a *cross-sequential design* consists of two or more cross-sectional studies conducted at two or more times of measurement. These multiple cross-sectional designs include the same age ranges; however, the participants are different in each wave of testing. For example, we might compare performances on intelligence tests for people between ages 20 and 50 in 1980 and then repeat the study in 1990 with a different group of people aged 30 to 60.

Table 1.5 also depicts the longitudinal sequential design. A *longitudinal sequential design* consists of two or more longitudinal designs that represent two or more cohorts. Each longitudinal design in the sequence begins with the same age range and follows people for the same length of time. For example, we may want to begin a longitudinal study of intellectual development with a group of 50-year-olds in 1980, using the 1930 cohort. We would then follow this cohort for a period of years. In 1990 we would begin a second longitudinal study on 50-year-olds, using the 1940 cohort, and follow them for the same length of time as we do the first cohort.

TABLE 1.5	Sequential Design			
	Time of Measurement			
Cohort	2000	2010	2020	2030
1950	50	60	70	80
1960	**40**	**50**	**60**	**70**
1970	30	**40**	50	**60**
1980	20	30	40	50

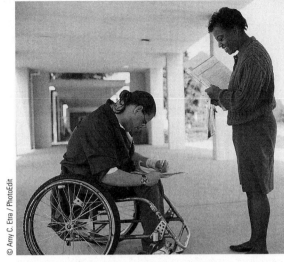

Before participating in any research, the participant must be told what the project entails.

Although sequential designs are powerful and provide by far the richest source of information about developmental issues, few researchers use them because they are costly. Trying to follow many people over long periods of time, generating new samples, and conducting complex data analyses are expensive and time-consuming. Clearly, this type of commitment to one project is not possible for most researchers.

EXTREME AGE GROUPS DESIGNS. Suppose you want to investigate whether people's ability to remember items at the grocery store differs with age. Your first impulse may be to gather a group of younger adults and compare their performance with that of a group of older adults. This approach, which is by far the most common one in adult development and aging research, is called an *extreme age groups design*. Typically, such studies compare samples obtained in convenient ways; younger adults usually are college students and older adults often are volunteers from senior centers or church groups.

Despite the fact that the extreme age groups design is very common (most of the studies cited in this book used this design), there are several problems with it (Hertzog & Dixon, 1996). Three concerns are key. First, the samples are not representative, so we must be very careful not to read too much into the results; findings from extreme age group studies may not generalize to people other than ones like those who participated. Second, age should be treated as a continuous variable, not as a category ("young" and "old"). Viewing age as a continuous variable allows

researchers to gain a better understanding of how age relates to any observed age differences. Finally, extreme age group designs assume that the measures used mean the same thing across both age groups. Measures may tap somewhat different constructs, so the reliability and validity of each measure should be checked in each age group.

Despite these problems, the extreme age group design can provide useful information if used carefully. Most importantly, this approach can point out issues that may provide fruitful avenues for subsequent longitudinal or sequential studies, in which case we can uncover information about age changes.

Conducting Research Ethically

Investigators conducting research on adults must be very careful about what they are doing and treat their research participants with respect. To ensure that this happens, many professional organizations, such as the American Psychological Association, and government research funding agencies, such as the National Institutes of Health, have adopted strict guidelines to protect research participants.

Studying Adult Development and Aging

Who was the investigator and what was the aim of the study? In the 1950s, little information was available about longitudinal changes in adults' intellectual abilities. What little there was showed a developmental pattern very different from the picture of across-the-board decline obtained in cross-sectional studies. To provide a more thorough picture of intellectual change, K. Warner Schaie began the Seattle Longitudinal Study in 1956.

How did the investigator measure the topic of interest? Schaie used standardized tests of primary mental abilities to assess a wide range of abilities such as logical reasoning and spatial ability.

Who participated in the study? Over the course of the study, more than 5000 individuals have been tested in six testing cycles (1956, 1963, 1970, 1977, 1984, and 1991). All participants were recruited through a very large

health maintenance organization in Seattle that is representative of the upper 75% of the socioeconomic spectrum.

What was the design of the study? To provide a thorough view of intellectual change over time, Schaie invented a new type of research design: the sequential design. Participants are tested every 7 years. Like most longitudinal studies, Schaie's sequential study encountered selectivity effects; that is, people who return over the years for retesting tend to do better initially than those who fail to return. However, an advantage of Schaie's sequential design is that by bringing in new groups of participants, he has been able to estimate the importance of selection effects, a major improvement over previous research.

Were there ethical concerns with the study? The most serious issue in any

study in which participants are followed over time is confidentiality. Because people's names must be retained for future contact, the researchers must be very careful about keeping personally identifiable information secure.

What were the results? Among the many important findings from the study are differential changes in abilities over time and cohort effects. As you can see in Figure 1.4, scores on tests of primary mental abilities improve gradually until the late 30s or early 40s. Small declines begin in the 50s, increase as people age into their 60s, and increase faster in the 70s (Schaie, 1995).

Cohort differences also were found. As you can see in Figure 1.5, more recently born younger and middle-aged cohorts performed better than older cohorts on some skills, such as inductive reasoning ability, but not

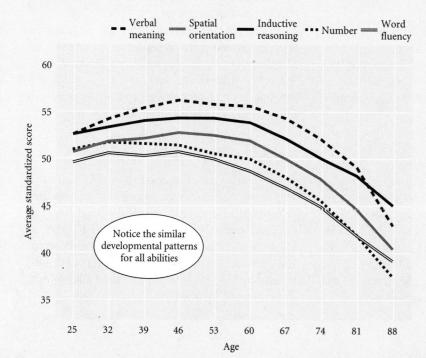

FIGURE 1.4 Longitudinal changes in intellectual functions from age 25 to age 88.

Source: Schaie, K. W. (1994). The course of adult intellectual development. *American Psychologist, 49,* 304–313. Copyright © 1994 by the American Psychological Association. Reprinted with permission.

others. An example of the latter is that older cohorts outperformed younger ones on number skills (Schaie, 1995). These cohort effects probably reflect differences in educational experiences; younger groups' education emphasized figuring things out on one's own, whereas older groups' education emphasized rote learning. Additionally, older groups did not have calculators or computers, so they had to do mathematical problems by hand.

Schaie uncovered many individual differences as well; some people showed developmental patterns closely approximating the overall trends, but others showed unusual patterns. For example, some individuals showed steady declines in most abilities beginning in their 40s and 50s, others showed declines in some abilities but not others, but some people showed little change in most abilities over a 14-year period. Such individual variation in developmental patterns means that average trends, like those depicted in the graphs, must be interpreted cautiously; they reflect group averages and do not represent the patterns shown by each person in the group.

Additionally, Schaie (1994) identified several variables that appear to reduce the risk of cognitive decline in old age:

Being free of cardiovascular and other chronic diseases

Living in favorable environmental conditions (such as good housing)

Remaining cognitively active through reading and lifelong learning

Having a flexible personality in middle age

Being married to a person with high cognitive status

Being satisfied with one's life achievements in middle age

What did the investigator conclude? Three points are clear. First, intellectual development during adulthood is marked by a gradual leveling off of gains, followed by a period of stability and then a time of gradual decline in most abilities. Second, these trends vary from one cohort to another. Third, individual patterns of change vary widely from person to person.

Overall, Schaie's findings indicate that intellectual development in adulthood is influenced by a wide variety of health, environmental, personality, and relationship factors. By attending to these influences throughout adulthood, we can at least stack the deck in favor of maintaining good intellectual functioning in late life.

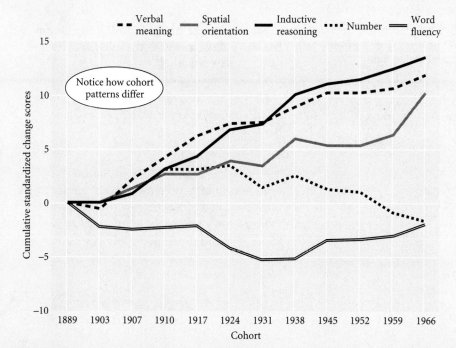

FIGURE 1.5 **Cohort differences in intellectual functions from birth cohorts between 1889 and 1966.**

Source: Schaie, K. W. (1994). The course of adult intellectual development. *American Psychologist, 49,* 304–313. Copyright © 1994 by the American Psychological Association. Reprinted with permission.

In general, investigators must submit their research proposals to ethics review panels before beginning the project. Review panels examine the proposal in detail. One requirement is that researchers obtain informed consent from human participants before collecting data from them; that is, investigators must tell potential participants the purpose of the project, what they will be asked to do, whether the project entails any risks, any benefits participants may receive, and any other relevant information the review panel deems appropriate. Only when the review panel has given the investigator permission to proceed is the researcher able to begin the project.

The requirement for informed consent is very important. If prospective participants cannot complete the informed consent procedure themselves, perhaps because they are incapacitated or because they have a condition, such as Alzheimer's disease, that causes intellectual impairment, someone else (usually a family member) must complete the process. However, researchers must take extra precautions to be sensitive to these individuals; for example, if it becomes apparent that the participant does not like the procedures, the researcher must stop collecting data from that individual.

These ethical principles provide important protections for participants and investigators alike. By treating research participants with respect, investigators are in a better position to make important discoveries about adult development and aging.

Concept Checks

1. What are the three major approaches to measuring a behavior or topic of interest?
2. What are the key differences between experimental, correlational, and case study designs?
3. What three basic effects are examined in all developmental research?
4. What are the advantages and disadvantages of cross-sectional, longitudinal, and sequential designs?
5. What are the limitations of the extreme age groups design?
6. What steps do researchers need to take before conducting a study involving human participants?

Putting It All Together

In this chapter, we encountered many of the basic issues and concepts underlying adult development and aging. Many myths and stereotypes about older adults exist, which can result in ageism. Like Roberto, we discovered that the number of older adults is increasing rapidly, especially in ethnic minority groups. Four major forces shape everyone's development, including Levar's granddaughter Devonna: biological, psychological, sociocultural, and life-cycle forces. However, Devonna will differ from Levar in her experience of normative age-graded, normative history-graded, and nonnormative influences. Four controversies also shape how we describe development: nature–nurture, stability–change, continuity–discontinuity, and universal versus context-specific development. Leah and Sarah's discussion about remembering grocery lists helped us discover the ways in which gerontologists conduct research about adult development and aging.

Summary

Perspectives on Adult Development and Aging

- Gerontology is the study of aging from maturity through old age, as well as the study of older adults as a special group.
- Myths of aging lead to negative stereotypes of older people, which can result in ageism, a form of discrimination against older people simply because of their age.

The Life-Span Perspective

- The life-span perspective divides human development into two phases: an early phase (childhood and adolescence) and a later phase (young adulthood, middle age, and old age).
- There are four key features of the life-span perspective: multidirectionality, plasticity, historical context, and multiple causation.

The Demographics of Aging

- The number of older adults in the United States and other industrialized countries is increasing rapidly because of better health care and declines in mortality during childbirth. The large numbers of older adults have important implications for human services.

- The number of older Hispanic American, Asian American, and Native American adults will increase much faster between now and 2050 than the number of European American and African American older adults.

- The educational level of older adults will continue to increase, so that by 2030 it is expected that 75% will have a college degree.

ISSUES IN STUDYING ADULT DEVELOPMENT AND AGING

The Forces of Development

- Development is shaped by four forces. Biological forces include all genetic and health-related factors. Psychological forces include all internal perceptual, cognitive, emotional, and personality factors. Sociocultural forces include interpersonal, societal, cultural, and ethnic factors. Life-cycle forces reflect differences in how the same event or combination of biological, psychological, and sociocultural forces affects people at different points in their lives.

- Normative age-graded influences are life experiences that are highly related to chronological age. Normative history-graded influences are events that most people in a specific culture experience at the same time. Nonnormative influences are events that may be important for a specific individual but are not experienced by most people.

Controversies in Development

- The nature–nurture controversy concerns the extent to which inborn, hereditary characteristics (nature) and experiential, or environmental, influences (nurture) determine who we are. The focus on nature and nurture must be on how they interact.

- The stability–change controversy concerns the degree to which people remain the same over time.

- The continuity–discontinuity controversy concerns competing views of how to describe change: as a smooth progression over time (continuity) or as a series of abrupt shifts (discontinuity).

- The universal versus context-specific development controversy concerns whether there is only one pathway of development or several. This issue becomes especially important in interpreting cultural and ethnic group differences.

The Meaning of Age

- Three types of aging are distinguished. Primary aging is normal, disease-free development during adulthood. Secondary aging is developmental changes that are related to disease. Tertiary aging is the rapid losses that occur shortly before death.

- Chronological age is a poor descriptor of time-dependent processes and serves only as a shorthand for the passage of calendar time. Time-dependent processes do not actually cause behavior.

- Perceived age is the age you think of yourself as being.

- Better definitions of age include biological age (where a person is relative to the maximum number of years he or she could live), psychological age (where a person is in terms of the abilities people use to adapt to changing environmental demands), and sociocultural age (where a person is in terms of the specific set of roles adopted in relation to other members of the society and culture).

RESEARCH METHODS

Measurement in Adult Development and Aging Research

- Measures used in research must be reliable (measure things consistently) and valid (measure what they are supposed to measure).

- Systematic observation involves watching people and carefully recording what they say or do. Two forms are common: naturalistic observation (observing people behaving spontaneously in a real-world setting) and structured observations (creating a setting that will elicit the behavior of interest).

- If behaviors are hard to observe directly, researchers often create tasks that sample the behavior of interest.

- Self-reports involve people's answers to questions presented in a questionnaire or interview about a topic of interest.

- Most of the research on adults has focused on middle-class, well-educated European Americans. This creates serious problems for understanding the development experiences of other groups of people.

General Designs for Research

- Experiments consist of manipulating one or more independent variables, measuring one or more dependent variables, and randomly assigning participants to the experimental and control groups. Experiments provide information about cause and effect.

- Correlational designs address relations between variables; they do not provide information about cause and effect but do provide information about the strength of the relation between the variables.

- Case studies are systematic investigations of individual people that provide detailed descriptions of people's behavior in everyday situations.

Designs for Studying Development

- Age effects reflect underlying biological, psychological, and sociocultural changes. Cohort effects are differences caused by experiences and circumstances unique to the generation to which one belongs. Time-of-measurement effects reflect influences of the specific historical time when one is obtaining information. Developmental research designs represent various combinations of age, cohort, and time-of-measurement effects. Confounding is any situation in which one cannot determine which of two or more effects is responsible for the behaviors being observed.

- Cross-sectional designs examine multiple cohorts and age groups at a single point in time. They can identify only age differences and confound age and cohort.

- Longitudinal designs examine one cohort over two or more times of measurement. They can identify age change but have several problems, including practice effects, dropout, and selective survival. Longitudinal designs confound age and time of measurement.

- Time lag designs examine multiple cohorts of same-aged people. They confound cohort and time of measurement, and they are rarely used.

- Sequential designs involve more than one cross-sectional (cross-sequential) or longitudinal (longitudinal sequential) design. Although they are complex and expensive, they are important because they help disentangle age, cohort, and time-of-measurement effects.

- The extreme age groups design compares younger and older adult samples of convenience. The design has three major limitations: Samples are not representative, age is not treated as a continuous variable, and measurement equivalence is not ensured.

Conducting Research Ethically

- Investigators must obtain informed consent from their participants before conducting research.

Review Questions

PERSPECTIVES ON ADULT DEVELOPMENT AND AGING

- What are the premises of the life-span perspective?

- How are population demographics changing around the world, and what difference does it make?

ISSUES IN STUDYING ADULT DEVELOPMENT AND AGING

- What are the four basic forces in human development?

- What are the major characteristics of normative age-graded, normative history-graded, and nonnormative influences?
- How do nature and nurture interact?
- What are the main issues in the stability–change controversy?
- What is the continuity–discontinuity controversy? What kinds of theories derive from each view?
- What is the universal versus context-specific development controversy, and how does it relate to sociocultural forces?
- In what ways can age be defined? What are the advantages and disadvantages of each definition?

RESEARCH METHODS

- What are the reliability and validity of a measure?
- What are the three main approaches scientists use to measure behavior in adult development and aging research? What are the strengths and weaknesses of each?
- How do we know whether a sample is representative?
- What is an experiment? What information does it provide?
- What is a correlational design? What information does it provide?
- What is a case study? What information does it provide?
- What are age, cohort, and time-of-measurement effects? How and why are they important for developmental research?
- What is a cross-sectional design? What are its advantages and disadvantages?
- What is a longitudinal design? What are its advantages and disadvantages?
- What differences are there between cross-sectional and longitudinal designs in terms of uncovering age differences and age changes?
- What is a time lag design?
- What are sequential designs? What different types are there? What are their advantages and disadvantages?

- What are the limitations of the extreme age groups design?
- What steps must researchers take to protect the rights of participants?

Integrating Concepts in Development

1. Analyze each of the four major controversies in development in terms of the four developmental forces. What real-world examples can you think of that are examples of each combination of controversy and force?

2. Using yourself as an example, figure out your age using chronological, perceived, biological, psychological, and sociocultural definitions. How do they differ? Why?

3. Using the Leah and Sarah vignette as an example, design cross-sectional, longitudinal, and sequential studies of two different styles of caring for people with Alzheimer's disease. What will you learn from each of the studies?

Key Terms

age effects One of the three fundamental effects examined in developmental research, along with cohort and time-of-measurement effects, which reflects the influence of time-dependent processes on development.

ageism The untrue assumption that chronological age is the main determinant of human characteristics and that one age is better than another.

biological forces One of four basic forces of development that includes all genetic and health-related factors.

case study An intensive investigation of individual people.

cohort effects One of the three basic influences examined in developmental research, along with age and time-of-measurement effects, which reflects differences caused by experiences and circumstances unique to the historical time in which one lives.

confounding Any situation in which one cannot determine which of two or more effects is responsible for the behaviors being observed.

continuity–discontinuity controversy The debate over whether a particular developmental phenomenon represents smooth progression over time (continuity) or a series of abrupt shifts (discontinuity).

correlational study An investigation in which the strength of association between variables is examined.

cross-sectional study A developmental research design in which people of different ages and cohorts are observed at one time of measurement to obtain information about age differences.

dependent variable Behaviors or outcomes measured in an experiment.

experiment A study in which participants are randomly assigned to experimental and control groups and in which an independent variable is manipulated to observe its effects on a dependent variable so that cause-and-effect relations can be established.

independent variable Variable manipulated in an experiment.

life-cycle forces One of the four basic forces of development that reflects differences in how the same event or combination of biological, psychological, and sociocultural forces affects people at different points in their lives.

life-span perspective A view of the human life span that divides it into two phases: childhood/adolescence and young/middle/late adulthood.

longitudinal study A developmental research design that measures one cohort over two or more times of measurement to examine age changes.

nature–nurture controversy A debate over the relative influence of genetics and the environment on development.

nonnormative influences Random events that are important to an individual but do not happen to most people.

normative age-graded influences Experiences caused by biological, psychological, and sociocultural forces that are closely related to a person's age.

normative history-graded influences Events experienced by most people in a culture at the same time.

primary aging The normal, disease-free development during adulthood.

psychological forces One of the four basic forces of development that includes all internal perceptual, cognitive, emotional, and personality factors.

reliability The ability of a measure to produce the same value when used repeatedly to measure the identical phenomenon over time.

secondary aging Developmental changes that are related to disease, lifestyle, and other environmental changes that are not inevitable.

self-reports People's answers to questions about a topic of interest.

sequential designs Types of developmental research designs involving combinations of cross-sectional and longitudinal designs.

sociocultural forces One of the four basic forces of development that includes interpersonal, societal, cultural, and ethnic factors.

stability–change controversy A debate over the degree to which people remain the same over time as opposed to being different.

systematic observation A type of measurement involving watching people and carefully recording what they say or do.

tertiary aging Rapid losses occurring shortly before death.

time lag study A developmental research design examining same-aged people from different cohorts.

time-of-measurement effects One of the three fundamental effects examined in developmental research, along with age and cohort effects, which result from the time at which the data are collected.

universal versus context-specific development controversy A debate over whether there is a single pathway of development or several.

validity The degree to which an instrument measures what it is supposed to measure.

Resources

READINGS

Baltes, P. B. (1987). Theoretical propositions of life-span developmental psychology: On the dynamics between growth and decline. *Developmental Psychology, 23*, 611–626. One of the great classics, a discussion of basic concepts underlying a life-span perspective; medium difficulty.

Baltes, P. B., Lindenberger, U., & Staudinger, U. M. (1998). Life-span theory in developmental psychology. In R. M. Lerner (Ed.), *Handbook of child psychology: Vol. 1. Theoretical models of human development* (5th ed., Editor-in-Chief: W. Damon, pp. 1029–1143). New York: Wiley. The definitive discussion of the life-span perspective and its influence on understanding adult development and aging; medium to difficult.

Berg, B. L. (1998). *Qualitative research methods for the social sciences* (3rd ed.). Boston: Allyn & Bacon. A more detailed discussion of observational, case study, and other nonexperimental research methods; easy to moderate difficulty.

Binstock, R. H. (1999). Public policy issues. In J. C. Cavanaugh & S. K. Whitbourne (Eds.), *Gerontology: An interdisciplinary perspective* (pp. 414–447). New York: Oxford University Press. An excellent discussion of the implications of populations changes in the United States; easy to moderate difficulty.

Cavanaugh, J. C., & Whitbourne, S. K. (1999). Research methods. In J. C. Cavanaugh & S. K. Whitbourne (Eds.), *Gerontology: An interdisciplinary perspective* (pp. 33–64). New York: Oxford University Press. A more detailed discussion of general research issues; moderate difficulty.

Sokolovsky, J. (Ed.). (1997). *The cultural context of aging.* New York: Bergin & Garvey. A general treatment of many aspects of aging in a cross-cultural perspective; easy to moderate difficulty.

WEB SITES

Statistical information about older adults on a variety of topics is collected annually by the U.S. government. In addition, several reports are available on such things as demographic projections and health. One good source is the Administration on Aging, which can be found at http://www.aoa.dhhs.gov.

AARP is the largest group of people dedicated to shaping and enriching the experience of aging for all. The organization produces numerous reports and engages in much advocacy work on behalf of midlife and older adults. The AARP home page can be found at http://www.aarp.org.

One of the best sites on the Web for starting a search for information about any aspect of aging is the Division of Adult Development and Aging (Division 20) of the American Psychological Association. The division maintains links to many other aging-related sites. The division home page can be found at http://aging.ufl.edu/adadivzo/apadivzo.htm

The Gerontological Society of America is an interdisciplinary professional organization that reflects all aspects of aging. The society publishes reports on various topics and sponsors an annual meeting. The society also has a policy institute. The society's home page can be found at http://www.geron.org.

SEARCH ONLINE WITH
INFOTRAC COLLEGE EDITION

For more information on the topics in this chapter, explore InfoTrac College Edition, your online library. Go to http://www.infotrac-college.com/wadsworth and use the passcode that came on the card with your book. Try these search terms: demographics, life-span development, research design.

PHYSICAL CHANGES

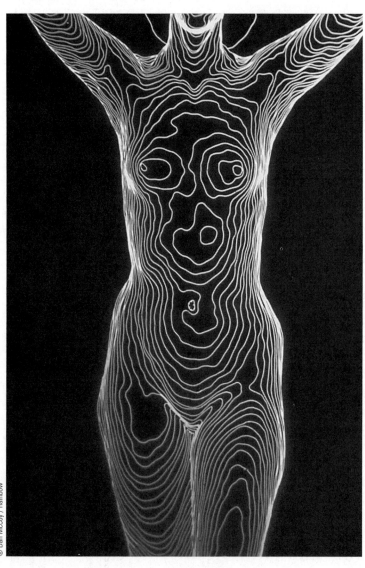

© Jeff Christensen / Gamma-Liaison

April 13, 1997, was a magical day. Millions of people watched as Tiger Woods rewrote the record book at the Masters golf tournament in Augusta, Georgia. At age 21, Woods was the youngest person ever to win the tournament, and he did it with the lowest score (270) and largest margin of victory (12 strokes) ever. He has gone on to become a consistently top-rated golfer, winning numerous tournaments, including the Grand Slam.

What's ahead for Tiger Woods? Although we can't predict how many and which tournaments he will win over the coming years, we can predict that eventually his abilities will begin to wane. By the time he's in his late 40s, it is likely that he will be less of a force on the PGA Tour. Indeed, the record for the oldest player to win the Masters was set by Jack Nicklaus, perhaps the greatest golfer of all time, who won at age 46. Recognizing that older players generally cannot compete with younger players, the PGA created the Senior Tour for professional golfers over age 50.

In this chapter, we will discover how physical abilities change across adulthood. We will focus on normative changes, ones that happen to each of us, including Tiger Woods. What makes Woods (and other professional athletes) different is that because they stay in great physical condition, the normative changes tend to happen more slowly.

Why Do We Age? Biological Theories of Aging

LEARNING OBJECTIVES

- How do rate-of-living theories explain aging?
- What are the major hypotheses in cellular theories of aging?
- How do programmed cell death theories propose that we age?
- How do the basic developmental forces interact in biological and physiological aging?

*N*olan Ryan was one of the greatest pitchers in the history of major league baseball, striking out more batters than any other pitcher. But of all his records, perhaps the most amazing aspect of his career was that he was still playing in his 40s, well past the age at which most other professional baseball players retire. Eventually, though, time caught up with him and he retired. Were it not for aging, who knows how long Nolan could have played? Why does everyone, including great baseball pitchers, grow old and eventually die?

Why are some athletes forced to retire early in their careers whereas others, such as Nolan Ryan, keep going far longer? For that matter, why do we age at all? After all, some creatures, such as lobsters, do not age as humans do. Scientists and philosophers have pondered the question of why people grow old and die for millennia. Their answers spurred researchers to create a collection of theories based on basic biological and physiological processes. The search has included many hypotheses, such as metabolic rates and brain sizes, that haven't proved accurate. But as scientists continue unlocking the keys to our genetic code, hope is rising that we may eventually have an answer. To date, though, no existing theory does a complete job at explaining all the normative changes we experience (Cavanaugh, 1999c; Cristofalo et al., 1999).

Before we explore some of the partial explanations from scientific research, complete the Discovering Development exercise. Compare the results of this exercise with some of the theories described next. What similarities and differences did you uncover?

Rate-of-Living Theories

One intriguing theory of aging postulates that people have only so much energy to expend in a lifetime. If we examine the metabolic rate of various animals and look for correlations with their life spans, we find some support for this idea. For example, insects' life spans can be increased by not allowing them to fly, and some mammals live longer when they are induced to hibernate (Cristofalo et al., 1999).

Some researchers extended this idea and wondered whether the number of calories one eats has an influence on aging. Evidence from experiments with rodents and rhesus monkeys suggests that reducing caloric intake lowers the risk of premature death, slows down a wide range of normative age-related changes, and in some cases results in longer life spans than do normal diets (Hayflick, 1996; Roth et al., 1995). Although controlled experimental evidence with humans is lacking, there are some suggestive cross-cultural findings. For example, Okinawans, who eat only 60% of the normal Japanese diet, have 40 times as many centenarians (people who are at least 100 years old) per capita as there are in the rest of Japan. Moreover, the Okinawan incidence of cardiovascular disease, diabetes, and cancer is half that in the rest of Japan (Monczunski, 1991).

A third variation of rate-of-living theories involves the hormonal regulatory system's adaptation to stress (Finch & Seeman, 1999). Although stress per se does not cause aging, the body's ability to deal with it undergoes significant decline with age. These changes have been shown to be related to several diseases common in later life, including atherosclerosis, hypertension, diabetes, osteoporosis, and cognitive deficits.

Cellular Theories

A second family of ideas points to causes of aging at the cellular level. One notion focuses on the number of times cells can divide, which presumably places limits on the life span of a complex organism. Cells grown in laboratory culture dishes undergo only a fixed number of divisions before dying, with the

What does the average person believe about how and why we age physiologically? To find out, list the various organ and body systems discussed in this chapter. Ask some people you know of different ages two sets of questions. First, ask them what they think happens to each system as people grow older. Then ask them what they think causes these changes. Compile the results from your interviews and compare them with what you discover in this chapter. To what extent were your interviewees correct in their descriptions? Where were they off base? Does any of the misinformation match up with the stereotypes of aging we considered in Chapter 1? Why do you think this might be the case? How accurate are people? Discover for yourself.

number of possible divisions dropping depending on the age of the donor organism; this phenomenon is called the Hayflick limit, after its discoverer, Leonard Hayflick (Hayflick, 1996). For example, cells from human fetal tissue are capable of 40 to 60 divisions; cells from a human adult are capable of only about 20. What causes cells to limit their number of divisions? *Evidence suggests that the tips of the chromosomes, called* **telomeres,** *play a major role* (Cristofalo et al., 1999; Mera, 1998). An enzyme called *telomerase* is needed in DNA replication to fully replicate the telomeres. But telomerase normally is not present in cells, so with each replication the telomeres become shorter. Eventually, the chromosomes become unstable and cannot replicate because the telomeres become too short (Hayflick, 1998). Some researchers believe that cancer cells proliferate so quickly in some cases because they can activate telomerase, meaning that the cancer cells may become functionally immortal and take over the organ system (Mera, 1998).

A second cellular theory is based on a process called **cross-linking,** *in which certain proteins in human cells interact randomly and produce molecules that are linked in such a way as to make the body stiffer* (Cavanaugh, 1999c). The proteins in question, which make up roughly one third of the protein in the body, are called collagen. Collagen in soft body tissue acts much like reinforcing rods in concrete. The more cross-links there are, the stiffer the tissue. For example, leather tanning involves using chemicals that create many cross-links to make the leather stiff enough for use in shoes and other products. As we age, the number of cross-links increases. This process may explain why muscles, such as the heart, and arteries become stiffer with age. However, few scientific data demonstrate that cross-linking impedes metabolic processes or causes the formation of faulty molecules that would constitute a fundamental cause of aging (Hayflick, 1998). Thus, even though cross-linking occurs, it probably is not an adequate explanation of aging.

A third type of cellular theory proposes that aging is caused by unstable molecules called **free radicals,** *which are highly reactive chemicals produced randomly in normal metabolism* (Cristofalo et al., 1999). When these free radicals interact with nearby molecules, problems may result. For example, free radicals may cause cellular damage, which in turn impairs the functioning of the organ, or may block the effects of important molecules. The most important evidence that free radicals may be involved in aging comes from research with substances that prevent the initial development of free radicals. These substances, called antioxidants, prevent oxygen from combining with susceptible molecules to form free radicals. Common antioxidants include vitamins A, C, and E and coenzyme Q. A growing body of evidence shows that ingesting antioxidants postpones the appearance of age-related diseases such as cancer, cardiovascular disease, and immune system dysfunction (Hayflick, 1996), but there is no evidence that taking antioxidants actually increases the life span (Cristofalo et al., 1999).

Programmed Cell Death Theories

What if aging were programmed into our genetic code? This possibility seems more likely as the explosion of knowledge about human genetics continues to unlock the secrets of our genetic code. Even when cell death appears random, researchers now believe that such losses may be part of a master genetic program (Bergeman, 1997; Cristofalo et al., 1999; Hayflick, 1998). Programmed cell death appears to be a function of physiological processes, the innate ability of cells to self-destruct, and the ability of dying cells to trigger key processes in other cells. At present, we do not know how this self-destruct program is activated, nor do we understand how it works. However, understanding programmed cell death may be the key to understanding how genes and physiological processes interact with psychological and sociocultural forces to produce aging (Bergeman, 1997).

It is possible that the other explanations we have considered in this section and the changes we examine throughout this text are the result of a genetic program. For example, there is evidence that osteoarthritis (Charles, 1998), changes in brain cells (Martin, 1998), Alzheimer's disease (Woodruff-Pak & Papka, 1999), certain types of memory (Johansson et al., 1999), and personality (Bouchard, 1997) have key genetic underpinnings. As genetics research continues, it is likely that we will have some exciting answers to the question Why do we age?

Implications of the Developmental Forces

Although we do not yet have one unified theory of biological and physiological aging, the picture is becoming clearer. We know that there clearly are genetic components, that the body's chemistry lab produces incorrect products at times, and that there are errors in the operation and replication of DNA (Hayflick, 1998). From the perspective of the basic developmental forces, the biological theories provide ways to describe the biological forces. As we examine specific body systems in this chapter and health-related processes in Chapter 3, we will begin to integrate the biological forces with the psychological, sociocultural, and life-cycle forces. In those discussions, notice how changes in body systems and diseases are influenced by these other factors.

The implication of this dynamic, interactive process is that the diagnosis and treatment of health-related concerns must also include many perspectives. It is not enough to have one's physical functioning checked to establish whether one is healthy. Rather, one needs not only a typical bodily physical but also a checkup of psychological and sociocultural functioning. Finally, the results of all these examinations must be placed in the context of the overall life span. Although we do not yet have a unified theory of biological and physiological aging and are not likely to in the near future (Cavanaugh, 1999c; Cristofalo et al., 1999; Hayflick, 1998), such a theory would have to account for a wide array of changes relating not only to biological forces but to other forces as well. Perhaps then we'll discover why Nolan Ryan was still throwing strikes when most of his peers were watching him on television.

CONCEPT CHECKS

1. What is the basic premise of all rate-of-living theories?
2. What are the major types of cellular theories? What are their similarities and differences?
3. What mechanism is thought to underlie programmed cell death?
4. How might the four developmental forces interact in the context of biological and physiological aging?

APPEARANCE AND MOBILITY

LEARNING OBJECTIVES

- How do our skin, hair, and voices change with age?
- What happens to our body build with age?
- What age-related changes occur in our ability to move around?

By all accounts, Kristina is extremely successful. She was a famous model in her late teens and 20s, and she learned enough about the business to start her own multinational modeling agency by the time she was 36. Kristina was very upset when she looked in the mirror the other day and saw a patch of gray hair. "Oh no," she exclaimed, "I can't be going gray! What am I going to do?"

Kristina's experience isn't unique. We all see the outward signs of aging first in the mirror: gray hair, wrinkled skin, and an expanding waistline or hips. These changes occur gradually and at different rates; some of us experience all the changes in young adulthood, whereas others don't have them until late middle or old age. How we perceive the person staring back at us in the mirror says a great deal about how we feel about aging; positive feelings about the signs of aging are related to positive self-esteem.

How easily we move our changing bodies in the physical environment is also a major component of adaptation and well-being in adulthood. If we cannot get around, we must depend on others, which lowers our self-esteem and sense of competence. Having a body that moves effectively also allows us to enjoy physical activities such as walking, swimming, and skiing.

Changes in Skin, Hair, and Voice

When we, like Kristina, see the first visible signs of aging, it makes no difference that these changes are universal and inevitable. Nor does it matter that our wrinkles are caused by a combination of changes in the structure of the skin and its connective and supportive tissue and the cumulative effects of exposure to sunlight. Normal as the loss of hair pigmentation is, we may still want to hide the gray (Whitbourne, 1999). What matters on that day is that we have seen our first wrinkle and gray hair.

CHANGES IN THE SKIN. Why does our skin wrinkle? Wrinkling is actually a complex, four-step process (Gilchrest, 1995). First, the outer layer of skin becomes thinner through cell loss, causing the skin to become more fragile. Second, the collagen fibers that make up the connective tissue lose much of their flexibility, making the skin less able to regain its shape after a pinch. Third, elastin fibers in the middle layer of skin lose their ability to keep the skin stretched

© Cleo / PhotoEdit

The signs of physical aging are first noticed in the mirror: gray or thinning hair and wrinkles.

out, resulting in sagging. Finally, the underlying layer of fat, which helps provide padding to smooth out the contours, diminishes.

It may surprise you to know that how quickly your face ages is under your control to a large extent. A major cause of the underlying changes that result in wrinkles is exposure to ultraviolet rays from the sun (Takema et al., 1994; Yang et al., 1995). Using sunscreens and sunblocks properly and limiting your exposure to sunlight may slow the development of these problems. The message is clear: Young adults who are dedicated sun-worshippers eventually pay a high price for their tans.

A lifetime of sun and normative age-related processes makes older adults' skin thinner and drier, gives it a leathery texture, makes it less effective at regulating heat or cold, and makes it more susceptible to cuts, bruises, and blisters. To counteract these problems, people should use skin moisturizers, vitamin E, and facial massages (Ditre et al., 1996; Iida & Noro, 1995; Nachbar & Korting, 1995). The coloring of light-skinned people undergoes additional changes with age. The number of pigment-containing cells in the outer layer decreases, and those that remain have less pigment, resulting in lighter skin. In addition, age spots (areas of dark pigmentation that look like freckles) and moles (pigmented outgrowths) appear more often. Some of the blood vessels in the skin may become dilated and create small, irregular red lines. Varicose veins may appear as knotty, bluish irregularities in blood vessels, especially on the legs (Gilchrest, 1995; Whitbourne, 1999).

CHANGES IN THE HAIR. Gradual thinning and graying of the hair of both men and women occur inevitably with age, although there are large individual differences in the rate of these changes. Hair loss is caused by destruction of the germ centers that produce the hair follicles, whereas graying results from a cessation of pigment production. Men usually do not lose facial hair as they age; you probably have seen many balding men with thick, bushy beards. Additionally, men often develop bushy eyebrows and hair growth inside the ears. In contrast, women often develop patches of hair on the face, especially on the chin (Whitbourne, 1999). This hair growth is related to the hormonal changes of the climacteric, discussed later in this chapter.

CHANGES IN THE VOICE. The next time you're in a crowd of people of different ages, close your eyes and listen to the way they sound. You probably will be fairly accurate in guessing how old the speakers are just from the quality of the voices you hear. Younger adults' voices tend to be full and resonant, whereas older adults' voices tend to be thinner or weaker. Age-related changes in one's voice include lowering of pitch, increased breathlessness and trembling, slower and less precise pronunciation, and decreased volume. Some researchers report that changes in the larynx (voice box), the respiratory system, and the muscles controlling speech cause these changes. However, other researchers contend that these changes result from poor health and are not part of normal aging. The question of whether changes in the voice are mostly normative or mainly the product of disease remains unresolved (Whitbourne, 1996a).

Changes in Body Build

If you have been around the same older people, such as your grandparents, for many years, you undoubtedly have noticed that the way their bodies look changed over time. Two changes are especially visible: a decrease in height and fluctuations in weight. Height remains fairly stable until the 50s, but between the mid-50s and mid-70s men lose about 1 inch and women lose about 2 inches (de Groot et al., 1996). This height loss usually is caused by compression of the spine from loss of bone strength, changes in the discs between the vertebrae in the spine, and changes in posture (Gerhart, 1995). We consider some specific aspects of changes in bone structure a bit later.

Weight gain in middle age followed by weight loss in later life is common. Typically, people gain weight between their 20s and their mid-50s but lose weight throughout old age. In part, the weight gain is caused by changes in body metabolism, which tends to slow down, and reduced levels of exercise, which in turn reduces the number of calories needed daily. Unfortunately, many people do not adjust their food intake to match these changes. The result is often tighter-fitting clothes. For men, this weight gain tends to be around the abdomen, creating middle-aged bulge. For women, this weight gain tends to be around the hips, giving women the familiar "pear-shaped" figure. By late life, though, the body loses both muscle and bone, which weigh more than fat, in addition to some fat, resulting in weight loss (Baumgartner et al., 1995). However, more recent cohorts of older women are showing less body fat (Rico et al., 1993), compared with more recent cohorts of older men, who are showing more (Grinker et al., 1995). These differences may be caused by changes in lifestyle and dietary habits.

Changes in Mobility

Being able to get around on one's own is an important part of remaining independent. As we will see, we all experience some normative changes that can affect our ability to remain mobile, but most of these changes do not inevitably result in serious limitations.

MUSCLES. Although the amount of muscle tissue in our bodies declines with age, this loss is hardly noticeable in terms of strength and endurance; even at age 70 the loss is no more than 20%. After that, however, the rate of change increases. By age 80 the loss in strength is up to 40%, and it appears to be more severe in the legs than in the arms and hands. However, some people retain their strength well into old age (Booth et al., 1994; Skelton et al., 1994). In one study, 15% of people over age 60 showed no loss of grip strength over a 9-year period (Kallman et al., 1990). Research evidence suggests that muscle endurance also diminishes with age but at a slower rate. Men and women show no differences in the rate of muscle change (Spirduso & MacRae, 1990).

BONES. You have probably seen commercials and advertisements aimed mostly at women for products that help maintain bone mass. If you surmise that such products reflect a serious and real health concern, you are correct. Normal aging is accompanied by the loss of bone tissue throughout the body. Bone loss begins in the late 30s, accelerates in the 50s (particularly in women), and slows by the 70s (Currey et al., 1996). The gender difference in bone loss is important. Once the process begins, women lose bone mass approximately twice as fast as men. The difference results from two factors. First, women have less bone mass than men in young adulthood, meaning that they start out with less ability to withstand bone loss before it causes problems. Second, the depletion of estrogen after menopause speeds up bone loss.

What happens to aging bones? The process involves a loss of bone mass inside the bone, which makes bones more hollow. In addition, bones tend to become porous. The changes result from body weight, genetics, and lifestyle factors such as smoking, alcohol use, and diet (Whitbourne, 1999). All these bone changes cause an age-related increase in the likelihood of fractures because hollow, porous bones are easier to break. Furthermore, broken bones in older people present more serious problems than in younger adults because they are more likely to be clean fractures that

are difficult to heal. Bones of younger adults fracture in such a way that there are many cracks and splinters to aid in healing. This is analogous to the difference in breaking a young, green tree branch (which is harder to do) and an old, dry twig.

Women are especially susceptible to severe bone degeneration, a disease called **osteoporosis,** *in which the loss of bone mass and increased porosity create bones that resemble laced honeycombs.* You can see the result in Figure 2.1. Eventually, people with osteoporosis tend to develop a distinct curvature in their spines, as shown in Figure 2.2.

Osteoporosis is the leading cause of broken bones in older women (Ebersole & Hess, 1998). The disease appears more often in fair-skinned, European American, thin, and small-framed women than in other groups; for example, rates are substantially lower among African American women. Evidence from bone scans suggests that at least 65% of all women over age 60 and almost all women over age 90 are affected; in all, more than 20 million women in the United States have osteoporosis, with millions more at risk. Osteoporosis is caused in part by low bone mass at skeletal maturity, deficiencies of calcium and vitamin D, estrogen depletion, and lack of weight-bearing exercise. Other risk factors include smoking, high-protein diets, and excessive alcohol, caffeine, and sodium intake.

The relationship between dietary calcium intake and osteoporosis is controversial (Aldwin & Gilmer, 1999). There is some evidence that calcium supplements after menopause may slow the rate of bone loss and delay the onset of osteoporosis, but benefits appear to be greater when the supplements are provided before menopause (Plosker & McTavish, 1996). The reasons why estrogen depletion affects bone loss are not fully understood, mainly because the effects must be indirect because there are no estrogen receptors in bone tissue. Although estrogen replacement therapy may slow bone loss, this approach must be used cautiously because of potential side effects (Kawas et al., 1997). (We explore hormone replacement therapy in detail later when we consider reproductive changes in women.) Additionally, estrogen therapy must be continued indefinitely because bone loss speeds up as soon as the therapy is stopped.

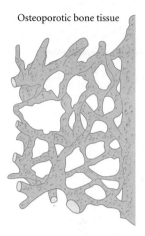
Osteoporotic bone tissue

Normal bone tissue

FIGURE 2.1 **Osteoporotic and normal bone structures. Notice how much mass the osteoporotic bone has lost.**

Data showing that vitamin D metabolism plays a causative role in osteoporosis are clear; however, whether supplementary dietary vitamin D retards bone loss is less certain. Some research shows that vitamin D administered after menopause slows bone loss, whereas other research does not (Dawson Hughes, 1996). However, the U.S. Food and Drug Administration endorses vitamin D supplements as a therapy for osteoporosis on the grounds that side effects are minimal and that there are some supportive data. Some evidence also supports the view that oral ingestion of magnesium, zinc, vitamin K, and special forms of fluoride may also be effective.

You may have heard some of the claims about using human growth hormone to treat various problems related to changes in the muscles and bones. Some researchers have found positive effects of human growth hormone in studies of normal aging (Welle et al., 1996). But most studies have failed to support the advertised benefits (Taaffe, et al., 1996) and some have found harmful side effects such as increased risk of breast cancer (Dorgan et al., 1997).

JOINTS. Many older adults complain of aching joints. They have good reason. Beginning in the 20s, the protective cartilage in joints shows signs of deteriora-

tion, such as thinning and becoming cracked and frayed. *Over time the bones underneath the cartilage become damaged, which can result in* **osteoarthritis,** *a disease marked by gradual onset and progression of pain and disability, with minor signs of inflammation* (Ettinger, 1995). The disease usually becomes noticeable in late middle age or early old age, and it is especially common in people whose joints are subjected to routine overuse and abuse, such as athletes and manual laborers. Thus, osteoarthritis is a wear-and-tear disease. Pain typically is worse when the joint is used, but skin redness, heat, and swelling are minimal or absent. Osteoarthritis usually affects the hands, spine, hips, and knees, sparing the wrists, elbows, shoulders, and ankles. Effective management approaches consist mainly of certain steroids and anti-inflammatory drugs, rest and nonstressful exercises that focus on range of motion, diet, and a variety of homeopathic remedies.

A second and more common form of arthritis is **rheumatoid arthritis,** *a more destructive disease of the joints that also develops slowly and typically affects different joints and causes different types of pain than osteoarthritis* (Ettinger, 1995). Most often, a pattern of morning stiffness and aching develops in the fingers, wrists, and ankles on both sides of the body. Joints

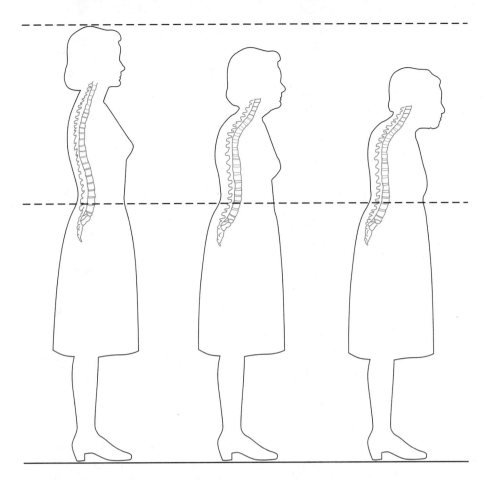

FIGURE 2.2 Changes in the curvature of the spine as a result of osteoporosis. These changes create the stooping posture common among older people with advanced osteoporosis.

Source: Ebersole, P., & Hess, P. (1998). *Toward healthy aging* (5th ed., p. 395). St. Louis: Mosby.

appear swollen. The typical therapy for rheumatoid arthritis consists of aspirin or other nonsteroidal anti-inflammatory drugs. Newer chemical therapies (such as methotrexate) and experimental drugs (such as cyclosporine) are showing promising results. Rest and passive range-of-motion exercises are also helpful. Contrary to popular belief, rheumatoid arthritis is not contagious, hereditary, or self-induced by any known diet, habit, job, or exposure. Interestingly, the symptoms often come and go in repeating patterns.

Psychological Implications

The appearance of wrinkles, gray hair, fat, and the like can have major effects on a person's self-concept (Whitbourne, 1999). Middle-aged adults may still think of themselves as young and may not appreciate being called old. Because U.S. society places high value on looking young, middle-aged and older adults, especially women, may be regarded as inferior on a number of dimensions, including intellectual ability. In contrast, middle-aged men with some gray hair often are considered distinguished, more experienced, and more knowledgeable than their younger counterparts.

Given the social stereotypes we examined in Chapter 1, many women (and increasingly, some men) use any available means to compensate for these changes. Some age-related changes in facial appearance can be disguised with cosmetics. Hair dyes can restore color. Surgical procedures such as facelifts can tighten sagging and wrinkled skin. But even plastic surgery only delays the inevitable; at some point everyone takes on a distinctly old appearance.

Losses in strength and endurance in old age have much the same psychological effects as changes in appearance (Whitbourne, 1999). In particular, these changes tell the person that he or she is not as capable of adapting effectively to the environment. Loss of muscle coordination (which may lead to walking more slowly, for example) may not be inevitable, but it can prove embarrassing and stressful. Exercise and resistance training can improve muscle strength, even up to age 90 (Fiatarone et al., 1990; Morganti et al., 1995; Shephard, 1997; Sinaki, 1996). Interestingly, the rate of improvement does not seem to differ with age; older adults get stronger at the same rate as younger adults.

The changes in the joints, especially in arthritis, have profound psychological effects (Whitbourne, 1999). These changes can severely limit movement, thereby reducing independence and the ability to complete normal daily routines. Moreover, joint pain is very difficult to ignore or disguise, unlike changes in appearance. Consequently, the person who can use cosmetics to hide changes in appearance cannot use the same approach to deal with constant pain in the joints. Older adults use a wide range of adaptive behaviors to cope (Gignac et al., 2000). For example, participation in an exercise program appears to have some benefit. Older adults who suffer bone fractures face several other consequences in addition to discomfort. For example, a hip fracture may force hospitalization or even a stay in a nursing home. For all fractures, the recovery period is much longer than that for a younger adult. Additionally, older people who witness friends or relatives struggling during rehabilitation may reduce their own activities as a precaution.

CONCEPT CHECKS

1. What changes occur with age in skin, hair, and voice?
2. What changes occur with age in muscles, bones, and joints?
3. What are the major psychological consequences of changes in appearance and mobility?

SENSORY SYSTEMS

LEARNING OBJECTIVES

- What age-related changes happen in vision?
- How does hearing change as people age?
- What age-related changes occur in people's senses of touch and balance?
- What happens to taste and smell with increasing age?

*B*ertha has attended Sunday services in her local AME church for 82 years. Over the past few years, though, she has experienced greater difficulty in keeping her balance as she walks down the steps from her row house to the sidewalk. Bertha is noticing that her balance problems occur even when she is walking on level ground. Because Bertha is afraid of falling and breaking a bone, she is concerned that she will have to stop attending her beloved church.

You have probably seen people like Bertha walking slowly and tentatively along the sidewalk. Why do people have these problems? If you think it is because the sensory system directly related to maintaining balance, the vestibular system, declines with age, you would only be partly correct. It turns out that keeping one's balance is a complex process in which we integrate input from several sources, such as vision and touch, as well as muscles, bones, and joints. In this section we discover the changes that occur in our sensory systems. These changes challenge our ability to interact with the world and communicate with others.

Vision

Have you ever watched middle-aged people try to read something that is right in front of them? If they do not already wear glasses or contact lenses, they typically move the material farther away so that they can see it clearly. This change in vision is one of the first noticeable signs of aging, along with the wrinkles and gray hair we considered earlier. Because we rely extensively on sight in almost every aspect of our waking life, its normative, age-related changes have profound and pervasive effects on people's everyday lives (Whitbourne, 1999).

How does eyesight change with age? The major changes are best understood by grouping them into two classes: changes in the structures of the eye, which begin in the 40s, and changes in the retina, which begin in the 50s (Kline & Schieber, 1985).

STRUCTURAL CHANGES IN THE EYE. Two major kinds of age-related structural changes occur in the eye. One is a decrease in the amount of light that passes through the eye, resulting in the need for more light to do tasks such as reading. As you might suspect, this change is one reason why older adults do not see as well in the dark, which may account in part for their reluctance to go places at night. One possible logical response to the need for more light would be to increase illumination levels in general. However, this solution does not work in all situations because we also become increasingly sensitive to glare (Whitbourne, 1999). Additionally, our ability to adjust to changes in illumination, called adaptation, declines. Going from outside into a darkened movie theater involves dark adaptation; going back outside involves light adaptation. Research indicates that the time it takes for both types of adaptation increases with age (Kline & Schieber, 1985). These changes are especially important for older drivers, who have more difficulty seeing after being confronted with the headlights of an oncoming car.

The other key structural changes involve the lens. As we grow older, the lens becomes more yellow, causing poorer color discrimination in the green–blue–violet end of the spectrum (Mancil & Owsley, 1988). Also, the lens's ability to adjust and focus declines as the muscles around it stiffen (Kupfer, 1995). *This is what causes difficulty in seeing close objects clearly (called* **presbyopia***), necessitating either longer arms or corrective lenses.* To complicate matters further, the time our eyes need to change focus from near to far (or vice versa) increases (Whitbourne,

1996a). This also poses a major problem in driving. Because drivers are constantly changing their focus from the instrument panel to other autos and signs on the highway, older drivers may miss important information because of their slower refocusing time (Panek & Rearden, 1986).

Besides these normative structural changes, some people experience diseases caused by abnormal structural changes. First, opaque spots called cataracts may develop on the lens, which limits the amount of light transmitted. Cataracts often are treated by surgical removal and use of corrective lenses. Second, the fluid in the eye may not drain properly, causing very high pressure; this condition, called glaucoma, can cause internal damage and loss of vision. Glaucoma is a fairly common disease in middle and late adulthood and is usually treated with eye drops.

RETINAL CHANGES. The second major family of changes in vision result from changes in the retina. The retina lines approximately two thirds of the interior of the eye. The specialized receptor cells in vision, the rods and the cones, are contained in the retina. They are most densely packed toward the rear and especially at the focal point of vision, a region called the macula. At the center of the macula is the fovea, where incoming light is focused for maximum acuity, as when one is reading. With increasing age the probability of degeneration of the macula increases (Kupfer, 1995). Macular degeneration involves the progressive and irreversible destruction of receptors from any of a number of causes. This disease results in the loss of the ability to see details; for example, reading is extremely difficult, and television often is reduced to a blur. Roughly 1 in 5 people over age 75, especially smokers and European American women, have macular degeneration, making it the leading cause of functional blindness in older adults.

A second age-related retinal disease is a byproduct of diabetes. Diabetes is accompanied by accelerated aging of the arteries, with blindness being one of the more serious side effects. Diabetic retinopathy, as this condition is called, can involve fluid retention in the macula, detachment of the retina, hemorrhage, and aneurysms (Kupfer, 1995). Because it takes many years to develop, diabetic retinopathy is more common among people who developed diabetes early in life.

The combined effects of the structural changes in the eye create two other types of changes. First, the ability to see detail and to discriminate different visual patterns, called acuity, declines steadily between ages 20 and 60, with a more rapid decline thereafter. Loss of acuity is especially noticeable at low light levels (Kline, 1994).

PSYCHOLOGICAL EFFECTS OF VISUAL CHANGES. Clearly, age-related changes in vision affect every aspect of older adults' daily lives. Research indicates that there can be as much as a sixfold decline in visual ability in everyday situations, depending on the skill needed (Kosnik et al., 1988; Schneider, 1996). Imagine the problems people experience performing tasks that most young adults take for granted, such as reading a book, watching television, reading grocery labels, or driving a car. Fortunately, some of the universal changes, such as presbyopia, can be corrected easily through glasses or contacts. Surgery to correct cataracts is now routine. The diseased lens is removed and an artificial one is inserted in an outpatient procedure that usually lasts about 30 minutes, with little discomfort. Patients usually resume their normal activities in less than a week and report much improved daily lives.

If you want to provide environmental support for older adults, taking their vision changes into account, you need to think through your intervention strategies carefully. For example, simply making the environment brighter may not be the answer. For increased illumination to be beneficial, surrounding surfaces must not increase glare. Using flat latex paint rather than glossy enamel and avoiding highly polished floors are two ways to make environments "older adult–friendly." There should be high contrast between the background and operational information on dials and controls, such as on stoves and radios. Older adults may also have trouble seeing some fine facial details. As Whitbourne (1996a) notes, some people may react to these changes by simply avoiding the kitchen or listening to their favorite music, or avoid social contact out of fear that they may not recognize a face.

Among people who have experienced substantial vision loss, it appears that conscientiousness predicts how they handle their vision loss. People high in conscientiousness perceive vision loss as a challenge to be overcome. As a result, they are more willing to invest the time and energy necessary to complete tasks and to learn alternative strategies (Casten et al., 1999). Visual problems also increase vulnerability to falls because the person may be unable to see hazards in his or her path or to judge distance very well. Thus, part of Bertha's concern about falling may be caused by changes in her ability to tell where the next step is or to see hazards along the sidewalk.

Hearing

Experiencing hearing loss is one of the most well-known normative changes with age (Whitbourne, 1999). A visit to any housing complex for older adults will easily verify this point; you will quickly notice that television sets and radios are turned up fairly loud in most of the apartments. Yet you don't have to be old to experience significant hearing problems. When it became difficult to hear what was being said to him, President Bill Clinton obtained two hearing aids. He was 51 years old at the time, and he attributed his hearing loss to too many high school bands and rock concerts when he was young. His situation is far from unique. Loud noise is the enemy of hearing at any age. You probably have seen people who work in noisy environments wearing protective gear on their ears so that they are not exposed to loud noise over extended periods of time.

But you can do serious damage to your hearing with short exposure too; in 1988, San Francisco punk rock bassist Kathy Peck was performing at the Oakland Coliseum and played so loud that she had ringing in her ears for 3 days and suffered permanent hearing loss. As a result, she founded Hearing Education and Awareness for Rockers (HEAR) shortly thereafter to educate musicians about the need to protect their ears (Soulsman, 1999). HEAR has picked up momentum ever since; in 1998 they distributed 60,000 pairs of free ear plugs to musicians and fans of the Lollapalooza Tour. You don't need to be at a concert to damage your hearing, either. Using headphones, especially at high volume, can cause the same serious damage and should be avoided. It is especially easy to cause hearing loss with headphones if you wear them while exercising; the increased blood flow to the ear during exercise makes hearing receptors more vulnerable to damage.

The cumulative effects of noise and normative age-related changes create the most common age-related hearing problem: reduced sensitivity to high-pitched tones, called **presbycusis,** *which occurs earlier and more severely than the loss of sensitivity to low-pitched tones* (Gulya, 1995). Research indicates that by the late 70s, roughly half of older adults have presbycusis. Men typically have greater loss than women, but this may be because of differential exposure to noisy environments. Hearing loss usually is gradual at first but accelerates during the 40s, a pattern seen clearly in Figure 2.3.

Presbycusis results from four types of changes in the inner ear (Gulya, 1995): sensory, consisting of atrophy and degeneration of receptor cells; neural, consisting of a loss of neurons in the auditory pathway in the brain; metabolic, consisting of a diminished supply of nutrients to the cells in the receptor area; and mechanical, consisting of atrophy and stiffening of the vibrating structures in the receptor area. Knowing the cause of a person's presbycusis is important because the different causes have different implications for other aspects of hearing (Whitbourne, 1996a). Sensory presbycusis has little effect on other hearing abilities. Neural presbycusis seriously affects the ability to understand speech. Metabolic presbycusis produces severe loss of sensitivity to all pitches. Finally, mechanical presbycusis also produces loss across all pitches, but the loss is greatest for high pitches.

Because hearing plays a major role in social communication, its progressive loss could have an equally important effect on social adjustment. Loss of hearing in later life can cause numerous adverse emotional reactions, such as loss of independence, social isolation, irritation, paranoia, and depression. Much research indicates hearing loss per se does not cause social maladjustment or emotional disturbance.

However, friends and relatives of an older person with hearing loss often attribute emotional changes to hearing loss, which strains the quality of interpersonal relationships (Whitbourne, 1996a). Thus, hearing loss may not directly affect older adults' self-concept or emotions, but it may negatively affect how they feel about interpersonal communication. By understanding hearing loss problems and ways to overcome them, those without hearing loss can play a large part in minimizing the effects of hearing loss on the older people in their lives.

Fortunately, many people with hearing loss can be helped through two types of amplification systems and cochlear implants, described in Table 2.1. Analog hearing aids are the most common and least expensive, but they provide the lowest-quality sound. Digital hearing aids include microchips that can be programmed for different hearing situations. Cochlear implants do not amplify sound; rather, a microphone transmits sound to a receiver, which stimulates auditory nerve fibers directly. Although technology continues to improve, none of these devices can duplicate our original equipment, so be kind to your ears.

Somesthesia and Balance

Imagine that you are with your lover right now. Think about how good it feels when you are caressed lovingly, the tingly sensations you may get. Thank your somesthetic system for that. Remember Bertha, the older woman worried about falling? Avoiding falls entails integrating much information about our body position to maintain balance.

SOMESTHESIA. As you've probably discovered, your lover's touch feels different on various parts of your body. That's because the distribution of touch receptors is not consistent throughout the body; the greatest concentrations are in the lips, tongue, and fingertips. Although it takes more pressure with age to feel a touch on the smooth (nonhairy) skin on the hand such as the fingertips (Stevens, 1992), touch sensitivity in the hair-covered parts of the body is maintained into later life (Whitbourne, 1996a).

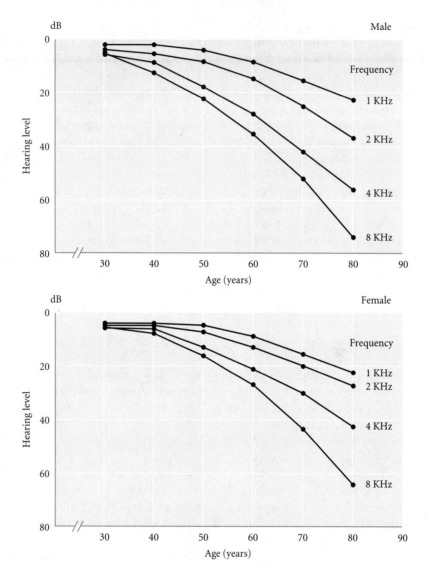

FIGURE 2.3 **Gender differences in hearing loss. Notice that the changes in men are greater.**

Source: Ordy, J. M., Brizzee, K. R., Beavers, T., & Medart, P. (1979). Age differences in the functional and structural organization of the auditory system in man. In J. M. Ordy & K. R. Brizzee (Eds.), *Sensory systems and communication in the elderly.* Copyright © Lippincott, Williams & Wilkins, 1979.

Older adults often report that they have more trouble regulating body temperature so that they feel comfortable. However, the research evidence to support this perception is conflicting. Some data suggest that the threshold for warmth increases somewhat (Whitbourne, 1996a). These data appear to conflict with lowered cold tolerance by older adults, which should create a much larger change in threshold.

TABLE 2.1	Helping People with Hearing Loss
Type of Device	**How It Works**
Analog hearing aid	Although there are various styles, the basic design is always the same. A mold is placed in the outer ear to pick up sound and send it through tubes to a microphone. The microphone sends the sound to an amplifier. The amplifier enhances the sound and sends it to the receiver. The receiver sends the amplified sound to the ear.
Digital hearing aid	These are similar to analog hearing aids, but digital aids use directional microphones to control the flow of sound. Compression technology allows the sound to be increased or decreased as it rises and falls naturally in the room. Microchips allow hearing aids to be programmed for different hearing situations. This technology also uses multiple channels to deliver sound with varying amplification characteristics.
Cochlear implant	The main difference between hearing aids and cochlear implants is that implants do not make the sound louder. Rather, the implant is a series of components. A microphone, usually mounted behind the ear on the scalp, picks up sound. The sound is digitized by microchips and turned into coded signals, which are broadcast via FM radio signals to electrodes that have been inserted into the inner ear during surgery. The electrodes stimulate the auditory nerve fibers directly.

However, the discrepancy may be caused by different age effects between temperature sensitivity and temperature regulation, but we do not know for certain (Whitbourne, 1996a).

Although there are many studies of age-related differences in sensitivity to pain, we still do not have a clear picture of how it changes in adulthood (Harkins & Kwentus, 1990; Portenoy, 1995). A major problem confronting researchers interested in pain threshold and pain tolerance (the highest level of pain that can be withstood) is that pain sensitivity varies across different locations on the body and with different types of stimulation. Moreover, experiencing pain is more than just a sensory experience; it involves cognitive, motivational, personality, and cultural factors as well. Although older adults complain more about pain, the research evidence is conflicting. Data showing everything from decreased sensitivity to increased sensitivity can be found (Harkins & Kwentus, 1990; Portenoy, 1995; Whitbourne, 1996a).

How is your body situated right now? Knowing this at any particular moment means that we have experienced our sense of body position, or kinesthesis. Kinesthesis involves sensory feedback about two

kinds of movements: passive movements and active movements. Passive movements are instigated by something (or someone) else, as when someone picks up your hand. Active movement is voluntary, as in walking.

Age-related changes in passive movements depend on the part of the body in question. For example, differences are not observed for passive movement of the big toe but are found for several joints, including the knees and the hips. However, age differences in active movements are not found. For example, judgments of muscle or tendon strain produced by picking up different weights do not differ with age (Ebersole & Hess, 1998).

Sensations from the skin, internal organs, and joints serve critical functions. They keep us in contact with our environment, help us avoid falling, help us communicate, and keep us safe. In terms of self-esteem, how well our body is functioning tells us something about how well we are doing. Losing bodily sensations can have major implications; loss of sexual sensitivity and changes in the ability to regulate one's body temperature affect the quality of life. How a person views these changes is critical for maintaining self-esteem. We can help by providing supportive environments that lead to successful compensatory behaviors.

BALANCE. Bertha, the older woman we met in the vignette, is concerned about losing her balance and falling. Bertha (and each of us) gets information about balance from the vestibular system, housed deep in the inner ear. The vestibular system is designed to respond to the forces of gravity as they act on the head and then to provide this information to the parts of the brain that initiate the appropriate movements so that we can maintain balance.

Dizziness (the vague feeling of being unsteady, floating, and lightheaded) and vertigo (the sensation that one or one's surroundings are spinning) are common experiences for older adults. Although age-related structural changes in the vestibular system account for some of the problems, they do not account entirely for increases in dizziness and vertigo. Loss of visual information makes it more difficult for older adults in particular to compensate successfully (Robin, 1995; Whitbourne, 1999). Also, it takes older adults longer to integrate all the sensory information coming to the brain to control posture (Whitbourne, 1999). And dizziness can be a side effect of certain medications and physical illnesses.

Because of these changes, the likelihood of falling increases with age. Falls may be life-threatening events, especially for those 75 and older, because of the increased risk of broken bones (Whitbourne, 1999). Environmental hazards such as loose rugs and slippery floors are more likely to be a factor for healthy, community-dwelling older adults, whereas disease is more likely to play a role in institutionalized people. Increases in body sway, the natural movement of the body to maintain balance, occur with increasing age. Connections between the degree of body sway and likelihood of falling have been shown, with people who fall often having more body sway (Robin, 1995; Whitbourne, 1996a).

Because fear of falling has a basis in reality, it is important that concerns not be taken lightly. Older adults can be taught to pay greater attention to other

© Peter Turnley / CORBIS

Keeping one's balance is a key concern among older adults.

cues, such as somesthetic ones. During times of dizziness or vertigo, people can learn to attend to the position of lower body limbs to better use this feedback in adjusting posture (Hu & Woollacott, 1994a, 1994b). People can also be trained to improve their balance through tai chi (Wolf et al., 1996; Wolfson et al., 1996), described in detail in the How Do We Know? feature. Any of these intervention programs can be of value in preventing falls.

Taste and Smell

TASTE. There is an expression "too old to cut the mustard," which dates back to when people made mus-

Who were the investigators, and what were the aims of the studies? Helping older adults improve their balance is an important way to help lower the risk of falling. Tai chi, an ancient Chinese martial art, enhances body awareness. Wolf et al. (1996) examined whether tai chi improves balance, and Wolfson et al. (1996) investigated whether older adults trained in tai chi continue to use it after intensive training ends.

How did the investigators measure the topic of interest? Wolf et al. measured several variables, including strength, flexibility, functioning, depression, and fear of falling. Wolfson et al. assessed loss of balance, stability, walking speed, and leg movements. Both sets of measures focused on participants' ability to maintain balance.

Who were the participants in the studies? Wolf et al. studied a total of 200 older adults; Wolfson et al. studied 110 older adults. All participants in both studies lived in the community.

What was the design of the studies? Both studies were experiments in a longitudinal design; participants were randomly assigned to experimental and control groups. Wolf et al. used a 15-week intervention and also assessed their participants before and immediately after the intervention and at a 4-month follow-up. Wolfson et al. used an intervention schedule of three times per week for 12 weeks, followed by long-term group instruction once per week for 6 months.

Were there ethical concerns with the study? Participants in both studies were provided with informed consent and were closely monitored by health care professionals throughout the studies, so there were no ethical concerns.

What were the results? Both studies showed significant improvements in balance after tai chi training. The measures indicated that leg motion improved, blood pressure was lower, and fear of falling was lower. Most important, performance on key balance measures showed that performance matched levels analogous to those of people 3 to 10 years younger. These significant gains lasted as long as 6 months after intensive training ended.

What did the investigators conclude? Both Wolf et al. and Wolfson et al. concluded that tai chi training not only provides important improvements in balance in older adults but also lowers their fear of falling. Because tai chi is a low-impact martial art, it is easily adapted for use by older adults.

---

tard at home by grinding mustard seed and adding just the right amount of vinegar ("cutting the mustard") to balance the taste. If too much vinegar was added, the concoction tasted terrible, so the balance was critical. Many families found that older members tended to add too much vinegar.

Despite the everyday belief that taste ability changes with age, we do not have much data documenting what actually happens. What we know is that the ability to detect different tastes declines gradually and that these declines vary a great deal from flavor to flavor and person to person (Meisami, 1994; Stevens et al., 1995). Whatever age differences we observe are not caused by a decline in the sheer number of taste buds; unlike those of other neural cells, the number of taste cells does not change appreciably across the life span (Whitbourne, 1996a).

Despite the lack of evidence of large declines in the ability to taste, there is little question that older adults complain more about boring food (Whitbourne, 1996a). The explanation may be that changes in the enjoyment of food are caused by psychosocial issues (such as personal adjustment), changes in smell (which we consider next), or disease. For instance, we are much more likely to eat a balanced diet and enjoy our food when we do not eat alone and when we get a whiff of the enticing aromas from the kitchen.

Physical Changes

SMELL. "Stop and smell the roses." "Ooh! What's that perfume you're wearing?" "Yuck! What's that smell?" There is a great deal of truth in the saying "the nose knows." Smell is a major part of our everyday lives. How something smells can alert us that dinner is cooking, warn of a gas leak or a fire, let us know that we are clean, or be sexually arousing. Many of our social interactions involve smell (or the lack of it). We spend billions of dollars making our bodies smell appealing to others. It is easy to see that any age-related change in sense of smell would have far-reaching consequences.

Researchers agree that the ability to detect odors remains fairly intact until the 60s, when it begins to decline, but there are wide variations across people and types of odors (Whitbourne, 1999). These variations could have important practical implications. A large survey conducted by the National Geographic Society indicated that older adults were not as able to identify particular odors as younger people. One of the odors tested was the substance added to natural gas that enables people to detect leaks, a potentially fatal problem.

Abnormal changes in the ability to smell are turning out to be important in the differential diagnosis of Alzheimer's disease (Meisami, 1994). According to several studies, people with Alzheimer's disease are able to identify only 60% of the odors identified by age-matched control participants; in more advanced stages of the disease, this was reduced to only 40% compared with controls. These changes give clinicians another indicator for diagnosing suspected cases of Alzheimer's disease.

The major psychological consequences of changes in smell concern eating, safety, and pleasurable experiences. Odors play an important role in enjoying food and protecting us from harm. Socially, decreases in our ability to detect unpleasant odors may lead to embarrassing situations in which we are unaware that we have body odors or need to brush our teeth. Social interactions could suffer as a result of these problems. Smells also play a key role in remembering past life experiences. Who can forget the smell of cookies baking in Grandma's oven? Loss of odor cues may mean that our sense of the past suffers as well.

CONCEPT CHECKS

1. What are the major structural changes with age in the eye? What functional effects do these changes have?
2. How does hearing change with age?
3. What changes occur with age in somesthesia and balance?
4. How do the abilities to taste and smell change with age?

VITAL FUNCTIONS

LEARNING OBJECTIVES

- What age-related changes occur in the cardiovascular system? What types of cardiovascular disease are common in adult development and aging? What are the psychological effects of age-related changes in the cardiovascular system?
- What structural and functional changes occur with age in the respiratory system? What are the most common types of respiratory diseases in older adults? What are the psychological effects of age-related changes in the respiratory system?

Steve is an active 73-year-old man who walks and plays golf regularly. He smoked earlier in his life, but he quit years ago. He also watches his diet to control fat intake. Steve recently experienced some chest pains and sweating but dismissed it as simply age-related. After all, he thought to himself, he takes care of himself. However, Steve's wife, Grace, is concerned that he may have a more serious problem.

Two of the systems that are essential to life are our cardiovascular system and our respiratory system; that's why they are called vital functions. Each undergoes important normative changes with age that can affect the quality of one's life. In this section, we'll find out whether Grace has reason to worry about Steve's symptoms. We'll also discover why figuring out the pattern of age-related changes in the respiratory system is very difficult. It is clear that age-related changes in the cardiovascular and respiratory systems are excellent examples of how the forces of development interact. On the biological front, we know that some cardiovascular and respiratory diseases have important genetic links. Psychologically, certain personality traits have been linked with increased risk of disease. Socioculturally, some cardiovascular and respiratory diseases are clearly tied to lifestyle. The impact of both cardiovascular and respiratory diseases also differs as a function of age. Let's explore in more detail how these various forces come together.

Cardiovascular System

The human heart is an amazing organ. In an average lifetime, the heart beats more than 3 billion times, pumping the equivalent of more than 900 million gallons of blood. Two important age-related structural changes in the heart are the accumulation of fat deposits and the stiffening of the heart muscle caused by tissue changes. By the late 40s and early 50s, the fat deposits in the lining around the heart may form a continuous sheet. Meanwhile, healthy muscle tissue is being replaced by connective tissue, which causes a thickening and stiffening of the heart muscle and valves. These changes reduce the amount of muscle tissue available to contract the heart. The net effect is that the remaining muscle must work harder. To top it off, the amount of blood that the heart can pump declines from roughly 5 liters per minute at age 20 to about 3.5 liters per minute at age 70 (Lakatta, 1995; Whitbourne, 1999).

The most important change in the circulatory system involves the stiffening (hardening) of the walls of the arteries. These changes are caused by calcification of the arterial walls and by replacement of elastic fibers with less elastic ones.

The combination of changes in the heart and the circulatory system results in a significant decrease in a person's ability to cope with physical exertion, especially aerobic exercise. By age 65, the average adult has experienced a 60–70% decline in the aerobic capacity since young adulthood. However, if you stay in good shape throughout adulthood, the decline is much less, perhaps as little as 20–25% (Trappe et al., 1996). This decline is one reason why older adults who are not in good shape are more likely to have heart attacks while performing moderately exerting tasks such as shoveling snow.

CARDIOVASCULAR DISEASE. In the United States, someone dies from cardiovascular disease every 33 seconds (American Heart Association, 1998). It is the leading cause of death in all ethnic groups in the United States (Figure 2.4) and in many other countries. The prevalence of cardiovascular disease increases dramatically with age. Note also that the rates for men are higher until old age. The good news is that deaths from cardiovascular disease have been declining in the United States, especially among men, since the 1970s (Siegler et al., 1999).

Why are there ethnic and gender differences? Ethnic differences may be caused by differential genetic predisposition, quality of health care, diet, and stress (American Heart Association, 1998). Although many people believe that gender differences can be traced to hormonal protection in premenopausal women caused by estrogen, the elimination of the gender gap by age 75 is not caused mostly by the lack of estrogen in postmenopausal women. Rather, the difference has more to do with the leveling off of death rates in men (Avis, 1999). However, menopause is associated with lower levels of HDL ("good") cholesterol and higher levels of LDL ("bad") cholesterol (Brown et al., 1993), so the full role of estrogen in cardiovascular disease has yet to be uncovered.

Several types of cardiovascular disease are noteworthy. **Congestive heart failure** *occurs when cardiac output and the ability of the heart to contract severely decline, making the heart enlarge, pressure in the veins increase, and the body swell.* Congestive heart failure is the most common cause of hospitalization for people over age 65. **Angina pectoris** *occurs when the oxygen supply to the heart muscle becomes insufficient, resulting in chest pain.* Angina may feel like chest pressure, a burning pain, or a squeezing that radiates from the chest to the back, neck, and arms (American Heart Association, 1999). In most cases the pain is induced by physical exertion and is relieved within 5 to 10 minutes by rest. The most common treatment of angina is nitroglycerine, although in some cases coronary arteries may need to be cleared through surgical procedures or replaced through coronary bypass surgery.

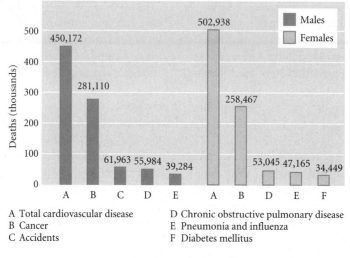

Leading causes of death for men and women in the United States (1997).

Source: American Heart Association. (1999). *2000 Heart and stroke statistical update* (p. 5).

Heart attack, called **myocardial infarction (MI),** *occurs when blood supply to the heart is severely reduced or cut off.* Mortality after a heart attack is much higher for older adults (Centers for Disease Control and Prevention, 2000). The initial symptoms of an MI are identical to those of angina but typically are more severe and prolonged; there may also be nausea, vomiting, severe weakness, and sweating, which Steve experienced. Thus, Grace is right to be concerned about Steve's symptoms. In as many as 25% of patients, however, chest pain may be absent. These "silent" heart attacks are more common in older adults, especially those with diabetes (American Heart Association, 1999). Treating heart attack victims of all ages includes careful evaluation and a prescribed rehabilitation program consisting of lifestyle changes in diet and exercise.

Atherosclerosis *is an age-related disease caused by the buildup of fat deposits on and the calcification of the arterial walls* (Aldwin & Gilmer, 1999). Much like sandbars in a river or mineral deposits in pipes, the fat deposits interfere with blood flow through the arteries. These deposits begin very early in life and continue throughout the life span. Some amount of fat

deposit inevitably occurs and is considered a normal part of aging. However, excess deposits may develop from poor nutrition, smoking, and other aspects of an unhealthy lifestyle.

When severe atherosclerosis occurs in blood vessels that supply the brain, neurons may not receive proper nourishment, causing them to malfunction or die, a condition called cerebrovascular disease. *When the blood flow to a portion of the brain is completely cut off, a* **cerebrovascular accident (CVA),** *or stroke, results.* Estimates are that someone in the United States has a CVA every 53 seconds, making stroke one of the most common forms of cardiovascular disease (American Heart Association, 1998). Causes of CVAs include clots that block blood flow in an artery or the actual breaking of a blood vessel, which creates a cerebral hemorrhage. The severity of a CVA and likelihood of recovery depend on the specific area of the brain involved, the extent of disruption in blood flow, and the duration of the disruption. Consequently, a CVA may affect such a small area that it goes almost unnoticed, or it may be so severe as to cause death.

The risk of a CVA increases with age; in fact, CVAs are among the leading causes of death among older adults in the United States (Centers for Disease Control and Prevention, 2000). In addition to age, other risk factors include being male, being African American, and having high blood pressure, heart disease, or diabetes. The higher risk among African Americans appears to be caused by a greater prevalence of hypertension in this population (American Heart Association, 1998).

Treatment of CVA has advanced significantly. The most important advance is use of the clot-dissolving drug *tissue plasminogen activator* (TPA) to treat CVAs. This is a major advance in medical therapy because physicians now have an approved treatment for CVAs caused by blood clots, which constitute 80% of all CVAs. Not every patient should receive TPA treatment, and TPA is effective only if given promptly. For maximum benefit, the therapy must be started within 3 hours after the onset of a stroke. Therefore, it is critical that caregivers, medical professionals, and the public recognize and respond to the onset of stroke (American Heart Association, 1999). Recovery from CVA depends on the severity of the stroke, area and extent of the brain affected, and patient age.

As we grow older, blood pressure tends to rise, mostly because of structural changes in the cardiovascular system. *When blood pressure increases become severe, defined as 140 mm Hg or more systolic pressure (the pressure during the heart's contraction phase) or 90 mm Hg or more diastolic pressure (the pressure during the heart's relaxation phase), the disease* **hypertension** *results* (American Heart Association, 1999). (So-called normal blood pressure is 120/80 mm Hg.) Roughly 25% of the population between ages 25 and 74 have some degree of hypertension. However, the rate is about 35% among African Americans, and twice as many African Americans die from hypertension as European Americans (Cooper et al., 1999). This difference may be caused by a genetic mutation affecting enzymes that help control blood pressure and by environmental factors related to stress, poor access to health care, and poverty.

Hypertension is a very serious matter. Older adults with hypertension have three times the risk of dying from cardiovascular disease, and it has important negative effects on cognitive abilities (Elias et al.,

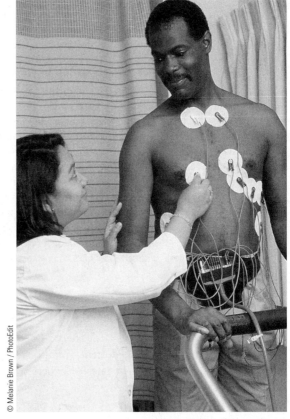

© Melanie Brown / PhotoEdit

African-American men are at especially high risk for hypertension.

1995). Because hypertension is a disease with no clear symptoms, most people with hypertension are not aware that they have a problem. Regular blood pressure monitoring is the only sure way to find out whether one has hypertension.

Some of the causes of hypertension are not purely physiological. For example, stress and high-sodium diets have been shown to cause hypertension in some people. Espino and Maldonado (1990) report that the rate of hypertension was higher among Mexican Americans who were more acculturated into the American lifestyle. In fact, degree of acculturation was a better predictor of hypertension than socioeconomic variables such as income. They speculate that with acculturation come higher levels of stress and the adoption of a less healthful diet that puts such people

As we have seen, telling the difference between normative age-related changes in the respiratory system and changes caused by living in a polluted environment is nearly impossible. This situation clearly demonstrates the interactive effects of the four developmental forces.

Biologically, it is certain that lung tissue deteriorates over time. So even if we were to live in completely unpolluted environments, everyone would experience decreases in the ability to take in air and efficiently exchange oxygen and carbon dioxide.

However, the sociocultural forces on individuals determine the rate of deterioration. Where we live in terms of industrial or other sources of pollution makes a huge difference, as do local government responses to it. Being poor in industrialized countries generally means living in more polluted environments, with less access to adequate health care. Psychological forces influence how people interpret and deal with issues relating to the environment and pollution as well as the direct impact of declining respiratory function on

cognitive and other abilities. Finally, when in one's life and for how long one lives in highly polluted environments matters. Obviously, the younger one is and the longer one lives in such environments, the more damage is done.

It is clear that pollution takes a terrible toll on respiratory function. The rapid rise in respiratory diseases over the past few decades is a direct indication of the problem (American Lung Association, 1998). Changes must be made to alter the outcome.

---

at risk. Similarly, Cooper and colleagues (1999) showed that people of African descent around the world differ significantly in their rates of hypertension, with those living in societies in which racism is a major social problem (especially the United States and the United Kingdom) having the highest rates.

Respiratory System

If you're like most younger and middle-aged adults, you probably don't pay much attention to your breathing unless you're gasping for breath after physical exertion. Many older adults notice their breathing a great deal more. Why? With increasing age, the rib cage and the air passageways become stiffer, making it harder to breathe. The lungs change in appearance over time, going gradually from their youthful pinkish color to a dreary gray, caused mainly by breathing in carbon particles (from air pollution). The maximum amount of air we can take into the lungs in a single breath begins to decline in the 20s, decreasing by 40% by age 85. And the rate at which we can exchange oxygen for carbon dioxide drops significantly as the membranes of the air sacs in the lungs deteriorate (Whitbourne, 1999).

One of the difficulties in understanding age-related changes in the respiratory system is that it is hard to know how much of the change is caused specifically by normative developmental factors and how much is caused by environmental factors. Take time to explore this problem in more detail by reading the Forces in Action feature.

RESPIRATORY DISEASES. *The most common and incapacitating respiratory disorder in older adults is* **chronic obstructive pulmonary disease** (COPD), *a family of diseases that includes chronic bronchitis and emphysema.* Between 1979 and the late 1990s, the death rate from COPD increased more than 40%, in part because of better diagnosis but most importantly because of greater long-term exposure to pollution. COPD is a progressive disease in which the prognosis is usually very poor (American Lung Association, 1998).

Emphysema *is the most serious type of COPD and is characterized by the destruction of the membranes around the air sacs in the lungs* (American Lung Association, 1998). This irreversible destruction creates holes in the lung, drastically reducing the ability to exchange oxygen and carbon dioxide. To make matters worse, the bronchial tubes collapse prematurely when the person exhales, thereby preventing the lungs from emptying completely. Emphysema is a very debilitating disease. In its later stages, even the smallest physical exertion causes a struggle for air. People with emphysema may have such poorly oxygenated blood that they become confused and disoriented. About 82% of the cases of emphysema are self-induced by smoking; the remaining cases are caused by a genetic deficiency of a protein known as α_1-antitrypsin. Although some drugs are available to help ease breathing, lung transplantation remains a treatment of last resort, especially in the genetic form of the disease (Cannon, 1996).

Chronic bronchitis can occur at any age, but it is more common in people over age 45, especially among people who are exposed to high concentrations of dust, irritating fumes, and air pollution. Treatment usually consists of medication to open bronchial passages (called bronchodilators) and a change of work environment. Similarly, asthma is another very common respiratory disease that is increasing in prevalence. Treatment for asthma also involves the use of bronchodilators.

CONCEPT CHECK

1. What are the major age-related changes in the cardiovascular system?
2. What are the major age-related changes in the respiratory system?

THE REPRODUCTIVE SYSTEM

LEARNING OBJECTIVES

- What reproductive changes occur in women?
- What reproductive changes occur in men?
- What are the psychological effects of reproductive changes?

Helen woke up in the middle of the night drenched in sweat. She'd been feeling fine when she went to bed after her 48th birthday party, so she wasn't sure what was the matter. When she visited her gynecologist later that day for her routine checkup, Helen was told that her experience probably was a sign that she was in the peri-

menopausal phase. Helen wonders what other things she'll experience.

As you probably surmised, Helen has begun going through a major biological process, called the **climacteric,** *during which she will pass from her reproductive to nonreproductive years. In Helen's case, she is entering the perimenopausal phase, which leads into* **menopause,** *the point at which her ovaries will stop releasing eggs. Men do not endure such sweeping biological changes but experience several gradual changes. As is true for Helen, many of the major changes in our reproductive system begin during middle age. These changes have important psychological implications because midlife is thought by many to be a key time for redefining ourselves. Let's see how the experience differs for women and men.*

Female Reproductive System

As Helen is beginning to learn firsthand, the major reproductive change in women during adulthood is the loss of the ability to bear children. This change begins in the 40s, as menstrual cycles become irregular, and by age 50 to 55 it is usually complete (Avis, 1999). This end of monthly periods is accompanied by decreases in estrogen and progesterone levels, changes in the reproductive organs, and changes in sexual functioning (Whitbourne, 1999).

A variety of physical and psychological symptoms may accompany perimenopause and menopause with decreases in hormonal levels (Avis, 1999; Planned Parenthood, 1998): hot flashes, night sweats, headaches, mood changes, difficulty concentrating, vaginal dryness, and a variety of aches and pains. Although many women report no symptoms at all, most women experience at least some, but there are large ethnic and cultural group differences. For example, studies of European American women reveal a decrease in reported physical symptoms after climacteric. In contrast, African American women reported more physical symptoms after climacteric than before. Although these differences could be a function of the different age groups included in the various studies, they also draw attention to the need to study the experiences of women

What women report about the experience of perimenopause and menopause is related to culture. American and Japanese women, for example, report different symptoms.

from different ethnic and racial backgrounds (Jackson et al., 1991).

Cultural differences are exemplified in Lock's (1991) classic study of Japanese women. Fewer than 13% of Japanese women whose menstrual periods were becoming irregular reported having hot flashes during the previous 2 weeks, compared with nearly half of Western women. In fact, fewer than 20% of Japanese women in the study had ever had a hot flash, compared with nearly 65% of Western women. However, Japanese women reported more headaches, shoulder stiffness, ringing in the ears, and dizziness than Western women. Why? The answer seems to be the power of sociocultural forces. In Japan, the government considers "menopausal syndrome" to be a modern affliction of women with too much time on their hands. With this official attitude, it is hard to know whether Japanese women actually experience menopause differently or may simply be reluctant to describe their true experience.

One way to address the symptoms associated with the climacteric is hormone replacement therapy. Many physicians also point out that having women take hormones after menopause may also provide some protection against cardiovascular disease, as described earlier in this chapter. However, as discussed in the Current Controversies feature, probably no other area of medical research has resulted in more contradictory data about the potentially serious side effects (or lack

For many years, women have had the choice of taking medications to replace the female hormones that are not produced naturally by the body after menopause. Hormone replacement therapy (HRT) reduces the physiological symptoms associated with the climacteric, delays the onset of osteoporosis, and may decrease the risk of cardiovascular disease and perhaps Alzheimer's disease (Aldwin & Gilmer, 1999; Avis, 1999). However, research also shows that if HRT is stopped, bone loss resumes, and the lowered risk of cardiovascular disease thought to be caused by HRT may in fact be caused by systematic differences between women who use HRT and those who do not; for example, women who use HRT tend to have lower cholesterol levels to begin with than women who do not use HRT (Avis, 1999; Johannes et al., 1994). Additionally, taking these drugs may not be risk free; some evidence of increased breast cancer risk in women taking replacement hormones has been reported based on combined analyses of small studies, but the extent of the risk for specific groups is unclear (Colditz et al., 1995). One of the main

problems is the lack of large-scale epidemiological data examining different types of hormone therapies; this issue is being addressed by the Women's Health Initiative.

One of the major problems in understanding the long-term effects of HRT is that much of the research focuses on estrogen-only drugs rather than the more commonly used estrogen—progestin combination. About the only long-term research on this combination comes from studies on contraception use; unfortunately, this research does not include older women, so we cannot be sure what the long-term consequences are for them (Avis, 1999).

A newer approach involves a class of compounds called *selective estrogen receptor modulators (SERMs),* which can be considered "designer estrogens" (Avis, 1999). SERMs have the protective properties of estrogen on bone tissue and the cardiovascular system but seem to block some estrogen effects on breast and uterine tissue. In essence, they have the advantages of traditional HRT with apparently none of the negative side effects. Two SERMs that are being intensively studied are tamoxifen, the

first SERM approved for clinical use, and raloxifene. Although both show promise, the potential of increased uterine cancer in the case of tamoxifen and increased hot flashes in the case of raloxifene indicate that neither is perfect (Avis, 1999; Walsh et al., 1998).

In sum women have difficult choices to make when deciding whether to use HRT to combat certain symptoms related to menopause and to protect themselves against other diseases. To date, research evidence about the long-term risks of HRT is mixed. The best course of action is to consult closely with one's physician to weigh the benefits and risks.

Search Online with
InfoTrac College Edition
For more information on these controversies, explore InfoTrac College Edition, your online library. Go to http://www.infotrac-college.com/wadsworth and use the passcode that came on the card with your book. Try these search terms: hormone replacement therapy; hormone therapy, subdivisions

thereof) than has work on hormone replacement therapy.

Women's genital organs undergo progressive change after menopause (Whitbourne, 1999). The vaginal walls shrink and become thinner, the size of the vagina decreases, vaginal lubrication is reduced and delayed, and some shrinkage of the external genitalia occurs. These changes have important effects on sexual activity, such as an increased possibility of

painful intercourse and a longer time and more stimulation needed to reach orgasm. Failure to achieve orgasm is more common than in a woman's younger years. However, maintaining an active sex life throughout adulthood lowers the degree to which problems are encountered.

Despite the physical changes, there is no physiological reason why most women cannot continue sexual activity and enjoy it well into old age. Whether

Physical Changes

this happens depends more on the availability of a suitable partner than on a woman's desire for sexual relations. This is especially true for older women. The AARP *Modern Maturity* sexuality study (AARP, 1999a) found that older married women were far more likely to have an active sex life than unmarried women. The primary reason for the decline in women's sexual activity with age is the lack of a willing or appropriate partner, not a lack of physical ability or desire (AARP, 1999a).

Male Reproductive System

Unlike women, men do not have a physiological (and cultural) event to mark reproductive changes. Men do not experience a complete loss of the ability to have children. However, men do experience a normative decline in the quantity of sperm (Lewis, 1995). Sperm production declines by approximately 30% between age 25 and 60 (Whitbourne, 1996a). However, even at age 80 a man is still half as fertile as he was at age 25 and is quite capable of fathering a child.

With increasing age the prostate gland enlarges, becomes stiffer, and may obstruct the urinary tract. Prostate cancer becomes a real threat during middle age; annual screenings are extremely important for men over age 50 (American Cancer Society, 1999b). The majority of men show a gradual reduction in testosterone levels after the mid-20s (Whitbourne, 1996a). However, some men who experience an abnormally rapid decline in testosterone production during their late 60s report symptoms similar to those experienced by some menopausal women, such as hot flashes, chills, rapid heart rate, and nervousness (Ebersole & Hess, 1998).

Men experience some physiological changes in sexual performance. By old age, men report less perceived demand to ejaculate, a need for longer time and more stimulation to achieve erection and orgasm, and a much longer resolution phase during which erection is impossible (Saxon & Etten, 1994). Older men also report more frequent failures to achieve orgasm and loss of erection during intercourse (AARP, 1999a). However, the advent of the drug Viagra, which helps men achieve and maintain an erection, has provided an easy-to-use medical treatment for erectile dysfunction.

As with women, as long as men enjoy sex and have a willing partner, sexual activity is a lifelong option. As for women, the most important ingredient of sexual intimacy for men is a strong relationship with a partner (AARP, 1999a).

Psychological Implications

Older adults say that engaging in sexual behavior is an important aspect of human relationships throughout adulthood (AARP, 1999a). Healthy adults at any age are capable of having and enjoying sexual relationships. Moreover, the desire to do so normally does not diminish. Unfortunately, one of the myths in our society is that older adults cannot and should not be sexual. Many young adults find it difficult to think about their grandparents in this way.

Such stereotyping has important consequences. What comes to mind when we see an older couple being publicly affectionate? Many people feel that such behavior is cute. But observers tend not to refer to their own or their peers' relationships in this way. Many nursing homes and other institutions actively dissuade their residents from having sexual relationships and may even refuse to allow married couples to share the same room. Adult children believe that their widowed parent does not have the right to establish a new sexual relationship. The message we are sending is that sexual activity is fine for the young but not for the old. The major reason why older women do not engage in sexual relations is the lack of a socially sanctioned partner. It is not that they have lost interest; rather, they believe that they are simply not permitted to express their sexuality any longer.

CONCEPT CHECK

1. What physical symptoms accompany age-related changes in women's reproductive system?
2. What are the major changes in men's reproductive system?
3. How does sexual activity change with age?

THE NERVOUS SYSTEM

LEARNING OBJECTIVES

- What major changes occur in neurons? How does neurons' ability to communicate with each other change with age? What are the psychological effects of changes in the brain?
- What major changes occur in the autonomic nervous system?

Jorge is an active 83-year-old former factory worker who lives with his wife, Olivia, in a crowded apartment in Los Angeles. Over the past few years, Jorge has had increasing difficulty handling the heat of southern California summers. Olivia has noticed that Jorge takes more naps during the day and sleeps poorly at night. Jorge and Olivia wonder whether there is something wrong with him.

Our brains are the most complex structures yet discovered in the universe. Everything that makes us individuals is housed there, and we are only now beginning to unlock its mysteries. The major challenge is that observing age-related changes in the brain is difficult. Usually we must rely on indirect evidence such as memory problems. However, advances in imaging are making it easier to watch ongoing brain activity in people of different ages.

In this section we consider the age-related changes that occur in the central nervous system (the brain and spinal cord) and the autonomic nervous system (nerves in the rest of the body). Understanding normative changes in the central nervous system sets the stage for understanding diseases such as Alzheimer's disease, discussed in Chapter 4, as well as many of the cognitive changes discussed in Chapters 6, 7, and 8. Jorge's experiences are related to changes in the autonomic nervous system; we'll discover whether Jorge's problems are normative.

Central Nervous System

If you ask older adults to describe their experience of changes in their central nervous system, it's likely that they will be hard pressed to do so. There are fewer obvious signs than there are with appearance or vision, for example. This is because the age-related changes in the brain that we will consider begin very subtly; they are often difficult to document because they are microscopic and are hard to tie to specific behaviors. *Changes in the brain occur mainly at the level of individual brain cells, called* **neurons.** Much of what we have learned over the past decade has come from highly sophisticated computer-enhanced imaging techniques and from careful research in neuroscience. In this discussion we consider primarily changes that are currently viewed as normative. Abnormal brain aging, such as that which occurs in Alzheimer's disease, is considered in more detail in Chapter 4.

As you can see in Figure 2.5, neurons have several parts that play specialized roles in receiving, conducting, and transmitting information. At the left end of the neuron in the figure are the *dendrites*, which pick up the chemical signals coming in from other nearby neurons much as TV antennae pick up signals from nearby stations. The signal is brought into the *cell body*, where it is converted into an electrochemical impulse and sent down the *axon* to the terminal branches. The *terminal branches*, shown at the right end of the drawing, act like transmitter stations. Chemicals called *neurotransmitters* are released at the terminal branches and carry the information signal to the next neuron's dendrites. The neurotransmitters are necessary for communication between neurons because neurons do not physically touch one another. The gap between the terminal branches of one neuron and the dendrites of another, across which neurotransmitters travel, is called the synapse.

We are born with roughly 1 trillion neurons of different sizes and shapes, which constitute all the neurons we will ever have. Neurons grow in size and complexity across the life span but, like heart muscle cells, cannot regenerate (Scheibel, 1996). Once a neuron dies it is lost forever.

Individual neurons undergo a wide variety of normative age-related changes. In most people, these changes produce little noticeable difference in behavior until very old age. However, when the changes are widespread and occur more rapidly, disease typically is present. One problem in differentiating between normal and abnormal brain aging is that many of the same changes underlie both; for example, the defin-

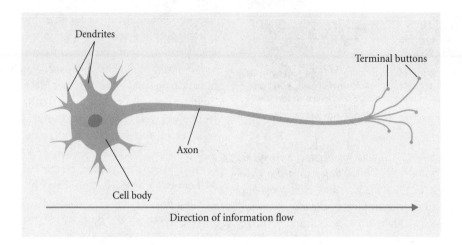

FIGURE 2.5 Diagram of a typical neuron.

ing characteristics of brain changes in Alzheimer's disease also are normative.

A second problem is that although we have documented many neuronal changes, we understand the implications of only a few. Tying specific brain changes to specific behaviors is very difficult. However, significant advances have been made using sophisticated brain imaging techniques.

STRUCTURAL CHANGES IN NEURONS. How does the structure of neurons change with age? The most important change in the cell body and axon involves changes in the fibers contained there. *Sometimes, for reasons we do not understand, neurons in certain parts of the brain develop* **neurofibrillary tangles,** *in which fibers in the axon become twisted together to form paired helical, or spiral, filaments* (Scheibel, 1996). Large concentrations of neurofibrillary tangles are associated with behavioral abnormalities and are one defining characteristic of Alzheimer's disease. However, some degree of tangling occurs normally as we age (Joynt, 1995; Scheibel, 1996). (This is an example of why it is sometimes difficult to tell the difference between normal and abnormal aging.)

Changes in the dendrites are complex. As some neurons deteriorate and die, there is a compensatory lengthening and increase in the number of dendrites of the remaining neurons (Ebersole & Hess, 1998; Scheibel, 1996). The new connections between the dendrites may make up for the loss of neurons, but only to a point. Eventually, the loss of neurons outpaces the ability of remaining neurons to make connections. The rate of this shift may be a difference between normal and abnormal aging, but additional research on this issue is necessary.

Damaged and dying neurons sometimes collect around a core of protein and produce **neuritic plaques.** Neuritic plaques have been found in samples taken at autopsy from various parts of the brain (Joynt, 1995). Although the number of neuritic plaques increases with age, large numbers of them are not observed in normal brain aging until around age 90 (Adams, 1980). Until then, high concentrations of neuritic plaques are considered characteristic of abnormal aging; for example, they are also indicative of Alzheimer's disease.

The normative loss and growth pattern in neurons may provide insight into abnormal brain aging. It could be that abnormal brain aging occurs when losses greatly outnumber gains before very old age. This is clearly the case in conditions such as Alzheimer's disease and related disorders, in which there is massive progressive loss of neurons in many areas of the brain.

CHANGES IN COMMUNICATION BETWEEN NEURONS. Because neurons do not physically touch one another, they must communicate by releasing neurotransmitters into the synapse. Are there age-related changes in neurotransmitters? Yes, and the changes help us understand why some older adults experience certain kinds of problems and diseases. Changes in the level of neurotransmitters affect the efficiency of information transmission between neurons. Age-related changes occur along several neurotransmitter pathways, which are groups of neurons that use the same neurotransmitter (Whitbourne, 1996a).

One pathway in the brain that is responsible for controlling motor movements uses the neurotransmitter dopamine. *As we age, the level of dopamine decreases; if this decline is extreme, we develop* **Parkinson's disease** (Ebersole & Hess, 1998). Parkinson's disease is characterized by tremors of the hands, arms, and legs, which decrease when one is performing voluntary tasks, and a shuffling walking style (Aldwin & Gilmer, 1999). Pope John Paul II, former boxer Muhammad Ali, actor Michael J. Fox, and attorney general Janet Reno all have Parkinson's disease.

Although there is no cure, the symptoms of Parkinson's disease can be alleviated by medications or surgery, and a gene believed responsible for a form of Parkinson's has been discovered that may result in future innovative treatments. One drug, L-dopa, is converted into the neurotransmitter dopamine, which helps restore the normal balance of the neurotransmitter (Ebersole & Hess, 1998). Drugs that mimic dopamine's role in the brain also allow patients to regain some of their lost muscle control. More recently, a new kind of drug called a catechol-O-methyltransferase (COMT) inhibitor (e.g., Tasmar) has been approved for use with L-dopa. COMT inhibitors block a key enzyme responsible for breaking down L-dopa before it reaches the brain, making L-dopa more effective. Patients with a stable response to L-dopa who took Tasmar experienced significant improvements in daily activities such as talking, writing, walking, and dressing (Henkel, 1998). Surgical interventions include "brain pacemakers," which consist of a wire surgically implanted deep within the brain and connected to a pulse generator, similar to a

Parkinson's disease has become better known because it has struck famous people, such as Michael J. Fox.

cardiac pacemaker, implanted near the collarbone. Whenever a tremor begins, a patient can activate the device by passing a hand-held magnet over the generator. Other surgical interventions include destroying certain parts of the brain that are overactive in Parkinson's disease (Henkel, 1998). Despite the range of therapies available to ease the disease's debilitating symptoms, however, treatments now on the market can neither replace the faulty nerve cells that cause the disease nor stop Parkinson's from progressing.

Age-related declines in the neurotransmitter acetylcholine are also well documented and are linked with memory problems in old age (Whitbourne, 1996a). Research interest in acetylcholine is spurred by its link to both Alzheimer's disease and Huntington's disease. Some researchers speculate that there are causal connections between these diseases and abnormally low levels of choline acetyltransferase, an enzyme responsible for synthesizing acetylcholine (Joynt, 1995). Much of the search for drugs to alleviate the symptoms of Alzheimer's focuses on this and other enzymes related to acetylcholine.

STUDYING BRAIN—BEHAVIOR RELATIONS: IMAGING TECHNIQUES. If we could peek inside a living, working brain, what would we find? The answer to this question turns out to be one of the most exciting avenues of research on brain development. Investigators can now use com-

TABLE 2.2	Brain Imaging Techniques
Type of Imaging	**Description**
Computed tomography (CT)	Images created by passing highly focused x-rays in various directions through the patient, with computers creating a three-dimensional image.
Magnetic resonance imaging (MRI)	Images produced by reorienting the body's molecules with large and very powerful magnets; detectors pick up radio frequencies that are shot through the body section under study. Can be used to study some physiological processes.
Positron emission tomography (PET)	Images created by injecting a radioactive isotope and passing positrons (subatomic particles) through the body from various directions, detecting them, and analyzing them. Very useful technique for studying brain activity, typically by examining glucose metabolism.

puter-enhanced images to assist in diagnosing disease and even to study the thinking brain. As described in Table 2.2, researchers use three main imaging techniques to do this: computed tomography (CT) scans, magnetic resonance imaging (MRI), and positron emission tomography (PET). CT and MRI are widely used not only in research but also in diagnosing brain diseases such as tumors and strokes. All three have provided fascinating insights into brain functioning.

Future insights into brain aging will come from neuroscience research using imagery techniques that examine relations with specific findings from molecular biological and genetic studies.

Autonomic Nervous System

Few changes occur in the autonomic nervous system as we age, but two tend to get people's attention: body temperature control and sleep. Jorge, whom we met in the vignette, is experiencing both of these changes.

REGULATING BODY TEMPERATURE. Every year, newscasts around the world report during cold or hot spells that more older adults die than people in other age groups. Why does this happen? We considered evidence earlier in this chapter that cold and warm temperature thresholds may change little. If they can feel cold and warm stimuli placed against them about as well as people of other age groups, what accounts for these deaths?

It turns out that older adults have difficulty telling that their core body temperature is low (Besdine, 1995; Taylor et al., 1995). In other words, older people are much less likely to notice that they are cold. To make matters worse, older adults also have slower vasoconstrictor response, which is the ability to raise one's core body temperature when the body's peripheral temperature drops (Besdine, 1995). Similarly, older adults have trouble responding to high heat because they do not sweat as much (Besdine, 1995). Even when they are hot, older adults are less likely to drink water because of lower thirst sensitivity (Phillips et al., 1991).

Taken together, the difficulties older adults have in regulating body temperature in extreme cold and heat are the primary reason why older adults are much more susceptible to hypothermia (body temperature below 95°F over a long period) and hyperthermia (body temperature above 98.6°F that cannot be relieved by sweating; Besdine, 1995). This is why social service agencies are especially mindful of older adults during major weather events.

SLEEP AND AGING. How did you sleep last night? If you are older, chances are that you had some trouble. In fact, sleep complaints are common in older adults (Vitiello, 1996; Whitbourne, 1999). These complaints most often concern difficulty in falling asleep, frequent or prolonged awakenings during the night, early morning awakenings, and a feeling of not sleeping very well. Effects of poor sleep are experienced the next day; moodiness, poorer performance on tasks involving sustained concentration, fatigue, and lack of motivation are some of the telltale signs.

Nearly every aspect of sleep undergoes age-related changes (Vitiello, 1996). It takes older adults longer to fall asleep, they are awake more at night, they are more easily awakened, and they experience major shifts in their sleep–wake cycles, called *circadian rhythms*. Across adulthood, circadian rhythms move from a two-phase pattern of sleep (awake during the day and sleep at night for most people) to a multiphase rhythm reminiscent of that of infants (daytime napping and shorter sleep cycles at night). These changes are related to the changes in regulating core body temperature discussed earlier. Other major causes of sleep disturbance include *sleep apnea* (stopping breathing for 5–10 seconds), periodic leg jerks, heartburn, frequent need to urinate, poor physical health, and depression (Herrera, 1995; Vitiello, 1996).

To compensate for changes in the quality of sleep, older adults often take daytime naps. Unfortunately, this strategy results in more disruptions of nighttime sleep (Vitiello, 1996). As a result, many older adults are prescribed sleeping pills or hypnotic sedatives. But these medications often do not help alleviate the problem, especially if used long term, because they may induce insomnia (Herrera, 1995; Vitiello, 1996). Among the most effective treatments of sleep problems are increasing physical exercise, reducing caffeine intake, avoiding daytime naps, and making sure that the sleeping environment is as quiet and dark as possible.

As we now know, Jorge's difficulty with heat and sleep reflect normative changes that occur with age. Olivia should be informed of these changes and encouraged to make sure Jorge drinks plenty of water and adopts good sleep habits.

Psychological Implications

Probably the worst stereotype about aging is that older adults "get senile." Older adults may even consider an insignificant memory lapse as evidence of impending senility, even though memory lapses normally occur throughout life (Cavanaugh et al., 1998).

But the term *senility* has no valid medical or psychological meaning, and its continued use simply perpetuates the myth that drastic mental decline is a product of normal aging (Qualls, 1999; Woodruff-Pak & Papka, 1999). It is not. The diseases involving loss of memory, emotional response, and bodily functions are dementias, and are discussed in Chapter 4. Dementia is not a part of normal aging; roughly 6–8% of people over age 65 have dementia, with the risk doubling about every 5 years (Qualls, 1999). People who develop dementia may show severe and progressive impairments of memory, judgment, comprehension, and motor functions. It is often the fear of developing dementia that makes people interpret the slightest mental or physical mistake as symptomatic.

Nevertheless, several aspects of psychological functioning are affected by normal brain aging, which may, in turn, affect adults' adaptation to the environment (Whitbourne, 1996a). For example, age-related declines in recent memory may be caused by neuronal losses. These changes make it more difficult for older adults to complete daily routines that demand remembering information over time, and older adults become less efficient at learning new facts and skills. In contrast, continued dendritic growth may be one reason why there is little evidence of age-related changes in experience-based problem solving, reasoning, and judgment until late in life (Schaie, 1995).

CONCEPT CHECKS

1. What structural changes occur in the neurons?
2. What changes occur with age in neurotransmitters?
3. What changes occur with age in the autonomic nervous system?
4. What is the worst stereotype about the psychological effects of brain aging?

PUTTING IT ALL TOGETHER

Although we cannot explain why physical changes occur with age, we have an increasingly accurate understanding of what these changes are. We know that Nolan Ryan represents the individual variation present in normative aging; although he lasted much longer than is typical in professional baseball, his skills nonetheless declined eventually. Kristina's experience in her mirror is a universal one: Someday we all will see our first wrinkles and gray hair. Changes in physical appearance are among the first signs of aging. Bertha's concern about falling is well founded; the normative changes in balance and in other sensory systems make falls a real issue for many older adults. Steve's chest pains and sweating are warning signs of cardiovascular disease, still the most common cause of death among older adults. Women in the United States like Helen who are entering perimenopause are likely to experience a cluster of symptoms including night sweats and hot flashes; however, Helen's counterparts in other parts of the world may report very different experiences. The normative changes that occur in the brain in many cases are not different from those seen in diseases such as Alzheimer's disease; the difference is in the degree of change. Sleep changes like those Jorge is experiencing are normative; changing one's sleep habits is one effective way to compensate for them. In Chapter 3, we will see how these physical changes are related to longevity, health, and diseases.

Summary

WHY DO WE AGE? BIOLOGICAL THEORIES OF AGING

Rate-of-Living Theories

- Rate-of-living theories are based on the idea that people are born with a limited amount of energy that can be expended at some rate.
- Metabolic processes such as eating fewer calories or reducing stress may be related to living longer.
- The body's declining ability to adapt to stress with age may also be a partial cause of aging.

Cellular Theories

- Cellular theories suggest that there may be limits on how often cells may divide before dying (called the Hayflick limit), which may partially explain aging. The shortening of telomeres may be the major factor.
- A second group of cellular theories relate to a process called cross-linking that results when certain proteins interact randomly and produce molecules that make the body stiffer. Cross-links interfere with metabolism.
- A third type of cellular theory proposes that free radicals, which are highly reactive chemicals produced randomly during normal cell metabolism, cause cellular damage. There is some evidence that ingesting antioxidants may postpone the appearance of some age-related diseases.

Programmed Cell Death Theories

- Programmed cell death theories are based on genetic hypotheses about aging. Specifically, there appears to be a genetic program that is triggered by physiological processes, the innate ability to self-destruct, and the ability of dying cells to trigger key processes in other cells.

Implications of the Developmental Forces

- Although biological theories are the foundation of biological forces, the full picture of how and why we age cannot be understood without considering the other three forces (psychological, sociocultural, and life cycle).

APPEARANCE AND MOBILITY

Changes in Skin, Hair, and Voice

- Normative changes with age in appearance include wrinkles, gray hair, and thinner and weaker voice.

Changes in Body Build

- Normative changes include decrease in height and increase in weight in midlife followed by weight loss in late life.

Changes in Mobility

- The amount of muscle decreases with age, but strength and endurance change only slightly.

- Loss of bone mass is normative; in severe cases, though, the disease osteoporosis may result, in which bones become brittle and honeycombed.
- Osteoarthritis and rheumatoid arthritis are two diseases that impair a person's ability to get around and function in the environment.

Psychological Implications

- Cultural stereotypes have an enormous influence on the personal acceptance of age-related changes in appearance.
- Loss of strength and endurance and changes in the joints have important psychological consequences, especially regarding self-esteem.

SENSORY SYSTEMS

Vision

- Several age-related changes occur in the structure of the eye, including decreases in the amount of light passing through the eye and in the ability to adjust to changes in illumination, yellowing of the lens, and changes in the ability to adjust and focus (presbyopia). In some cases these changes result in various diseases, such as cataracts and glaucoma.
- Other changes occur in the retina, including degeneration of the macula. Diabetes also causes retinal degeneration.
- The psychological consequences of visual changes include difficulties in getting around. Compensation strategies must take several factors into account; for example, the need for more illumination must be weighed against increased susceptibility to glare.

Hearing

- Age-related declines in the ability to hear high-pitched tones (presbycusis) are normative.
- Exposure to noise speeds up and exacerbates hearing loss.
- Psychologically, hearing losses can reduce the ability to have satisfactory communication with others.

Somesthesia and Balance

- Changes in sensitivity to touch, temperature, and pain are complex and not understood; age-related trends are unclear in most cases.

- Dizziness and vertigo are common in older adults and increase with age, as do falls. Changes in balance may result in greater caution in older adults when walking.

Taste and Smell

- Age-related changes in taste are minimal. Many older adults complain about boring food; however, these complaints appear to be largely unrelated to changes in taste ability.
- The ability to detect odors declines rapidly after age 60 in most people. Changes in smell are primarily responsible for reported changes in food preference and enjoyment.

VITAL FUNCTIONS

Cardiovascular System

- Some fat deposits in and around the heart and inside arteries are a normal part of aging. Heart muscle gradually is replaced with stiffer connective tissue. The most important change in the circulatory system is the stiffening (hardening) of the walls of the arteries.
- Overall, men have a higher rate of cardiovascular disease than women. Several diseases increase in frequency with age: congestive heart failure, angina pectoris, myocardial infarction, atherosclerosis (severe buildup of fat inside and the calcification of the arterial walls), cerebrovascular disease (cardiovascular disease in the brain), and hypertension (high blood pressure).

Respiratory System

- The amount of air we can take into our lungs and our ability to exchange oxygen and carbon dioxide decrease with age. Declines in the maximum amount of air we can take in also occur.
- Chronic obstructive pulmonary disease (COPD), such as emphysema, increases with age. Emphysema is the most common form of age-related COPD; although most cases are caused by smoking, a few are caused by secondhand smoke, air pollution, or genetic factors. Chronic bronchitis also becomes more prevalent with age.

THE REPRODUCTIVE SYSTEM

Female Reproductive System

- The transition from childbearing years to the cessation of ovulation is called the climacteric; menopause is the point at which the ovaries stop releasing eggs. A variety of physical and psychological symptoms accompany menopause (e.g., hot flashes), including several in the genital organs; however, women in some cultures report different experiences.

- Hormone replacement therapy remains controversial because of conflicting results about its long-term effects.

- No changes occur in the desire to have sex; however, the availability of a suitable partner for women is a major barrier.

Male Reproductive System

- In men, sperm production declines gradually with age. Changes in the prostate gland occur and should be monitored through yearly examinations.

- Some changes in sexual performance, such as increased time to erection and ejaculation and increased refractory period, are typical.

Psychological Implications

- Healthy adults of any age are capable of engaging in sexual activity, and the desire to do so does not diminish with age. However, societal stereotyping creates barriers to free expression of such feelings.

THE NERVOUS SYSTEM

Central Nervous System

- Neurons are the basic cells in the brain. Some neurons develop neurofibrillary tangles, new fibers produced in the axon that are twisted. Large numbers of these are associated with Alzheimer's disease. Some neurons lose dendrites with age, whereas others gain dendrites. Damaged or dying neurons sometimes become surrounded by protein and form neuritic plaques. Large numbers of plaques are associated with Alzheimer's disease.

- Several neurotransmitter levels decrease with age, including those of dopamine, acetylcholine, and serotonin. Some diseases, such as Parkinson's, Alzheimer's, and Huntington's, are related to changes in neurotransmitter levels.

- Three types of brain imaging are used in research: computed tomography (CT), magnetic resonance imaging (MRI), and positron emission tomography (PET). Each provides important information about brain structures. CT and MRI scans are used most often in routine diagnosis of brain diseases. PET scans also provide information on brain metabolism.

Autonomic Nervous System

- Regulating body temperature becomes increasingly problematic with age. Older adults have difficulty telling when their core body temperature drops, and their vasoconstrictor response diminishes. When they become very hot, older adults are less likely to drink water.

- Sleep patterns and circadian rhythms change with age. Older adults are more likely to compensate by taking daytime naps, which exacerbates the problem. Effective treatments include exercising, reducing caffeine, avoiding daytime naps, and making the sleep environment as quiet and dark as possible.

Psychological Implications

- The term *senility* no longer has medical meaning, nor do all (or even most) older adults become "senile." However, many people remain concerned about this issue. Brain changes underlie many behavioral changes, including memory.

Review Questions

BIOLOGICAL THEORIES OF AGING

- What biological theories have been proposed to explain aging? What are their similarities and differences?

- Why do some people argue that diets high in antioxidants can prolong life?
- What are some of the sociocultural forces that operate on the biological theories? What are some examples of these forces?

APPEARANCE AND MOBILITY

- What age-related changes occur in appearance?
- How does body build change with age?
- How do muscle and bone tissue change with age?

SENSORY SYSTEMS

- What age-related changes occur in vision? What are the psychological effects of these changes?
- What age-related changes occur in hearing? What are the psychological effects of these changes?
- What age-related changes occur in somesthesia and balance?
- What age-related changes occur in taste and smell?

VITAL FUNCTIONS

- What changes occur with age in the cardiovascular system? What gender differences have been noted? Which cardiovascular diseases increase in frequency with age?
- What changes occur with age in the respiratory system? How are respiratory diseases related to age?

THE REPRODUCTIVE SYSTEM

- What age-related changes occur in women's and men's reproductive ability?
- How does interest in sexual activity change with age? What constraints operate on men and women?

THE NERVOUS SYSTEM

- What structural changes occur with age in the neuron? How are these changes related to diseases such as Alzheimer's?
- What changes occur with age in neurotransmitters?
- What types of brain imaging techniques are used, and what structures and processes do they measure?

- What changes occur in people's ability to regulate body temperature?
- How does sleep change with age?

Integrating Concepts in Development

- How do the various biological theories of aging match with the major age-related changes in body systems? Which theories do the best job? Why?
- Given what you now know about normative changes in appearance, what would you say about the stereotypes of aging you identified in the Discovering Development exercise you did in Chapter 1?
- Why do you think that the rates of death from cardiovascular disease are so much higher in industrialized countries?
- How might the age-related changes in the respiratory system be linked with societal policies on the environment?
- What changes in memory and intelligence would you expect based on the changes in the nervous system? (Check your answer against the descriptions of these changes in Chapters 6, 7, and 8.)

Key Terms

angina pectoris A painful condition caused by temporary constriction of blood flow to the heart.

atherosclerosis A process by which fat is deposited on the walls of arteries.

cerebrovascular accident (CVA) An interruption of the blood flow in the brain.

chronic obstructive pulmonary disease (COPD) A family of age-related lung diseases that block the passage of air and cause abnormalities inside the lungs.

climacteric The transition during which a woman's reproductive capacity ends and ovulation stops.

congestive heart failure A condition occurring when cardiac output and the ability of the heart to contract severely decline, making the heart enlarge, increasing pressure to the veins, and making the body swell.

cross-linking Random interaction between proteins that produce molecules that make the body stiffer.

emphysema Severe lung disease that greatly reduces the ability to exchange carbon dioxide for oxygen.

free radicals Deleterious and short-lived chemicals that cause changes in cells that are thought to result in aging.

hypertension A disease in which one's blood pressure is too high.

menopause The cessation of the release of eggs by the ovaries.

myocardial infarction A heart attack.

neuritic plaques A normative change in the brain involving amyloid protein collecting on dying or dead neurons. Large numbers of neuritic plaques is a defining characteristic of Alzheimer's disease.

neurofibrillary tangles A normative age-related change in the brain involving the production of new fibers in the neuron. Large numbers of neurofibrillary tangles is a defining characteristic of Alzheimer's disease.

neurons The basic cells in the brain.

osteoarthritis A form of arthritis marked by gradual onset and progression of pain and swelling, caused primarily by overuse of a joint.

osteoporosis A degenerative bone disease more common in women in which bone tissue deteriorates severely to produce honeycomblike bone tissue.

Parkinson's disease A brain disease caused by an extreme drop in the neurotransmitter dopamine.

presbycusis A normative age-related loss of the ability to hear high-pitched tones.

presbyopia The normative age-related loss of the ability to focus on nearby objects, usually resulting in the need for glasses.

rheumatoid arthritis A destructive form of arthritis involving more swelling and more joints than osteoarthritis.

telomeres Tips of the chromosomes that shorten with each replication.

Resources

READINGS

Clark, W. R. (1999). *A means to an end: The biological basis of aging and death.* New York: Oxford University Press. Good general overview of biological aging; moderate difficulty.

Hayflick, L. (1996). *How and why we age* (2nd ed.). New York: Ballantine. One of the best general overviews of biological theories and research by one of the leading researchers in the field; easy to moderate.

Kirkwood, T. B. L. (1999). *The time of our lives: The science of human aging.* New York: Oxford University Press. A very readable account of the biological and physical changes that occur with age; easy reading.

Medina, J. (1996). *The clock of ages: Why we age–how we age–winding back the clock.* New York: Cambridge University Press. Overview of topics covered in this chapter; moderate difficulty.

Whitbourne, S. K. (1996). *The aging individual.* New York: Springer. A more advanced overview of biological and physiological changes, but with excellent discussions of the psychological effects of these changes; medium to difficult.

WEB SITES

Lighthouse International is a leading resource worldwide for information on visual impairment and intervention. Their Web site provides a wide variety of information and resources and summaries of legislative and advocacy activities. The Lighthouse International home page can be found at http://www.lighthouse.org.

The American Heart Association provides a wide range of information, including risk assessments, on its Web site. Information includes preventive measures, diet recommendations, and basic information about cardiovascular and circulatory diseases. Additionally, you can access the American Stroke Association site.

The Heart Association home page can be found at http://www.americanheart.org.

The National Institute on Aging (NIA) publishes several informative brochures and reports about many aspects of physical aging, such as menopause, cardiovascular disease, and sensory changes. All the information is based on scientific research. The NIA Health Information home page can be found at http://www.nih.gov/nia/health/.

SEARCH ONLINE WITH

INFOTRAC COLLEGE EDITION

For more information on the topics in this chapter, explore InfoTrac College Edition, your online library. Go to http://www.infotrac-college.com/wadsworth and use the passcode that came on the card with your book. Try these search terms: molecular aging; skin aging; aging, causes of.

LONGEVITY, HEALTH, AND FUNCTIONING

© Jacques M. Chenet / Liaison Agency

"When you get real old, honey," said Elizabeth (Bessie) Delany, "you lay it all on the table. There's an old saying: Only little children and old folks tell the truth." And tell the truth she did. Along with her sister Sarah (Sadie), Bessie Delany told the story of more than 100 years of living through segregation, discrimination, the civil rights movement, and the women's movement. They were born more than a decade before the first airplane flew, and they lived to see men walk on the moon. Each of them rose to professional prominence, Bessie as the second African American woman to be licensed as a dentist in New York, Sadie as the first African American to teach domestic science on the high school level in New York City public schools. They never married. Their story became two best-selling books and a highly successful Broadway play.

Sadie and Bessie Delany were blessed with very long, full lives. Sadie died in 1999 at age 109, and Bessie died in 1995 at age 104. They certainly had excellent genes, but there's more to living a long and healthy life than that. We'll discover in this chapter that longevity depends on a complex set of variables. Sadie and Bessie's good health meant that they enjoyed good quality of life and avoided chronic disease. Compared with most older adults, they had little experience with medications, a potential source of problems for many older people. That Sadie and Bessie were independent puts them in the majority of older adults who are not disabled.

Will you live to be 100 years old? If you are lucky enough to experience the right confluence of genetics, psychological characteristics, and socioeconomic factors and avoid key events at particular points in your life, you just might. Whether your life will be a big hit remains to be seen.

HOW LONG WILL WE LIVE?

LEARNING OBJECTIVES

- What are the average and maximum longevity for humans?
- What genetic and environmental factors influence longevity?
- What ethnic factors influence average longevity?
- What factors create gender differences in average longevity?

Susie is a 51-year-old Chinese American living in San Francisco. Susie's mother (age 76), father (age 77), and grandmother (age 103), who are all in excellent health, live with her and her husband. Susie knows that several of her other relatives have lived long lives but wonders whether this has any bearing on her own life expectancy.

As we saw in Chapter 1, many more people are living to old age today than ever before. Like Susie, people today have already seen far more older adults than their great-great-grandparents did. The tremendous increase in the number of older adults has focused renewed interest in life expectancy. Susie's question about her own longevity exemplifies this interest. Knowing how long we are likely to live is important not only for us but also for government agencies, service programs, the business world, and insurance companies. Why? The length of life has an enormous impact on just about every aspect of life, from decisions about government health care programs (much higher costs to care for more chronically ill people) to retirement policy (debates over the age at which people may collect maximum retirement benefits) to life insurance premiums (longer lives on average mean cheaper rates for young adults). Longer lives have forced change in all these

areas and will continue to do so for the next several decades.

Life expectancy can be examined from the perspective of the basic developmental forces because how long we live depends on complex interactions between biological, psychological, socioeconomic, and life-cycle forces. For example, some people, like Susie, have many relatives who live to very old age, whereas others have relatives who die young. Tendencies toward long lives (or short ones, for that matter) tend to run in families. As we will see, our "long-life genes" play a major role in governing how long we are likely to live.

But the world in which we live can affect how long we live, too. Environmental factors such as disease and toxic chemicals modify our genetic heritage and shorten our lifetime, sometimes drastically. By the same token, environmental factors such as access to high-quality medical care can sometimes offset genetic defects that would have caused early death, thereby increasing our longevity. In short, no single developmental force can account for the length of life. Let's begin our exploration of how long we live with a discussion of the concept of longevity. To get started, complete the exercise in the Discovering Development feature and see how long you might live. When you have finished, continue reading to discover the research base behind the numbers.

Average and Maximum Longevity

The number of years one lives, as jointly determined by genetic and environmental factors, is called longevity. Researchers distinguish between two different types of longevity: average longevity and maximum longevity. **Average longevity** *is commonly called average life expectancy and refers to the age at which half of the individuals who are born in a particular year will have died.* Average longevity is affected by both genetic and environmental factors. For people in the United States, average longevity has been increasing steadily since 1900; recent estimates are presented in Figure 3.1. Note in the figure that the most rapid increase in average longevity occurred in the first half of the 20th

Did you ever speculate about how long you might live? Are you curious? If you'd like a preview of several of the key influences on how long we live, try completing the questions at http://www.beeson.org/livingto100. Take notes about why you think each question is being asked. Once you're finished, submit your form. Take time to read about each of the topics, then read more about them in the text. Will you live to be 100? Only time will tell.

century. These increases in average longevity were caused mostly by declines in infant mortality rates through the elimination of diseases such as smallpox and polio and through better health care. The decrease in the number of women who died during childbirth was especially important in raising average life expectancies for women. All of these advances in medical technology and improvements in health care mean that more people survive to old age, thereby increasing average longevity in the general population.

Average longevity can be computed for people at any age. The most common method is to compute average longevity at birth, which is the projected age at which half of the people born in a certain year will have died. This computation takes into account peo-

ple who die at any age, from infancy onward. Thus, an average longevity of 78 years at birth means that 78 years after a group of people are born, half of them will still be alive. When average longevity is computed at other points in the life span, the calculation is based on all the people who are alive at that age; people who died earlier are not included. For example, computing the average longevity for people currently 40 years old would provide a predicted age at which half of those people will have died. People born into the same birth cohort but who died before age 40 are not counted. Eliminating those who die at early ages from the computation of average longevity at a specific age makes projected average longevity at age 65 longer than it was at birth.

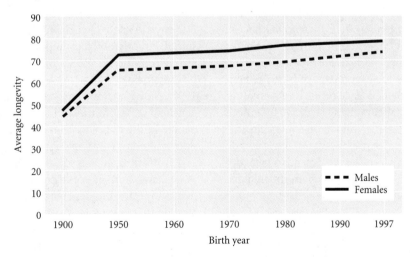

FIGURE 3.1 **Average longevity at birth in the United States.**

Source: National Center for Health Statistics, 1999.

Maximum longevity *is the oldest age to which any individual of a species lives.* Although the biblical character Methuselah is said to have lived to the ripe old age of 969 years, modern scientists are more conservative in their estimates of a human's maximum longevity. Even if we were able to eliminate all diseases, most researchers estimate the limit to be somewhere around 120 years because key body systems such as the cardiovascular system have limits on how long they can last (Hayflick, 1998). Whether this estimate of maximum longevity will change as new technologies produce better artificial organs remains to be seen. An important issue is whether extending the life span indefinitely would be a good idea.

Because maximum longevity of different animal species varies widely, scientists have tried to understand these differences by considering important biological functions such as metabolic rate or brain size (Hayflick, 1996). Just as with biological theories of aging, none of these explanations has met with complete success (Cristofalo et al., 1999; Hayflick, 1998). For example, why the giant tortoises of the Galapagos Islands typically live longer than we do remains a mystery.

Increasingly, researchers are differentiating **active life expectancy** from **dependent life expectancy;** *the difference is between living to a healthy old age (active life expectancy) and simply living a long time (dependent life expectancy).* Said another way, it is the difference between adding years to life and adding life to years. One's active life expectancy ends at the point when one loses independence or must rely on others for most activities of daily living (e.g., cooking meals, bathing). The remaining years of one's life constitute living in a dependent state. How many active and dependent years one has in late life depends a great deal on the interaction of genetic and environmental factors, to which we now turn.

Genetic and Environmental Factors in Average Longevity

Let's return to Susie, who wonders whether she can expect to live a long life. What influences how long we will live on average? Our average longevity is influenced most by genetic, environmental, ethnic, and gender factors. Clearly, these factors interact; being from an ethnic minority group, for example, often means that one has a higher risk of exposure to a harmful environment. But it is important to examine each of these factors and see how they influence our longevity. Let's begin with genetic and environmental factors.

GENETIC FACTORS. We have known for a long time that a good way to increase one's chances of a long life is to come from a family with a history of long-lived individuals (Hayflick, 1998). For example, if your mother lives to at least age 80, roughly 4 years are added to your average longevity (Woodruff-Pak, 1988). Alexander Graham Bell (the same guy who received the credit for inventing the telephone) was one of the first people to demonstrate systematically the benefits of coming from a long-lived family. Bell considered 8,797 of William Hyde's descendants and found that children of parents who had lived beyond 80 survived about 20 years longer than children whose parents had both died before they were 60. Thus, Susie's long-lived family sets the stage for Susie to enjoy a long life herself.

One exciting line of contemporary research, the Human Genome Project, is attempting to map all our genes. As noted in Chapter 2, this research and its spinoffs in microbiology and behavior genetics have already produced some astounding results in terms of genetic linkages to disease and aging (Bergeman, 1997). Some attempts are even being made to treat genetic diseases by implanting "corrected" genes into people in the hopes that the good genes will reproduce and eventually wipe out the defective genes.

Payoffs from such research are already helping us understand how increasing numbers of people are living to 100 or older. For example, Perls (1995) showed that genetic factors play a major role in determining how well older people cope with disease. The oldest-old, such as Susie's grandmother, are hardy because they have a high threshold for disease and show slower rates of disease progression than their peers who develop chronic diseases at younger ages and die earlier.

Both positive and negative aspects of aging can be transmitted through genes. Genetic research often uses families to identify markers for specific diseases.

ENVIRONMENTAL FACTORS. Although heredity is a major determinant of longevity, environmental factors also affect the life span (Bergeman, 1997; Hayflick, 1998). Some environmental factors are more obvious; diseases, toxins, lifestyle, and social class are among the most important. Diseases, such as cardiovascular disease and Alzheimer's disease, and lifestyle issues, such as smoking and exercise, receive a great deal of attention from researchers. Environmental toxins, encountered mainly as air and water pollution, are a continuing problem. For example, toxins in fish, bacteria and cancer-causing chemicals in drinking water, and airborne pollutants are major agents in shortening longevity.

The impact of social class on longevity results from the reduced access to goods and services, especially medical care, that characterizes most ethnic minority groups, the poor, and many older adults (National Center for Health Statistics, 1999). Most of these people have little or no health insurance, and many cannot afford the cost of a more healthful lifestyle. For example, lead poisoning from old water pipes, air pollution, and poor drinking water are serious problems in large urban areas, but many people simply cannot afford to move.

How environmental factors influence average life expectancy changes over time. For example, acquired immunodeficiency syndrome (AIDS) became a factor in longevity during the 1980s and continues to kill millions of people around the world. In contrast, the life expectancy impact of cardiovascular diseases is lessening somewhat as the rates of those diseases decline.

The sad part about most environmental factors is that we are responsible for them. Denying adequate health care to everyone, continuing to pollute our environment, and failing to address the underlying causes of poverty have undeniable consequences: They needlessly shorten lives and dramatically increase the cost of health care.

Ethnic Differences in Average Longevity

People in different ethnic groups do not have the same average longevity at birth. For example, African Americans' average longevity at birth is roughly 6.5 years lower for men and about 5 years lower for women than it is for European Americans (Centers for Disease Control and Prevention, 2000). Why do such large differences exist? The most important reasons are the substantial differences in most environmental variables between European Americans and other ethnic groups.

When examined carefully, ethnic differences in average longevity are quite complex (Go et al., 1995). Because people in ethnic minority groups are at greater risk for disease (e.g., sickle cell anemia) and other hazards (e.g., homicide), have much less access to good health care, and live less healthful lifestyles for economic reasons, people of ethnic minorities die earlier than their European American counterparts. However, those from ethnic minority groups who survive to old age may live longer on average than European Americans. The reason for the switch in average longevity advantage has to do mainly with the kinds of people from ethnic minority groups who survive to old age. Like Susie's mother and grandmother, they tend to be healthier because they typically have made it to old age without the assistance of high-quality medical care. Such people undoubtedly have a genetic advantage. However, until all people have equal access to health care and have equal opportunities to engage in healthful lifestyles, the degree to which genetic factors account for differences in average longevity will remain unknown.

Environmental influences are also key in understanding differences in average longevity at birth around the world. These differences between developing and industrialized countries are dramatic. But even among industrialized nations, there are important differences depending on when you make the comparisons. Because older European Americans tend to have the best health care in the world, they have a greater average longevity at age 80 than people in Sweden and Japan, although people in these countries have longer average longevity at birth (Manton & Vaupel, 1995).

Gender Differences in Average Longevity

If you have ever visited a senior center or a long-term care facility, you probably wondered, "Where are all the very old men? Why do women tend to live longer than men?" As Hayflick (1996) notes, the short (but accurate) answer to the question of why women live longer is that we do not know for sure. Surprisingly, this difference has resulted in little research, despite the social, economic, and political effects of this gender difference.

If we consider average longevity from birth in the United States, females have nearly a 7-year edge over males. This difference closes during adolescence and increases in favor of females for much of adulthood, with the gap narrowing somewhat in very old age. The visible result of these differences is much more striking when considered in terms of the ratio of men to women at various ages. At birth, there are roughly 106 boys for every 100 girls; however, more male babies die in infancy or are stillborn. Increased vulnerability of males to disease continues throughout life. Between ages 65 and 69, the ratio drops to 81 men for every 100 women. The differential increases rapidly; between ages 80 and 84, the ratio is roughly 53 to 100, and by age 100 it is down to approximately 27 to 100.

These differences are fairly typical of most industrialized countries but not of developing countries. Indeed, the female advantage in average longevity in the United States became apparent only in the early 20th century (Hayflick, 1996). Why? Until then, so many women died in childbirth that their average longevity as a group was reduced to that of men.

Death in childbirth still partially explains the lack of a female advantage in developing countries today; however, part of the difference in some countries also results from infanticide of baby girls. Socioeconomic factors such as access to health care, work and educational opportunities, and athletics also help account for the emergence of the female advantage in industrialized countries (Hayflick, 1998).

Many ideas have been offered to explain the significant advantage women have over men in average longevity in industrialized countries (Hayflick, 1996). Overall, men's rates of dying from the top 15 causes of death are significantly higher than women's at nearly every age, and men are also more susceptible to infectious diseases. These differences have led some to speculate that perhaps there is no fundamental biological difference in longevity but rather a much greater susceptibility in men of contracting certain fatal diseases (Hayflick, 1996).

Other researchers disagree; they argue that there are potential biological explanations. These include the fact that women have two X chromosomes, compared with one in men; men have a higher metabolic rate; women have a higher brain-to-body weight ratio; and women have lower testosterone levels. However, none of these explanations has sufficient scientific support to explain why most women in industrialized countries can expect, on average, to outlive most men (Hayflick, 1996).

Despite their longer average longevity, women do not have all the advantages. Interestingly, older men who survive beyond age 90 are the hardiest segment of their birth cohort in terms of performance on cognitive tests (Perls, 1995). Between ages 65 and 89, women score higher on cognitive tests; beyond age 90, men do much better.

CONCEPT CHECKS

1. What are some of the main reasons that average longevity increased during the 20th century?

2. What evidence is there that genetics influences average longevity? What are the key environmental influences on average longevity?

3. What are some of the reasons for ethnic differences in average longevity?

4. What explanations have been offered to account for women's longer average longevity?

HEALTH AND ILLNESS

LEARNING OBJECTIVES

- What are the key issues in defining health and illness?
- How is the quality of life assessed?
- What normative age-related changes occur in the immune system?
- What are the developmental trends in chronic and acute diseases?
- What are the key issues in stress across adulthood?

*R*osa *is a 72-year-old immigrant from Mexico living in a small apartment in a large city in the southwestern United States. For most of her life she has been very healthy, but lately she has noticed that it is getting harder to get up every morning. Additionally, when she gets a cold it takes her longer to recover than when she was younger. Rosa wonders whether these problems are typical or whether she is experiencing something unusual.*

Each of us has had periods of health and of illness. Most people are like Rosa—healthy for nearly all our lives. In this section, we will tackle the difficult issue of defining health and illness. We will consider quality of life, an increasingly important notion as medical technology keeps people alive longer. We will see how the differences between acute and chronic disease become more important with age. Because our immune system plays such a central role in health and illness, we will examine key age-related changes in it. Finally, we will consider how stress can affect our health.

Defining Health and Illness

What does the term *health* mean to you? The total lack of disease? Complete physical, mental, and social well-being? Actually, scientists cannot agree on a comprehensive definition, largely because what we include in the term keeps broadening (Pender, 1996). Many people now include biological, psychological, sociocultural, spiritual, and environmental components. Change in any one of these aspects affects people's health. *Still, most researchers define* **health** *as the absence of acute and chronic physical or mental disease and impairments* (Deeg et al., 1996). **Illness** *is the presence of a physical or mental disease or impairment.*

Think for a moment about your health. How would you rate it? Although this question looks simple, how people answer it turns out to be predictive of illness and mortality (Idler & Benyamini, 1997). Why? There are several possibilities (Wolinsky & Tierney, 1998). One is that self-rated health captures more aspects of health than other measures. A second possibility is that poor self-rated health reflects respondents' belief that they are on a downward trajectory in functioning. A third is that people's self-ratings affect their health-related behaviors, which in turn affect health outcomes. Finally, self-rated health may actually represent an assessment of people's internal and external resources that are available to support health.

Research data support all these ideas. However, there are important gender and cultural differences. For example, research reveals that self-rated health is roughly comparable across cultures (Jylhä et al., 1998). However, in some studies self-rated health predicts mortality better in men than in women in cross-cultural samples in France (Helmer et al., 1999), Finland, and Italy (Jylhä et al., 1998), but it predicts mortality better in women than in men in an Australian sample (Simons et al., 1996).

An important developmental issue is whether self-ratings of health differ with age. For many years, it appeared that they did, although in a counterintuitive way: Many studies showed that the old-old had more positive ratings than other age groups. However, Roberts (1999) carefully examined 17 previous studies and found that the way in which people were asked to rate their health, as well as how the age groups were defined and the samples obtained, created a bias favoring the oldest age group. This finding points out the importance of paying close attention to the research design issues discussed in Chapter 1.

Clearly, the relationship between self-rated health and health outcomes is complex. As we consider other elements of health, we will gain additional insights into this relationship. Additionally, in Chapter 5 we see how certain interventions can influence both the perceptions of one's health and health outcomes.

Quality of Life

One of the primary goals of people across adulthood is to have high quality of life. But what does that mean? Precise definitions are hard to find. Most people would find it easier to say what quality of life is not: being dependent on a respirator while in a permanent vegetative state is one common example. Researchers have found it easier to approach quality-of-life issues this way as well. In terms of the framework used in this text, quality of life is a multidimensional concept encompassing biological, psychological, and sociocultural domains at any point in the life cycle (Birren et al., 1991).

Most research on quality of life has focused on two areas: quality of life in the context of specific diseases or conditions and quality of life relating to end-of-life issues. We briefly lay out the issues here and return to them as we discuss specific situations in this chapter and in Chapters 5 (interventions that increase quality of life) and 13 (end-of-life issues).

In many respects, quality of life is a subjective judgment that can be understood in the context of broader models of adult development and aging. One such model describes ways in which people select domains of relative strength, optimize their use of these strengths, and compensate for age-related changes (Baltes et al., 1998; Freund & Baltes, 1998). From this perspective, quality of life is a successful use of selection, optimization, and compensation to manage one's life, resulting in successful aging.

If we apply this notion to health, then quality of life is the ability to manage illness (Brod et al., 1999). Albert (1997) argues that health-related quality of life includes both physical and mental health. In general, research on health-related quality of life addresses a critical question (Lawton et al., 1999): To what extent does distress from illness or side effects associated with treatment reduce the person's wish to live? Lawton and colleagues (1999) show that the answer to this question depends a great deal on a person's *valuation of life,* the degree to which a person is attached to his or her present life. How much one enjoys life, has hope about the future, and finds meaning in everyday events, for example, has a great deal of impact on how long that person would like to live.

Narrowing the focus of quality of life as it relates to specific conditions brings us to the domains of physical impairment or disability and of Alzheimer's disease. Quality of life in the former context includes issues of environmental design that improves people's functioning and well-being (Lawton, 1999). We examine environmental influences in Chapter 5. Quality of life is more difficult to assess in people with Alzheimer's disease, although advances are being made (Brod et al., 1999; Rabins et al., 1999). We consider this issue in Chapter 4 when we focus on Alzheimer's disease.

Changes in the Immune System

Every day, we are threatened by invaders: bacterial, viral, and parasitic infections (as well as their toxic byproducts) and abnormal cells such as precancerous and tumor cells. Our bodies have a highly advanced defense system against foreign invaders: our immune system. This is a highly complex system of interacting parts that we are just beginning to comprehend (Aldwin & Gilmer, 1999). For example, one great mystery is how the immune system learns to differentiate self from invader. Researchers think that it involves recognizing certain substances, called *antigens,* on the surface of invading bacteria and cells that have been taken over by viruses. Regardless how it actually happens, once the immune system has learned to recognize the invader, it creates a defense against it.

How does the defense system work? The immune system is composed of three major types of cells that form a network of interacting parts: cell-mediated immunity (consisting of thymus-derived, or *T-lymphocytes*), humoral immunity (*B-lymphocytes*), and nonspecific immunity (*monocytes* and *polymorphonuclear neutrophil leukocytes;* Miller, 1996a). The primary job of the two types of lymphocytes is to defend against malignant (cancerous) cells, viral infection, fungal infection, and some bacteria. Natural killer (NK) cells are a subpopulation of lymphocytes that provide a broad surveillance system to prevent tumor growth and our primary defense against cancer, although how this happens is not fully understood (Aldwin & Gilmer, 1999; Kutza et al., 1995). NK cells also help fight viral infections and parasites and may have a role in multiple sclerosis, a disease that typically manifests itself during young adulthood and early middle age (Adler & Nagel, 1994). Additionally, there are five major types of antibodies called immunoglobulins (IgA, IgD, IgE, IgG, and IgM), each of which performs a specialized function. For example, IgE mediates allergies and asthma, and IgG (also called γ-globulin) helps fight hepatitis.

How does aging affect the immune system? Researchers are only beginning to understand this process, and little direct evidence is available. Moreover, the immune system is sensitive to a wide variety of lifestyle and environmental factors, such as diet, stress, exercise, and disease, making it very difficult to isolate changes caused by aging alone. Furthermore, conflicting data are obtained depending on what part of the body is examined, even in the same person over time (Miller, 1996b). However, because older adults are more susceptible to certain infections and have a much higher risk of cancer (both of which are discussed in more detail later in this chapter), most researchers believe that the immune system changes with age.

Research evidence suggests that the total number of T-lymphocytes probably does not change with age, at least not until age 90, although the balance in the types of T-lymphocytes appears to change (Lehtonen et al., 1990; Miller, 1996a, 1996b). Specifically, older adults have fewer immature T-lymphocytes and more mature ones. Because it is the immature cells that "learn" to fight new invaders, this balance shift may explain why older adults' immune systems are less effective when exposed to new strains of bacteria or viruses (Aldwin & Gilmer, 1999). Likewise, the total concentration of indicators of B-lymphocytes and NK cells changes little with age (Aldwin & Gilmer, 1999; Miller, 1996a, 1996b).

What is much clearer is that major changes occur in how well lymphocytes work (Aldwin & Gilmer, 1999; Ebersole & Hess, 1998; Miller, 1996a, 1996b). For one thing, older adults' immune systems take longer to build up defenses against specific diseases,

even after an immunization injection. This is probably caused by the changing balance in T-lymphocytes and could partially explain why older adults need to be immunized earlier against specific diseases such as influenza. Similarly, B-lymphocytes decrease in functioning. Research examining the administration of substances such as growth hormones to older adults to stimulate lymphocyte functioning indicates that some specific lymphocyte functioning returns to normal (Adler & Nagel, 1994). This process for T- and B-lymphocytes is described in Figure 3.2.

The changes in immune system function have important implications (Aldwin & Gilmer, 1999; Miller, 1996a). Older adults become more prone to serious consequences from illnesses that are easily defeated by younger adults. Additionally, various forms of leukemia, which are cancers of the immune cells, increase with age along with other forms of cancer. *Finally, the immune system can begin attacking the body itself in a process called* **autoimmunity.** Autoimmunity results from an imbalance of B- and T-lymphocytes giving rise to autoantibodies and is responsible for several disorders, such as rheumatoid arthritis (Ebersole & Hess, 1998).

A growing body of evidence is pointing to key connections between our immune system and our psychological state. For example, Cohen and Herbert (1996) showed how our psychological state, or a characteristic such as our attitude, can begin a series of neurological, hormonal, and behavioral responses that directly change the immune system and make us more likely to become ill.

Psychoneuroimmunology *is the study of the relations between psychological, neurological, and immunological systems that raise or lower our susceptibility to and ability to recover from disease.* The focus of much of this research has been on identifying the psychological triggers that start the process and result in cancer. Two general types of investigations have been conducted (Cohen & Herbert, 1996): predicting which healthy older adults are likely to eventually get cancer and predicting those who will live longer after being diagnosed with cancer. So far, findings are mixed. Some results show that having a positive attitude and a good social support system predict longer

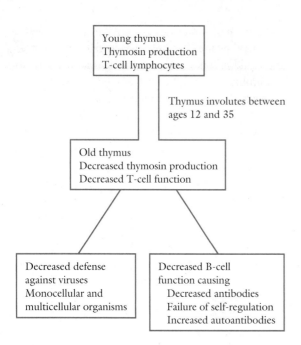

FIGURE 3.2 Process of aging of the immune system.

Source: Ebersole, P., & Hess, P. (1998). *Toward healthy aging: Human needs and nursing response* (5th ed., p. 41). St. Louis: Mosby.

life for middle-aged patients with cancer but not for older ones (Schulz et al., 1996). To make matters more complicated, some evidence suggests that the effects of social support are more important for women than for men. Interestingly, factors such as depression have not yet been shown to have strong effects (Cohen & Herbert, 1996).

AIDS AND OLDER ADULTS. An increasing number of older adults have AIDS; the Centers for Disease Control and Prevention (1999) estimate that roughly 4,000 people over age 65 have AIDS in the United States. These are people who contracted the human immunodeficiency virus (HIV) during middle age and survived to later life and people who contracted the disease as older adults. Unfortunately, because of the social stereotype that older adults are not sexually active, many physicians do not test older patients (Hooyman & Kiyak, 1999).

Although older men are at higher risk for AIDS, older women also are at significant risk. For men, the most common risk factor is homosexual or bisexual behavior. In contrast, AIDS usually is transmitted to older women through heterosexual contact with infected partners. Older adults may be more susceptible to HIV infection because of the changes in the immune system discussed earlier. For women, the thinning of the vaginal wall with age makes it more likely that it will tear, making it easier for the HIV to enter the bloodstream. Older adults' lower frequency of condom use also raises the risk (Gaerta et al., 1996). Once they are infected, the progression from HIV-positive status to AIDS is more rapid among older adults. Once they are diagnosed with AIDS, older adults' remaining life span is nearly a year shorter than it is for newly diagnosed young adults.

It is clear that older adults need to be educated about their risk for HIV and AIDS. Few media stories about the problem focus on older adults, so they may mistakenly believe that they have nothing to worry about. They are less likely to raise the issue with a physician, less likely to be tested, and, if diagnosed, less likely to seek support groups. We must change ageist attitudes toward older adults and sexuality to ensure that people of all ages are educated and screened (Emlet, 1997).

Chronic and Acute Diseases

Rosa, the immigrant from Mexico, is typical of older adults: She is beginning to experience some recurring health difficulties and finding out that she does not recover as quickly from even minor afflictions. You probably have had several encounters with illnesses that come on quickly, last a few days, then abate. You may have also experienced conditions that tend to last much longer, with long-term consequences. Your experience reflects the difference between acute and chronic diseases (Rush-Presbyterian St. Luke's Medical Center, 1998). **Acute diseases** *are conditions that develop over a short period of time and cause a rapid change in health.* We are all familiar with acute diseases, such as colds, influenza, and food poisoning. Most acute diseases are cured with medications (such as antibiotics for bacterial infections) or allowed to run their course (the case with most viral infections). *In contrast,* **chronic diseases** *are conditions that last a* longer period of time (at least 3 months) and may be accompanied by residual functional impairment that necessitates long-term management. Chronic diseases include arthritis and diabetes mellitus.

What do you think happens to the incidence of acute and chronic diseases as people age? If you said that the rates of acute disease go down whereas the rates of chronic diseases go up, you are correct. Contrary to what many people believe, older adults have fewer colds, for example, than younger adults. However, when they do get an acute disease, older adults tend to get sicker and take longer to recover (National Center for Health Statistics, 1999). Thus, although they get fewer acute infections, older people may actually spend more days feeling sick than their younger (and, based on frequency of occurrence, "sicker") counterparts. This is probably why many people mistakenly believe that the rates of acute disease increase with age.

Because they have more problems fighting acute infections, older adults are more at risk from dying of an acute condition. For example, the rate of respiratory infection is about the same for younger and older adults, but people over age 65 account for roughly 90% of deaths from pneumonia and influenza. For these reasons, health professionals strongly recommend that older adults be vaccinated against pneumonia and influenza; these shots reduce the risk of pneumonia by about two thirds and influenza by half (National Center for Health Statistics, 1999).

Until the 1990s, chronic disease was simply viewed as a part of aging. With the publication in 1991 of the historic document *Healthy People 2000: National Health Promotion and Disease Prevention* (USDHHS, 1991), the view shifted dramatically to one of prevention and wellness. As we see a bit later in this chapter, advances in managing chronic conditions have been made.

The Role of Stress

You know what it feels like to be stressed. Whether it's from the upcoming exam in this course, the traffic jam you sat in on your way home yesterday, or the demands your children place on you, stress seems to be everywhere. There is plenty of scientific evidence that over the long term, stress is very bad for your health. But despite thousands of scientific studies, scientists still cannot agree on a formal definition of *stress*. To some, stress is a property of specific events, such as the death of a partner (McLeod, 1996). In this approach, events vary in how stressful they are, but everyone who experiences a particular event comes under the same level of stress. To others, stress is a result of people's evaluation of events in the context of the various resources they have (Cohen et al., 1995; Lazarus & Folkman, 1984). This approach emphasizes that stress is defined by the person and that no two people experience the same event in exactly the same way.

Because the second view is the most widely used approach for studying stress and the ways in which people deal with it, we examine it in more detail. Although there are several variations on this approach, we focus on Richard Lazarus and Susan Folkman's framework as the best-researched representative of the view that whether a person feels stressed depends on how he or she evaluates the situation at hand. Let's see how this decision occurs.

THE STRESS AND COPING PARADIGM. Suppose you are stuck in a traffic jam. Depending on whether you are late for an appointment or have plenty of time on your hands, you will probably feel very different about your situation. *The* **stress and coping paradigm** *views stress not as an environmental stimulus or as a response but as the interaction of a thinking person and an event* (Lazarus, 1984; Lazarus et al., 1985; Lazarus & Folkman, 1984). How we interpret an event such as being stuck in traffic is what matters, not the event itself or what we do in response to it. Put more formally, stress is "a particular relationship between the person and the environment that is appraised by the person as taxing or exceeding his or her resources and endangering his or her well-being" (Lazarus & Folkman, 1984, p. 19). Note that this definition states that stress is a transactional process between a person and the environment, that it takes into account personal resources, that the person's appraisal of the situation is key, and that unless the situation is considered to be threatening, challenging, or harmful, stress does not result. A diagram of the transactional model is shown in Figure 3.3.

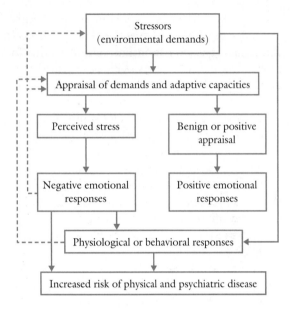

FIGURE 3.3   An example of a transactional model of stress.

From *Measuring stress: A guide for health and social scientists,* edited by Sheldon Cohen, Kessler, and Gordon, copyright © 1995 by Oxford University Press, Inc. Used by permission of Oxford University Press, Inc.

What exactly does this definition mean? Think about our traffic jam example. The transactional model of stress says that each time you are in a traffic jam you make a separate judgment as to whether it is stressful depending on the resources you have and your interpretation of them. The resources a person has include such things as the cumulative experience of dealing with similar situations (traffic jams) before, knowledge or access to information about the event, the ability to get help if necessary, and the time necessary to engage in any actions necessary to address the situation. Clearly, these resources vary a great deal from person to person and reflect the influence of biological (e.g., genetic), psychological (e.g., personality), sociocultural (e.g., ethnicity), and life-cycle (e.g., life-stage) forces. These differences in resources are extremely important in understanding why some people have little trouble dealing with very difficult events (e.g., a severe illness) whereas other people seem to have trouble with seemingly routine events

(e.g., calming a crying child). Recognizing these differences, let's begin our closer look at the stress and coping paradigm with the concept of appraisal.

APPRAISAL. Lazarus and Folkman (1984) describe three types of appraisals of stress. **Primary appraisal** *categorizes events into three groups based on the significance they have for our well-being: irrelevant, benign or positive, and stressful.* Irrelevant events are ones that have no bearing on us personally; hearing about a typhoon nowhere near land in the South Pacific while sitting in your living room in Boston is an example. Benign or positive events are ones that have good effects, such as a long-anticipated pay increase. Finally, stressful events are ones, such as an upcoming operation or test, that are appraised as harmful, threatening, or challenging.

Primary appraisals act as a filter for events we experience. Specifically, any event that is appraised as either irrelevant or as benign or positive is not stressful. In a real sense, we decide which events are potentially stressful and which ones are not. This is an important point for two reasons. First, it means we can effectively sort out the events that may be problems and those that are not, allowing us to concentrate on dealing with life's difficulties more effectively. Second, it means that we could be wrong about our reading of an event. A situation that may appear at first blush to be irrelevant, for example, may actually be very important, or a situation deemed stressful initially may turn out not to be. Such mistakes in primary appraisal could set the stage for real (or imagined) crises later on.

If a person believes that an event is stressful, a second set of decisions, called secondary appraisal, is made. **Secondary appraisal** *evaluates our perceived ability to cope with harm, threat, or challenge.* Secondary appraisal is the equivalent of asking three questions: "What can I do?" "How likely is it that I can use one of my options successfully?" and "Will this option reduce my stress?" How we answer these questions sets the stage for addressing them effectively. For example, if you believe that there is something you can do in a situation that will make a difference, then your perceived stress may be reduced and you may be able to deal with the event successfully. In contrast, if you believe that there is little that you can do to address the situation successfully or reduce your feelings of stress, then you may feel powerless and ineffective, even if others around you believe that there are steps you could take. What matters in secondary appraisals (and all other decisions in this framework) is what you think is true, not what others think.

After you make a decision about an event and reach a preliminary conclusion about what you should do about it (if anything), the situation continues to play itself out. As the event continues to unfold, you begin to get an idea as to whether your primary (and secondary, if necessary) appraisal was accurate. If it was, then you would probably stick with your original evaluation. However, sometimes you learn additional information or experience another situation that indicates that you should reappraise the original event. **Reappraisal** *involves making a new primary or secondary appraisal resulting from changes in the situation.* For example, you may initially dismiss an accusation that your partner is cheating on you (i.e., make a primary appraisal that the event is irrelevant), but after being shown pictures of your partner in a romantic situation with another person, you reappraise the event as stressful. Reappraisal can either increase stress (if your partner had initially denied the encounter) or lower stress (if you discovered that the photographs were fakes).

The three types of appraisals demonstrate that determining whether an event is stressful is a dynamic process. Initial decisions about events may be upheld over time, or they may change in light of new information or personal experience. Thus, different events may be appraised in the same way, and the same event may be appraised differently at any two points in time. This dynamic process helps explain why people react the way they do over the life span. For example, as our physiological abilities change with increasing age, we may have fewer physical resources to handle particular events. As a result, events that were appraised as not stressful in young adulthood may be appraised as stressful in late life.

COPING. During the secondary appraisal of an event labeled stressful in primary appraisal, we may believe that there is something we can do to deal with the event effectively. *Collectively, these attempts to deal with stressful events are called* **coping.** Lazarus and Folkman (1984) view coping more formally as a complex, evolving process of dealing with stress that is learned. Much like appraisals, coping is seen as a dynamic, evolving process that is fine-tuned over time. Our first attempt might fail, but if we try again in a slightly different way we may succeed. Coping is learned, not automatic. That is why we often do not cope very well with stressful situations we are facing for the first time (such as the end of our first love relationship). The saying "practice makes perfect" applies to coping, too. Also, coping takes time and effort. Finally, coping entails only managing the situation; we need not overcome or control it. Indeed, many stressful events cannot be fixed or undone; many times the best we can do is to learn to live with the situation. It is in this sense that we may cope with the death of a spouse.

The ways in which people cope can be classified in several different ways. At a general level we can distinguish between problem-focused coping and emotion-focused coping. *Problem-focused coping* involves attempts to tackle the problem head-on. Taking medication to treat a disease and spending more time studying for an examination are examples of problem-focused coping with the stress of illness or failing a prior test. In general, problem-focused coping entails doing something directly about the problem at hand. *Emotion-focused coping* involves dealing with one's feelings about the stressful event. Allowing oneself to express anger or frustration over becoming ill or failing an exam is an example of this approach. The goal here is not necessarily to eliminate the problem, although this may happen. Rather, the purpose may be to help oneself deal with situations that are difficult or impossible to tackle head-on.

Several other behaviors can also be viewed in the context of coping. Many people believe that their relationship with God is an important aspect of coping (Ishler et al., 1995). Psychoanalytic researchers point to Freud's notion of defense mechanisms as behav-

Religiosity and spirituality are important aspects of a person's lifestyle that must be considered in holistic approach to health and wellness.

iors that may be used to reduce stress. In short, people use many different types of behaviors when they feel stressed.

How well we cope depends on several factors. For example, healthy, energetic people are better able to cope with an infection than frail, sick people. Psychologically, a positive attitude about oneself and one's abilities is also important. Good problem-solving skills put one at an advantage by creating several options with which to manage the stress. Social skills and social support are important in helping one solicit suggestions and assistance from others. Finally, financial resources are important; having the money to pay a mechanic to fix your car allows you to avoid the frustration of trying to do it yourself.

AGING AND THE STRESS AND COPING PARADIGM. Two important age-related differences in the stress and coping paradigm are the sources of stress and coping strategies. Age-related differences have been described for the kinds of things people report as everyday stresses (Aldwin et al., 1996a; Folkman et al., 1987). Younger adults experience more stress in the areas of finance, work, home maintenance, personal life, family, and friends than do older adults. These differences probably exist because young adults are likely to be parents of small children and are likely to be employed; parenting and work roles are less salient to retired older

adults. The stresses reported frequently by older adults may be more age related than role related. That is, environmental stress may be caused by a decreased ability to get around rather than by a specific role.

There is some evidence that the old-old report having fewer stressors in the past week than any other age group (Aldwin et al., 1996a). Why this is the case is unclear. It may be that in late life people begin to narrow their focus and thus have fewer areas of life that could produce stress. Or, as we will see in Chapter 10, the old-old may adopt a more philosophical outlook on life and not let things bother them as much.

Age differences in coping strategies across the life span are striking and consistent (Diehl et al., 1996). One key difference is that older adults are more likely to use past experience in coping as a guide (Aldwin et al., 1996b). This results in different coping styles. For example, Blanchard-Fields and her colleagues have shown that younger adults tend to use defensive coping styles much of the time, whereas older adults choose coping strategies on the basis of whether they feel in control of the situation (Blanchard-Fields & Irion, 1988). Even when people are faced with similar problems, age differences in coping style are apparent. For example, Felton and Revenson (1987) report that when trying to cope with their chronic illnesses, middle-aged adults are more likely to use interpersonal strategies such as information seeking than are older adults. One way to interpret these differences is as a shift in "management strategies" (Aldwin et al., 1996b). As people age, they become better at managing their lives so as to avoid problems in the first place, so they don't need to cope with stress.

But becoming better at managing life does not mean that older adults are willing to give up meaningful roles when they encounter stressful events. As discussed in the How Do We Know? feature, older adults may become more committed to highly cherished roles when stressful life events arise (Krause, 1999).

EFFECTS OF STRESS ON HEALTH. How does stress affect us? If the stress is short, such as being stuck in a traffic jam for an hour when we're already late in an

CHAPTER 3

Who was the investigator, and what was the aim of the study? How older adults cope with the effects of stressful events related to highly valued roles (such as parent, spouse, provider, and homemaker) has been debated for years. Neal Krause (1999) decided to see which of two theoretical views did a better job of explaining how this coping occurs. Specifically, he examined whether older adults would tend to devalue a highly salient role in which they experienced a stressful event as a way to deal with it.

How did the investigator measure the topic of interest? To get a broad assessment of the key variables, Krause used several self-report measures. The *salient role devaluation* measure assessed whether people's most salient role was the same at two times of measurement. The *stress in most highly valued role* measure assessed whether a highly stressful event related to the most salient role at the first time of measurement occurred. The *stress in other roles* measure assessed the number of stressful events associated with roles other than the most salient one. The *role-specific self-esteem* measure assessed the degree to which people believed they were useful, worthwhile, and successful. The *global self-esteem* measure assessed whether people feel self-worth, have good qualities, and have a positive attitude toward themselves. Additionally, participants were asked their age and educational level.

Who were the participants in the study? The sample was drawn from all eligible adults in the Health Care Finance Administration (HCFA) Medicare Beneficiary Eligibility List. Two groups of people are not included in the list: those without Social Security numbers and people over 100 years of age (HCFA does not release information about such people). The sample was a random selection from this master list of people over age 65 who were not working for pay and who lived in the contiguous United States (i.e., residents of Alaska and Hawaii were excluded). At Time 1, 1,103 people were interviewed. At Time 2, 605 of these people were successfully reinterviewed. Of the others, 173 had died, 33 had moved to a nursing home, 75 refused to participate again, 98 could not be located, and 119 were too ill to participate. A total of 589 adults had usable data from both interviews, so these were the people whose data were analyzed.

What was the design of the study? Krause used a longitudinal design with two times of measurement: 1992–1993 and 1996–1997.

Were there ethical concerns in the study? Because people had the right to not participate, there were no ethical concerns with the study.

What were the results? Because of the problems inherent in longitudinal designs (see Chapter 1), Krause checked for systematic differences in participants in the Time 1 and Time 2 samples. He found that the people not completing the interview at Time 2 were more likely to be older and male, have less education, and have lower self-rated health. However, no differences directly related to stress were found, meaning that the findings can be interpreted in a straightforward manner.

Three important results emerged. First, when one or more undesirable events are encountered in the most highly valued role, older adults are about 33% less likely to devalue that role in the follow-up interview. Second, feelings of self-worth associated with the role valued most highly exert a significant effect in keeping that role salient at the follow-up interview. Third, the effect of self-worth is slightly greater than the effect of stress in keeping highly salient roles salient.

What did the investigator conclude? The findings clearly indicate that rather than turning away from highly valued roles when stressful events occur, older adults actually become more committed to them. Why people choose this course remains to be explained.

otherwise relaxed day, the answer is that it probably will have little effect other than on our temper. But if the stress is continuous, or chronic, then the picture changes dramatically. Chronic stress has several potentially serious effects (Davis et al., 2000), including immune system suppression leading to increased susceptibility to viral infections, increased risk of atherosclerosis and hypertension, and impaired memory and cognition. In women, chronic stress can also inhibit menstruation, and they react to a wider range of outside stressors than do men.

Researchers are divided on whether these effects of chronic stress change with age. Some evidence suggests that hormonal reactions increase with age (Gotthardt et al., 1995), whereas other studies show no difference (Nicolson et al., 1997; Soederberg Miller & Lachman, 1999). Part of the discrepancy may result from the variability in hormonal changes across individuals in how people respond to stress, and part may result from the apparent reduction in the number of events older people label as stressful. Most data indicate that adults of all ages tend to return to prestress levels of functioning in roughly the same ways (Soederberg Miller & Lachman, 1999).

CONCEPT CHECKS

1. How do researchers define *health?* What are the problems with these definitions?
2. How is *quality of life* defined?
3. What are the major age-related changes in immune system functioning?
4. What are the differences between chronic and acute diseases?
5. What is the stress and coping paradigm? What are the key age-related changes that occur?

COMMON CHRONIC CONDITIONS AND THEIR MANAGEMENT

LEARNING OBJECTIVES

- What are the most important issues in chronic disease?
- What are some common chronic conditions across adulthood?
- How can people manage chronic conditions?

Moses is a 75-year-old African American man who worked as a lawyer all his life. Recently, he was diagnosed as having prostate cancer. Moses has heard about several treatment options, such as surgery and radiation therapy, and he is concerned about potential side effects, such as impotence. Moses wonders what he should do.

Every day, millions of older adults get up in the morning and face another day of dealing with chronic disease. Although medical advances are made every year, true cures for these conditions probably are not imminent. We considered some chronic diseases in Chapter 2 in the context of discussing age-related changes in major body systems; arthritis and cardiovascular disease were among them.

In this section we will consider other chronic conditions, such as diabetes and cancer. We will see that Moses' concern about how to deal with his prostate cancer is one facing many people. As Moses will discover, in many situations there is no clear-cut "right" way to proceed. We will also examine some ways to help alleviate the effects of some chronic conditions and consider some ways in which we may be able to prevent such diseases or at least reduce our chances of getting them.

General Issues in Chronic Conditions

Having a chronic disease does not mean that one becomes incapacitated. Even though the type and severity of chronic conditions vary across people, most older adults manage to accomplish the necessary tasks of daily living despite having a chronic condition. Only about 2% of older adults with chronic conditions are bedridden (Hooyman & Kiyak, 1999).

Although most people manage to accomplish the necessary tasks of daily living, they may experience limitations. Chronic conditions can make life unpleasant and in some cases can increase susceptibility to other diseases. Understanding chronic conditions requires understanding how the four developmental forces interact.

We saw in Chapter 2 that researchers are beginning to understand genetic connections with such chronic conditions as cardiovascular disease and cancer. Other biological aspects include the changes in physical systems with age, including the immune system, that can set the stage for chronic conditions. Psychological aspects key to chronic disease include the coping skills people bring to bear on their conditions; we consider some of these later in this chapter.

Sociocultural factors include the lack of adequate health care, which creates barriers to treatment. The ethnic group differences in some chronic conditions, such as hypertension, are also important to keep in mind. Finally, life-cycle factors help us understand why reactions to the same chronic condition varies with the age of onset. Moreover, some conditions such as rheumatoid arthritis can occur at any point in adulthood, whereas others such as prostate cancer tend to occur most after midlife.

As the number of older adults increases rapidly, so will the extent of chronic conditions as health problems. This will necessitate a fundamental change in health care, reflecting a shift from an acute care focus to one that focuses much more on managing chronic conditions. Let's consider some of the most common chronic conditions.

Common Chronic Conditions

What are the most common chronic conditions experienced by older adults? Arthritis and various forms of cardiovascular disease are the most prevalent (National Center for Health Statistics, 1999). Four others are also extremely important: diabetes, cancer, incontinence, and stress.

ARTHRITIS. We saw in Chapter 2 that osteoarthritis and rheumatoid arthritis afflict many adults. It is estimated that everyone over age 60 shows some physical evidence of one form of arthritis, with at least 70% of these people reporting pain (National Center for Health Statistics, 1999). Because it is so common, most people assume that arthritis is simply a part of normal aging and further assume they must simply learn to live with it. Consequently, many people fail to seek appropriate therapy.

Rheumatoid arthritis is not strictly an age-related condition; in fact, many young and middle-aged adults have symptoms. The cause of rheumatoid arthritis remains unknown. In contrast, osteoarthritis is age-related, with symptoms usually not beginning until later in life. Genetic and environmental factors (such as overuse) have been identified.

The primary problem facing people with arthritis is pain. Strangely, the pain often is variable; people have both good days and bad days. In most cases, people with arthritis structure their days around these variations, doing more when they can. However, reducing physical activity has a paradoxical effect. Movement stimulates the secretion of synovial fluid, which lubricates the surfaces between and increases blood flow to the joints. Movement also keeps muscles toned and limber. All are important in keeping joints flexible; refraining from movement ultimately makes the joints hurt worse. Lack of movement over long periods of time can eventually result in the joints "freezing" in place, a conditions called *contracture*. Thus, people with arthritis must be encouraged to keep moving; the pain accompanying the arthritis is lower than that which would result from a contracture.

CARDIOVASCULAR AND CEREBROVASCULAR DISEASE. As noted in Chapter 2, a range of cardiovascular diseases occur with age. Most of these can be managed effectively through lifestyle interventions. Another chronic cardiovascular condition that is discussed much less often is *hypotension*, or low blood pressure. Symptoms of hypotension include dizziness or lightheadedness when you stand up quickly. Hypotension often is related to anemia and is very common in older adults. Although hypotension per se is not a dangerous condition, the resulting dizziness can increase the likelihood of falls.

Cerebrovascular accidents (CVAs) often create chronic conditions by causing brain damage. As noted in Chapter 2, quick intervention is important, but in many cases such interventions merely limit the spread of damage rather than prevent it. Because of advances in intervention, the death rate from CVA has dropped 40% over the past two decades (Gorelick et al., 1996). Depending on where in the brain the damage occurs, people experiencing CVAs may face months or years of rehabilitation. Despite major advances in therapy, roughly half of all patients who suffered motor impairments still have residual motor difficulties 1 year after their CVA (Gresham et al., 1995). Consequently, rehabilitation must also address the psychological implications of the loss of functioning.

DIABETES MELLITUS. *The disease* **diabetes mellitus** *occurs when the pancreas produces insufficient insulin.* The primary characteristic of diabetes mellitus is above-normal sugar (glucose) in the blood and urine caused by problems in metabolizing carbohydrates. People with diabetes mellitus can go into a coma if the level of sugar gets too high, and may lapse into unconsciousness if it gets too low.

There are three groups of older adults with diabetes: those who developed diabetes as children, adolescents, or young adults; those who developed diabetes in late middle age and also typically developed cardiovascular problems; and those who develop diabetes in late life and usually show mild problems. This last group includes the majority of older adults with diabetes mellitus.

In adults, diabetes mellitus often is associated with obesity. The symptoms of diabetes seen in younger people (excessive thirst, increased appetite and urination, fatigue, weakness, weight loss, and impaired wound healing) may be far less prominent or absent in older adults. As a result, diabetes mellitus in older adults often is diagnosed during other medical procedures, such as eye examinations or hospitalizations for other conditions. Overall, diabetes is more common among older adults, members of minority groups, and women (National Academy on an Aging Society, 2000a).

The chronic effects of increased glucose levels may result in complications. The most common long-term effects include nerve damage, diabetic retinopathy (discussed in Chapter 2), kidney disorders, CVAs, cognitive dysfunction, damage to the coronary arteries, skin problems, and poor circulation in the arms and legs, which may lead to gangrene. Diabetes also increases the chance of developing atherosclerosis and coronary heart disease.

Although it cannot be cured, diabetes can be managed effectively through a low-carbohydrate and low-calorie diet, exercise, proper care of skin, gums, teeth, and feet, and medication (insulin). For older adults, it is important to address potential memory difficul-

ties with the daily testing and management regimens. Education about diabetes mellitus was added to Medicare coverage in 1997, making it easier for older adults to learn how to manage the condition.

CANCER. Cancer is the second leading cause of death in the United States, behind cardiovascular disease. Every year roughly 1,250,000 people are diagnosed as having cancer, and more than 565,000 die (American Cancer Society, 1999a). Over the life span, nearly one in every two American men and one in three American women will develop cancer (American Cancer Society, 1999a). Some researchers argue that as the rates of cardiovascular disease continue to decline, cancer will become the leading cause of death in the United States (Manton et al., 1991). There is evidence that cancer is present in many people whose cause of death is officially listed as some other disease, such as pneumonia.

One unfortunate aspect of these statistics is that many current deaths caused by cancer are preventable. Some forms of cancer, such as lung and colorectal cancer, are caused in large part by unhealthful lifestyles. The American Cancer Society (1999a) estimates that cancers caused by smoking and excessive alcohol consumption alone account for nearly 200,000 deaths each year. Most skin cancers can be prevented by limiting exposure to the sun's ultraviolet rays. Clearly, changes in lifestyle would have a major impact on cancer rates.

The risk of getting cancer increases markedly with age (National Center for Health Statistics, 1999). Figure 3.4 depicts the incidence rates for cancer as a function of age. As can be seen, the largest number of cases occurs in the age group 60 to 79. Notice that after age 40 the incidence rate increases sharply. For example, the incidence of cancer at age 50 is only about 400 cases per 100,000 people; by age 70, however, it has increased to more than 1,500 cases. Overall, half of all cancer occurs in people over age 65.

The incidence and mortality rates of some common forms of cancer are shown in Table 3.1. Notice that prostate cancer is the most common form of cancer in men and breast cancer is the most common form in women in all ethnic groups (American Can-

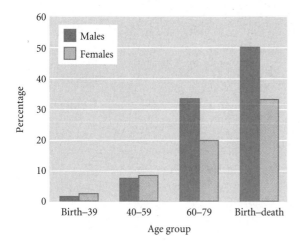

FIGURE 3.4 Cancer incidence rates as a function of age.

Source: National Cancer Institute; National Center for Health Statistics, 1999.

cer Society, 1999a; National Center for Health Statistics, 1999). Gender differences are apparent in some forms of cancer; for example, lung and colorectal cancers are more common in men (American Cancer Society, 1999a). Death rates from various forms of cancer differ: Lung cancer kills more than twice as many men as prostate cancer and 25% more women than breast cancer (in women). Five-year survival rates for these cancers also differ dramatically. Whereas only 14% of patients with lung cancer are still living 5 years after diagnosis, an average of 85% of patients with breast cancer and 93% of patients with prostate cancer are (American Cancer Society, 1999a).

Why older people have a much higher incidence of cancer is not really understood. Part of the reason is the cumulative effect of poor health habits over a long period of time, such as cigarette smoking and poor diet. In addition, the cumulative effects of exposure to pollutants and cancer-causing chemicals are partly to blame. As noted earlier in this chapter, some researchers believe that normative age-related changes in the immune system, resulting in a decreased ability to inhibit the growth of tumors, may also be responsible.

Research in molecular biology and microbiology is increasingly pointing to genetic links (Bergeman, 1997). The National Cancer Institute initiated the Cancer Gene Anatomy Program (CGAP; http://www.ncbi.nlm.nih.gov/CGAP/) to develop a comprehensive list of all genes responsible for cancer. For example, two breast cancer susceptibility genes have been identified: BRCA1 on chromosome 17 and BRCA2 on chromosome 13. When a woman carries a mutation in either BRCA1 or BRCA2, she is at a greater risk of being diagnosed with breast or ovarian cancer at some point. Similarly, a potential susceptibility locus for prostate cancer has been identified on chromosome 1, called HPC1, which may account for about 1 in 500 cases of prostate cancer. Although genetic screening tests for breast and prostate cancer for the general population are not yet warranted, such tests may one day be routine. Genetics also is providing much of the exciting new research on possible treatments by giving investigators new ways to fight the disease.

Age-related tissue changes have been associated with the development of tumors, some of which become cancerous; some of these may be genetically linked as well. The discovery that the presence of telomerase causes cells to grow rapidly and without limits on the number of divisions they can undergo provides additional insights into how cancer develops (Mera, 1998). What remains to be seen is how these genetic events interact with environmental factors, such as viruses or pollutants. Understanding this interaction process, predicted by the basic developmental forces, could explain why there are great interindividual differences in when and how cancer develops.

The most effective way to address the problem of cancer is through increased use of screening techniques and preventive lifestyle changes. The American Cancer Society strongly recommends these steps for people of all ages, but older adults need to be especially aware of what to do. Table 3.2 contains guidelines for the early detection of some common forms of cancer.

As Moses is learning, one of the biggest controversies in cancer prevention concerns screening and

Incidence	White	African American	Asian/Pacific Islander	Native American	Hispanic[†]
All sites					
Males	485.6	605.1	324.1	180.1	331.2
Females	352.0	336.1	243.4	135.9	244.9
Total	405.2	445.8	277.9	153.8	278.1
Breast (female)	113.2	99.0	71.4	31.9	69.3
Colon and rectum					
Males	53.8	59.4	47.2	21.9	35.6
Females	37.2	45.5	31.2	NC	24.3
Total	44.3	51.2	38.3	16.4	29.1
Lung and bronchus					
Males	74.3	114.4	52.4	25.1	40.0
Females	43.3	46.4	22.4	14.1	19.8
Total	56.4	75.0	35.8	18.8	28.2
Prostate	150.3	224.3	82.2	46.4	104.4

Mortality	White	African American	Asian/Pacific Islander	Native American	Hispanic[‡]
All sites					
Males	210.1	311.4	129.9	122.8	132.6
Females	140.1	168.8	83.9	88.8	86.5
Total	168.2	224.8	104.0	103.0	105.3
Breast (female)	26.0	31.5	11.6	11.7	15.3
Colon and rectum					
Males	21.8	28.0	13.6	10.5	13.2
Females	14.6	20.1	9.0	8.7	8.5
Total	17.6	23.3	11.0	9.6	10.5
Lung and bronchus					
Males	70.7	102.0	35.14	0.0	32.4
Females	33.6	32.7	15.0	19.6	11.0
Total	49.4	61.0	23.9	28.5	20.1
Prostate	24.1	55.0	10.9	14.2	16.8

*Per 100,000, age-adjusted to the 1970 U.S. standard population.

[†]Hispanic is not mutually exclusive from white, African American, Asian/Pacific Islander, and Native American.

NC = Statistic not calculated. Rate based on fewer than 10 cases per year within the time interval.

Note: Incidence data are from the 11 SEER areas; mortality data are from all states except Connecticut, Oklahoma, Louisiana, and New Hampshire. Data Sources: Incidence Rates Mortality Rates–Vital Statistics of the United States, 1998,—NCI Surveillance, Epidemiology, and End Results Program, 1998.

treatment for prostate cancer. The Current Controversies summarizes the issues: lack of data about the causes and the course of the disease and disagreement over treatment approaches. This controversy mirrors similar debates over the treatment of breast cancer, contrasting the relative merits of radical mastectomy (removal of the breast and some surrounding tissue) with lumpectomy (removal of the cancer-

TABLE 3.2 **Summary of American Cancer Society (ACS) Recommendations for Early Cancer Detection in Asymptomatic People**

Site	Recommendation
Cancer-related checkup	A cancer-related checkup is recommended every 3 years for people aged 20–40 and every year for people age 40 and older. This exam should include health counseling and, depending on a person's age, might include examinations for cancers of the thyroid, oral cavity, skin, lymph nodes, testes, and ovaries, as well as for some nonmalignant diseases.
Breast	Women 40 and older should have an annual mammogram and an annual clinical breast exam (CBE) performed by a health care professional and should perform monthly breast self-examination. The CBE should be conducted close to the scheduled mammogram. Women ages 20–39 should have a clinical breast exam performed by a health care professional every 3 years and should perform monthly breast self-examination.

Colon and rectum	Men and women aged 50 or older should follow one of the examination schedules below:
	    A fecal occult blood test every year and a flexible sigmoidoscopy every 5 years.*
	    A colonoscopy every 10 years.*
	    A double-contrast barium enema every 5–10 years.*

Prostate	The ACS recommends that both the prostate-specific antigen blood test and the digital rectal examination be offered annually, beginning at age 50, to men who have a life expectancy of at least 10 years and to younger men who are at high risk. Men in high-risk groups such as those with a strong familial predisposition (i.e., two or more affected first-degree relatives) or African Americans, may begin at a younger age (i.e., 45 years).
Uterus	**Cervix:** All women who are or have been sexually active or who are 18 and older should have an annual Pap test and pelvic examination. After three or more consecutive satisfactory examinations with normal findings, the Pap test may be performed less frequently. Discuss the matter with your physician. **Endometrium:** Women at high risk for cancer of the uterus should have a sample of endometrial tissue examined when menopause begins.

*A digital rectal exam should be done at the same time as sigmoidoscopy, colonoscopy, or double-contrast barium enema. People who are at moderate or high risk for colorectal cancer should talk with a doctor about a different testing schedule. Reprinted by permission of the American Cancer Society, Inc.

ous tumor only) and how chemotherapy, radiation, and drugs such as tamoxifen fit into the overall treatment approach.

In general, cancer treatment involves five major approaches that are typically used in combination (American Cancer Society, 1999a): surgery, chemotherapy, radiation, hormonal therapy, and immunological therapy. In addition, numerous alternative therapies, such as herbal approaches, exist. Contin-

ued advances in genetic research probably will result in genetically engineered medications designed to attack cancer cells. As with any health care decision, people with cancer need to become as educated as possible about the options.

INCONTINENCE. *For many people, the loss of the ability to control the elimination of urine and feces on an occasional or consistent basis, called* **incontinence,** *is a*

Roughly the size of a walnut and weighing about an ounce, the prostate gland is an unlikely candidate to create a major medical controversy. The prostate is located in front of the rectum and below the bladder and wraps around the urethra (the tube carrying urine out through the penis). Its primary function is to produce fluid for semen, the liquid that transports sperm. In half of all men over age 60, the prostate tends to enlarge, which may produce such symptoms as difficulty in urinating and frequent nighttime urination.

Enlargement of the prostate can happen for three main reasons: prostatitis (an inflammation of the prostate that is usually caused by an infection), benign prostatic hyperplasia (BPH), and prostate cancer. BPH is a noncancerous enlargement of the prostate that affects the innermost part of the prostate first. This often results in urination problems as the prostate gradually squeezes the urethra, but it does not affect sexual functioning. Prostate cancer often begins on the outer portion of the prostate, which seldom causes symptoms in the early stages. Each year, more than 200,000 men in the United States are diagnosed with prostate cancer; 35,000 die. For reasons we do not yet understand, African American men like Moses have a 40% higher chance of getting prostate cancer. Additionally, a genetic link is clear: A man whose brother has prostate cancer is four times more likely to get prostate cancer than a man with no brothers having the disease.

Part of the controversy surrounding prostate cancer relates to whether early detection reduces mortality from the disease. The American Cancer Society (ACS; 1999b), the National Comprehensive Cancer Network (NCCN), the Prostate Health Council, and other groups have conducted aggressive campaigns to encourage men over age 50 (age 40 in high-risk groups) to undergo two diagnostic tests annually: the digital rectal examination (DRE, in which a physician examines the prostate by touch) and the prostate-specific antigen (PSA) blood test. In sharp contrast to clear evidence that early detection of breast cancer in women reduces mortality by at least 30% among older women, no similar statistics exist for prostate cancer. This lack of data led the U.S. Preventive Services Task Force, the Canadian Task Force on the Periodic Health Examination, and others to recommend abandoning routine

---

source of great concern and embarrassment. As you can imagine, incontinence can result in social isolation and lower quality of life if no steps are taken to address the problem.

Urinary incontinence, the most common form, increases with age (Aldwin & Gilmer, 1999; Whitbourne, 1999). Among community-dwelling older adults, roughly 20% of women and 10% of men experience urinary incontinence. But rates are much higher if the person has dementia and is living in the community (about 35%) or if the person is living in a nursing home (roughly 70%).

Urinary incontinence occurs for five major reasons (Ebersole & Hess, 1998). *Stress incontinence* happens when pressure in the abdomen exceeds the ability to resist urinary flow. This may occur when a person coughs, sneezes, or lifts a heavy object. *Urge incontinence* usually is caused by a central nervous system problem after a CVA or urinary tract infection. People feel the urge to urinate but cannot make it to a toilet quickly enough. *Overflow incontinence* results from improper contraction of the kidneys, causing the bladder to become overdistended. Certain drugs, tumors, and prostate enlargement are common causes of overflow incontinence. *Functional incontinence* occurs when the urinary tract is intact but because of physical disability or cognitive impairment the person is unaware of the need to urinate. *Iatrogenic incontinence* usually is caused by medication side effects. Changing the dosage often solves the problem.

Most types of incontinence can be alleviated with interventions. Among the most effective are behavioral interventions, which include diet changes, relearning to recognize the need to toilet, and Kegel exercises for improved pelvic muscle control (Burgio et

prostate cancer screening because of the cost and the uncertain benefits associated with it.

The ACS and the NCCN (1999) jointly created a guide to prostate cancer screening and treatment to help men negotiate the confusing state of affairs. Although not a replacement for physician input, the screening and treatment charts can be very useful in sorting through the various options.

The sharp division among medical experts highlights the relation between carefully conducted research and public health policy. At present, there has been no systematic comparison of various treatment options (which include surgery, radiation, hormones, and drugs), nor do we fully understand the natural course of prostate cancer in terms of which types of tumors spread to other organs and which ones do not (American Cancer Society and National Comprehensive Cancer Network, 1999; Calciano et al., 1995). Given that some of the side effects of surgery include urinary incontinence and impotence and that some of the other therapies may produce other unpleasant effects, there is debate on whether the disease should be treated at all in most patients (ACS and NCCN, 1999).

At present, men who experience prostate-related symptoms are left to decide for themselves what to do. Many men opt for immediate treatment and learn how to live with the subsequent side effects. Support groups for men with prostate cancer are becoming more common, and many encourage the patient's partner to participate. The controversy surrounding early screening and detection of prostate cancer is unlikely to subside soon because the necessary research concerning effective treatment and survival will take years to conduct. Until then, if you or someone you know is over 50 or is in a high-risk group, the decision still must be made. Talk at length with a physician who is up-to-date on the topic and educate yourself about the alternatives.

Search Online with InfoTrac College Edition For more information on these controversies, explore InfoTrac College Edition, your online library. Go to http://www.infotrac-college.com/ wadsworth and use the passcode that came on the card with your book. Try this search term: prostate cancer.

al., 1994; Ebersole & Hess, 1998). Certain medications and surgical intervention may be needed in some cases. Numerous products such as protective undergarments and padding also are available to help absorb leaks. All these options help alleviate the psychological and social effects of incontinence and help people live better lives (Burgio et al., 2001).

Managing Pain

One of the most unpleasant aspects of many chronic diseases is pain. Pain is disruptive, saps energy, negatively affects quality of life, and can lead to an ever-intensifying cycle of pain, anxiety, and anguish. Pain is also one of the most common complaints of older adults and is responsible for depression, sleep disorders, decreased social interaction, impaired mobility, and increased health care costs (Sarvis, 1995).

Unfortunately, many myths exist about pain in older adults. These myths involve stereotypes about aging and about medical conditions. Failure to understand pain in older adults can lead to a failure to provide adequate steps to relieve pain.

How do people manage pain? Perhaps the most important step is to understand that pain is not a necessary part of treatment, people can control their pain, no one approach is likely to be sufficient, and asking for pain relief is to be expected. There are two general pain management techniques: pharmacological and nonpharmacological (Ebersole & Hess, 1998). These approaches often are used together for maximum pain relief.

Pharmacological approaches to pain management include nonnarcotic and narcotic medications. Nonnarcotic medications are best for mild to moderate pain, whereas narcotic medications are best for severe pain. Nonnarcotic medications include nonsteroidal antiinflammatory drugs (NSAIDs), such as ibuprofen, and acetaminophen. However, these drugs must be used with caution because they may cause toxic side effects in older adults. Narcotic drugs that work well in older adults include morphine and codeine; other commonly used drugs, such as meperidine and pentazocine should be avoided because of age-related changes in metabolism. All these medications must be monitored very closely.

Nonpharmacological pain control includes a variety of approaches, all of which are effective with some people; the trick is to keep trying until the best approach is found. Common techniques include the following:

Deep and superficial stimulation of the skin through therapeutic touch, massage, vibration, heat, cold, and various ointments

Electrical stimulation over the pain site or to the spine

Acupuncture and acupressure

Biofeedback, in which a person learns to control and change the body processes responsible for the pain

Distraction techniques that draw a person's attention away from the pain

Relaxation, meditation, and imagery approaches that rid the mind of tension and anxiety

Hypnosis, either self-induced or induced by another person

Like other treatments, nonpharmacological interventions have both advantages and disadvantages. The best approach is to try various techniques until the best relief is obtained.

The most important point is that pain is not a necessary part of growing old or having a disease. Pain relief is an important part of recovery and should be included in any treatment regimen for adults of all ages.

CONCEPT CHECKS

1. What are the most important things to consider in chronic diseases?

2. What are some of the most common chronic conditions in older adults?

3. How is pain managed?

PHARMACOLOGY AND MEDICATION ADHERENCE

LEARNING OBJECTIVES

- What are the developmental trends in using medication?
- How does aging affect the way the medications work?
- What are the consequences of medication interactions?
- What are the important medication adherence issues?

*L*ucy is an 80-year-old woman who has several chronic health problems. As a result, she takes 12 medications every day. She must be very careful about following the regimen very carefully; some of her medications must be taken with food, some on an empty stomach, and some at bedtime. Lucy's daughter is concerned that Lucy may experience serious problems if she fails to take her medications properly.

One of the most important health issues for older adults is the use of both prescription and over-the-counter medications. In fact, older adults take roughly half of all drugs prescribed in the United States, and more than one third take at least three prescribed drugs (Park et al., 1992). When over-the-counter drugs are included, most older adults take several medications every day. Like Lucy, most people take these drugs to relieve pain or related problems resulting from chronic conditions.

Patterns of Medication Use

The explosion of new medications over the past two decades has created many options for physicians in treating disease, especially chronic conditions. Consequently, the average number of medications a typical older adult takes has increased. In the United States, people over age 60 take nearly 50% of all prescription and over-the-counter medications, far

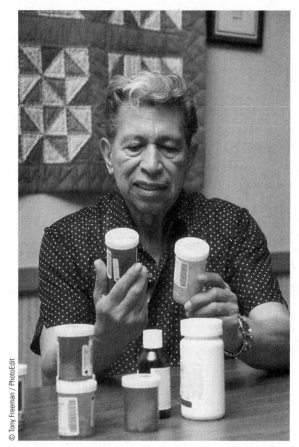

Because most older adults take several medications, understanding how they interact is critical.

age was a matter of extensive congressional debate in the Medicare reform legislation of the late 1990s.

As even more medications are developed and approved, the use of multiple medications will continue. When used appropriately, medications can improve people's lives; when used inappropriately, they can cause harm. Understanding how medications work and how these processes change with age is extremely important.

Developmental Changes in How Medications Work

When Lucy takes her medications every day, what happens? Understanding how medications work involves examining developmental changes in absorption, distribution, metabolism, and excretion of medications (Cusack, 1995).

Absorption is the time needed for one of Lucy's medications to enter the bloodstream. For drugs taken orally, a key factor is the time it takes for the medication to go from the stomach to the small intestine, where maximum absorption occurs. This transfer may take longer than expected in older adults, resulting in too little or too much absorption, depending on the drug. However, once in the small intestine, absorption appears to be no different in older, middle-aged, or younger adults (Hess & Lee, 1998).

Once in the bloodstream, the medication is *distributed* throughout the body. How well distribution occurs depends on the adequacy of the cardiovascular system. Maximal effectiveness of a drug depends on the balance between the portions of the drug that bind with plasma protein and the portions that remain free. As we grow older, more portions of the drug remain free; this means that toxic levels of a drug can build up more easily in older adults. Similarly, drugs that are soluble in water or fat tissue can also build up more easily in older adults because of age-related decreases in total body water or possible increases in fat tissue. The effective dosage of a drug depends critically on the amount of free drug in the body; thus, whether the person is young or old, thin or obese, is very important to keep in mind (Hess & Lee, 1998).

more than any other age group (Hess & Lee, 1998). This translates into about six or seven medications per older adult; Lucy takes more than the average.

Although advances in medication are highly desirable, there are hidden dangers for older adults. Until the late 1990s, clinical trials of new medications were not required to include older adults. Thus, for most of the medications on the market, it is unclear whether they work to the same degree as they do for younger or middle-aged adults. Additionally, many of these newer, often more effective medications are very expensive. The lack of prescription drug insurance for most older Americans means that many cannot afford them; including such insurance cover-

Getting rid of medications in the bloodstream is partly the job of the liver, a process called drug *metabolism.* There is much evidence that this process is slower in older adults, meaning that drugs stay in the body longer as people grow older (Cusack, 1995) Slower drug metabolism can also create the potential for toxicity if the medication schedule does not take this into account.

Sometimes drugs are decomposed into other compounds to help eliminate them. Drug *excretion* occurs mainly through the kidneys in urine, although some elimination through feces, sweat, and saliva occurs. Changes in kidney function with age, related to lower total body water content, are common. This means that drugs often are not excreted as quickly by older adults, again setting the stage for possible toxic effects (Hess & Lee, 1998).

What do these changes mean? Most important, the dosage of a drug needed to get the desired effect may be different for older adults than for middle-aged or younger adults. In many cases, physicians recommend using one third to one half the usual adult dosage when the difference between the effective dosages and toxic dosages is small or there is a high rate of side effects (Cusack, 1995). Additionally, because of age-related physiological changes, several drugs are not recommended for use by older adults.

Medication Side Effects and Interactions

Because of their high rate of medication use, older adults also have the highest risk of adverse drug effects (Kane et al., 1994). In part, these problems result from physiological changes that occur with age in how drugs are absorbed into the body, how long they remain, and how well they work. For example, changes in the stomach may slow down the rate at which drugs enter the body, meaning that achieving the effective level of the drug in the body may take longer to occur. Changes in liver and kidney functioning affect how rapidly the drug is removed and excreted from the body, meaning that levels of the drug may remain high for longer periods of time.

As we have seen, age-related increases in the frequency of chronic conditions means that older adults are likely to have more than one medical problem for which they take medications. In this regard, Lucy is fairly typical. *Treating multiple conditions results in* **polypharmacy,** *the use of multiple medications.* Polypharmacy is potentially dangerous because many drugs do not interact well; the action of some drugs is enhanced when used in combination with others, whereas other drugs may not work at all when used in combination. Drug interactions may create secondary medical problems that in turn need to be treated, and the primary condition may not be treated as effectively. Moreover, drug interactions can produce symptoms that appear to be caused by other diseases; in some cases they may cause confusion and memory loss that mimics Alzheimer's disease. Lucy's daughter is correct in worrying about her mother taking her medications as prescribed. Analyzing a person's medication regimen, including both prescription and over-the-counter medications, and asking the patient or caregiver to describe how they are taken is important in diagnosing health problems.

Given the high level of medication use among older adults, what can be done to minimize drug interaction effects? Physicians play a key role, but other health care professionals must also be alert because older adults typically go to more than one physician. Accurate medication histories including all types of medicines are essential. Inappropriate use of drugs, such as antipsychotics to control behavior, must also be monitored.

Adherence to Medication Regimens

The likelihood of adverse drug reactions increases as the number of medications increases. Taking more drugs also means that keeping track of each becomes more difficult. (Imagine having to keep track of six different medications, each of which has a different schedule.) Medication adherence (taking medications correctly) becomes less likely the more drugs people take and the more complicated the regimens are. Combined with sensory, physical, and cognitive changes in older adults, medication adherence is a significant problem in this age group (Park et al., 1992). The oldest old are especially at risk; the most common problem is that they simply forget to take the medication. (We consider ways to help people remember to take their medications in Chapter 7.)

What factors can increase compliance? In general, a belief that the disease for which the medications are being taken is serious, good communication between the patient and the physician, reminder cards or organized pill boxes, and discussions with the patient about the importance of compliance appear to be the best approaches (Cusack, 1995).

The best approach, of course, is to keep the number of medications to a minimum (Monane et al., 1993). If the use of drugs is determined to be essential, then periodic reevaluations should be conducted and the medication discontinued when possible. Additionally, the lowest effective dosage should be used. In general, medication use by older adults should get the same careful consideration as by any other age group.

CONCEPT CHECKS

1. How many medications does the average older adult take?
2. What changes occur with age in the ways in which medications work?
3. What side effect and drug interaction concerns do older adults face?
4. How can compliance to medication regimens be improved?

FUNCTIONAL HEALTH AND DISABILITY

LEARNING OBJECTIVES

- What is functional health?
- What factors are important to include in a model of disability in late life?
- What causes functional limitations and disability in older adults?

*B*rian is a 68-year-old former welder who retired 3 years ago. He and his wife, Dorothy, had planned to travel in their RV and see the country. But Brian's arthritis has been getting worse lately and he is having increasing difficulty getting around and doing basic daily tasks. Brian and Dorothy wonder what the future holds for them.*

Brian and Dorothy are not alone. Many couples plan to travel or to do other activities after they retire, only to find health issues complicating the situation. As the focus on health has shifted over the past several decades to chronic disease, researchers have increasingly focused on how well people can function in their daily lives. In this section, we examine how functional health is determined and how disability occurs.

A Model of Disability in Late Life

As we saw earlier in this chapter, one of the defining characteristics of a chronic condition is that it lasts a long time. This means that for most adults, the time between the onset of a chronic condition and death is long, measured in years and even decades. Chronic diseases typically involve some level of discomfort, and physical limitations are common, everyday issues for most people, as they are for Brian. Over the course of the disease, these problems usually increase, resulting in more efforts by patients and health care workers to try to slow the progress of the disease. In many cases, these efforts allow people to resume such activities as daily walks and shopping and to feel optimistic about the future (Verbrugge, 1994).

In the context of chronic conditions, **disability** *is the effects of chronic conditions on people's ability to engage in activities that are necessary, expected, and personally desired in their society* (Verbrugge, 1994). When people are disabled as a result of a chronic condition, they have difficulty doing daily tasks, such as household chores, personal care, job duties, active recreation, socializing with friends and family, and errands. One of the most important research efforts related to health and aging is understanding how disability results from chronic conditions and what might be done to help prevent it.

Verbrugge and Jette (1994) have proposed an excellent and comprehensive model of disability resulting from chronic conditions, which is shown in Figure 3.5. The model consists of four main parts. The main pathway is an adaptation of frameworks

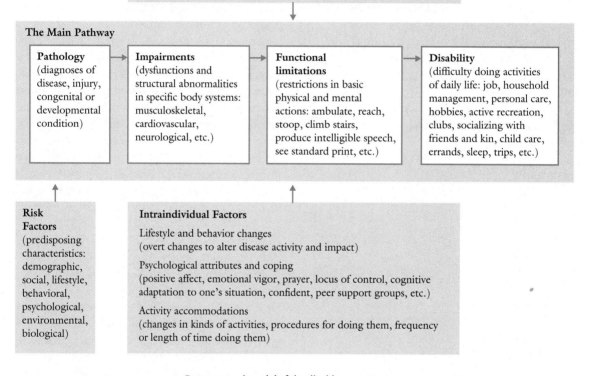

Extraindividual Factors

Medical care and rehabilitation
(surgery, physical therapy, speech therapy, counseling, health education, job retraining, etc.)

Medications and other therapeutic regimens
(drugs, recreational therapy, aquatic exercise, biofeedback, meditation, rest, energy conservation, etc.)

External supports
(personal assistance, special equipment and devices, standby assistance and supervision, day care, respite care, meals on wheels, etc.)

Built, physical, and social environment
(structual modifications at job and home, access to buildings and public transportation, improvement of air quality, reduction of noise and glare, health insurance and access to medical care, laws and regulations, employment discrimination, etc.)

The Main Pathway

Pathology
(diagnoses of disease, injury, congenital or developmental condition)

→

Impairments
(dysfunctions and structural abnormalities in specific body systems: musculoskeletal, cardiovascular, neurological, etc.)

→

Functional limitations
(restrictions in basic physical and mental actions: ambulate, reach, stoop, climb stairs, produce intelligible speech, see standard print, etc.)

→

Disability
(difficulty doing activities of daily life: job, household management, personal care, hobbies, active recreation, clubs, socializing with friends and kin, child care, errands, sleep, trips, etc.)

Risk Factors
(predisposing characteristics: demographic, social, lifestyle, behavioral, psychological, environmental, biological)

Intraindividual Factors

Lifestyle and behavior changes
(overt changes to alter disease activity and impact)

Psychological attributes and coping
(positive affect, emotional vigor, prayer, locus of control, cognitive adaptation to one's situation, confident, peer support groups, etc.)

Activity accommodations
(changes in kinds of activities, procedures for doing them, frequency or length of time doing them)

FIGURE 3.5 **A model of the disablement process.**

Source: Verbrugge, L. M., & Jette, A. M. (1994). The disablement process. *Social Science and Medicine, 38,* 4.

proposed by the World Health Organization (1980) and the U.S. Academy of Science's Institute of Medicine (Pope & Tarlov, 1991), both of which were based on work by sociologist Saad Nagi (1965, 1991). This pathway emphasizes the relations between pathology (the chronic conditions a person has), impairments of organ systems (such as muscular degeneration), functional limitations in the ability to perform activities (such as restrictions in one's mobility), and disability.

The model also includes risk factors and two types of intervention strategies: environmental and health care (*extraindividual factors*) and behavioral and personality (*intraindividual factors*). Risk factors are long-standing behaviors or conditions that increase one's chances of functional limitation or disability. Examples of risk factors include low socioeconomic status, chronic health conditions, and health-related behaviors such as smoking. Extraindividual factors include interventions such as surgery, medication, social support services (e.g., meals on wheels), and physical environmental supports (e.g., wheelchair ramps). The presence of these factors often helps people maintain their independence and may make the difference between living at home and living in a long-term care facility. Intraindividual factors include such things as beginning an exercise program, keeping a positive outlook, and taking advantage of transportation programs to increase mobility. Femia, Zarit, and Johansson (2001) validated Verbrugge and Jette's (1994) model in a study of older adults over age 79 in Sweden. Among the most important results were the mediating role of psychosocial factors on risk factors for disability.

Both extraindividual and intraindividual interventions are aimed at reducing the restrictions and difficulties resulting from chronic conditions. Unfortunately, sometimes they do not work as intended and may even create problems of their own. For example, a prescribed medication may produce negative side effects that, instead of alleviating the condition, create a new problem. Or social service agencies may have inflexible policies about when a particular program is available, which may make it difficult for a person who needs the program to participate in it. Situations such as these are called *exacerbators* because they make the situation worse than it was originally. Although they may be unintended, the results of exacerbators can be serious and necessitate additional forms of intervention.

One of the most important aspects of Verbrugge and Jette's (1994) model is the emphasis on the fit between the person and the environment. When a person's needs are met by the environment, the person's quality of life and adaptation are optimal. We take a close look at this principle in Chapter 5 when we examine theoretical models of person–environment fit in detail.

Determining Functional Health Status

How can we determine where a person is along Verbrugge and Jette's continuum? The answer to this question describes a person's functional health status, that is, how well the person is functioning in daily life. In making these assessments, it is essential to differentiate the tasks a person reports he or she can do, tasks a person can demonstrate in a laboratory or clinic that simulates the same tasks at home, and tasks the person actually does at home (Glass, 1998). To determine functional health status accurately, we must ensure that the assessment tool used measures a person's true functional level.

In many cases, assessing functional health status is done for a very practical reason: to identify older adults who need help with everyday tasks. **Frail older adults** *are those who have physical disabilities, are very ill, and may have cognitive or psychological disorders who need assistance with everyday tasks.* They constitute a minority of older adults, but the size of this group increases a great deal with age, as shown in Figure 3.6.

Frail older adults are people whose competence is declining. However, they do not have one specific problem that differentiates them from their active, healthy counterparts (Guralnick & Simonsick, 1993; Strawbridge et al., 1998). To identify the areas in which people experience limited functioning, researchers developed observational and self-report techniques to measure how well people can accomplish daily tasks.

Everyday competence assessment consists of examining how well people can complete activities of daily living and instrumental activities of daily living (Diehl, 1998). **Activities of daily living (ADLs)** *include basic self-care tasks such as eating, bathing, toileting, walking, or dressing.* A person can be considered frail if he or she needs help with one or more of

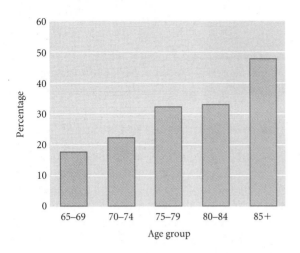

FIGURE 3.6 **Percentage of adults with disabilities as a function of age.**

Source: National Center for Health Statistics, 1999.

these tasks. **Instrumental activities of daily living (IADLs)** *are actions that entail some intellectual competence and planning.* Which activities constitute IADLs vary widely across cultures. For example, for most adults in Western culture IADLs would include shopping for personal items, paying bills, making telephone calls, taking medications appropriately, and keeping appointments. In other cultures, IADLs might include caring for animal herds, making bread, threshing grain, and tending crops.

The number of older adults who need assistance with ADLs and IADLs increases with age (Administration on Aging, 1999b; Crimmins et al., 1997). Less than 5% of adults aged 65–74 need ADL assistance, whereas 20% of those over age 85 need help (Administration on Aging, 1999b). Chronic conditions and poor health exacerbate the problem. One extensive study of people's functioning the year before death showed that 70% of them needed help with some ADLs, all people over age 85 needed some assistance, and roughly half needed help with all ADLs (Lentzner et al., 1992).

Similar results are reported for IADLs. There is some evidence that more recent cohorts have less need for assistance in some areas, especially because of declining rates of cardiovascular disease (Crimmins et al., 1997; Reynolds et al., 1998). However, more recent cohorts may also be at higher risk for disabilities related to asthma and muscle and skeletal problems (Reynolds et al., 1998).

Although frailty becomes more likely with increasing age, especially during the last year of life, there are many ways to provide a supportive environment for frail older adults. We take a closer look at some of them in Chapter 5.

What Causes Functional Limitations and Disability in Older Adults?

As you were reading about the Verbrugge and Jette (1994) model, you may have been thinking about Brian's situation and those of other adults you know. If you and your classmates created a list of all the conditions you believe cause functional limitations and disabilities in older adults, the list undoubtedly would be long. (Try it and see for yourself.) Indeed, over the years researchers have discovered the same thing and have reported numerous conditions that cause these problems (Boult et al., 1994). But by strategically combining a large representative sample of conditions with sophisticated statistical analyses, this list can be shortened greatly. If these steps are taken, what conditions best predict future problems in functioning?

One answer to this question comes from Boult and colleagues' (1994) research, which was designed to identify chronic medical conditions that result in severe functional limitations. They studied nearly 7,000 noninstitutionalized people over age 70 living in the United States at two points in time (1984 and 1988). At each point in time they classified people as being functionally intact, functionally limited because of their inability to perform at least one of seven target activities, or deceased. An important aspect of this investigation was that the researchers took exercise habits and demographic, socioeconomic, and psychosocial factors into account. Although the study was not designed as a direct test of the Verbrugge and Jette (1994) model, all these factors are considered important in it.

Boult and associates (1994) reported that two chronic conditions were strong predictors of functional limitations: cerebrovascular disease and arthritis. Additionally, the findings suggested that coronary artery disease may also be a predictor, but the statistical evidence for this was weaker. The authors concluded that focusing attention on identifying these conditions as early as possible may reduce the incidence of severe functional limitations in older adults. Because Brian has arthritis, it is a good bet that he will experience greater disability in the future.

In addition to specific chronic diseases, several additional predictive factors for subsequent disability have been identified. In a longitudinal study over three decades, Strawbridge and colleagues (1998) found that smoking, heavy drinking, physical inactivity, depression, social isolation, and fair or poor perceived health also predicted who would become disabled in some way.

HOW IMPORTANT ARE SOCIOECONOMIC FACTORS? Once we have identified the specific conditions that are highly predictive of future functional limitations, an important question is whether the appropriate intervention and prevention programs should be targeted at particular groups of people. That is, would people who are well educated and have high incomes have the same rate of key chronic conditions as people in lower socioeconomic groups? If not, then people with different socioeconomic backgrounds have different needs.

Reed and colleagues (1995) tackled this question by comparing roughly 2,000 residents of Marin County, California, over age 65 with the total U.S. population in the same age group. The researchers chose Marin County because it is among the most affluent in California and because it could be viewed as a healthy community environment. Their findings came as a surprise. As expected, residents of Marin County lived on average longer than the typical American. However, despite their privileged status, the Marin County Residents had the same prevalence of disease and disability as the U.S. population at large.

The implications of these findings, if further research substantiates them, are sobering. Because of

Although many older people have disabilities, they continue to participate in a variety of activities.

their greater average longevity, people from affluent communities can expect to spend a longer period of their later lives living with disabilities and in need of medical care (Reed et al., 1995); they will have longer dependent life expectancy. This is especially true for women because of their greater average longevity. Chronic conditions do not appear to be postponed in affluent people; indeed, such people may simply live with disabilities for a longer period of time.

DO GENDER AND ETHNICITY MATTER? Throughout this and previous chapters, we have encountered important differences between men and women and between various ethnic groups. Thus, we might expect such differences in the area of disability. This is the case, particularly when it comes to cross-cultural comparisons involving developing countries that focus on adults' abilities to perform routine tasks, an important component in the model of health we examined earlier in this section.

In one of the few studies in this area, Rahman and colleagues (1994) compared representative samples of men and women in the United States, Jamaica, Malaysia, and Bangladesh. In making their comparisons, Rahman and colleagues made corrections for gender differences in mortality and socioeconomic differences. Two of their findings are noteworthy. First, women's self-reported health was worse in all the countries studied. Second, self-reported health

We have seen that the incidence of disability as defined by the need for assistance with ADLs and IADLs increases dramatically with age. An important question is: Who is most at risk? The answer can be found in applying the developmental forces to the disablement process.

Clearly, biological forces play a major role. We have seen in this chapter and in Chapter 2 that genetics plays a major role in determining who will get a specific inheritable disease. This is especially important in certain chronic conditions such as cardiovascular disease and cancer. As our knowledge about human genetics continues to improve, it is likely that many more connections will be found.

Psychological forces also play a role. We saw in our consideration of stress and changes in the immune system that psychological characteristics predict negative health outcomes. In addition, disability itself is a strong predictor of depression in later life. Psychological factors are also key in understanding who is in the best position to deal with chronic disease and halt the progression toward disability.

Sociocultural factors often are overlooked in considering disability. But people who have limited access to health care are at a serious disadvantage because they may not be able to take advantage of the many advances in treatment. This is especially true for poor ethnic minorities in the United States and poor people worldwide. We have noted several areas in which ethnicity could be responsible for the development of disability in older adults.

As can be surmised from the statistics, the time in one's life cycle at which a problem occurs is critical. In part, the role of life-cycle forces depends on the operation of myths and stereotypes about older adults. To the extent that people (including physicians) believe that disability is a normal part of aging, intervention is less likely. Additionally, when a problem occurs in later life, it is probable that the person will have fewer biological, psychological, and sociocultural resources to bring to bear.

Taken together, the four developmental forces point out that disability results from a complex, multidimensional process. People who have genetic predispositions, have negative attitudes about their well-being, are poor or from an ethnic minority group, and are among the old-old are at higher risk.

---

problems were much more prevalent in the developing countries than in the United States.

Rahman et al.'s (1994) findings indicate that gender makes a difference in health and that the differences between men and women hold up across selected cultures. Although access to health care and lifestyle factors are likely explanations, it is too early to know for certain how these factors create the observed differences.

Of additional concern to researchers is whether ethnic groups differ from each other. In a large study of more than 5,100 older African American and European American men and women, Johnson and Wolinsky (1994) used the concepts of pathology, functional limitation, and disability to predict people's perceived health. Several of their findings are important. First, they discovered that the components of some scales used to measure such things as ability to care for oneself had different measurement properties for each group (e.g., African American men versus women, European American men versus women, African Americans versus European Americans). This means that the scales may be measuring different things in different groups, making it very difficult to generalize findings from one group to another. However, some scales (e.g., lower body disabilities) were equally valid across ethnic groups.

Second, Johnson and Wolinsky found several gender differences, especially in the European American group. For both ethnic groups, women's perceived health status was predicted by both the ability to perform several basic functions (e.g., personal care) and disability involving body mobility, whereas men's perceived health status was predicted mainly by ability to perform basic functions. In the European American group, ability to perform complex daily tasks, such as managing money, was more predictive of men's than of women's perceived health status.

Rahman et al.'s (1994) cross-cultural findings and Johnson and Wolinsky's (1994) results point to important gender, ethnic, and cultural differences in health, as well as differences in which specific aspects of chronic conditions, functional limitations, and disabilities predict what people perceive their health status to be. Such differences must be taken into account in designing intervention programs; a one-size-fits-all approach will not be equally successful across these different groups of people. These issues are discussed from a developmental forces perspective in the Forces in Action feature.

CONCEPT CHECKS

1. What factors should be included in a model of adults' disability?
2. How is functional health determined? What are the major issues in ADLs and IADLs?
3. What are the primary causes of disability in older adults?

PUTTING IT ALL TOGETHER

If we had a choice, each of us would like to live a healthy, productive life; many of us would also like to live a long time if we stay healthy. Susie's long-lived relatives indicate that she has a good chance at longevity because genetics are an important predictor. Rosa's experience of increasing health concerns typifies the experience of many older adults: Chronic diseases increase in frequency with age. Moses's diagnosis of prostate cancer reflects ethnic differences in the rates of certain diseases and the controversies that surround treatment (and even preventive health care) in some areas. Lucy's complex medication regimen reminds us that older adults on average take several medications every day, raising concerns about compliance and health problems caused by medication interactions. Brian's difficulties with some routine tasks shows us that we must be aware of the potential some older adults have for developing disabilities. For us to live long, healthy, productive lives, we must negotiate through a series of potential health problems. It can be done, but we must stay on guard.

Summary

How Long Will We Live?

Average and Maximum Longevity

- Average longevity is the age at which half of the people born in a particular year will have died. Maximum longevity is the longest time a member of a species lives. Active longevity is the time during which people are independent. Dependent life expectancy is the time during which people rely on others for daily life tasks.

- Average longevity increased dramatically in the first half of the 20th century, but maximum longevity remains at about 120 years. This increase resulted mainly from the elimination of many diseases and a reduction in deaths during childbirth.

Genetic and Environmental Factors in Average Longevity

- Having long- or short-lived parents is a good predictor of your own longevity.

- Living in a polluted environment can dramatically shorten longevity; being in a committed relationship lengthens it. Environmental effects must be considered in combination.

Ethnic Differences in Average Longevity

- Different ethnic groups in the United States have different average longevity. However, these differences result primarily from differences in nutrition, health care, stress, and financial status. In late life, people in some ethnic minority groups live longer than European Americans.

Gender Differences in Average Longevity

- Women tend to live longer than men, partly because men are more susceptible to disease and environmental influences. Numerous hypotheses have been offered for this difference, but none have been supported strongly.

Health and Illness

Defining Health and Illness

- Health is the absence of acute and chronic physical or mental disease and impairments.

Illness is the presence of a physical or mental disease or impairment.

- Self-rated health is a good predictor of illness and mortality. However, gender and cultural differences have been found.

Quality of Life

- Quality of life is a multidimensional concept encompassing biological, psychological, and sociocultural domains at any point in the life cycle.
- In the context of health, people's valuation of life is a major factor in quality of life.

Changes in the Immune System

- The immune system is composed of three major types of cells that form a network of interacting parts: cell-mediated immunity (consisting of thymus-derived, or T-lymphocytes), humoral immunity (B-lymphocytes), and nonspecific immunity (monocytes and polymorphonuclear neutrophil leukocytes). Natural killer (NK) cells are also important components.
- The total number of lymphocytes and NK cells does not change with age, but how well they function does.
- The immune system can begin attacking itself, a condition called autoimmunity.
- Psychoneuroimmunology is the study of the relations between psychological, neurological, and immunological systems that raise or lower our susceptibility to and ability to recover from disease.
- HIV and AIDS are growing problems among older adults.

Chronic and Acute Diseases

- Acute diseases are conditions that develop over a short period of time and cause a rapid change in health. Chronic diseases are conditions that last a longer period of time (at least 3 months) and may be accompanied by residual functional impairment that necessitates long-term management.
- The incidence of acute disease drops with age, but the effects of acute disease worsen. The incidence of chronic disease increases with age.

The Role of Stress

- The stress and coping paradigm views stress not as an environmental stimulus or as a response but as the interaction of a thinking person and an event.
- Primary appraisal categorizes events into three groups based on the significance they have for our well-being: irrelevant, benign or positive, and stressful. Secondary appraisal assesses our ability to cope with harm, threat, or challenge. Reappraisal involves making a new primary or secondary appraisal resulting from changes in the situation.
- Attempts to deal with stressful events are called coping. Problem-focused coping and emotion-focused coping are two major categories. People also use religion as a source of coping.
- There are developmental declines in the number of stressors and in the kinds of coping strategies people use.
- Stress has several negative consequences for health.

COMMON CHRONIC CONDITIONS AND THEIR MANAGEMENT

General Issues in Chronic Conditions

- Chronic conditions are the interaction of biological, psychological, sociocultural, and life-cycle forces.

Common Chronic Conditions

- Arthritis is the most common chronic condition. Arthritis and osteoporosis can cause mild to severe impairment.
- Cardiovascular and cerebrovascular diseases can create chronic conditions after stroke.
- Diabetes mellitus occurs when the pancreas produces insufficient insulin. Although it cannot be cured, it can be managed effectively. However, some serious problems, such as diabetic retinopathy, can result.
- Many forms of cancer are caused by lifestyle choices, but genetics also plays an important role. The risk of getting cancer increases markedly with age. Prostate and breast cancer involve difficult treatment choices.

- For many people, the inability to control the elimination of urine and feces on an occasional or consistent basis, called incontinence, is a source of great concern and embarrassment. Effective treatments are available.

Managing Pain

- Effective pain management occurs through pharmacological and nonpharmacological approaches. Pain is not a normal outcome of aging and is not to be dismissed.

PHARMACOLOGY AND MEDICATION ADHERENCE

Patterns of Medication Use

- Older adults use nearly half of all prescription and over-the-counter drugs. The average older adult takes six or seven medications per day.

Developmental Changes in How Medications Work

- The speed with which medications move from the stomach to the small intestine may slow with age. However, once drugs are in the small intestine, absorption rates are the same across adulthood.
- The distribution of medications in the bloodstream changes with age.
- The speed of drug metabolism in the liver slows with age.
- The rate at which drugs are excreted from the body slows with age.

Medication Side Effects and Interactions

- Older adults are more prone to harmful medication side effects.
- Polypharmacy is a serious problem in older adults and may result in serious drug interactions.

Adherence to Medication Regimens

- Polypharmacy leads to lower rates of correct adherence to medication regimens.
- Use of structured pill boxes, a belief that the disease for which the medications are being taken is serious, good communication between the patient and the physician, reminder cards or organized pill boxes, and discussions with the patient about the importance of compliance appear to be the best ways to improve adherence.

FUNCTIONAL HEALTH AND DISABILITY

A Model of Disability in Late Life

- Disability is the effects of chronic conditions on people's ability to engage in activities in daily life.
- A model of disability includes pathology, impairments, functional limitations, disability, risk factors, extraindividual factors, and intraindividual factors. This model includes all four main developmental forces.

Determining Functional Health Status

- Frail older adults are those who have physical disabilities, are very ill, and may have cognitive or psychological disorders and who need assistance with everyday tasks.
- Activities of daily living (ADLs) include basic self-care tasks such as eating, bathing, toileting, walking, and dressing.
- Instrumental activities of daily living (IADLs) are actions that entail some intellectual competence and planning.
- Rates of problems with ADLs and IADLs increase dramatically with age.

What Causes Functional Limitations and Disability in Older Adults?

- The chronic conditions that best predict future disability are arthritis and cerebrovascular disease. Other predictors include smoking, heavy drinking, physical inactivity, depression, social isolation, and fair or poor perceived health.
- Being wealthy helps increase average longevity but does not protect one from developing chronic conditions, meaning that such people may experience longer periods of disability late in life.
- Women's health generally is poorer across cultures, especially in developing countries.
- Ethnic group differences are also important. The validity of measures of functioning sometimes differ across ethnicity and gender.

Review Questions

HOW LONG WILL WE LIVE?

- What is the difference between average longevity and maximum longevity?

- What genetic and environmental factors influence average longevity?
- What ethnic and gender differences have been found?

Health and Illness

- How are the definitions of health and illness linked?
- How is the quality of life defined generally and in relation to health?
- What are the major age-related changes in the immune system? How do they affect health and illness?
- What is the difference between acute and chronic diseases? How do the rates of each change with age?
- How does the stress and coping paradigm explain the experience of stress? What age-related changes occur in the process?

Common Chronic Conditions and Their Management

- What are the general issues to consider in managing chronic disease?
- What are some common chronic diseases experienced by older adults?
- How is pain managed?

Pharmacology and Medication Adherence

- What is the typical pattern of medication use in older adults?
- What changes occur with age that influence how well medications work?
- What are the major risks for side effects and drug interactions?
- How can adherence to medication regimens be improved?

Functional Health and Disability

- What are the key components in a model of disability in older adults?
- What are ADLs and IADLs? How does the number of people needing assistance change with age?
- What conditions result in disability most often?
- How do socioeconomic status, ethnicity, and gender affect health and disability?

Integrating Concepts in Development

- What physiological changes described in Chapter 2 are important in understanding health?
- Based on information in Chapters 2 and 3, how might a primary prevention program be designed to prevent cardiovascular disease? (Compare your answer with the intervention types described in Chapter 5.)
- How do the ethnic differences in average longevity and in health relate to the diversity issues we examined in Chapter 1?

Key Terms

active life expectancy The age to which one can expect to live independently.

activities of daily living (ADLs) Basic self-care tasks such as eating, bathing, toileting, walking, and dressing.

acute diseases Conditions that develop over a short period of time and cause a rapid change in health.

autoimmunity The process by which the immune system begins attacking the body.

average longevity The length of time it takes for half of all people born in a certain year to die.

chronic diseases Conditions that last a longer period of time (at least 3 months) and may be accompanied by residual functional impairment that necessitates long-term management.

coping In the stress and coping paradigm, any attempt to deal with stress.

dependent life expectancy The age to which one can expect to live with assistance.

diabetes mellitus A disease that occurs when the pancreas produces insufficient insulin.

disability The effects of chronic conditions on people's ability to engage in activities that are necessary, expected, and personally desired in their society.

frail older adults Older adults who have physical disabilities, are very ill, and may have cognitive or psychological disorders and who need assistance with everyday tasks.

health The absence of acute and chronic physical or mental disease and impairments.

illness The presence of a physical or mental disease or impairment.

incontinence The loss of the ability to control the elimination of urine and feces on an occasional or consistent basis.

instrumental activities of daily living (IADLs) Actions that entail some intellectual competence and planning.

maximum longevity The maximum length of time an organism can live, roughly 120 years for humans.

polypharmacy The use of multiple medications.

primary appraisal First step in the stress and coping paradigm in which events are categorized into three groups based on the significance they have for our well-being: irrelevant, benign or positive, and stressful.

psychoneuroimmunology The study of the relations between psychological, neurological, and immunological systems that raise or lower our susceptibility to and ability to recover from disease.

reappraisal In the stress and coping paradigm, this step involves making a new primary or secondary appraisal resulting from changes in the situation.

secondary appraisal In the stress and coping paradigm, an assessment of our perceived ability to cope with harm, threat, or challenge.

stress and coping paradigm A model that views stress not as an environmental stimulus or as a response but as the interaction of a thinking person and an event.

Resources

READINGS

Numerous well-written pamphlets on topics related to cancer prevention, assessment, and treatment can be obtained from your local chapter of the American Cancer Society. These pamphlets are easy to read yet provide up-to-date information on technical topics.

Dychtwald, K. (1999). *Healthy aging: Challenges and solutions.* Gaithersburg, MD: Aspen. A good overview of the health issues facing the United States in the next few decades. Easy reading.

Kane, R. L., Evans, J. G., & Macfadyen, D. (1990). *Improving the health of older people: A world view.* Oxford, England: Oxford University Press. Presents a readable description of international perspectives on health promotion and aging. One of the few works in this area.

Kane, R. L., Ouslander, J. G., & Abrass, I. B. (1999). *Essentials of clinical geriatrics* (4th ed.). New York: McGraw-Hill. Latest revision of a useful guide to health and aging. Moderately difficult.

Perls, T. T., Silver M. H., & Lauerman, J. F. (1999). *Living to 100.* New York: Basic Books. An easy to read discussion of healthy habits to follow to increase your life expectancy.

WEB SITES

The American Cancer Society maintains an excellent site that has a range of information for laypeople and professionals. Especially useful are their reports and treatment and prevention guidelines. Their home page can be found at http://www.cancer.org.

The National Center for Chronic Disease Prevention and Health Promotion has a very informative Web site concerning all aspects of chronic disease. This center is part of the Centers for Disease Control and Prevention. The home page can be found at http://www.cdc.gov/nccdphp/.

RxList provides an online index to medications that includes information about how the drugs are used, usual dosage, side effects, and other useful data. Also included in the Web site is a discussion list for commonly prescribed medications. Although this site is not a replacement for physicians or pharmacists, it can be used to gather information about medications. The home page can be found at http://www.rxlist.com.

SEARCH ONLINE WITH
INFOTRAC COLLEGE EDITION

For more information on the topics in this chapter, explore InfoTrac College Edition, your online library. Go to http://www.infotrac-college.com/wadsworth and use the passcode that came on the card with your book. Try these search terms: aging, healthy aspects; longevity; longevity, health aspects.

CLINICAL ASSESSMENT, MENTAL HEALTH, AND MENTAL DISORDERS

© AP / Wide World Photos

Ronald Reagan was the oldest man ever elected as President of the United States, serving from 1981 to 1989. As a former well-known actor and two-term governor of California, Reagan had broad experience in the limelight. Enormously popular during his tenure, Reagan presided over the United States at a time of major global change. Shortly after he left office, however, Reagan began to experience serious memory difficulties along with other serious problems. Eventually he was diagnosed with Alzheimer's disease, and he slowly deteriorated as the disease progressed.

In this chapter, we consider situations like President Reagan's when the aging process goes wrong. Such problems happen to families every day across all demographic categories. Certainly, Alzheimer's disease is not part of normal aging, nor are the other problems we consider.

This chapter is about the people who do not make it through adulthood to old age in the usual way. A minority of adults develop mental health difficulties that cause them problems in their daily lives and sometimes rob them of their dignity. We consider how mental health is defined and how these problems are assessed and treated. We focus on several specific problems, including depression, delirium, dementia, anxiety disorders, psychotic disorders, and substance abuse. As we consider different types of mental disorders, we note how each is diagnosed, what is known about causes, and what effective treatments are available.

Mental Health and the Adult Life Course

LEARNING OBJECTIVES

- How are mental health and psychopathology defined?
- What are the key dimensions used for categorizing psychopathology?
- Why are ethnicity and aging important variables to consider in understanding mental health?

Janet lives alone in a small apartment. Lately, some of her neighbors have noticed that Janet doesn't come to church services as regularly as she used to. Janet's friend Betty noticed that Janet cries a lot when she's asked whether anything is wrong, and sometimes she seems very confused. Betty also notes that several of Janet's friends have died recently but still wonders whether something more serious is wrong with her.

Situations like Janet's are common. Like Betty, we could think that Janet is simply trying to deal with the loss of friends and is simply experiencing grief. But there may be something more serious the matter; Janet's confusion may be out of the ordinary. Janet's situation points out the difficulty in knowing exactly where mental health ends and mental illness or mental disorder begins. What distinguishes the study of mental disorders, or psychopathology, in adulthood and aging is not so much the content of the behavior as its context, that is, whether it interferes with daily functioning. To understand psychopathology as it is manifested in adults of different ages, we must see how it fits into the life-span developmental perspective outlined in Chapter 1.

Defining Mental Health and Psychopathology

The difference between mental health and mental disorder has never been clearly stated (Qualls, 1999). Most scholars avoid the issue entirely or try simply to say what mental health or psychopathology is not. What constitutes normal or abnormal behavior is hard to define precisely because expectations and standards for behavior change over time, over situations, and across age groups (Birren & Renner, 1980; VandenBos, 1999). Thus, what is considered mental health depends on the circumstances under consideration. Birren and Renner (1980) summarize several arguments about the nature of mental health and argue that mentally healthy people have the following characteristics: a positive attitude toward self, an accurate perception of reality, a mastery of the environment, autonomy, personality balance, and growth and self-actualization.

One could argue that to the extent these characteristics are absent, mental disorder or psychopathology becomes more likely. In that case, we would consider behaviors that are harmful to oneself or others, lower one's well-being, and are perceived as distressing, disrupting, abnormal, or maladaptive. Although this approach is used frequently with younger or middle-aged adults, it presents problems when applied to older adults (Smyer & Qualls, 1999). Some behaviors that would be considered abnormal under this definition may actually be adaptive under some circumstances for many older people (such as isolation, passivity, or aggressiveness). Consequently, an approach to defining abnormal behavior that emphasizes considering behaviors in isolation and from the perspective of younger or middle-aged adults is inadequate for defining abnormal behaviors in older adults. For example, because of physical, financial, social, health, or other reasons, some older adults do not have the opportunity to master their environment. Depression or hostility may be an appropriate and justified response to such limitations. Moreover, such responses may help them deal with their situation more effectively and adaptively. Figure 4.1 compares the most common forms of mental disorder as a function of age.

The important point in differentiating normal from abnormal behavior (or mental health from psychopathology) is that behaviors must be interpreted in context. In other words, we must consider what else is happening and how the behavior fits the situation in addition to such factors as age and other personal characteristics.

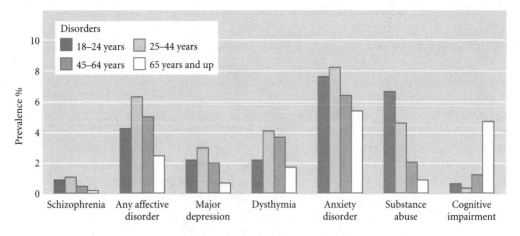

FIGURE 4.1 Prevalence of various mental disorders as a function of age.

Source: Rabins, P. V. (1992). Prevention of mental disorder in the elderly: Current perspectives and future prospects. *Journal of the American Geriatrics Society, 40,* 728.

A Multidimensional Life-Span Approach to Psychopathology

Suppose two people, one young and one old, came into your clinic, each complaining about a lack of sleep, changes in appetite, a lack of energy, and feeling down. What would you say to them?

If you evaluate them in identical ways, you might be headed for trouble. Just as we have seen in other chapters that older and younger adults may think differently or view themselves differently, the meaning of their symptoms and complaints may also differ, even though they appear to be the same. This point is not always incorporated into views of psychopathology. For example, some approaches assume that the same underlying cause is responsible for abnormal or maladaptive behavior regardless of age and that the symptoms of the mental disease are fairly constant across age. Although such models often are used in clinical diagnosis, they are inadequate for understanding psychopathology in old age. Viewing adults' behavior from a life-span developmental forces perspective makes a big difference in how we approach psychopathology. Let's see why.

BIOLOGICAL FORCES. Various chronic diseases, functional limitations, and other ailments can change behavior. Because health problems increase with age (see Chapters 2 and 3), we must be more sensitive to them when dealing with older adults. In addition, genetic factors often underlie important problems in old age. For example, the evidence is growing that Alzheimer's disease has a genetic component. Physical problems may provide clues about underlying psychological difficulties; for example, marked changes in appetite may be a symptom of depression. Moreover, some physical problems may present themselves as psychological ones. For example, extreme irritability can be caused by thyroid problems, and memory loss can result from certain vitamin deficiencies. In any case, physical health and genetic factors are very important dimensions to take into account in diagnosing psychopathology in adults and should be among the first avenues explored.

PSYCHOLOGICAL FORCES. Psychological forces across adulthood are key for understanding psychopathology. As we will see in Chapters 6, 7, and 8, several important changes in attention, memory, and intellectual performance must be considered carefully in interpreting behavior. Normative changes with age in these abilities can mimic certain mental disorders; likewise, these changes can make it more difficult to tell when an older adult has a given type of psychopathology.

Additionally, the nature of a person's relationships with other people, especially family members and friends, is a key dimension in understanding how psychopathology is manifested in adults of different ages. Important developmental differences occur in the interpersonal realm; for example, younger adults are more likely to be expanding their network of friends, whereas older adults are more likely to be experiencing losses. Chapter 11 summarizes developmental changes in key relationships that may influence adults' interpretation of symptoms.

SOCIOCULTURAL FORCES. The social norms and cultural factors we all experience also play a key role in helping define psychopathology. They influence people's behaviors and affect our interpretation of them. For example, an older woman who lives alone in a high-crime area may be highly suspicious of other people. To label her behavior "paranoid" may be inappropriate because her well-being may depend on maintaining a certain level of suspicion of others' motives toward her. Because customs differ across cultures, behaviors that may be normative in one culture may be viewed as indicating problems in another. In short, we must ask whether the behavior we see is appropriate for a person in a particular setting.

LIFE-CYCLE FACTORS. How one behaves at any point in adulthood is strongly affected by one's past experiences and the issues one is facing. These life-cycle factors must be taken into account in evaluating adults' behaviors. For example, a middle-aged woman who wants to go back to school may not have an adjustment disorder; she may simply want to develop a new aspect of herself. Likewise, an older man who provides vague answers to personal questions may not be resistant; he may simply be reflecting his generation's reluctance to disclose one's inner self to a stranger.

Most important, the meaning of particular symptoms may change with age. For example, problems with early morning awakenings may indicate depression in a young adult but may simply be a result of normal aging in an older adult (see Chapter 2).

Ethnicity, Aging, and Mental Health

As we encountered first in Chapter 1 and have seen elsewhere in the text, sociocultural influences are a major and often overlooked factor in understanding people's behavior and developmental history. Mental health is no exception; in fact, sociocultural influences must be considered in evaluating people's behavior and designing effective ways to treat problems (Jackson et al., 1995). For example, by the time most people of color reach old age in the United States, they have experienced a lifetime of inadequate health care, greater exposure to environmental risks, and the stress of prejudice and discrimination (Jackson, 1993). Many personally experienced discrimination, and, in the case of Japanese Americans, even internment camps that affect their trust of the health care system (Haley et al., 1998). Let's look more closely at the key issues.

In neither the general nor the ethnic populations do most people have mental disorders (Jackson et al., 1995). Still, very little is known about the nature and extent of the difficulties people face in ethnic populations, especially for groups other than African Americans. Neither positive mental health nor psychopathology has been adequately defined in any group, and no current approach takes social context into account in such a way as to be sensitive to contextual differences in ethnic communities. For example, although many explanations of deviant and antisocial behavior are grounded in the oppressive life conditions that characterize many ethnic communities, the conceptualization of positive mental health for older ethnic groups does not take the lifetime accumulation of such effects into account (Jackson et al., 1995). However, such sensitivity to conditions does not preclude finding commonalities across ethnic groups; indeed, identifying such commonalities would be an excellent place to start.

What little data we have suggest both similarities and differences in the incidence of specific types of psychopathology across different ethnic groups. Most epidemiological studies of the prevalence and incidence of mental disorders in young adults show little difference across ethnic groups (Jackson et al., 1995). However, a much more complex picture emerges when older adults are studied (Stanford and DuBois, 1992). For example, among Hispanic older adults, men show higher rates of alcohol abuse, whereas women have higher rates of phobia and panic disorders. Native American men also have high rates of alcohol abuse. Rates of depression are lower among older African Americans (Moulton, 1997).

The complicated relations between age, ethnicity, and risk of developing a mental disorder merely emphasize the importance of including age and ethnicity in studies of psychopathology. Clearly, a life-course perspective that includes ethnicity would be the best approach. But even if such a framework were adopted, we would still be faced with another problem: appropriate assessment of functioning.

People have different ways of describing how they feel. Such differences are amplified by ethnic and cultural differences in what one is supposed to reveal to strangers about one's inner self. Placed in a context of important differences in social stressors, physical health, and age, assessing mental health in older ethnic adults is a daunting task. Currently, there is disagreement in the literature over some key issues. For example, do ethnicity and social class change the relation between chronic stressors and mental health? To what extent do social support, religiosity, and the family support system buffer people against stress differently across ethnic groups? Answers to these questions are difficult, and the few studies that address them provide inconclusive results (Jackson et al., 1995).

What can be done to determine the ways in which ethnicity influences mental health? Jackson et al. (1995) argue that researchers should adopt an ethnic research matrix that takes as its defining elements ethnicity, national origin, racial group membership, gender, social and economic statuses, age, accultura-

tion, coping reactions, and mental health outcomes (e.g., psychopathology, positive adjustment). Only by adopting this comprehensive approach can we understand what, how, and when aspects of race, ethnicity, age, and the life course influence mental health.

CONCEPT CHECKS

1. How is psychopathology defined?
2. What biological factors are important to consider in psychopathology?
3. What is known about the role of ethnicity and aging in mental health?

DEVELOPMENTAL ISSUES IN ASSESSMENT AND THERAPY

LEARNING OBJECTIVES

- What key areas are included in a multidimensional approach to assessment?
- What factors influence the assessment of adults?
- How are mental health issues assessed?
- What are some major considerations for therapy across adulthood?

Juan is a 76-year-old World War II veteran who lives in California. Over the past year, his wife, Rocio, has noticed that Juan's memory isn't quite as sharp as it used to be; Juan also has less energy, stays home more, and does not show as much interest in playing dominos, a game at which he excels. Rocio wonders what might be wrong with Juan.

Many adults can relate to Rocio because they are concerned about someone they know. Whether the person is 25 or 85, being able to determine whether memory problems, energy loss, social withdrawal, or other areas of concern really indicate an underlying problem is important. As you might suspect, health care professionals should not use identical approaches to assess and treat adults of widely different ages. In this section, we consider how assessment methods and therapies must take developmental differences into account.

Areas of Multidimensional Assessment

What does it mean to assess someone? Assessment makes it possible to describe the behavior or other characteristics of people in meaningful ways (Edelstein & Kalish, 1999). Assessment is a formal process of measuring, understanding, and predicting behavior. It involves gathering medical, psychological, and sociocultural information about people through various means, such as interviews, observation, tests, and clinical examinations.

As we noted in Chapter 1, two central aspects of any assessment approach are reliability and validity. Without these psychometric properties, we cannot rely on the assessment method to provide good information. Additionally, any assessment method must be of practical use in determining the nature of the problem and choosing the appropriate treatment.

A multidimensional assessment approach is most effective (Edelstein & Kalish, 1999; Hestad et al., 1999; Segal et al., 1999). Multidimensional assessment often is done by a team of professionals; for example, a physician may examine the medication regimen, a psychologist the cognitive functioning, a nurse the daily living skills, and a social worker the economic and environmental resources. Let's consider Juan's situation as an example.

A thorough assessment of Juan's physical health is essential, as it is for adults of all ages, especially for older adults. Many physical conditions can create (or hide) mental health problems, so it is important to identify any underlying issues. Laboratory tests can also be ordered that can provide additional clues to the presence or even the cause of the problem.

Establishing Juan's cognitive ability is also key. Complaints of cognitive problems increase across adulthood, so it is important to determine the extent to which abnormal changes in older people are discriminated from normative change. Adults of all ages can be given intelligence tests, neuropsychological examinations, and mental status examinations. **Mental status exams** *are especially useful as quick screening measures of mental competence that are used to screen for cognitive impairment;* one commonly used instrument, the Mini Mental Status Exam, is shown in

Table 4.1. If Juan's score on these brief measures indicates potential problems, more complete follow-up assessments would be used.

Psychological functioning typically is assessed through interviews, observation, and tests or questionnaires. Usually, a clinician begins with an interview of Juan and brief screening instruments and follows up, if necessary, with more thorough personality inventories or more detailed interviews.

How well Juan functions in his daily life is also assessed carefully. Usually, this entails determining whether he has difficulty with activities of daily living and instrumental activities of daily living (see Chapter 3). Also assessed is the person's decision-making capacity; each state has legal standards guiding the competency assessment.

Social factors in Juan's life such as social support constitute the final area of assessment. Rook (1994) describes three dimensions of social functioning: ties with one's social network, the content of interactions with members of the social network, and the number and quality of interactions with network members. Addressing all areas of Juan's physical, cognitive, psychological, and social functioning will help determine whether Rocio has reason to be concerned.

Factors Influencing Assessment

Health care professionals' preconceived ideas about the people they assess may have negative effects on the assessment process (Edelstein & Kalish, 1999). Two areas of concern are biases (negative or positive) and environmental conditions (where the assessment occurs, sensory or mobility problems, and health of the client).

Many types of bias have been documented as affecting the assessment process (Edelstein & Kalish, 1999; James & Haley, 1995). Negative biases about people are widespread and include racial, ethnic, and age stereotypes. For example, clinicians may hold negative biases against younger adults of ethnic minorities and more readily "diagnose" problems that do not truly exist. Likewise, because of ageism, older adults may be "diagnosed" with untreatable problems such as Alzheimer's disease rather than treatable

TABLE 4.1 The Mini Mental Status Exam

Maximum Score	Score	
		Orientation
5	( )	What is the (year) (season) (date) (day) (month)?
5	( )	Where are we (state) (country) (town) (hospital) (floor)?
		Registration
3	( )	Name three objects; take 1 second to say each. Then ask the patient all three after you have said them.
		Give one point for each correct answer. Then repeat them until he or she learns all three. Count trials and record.
		Attention and Calculation Trial
5	( )	Serial 7s. Give one point for each correct. Stop after five answers. Alternatively spell *world* backwards.
		Recall
3	( )	Ask for three objects repeated earlier. Give one point for each correct.
		Language Trial
9	( )	Name a pencil and a watch (2 points).
		Repeat the following: "No ifs, ands, or buts" (1 point).
		Follow a three-stage command: "Take a paper in your right hand, fold it in half, and put it on the floor" (3 points).
		Read and obey the following:
		"Close your eyes" (1 point).
		"Write a sentence" (1 point).
		"Copy design" (1 point).
		Assess level of consciousness along a continuum.
		Alert Drowsy Stupor Coma
	Total ( )	

Source: Folstein, M. F., Folstein, S., & McHugh, P. R. (1975). Mini-mental state: A practical method for grading the cognitive state of patients for the clinician. *Journal of Psychiatric Research, 12,* 189–198.

problems such as depression (see Chapter 1). In contrast, positive biases about certain people also works against accurate assessment. For example, a belief that women do not abuse alcohol may result in a misdiagnosis; beliefs that older adults are "cute" may mitigate against accurate assessment of abilities. Clearly, the best defense against bias is for clinicians to be fully educated about their prospective clients.

The environmental conditions in which the assessment occurs can also work against accurate outcomes. Clinicians do not always have the option of selecting an ideal environment; rather, assessments sometimes occur in hallways, with a bedridden patient, or in a noisy emergency room. People with sensory or motor difficulties must be accommodated with alternative assessment formats. The patient's physical health may also complicate assessment; in many cases with older adults, it can also create a negative bias (James & Haley, 1995).

Taken together, clinical assessment is an excellent example of how the forces of development come together. As described in the Forces in Action feature,

As described in the text, accurate clinical assessment is a complex undertaking. We can use the forces of development as a framework to create the ideal assessment approach. Biological forces play a role through physical health, physical changes with age, and genetics. Each of these aspects must be thoroughly examined. In later sections, we will encounter types of mental disorders that have strong connections to each.

Psychological forces in mental disorders involve primarily cognitive functioning, social cognition, and personality. We will see that each is a defining characteristic of some types of mental disorders. Clinical assessment depends critically on accurate and unbiased assessment of these dimensions.

Sociocultural forces exert their influence through social class, ethnicity, and social network. Social class and ethnicity are important because they often determine the access people have to good mental and physical health care. In part, the ethnic differences that exist in some forms of mental disorders can be traced to these variables. Social class and ethnicity also play into clinicians' biases toward certain types of clients, which in turn results in inaccurate assessment.

Life-cycle forces are key to assessment in that the symptoms demonstrated for a particular disorder often change with age. Sensitivity and awareness of such changes is necessary for treatable conditions to be correctly diagnosed. Normative changes with age in functioning must also be taken into account for accurate diagnosis.

---

only when all four forces are considered can mental health problems be assessed accurately.

Assessment Methods

How are adults assessed? In terms of cognitive, psychological, and social assessments, there are six primary methods (Edelstein & Kalish, 1999): interview, self-report, report by others, psychophysiological assessment, direct observation, and performance-based assessment.

Clinical interviews are the most widely used assessment method (Edelstein & Semenschuck, 1996). They are useful because they provide both direct information in response to the questions and nonverbal information such as emotions. Interviews can be used to obtain historical information, determine appropriate follow-up procedures, build rapport with the client, obtain the client's informed consent to participate in the assessment, and evaluate the effects of treatment. All these tasks are important with adults of all ages. When interviewing older adults, though, it is important to use somewhat shorter sessions, learn something about the social history of the cohort, and be aware of sensory deficits and cognitive and medical conditions that may interfere with the interview.

As described in Chapter 1, self-report instruments include a wide array of measures in which the client responds to surveys and questionnaires. Many commonly used assessment measures are presented in a self-report format. As noted in Chapter 1, a major concern is the reliability and validity of these measures with older adults.

Family members and friends are an important source of information. In some cases, such as Alzheimer's disease, discrepancies between the client's and others' description of the problem can be diagnostic. Such sources also are valuable if the client is unlikely or unable to tell the whole story. Such information can be obtained through interviews or self-report.

Psychophysiological assessment examines the relation between physical and psychological functioning. One common psychophysiological measure is the electroencephalogram (EEG), which measures brain wave activity. Other measures include heart rate, muscle activity, and skin temperature. Such measures provide a way to measure the body's reaction to certain stimuli, especially when the client gets anxious or fearful in response to them.

In some cases it is possible to observe the client through systematic or naturalistic observation (see

Psychotherapy has been shown to be as effective with older adults
as with younger adults.

Chapter 1). Direct observation is especially useful when the problem involves specific behaviors, as in eating disorders. A variety of techniques exist for structuring observations, and they can be used in a wide array of settings, from homes to nursing homes.

Finally, performance-based assessment involves giving clients a specific task to perform. This approach underlies much cognitive and neuropsychological assessment. For example, a person's memory is assessed by giving him or her a list of items to remember and then testing retention. Some neuropsychological tests involve drawing or copying pictures.

Developmental Issues in Therapy

Assuming that Juan is assessed properly and is found to have a mental disorder, what next? How can he be helped? Therapy for mental disorders generally involves two approaches (Smyer & Qualls, 1999): medical treatment and psychotherapy. Medical treatment most often involves the use of various medications, which are based on the underlying physiological causes of the disorders. Psychotherapy usually involves talking to a clinician or participating in a group. In either case, it is essential to take into account developmental differences in people as they age.

As we saw in Chapter 3, the ways in which medications work change with age. The effective dosage of a specific medication may be very different for younger, middle-aged, and older adults. In some cases, medications that work in one age group do not work for others.

In terms of psychotherapy, adults of different ages deal with different major developmental issues (Zarit & Knight, 1996). As we will see in more detail in Chapter 10, various hypotheses suggest that as adults age, different life issues become central. For example, according to Erikson (1982), young adults deal with forming intimate relationships with others, middle-aged adults grapple with passing on their experience to younger generations, and older adults struggle with the meaning of their lives. Such issues often are the major issue when people enter therapy. Thus, clinicians must be sensitive to the primary developmental issues facing people of different ages to make sense of their problems.

Another major issue in psychotherapy is establishing whether a particular psychotherapeutic approach is effective (Gatz et al., 1998). A set of criteria was developed by the Division of Clinical Psychology of the American Psychological Association (Division 12) for "well established" and "probably efficacious" treatments (Chambless et al., 1996). The criteria are strict. Although such "pure-form interventions" may not translate perfectly into real-world settings because clients often have more complex problems than those examined in research settings (Goldfried & Wolfe, 1998), the criteria do provide a benchmark by which to judge. The psychotherapeutic approaches that meet the standard appear to be effective for a wide range of ages and are the psychotherapies of choice (Gatz et al., 1998).

CONCEPT CHECKS

1. What are the major areas of thorough clinical assessment?
2. What factors must be considered in conducting clinical assessment?
3. What are the major clinical assessment techniques?
4. What developmental factors must be considered in therapy?

THE BIG THREE: DEPRESSION, DELIRIUM, AND DEMENTIA

LEARNING OBJECTIVES

- What are the most common characteristics of people with depression? How is depression diagnosed? What causes depression? What is the relation between suicide and age? How is depression treated?
- What is delirium? How is it assessed and treated?
- What is dementia? What are the major symptoms of Alzheimer's disease? How is it diagnosed? What causes it? What intervention options are there? What are some other major forms of dementia? What do family members caring for patients with dementia experience?

*L*ing has lived in the same neighborhood in New York for all of her 74 years. Her son, who visits her every week, has started noticing that Ling's memory problems have gotten much worse, her freezer is empty, and her refrigerator has lots of moldy food. When he investigated further, he found that her bank accounts were in disarray. Ling's son wonders what could be wrong with her.

Ling's behaviors certainly do not appear to be typical of older adults. Unfortunately, Ling is not alone in experiencing difficulties; many older adults have similar problems. In this section, we consider three of the most common difficulties: depression, delirium, and dementia. As we will see, both depression and delirium are treatable; the most common form of dementia, Alzheimer's disease, is not. The three conditions are connected by overlapping symptoms and the possibility that they may coexist. Let's consider each in detail.

Depression

Depression is one of the most common mental disorders and one of the most treatable (Gatz et al., 1996; Smyer & Qualls, 1999). Estimates from several large epidemiological surveys indicate that at any time, 2–5% of adults of all ages have a clinical depressive disorder (depression that meets strict diagnostic criteria) and that roughly 15% of all community residents have some depressive symptoms; for older adults only the estimates are about 1–2% with clinical depression and 16% with symptoms above the clinical cutoff (Kasl-Godley et al., 1999; Schneider, 1995; Smyer & Qualls, 1999). There is increasing evidence that depression is a major mental health problem among older adults that has been badly underdiagnosed and undertreated (Friedhoff, 1994). In part, this is because of important differences in symptoms between younger and older adults.

Contrary to popular belief, the rate of clinical depression actually declines across adulthood, as shown in Figure 4.2 (Gatz, 2000; Qualls, 1999). Young adults are at the most risk. However, if we consider people's reports of symptoms of depression, a different picture emerges. In this case, the highest rates occur in younger adults and people over age 75, with middle-aged adults having a lower rate (Gatz et al., 1996). Importantly, there is also evidence of a cohort effect, with more recent-born cohorts showing higher rates of depression. If this trend continues, future groups of older adults may have higher rates of depression than current older adults (Gatz et al., 1996).

Finally, depression commonly accompanies other chronic conditions. For example, research indicates that 33% of people with diabetes also show symp-

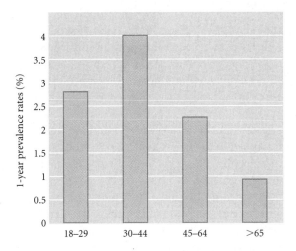

FIGURE 4.2 **Prevalence of major depressive disorder as a function of age.**

Adapted with the permission of The Free Press, a division of Simon & Schuster, Inc., from *Psychiatric Disorders in America: The Epidemiologic Catchment Area Study* by Lee N. Robins and Darrel A. Regier. Copyright © 1991 by Lee Robins and Darrel A. Regier.

toms of depression, as do 42% of people with cancer and 45% of people who have had a recent heart attack (National Academy on an Aging Society, 2000c).

GENERAL SYMPTOMS AND CHARACTERISTICS OF PEOPLE WITH DEPRESSION. *The most prominent feature of clinical depression is* **dysphoria,** *that is, feeling down or blue.* There are important developmental differences in how this feature is expressed (Gatz, 2000). Older adults may not label their down feelings as depression but rather as pessimism or helplessness (Reifler, 1994). Indeed, a large community study of more than 6,500 adults revealed that older adults were much less likely to endorse statements relating to dysphoria (Gallo et al., 1994). Additionally, older adults are more likely to show signs of apathy, subdued self-deprecation, expressionlessness, and changes in arousal than are younger people (Reifler, 1994). It is common for depressed older adults to withdraw, not speak to anyone, confine themselves to bed, and not take care of bodily functions. Younger adults may engage in some of these behaviors but to a much lesser extent.

The second major component of clinical depression is the accompanying physical symptoms. These include insomnia, changes in appetite, diffuse pain, troubled breathing, headaches, fatigue, and sensory loss (Smyer & Qualls, 1999). The presence of these physical symptoms in older adults must be evaluated carefully. As noted in Chapter 2, some sleep disturbances may reflect normative changes that are unrelated to depression; however, regular early morning awakening is consistently related to depression, even in older adults (Rodin et al., 1988). Alternatively, the physical symptoms may reflect an underlying physical disease that is manifested as depression. Indeed, many older adults admitted to the hospital with depressive symptoms turn out to have previously undiagnosed medical problems that are uncovered only after thorough blood and metabolic tests (Smyer & Qualls, 1999). A list of some of the most common diseases that are often accompanied by depression can be seen in Table 4.2.

The third primary characteristic is that the symptoms must last at least 2 weeks. This criterion is used to rule out the transient symptoms that are common to all adults, especially after a negative experience such as receiving a rejection letter from a potential employer or getting a speeding ticket.

Fourth, other causes for the observed symptoms must be ruled out. For example, other health problems, neurological disorders, medications, metabolic conditions, alcoholism, or other forms of psychopathology can cause depressive symptoms. These causes influence appropriate treatment decisions.

Finally, the clinician must determine how the person's symptoms are affecting his or her daily life. Is the ability to interact with other people impaired? Can he or she carry out domestic responsibilities? What about effects on work or school? Is the person taking any medication? Clinical depression involves significant impairment in daily living.

Although the primary risk factors for depression do not change with age, some important personal characteristics do. Being female, unmarried, widowed, or recently bereaved; experiencing stressful life events; and lacking an adequate social support network are more common among older adults with

TABLE 4.2	Physical Illnesses That Cause Depression in Older Adults

Coronary artery disease
Hypertension, myocardial infarction, coronary artery bypass surgery, congestive heart failure

Neurologic disorders
Cerebrovascular accidents, Alzheimer's disease, Parkinson's disease, amyotrophic lateral sclerosis, multiple sclerosis, Binswanger's disease

Metabolic disturbances
Diabetes mellitus, hypothyroidism or hyperthyroidism, hypercortisolism, hyperparathyroidism, Addison's disease, autoimmune thyroiditis

Cancer
Pancreatic, breast, lung, colonic, and ovarian carcinoma; lymphoma, and undetected cerebral metastasis

Other conditions
Chronic obstructive pulmonary disease, rheumatoid arthritis, deafness, chronic pain, sexual dysfunction, renal dialysis, chronic constipation

Source: Sunderland, T., Lawlor, B. A., Molchan, S. E., & Martinez, R. A. (1988). Depressive syndromes in the elderly: Special concerns. *Psychopharmacology Bulletin, 24,* 567–576.

depression than younger adults (Zisook & Schucter, 1994). Subgroups of older adults who are at greater risk include those with chronic illnesses (of whom up to half may have major depression), nursing home residents, and family caregivers (of whom up to 40% may have major depression; Schneider, 1995).

Rates of clinical depression vary across ethnic groups (Haley et al., 1998). Older people of ethnic minorities who are not highly acculturated in the United States tend to show higher rates of depression; this is especially true for Chinese Americans and Mexican Americans (Lam et al., 1997). Hispanic Americans have a higher rate of depression overall, with some estimates indicating that up to one-fourth of older Hispanics have depression or related disor-

der, possibly caused by poor health in general (Bastida & Gonzalez, 1995). Older African Americans have lower rates of depression than European Americans (Moulton, 1997). Clearly, the pattern of ethnic differences indicates that the reasons for them are complex and not well understood.

GENDER AND DEPRESSIVE SYMPTOMS. Women tend to be diagnosed as being depressed more often than men (Gatz et al., 1996). This has led some researchers to focus specifically on women's experience of depression to identify the kinds of symptoms they have. In a series of studies, Newmann, Engel, and Jensen (1990, 1991) looked at the patterns of symptoms women report and how these symptoms change over time. They found two different depressive syndromes and four different but related forms of psychological distress.

The two depressive syndromes differ on whether two key symptoms are present: dysphoria and feelings of guilt or self-blame. They are present in classic clinical depression but appear to be absent in a version of depression that at one time was called masked depression but is now called the *depletion syndrome of the elderly* (Kasl-Godley et al., 1999). Several other symptoms described earlier are common to the two different types (such as feeling worthless, losing interest in things, and having various physical symptoms). Interestingly, four limited forms of psychological distress were found, each independent of the others: sleep disturbances, loss of energy, loneliness, and self-deprecating attitude. These results clearly show that the symptoms of depression, as well as the syndrome itself, are far more complicated than most people imagine.

In their second study, Newmann and colleagues (1991) showed that the classic depressive syndrome declines in frequency with age, whereas the depletion syndrome increases. These findings imply that the age-related declines in the frequency of severe depression discussed earlier probably reflect classic depression. Moreover, these results point to the need for very careful diagnosis of depression in women.

ASSESSMENT SCALES. Numerous scales are used to assess depression, but because most were developed on

Contrary to myth, the rate of depression actually declines with age.

younger and middle-aged adults, they are most appropriate for these age groups. The most important difficulty in using these scales with older adults is that they all include several items assessing physical symptoms. For example, the Beck Depression Inventory (Beck, 1967) contains items that focus on feelings and physical symptoms. Although the presence of such symptoms usually is indicative of depression in younger adults, as we noted earlier such symptoms may not be related to depression at all in older adults. More recently, scales such as the Geriatric Depression Scale (Yesavage et al., 1983) aimed specifically at older adults have been developed. Physical symptoms are omitted, and the response format is easier for older adults to follow.

An important point to keep in mind about these scales is that the diagnosis of depression should never be made on the basis of a test score alone. As we have seen, the symptoms observed in clinical depression could be indicative of other problems, and symptom patterns are very complex. Moreover, there is some evidence of gender bias; in one study, both the Geriatric Depression Scale and the Beck Depression Inventory were more accurate in diagnosing depression in older women than in older men (Allen-Burge et al., 1994). Only by assessing many aspects of physical and psychological functioning can a clinician make an accurate assessment.

CAUSES OF DEPRESSION. Several theories about the causes of depression have been proposed. They can be grouped into two main categories: biological theories and psychosocial theories.

Biological theories focus most on genetic predisposition and changes in neurotransmitters (Qualls, 1999). The genetic evidence is based on several studies that show higher rates of depression in relatives of depressed people than would be expected given base rates in the population. This genetic link is stronger in early-onset depression than it is in depression that has its onset in late life (Kasl-Godley et al., 1999), but the link still accounts for 30% of the variance in depression in older twins (Gatz et al., 1992).

There is substantial research evidence that severe depression is linked to the ineffective use of neurotransmitters such as norepinephrine and serotonin (Qualls, 1999). These links are the basis for the medications developed to treat depression. As we saw in Chapter 2, the levels of these neurotransmitters change with age. This would lead to the prediction that the rates of depression should increase with age. But because the rate of clinical depression actually declines, the neurotransmitter link does not explain the data very well. Other physiological theories of depression cite abnormal brain function and physical illness.

The most common theme of psychosocial theories of depression is loss (Cohler, 1993; Gaylord & Zung, 1987). Bereavement is the type of loss that has received the most attention, but the loss of anything considered personally important could also be a trigger. Moreover, these losses may be real and irrevocable, threatened and potential, or imaginary and fantasized. The likelihood that these losses will occur varies with age. Middle-aged adults are more likely to experience the loss of physical attractiveness, for example, whereas older adults are more likely to experience the loss of a loved one.

A different approach is taken in behavioral and cognitive–behavioral theories of depression. The behavioral approach argues that people with depression engage in fewer pleasant activities and receive less pleasure from them than do nondepressed people (Smyer & Qualls, 1999). This link between behaviors and mood is the basis for various therapeutic interventions. The cognitive–behavioral approach emphasizes internal belief systems, which focuses on how people interpret uncontrollable events (Beck, 1967). The idea underlying this approach is that experiencing unpredictable and uncontrollable events instills a feeling of helplessness, which results in depression. Additionally, perceiving the cause of negative events as some inherent aspect of the self that is permanent and pervasive also plays an important role in causing feelings of helplessness and hopelessness. In short, according to the cognitive–behavioral approach, people who are depressed believe that they are personally responsible for their plight, that things are unlikely to get better, and that their whole life is a shambles.

An alternative psychosocial explanation argues that whether a person experiences depression depends on a balance among biological dispositions, stress, and protective factors (Gatz, 2000). Developmentally, biological factors become more important with age, whereas stress factors diminish. Protective factors, such as psychological coping skills, also improve, which may account in part for the decreased incidence of depression in later life.

TREATMENT OF DEPRESSION. As we have seen, depression is a complex problem that can result from a wide variety of causes. However, an extremely crucial point is that all forms of depression benefit from some form of therapy and that they are quite effective (Scogin & McElreath, 1994). For the severe forms, medications may be needed. In some cases of severe, long-term depression, electroconvulsive

therapy may be needed. For the less severe forms of depression, and usually in conjunction with medication for severe depression, there are various forms of psychotherapy. A summary of the various treatment options is presented in Table 4.3.

Three families of drugs are used to combat severe depression. The first-line medications to treat depression are called selective serotonin reuptake inhibitors (SSRIs; Newhouse, 1996). SSRIs gained wide popularity beginning in the late 1980s because they have the lowest overall rate of side effects of all antidepressants. SSRIs work by boosting the level of serotonin, a neurotransmitter involved in regulating moods. One of the SSRIs, Prozac, became controversial because it was linked in a small number of cases with the serious side effect of high levels of agitation. Drugs such as fluoxetine HCl (Prozac) make people "not sad," which is different from making people happy. Other SSRIs, such as sertraline (Zoloft) and nefazodone HCl (Serzone), appear to have fewer adverse reactions and are widely prescribed.

Other commonly used medications are the heterocyclic antidepressants (HCAs). Although HCAs are effective in at least 70% of cases, they are most effective with younger and middle-aged people. The main problem with HCAs in older adults is that they are more likely to have other medical conditions or to be taking other medications that preclude the use of HCAs. For example, people who are taking antihypertensive medications or who have any of a number of metabolic problems should not take the tricyclic HCAs (Buffum & Buffum, 1998). Moreover, the risk of side effects beyond dry mouth is much greater in older adults, although some of the newer HCAs have significantly lower risk. Because HCAs must be taken for roughly a week before the person feels relief, compliance with the therapy sometimes is difficult.

A third group of drugs that relieve depression is the monoamine oxidase (MAO) inhibitors, so named because they inhibit MAO, a substance that interferes with the transmission of signals between neurons. MAO inhibitors generally are less effective than the tricyclics and can produce deadly side effects (Buffum & Buffum, 1998). Specifically, they interact with foods that contain tyramine or dopamine—mainly

TABLE 4.3   Summary of Depression Treatment Options

Treatment	Efficacy	Comments
Antidepressant medications	Numerous (more than 30) randomized, placebo-controlled trials of several tricyclics, bupropion, trazodone, and others. Trial results are for acute treatment responses.	Adequate dosages, plasma levels, and treatment duration are essential to maximize response. Response may take 6 to 12 weeks, somewhat longer than in younger patients. Side effects may limit use.
Augmentation of antidepressants with lithium, thyroid medications, carbamazepine	Patients nonresponsive to several weeks of treatment with standard antidepressant medications may respond rapidly after these medications are added. Evidence is based on case series and reports.	May be useful in patients who are not responding or only partially responding to standard antidepressant medications. Constitutes acceptable clinical practice.
Electroconvulsive therapy	Clearly effective in severe depression; depression with melancholia, and depression with delusions and when antidepressants are not fully effective. Sometimes combined with antidepressants.	In medication-resistant patients, acute response rate is approximately 50%. Relapse rate is high, necessitating attention to maintenance antidepressant treatment. Effects are more favorable with increasing age.
Psychotherapy	More effective treatment than waiting list, no treatment, or placebo; equivalent to antidepressant medications in geriatric outpatient populations generally, with both major or minor depression. About half of studies are group interventions. Therapy orientations were cognitive, interpersonal, reminiscence, psychodynamic, and eclectic.	Studies have been in older outpatients who were not significantly suicidal and for whom hospitalization was not indicated. There is no evidence of efficacy in severe depression. Distribution of responses may be different from the response to medication.
Combined antidepressant medication and psychotherapy	Effective in outpatients using manual-based therapies; the relative contributions of each component are not well understood.	Combined therapy has not been adequately studied in older adults.

Source: U.S. Public Health Service (1993).

cheddar cheese but also others, such as wine and chicken liver—to create dangerously and sometimes fatally high blood pressure. MAO inhibitors are used with extreme caution, usually only after SSRIs and HCAs have proved ineffective.

If periods of depression alternate with periods of mania or extremely high levels of activity, a diagnosis of bipolar disorder is made (American Psychiatric Association, 1994). Bipolar disorder is characterized by unpredictable, often explosive mood swings as the person cycles between extreme depression and extreme activity. The drug therapy of choice for bipolar disorder is lithium (Buffum & Buffum, 1998), which came into widespread use in the early 1970s. Lithium is very effective in controlling the mood swings, although we do not completely understand why it works. The use of lithium must be monitored very closely because the difference between an effective dosage and a toxic dosage is very small. Because lithium is a salt, it raises blood pressure, making it dangerous for people who have hypertension or kidney disease. The effective dosage for lithium decreases with age; physicians unaware of this change run the risk of inducing an overdose, especially in older adults (Buffum & Buffum, 1998). Compliance is also a problem because no improvement is seen for 4–10 days after the initial dose and because many people with bipolar disorder do not like having their moods controlled by medication.

Electroconvulsive therapy (ECT) is an effective treatment for severe depression, especially in people whose depression has lasted a long time, who are suicidal, who have serious physical problems caused by their depression, and who do not respond to medications (Smyer & Qualls, 1999). Unlike antidepressant medications, ECT has immediate effects. Usually, only a few treatments are needed, compared with long-term maintenance schedules for drugs. But ECT also has some side effects. Memory of the ECT treatment itself is lost. Memory of other recent events is temporarily disrupted, but it usually returns within a week or two. Older adults who receive ECT are at risk of heart attacks (Rice et al., 1994), but overall it is effective when other treatments fail (Sackeim, 1994).

Psychotherapy is a treatment approach based on the idea that talking to a therapist about one's problems can help. Often, psychotherapy can be very effective by itself in treating depression. In cases of severe depression, psychotherapy may be combined with drug or ECT therapy. Of the more than 100 different types of psychotherapy, two general approaches seem to work best for depression: **behavior therapy,** *which focuses on attempts to alter current behavior without necessarily addressing underlying causes,* and **cognitive therapy,** *which attempts to alter the ways people think.*

The fundamental idea in behavior therapy is that depressed people receive too few rewards or reinforcements from their environment (Lewinsohn, 1975). Thus, the goal of behavior therapy is to get them to increase the good things that happen to them. Often, this can be accomplished by having people increase their activities; if they do more, the likelihood is that more good things will happen. Additionally, behavior therapy seeks to get people to decrease the number of negative thoughts they have because depressed people tend to look at the world pessimistically. They get little pleasure out of activities that nondepressed people enjoy a great deal: seeing a funny movie, playing a friendly game of volleyball, or being with a lover.

To get activity levels up and negative thoughts down, behavior therapists usually assign tasks that force clients to practice the principles they are learning during the therapy sessions. This may involve going out more to meet people, joining new clubs, or just learning how to enjoy life. Family members are instructed to ignore negative statements made by the depressed person and to reward positive self-statements with attention, praise, or even money.

Cognitive therapy for depression is based on the idea that depression results from maladaptive beliefs or cognitions about oneself. From this perspective, a depressed person views the self as inadequate and unworthy, the world as insensitive and ungratifying, and the future as bleak and unpromising (Beck et al., 1979). In cognitive therapy the person is taught how to recognize these thoughts, which have become so automatic and ingrained that other perspectives are not seen. Once this awareness has been achieved, the person learns how to evaluate the self, world, and future more realistically. These goals may be accomplished through homework assignments similar to those used in behavior therapy. These often involve reattributing the causes of events, examining the evidence before drawing conclusions, listing the pros and cons of maintaining an idea, and examining the consequences of that idea. Finally, people are taught to change the basic beliefs that are responsible for their negative thoughts. For example, people who believe that they have been failures all their lives or that they are unlovable are taught how to use their new-found knowledge to achieve more realistic appraisals of themselves.

Two versions of psychoanalytic therapy particularly useful with older adults are life review therapy and reminiscence. The goal of both therapies is to use the memories of previous events and relationships as ways to confront and resolve conflicts. Life review therapy and reminiscence can be done individually or in groups, and they can be unstructured or structured (by using particular topics as triggers). Although both approaches have become very popular and are claimed to be effective, why they work and how remembering the past relates to specific cognitive and emotional processes are unknown (Smyer & Qualls, 1999).

Delirium

A **delirium** *is characterized by a disturbance of consciousness and a change in cognition that develop over a short period of time* (American Psychiatric Association, 1994). The changes in cognition can include difficulties with attention, memory, orientation, and language. Delirium can also affect perception, the sleep–wake cycle, personality, and mood. Although the onset of delirium usually is rapid, its course can vary a great deal over the course of a day (Qualls, 1999).

Delirium can be caused by any of a number of medical conditions (such as stroke, cardiovascular disease, metabolic condition), medication side effects, substance intoxication or withdrawal, exposure to toxins, or any combination of factors (Smyer & Qualls, 1999). Because they take more medications on average than other age groups, older adults are particularly susceptible to delirium. In the general community, the rate of delirium in people over age 55 is low (between 0.4–1.1%), but among people who are ill the rate is much higher, with as many as 50% of postoperative patients experiencing delirium (Qualls, 1999).

Assessment and treatment of delirium focus on the physiological causes. In general, the most important aspect of diagnosis is differentiating delirium from depression and dementia. The key features of each is shown in Table 4.4. The severity of delirium is related to the level of underlying physiological problem. In many cases, delirium is accompanied by severe misinterpretations of the environment and confusion, which is best alleviated by having one reliable family member or friend provide reassurance to the patient (Ebersole & Hess, 1998).

If the cause of the delirium can be identified and addressed, most cases of delirium can be cured. In some cases, however, delirium can be fatal or result in permanent brain damage (Ebersole & Hess, 1998).

Dementia

Probably no other condition associated with aging is more feared than dementia, a family of disorders. In dementia one can literally lose one's mind, being reduced from a complex, thinking, feeling human being to a confused, vegetative victim unable even to recognize one's spouse and children. Dementias serious enough to impair independent functioning affect roughly 4 million Americans, or 6–8% of people over age 65 (Smyer & Qualls, 1999). These rates vary tremendously with age, however. Fewer than 1% of the people are afflicted at age 65, but the incidence rises sharply to as many as 50% in some studies of those over age 85 (Gatz et al., 1996). Estimates are that the number of people with dementia will roughly triple by the mid-21st century unless a cure or prevention is found (Alzheimer's Association, 1999).

Although there is a real basis for fearing dementia, most older adults are not demented. For many people, the fear of dementia is the most serious problem, leading them to consider every lapse of memory a symptom. It is hard to know how many older adults have unstated fears because they can no longer remember things in the same ways they did when they were younger. But as noted in Chapter 7, memory abilities show some normative changes with age. Consequently, what many people believe are signs that they are becoming demented are actually quite normal.

THE FAMILY OF DEMENTIAS. **Dementia** *is not a specific disease but rather a family of diseases that are characterized by cognitive and behavioral deficits involving some form of permanent damage to the brain.* About a dozen

Clinical feature	Delirium	Dementia	Depression
Onset	Acute or subacute, depends on cause, often at twilight or in darkness	Chronic, generally insidious, depends on cause	Coincides with major life changes, often abrupt
Course	Short, diurnal fluctuations in symptoms, worse at night, in darkness, and on awakening	Long, no diurnal effects, symptoms progressive yet stable over time	Diurnal effects, typically worse in the morning, situational fluctuations, but less than with delirium
Progression	Abrupt	Slow but uneven	Variable, rapid or slow but even
Duration	Hours to less than 1 month, seldom longer	Months to years	At least 6 weeks, can be several months to years
Awareness	Reduced	Clear	Clear
Alertness	Fluctuates, lethargic or hypervigilant	Generally normal	Normal
Attention	Impaired, fluctuates	Generally normal	Minimal impairment, but is easily distracted
Orientation	Generally impaired, severity varies	Generally normal	Selective disorientation
Memory	Recent and immediate impaired	Recent and remote impaired	Selective or patchy impairment, islands of intact memory
Thinking	Disorganized, distorted, fragmented, incoherent speech, either slow or accelerated	Difficulty with abstraction, thoughts impoverished, judgment impaired, words difficult to find	Intact but with themes of hopelessness, helplessness, or self-deprecation
Perception	Distorted, illusions, delusions, and hallucinations, difficulty distinguishing between reality and misperceptions	Misperceptions usually absent	Intact, delusions and hallucinations absent except in severe cases
Psychomotor behavior	Variable, hypokinetic, hyperkinetic, and mixed	Normal, may have apraxia	Variable, psychomotor retardation or agitation
Sleep–wake cycle	Disturbed, cycle reversed	Fragmented	Disturbed, usually early morning awakening
Associated features	Variable affective changes, symptoms of autonomic hyperarousal, exaggeration of personality type, associated with acute physical illness	Affect tends to be superficial, inappropriate, and labile, attempts to conceal deficits in intellect, personality changes, aphasia, agnosia may be present, lacks insight	Affect depressed, dysphoric mood, exaggerated and detailed complaints, preoccupied with personal thoughts, insight present, verbal elaboration
Assessment	Distracted from task, numerous errors	Failing highlighted by family, frequent "near miss" answers, struggles with test, great effort to find an appropriate reply, frequent requests for feedback on performance	Failings highlighted by individual, often answers "don't know," little effort, often gives up, indifferent toward test, does not care or attempt to find answer

Source: Foreman, M. D., Fletcher, K., Mion, L. C., et al. (1996). Assessing cognitive function. *Geriatric Nursing, 17,* 228.

forms of dementia have been identified. Dementia involves severe cognitive and behavioral decline and is not caused by a rapid onset of a toxic substance or by infection (American Psychiatric Association, 1994). If delirium is present, dementia cannot be diagnosed.

We focus on several types of dementias that are irreversible and degenerative. The most common and widely known of these is Alzheimer's disease, but others are important as well: vascular dementia, Parkinson's disease, Huntington's disease, alcoholic dementia, and AIDS dementia complex.

ALZHEIMER'S DISEASE. **Alzheimer's disease** *is the most common form of progressive, degenerative, and fatal dementia, accounting for perhaps as many as 70% of all cases of dementia* (Fromholt & Bruhn, 1999). We have only recently realized how common Alzheimer's disease is, however. When Alois Alzheimer first described the sequence of changes in 1907, he was referring to a person 51 years old. For the next 60 years physicians believed that the disease was very rare. It was not until Tomlinson, Blessed, and Roth (1970) showed that the same kinds of changes occurred in both early-onset and late-onset forms of the disease that physicians realized that age was not a factor. As a result, almost all that we know about Alzheimer's disease has been learned since 1970, with new discoveries coming almost daily.

NEUROLOGICAL CHANGES IN ALZHEIMER'S DISEASE. The changes in the brain that characterize Alzheimer's disease are microscopic. This means that definitive diagnosis of the disease can be done only at autopsy (Ebersole & Hess, 1998). These progressive changes eventually cause so much brain destruction that the person dies. The microscopic changes that define Alzheimer's disease are rapid cell death, neurofibrillary tangles, and neuritic plaques. Several changes in neurotransmitter levels also are observed. Rapid cell death occurs most in the hippocampus (a structure in the brain most closely involved in memory), the cortex (the outer layer of the brain in which our higher-level cognitive abilities reside), and the basal forebrain (the lower portion of the front of the brain). This cell death occurs at a rate much greater than normal.

Neurofibrillary tangles (see Chapter 2) are accumulations of pairs of filaments in the neuron that become wrapped around each other; when examined under a microscope, these paired filaments look like intertwined spirals. Neurofibrillary tangles occur in several areas of the brain, and the number of tangles is directly related to the severity of symptoms (Scheibel, 1996). *Neuritic plaques (see Chapter 2) are spherical structures consisting of a core of* **amyloid,** *a protein, surrounded by degenerated fragments of dying or dead neurons.* The plaques also are found in various parts of the brain and are related to the severity of the disease (Scheibel, 1996). Degeneration of neurons in some areas of the brain results in the formation of vacuoles, or spaces that become filled with fluid and granular material.

Although the changes occurring in the brains of people with Alzheimer's disease are substantial, we must use caution in assuming that they represent qualitative differences from normal aging. They may not. As we saw in Chapter 2, all the changes seen in Alzheimer's disease, including the structural and neurotransmitter changes, are also found in normal older adults. To be sure, the changes in Alzheimer's disease are much greater. But the important point is that Alzheimer's disease may be merely an exaggeration of normal aging and not something qualitatively different from it.

SYMPTOMS AND DIAGNOSIS. The major symptoms of Alzheimer's disease are gradual changes in cognitive functioning: declines in memory, learning, attention, and judgment; disorientation in time and space; difficulties in word finding and communication; declines in personal hygiene and self-care skills; inappropriate social behavior; and changes in personality (American Psychiatric Association, 1994; Smyer & Qualls, 1999). These symptoms tend to be vague in the beginning, and they mimic other psychological problems such as depression or stress reactions. For example, an executive may not be managing as well as she once did and may be missing deadlines more often. Slowly, the symptoms get worse. This executive, who once could easily handle millions of dollars, can no longer add two small numbers. A homemaker cannot set the table. A person who was previously outgoing is now quiet and withdrawn; a gentle person is now hostile and aggressive. Emotional problems become increasingly apparent, including depression, paranoia, and agitation. Wandering becomes a serious problem, especially because the person may have no idea where he or she is or how to get home, thus posing a genuine safety concern. As the disease progresses, the patient becomes incontinent and more and more dependent on others for care, eventually becoming completely incapable of even such simple tasks as dressing and eating. *In general, the symptoms associated with Alzheimer's disease are worse in the evening than in the morning, a phenomenon that caregivers call* **sundowning.**

The rate of deterioration in Alzheimer's disease varies widely from one patient to the next, although progression usually is faster when onset occurs earlier in life (Wilson et al., 2000). However, we can identify a series of stages that the patient goes through (Reisberg et al., 1982). Many diseases cause problems similar to those observed in the early stages of Alzheimer's disease. In fact, fewer than 10% of those who show mild cognitive impairment go on to develop more serious cognitive impairment within several years of the clinical evaluation (Reisberg et al., 1985).

Although a definitive diagnosis of Alzheimer's disease depends on an autopsy, the number and severity of behavioral changes allow clinicians to make increasingly accurate early diagnosis (Qualls, 1999). For this earlier diagnosis to be accurate, however, it must be comprehensive and broad. Figure 4.3 provides an overview of the process that should be used to differentiate Alzheimer's disease from other conditions. Note that a great deal of the diagnostic effort goes into ruling out other possible causes for the observed cognitive deficits: All possible treatable causes for the symptoms must be eliminated before a diagnosis of Alzheimer's disease can be made. Unfortunately, many clinicians do not conduct such thorough diagnoses; nearly half the cases of dementia are missed by general practice physicians (Boise et al., 1999).

As noted in Figure 4.3, the clinical diagnosis of Alzheimer's disease consists of carefully noting the history of the symptoms, documenting the cognitive impairments, conducting a general physical exam and neurological exam, performing laboratory tests to rule out other diseases, obtaining a psychiatric evaluation, performing neuropsychological tests, and assessing functional abilities.

Searching for a Cause. We do not know for certain what causes Alzheimer's disease. There are many hypotheses, as described in Table 4.5. At present, the main focus of research is on a genetic link (Sherrington et al., 1995). The strong possibility that at least some forms of Alzheimer's disease are inherited is a major concern of patients' families. The research evidence to date strongly indicates that genetic factors may be a powerful determinant of Alzheimer's disease, and possible markers on chromosomes have been found (Sherrington et al., 1995). Genetic research has identified links to both early-onset and late-onset of Alzheimer's disease.

For early-onset Alzheimer's disease, genetic mutations have been identified in three different genes (Gatz et al., 1997). All of them show an autosomal dominant inheritance pattern. *An* **autosomal dominant pattern** *is one in which only one gene from one parent is necessary to produce the disease; this means that there is a 50% chance that the child of an affected parent will have the disorder.* An autosomal dominant pattern for Alzheimer's disease makes sense because we know that at least two other forms of dementia, Pick's disease and Huntington's disease, are autosomal dominant. The first relates to chromosome 21 and stems from a linkage between Alzheimer's disease and Down syndrome. Almost all people with Down syndrome over age 40 develop severe cognitive impairments and brain changes like those in Alzheimer's disease, leading some researchers to hypothesize a linkage between the two diseases (Kosik, 1992). However, subsequent evidence showed that this was not likely to be the case. The genes responsible for Down syndrome and for the production of amyloid precursor protein (which underlies the production of amyloid) are on different sections of chromosome 21

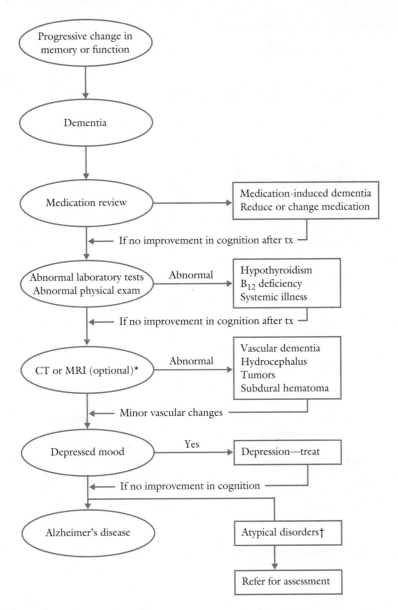

CHAPTER 4

*It is required in patients with focal signs, rapid progression, and headache.
†This category contains rare dementias (e.g., frontotemporal degenerations, Jakob–Creutzfeldt disease, Parkinson's disease, and other movement disorders that present with dementias) that should be considered when unusual clinical features are present or a rapidly progressive course is noted.

FIGURE 4.3 **Differential diagnosis and Alzheimer's disease algorithm.**

Source: Alzheimer's Association online document. Developed and endorsed by the TriAD Advisory Board. Copyright 1996 Pfizer Inc. and Esai Inc. with special thanks to J. L. Cummings. Algorithm reprinted from TriAD, *Three for the Management of Alzheimer's Disease,* with permission.

TABLE 4.5   Hypotheses of the Cause of Alzheimer's Disease

Factors	Action or Hypothesis	Results	Progress
Neurotransmitters			
Acetylcholine	Acetylcholine levels drop by about 90%.	Decline in memory.	Drug therapies aimed at postsynaptic receptor sites: vitamin E and Deprenyl being tested in clinical trials.
Serotonin, somatostatin, noradrenaline	Levels lower than normal.	Sensory disturbance, aggressive behavior, neuron death.	
Phospholipids	Shape and action of the receptors may play role.	Abnormalities transmit garbled messages from one neuron to another because of dysfunction or blockage of relay points.	
Beta amyloid	Forms insoluble plaque.	Possible neuron death.	Studies link the disruption of K^+ and Ca^{++} levels; link between cholinergic neuron death and beta amyloids.
Tau	Neurofibrillary tangles.	Twisted paired helical filaments destabilize the microtubule structure.	
Genes			
1, 14, 19 (Apo E4)	Protein and amyloid become insoluble, leading to deposition of plaque. Tau protein allows structure of microtubules to become undone, causing tangles.	Linked to late onset of Alzheimer's; increases deposits of beta amyloid. Directly regulates apolipoprotein (Apo E4) and quickly binds with beta amyloid.	How tau and beta amyloids react to APP.
21	Neurons with short dendrites; carries code for mutated amyloid precursor protein (APP) familial Alzheimer's disease.	Early Alzheimer's.	Supports theory that beta amyloids play a role in Alzheimer's disease; also gene found in Down's syndrome.
Metabolism			
Glucose and O_2 molecules	Altered glucose metabolism.	Dramatic decline in glucose and oxygen as neurons degenerate and die or neuron degeneration causes glucose decline.	Neurons having problems with metabolism react abnormally to another neurotransmitter, glutamate.

continued

TABLE 4.5   Hypotheses of the Cause of Alzheimer's Disease continued

Factors	Action or Hypothesis	Results	Progress
Metabolism-cont'd Calcium	A rise in Ca^{++} level inside the cell.	Series of cascades of biochemical events, allowing a rise in calcium channels admit in excess Ca^{++}.	
	Levels rise because of energy level crisis in neurons.	A defect in structure leads to an increase in storage or pumping calcium out. Chronically high levels of neurotransmitter glutamate disrupts metabolism, causing an influx of Ca^{++}.	
	Hormone glucocorticoid.	Neuron death and dysfunction caused in hippocampus.	
Environment Aluminum	Trace metal in brain.	Turns up in more than normal amounts in many brain autopsies of patients with Alzheimer's.	Nothing confirmed.
Zinc	Too little or too much.	Found on brain autopsy of patients with Alzheimer's.	
Food borne poisons	Food toxins.	Causes soluble beta amyloid of the cerebral spinal fluid to clump together, similar to plaque of patients with Alzheimer's; may cause neurologic damage and enhance the action of neurotransmitter glutamate.	Current studies are looking at this.
Viruses	A virus or other infection.		

Source: National Institute on Aging (1995).

(Raeburn, 1995; Sherrington et al., 1995). The second, presenilin-1 (PS-1), is located on chromosome 14 (Sherrington et al., 1995). The third is located on chromosome 1 and probably is related to the protein on the neuronal membrane (Gatz et al., 1997).

Although these results are important, most cases of Alzheimer's disease are late onset. The most promising work with this form has noted links between the genetic markers and the production of amyloid protein, the major component of neuritic plaques (Raeburn, 1995). Much of this research focuses on apolipoprotein E4 (apo E4), associated with chromosome 19, which may play a central role in creating neuritic plaques. Interestingly, another version, apo E2, seems to have the reverse effect: It decreases the risk of Alzheimer's disease (Gatz et al., 1997). Researchers are also looking for relationships between apolipoprotein E and cognitive functioning (Riley et al., 2000).

Even if a specific gene is identified for each type of Alzheimer's disease, many questions about the cause of Alzheimer's disease will remain. Why does it take so long for the genetic defect to appear? What mechanism starts it? Why is there so much variation when it appears? Answers to these questions will help us understand how Alzheimer's disease develops.

If an autosomal dominant pattern were responsible, what would this mean for the relatives of people with Alzheimer's disease? Actually, it would depend on the relative's age. Even though the risk would always be greater, even at age 65 this increased risk would have little practical significance because the overall incidence of Alzheimer's disease at this age is low. But by age 80 the risk to first-degree relatives is roughly 25%, compared with 6% in the general population (Breitner, 1988). Although these numbers are not reassuring, they are much lower than the risk for many other autosomal dominant genetic diseases, such as Huntington's disease.

Tests can be developed to detect genes that transmit diseases via an autosomal dominant pattern. Such a test already exists for Huntington's disease. As discussed in the Current Controversies feature, however, taking the test is not an easy decision, even when there is a high risk of passing the disease on to one's children.

INTERVENTION STRATEGIES. Alzheimer's disease is incurable. However, much research has been done to find ways to alleviate the cognitive deficits and behavioral problems that characterize the disease.

Much of the recent research has focused on various drugs that could improve memory (Schneider, 1995). These drugs include a wide variety of compounds aimed at improving cerebral blood flow or levels of various neurotransmitters. Although some drugs, such as tacrine (Cognex) and donepezil (Aricept), have been reported to improve cognitive functioning, these successes often have been achieved with carefully selected patients on carefully selected tests, and none of the drugs has shown reliable improvements in a wide variety of patients (Schneider, 1995).

In contrast to the poor picture for improving cognitive performance, improving other behavioral problems is possible. Drugs that are used primarily in younger patients to treat schizophrenia, such as thioridazine and haloperidol, are effective in alleviating the severe psychiatric symptoms that develop during the course of Alzheimer's disease (Schneider, 1995). Similarly, antidepressants are effective in alleviating the depressive symptoms that typically accompany the early stages of the disease (Ebersole & Hess, 1998), and sedatives may be effective for sleep disturbances. However, these medications should be used with caution because dosage levels for older adults may be far lower than those for younger patients, and side effects may be much more serious (Hess & Lee, 1998).

More recent research has begun looking for ways to prevent, or at least delay, the onset of Alzheimer's disease. Some of the substances being examined include vitamin E, melatonin, and estrogen. The case of estrogen is especially interesting because some research indicates that estrogen loss after menopause is related to memory loss (Sherwin, 1997).

CARING FOR PATIENTS WITH DEMENTIA AT HOME. The changes in a person who has a form of dementia are devastating to the patient and the whole family (Aneshensel et al., 1995). Watching a spouse, parent, or sibling go from being an independent, mature adult to being a helpless shell who is oblivious to his or her surroundings is extremely difficult.

Despite these formidable emotional issues, most patients with dementia (as well as other impairments) are cared for by their family members at home (National Academy on an Aging Society, 2000b). At least 75% of caregivers are women; in order of frequency, caregivers are most likely to be a spouse, daughter, sister, daughter-in-law, niece, granddaughter, or friend

When scientists discovered that they could determine whether someone was carrying the gene for Huntington's disease (also called *Huntington's Chorea*), they thought it would be a welcome relief to thousands of families. After all, Huntington's disease is a terrible scourge of adults in their 30s, 40s, and 50s, eventually institutionalizing most and killing them all. As noted in the text, those who have one parent with the disease run a 50–50 chance of having it themselves and, if they have children, of passing it on to them. So it seemed likely that the ability to determine in advance who would develop or escape the disease would be welcomed by affected families, allowing them to plan more practically about having children, choosing jobs, obtaining insurance, organizing finances, and pursuing social and leisure interests.

But the scientists were wrong. Only a small fraction of those at risk and close enough to obtain the test have done so. Why? The answer is not with the test, which involves a genetic analysis of blood samples taken from the person being tested and from six or so family members. Perhaps the answer lies in the fact that a positive result on the test means a high probability of developing the disease. In short, one learns that one faces a long, terrible death. The test is 99% accurate.

Samuel L. Baily, former chairman of the National Huntington's Disease Association, chose not to have the test even though his mother died from Huntington's disease at age 58, 8 years after she was diagnosed. Baily, symptom-free at age 52, said that he would rather just take his chances with the disease, which also killed his maternal grandfather. He prefers to live with the hope of not getting it than with the knowledge that he will.

Others choose a different course. Karen Sweeney, 28, who is married and has four children, told interviewers that she had to know. The stress of knowing that her mother and grandfather both died from the disease had taken its toll on her and on her marriage. After moving to Baltimore to be eligible for the Johns Hopkins testing program, Karen and her husband went through extensive counseling before the test.

For Karen, the news was good: no Huntington's.

Certainly, Huntington's disease and all other forms of dementia are terrible diseases. With research rapidly advancing on Alzheimer's disease, it is likely that a test for a genetic marker for it will be developed in the next decade. It is also likely that a test will be available before there is a cure. If you had relatives who had died from Alzheimer's disease or Huntington's disease, if you were planning to have a family, and if a test were available, what would you do? What ethical issues are raised by the availability of such tests?

Search Online with InfoTrac College Edition For more information on these controversies, explore InfoTrac College Edition, your online library. Go to http://www.infotrac-college.com/wadsworth and use the passcode that came on the card with your book. Try these search terms: Alzheimer's disease, genetic aspects; genetic screening; Huntington's Chorea.

(Cavanaugh, 1999a). Caregivers tend to be of moderate financial means, with about one-third being poor (Query & Flint, 1996).

One useful way to conceptualize family caregiving is as an unexpected career (Aneshensel et al., 1995). The caregiving career begins with the onset of the illness and moves through a number of separate steps. Note that the process does not end with the placement of the affected family member in a nursing home, or even with that person's death. Rather,

Aneshensel et al. (1995) point out that the career continues through the bereavement and social readjustment period, at which point one may continue with life. Note that the kind of caregiving changes, from the comprehensive caregiving, which covers all aspects of the process, to sustained caregiving in the home to foreshortened caregiving in the nursing home to withdrawal from caregiving.

Because the majority of people with dementia have Alzheimer's disease, most of the research focuses on caregivers of these patients. However, the discussion in this chapter applies to caregivers of all patients with dementia. Let's consider some behavioral intervention strategies that work.

EFFECTIVE BEHAVIORAL STRATEGIES. Many actions can be taken to improve the lives of people with dementia. Key steps to be taken once a diagnosis is made include obtaining accurate information about the disease, involving the patient as much as possible in decisions, identifying the primary caregiver, reassessing the patient's living situation, setting realistic goals, making realistic financial plans, identifying a source of regular medical care, maximizing the patient's opportunity to function at his or her optimal level, making realistic demands of the patient, and using outside services as needed. The goal of these early steps is to build a broad support network of relatives, medical personnel, and service providers that may be needed later. The new responsibilities of family members require changes in daily routines; people adjust to these roles at different rates.

Caregivers must rethink many behaviors and situations that they take for granted when they find themselves caring for a patient with Alzheimer's disease. Dressing, bathing, and grooming become more difficult or even aversive to the patient. Use of Velcro fasteners, joining the patient during a bath or shower, and other such changes may be necessary. Nutritional needs must be monitored because patients may forget that they have just eaten or may forget to eat. Medications must be used with caution. Changes in personality and sexual behavior must be viewed as part of the disease. Sleeplessness can be addressed by establishing consistent bedtimes, giving warm milk or tryptophan, and limiting caffeine intake. Wandering is an especially troublesome problem because it is difficult to control; making sure that the patient has an identification bracelet with the nature of the problem on it and making the house accident-proof are two preventive steps. In severe cases of wandering it may be necessary to use restraints under the direction of a health care professional. Incontinence,

which usually occurs late in the disease, is a troubling and embarrassing issue for the patient; use of special undergarments or medications to treat the problem are two options. Incontinence is not necessarily related to Alzheimer's disease; for example, stress incontinence, which is fairly common among older women, is unrelated to dementia.

One of the most difficult issues caregivers face concerns taking things away from the patient and restricting activity. Early in the disease the patient experiences problems handling finances. It is not uncommon for patients to spend hundreds or even thousands of dollars on strange items, to leave the checkbook unbalanced and bills unpaid, and to lose money. Although the patient can be given some money to keep, someone else must handle the day-to-day accounts. Traveling alone is another sticky issue. Families of patients with dementia often do not recognize their loved one's deteriorating condition until a calamity occurs. Families should limit solo excursions to places within walking distance; all other trips should be made with at least one family member along. Driving often is a contentious issue, especially if the patient does not recognize his or her limitations. Once it is clear that the patient cannot drive, the family must take whatever steps are necessary. In some cases this entails simply taking the car keys, but in others it becomes necessary to disable the car. Suggesting that the patient could be chauffeured is another alternative.

How can family members and health care professionals deal with the behavioral and cognitive problems experienced by people with Alzheimer's disease? One successful approach for dealing with difficult behavior is a technique called differential reinforcement of incompatible behavior (DRI) (Burgio et al., 1995). In DRI, caregivers reduce the incidence of difficult behavior by rewarding him or her for engaging in appropriate behaviors that cannot be done at the same time as the problem behaviors. For example, a person who throws food during dinner could be rewarded for sitting quietly and eating. The DRI technique is easily learned, has no side effects, and can be

Most people with Alzheimer's disease are cared for by a family member.

as effective as or more effective than medical treatments (Burgio, 1996).

Behavioral interventions for cognitive problems can be as simple as labeling cabinets, as mentioned earlier, or can be based on more formal approaches. Two that are extremely effective are spaced retrieval, a technique that helps patients with Alzheimer's disease learn and remember new information (Brush & Camp, 1998), and techniques based on the Montessori method, a teaching approach first developed for use with children (Camp, 1999). As described in the How Do We Know? feature, spaced retrieval works well even with people whose dementia has progressed to moderately severe levels. Montessori-based techniques allow young children and people with advanced Alzheimer's disease to interact in an intergenerational format. A key benefit of these techniques is an increase in social contact and significant decrease in problem behaviors among patients with Alzheimer's disease.

Caregiving is very stressful for families. Two options for caregivers are respite care and adult day care. Respite care is designed to allow family members to get away for a time. It can consist of in-home care provided by professionals or temporary placement in a residential facility. In-home care typically is used to allow caregivers to do errands or to have a few hours free, whereas temporary residential placement is reserved for a more extended respite, such as a weekend. Respite care is a tremendous help to caregivers. In one study there was marked improvement in family members' reports of problems after a

Who were the investigators, and what was the aim of the study? Alzheimer's disease is marked by progressive and severe memory loss. But can memory problems be remediated using implicit internal memory strategies? Cameron Camp and Leslie McKitrick (1991) decided to find out by using a technique called spaced retrieval.

How did the investigators measure the topic of interest? The secret to spaced retrieval is progressively increasing the amount of time between the recall of the target information (e.g., a person's name). For example, the instructor shows the client a picture of a person and says the person's name. After an initial recall interval of 5 seconds, the instructor asks the client to remember the name. As long as the client remembers correctly, recall intervals are increased to 10, 20, 40, 60, 90, 120, 150 seconds, and so on. If the client forgets the target information, the correct answer is provided, and the next recall interval is decreased to the length of the last correct trial. During the interval, the instructor engages the client in conversation to prevent active rehearsal of the information.

Who were the participants in the study? Camp and McKitrick tested people who had been diagnosed as probably having Alzheimer's disease who were also in an adult day care center.

What was the design of the study? The study used a longitudinal design so that Camp and McKitrick could track participants' performance over several weeks.

Were there ethical concerns with the study? Having people with Alzheimer's disease as research participants raises important informed consent issues. Because of their serious cognitive impairments, these people may not fully understand the procedures. Thus, family members such as spouses or adult child caregivers are also asked to give informed consent. Additionally, researchers must pay careful attention to participants' emotions; if participants become agitated or frustrated, the training or testing session must be stopped. Camp and McKitrick took all these precautions.

What were the results? Spaced retrieval worked well: Even people who earlier could not retain information for more than 60 seconds could remember names taught through this technique for very long periods (e.g., 5 weeks or more). Learning the staff names usually involved a few failures, but with additional practice success occurred. For example, one participant looked sternly at the researchers who had come to her day care center. "I know you're going to ask me for Jane's name." Yet only a month before, Iris could not remember Jane's name; in fact, she seemed incapable of learning it at all using rote rehearsal. Most important, the new learning did not interfere with other information in long-term memory.

What did the investigators conclude? It appears that many types of information can be taught, making spaced retrieval a flexible intervention. Spaced retrieval can be used in almost any setting, such as game playing or normal conversation, making it comfortable and nonthreatening to the client.

Although more work is needed to continue refining the technique, spaced retrieval is one of the most promising nondrug memory interventions for people with cognitive impairments.

2-week respite (Burdz et al., 1988). Adult day care provides placement and programming for frail older adults during the day. This option is used most often by adult children who are employed. The demand for respite and adult day care far exceeds their availability, making them limited options. An additional problem is that many insurance programs do not pay for these services, making them too expensive for caregivers with limited finances. Even when services are available, however, many families do not use them until their informal support system begins to break down (Caserta et al., 1987).

In general, family members must change their entire daily routines to care for a patient with dementia. Such complete alterations in habits, coupled with watching the deterioration in their loved one, create an extremely stressful situation. We consider the stresses of family caregiving in Chapter 11.

OTHER FORMS OF DEMENTIA. As we have noted, dementia is a family of different diseases. We consider several of them briefly.

VASCULAR DEMENTIA. Until it was discovered that Alzheimer's disease was not rare, most physicians and researchers believed that most cases of dementia resulted from cerebral arteriosclerosis and its consequent restriction of oxygen to the brain. As described in Chapter 2, arteriosclerosis is a family of diseases that, if untreated, may result in heart attacks or strokes. For the present discussion it is the stroke, or cerebrovascular accident (CVA), that concerns us. CVAs (see Chapter 2) result from a disruption of the blood flow, called an infarct, which may be caused by a blockage or hemorrhage.

A large CVA may produce severe cognitive decline, but this loss is almost always limited to specific abilities. This pattern is different from the classic, global deterioration seen in dementia. *However, a series of small CVAs can produce this global pattern of cognitive decline, which results in a condition called* **vascular dementia** (Smyer & Qualls, 1999). Vascu-

lar dementia accounts for 10–15% of all cases of dementia.

The course of multi-infarct dementia is very different from that seen in Alzheimer's disease (Smyer & Qualls, 1997). Vascular dementia may have a sudden onset after a CVA, and its progression is described as stepwise. This is in contrast to the slow onset and gradual progression of Alzheimer's disease. The symptom pattern in vascular dementia is highly variable, especially early in the disease. Again, this is in contrast to the similar cluster of cognitive problems shown by Alzheimer's disease patients.

The steps in diagnosing multi-infarct dementia are similar to those for Alzheimer's disease. Evidence of CVAs from diagnostic imaging (CT or MRI) and a history of cerebrovascular disease usually are the key factors (Ebersole & Hess, 1998). In a small percentage of cases, however, evidence of both Alzheimer's disease and multi-infarct dementia is found.

PARKINSON'S DISEASE. *A cluster of characteristic motor problems defines* **Parkinson's disease:** *very slow walking, stiffness, difficulty getting in and out of chairs, and a slow tremor.* These behavioral symptoms are caused by a deterioration of the neurons in the midbrain that produce the neurotransmitter dopamine (Lieberman, 1974). Administration of the drug L-dopa greatly alleviates these behavioral problems.

The connection between Parkinson's disease and dementia was not generally recognized until the late 1970s. Researchers estimate that 14–40% of people with Parkinson's disease will develop dementia (Raskind & Peskind, 1992). Although early research proposed that the dementia associated with Parkinson's disease was the same as in Alzheimer's disease, more recent research indicates that the two are different. In particular, examination of brain tissue at autopsy reveals that a structural change called Lewy bodies is much more common in dementia associated with Parkinson's disease (Raskind & Peskind, 1992).

HUNTINGTON'S DISEASE. Huntington's disease is an autosomal dominant disorder that usually begins between ages 35 and 50. The disease generally manifests itself through involuntary flicking movements of the arms and legs; the inability to sustain a motor act such as sticking out one's tongue; prominent psychiatric disturbances such as hallucinations, paranoia, and depression; and clear personality changes, such as swings from apathy to manic behavior (Ebersole & Hess, 1998). Cognitive impairments typically do not appear until late in the disease. The onset of these symptoms is very gradual. The course of Huntington's disease is progressive; patients ultimately lose the ability to care for themselves physically and mentally. Walking becomes impossible, swallowing is difficult, and cognitive loss becomes profound. Changes in the brain thought to underlie the behavioral losses include degeneration of the caudate nucleus and the small-cell population, as well as substantial decreases in the neurotransmitters γ-aminobutyric acid (GABA) and substance P. Although antipsychotic medications sometimes are used to control the psychiatric disturbances and agitated behaviors, they are only partially effective (Burgio, 1996). As noted earlier, a test is available to determine whether one has the marker for the Huntington's disease gene.

ALCOHOLIC DEMENTIA. One of the consequences of long-term chronic alcoholism is Wernicke–Korsakoff syndrome. This disease, caused by a chronic deficiency of thiamine, causes major losses of memory and other cognitive functioning. The condition is treatable if the vitamin deficiency is detected early in the process, and cessation of excessive alcohol consumption usually is associated with improved cognitive functioning as well.

AIDS DEMENTIA COMPLEX. This disease arises as a predictable part of acquired immunodeficiency syndrome (AIDS; see Chapter 3; Raskind & Peskind, 1992). A protein called gp 120, which is a byproduct of the human immunodeficiency virus (HIV), is responsible for the death of neurons, which in turn causes dementia. Early symptoms of AIDS dementia

complex (ADC) include the inability to concentrate, problems performing complex sequential mental tasks, and memory loss in tasks demanding concentrated attention. Motor symptoms include clumsiness and weakness in the arms and legs. Behavioral changes include apathy, loss of spontaneity, depression, social withdrawal, and personality changes. Mental performance and motor problems continue to deteriorate as ADC progresses, and incontinence eventually occurs. In the terminal phase of ADC, patients are bedridden, stare vacantly, and have minimal social and cognitive interaction (Ebersole & Hess, 1998). Because HIV infection is largely preventable, ADC can be reduced through the practice of safe sex.

CONCEPT CHECKS

1. How does depression in older adults differ from depression in younger adults? How do these differences affect treatment?

2. What are the characteristics of delirium?

3. What are the underlying causes and changes in Alzheimer's disease? What can be done to help patients?

OTHER MENTAL DISORDERS AND CONCERNS

LEARNING OBJECTIVES

- What are the symptoms of anxiety disorders? How are they treated?
- What are the characteristics of people with psychotic disorders?
- What are the major issues involved with substance abuse?

*D*aisy forces herself to do her daily routine. She is shaky all the time because she just doesn't feel safe. Her neighborhood is deteriorating and she is afraid of what the teenagers will do to her. She imagines all sorts of horrible things that they could do to her. Her worst fear is that no one would know. Her heart races when she thinks about it. She rarely goes *out now, and she has convinced her son to bring her groceries and other supplies.*

Daisy's feelings indicate that people have difficulties for many reasons. She is clearly afraid, which could reflect a realistic assessment of her neighborhood. But her feelings also make her heart race, which is unusual. In this section, we examine three disorders that are receiving increased attention: anxiety disorders, psychotic disorders, and substance abuse.

Anxiety Disorders

Imagine that you are about to give a speech before an audience of 500 people. In the last few minutes before your address, you begin to feel nervous, your heart starts to pound, and your palms get sweaty. (You now have something in common with Daisy's reactions.) These feelings, common even to veteran speakers, are similar to those experienced by people with anxiety disorders: a group of conditions that are based on fear or uneasiness. Anxiety disorders include anxiety states, in which feelings of severe anxiety occur with no specific trigger; phobic disorders, characterized by irrational fears of objects or circumstances; and obsessive–compulsive disorders, in which thoughts or actions are performed repeatedly to lower anxiety. Anxiety disorders are diagnosed in as many as 33% of older adults according to some estimates, although the exact numbers are debated (Scogin, 1999; Smyer & Qualls, 1999). Still, the rates of anxiety disorders are thought to decline somewhat from their peak in young adulthood.

SYMPTOMS AND DIAGNOSIS OF ANXIETY DISORDERS. Common to all the anxiety disorders are physical changes that interfere with social functioning, personal relationships, or work. These physical changes include dry mouth, sweating, dizziness, upset stomach, diarrhea, insomnia, hyperventilation, chest pain, choking, frequent urination, headaches, and a sensation of a lump in the throat (Scogin, 1999). These symptoms occur in adults of all ages, but they are particularly common in older adults because of loss of health, re-

location stress, isolation, fear of losing control over their lives, or guilt resulting from feelings of hostility toward family and friends.

An important issue concerning anxiety disorders in older adults is that anxiety may be an appropriate response to the situation. For example, helplessness anxiety such as Daisy is experiencing is generated by a potential or actual loss of control or mastery (Verwoerdt, 1981). Additionally, a series of severe negative life experiences may result in a person's reaching the breaking point and appearing highly anxious. Many older adults who show symptoms of anxiety disorder have underlying health problems that may be responsible for the symptoms. In all cases the anxious behavior should be investigated first as an appropriate response that may not warrant medical intervention. The important point is to evaluate the older adult's behavior in context.

These issues make it difficult to diagnose anxiety disorders, especially in older adults (Tice & Perkins, 1996; Scogin, 1999). The problem is that there usually is nothing specific that a person can point to as the specific trigger or cause. Additionally, anxiety in older adults often accompanies an underlying physical disorder or illness. These secondary causes of anxiety must be disentangled from the anxiety symptoms so that each may be dealt with appropriately.

TREATING ANXIETY DISORDERS. Both drug therapy and psychotherapy are used to treat anxiety disorders. Benzodiazepines are the most widely prescribed medications for anxiety, and include such drugs as diazepam (Valium), chlordiazepoxide HCl (Librium), oxazepam (Serax), and lorazepam (Ativan) (Smyer & Qualls, 1999). Although benzodiazepines are effective with adults of all ages, they must be used very carefully with older adults. Effective dosage levels are lower in older adults, and the potential for side effects is much greater. Most important, these drugs can cause decreased cognitive functioning, which may be mistaken for early dementia. In general, the benzodiazepines may cause drowsiness, loss of coordination, headaches, and lower energy levels. Moreover, because of the potential for addiction, the long-term use of these drugs should be avoided.

In most cases the treatment of choice for anxiety disorders is psychotherapy. A broad range of approaches is effective with adults of all ages (Niederehe & Schneider, 1998). These include relaxation training, substituting rational for irrational thoughts, and gradual exposure to images or real situations that generate anxiety. The advantage of these psychotherapeutic techniques is that they usually involve only a few sessions, have high rates of success, and offer clients procedures that they can take with them. Best of all, they have no long-term side effects, unlike their medical counterparts.

Psychotic Disorders

Some forms of psychopathology, called psychoses, involve losing touch with reality and the disintegration of personality. Two behaviors that occur in these disorders are delusions, which are belief systems not based on reality, and hallucinations, which are distortions in perception.

Although the development of psychotic disorders is rare across adulthood, the number of new cases declines with age (Jeste et al., 1995). The behaviors present in psychotic disorders are commonly manifested as secondary problems in other disorders, especially in dementia (Rabins, 1992). Indeed, psychotic symptoms are an important aspect of the diagnosis of some of these other disorders and can be managed in the same way.

SCHIZOPHRENIA. Schizophrenia is characterized by the severe impairment of thought processes, including the content and style of thinking, distorted perceptions, loss of touch with reality, a distorted sense of self, and abnormal motor behavior (American Psychiatric Association, 1994). People with schizophrenia may show these abnormal behaviors in several ways: loose associations (such as saying that they have a secret meeting with the president of the United States in the local bowling alley),

hearing voices that tell them what to do, believing that they can read other people's minds, believing that their body is changing into something else, or sometimes having bizarre delusions (for example, that they are Jesus or that they are being spied on). Additionally, schizophrenic people tend to show very little or highly inappropriate emotionality (laughing hysterically at the news of a major tragedy, for instance). They are often confused about their own identity, have difficulty working toward a goal, and tend to withdraw from social contact.

The second hallmark symptom of schizophrenia is delusions, or well-formed beliefs not based in reality. Most often, these delusions involve persecution ("People are out to get me"). The distinction between paranoid disorders and schizophrenia is fuzzy; indeed, one type of schizophrenia is called paranoid type schizophrenia. In general, hallucinations, loose associations, and absent or inappropriate emotions do not occur in paranoid disorders (American Psychiatric Association, 1994).

The beliefs underlying delusions can result in anger, resentment, or even violent acts. Because people with psychoses are extremely suspicious and rarely seek help on their own, such people tend to come to the attention of authorities after having repeated run-ins with the police or neighbors, starting legal proceedings against others on mysterious grounds, or registering complaints about fictitious or distorted events.

The onset of schizophrenia occurs most often between ages 16 and 30, and only about 30% of cases occur after age 40 (Smyer & Qualls, 1999). The symptoms of schizophrenia also differ by age; for example, older adults show less thought disorder and less flattening of their emotions than younger adults (Rabins, 1992). Some researchers disagree, however, maintaining that there are few differences with age in the numbers of people who experience schizophrenic symptoms and no differences in the nature of the symptoms (Blazer et al., 1988). More research is needed to clarify the issue.

Longitudinal research indicates that the natural course of schizophrenia is improvement over the adult life span (Smyer & Qualls, 1999). Studies show that the first 10 years of the disorder are marked by cycles of remission and worsening, but symptoms generally lessen in more than half of people with schizophrenia in later life. This may be caused by a rebalancing of the neurotransmitters dopamine and acetylcholine, which are heavily weighted toward dopamine in younger adults with schizophrenia. Additional rebalancings of other neurotransmitters may also play a role.

TREATING SCHIZOPHRENIA. Traditionally, treatment of schizophrenia has emphasized medication. Drug therapy consists of antipsychotics, medications that are believed to work on the dopamine system (see Chapter 2). Some of the more commonly used antipsychotics are haleperidol (Haldol), chlorpromazine HCl (Thorazine), and thioridazine HCl (Mellaril). These medications must be used with extreme caution in adults of all ages because of the risk of serious toxic side effects, especially the loss of motor control. Despite these risks antipsychotics often are used in nursing homes and other institutions as tranquilizing agents to control difficult patients.

In general, people with schizophrenia are difficult to treat with psychotherapy. The severe thought disturbances characteristic of schizophrenia make it difficult for therapists to work with clients. Because of their extreme suspiciousness, paranoid people may be reluctant to cooperate in psychotherapy. If these barriers can be overcome, however, there is some evidence that supportive therapy may be effective (Karon & VandenBos, 1999). The goals of therapy for such people tend to be adaptive rather than curative, helping these people adapt to daily living rather than attempting to cure them.

Substance Abuse

Although you might think that substance abuse is primarily a problem of adolescents and young adults, many older adults have the problem (Lisansky Gomberg & Zucker, 1999). However, with the exception of alcohol, the substances most likely to be abused by young and old are different. Young adults tend to abuse illicit substances (e.g., cocaine, marijuana), whereas older adults are more likely to abuse prescription and over-the-counter medications (Lisansky Gomberg & Zucker, 1999; Smyer & Qualls, 1999).

Because of the differences in the types of substances abused by younger and older adults, it is very difficult to compare estimates of the extent of the problem. Alcohol provides the only common basis for comparison. What constitutes alcoholism? Alcoholism, also known as alcohol dependence, is a disease that includes alcohol craving and continued drinking despite repeated alcohol-related problems, such as losing a job or getting into trouble with the law. Alcoholism includes four symptoms: craving, impaired control, physical dependence, and tolerance.

As you can see in Figure 4.4, the prevalence of alcohol dependency drops significantly with age for both men and women. However, there are gender and ethnic group differences. For example, rates for men are 1.5–2 times as high as those for women, depending on age. European Americans also have higher rates of alcohol dependence than African Americans (National Institute on Alcohol Abuse and Alcoholism, 1995). Two patterns of onset are evident with older people with alcohol dependency: early-onset (young adulthood or middle age) lifelong problem drinking and late-onset problem drinking (Smyer & Qualls, 1999). Left untreated, alcohol dependency does not improve over time.

As we saw in Chapter 3, older adults are especially at risk for abusing medications because they take more of them than any other age group on average. This problem is greatly overlooked and can result in serious health problems (Lisansky Gomberg & Zucker, 1999). It is very difficult to determine the extent to which medication abuse is intentional or caused by memory problems, failure to understand instructions, or some other reason.

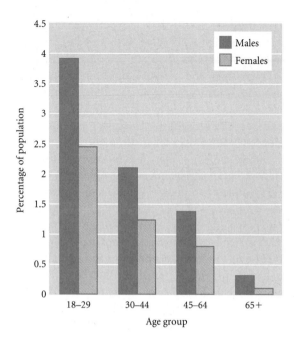

FIGURE 4.4 **Prevalence of alcohol dependency as a function of age.**

Source: National Institute on Alcohol Abuse and Alcoholism, 2000.

Treatment for substance abuse in all age groups focuses on three goals (Smyer & Qualls, 1999): stabilization and reduction of substance consumption, treatment of coexisting problems, and arrangement of appropriate social interventions. Older adults often respond better to education programs rather than direct confrontation to reduce their denial of their problem. Addressing other problems, such as depression and anxiety, may be effective in helping people use substances more appropriately. Training in self-management techniques to improve coping skills can also help, especially in cases of abuse involving pain medications (Dupree & Schonfeld,

1996). Although adults of all age groups can respond to treatment, success rates often are low, and older adults take longer to withdraw from substances than younger adults (Lisansky Gomberg & Zucker, 1999). Take the time to complete the Discovering Development feature. Finding out the treatment options in your area may enable you to help a friend; the lack of certain types of treatment options may also surprise you.

CONCEPT CHECKS

1. What are the major symptoms and treatment options for anxiety disorders?
2. What are the primary characteristics of psychoses? How do they differ with age?
3. What are the major considerations concerning substance abuse in older adults?

PUTTING IT ALL TOGETHER

In this chapter, we have encountered people who illustrate some of the problems faced by a minority of older adults. Janet exemplifies older adults who have difficulty dealing with the loss of her social network; her friend Betty shows that often it is acquaintances and family members who first notice difficulties. Juan's memory problems illustrate the kinds of problems clinicians must evaluate carefully to distinguish between normal and abnormal changes with age. Ling's difficulties with everyday tasks, coupled with cognitive declines, are an example of the kinds of behaviors that could be associated with dementia, but they must be assessed carefully to rule out severe depression. Daisy's growing uneasiness at leaving her home illustrates how realistic concerns can sometimes escalate into more serious problems. Taken together, these cases show that some older adults experience serious problems as they age, and they need thorough assessment that takes developmental issues into account.

One of the most controversial topics regarding substance abuse is how to deal with people who have the problem. If they use illicit drugs, should they be treated or jailed? If treatment is the choice, should they be placed in inpatient facilities or in outpatient programs? These decisions have become both political and sensitive. Many politicians have built their careers on being perceived as "tough on drugs" and have voted to curtail or eliminate treatment options for drug offenders. The rise of health management organizations has resulted in the near elimination of inpatient treatment facilities in favor of the less expensive outpatient programs.

A very enlightening exercise is to find out what treatment options are available in your area for people who have substance abuse problems. Find out whether there are any inpatient programs, which outpatient programs are available, and how long one has to wait to receive treatment. Also, find out the costs of the various programs and whether various health insurance policies cover the treatments.

Gather the information from several geographic regions and compare program availability. Think about what you would do if you were poor and needed help in your area. What do you think should be done to address the problem?

Summary

MENTAL HEALTH AND THE ADULT LIFE COURSE

Defining Mental Health and Psychopathology

- Definitions of mental health must reflect appropriate age-related criteria.
- Behaviors must be interpreted in context. Mentally healthy people have positive attitudes, accurate perceptions, environmental mastery, autonomy, personality balance, and personal growth.

A Multidimensional Life-Span Approach to Psychopathology

- Considering key biological, psychological, sociocultural, and life-cycle factors is essential for accurate diagnosis of mental disorders.
- Diagnostic criteria must reflect age differences in symptomatology.

Ethnicity, Aging, and Mental Health

- Little research has been done to examine ethnic differences in the definition of mental health and psychopathology in older adults.

- There is some evidence of different incidence rates across groups.

DEVELOPMENTAL ISSUES IN ASSESSMENT AND THERAPY

Areas of Multidimensional Assessment

- Accurate assessment depends on measuring functioning across a spectrum of areas, including medical, psychological, and social.

Factors Influencing Assessment

- Negative and positive biases can influence the accuracy of assessment.
- The environmental conditions under which the assessment is made can influence its accuracy.

Assessment Methods

- Six assessment techniques are used most: interview, self-report, report by others, psychophysiological assessment, direct observation, and performance-based assessment.

Developmental Issues in Therapy

- The two main approaches are medical therapy (usually involving drugs) and psychotherapy.

- With psychotherapy, clinicians must be sensitive to changes in the primary developmental issues faced by adults of different ages.

- Clear criteria have been established for determining "well established" and "probably efficacious" psychotherapies.

THE BIG THREE: DEPRESSION, DELIRIUM, AND DEMENTIA

Depression

- Depression is the most common mental disorder in adults, but it declines in frequency with age. Gender and ethnic differences in rates have been noted.

- Common features of depression include dysphoria, apathy, self-deprecation, expressionlessness, changes in arousal, withdrawal, and several physical symptoms. Additionally, the problems must last at least 2 weeks, not be caused by another disease, and negatively affect daily living. Clear age differences exist in the reporting of symptoms. Some assessment scales are not sensitive to age differences in symptoms.

- Possible biological causes of severe depression are neurotransmitter imbalance, abnormal brain functioning, or physical illness. Loss is the main psychosocial cause of depression. Internal belief systems also are important.

- Three families of drugs (SSRIs, HCAs, and MAO inhibitors), electroconvulsive therapy, and various forms of psychotherapy are all used to treat depression. Older adults benefit most from behavior and cognitive therapies.

Delirium

- Delirium is characterized by a disturbance of consciousness and a change in cognition that develop over a short period of time.

- Delirium can be caused by a number of medical conditions, medication side effects, substance intoxication or withdrawal, exposure to toxins, or any combination of factors. Older adults are especially susceptible to delirium.

- Most cases of delirium are cured, but some may be fatal.

Dementia

- Dementia is a family of disorders. Most older adults do not have dementia, but rates increase significantly with age.

- Alzheimer's disease is a progressive, fatal disease that is diagnosed at autopsy through neurological changes including neurofibrillary tangles and neuritic plaques.

- Major symptoms of Alzheimer's disease include gradual and eventually pervasive memory loss, emotional changes, and eventual loss of motor functions.

- Diagnosis of Alzheimer's disease consists of ruling out all other possible causes of the symptoms. This involves thorough physical, neurological, and neuropsychological exams.

- Current research suggests that Alzheimer's disease may be genetic, perhaps with an autosomal dominant inheritance pattern, although other hypotheses have been proposed.

- Although no cure for Alzheimer's disease is available, interventions to relieve symptoms are advisable and possible, including various drug and behavioral interventions. Dealing with declining functioning is especially difficult. Respite and adult day care are two options for caregivers.

- Vascular dementia is caused by several small strokes. Changes in behavior depend on where in the brain the strokes occur.

- Characteristic symptoms of Parkinson's disease include tremor and problems with walking. Treatment is done with drugs. Some people with Parkinson's disease develop dementia.

- Huntington's disease is a genetic disorder that usually begins in middle age with motor and behavioral problems.

- Alcoholic dementia (Wernicke–Korsakoff syndrome) is caused by a thiamine deficiency.

- AIDS dementia complex results from a byproduct of HIV. Symptoms include a range of cognitive and motor impairments.

Other Mental Disorders and Concerns

Anxiety Disorders

- Anxiety disorders include panic, phobia, and obsessive–compulsive problems. Symptoms include a variety of physical changes that interfere with normal functioning. Context is important in understanding symptoms. Both drugs and psychotherapy are used to treat anxiety disorders.

Psychotic Disorders

- Psychotic disorders involve personality disintegration and loss of touch with reality. One major form is schizophrenia; hallucinations and delusions are the primary symptoms.
- Schizophrenia is a severe thought disorder with an onset usually before age 45, but it can begin in late life. People with early-onset schizophrenia often improve over time as neurotransmitters become more balanced. Treatment usually consists of drugs; psychotherapy is not often effective alone.

Substance Abuse

- With the exception of alcohol, the substances most likely to be abused vary with age; younger adults are more likely to abuse illicit substances, whereas older adults are more likely to abuse prescription and over-the-counter medications.
- Alcohol dependency declines with age from its highest rates in young adulthood. Older adults take longer to withdraw, but similar therapies are effective in all age groups.

Review Questions

Mental Health and the Adult Life Course

- How do definitions of mental health vary with age?
- What are the implications of adopting a multidimensional model for interpreting and diagnosing mental disorders?

- Why are ethnicity and gender important considerations in understanding mental health?

Developmental Issues in Assessment and Therapy

- What is multidimensional assessment? How is it done?
- What major factors affect the accuracy of clinical assessment?
- How do the developmental forces influence assessment?
- What are the main developmental issues clinicians must consider in selecting therapy?

The Big Three: Depression, Delirium, and Dementia

- How do the rate of depression vary with age, gender, and ethnicity?
- What symptoms are associated with depression? How do they vary with age?
- What biological causes of depression have been proposed? How are they related to therapy?
- How is loss associated with depression?
- What treatments for depression have been developed? How well do they work with older adults?
- What is delirium? What causes it? Why are older adults more susceptible?
- What is Alzheimer's disease? How is it diagnosed?
- What causes Alzheimer's disease? What interventions are available?
- What other types of dementia have been identified? What are their characteristics?

Other Mental Disorders and Concerns

- What symptoms are associated with anxiety disorders? How are anxiety disorders treated?
- What are psychoses? What are their major symptoms? What treatments are most effective for schizophrenia?
- What developmental differences have been noted regarding substance abuse? How is alcohol dependency defined?

Integrating Concepts in Development

- Why is it so difficult to diagnose mental disorders in older adults? What concepts from Chapters 2 and 3 provide major reasons?
- Why do you think people with Alzheimer's disease might experience hallucinations and delusions?
- Why is there a connection between depression and dementia?
- What would studying people with Alzheimer's disease tell us about normal memory changes with age?

Key Terms

Alzheimer's disease An irreversible form of dementia characterized by progressive declines in cognitive and bodily functions, eventually resulting in death; it accounts for about 70% of all cases of dementia.

amyloid A type of protein involved in the formation of neuritic plaques both in normal aging and in Alzheimer's disease.

autosomal dominant pattern A type of genetic transmission in which only one gene from one parent is necessary for a person to acquire a trait or a disease.

behavior therapy A type of psychotherapy that focuses on and attempts to alter current behavior. Underlying causes of the problem may not be addressed.

cognitive therapy A type of psychotherapy aimed at altering the way people think as a cure for some forms of psychopathology, especially depression.

delirium A disorder characterized by a disturbance of consciousness and a change in cognition that develop over a short period of time.

dementia A family of diseases characterized by cognitive decline. Alzheimer's disease is the most common form.

dysphoria Feeling down or blue, marked by extreme sadness; the major symptom of depression.

mental status exam A short screening test that assesses mental competence, usually used as a brief indicator of dementia or other serious cognitive impairment.

Parkinson's disease A form of dementia marked by tremor and difficulty walking.

sundowning The phenomenon in which people with Alzheimer's disease show an increase in symptoms later in the day.

vascular dementia A form of dementia caused by a series of small strokes.

Resources

Readings

Bellenir, K. (1999). *Alzheimer's disease sourcebook: Basic consumer health information about Alzheimer's disease, related disorders, and other dementias.* Detroit: Omnigraphics. Good overview of Alzheimer's disease, Parkinson's disease, AIDS dementia complex, Huntington's disease, and others. Moderately difficult reading.

Davies, H. D., & Jensen, M. P. (1998). *Alzheimer's: The answers you need.* Forest Knolls, CA: Elder Books. Written in a question-and-answer format for people with early-stage Alzheimer's disease and their caregivers, this short book takes a different approach to covering basic information about the disease. Easy reading.

Gatz, M., Fiske, A., Fox, L. S., Kaskie, B., Kasl-Godley, J. E., McCallum, T. J., & Loebach Wetherell, J. (1998). Empirically validated psychological treatments for older adults. *Journal of Mental Health and Aging, 4,* 9—46. A comprehensive discussion of the best forms of psychotherapy for older adults across a variety of mental disorders. Easy to moderate difficulty.

McGowin, D. F. (1994). *Living in the labyrinth: A personal journey through the maze of Alzheimer's.* Cambridge, MA: Mainsail. A personal account of Alzheimer's disease that makes fascinating reading. Easy reading.

Thompson, T. (1996). *The beast: A journey through depression.* New York: Penguin. A moving firsthand account of living with depression. Easy reading.

Zarit, S. H., & Zarit, J. M. (1998). *Mental disorders in older adults: Fundamentals of assessment and treatment.* New York: Guilford. A comprehensive overview of mental health issues in older adults. Easy to moderate difficulty.

Web Sites

The Alzheimer's Association Web site has a wide range of information on the disease, including current research information, tips for caregivers, and links

to local chapters. Its home page can be found at
http://www.alz.org.

The National Institute on Alcohol Abuse and
Alcoholism provides many useful summaries, data, and
links to other good Web sites. The home page can be
found at http://www.niaaa.nih.gov.

PlanetRx maintains a useful site dedicated to research
and treatment of depression. It contains information
written in easy-to-understand formats. Their home page
can be found at http://www.depression.com/.

SEARCH ONLINE WITH
INFOTRAC COLLEGE EDITION

For more information on the topics in this
chapter, explore InfoTrac College Edition, your online
library. Go to http://www.infotrac-college.com/
wadsworth and use the passcode that came on the
card with your book. Try these search terms: aged—
psychology and mental health, geriatric psychiatry,
cognition disorders in old age, depression in old age,
schizophrenia in old age, Alzheimer's disease.

PERSON–ENVIRONMENT INTERACTIONS AND OPTIMAL AGING

© 1994 Priscilla Smith

Look carefully at the photos. Would you suspect that these people are at least in their 70s? Having good-looking bodies and being in great physical shape are not something most people think of when they consider older adults. But these people compete in the Senior Olympics, which brings together the best older athletes (some of whom competed in the Olympics when they were younger). They are examples of successful physical aging; of course, we know that other older adults experience problems.

Senior Olympians and all other adults are products of the interactions between the person and the environment. As obvious as this statement seems, only in the last few decades have the living environments in which people operate been studied systematically. And only more recently have researchers in adult development given them much thought. The principal concern in the field of environmental psychology has been the interaction of people with settings in which they live. The basic assumption is that "a person's behavioral and psychological state can be better understood with knowledge of the context in which the person behaves" (Lawton, 1980, p. 2).

In this chapter we explore how differences in the interaction between personal characteristics and the living environment can have profound effects on our behavior and our feelings about ourselves. Several theoretical frameworks are described that can help us understand how to interpret person–environment interactions in a developmental context. Because some people do not live in the community, we take a close look at long-term care facilities, especially nursing homes. Finally, we consider how person–environment interactions shape optimal aging and examine how people's lives can be enhanced. Even though we must sometimes consider the person separately from the environment, keep in mind throughout the chapter that in the end it is the interaction of the two that we want to understand.

DESCRIBING PERSON–ENVIRONMENT INTERACTIONS

LEARNING OBJECTIVES

- What is the competence and environmental press model?
- What is the congruence model?
- What are the major aspects of stress and coping theory relating to person–environment interactions?
- What is the loss continuum concept?
- What are the common themes in the theories of person–environment interactions?

Hank has lived in the same poor neighborhood all of his 75 years. Hank has been living alone for the past several months, ever since his wife, Marilyn, had a stroke and was placed in a nursing home. Hank's oldest daughter has been concerned about her father and has been pressing him to move in with her. Hank is reluctant: He likes knowing his neighbors, shopping in familiar stores, and being able to do what he wants. And he wonders how well he could adapt to living in a new neighborhood after all these years. He realizes that it might be easier for him to cope if he lived with his daughter, but it's a tough decision.

To appreciate the roles different environments play in our lives, we need a framework for interpreting how people interact with them. Theories of

person–environment interactions help us understand how people view their environments and how these views may change as people age. These views have been described since the 1930s in social psychology, but until the 1970s they had little impact on the study of adults (Hooyman & Kiyak, 1999). We consider four that have affected views of adult development and aging: competence and environmental press, congruence, stress and coping, and the loss continuum concept.

All these theories can be traced to a common beginning. Many years ago Kurt Lewin (1936) conceptualized person–environment interactions in the equation $B = f(P, E)$. *This relationship defining* **person–environment interactions** *means that behavior* (B) *is a function of both the person* (P) *and the environment* (E). More recent theorists have taken Lewin's equation and described the components in the equation in more detail. Specifically, their speculations concern the characteristics of people and environments that combine to form behavior.

Most of these models emphasize the importance of people's perceptions of their environments. That is, although objective aspects of environments (e.g., crime, housing quality) are important, personal choice plays a major role. For example, many people deliberately choose to live in New York or Atlanta, even though crime rates in those cities are higher than in Selma or Walla Walla. The importance of personal perception in environments is similar to the role of personal perception in social cognition and in concepts such as personal control (see Chapter 9). As we will see, these ideas, especially the notion of personal control, have been included in many approaches to understanding person–environment interactions.

Competence and Environmental Press

One way to express the person–environment interaction is by focusing on competence and environmental press (Lawton, 1982; Lawton & Nahemow, 1973). **Competence** *is the theoretical upper limit of a person's capacity to function.* Lawton and Nahemow (1973) believe that competence involves five domains: biological health, sensory–perceptual functioning, motor skills, cognitive skills, and ego strength. These domains are thought to underlie all other abilities, and they are lifelong. Unfortunately, the components of competence are not easy to measure. The problem is that most measures of the components involve the environment in some way. As noted in Chapter 2, for example, biological health is strongly related to the type of environment in which we live. Thus, in most research one must settle for a rough approximation of a person's true competence. Hank, the man we met in the vignette, would have good competence in this approach.

Environments can be classified on the basis of the varying demands they place on the person, a notion called **environmental press.** Lawton borrowed the concept of environmental press from Murray (1938). Environmental press can include any combination of three types of demands: physical, interpersonal, or social. Physical demands include such things as having to walk three flights of stairs to one's apartment. Interpersonal demands include the various pressures we feel to get along with other people. Social demands include such things as the local laws or social customs that affect our lives. Hank's current environment puts a low to moderate level of demands on him; if he moves, though, the demands will be higher because he will be less familiar with it.

Lawton and Nahemow's (1973) model is a combination of these ideas. They assert that behavior is a result of a person of a particular competence level acting in an environment of a specific press level. Furthermore, behavior is placed on a continuum from positive to negative and is thought to be manifested at two levels: observable behavior and affect, or feelings. These elements are represented schematically in Figure 5.1.

Low to high competence is represented on the vertical axis, and the horizontal axis represents weak to strong press level. Points in the graph show various combinations of person–environment interactions. Most important, the shaded areas demonstrate that adaptive behavior and positive affect result from many different combinations of competence and press levels, not just one. As one moves farther away from these areas—because of a change in press level,

for example—behavior becomes increasingly maladaptive, and affect becomes more negative. Notice that maladaptive behavior and negative affect also result from many combinations of competence and press levels. *Finally, the shaded area labeled* **adaptation level** *represents points where press is in balance for particular levels of competence.* The adaptation level is where behavior and affect are normal, so we are usually unaware of them. Awareness increases as we move away from adaptation level.

As an example of Lawton and Nahemow's model, consider Rick. Rick works in a store in an area of Omaha, Nebraska, where the crime rate is moderately high, representing a moderate level of environmental press. Because he is very good at self-defense, he has high competence; thus, he manages to cope. Because the Omaha police chief wants to lower the crime rate in that area, he increases patrols, thereby lowering the press level. If Rick maintains his high competence, maladaptive behavior may result because he has more competence than is optimal for the new environment. But if instead of the police a street gang moved in, he would have to increase his competence and be more prepared to maintain his adaptation level. Other changes in the environment (such as arson threats) or in his competence (such as a broken arm) would create other combinations.

Before leaving Lawton and Nahemow's model, we need to note an important implication for aging. The less competent the person is, the greater the impact of environmental factors. To the extent that people experience declines in health, sensory processes, motor skills, cognitive skills, or ego strength, they are less able to cope with environmental demands. For example, personal competence predicts how well older adults adapt after being discharged from a hospital (Lichtenberg et al., 2000). Thus, for older adults to maintain good adaptational levels, changes to lower environmental press or raise competence are needed. This point is made clearer in the Discovering Development feature. Take some time and complete it.

The competence and environmental press model has been the basis for interventions with people who have severe cognitive impairments, such as those of Alzheimer's disease (Smyer & Qualls, 1999). To manage severe cognitive impairment effectively, care-

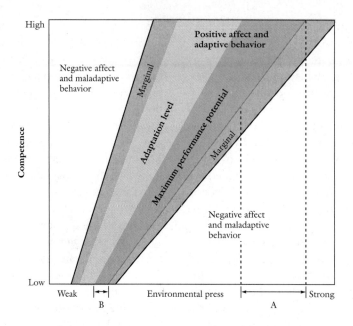

FIGURE 5.1 Behavioral and affective outcomes of person–environment interactions based on the competence and environmental press model. This figure indicates that a person of high competence will show maximum performance over a larger range of environmental situations than will a less competent person. The range of optimal environments occurs at higher level of environmental press (A) for the most competent person than it does for the least competent person (B).

Lawton, M. P. & L. Nahemow, "Ecology of the Aging Process" in C. Eisdorfer & M. P. Lawton (Eds.) *The Psychology of Adult Development and Aging,* p. 661. Copyright © 1973 by the American Psychological Association. Reprinted with permission.

givers must identify the right level of environmental support based on the patient's level of competence. For example, people with mild cognitive impairment may be able to live independently, but as the impairment increases additional levels of support are needed. The model has provided the basis for designing special care units for people with Alzheimer's disease. In these units, special environmental supports, such as color-coded room doors, help people with dementia identify where they belong.

Similarly, interventions for adults with physical disabilities and people living in senior housing communities can also be based on the competence and environmental press model. For example, providing tactile and other sensory supports helps people with disabilities. Research also shows that how public and private spaces are arranged affects the frequency and value of social interactions in housing complexes (Morse & Wisocki, 1991).

The Congruence Model

Another way to consider how people and environments interact is to look for the best fit for a specific person in a particular environment. This is what Kahana (1982) focuses on in her congruence model. Kahana includes the ideas of competence and environmental press but applies them differently. In Kahana's view people vary in their needs, and environments differ in their ability to satisfy them. *According to the* **congruence model,** *people with particular needs search for the environments that meet them best.* To the extent that a match exists, the person feels content and satisfied; when a mismatch occurs, stress and discomfort result.

Lawton and Nahemow's competence and environmental press model has wide applicability, as the examples of Hank and Rick in the text indicate. It provides an excellent introduction to the importance of considering people's capabilities and the environmental demands made of them. To understand how the model works, consider yourself. Make a list of the different aspects of your life, such as school, social activities, work, and so forth. Think about each of these areas, and rate yourself in terms of your abilities. For example, in the case of school, consider each course you are taking and rate how capable you are in each. Then consider the number and kinds of demands made on you in each area. For instance, in the case of school, think about the many demands put on you in each course. Now look at how your rating of your competence intersects with the kinds and number of demands. Does it place you in the position of feeling bored? In this case, you would fall in the left side of the graph. Are you feeling stressed out and under pressure? Then you would fall on the right side of the graph. Feeling just about right? You've experienced your adaptation level. Doing this analysis for the various aspects of your life may help you understand why you feel more competent in some areas than in others.

Congruence between the person and the environment is especially important when personal or environmental options are limited. Limitations can occur for three reasons: Environmental characteristics are restricted, as when public transportation is unavailable for going shopping; a person's freedom is limited, as when he or she must always eat at the same time every day; and one believes that one has limited freedom, as when one thinks that there is no way to get around despite a reliable bus system. By these criteria, Hank fits well with his current environment because he has ready access to all his basic necessities. Restricted environments are exemplified most clearly by long-term care facilities such as nursing homes and hospitals. Limits on individual freedom can result from age-related declines in competence. Self-perceptions of limited freedom reflect the belief that one's life is controlled by external forces, in the ways described in Chapter 9.

When applied specifically to the older adult, Kahana's congruence model shows that several points should be considered in optimizing the person–environment fit (Kahana & Kahana, 1983). One must consider not only the kind of situation, such as whether the person is in a single-family, congregate, or institutional living arrangement, but also personal factors. Personal factors are very important because people vary in their needs. Some of us value autonomy and independence highly, for example, whereas others place less importance on them. When designing programs and interventions for adults, we must be careful to take these individual differences into account. Otherwise, we may unintentionally increase the discrepancy between the person and the environment, resulting in increases in stress for the people we intended to help.

Kahana's model is especially useful in institutional settings such as nursing homes and hospitals. Indeed, most of the research that has examined issues such as autonomy has been done in long-term care facilities (Collopy, 1988; Hofland, 1988). This makes sense when one realizes that it is in these settings that difficult decisions are most often made that involve trade-offs between personal freedom and institutional requirements (Collopy, 1988). The importance of person–environment fit also lies in its ability to account for differences in competence between adults that cannot be attributed to problems with cognition or related abilities (Schaie & Willis, 1999). We return to Kahana's congruence model later when we focus on nursing homes.

Stress and Coping Framework

As you know from your own experience, sometimes your interaction with the environment is stressful. Schooler (1982) has applied Lazarus's cognitive theory of stress and coping, described in Chapter 3, to

Living independently is the clear preference of most older adults.

© Catherine Karnow / CORBIS

the understanding of the older person's interaction with the environment. The basic premise of Lazarus's theory is that people evaluate situations to assess their potential threat value. Situations can be evaluated as harmful, beneficial, or irrelevant. When situations are viewed as harmful or threatening, people also establish the range of coping responses that they have at their disposal for avoiding the harmful situation. This process results in a coping response. Outcomes of coping may be positive or negative depending on many contextual factors.

Schooler (1982) argues that this perspective is especially helpful in understanding older adults like Hank because of their greater vulnerability to social and physical hazards. To test his ideas, Schooler evaluated retest data on a sample of 521 people drawn from a national sample of 4,000 older adults living in long-term care facilities. In particular, he examined the impact of three potential stressors (environmental change, residential mobility, and major life events) on health or morale. He also examined the buffering, or protective, effects of social support systems and ecological factors on the relationships between the stressors and outcomes. Consistent with the theory, Schooler showed that the presence of social support systems affected the likelihood that particular situations would be defined as threatening. For example, living alone is more likely to be viewed as stressful when one has little social support than when one has many friends who live nearby.

Schooler's work provides an important theoretical addition because it deals with the relation between everyday environmental stressors and the adaptive response of community-dwelling individuals. However, more research must be done, especially in the area of understanding how the threat appraisal process varies with age across different environmental contexts.

The Loss Continuum Concept

Pastalan (1982) views aging as a progressive series of losses that reduce one's social participation. *This* **loss continuum** *includes children leaving, loss of social roles, loss of income, death of spouse or close friends and relatives, loss of sensory acuity, and loss of mobility caused by poorer health.* Hank has experienced the loss of Marilyn's companionship at home, illustrating that loss can occur in ways other than death. Because these losses reduce people's ability to partake fully in community resources, their own home and immediate neighborhood take on far greater importance. This increase in importance means that older adults are especially sensitive to even small environmental changes (Regnier, 1983; Rowles & Ohta, 1983).

The importance of the immediate neighborhood in the loss continuum concept is illustrated by the fact that a one-block radius around homes in cities is critical. Beyond this radius the rate at which older people make trips for shopping or other purposes drops sharply (Silverman, 1987). Consequently, well-planned environmental changes, even those on a small scale, can have significant payoffs for older adults. Pastalan (1982) views his approach as less a theory than a guide to practical change to facilitate older adults' maintenance of competence and independence.

Common Theoretical Themes and Everyday Competence

The four theories we have considered have much in common. Most important, all of them agree that the focus must be on the interaction between the person and the environment, not on one or the other. Another important common theme is that no one environment meets everyone's needs. Rather, a range of potential environments may be optimal.

Several researchers have built on these ideas and focused on people's everyday competence (Diehl, 1998). **Everyday competence** *is a person's potential ability to perform a wide range of activities considered essential for independent living.* It is not the person's actual ability to perform the task. Everyday competence also involves a person's physical, psychological, and social functioning, which interact in complex ways to create the person's day-to-day behavior (Diehl, 1998). Within each of these domains, a person's behavior involves many elements. For example, an older person's competence in the psychological domain includes cognitive problem-solving abilities, beliefs about personal control and self-efficacy, and styles of coping (McAvay et al., 1996; Mendes de Leon et al., 1996).

Although everyday competence is most often considered in the context of activities of daily living (ADLs) and instrumental activities of daily living (IADLs; see Chapter 3), it can also be considered more broadly as described here. The reason is that a behavior must not be viewed in isolation; behavior is expressed in a particular environmental context. In particular, researchers and clinicians need to be sensitive to cultural and contextual differences in everyday competence across different environments (Diehl, 1998).

Based on these ideas, Willis (1991, 1996a; Schaie & Willis, 1999) developed a model of everyday competence that incorporates all the key ideas discussed earlier.

Willis distinguishes between antecedents, components, mechanisms, and outcomes of everyday competence. Antecedents include both individual (e.g., health, cognition) and sociocultural (e.g., cultural stereotypes, social policy, health care policy) factors. These influence the intraindividual and contextual components, the particular domains and contexts of competence. Which components are most important or exert the most influence depends on the overall conditions under which the person lives. These elements of the model reflect the basic ideas in both the competence and environmental press model and the person–environment model we considered earlier. The mechanisms involve factors that moderate the way in which competence is actually expressed; for example, whether one believes that he or she is in control of the situation influences how competent the person turns out to be. Finally, the model proposes that the primary outcomes of everyday competence are psychological and physical well-being, which are two of the major components of successful aging.

Understanding the complexities of everyday competence is important as a basis for considering whether people, especially some older adults, are capable of making certain decisions for themselves. This issue often arises in terms of competence to make key health care and other decisions, a topic we consider in more detail later in this chapter. Willis's model also points out that the health outcomes of one episode of everyday competence are the antecedents for the next, illustrating how future competence is related to current competence.

CONCEPT CHECKS

1. What do the terms *competence, environmental press,* and *adaptation level* mean?
2. What are the basic components of the congruence model?
3. What are the main aspects of Schooler's stress and coping theory?
4. What is the loss continuum concept?
5. How can everyday competence be modeled?

LIVING IN LONG-TERM CARE FACILITIES

LEARNING OBJECTIVES

- What are the major types of long-term care facilities?
- What are the characteristics of the typical nursing home resident?
- What are the main ways of understanding the key characteristics of nursing homes?
- How can a nursing home be a home?
- How should people communicate with nursing home residents?
- How is decision-making capacity assessed?

The last place Maria thought she would end up was a bed in one of the local nursing homes. "That's a place where old people go to die," she used to say. "It's not gonna be for me." But here she is. Maria, 84 and living alone, fell and broke her hip. She needs to stay for a few weeks while she recovers. She hates the food; "tasteless goo," she calls it. Her roommate, Arnetta, calls the place a "jail." Arnetta, 79 and essentially blind, has Alzheimer's disease.

Maria and Arnetta may be the kind of people you think of when you conjure up images of nursing homes. To be sure, you will probably find some people like them there. But for each Maria or Arnetta, there are many more who come to terms with their situation and struggle to make sense of their lives. Nursing homes are indeed places where people who have very serious health problems go, and for many it is their final address. Yet if you visit a nursing home, you will find many inspiring people with interesting stories to tell.

There are many misconceptions about nursing homes. The first is that most older people end up in one. That perception clearly is not true. At any moment about 4.5% of the population over 65 is living in a facility of this type (National Center for Health Statistics, 1999). This may seem to be a small number of people, especially in view of the dominant stereotype of disability and sickness in old age. However, estimates of an older person's chance of spending any time in a nursing home are 30% for men and 50% for women (Hooyman & Kiyak, 1999). Thus, the number of people who are potentially affected by long-term care facilities is large.

You may be surprised to learn that the nursing home placement rate in the United States is lower than in many developed countries; for example, the rates in Canada, Sweden, and Switzerland are at least twice that in the United States (Hooyman & Kiyak, 1999).

Long-term care settings are very different environments from those we have considered so far. The residents of such facilities differ in many respects from their community-dwelling counterparts. Likewise, the environment itself is very different from neighborhood and community contexts. But because many aspects of the environment in these facilities are controlled, they offer a unique opportunity to examine person–environment interactions in more detail.

In this section we examine types of long-term care settings, the typical resident, the psychosocial environment in the facilities, and residents' ability to make decisions for themselves. Because almost all the adult developmental research in this field focuses on older adults, we concentrate on their experiences.

Types of Long-Term Care Facilities

The main types of long-term care facilities for older adults are nursing homes, assisted living, and adult foster homes (also called adult family homes). Nursing homes house the largest number of older residents of long-term care facilities. They are governed by state and federal regulations that establish minimum standards of care. Two levels of care in nursing homes are defined in U.S. federal regulations (Ebersole & Hess, 1998). Skilled nursing care consists of 24-hour care including skilled medical and other health services, usually from nurses. Intermediate care is also 24-hour care including nursing supervision, but at a less intense level. In actual practice the major differences between the two are the types and numbers of health care workers on the staff. Perhaps for this reason, the distinction between skilled and intermediate care often is blurred.

Assisted living facilities *provide a supportive living arrangement for people who need assistance with personal care (such as bathing or taking medications), but who are not so impaired physically or cognitively that they need 24-hour care* (Kane & Wilson, 1993). Most assisted living facilities are smaller than nursing homes. They provide congregate meals, housekeeping, laundry, and help with some activities of daily living. Most facilities have a nurse, social worker, and one or more case managers. Costs are usually lower than nursing homes.

Adult foster care *or adult family homes are another alternative to nursing homes for adults who do not need 24-hour care.* These facilities may also be regulated by states; however, no federal guidelines for these types of facilities exist. They are usually very small, housing five or six clients on average, and they house people

Most residents of nursing homes are very old European American women in poor health who are widowed or lived alone.

who need assistance with daily needs because of disabilities or chronic disorders such as arthritis but who otherwise are in fairly good health. The quality of care in these facilities varies widely.

Because they contain the majority of older adults who live in long-term care facilities, nursing homes have been the setting for almost all research on the effects of placement in these settings. For this reason nursing homes are the focus of the remainder of this section. Caution should be exercised in generalizing the results from nursing home research to other types of facilities. Differences in structure, staffing, and resident characteristics make such comparisons difficult. Therefore, we need more research on the experience of older residents in other types of facilities and on how these experiences compare with those of nursing home residents. Additionally, as noted in the Current Controversies feature, funding for nursing homes will be an increasingly important issue in the coming decades.

Who Is Likely to Live in Nursing Homes?

Who is the typical resident of a nursing home? She is very old, European American, financially disadvantaged, probably widowed or divorced, and possibly

without living children, and she has lived in the nursing home for more than a year. Maria and Arnetta, whom we met in the vignette, reflect these characteristics. Major risk factors are summarized in Table 5.1. Figure 5.2 shows the average age, gender, and race breakdown of the typical nursing home in the United States. Note that the characteristics of the typical nursing home resident are not similar to the population at large, as discussed in Chapter 1. For example,

TABLE 5.1	**Characteristics of People Most Likely to Be Placed in a Nursing Home**

Over age 85
Female
Recently admitted to a hospital
Lives in retirement housing rather than being a homeowner
Unmarried or live alone
Has no children or siblings nearby
Has some cognitive impairment
Has one or more problems with instrumental activities
   of daily living

Source: Freedman, V. A. (1996). Family structure and the risk of nursing home admission. *Journal of Gerontology: Social Sciences, 51B,* S61–S69.

The current system of financing long-term care in the United States is in very serious trouble. Nursing home costs average between $35,000 and $50,000 per year and are by far the leading catastrophic health care expense. In 1999, the Health Care Financing Administration estimated that national expenditures for nursing homes would be around $90 billion, growing to $151 billion by 2008. Contrary to popular belief, Medicare does not cover nursing home care but does have limited nursing home and home care benefits for people who need skilled nursing services and who meet other criteria. Private insurance plans currently pay only around 1–2% of the costs nationally. More than half the expense is paid for directly by nursing home residents. When residents become totally impoverished (a definition that varies widely from state to state), they become dependent on Medicaid, which pays about one-third of the total. (In 1998, the total Medicaid expenditures for skilled nursing home care alone were roughly $34.3 billion.) Given these expenses and the lack of insurance coverage, how will we be able to finance the long-term health care system?

One option is through the private sector. This approach includes long-term care insurance, individual retirement accounts for long-term care, health maintenance organizations, and alternative housing arrangements such as congregate housing. Many of these options place the burden on individuals to come up with ways of financing their own care. The Brookings Institution estimates that by 2018 private long-term care insurance will be affordable by as many as 45% of older adults. However, these projections also indicate that at best private insurance will lower Medicaid expenditures by only 2–5%. Such modest reductions in public support would also accompany individual retirement accounts, alternative housing, health maintenance organizations, and other options. Consequently, large subsidies from government will still be needed for long-term care regardless of what the private sector does.

Given that government subsidies for long-term care will be needed for the foreseeable future, the question becomes how to finance them. Under the current Medicaid system, older adults are not protected from becoming impoverished. Moreover, as the system is designed, a majority of people needing care ultimately will qualify for the program once their savings are depleted. With the aging of the baby-boom generation, Medicaid costs probably will skyrocket. If we want to continue the program in its current form, additional revenues are needed, perhaps in the form of taxes.

The questions facing us are whether we want to continue forcing older adults to become totally impoverished when they need long-term care, whether we want the government to continue subsidy programs, and whether we would be willing to pay higher taxes for this subsidy. How we answer these questions will have a profound impact on the status of long-term care over the next few decades.

Search Online with InfoTrac College Edition For more information on these controversies, explore InfoTrac College Edition, your online library. Go to http://www.infotrac-college.com/wadsworth and use the passcode that came on the card with your book. Try these search terms: long-term-care insurance; long-term-care facilities, finance; Medicare.

men are underrepresented in nursing homes, as are minorities. Burr (1990) reports that the nursing home placement rates for older unmarried adults are converging for African Americans and European Americans, and the reasons for doing so are essentially the same (e.g., poor health).

One important reason why certain demographic groups are not living in nursing homes is their cost.

A typical nursing home can cost $35,000–$50,000 and more depending on the type of facility and location (National Center for Health Statistics, 1999). Programs such as Medicare, Medicaid, and private long-term care insurance pay a portion of the cost, but most people face huge expenses. These costs often mean that poor and middle-income people cannot afford nursing homes.

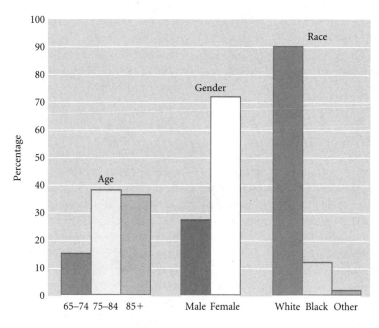

FIGURE 5.2 Demographic characteristics of nursing home residents over age 65.

Source: National Center for Health Statistics, 1997.

What are the problems of typical nursing home residents? For the most part, the average nursing home resident is clearly impaired, both mentally and physically. Indeed, the main reason for placing almost 80% of nursing home residents is health. Estimates are that nearly 80% of residents have mobility problems, and more than one third have mobility, eating, and incontinence problems (National Center for Health Statistics, 1999).

Clearly, frail older people and their relatives do not see nursing homes as an option until other avenues have been explored. This may account for the numbers of truly impaired people who live in nursing homes; the kinds and amount of problems make life outside the nursing home very difficult for them and their families. In fact, the best predictor of placement in a nursing home is the absence of a viable social support system; roughly 25% of nursing home placements occur upon the death or serious illness of the primary caregiver (Tennstedt et al., 1993). For these reasons, the decision to enter a nursing home often is made quickly in reaction to a crisis, such as a person's impending discharge from a hospital or other health emergency (Hooyman & Kiyak, 1999).

Characteristics of Nursing Homes

We can examine nursing homes on two dimensions: physical and psychosocial. Physical characteristics include factors such as size, staff-to-resident ratio, numbers and types of activities, and certification requirements. These characteristics are regulated by various government agencies. Unfortunately, very little research has been done comparing facilities on these dimensions, so we do not have a good idea of how much variance exists on these dimensions across nursing homes and when differences become important.

More is known about the effects of these dimensions on residents' psychosocial well-being. In this arena, the various approaches to person–environment interactions provide useful frameworks for understanding the psychosocial aspects of nursing homes.

Several researchers have conceptualized the effects of the institutional environment on residents. We are already familiar with Kahana's ideas; the previous discussion is expanded here. A second investigator, Moos, has taken a somewhat different approach that emphasizes measurement; we also consider his views in detail. Finally, we consider some work by Langer from a social psychological perspective.

THE CONGRUENCE APPROACH. In describing her congruence theory, Kahana (1982) also discusses several dimensions along which person–environment congruence can be classified. She is especially interested in describing facilities, so most of her research is aimed at documenting her dimensions in these settings.

Kahana's approach emphasizes that personal well-being is the product not just of the characteristics of the facility and of the person but also of the congruence between the person's needs and the ability of the facility to meet them. People whose needs are congruent with the control provided by the facility should have the highest well-being. However, any number of factors could be important in determining congruence, as is demonstrated by the large number of subdimensions in the congruence model.

The basic tenets of Kahana's approach have been translated into interventions in institutional settings (Zarit et al., 1999). Nursing homes are based on the medical tradition that defines residents as "sick" patients who are helpless and dependent on the staff to make decisions for them (Baltes, 1994). For some residents, this means that the environment assumes a lower level of functioning than they are capable of. This point is very important. Research shows that as many as 80% of dependent behaviors nursing home residents demonstrated were the result of residents being compliant with instructions from staff, not because they were actually dependent (Zarit et al., 1999). Residents also are fully aware that they are not performing behaviors they are competent to perform (Wahl, 1991). We return to this issue a bit later when we examine some different interventions that enhance resident's self-efficacy and competence.

MOOS'S APPROACH. A second way to examine the person–environment interaction in long-term care facilities has been offered by Moos and Lemke (1984, 1985). They believe that facilities can be evaluated in physical, organizational, supportive, and social climate terms. Each of these areas is thought to have an effect on residents' well-being.

Several scales have been developed to assess facilities on these dimensions. The Multiphasic Environmental Assessment Procedure (MEAP), one of the most comprehensive, assesses four aspects of the facility: physical and architectural features, administrative and staff policies and programs, resident and staff characteristics, and social climate. Each area is measured by separate multidimensional scales. Information from the MEAP provides a complete picture that allows a judgment to be made about how well the facility meets residents' needs.

Moos's approach enables us to measure and examine separate dimensions of the person–environment interaction independently. For one thing, it establishes areas of strength and weakness so that appropriate programs can be devised. This research has resulted in the publication of various guides to selecting nursing homes. For example, the Health Care Financing Administration (HCFA) publishes the very useful document *Your Guide to Choosing a Nursing Home*, available through the Web site listed at the end of the chapter. Such guides provide information about the questions one should ask, residents' rights, and sources of additional information.

SOCIAL PSYCHOLOGICAL PERSPECTIVES. As we have seen, nursing homes traditionally are based on a medical model that keeps residents dependent. What would happen if there were better congruence between residents' abilities and the nursing home environment? Could residents' self-efficacy be improved? If so, what would happen to their health?

Langer decided to find out. She believed that the important factor in residents' well-being is the degree to which they perceive that they are in control of their lives (Langer, 1985). To demonstrate her point, she conducted an ingenious experiment that is now one of the classic studies in gerontology. One group of nursing home residents was told that staff members were there to care for them and to make decisions for them about their daily lives. In contrast, a second group of residents was encouraged to make their own decisions about meals, recreational activities, and so forth. The second group showed greater well-being and higher activity levels than the first group (Langer & Rodin, 1976). These differences were still seen 18 months later; in fact, the second group also seemed to have lower mortality rates (Rodin & Langer, 1977).

Based on her findings, Langer became convinced that making residents feel competent and in control were key factors in promoting positive person–environment interactions in nursing homes. Langer (1985) points to several aspects of the nursing home environment that fail in this regard. First, the decision to place a person in a nursing home often is made by people other than the person involved. Staff members may communicate their belief that the resident is incapable of making decisions or may treat him or her like a child rather than like an adult who is moving to a new home.

Second, the label "nursing home resident" may have strong negative connotations. This is especially true if as a younger adult the person had negative ideas about why people go to nursing homes. A long history of social psychological research shows that the person may begin to internalize these stereotypical beliefs, even if they are unwarranted (Kelley, 1967). Other labels such as *patient* may have similar effects.

Third, what staff consider simply the demonstration of tender loving care may reinforce the belief in one's incompetence. That is, in helping people perform basic tasks such as getting dressed, we run the risk of increasing their level of incompetence and dependence on others. Again, providing assistance where none is needed may be a way in which the staff communicates its belief that the resident cannot fend for himself or herself at all.

The physical aspects of the environment may also reinforce the belief of no control. To the extent that the environment is unfamiliar or is difficult to nego-

tiate, people living in it may feel incompetent. Mastering the environment increases feelings of control, but if this process is not allowed or is made too easy, the outcome may be negative.

Finally, Langer (1985) argues that routine is also detrimental to well-being. If the environment is too predictable, there is little for people to think about; in Langer's terms, we become mindless. In this state we are typically not aware of what we do; we behave as if we were on automatic pilot. If nursing home environments promote mindlessness, then residents behave automatically and have difficulty remembering what happened even a short time before. When this occurs, the staff may view the person as incompetent. But because we all engage in mindless activity (e.g., performing a series of complex but automatic functions while driving) about which we have no recollection (one often cannot recall anything about driving the last several miles), we cannot justify this same mindlessness as indicative of incompetence in older adults.

Other researchers have replicated Langer's basic findings in nursing homes (Schulz & Hanusa, 1979) and retirement communities (Slivinske & Fitch, 1987). Buschmann and Hollinger (1994) found that providing affective social support through touching is an effective substitute for residents' inability to control their environment. Whether the benefits of increased control last over the long run is still an open issue. Whether we should treat nursing home residents with respect is not.

Can a Nursing Home Be a Home?

One key aspect of nursing homes has been largely overlooked: To what extent do residents consider a nursing home to be home? This gets to the heart of what makes people feel that the place in which they live is more than just a dwelling. On the surface, it appears that nursing homes are full of barriers to this feeling. After all, they may have regulations about the extent to which residents may bring their own furnishings and other personal effects with them, and residents are in an environment that has plenty of structural reminders that this is not a house in suburbia. Not having one's own refrigerator, for example, means that one can no longer invite friends over for a home-cooked meal (Shield, 1988).

Can nursing home residents move beyond these barriers and reminders and achieve a sense of home? Apparently so, but with some very important qualifications. Groger (1995) interviewed 20 older African American adults, 10 who lived in nursing homes and 10 who were home care clients. Groger's analysis of her interviews revealed that nursing home residents can indeed feel at home. The circumstances that foster this feeling include having the time to think about and participate in the placement decision, even if only minimally; having prior knowledge of, and positive experience with, a specific facility; defining home predominantly in terms of family and social relationships rather than in terms of place, objects, or total autonomy; and being able to establish some kind of continuity between home and nursing home either through activities or through similarities in living arrangements.

Groger (1995) also reports that getting nursing home residents to reminisce about home may actually facilitate adjustment. Some residents concluded that the nursing home was home only after long and detailed reflection on their prior home. Additionally, it may be easier for nursing home residents to feel at home on some days than others and from one situation to another, depending on the events or stimuli at the time.

Helping nursing home residents feel at home is an important issue that must be explored in more detail. Perhaps having people think about what constitutes a home before and after placement may make the transition from community to the facility easier to face. For those who need the care provided in a nursing home, anything that can be done to ease the transition would be a major benefit.

Communicating with Residents

Have you ever been to a nursing home? If so, one of the things you may have found difficult is talking with the residents, especially when interacting with residents who are cognitively impaired. Unfortu-

nately, this uneasiness often results in people relying on stereotypes of older adults in general and nursing home residents in particular in speaking to them, which results in inappropriate communication styles.

The communication style most people adopt is one in which younger adults overaccommodate their speech based on their stereotyped expectations of dependence and incompetence. This style is described as a general "communication predicament" of older adults (Ryan et al., 1986). Such speech conveys a sense of declining abilities, loss of control, and helplessness, which, if continued, may cause older adults to lose self-esteem and withdraw from social interactions. As time goes on, older adults who are talked to in this way may even begin behaving in ways that reinforce the stereotypes.

Inappropriate speech to older adults that is based on stereotypes of incompetence and dependence is called **patronizing speech.** Patronizing speech is slower speech marked by exaggerated intonation, higher pitch, increased volume, repetitions, tag and closed-end questions, and simplification of vocabulary and grammar. Speaking in this way can be conceptualized as "secondary baby talk," which is baby talk inappropriately used with adults (Ryan et al., 1993). *Secondary baby talk, also called* **infantilization,** *also involves the unwarranted use of a person's first name, terms of endearment, simplified expressions, short imperatives, an assumption that the recipient has no memory, and cajoling as a way to demand compliance* (Whitbourne et al., 1995).

Whitbourne and colleagues (1995) showed that infantilizing speech is viewed extremely negatively by some older adults. They found that community-dwelling older adults rated infantilizing speech especially negatively and were particularly resentful of its intonation aspects as indicative of a lack of respect. Nursing home residents were less harsh in their judgments, giving support to the idea that being exposed to infantilizing speech lowers one's awareness of its demeaning qualities. Whitbourne and colleagues also found no evidence that infantilizing speech is high in nurturance, as some previous authors had suggested. Similarly, Harwood and colleagues (1997) demonstrated that adults to whom patronizing speech is di-

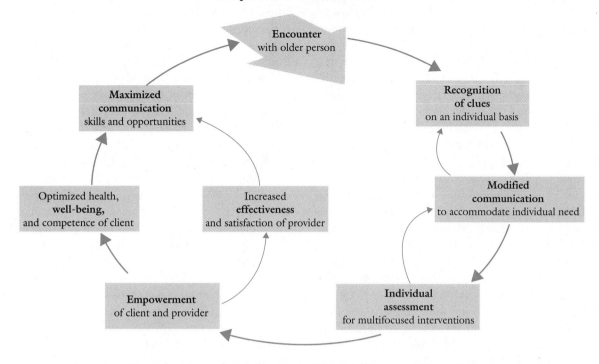

FIGURE 5.3 The communication enhancement model. Note that this model is dynamic in that there are opportunities to modify communication interactions and to have the outcomes of one interaction serve as input for another.

Source: Ryan, E. B., Meredith, S. D., MacLean, M. J., & Orange, J. B. (1995). Changing the way we talk with elders: Promoting health using the communication enhancement model. *International Journal of Aging and Human Development, 41,* 96.

rected are more likely to be blamed for accidents, especially when the target is an older adult.

How should people talk to older adults, especially those living in nursing homes? Ryan and her colleagues (1995) propose the communication enhancement model as a framework for appropriate exchange. This model is based on a health promotion model, which seeks opportunities for health care providers to optimize outcomes for older adults through more appropriate and effective communication. As you can see in Figure 5.3, this model emphasizes that communication with older adults must be based on recognizing individualized cues, modifying communication to suit individual needs and situations, appropriately assessing health and social prob-

lems, and empowering both older adults and health care providers.

What happens when residents respond in different ways to a staff member's patronizing speech? Ryan and colleagues (2000) examined what happened when nursing home residents responded passively, assertively, or humorously to a nurse's patronizing speech, which was then either maintained or changed to reflect more respect for the resident. Details of the study are provided in the How Do We Know? feature. The interchanges were rated by nursing home residents, staff, and community-residing older adults. Patronizing speech was rated negatively by everyone (but was less so by the nursing home residents). The nurse who continued to speak patronizingly when the resident responded assertively was rated most negatively, but residents were the most reluctant to endorse this way of responding. Humorous responses were rated in between, making it perhaps a safer alternative for residents to use to express opposition to a request yet still maintain an appearance of cooperation. Taken together, these results show the degree to which patronizing speech is disliked by community-dwelling older adults but accepted as expected by nursing home residents.

Ryan and colleagues' model and research can be readily applied to interactions with older adults from different ethnic groups and with older adults who have cognitive impairments. For example, an analysis of intergenerational communication comparing Western and Eastern cultures showed complex cultural variability, including the occurrence of less positive perceptions of conversations in some cases from respondents in Korea, Japan, China, Hong Kong, and the Philippines than in some Western countries (Williams et al., 1997). In general, an approach to communication based on the model promotes mental, social, and physical well-being among older adults and counters the fostering of dependence that follows from the traditional medical model discussed earlier. Most important, it reminds us that we must speak to all older adults in a way that conveys the respect they deserve.

Decision-Making Capacity and Individual Choices

Providing high-quality care for nursing home residents means putting into practice the various competency-enhancing interventions we have considered relating to personal control and communication. Doing so means that residents participate in making decisions about their care. But how can we make sure that residents understand what they are being asked to decide, especially when a majority of them have cognitive impairment?

The need to address this question became apparent in 1991 with the enactment of the Patient Self-Determination Act (PSDA). This law mandated that all facilities receiving Medicare and Medicaid funds comply with five requirements regarding advance care planning (Smyer & Allen-Burge, 1999): providing written information to people at the time of their admission about their right to make medical treatment decisions and to formulate advance directives (i.e., decisions about life-sustaining treatments and who could make medical decisions for them if they were incapacitated), maintaining written policies and procedures regarding advance directives, documenting the completion of advance directives in the person's medical chart, complying with state law regarding the implementation of advance directives, and providing staff and community education about advance directives.

The PSDA mandates work well with most people. However, assessing a person's capacity to make medical decisions is a tremendous challenge for medical ethics (American Geriatrics Society Ethics Committee, 1996). In theory, advance directives enable people to choose the type of medical treatment they prefer in advance of a medical crisis. However, numerous studies show that the theory does not hold up well in practice: Most people, especially older adults, engage in informal advance care planning, preferring to allow family members to make decisions for them when the need arises and to give them leeway in interpreting advance directives even when they exist (Smyer & Allen-Burge, 1999). Thus, it is unlikely that a person being admitted to a nursing home will have completed a formal advance directive. Because placement in a nursing home is already stressful and likely to occur in the context of a medical crisis, the new resident is unlikely to understand the information presented as mandated by the PSDA. To make matters worse, if the new resident is cognitively impaired, he or she may be unable to act in his or her own behalf in communicating end-of-life wishes. Research clearly shows that even people with nondocumented mild cognitive impairment

Who were the investigators, and what was the aim of the study? Older adults who live in nursing homes face many difficulties with the way people talk to (or about) them. The concept of patronizing speech, discussed in the text, captures the essence of the problem. Ryan and colleagues (2000) decided to see how different groups of people (nursing home resident, staff, and community-residing older adults) respond when a nurse talks in a patronizing way to a resident, who then responds.

How did the investigators measure the topic of interest? A written description of the context of an interaction between a nurse and a resident of a fictitious Canadian nursing home was followed by an audiotape of a conversation in which the nurse reminded the resident that it was time to go to a craft activity. Respondents then answered a questionnaire based on the kind of response the resident gave to the nurse. Respondents rated the nurse and the resident separately on a list of 12 adjectives rating her competence ("From this conversation, I would say the nurse [resident] is [competent, respectful, likeable, and helpful]"), manner ("From this conversation, I would say the nurse [resident] is trying to be [polite, cooperative, in control]"), and similar ratings for control adjectives and appropriateness adjectives.

Who were the participants in the study? In Study 1, participants were 48 nursing home residents with no known cognitive impairment and 48 staff members. In Study 2, participants were 49 nursing home

residents with no known cognitive impairment, 48 staff, and 48 community-residing older adults. Staff members were about 40 years younger than residents in both studies and about 33 years younger than the community residents in Study 2.

What was the design of the study? For the major project in Study 2, the design examined three groups (nursing home residents, staff, and community-residing older adults), three response styles by the resident (passive, assertive, and humorous), and two further styles by the nurse (continuing to patronize or shift to accommodating). The conversation scripts had three different responses from the resident to the nurse's patronizing statement ("Did we forget again, sweetie? It's time for crafts!"). In one, the resident gave a passive response to the request ("I know it's time to go. I'd rather not, but if you insist, I'll go."). In a second, the resident gave an assertive response ("I've already planned to watch my favorite TV program, so I won't have time to go today."). The third version had a humorous response ("I think I'll just pass today. I've made more crafts in my lifetime than an overachieving Girl Guide group at Christmas."). Additionally, there were two different versions of what the nurse said next: either continuing to be patronizing ("Now, now, I just know we'll have a nice time. It's important that we get out of our room for awhile, dear. You just have to give it a try!") or shifting to an accommodating style ("I can see

that you are not eager today. But it is important for you to get out of your room for awhile. Mrs. Brown, please consider joining us.").

Were there ethical concerns with the study? All participants were volunteers. Nursing home residents were screened for cognitive impairments. Because all participants were given the opportunity to withdraw and were given informed consent, there were no ethical concerns.

What were the results? The nurse who shifted to an accommodating style was rated more positively, and respondents could clearly describe the differences between the nurse's responses. However, nursing home residents were much more tolerant of patronizing speech. Patronizing speech was rated more negatively when the resident responded assertively, perhaps because the patronizer appears less appropriate. Interestingly, the assertive response did not elicit higher competency ratings.

What did the investigators conclude? The findings are consistent with previous data showing that patronizing speech is not viewed positively. However, this study marked the first time that this rating was obtained as a direct result of a speaker shifting styles. However, the tolerance of patronizing speech by nursing home residents and the failure to rate assertive responses as reflecting higher competence is troubling and shows the degree to which a culture of dependency pervades many nursing homes.

do not understand the information presented to them under PSDA guidelines (Frank et al., 1999).

Assessing a nursing home resident's ability to make medical treatment decisions can be conceptualized as a problem involving the fit between the legislative intent and the resident's capacity (Smyer & Allen-Burge, 1999). Several researchers have tackled the problem of how to assess decision-making capacity with varying results. One approach emphasizes maintaining autonomy and informed consent (Lidz et al., 1988), whereas a second takes a more legalistic approach (Marson et al., 1996). In either case, a careful assessment of the resident is necessary. Some research indicates that a mental status exam is a good initial step (Pruchno et al., 1995).

Still, many problems remain. No uniform approach to determining residents' competence exists. States also differ in terms of the criteria needed to demonstrate competence (which is usually approached from the opposite side: what it takes to establish incompetence). To complicate matters further, research also shows lack of agreement between what residents want and what their families think they would want, which also varies with ethnicity (Allen-Burge & Haley, 1997; Smyer & Allen-Burge, 1999). Resolving the problem will involve using the various approaches we have considered for determining person–environment interactions, combined with strong clinical assessment (see Chapter 4), in the context of specific treatment goals. Quality-of-life considerations are paramount (Lawton, 1996). Clearly, it takes an interdisciplinary team of professionals, residents, and family members working together to create an optimal solution.

CONCEPT CHECKS

1. What are the various types of long-term care facilities?
2. What are the characteristics of the typical nursing home resident?
3. What are the major points of the various approaches to describing the characteristics of nursing homes?
4. Under what conditions can a nursing home be a home for its residents?
5. What is the communication enhancement model?
6. What are the issues concerning decision-making capacity in nursing home residents?

OPTIMAL AGING

LEARNING OBJECTIVES

- What are the major strategies for maintaining and enhancing competence?
- What are the primary considerations in designing health promotion and disease prevention programs?
- What are the principal lifestyle factors that influence competence?

Jack had heard about the many things that were available on the Web, but like many older adults he was a little reluctant to tackle it. But after he purchased his first home computer at age 68, he began his surfing career. Now at age 73, he's a veteran with a wide array of bookmarked sites, especially those relating to health issues. He also communicates by e-mail, and he designed the community newsletter using his word-processing program.

Although most older adults are not as computer literate as Jack, increasing numbers of them are discovering that computers can be a major asset. Many take advantage of the growing resources available on the Web, including sites dedicated specifically to older adults. E-mail enables people of all ages to stay in touch with friends and family, and the growing success of e-commerce makes it easier for people with limited time or mobility to purchase goods and services. A survey conducted by AARP (AARP, 1999b) indicates that older adults have used computers to cut their phone bills by using e-mail, chat online with others, make new friends, and fill their free time. Research also shows that computer usage across adulthood among college faculty shows that older faculty are less comfortable using computers in general but are willing to learn how (Rousseau & Rogers, 1998).

The use of computers is one way in which technology can be used to enhance the competence of older adults. In this section, we consider the general topic of how to maintain and enhance competence through a variety of interventions. How to grow old successfully is a topic of increasing concern, especially given the demographic changes we considered in Chapter 1. Let's begin by taking a look at a useful framework for optimal aging.

Many older adults become computer literate to keep in touch with family members and take advantage of information available on the Web.

A Framework for Maintaining and Enhancing Competence

The life-span perspective we considered in Chapter 1 is an excellent starting point for understanding how to maintain and enhance people's competence. In this perspective, the changes that occur with age result from multiple biological, psychological, sociocultural, and life-cycle forces. Mastering tasks of daily living and more complex tasks (such as personal finances) contributes to a person's overall sense of competence (Willis, 1996a). How can this sense be optimized for successful aging?

The answer lies in applying three key adaptive mechanisms for aging: selection, optimization, and compensation (Baltes & Baltes, 1990; Marsiske et al., 1996; see Chapter 8 for a more detailed discussion). This framework helps address what Bieman-Copland, Ryan, and Cassano (1998) call the social facilitation of the nonuse of competence: the phenomenon of older people intentionally or unintentionally failing to perform up to their true level of ability because of the operation of social stereotypes that limit what older adults are expected to do. Instead of behaving at their true ability level, older adults behave in ways they believe to be typical or characteristic of their age group (Heckhausen & Lang, 1996). This phenomenon is the basis for the communication patterns we considered earlier in this chapter.

A key issue in the powerful role of stereotypes is to differentiate usual from successful aging (Rowe & Kahn, 1998). As shown in Figure 5.4, successful aging involves avoiding disease, being engaged with life, and maintaining high cognitive and physical functioning. It is a very individualized and subjective notion that is reached when a person achieves his or her desired goals with dignity and as independently as possible (Bieman-Copland et al., 1998).

The life-span perspective can be used to create a formal model for successful aging. Introduced by Bieman-Copland and colleagues (1998) based on ideas first presented by Baltes and Baltes (1990), the model shows how core assumptions about aging influence the basic premises of successful aging, which in turn creates antecedents, mechanisms, and outcomes. (You are already familiar with much of this model; it is the basis for the everyday competence model we considered earlier in this chapter.) The core assumptions recognize that aging is a complex process that involves increasing specialization and is influenced by factors unrelated to age. The basic premises of successful aging include keeping a balance between the various gains and losses that occur over time and keeping the influence of nonaging factors to a minimum. In short, these premises involve paying attention to both internal and external factors impinging on the person. The antecedents include all the changes that happen to a person. The mechanisms in the model are the selection, optimization, and compensation processes that shape the course of development. Finally, the outcomes of the model denote that enhanced competence, quality of life, and future adaptation are the visible signs of successful aging.

Using the model, various types of interventions can be created to help people age successfully. In general, such interventions focus on the individual or aspects of tasks and the physical and social environment (Bieman-Copland et al., 1998).

When designing interventions aimed primarily at the person, it is important to understand the target person's goals (rather than the goals of the researcher). For example, in teaching older adults how to use automatic teller machines (ATMs), it is essen-

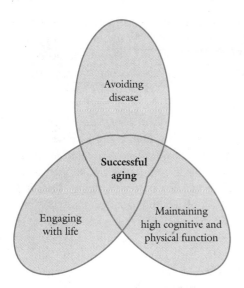

FIGURE 5.4 Components of successful aging.

From *Successful Aging* by John Wallis Rowe and Robert L. Kahn, copyright © 1998 by John Wallis Rowe, M.D., and Robert L. Kahn, Ph.D. Used by permission of Pantheon Books, a division of Random House, Inc.

Adopt a healthful lifestyle. Make it part of your daily routine.

Stay active cognitively. Keep an optimistic outlook and maintain your interest in things.

Maintain a social network and stay engaged with others.

Maintain good economic habits to avoid financial dependency.

tial to understand the kinds of concerns and fears older adults have and ensure that the training program address them (Rogers et al., 1997).

Interventions aimed at redesigning tasks or aspects of the environment must take the target person's abilities into account. For example, training older adults to use ATMs should take into account changes in vision and cognition that can affect the effectiveness of the instructional program (Rogers & Fisk, 1997; Rogers et al., 1996). We saw earlier that modifying the social environment can enhance nursing home residents' sense of control and possibly lengthen their lives.

In the remainder of this section, we consider a range of interventions aimed at enhancing optimal or successful aging. We examine programs for promoting health and preventing disease next, followed by specific aspects of lifestyle that influence successful aging.

Health Promotion and Disease Prevention

By now you're probably wondering how to promote successful aging. You may not be surprised to learn that there is no set of steps or magic potion you can take to guarantee that you will age optimally. But research is showing that there are some steps you can take to maximize your chances (Gatz & Zarit, 1999). As you can see in Table 5.2, most of them are not complex. But they do capture the results of applying the model for maintaining and enhancing competence we examined at the beginning of the section. The key strategies are sound health habits; good habits of thought, including an optimistic outlook and interest in things; a social network; and sound economic habits.

These simple steps are difficult in practice, of course. Nevertheless, they will help maximize the chances of aging successfully. Setting up this favorable outcome is important. Because of the demographic shifts in the population, health care costs for older adults in most developed countries are expected to skyrocket during the first half of the 21st century. Minimizing this increase is key.

In anticipation of these changes, the U.S. Department of Health and Human Services created a national initiative to improve the health of all Americans through a coordinated and comprehensive emphasis on prevention. The basis of this effort was *Healthy People 2000: National Disease Prevention and Health Promotion Objectives.* Now updated with new targets for the year 2010, the report set three broad goals: increase the length of healthy life, reduce health disparities among Americans, and achieve access to preventive services for all.

Although significant gains were made in the 1990s, they were not universal. Many members of ethnic minority groups and the poor still have not

Given that the U.S. government has not yet solved all the problems surrounding health promotion and disease prevention, how can future efforts be designed to maximize success? The answer lies in ensuring that the programs are grounded in the four developmental forces.

Any health promotion and disease prevention program must take biological forces into account. Although you may think that this is obvious, many programs currently offered to older adults are based on programs originally designed for younger adults (Ward-Griffin & Ploeg, 1997). Clearly, there are important developmental changes in bone structure, endurance, and so forth that must be taken into account.

Psychological forces are also key. Programs that include complicated instructions or regimens are less likely to be used by older adults, whose short-term memory skills may be taxed beyond their limits. Indeed, some effective interventions have been based entirely on simplifying instructions and replacing words with icons (Morrow et al., 1996, 1998). Additionally, even when older adults take notes they do not remember medical messages as well as younger adults, indicating that extra care must be taken to ensure that they understand all the key elements (Morrow et al., 1999).

Programs designed for one ethnic group or social class may not be applicable to others. However, little emphasis has been given to the importance of sociocultural forces on health promotion. As noted in the text, part of the lack of success of the U.S. initiatives is the failure to design programs that address ethnic- and class-specific needs.

Finally, programs that appeal to people at one point in the life cycle may not be as attractive to them at different times in their lives. For example, although younger adults may be attracted to high-energy exercise programs, older adults tend not to be. Thus, programs must take the preferences of people at different times in their lives into account.

It is clear that designing successful health promotion and disease prevention programs is a difficult task. No one-size-fits-all program can be created that will work with everyone. From a life-span perspective, it is necessary to fine tune programs based on a careful analysis of people's developmental status.

---

seen significant improvements in their lives. With this in mind, there has been a shift in focus from one that included only prevention to one that also includes optimum health practices.

The U.S. government allocates funds appropriated by the Older Americans Act through the Administration on Aging (AoA) to help support programs aimed at improving the health of older adults. These funds support a wide variety of programs, including health risk assessments and screenings, nutrition screening and education, physical fitness, health promotion programs on chronic disabling conditions, home injury control services, counseling regarding social services, and follow-up health services. One of the goals of these low-cost programs is to address the lack of awareness many people have about their own chronic health problems; for example, the AoA estimates that half of those with diabetes mellitus, more than half with hypertension, and 70% of those with high cho-lesterol levels are unaware that they have serious conditions. Health promotion and disease prevention programs such as those sponsored by the AoA could reduce the cost of treating the diseases through earlier diagnosis and better prevention education.

The kinds of programs envisioned by *Healthy People 2000* and the AoA represent a shift in focus from one aimed at individual responsibility for health behaviors to a social system approach (Ward-Griffin & Ploeg, 1997). Research indicates that such programs can be implemented successfully at senior centers and include a broad spectrum of topics, from exercise to nutrition counseling to home safety (Wallace et al., 1998). Additionally, it reflects a realization that health promotion and disease prevention programs can and must include adults of all ages and, as discussed in the Forces in Action feature, be grounded in the four developmental forces. As we will see a bit later, there are key issues that must be considered in designing successful programs for older adults. First, though, we consider some specific issues in prevention, with a focus on different types of programs.

ISSUES IN PREVENTION. In Chapter 3, we saw that Verbrugge and Jette's (1994) theoretical model offers a comprehensive account of disability resulting from chronic conditions and provides much guidance for research. Another benefit of the model is that it also provides insight into ways to intervene so that disability can be prevented or its progress slowed. Prevention efforts can be implemented in many ways, from developing vaccines that immunize people against certain diseases to programs that transport people to supermarkets so that otherwise homebound people can do their grocery shopping (German, 1995).

Traditionally, three types of prevention have been discussed: primary, secondary, and tertiary; more recently, the concept of quaternary prevention has been added (Verbrugge, 1994). A brief summary is presented in Table 5.3. **Primary prevention** *is any intervention that prevents a disease or condition from occurring.* Examples of primary prevention include immunizing against illnesses such as polio and influenza or controlling risk factors such as serum cholesterol levels and cigarette smoking in healthy people.

Secondary prevention *is instituted early after a condition has begun (but may not yet have been diagnosed) and before significant impairments have occurred.* Examples of secondary intervention include cancer and cardiovascular disease screening and routine medical testing for other conditions. These steps help reduce the severity of the condition and may even reduce mortality from it. In terms of the main pathway in Verbrugge and Jette's (1994) model, secondary prevention occurs between pathology and impairments.

Tertiary prevention *involves efforts to avoid the development of complications or secondary chronic conditions, manage the pain associated with the primary chronic condition, and sustain life through medical intervention.* Some chronic conditions have a high risk of creating additional medical problems; for example, being bedridden as a result of a chronic disease

often is associated with getting pneumonia. Tertiary prevention involves taking steps such as sitting the person up in bed to lower the risk of contracting additional diseases. In terms of the model, tertiary interventions are aimed at minimizing functional limitations and disability.

Historically, tertiary prevention efforts have not focused on functioning but rather on avoiding additional medical problems and sustaining life (Verbrugge, 1994). Consequently, the notion of quaternary prevention has been developed to address functional issues. **Quaternary prevention** *is efforts specifically aimed at improving the functional capacities of people who have chronic conditions.* Like tertiary prevention, quaternary prevention focuses on the functional limitations and disability components of the model. Some examples of quaternary prevention are cognitive interventions to help people with Alzheimer's disease remember things or occupational therapy to help people maintain their independence.

Although prevention has a long and well-documented history with younger and middle-aged adults, it is a newer approach with older adults (German, 1995). Although most efforts with older adults to date have focused on primary prevention, increasing attention is being paid to secondary prevention through screening for early diagnosis of diseases such as cancer and cardiovascular disease. Consequently, few systematic studies of the benefits and outcomes of tertiary and quaternary prevention efforts have been done (German, 1995). Part of the reason for this is that older adults who have chronic conditions may perceive that tertiary and quaternary prevention programs are intended for younger adults and not participate in them (German, 1995). However, the number of such programs being conducted in local senior centers and other settings attractive to older adults is increasing steadily, which should result in higher participation rates. The stakes are high. Because tertiary and quaternary prevention programs are aimed at maintaining functional abilities and minimizing disability, they can be effective, lower-cost alternatives for addressing the needs of older adults with chronic conditions (German, 1995).

TABLE 5.3	Types of Prevention Interventions	
Type of Prevention	Description	Examples
Primary	Any intervention that prevents a disease or condition from occurring	Immunizations against diseases, healthful diet
Secondary	Program instituted early after a condition has begun (but may not yet have been diagnosed) and before significant impairments have occurred	Cancer screening, other medical tests
Tertiary	Efforts to avoid the development of complications or secondary chronic conditions, manage the pain associated with the primary chronic condition, and sustain life through medical intervention	Moving a bedridden person to avoid sores, getting a patient out of bed to improve mobility after surgery
Quaternary	Efforts specifically aimed at improving the functional capacities of people who have chronic conditions	Cognitive interventions for people with Alzheimer's disease, rehabilitation programs after surgery

One of the interesting aspects of this approach is that most prevention programs can be applied at any stage. For example, a nutritional program aimed at lowering fat intake can be implemented as a primary prevention for healthy people to stay that way or as a tertiary or quaternary prevention for people with diagnosed cardiovascular disease. We now turn to some of these programs.

Lifestyle Factors

Most attention in health promotion and disease prevention programs is on tackling a handful of behaviors that have tremendous payoff, such as keeping fit and eating well. In turn, these programs educate adults about good health care practices and help identify conditions such as hypertension, high cholesterol levels, and elevated blood sugar levels, which, if left untreated, can cause atherosclerosis, heart disease, strokes, diabetes mellitus, and other serious conditions. Additionally, these programs draw attention to smoking cessation, drug and alcohol abuse and dependence, medication management, and accident prevention.

STAYING FIT. Do you exercise regularly? If so, you know firsthand that people of all ages can improve the quality of their lives through lifelong moderate physical exercise (Surgeon General, 1996). Regular moderate exercise can help prevent, delay the onset of, or ease several diseases and chronic conditions, including osteoporosis, heart disease, hypertension, atherosclerosis, stroke, diabetes mellitus, and some forms of cancer.

Despite all these benefits, fitness programs are among the most difficult to implement with adults, especially older adults. Older adults often must be convinced that they are capable of exercise and that they will benefit from it. Research results from successful exercise programs indicate that older adults must be convinced of the intrinsic benefits of exercise, and the aspects of exercise most valued by individual participants must be emphasized (Caserta & Gillett, 1998). Many older women feel physically vulnerable, and may not know the true risks and benefits of exercise; so they may need better information (Cousins, 2000). Additional keys to successful programs include proper instruction on how to exercise safely and effectively and information about access to convenient fitness programs.

Person–Environment Interactions and Optimal Aging

One of the most popular and successful exercise programs is one of the easiest: walking. Research comparing walking with more vigorous forms of exercise in middle-aged and older women shows that brisk walking can significantly reduce coronary heart disease even in women who begin exercising during midlife or old age (Manson et al., 1999). Among older adults, one major barrier to walking as exercise is the lack of safe and inexpensive places to go. Communities and businesses can help address this issue by creating walking clubs in shopping malls and other indoor places. Most enclosed malls now open their doors during the early morning for walkers, and some have used such programs to provide business opportunities for food vendors.

Psychological outcomes have also been associated with exercise. For example, McAuley and colleagues (1999) found that continuing to exercise over time can improve older adults' self-efficacy; however, this effect is not equivalent for all forms of exercise. It also appears that middle-aged men who exercise tend to do so because they recognize the effects of aging (Skultety et al., 1999). Other studies have related exercise to enhancing independence and mood and relieving mild depression (Shephard, 1997).

As a way to promote exercise in older adults, in 1998 the National Institute on Aging published *Exercise: A Guide from the National Institute on Aging,* a free manual. Based on research evidence, it is intended to help people design their own individualized exercise programs to maximize the likelihood that they will keep at them. Examples in the brochure include simple stretching, balance, and strength training exercises that people can do at home with equipment as simple as a chair and milk bottles filled with sand. Such attempts to tailor exercise programs to individual needs and preferences may result in higher success rates in getting older adults to be physically active.

EATING RIGHT. Ever since you were a child you've undoubtedly heard people telling you to eat a balanced diet. For better or worse, the same advice you heard applies across adulthood; in general the same nutritional guidelines developed for younger adults apply

Maintaining an active exercise program is one of most important elements of wellness and disease prevention.

into late life, with a few modifications (Rowe & Kahn, 1998). Because of the slowing of metabolic rates with age, older adults need fewer calories than younger adults. Older adults also are at higher risk for dehydration, so they should drink more water. And older adults need more protein.

For many older adults, though, eating right presents major problems. Some cannot afford the proper foods, others cannot get to the grocery store to buy them, and still others cannot prepare the proper meals. For these reasons, the Older Americans Act provides funds for various meals and nutritional education programs around the United States for more than 3.2 million older adults. Although many more people need nutritional assistance than the programs currently serve, these programs have made a substantial difference for many.

An important issue related to diet is obesity, a growing problem in the United States. One good way to assess your own status on this dimension is to compute your body mass index. **Body mass index (BMI)** *is a ratio of body weight and height and is related to total body fat.* Table 5.4 describes how to compute BMI. In 1995, the National Institutes of Health and the American Health Foundation issued guidelines that define healthy weight as a BMI below 25.

BMI is related to risk of serious medical conditions and mortality; the higher the BMI, the higher the risk. Figure 5.5 depicts the increased risk for several diseases and mortality associated with increased

TABLE 5.4	Determining Your Body Mass Index

The body mass index (BMI) is calculated as follows:

$$BMI = w/h^2$$

Where w = weight in kilograms (or pounds divided by 2.2)

h = height in meters (or inches divided by 39.37)

BMI. However, lowering your BMI is not necessarily a good thing. Low BMIs may indicate malnutrition, which is also related to increased mortality. Along these lines, Landi and colleagues (1999) report that low BMI is an important predictor of mortality among older community-dwelling adults and can be used as a quick determination of malnutrition.

In sum, eating the right diet is an important component in maintaining one's health. Using BMI as a benchmark can help people monitor how well they are doing. Combined with staying fit, eating right can help you stay healthy longer.

CONCEPT CHECKS

1. What are the key aspects of a life-span model for maintaining and enhancing competence?
2. What are the major elements in health promotion and disease prevention programs? What are the four types of prevention?
3. What are the key aspects of staying fit and eating right in late life?

PUTTING IT ALL TOGETHER

In this chapter, we considered how people and environments interact and focused on two contexts: nursing homes and optimal aging. We met Hank, who reminds us that adaptation to a particular environment may be the ideal situation for an older adult; changing locations may create significant disruption and produce more problems than it solves. Maria and Arnetta represent the typical nursing home resident, whose fit

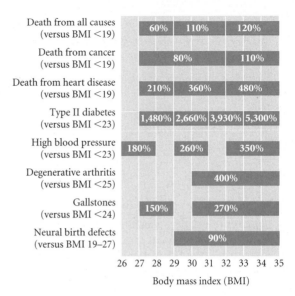

FIGURE 5.5 Increased risk of mortality and disease as related to body mass index.

Source: National Institutes of Health, 1999.

with their environment is especially important. How staff interact with them could produce dependence or promote their self-efficacy and sense of personal control. Jack represents a new generation of older adults who work to maintain their competence. Staying fit and eating a good diet can go a long way to help ensure health and prevent disease. Taken together, the topics we examined in this chapter represent a complex interaction of the four basic developmental forces that, when used to build appropriate interventions, can enhance older adults' competence.

Summary

DESCRIBING PERSON–ENVIRONMENT INTERACTIONS

- Behavior is viewed as a function of both the person and the environment.
- Person–environment interaction refers to the fact that behavior is a function of both the person and the environment.

Person–Environment Interactions and Optimal Aging

Competence and Environmental Press

- Competence is the upper limit on one's capacity to function.
- Environmental press reflects the demands placed on a person.
- Lawton and Nahemow's model establishes points of balance between the two, called adaptation levels. One implication of the model is that the less competent a person is, the more impact the environment has.

The Congruence Model

- Kahana's congruence model proposes that people search for environments that best meet their needs. Congruence between the person and the environment is especially important when either personal or environmental options are limited.
- The congruence model helps focus on individual differences and on understanding adaptation in nursing homes and other long-term care facilities.

Stress and Coping Framework

- Schooler applied Lazarus's model of stress and coping to person–environment interactions. Schooler claims that older adults' adaptation depends on their perception of environmental stress and their attempts to cope. Social systems and institutions may buffer the effects of stress.

The Loss Continuum Concept

- The loss continuum concept is based on the view of aging as a progressive series of losses that reduces one's social participation. Thus, home and neighborhood take on more importance. This approach is a guide to helping older adults maintain competence and independence.

Common Theoretical Themes and Everyday Competence

- All theories agree that the focus must be on interactions between the person and the environment. No single environment meets everyone's needs.
- Everyday competence is a person's potential ability to perform a wide range of activities considered essential for independent living.

LIVING IN LONG-TERM CARE FACILITIES

- At any given time, only about 4.5% of older adults are in long-term care facilities. Such facilities are excellent examples of the importance of person–environment fit.

Types of Long-Term Care Facilities

- Nursing homes, assisted living facilities, and adult foster homes are the main types of facilities in which older adults live.
- A distinction within nursing homes is between skilled nursing care and intermediate care.

Who Is Likely to Live in Nursing Homes?

- The typical resident is female, European American, very old, financially disadvantaged, widowed or divorced, possibly without living children, and has lived in the nursing home for more than 1 year.
- Placement in nursing homes is seen as a last resort and is often based on the lack of other alternatives, lack of other caregivers, or policies governing the level of functioning needed to remain in one's present housing. It often occurs quickly in the context of a medical crisis.

Characteristics of Nursing Homes

- Kahana's congruence model emphasizes the importance of fit between the person and the nursing home. This model discusses seven environmental and individual dimensions. Members of residents' social network are especially important.
- Moos's approach emphasizes evaluating physical, organizational, supportive, and social climate aspects.
- Langer emphasizes the importance of a sense of personal control in maintaining well-being and even staying alive. Control interventions can also help address depression.

Can a Nursing Home Be a Home?

- Residents of nursing homes can come to the conclusion that this can be home. Home is more than simply a place to live: Coming to the feeling that one is at home sometimes entails reflection on what one's previous home was like and recognizing that a nursing home can have some of the same characteristics.

Communicating with Residents

- Inappropriate speech to older adults is based on stereotypes of dependence and lack of abilities. Patronizing and infantilizing speech are examples of demeaning speech, which are rated very negatively by older adults. The communication enhancement model has been proposed as a framework for appropriate exchange. This model is based on a health promotion model that seeks opportunities for health care providers to optimize outcomes for older adults through more appropriate and effective communication.

Decision-Making Capacity and Individual Choices

- The Patient Self-Determination Act (PSDA) requires people to complete advance directives when admitted to a health care facility. A major ethical issue concerns how to communicate this information to people with cognitive impairment in nursing homes.

OPTIMAL AGING

A Framework for Maintaining and Enhancing Competence

- A life-span perspective on competence emphasizes core assumptions about aging, basic premises of successful aging, antecedents or personal characteristics, mechanisms (selection, optimization, and compensation), and outcomes (enhanced competence, quality of life, and future adaptation). This model serves as the basis for intervention programs.

Health Promotion and Disease Prevention

- The key strategies for health promotion and disease prevention programs are sound health habits; good habits of thought, including an optimistic outlook and interest in things; a social network; and sound economic habits.

- There are four basic types of prevention: primary, secondary, tertiary, and quaternary.

Lifestyle Factors

- Staying fit with regular exercise can prevent, delay the onset of, or ease several diseases and chronic conditions. Exercise programs also have psychological benefits. Fitness programs must be based on individual needs and interests to be maximally successful.

- Eating a healthful and balanced diet is an important component of a healthful lifestyle. Most nutritional needs remain the same across adulthood, although older adults need fewer calories, more water, and more protein. Body mass index is a predictor of health and mortality.

Review Questions

DESCRIBING PERSON–ENVIRONMENT INTERACTIONS

- What are person–environment interactions?

- Describe Lawton and Nahemow's theory of environmental press. In their theory, what is adaptation level?

- Describe Kahana's congruence model. In what settings is this model especially appropriate?

- Describe the application of the stress and coping model to person–environment interactions. What kinds of things buffer stress?

- Describe the loss continuum concept.

- What are the common themes expressed by the various theories of person–environment interactions?

- What are the key components of everyday competence?

LIVING IN LONG-TERM CARE FACILITIES

- How many older adults live in long-term care facilities at any given time?

- What types of facilities house older adults?

- Who is most likely to live in a nursing home? Why?

- How have the characteristics of nursing homes been studied? How do Kahana's approach, Moos's approach, and Langer's approach differ?

- How does a resident of a nursing home come to view it as a home?

- What are the characteristics of inappropriate speech aimed at older adults? What is an alternative approach?
- How does the Patient Self-Determination Act relate to residents' decision-making capacity?

OPTIMAL AGING

- What are the components of a life-span perspective model that describes how competence is maintained and enhanced?
- How are successful health promotion and disease prevention programs designed?
- What are the key considerations for older adults in staying fit and eating properly?

Integrating Concepts in Development

- What do the demographics about the aging of the population imply about the need for long-term care through the first few decades of the 21st century?
- How do the theories of person–environment interaction include the basic developmental forces?
- How do the elements of the model for maintaining and enhancing competence reflect research findings on physical and mental health?

Key Terms

adaptation level In Lawton and Nahemow's model, the point at which competence and environmental press are in balance.

adult foster care Also called adult family homes, housing options that provide an alternative to nursing homes for adults who do not need 24-hour care.

assisted living facilities Housing options for older adults that provide a supportive living arrangement for people who need assistance with personal care (such as bathing or taking medications) but who are not so impaired physically or cognitively that they need 24-hour care.

body mass index (BMI) A ratio of body weight and height that is related to total body fat.

competence In Lawton and Nahemow's model, the theoretical upper limit of a person's ability to function.

congruence model In Kahana's model, the notion that people need to find the environment in which they fit and that meets their needs the best.

environmental press In Lawton and Nahemow's model, the demands put on a person by the environment.

everyday competence A person's potential ability to perform a wide range of activities considered essential for independent living.

infantilization Also called secondary baby talk, a type of speech that involves the unwarranted use of a person's first name, terms of endearment, simplified expressions, short imperatives, an assumption that the recipient has no memory, and cajoling as a means of demanding compliance.

loss continuum A theory of person–environment interactions based on the notion that social participation declines as personal losses increase.

patronizing speech Inappropriate speech to older adults that is based on stereotypes of incompetence and dependence.

person–environment interactions The interface between people and the world in which they live that forms the basis for development, meaning that behavior is a function of both the person and the environment.

primary prevention Any intervention that prevents a disease or condition from occurring.

quaternary prevention Efforts specifically aimed at improving the functional capacities of people who have chronic conditions.

secondary prevention Program instituted early after a condition has begun (but may not yet have been diagnosed) and before significant impairments have occurred.

tertiary prevention Efforts to avoid the development of complications or secondary chronic conditions, manage the pain associated with the primary chronic condition, and sustain life through medical intervention.

Resources

READINGS

Binstock, R. H., Cluff, L. E., & Von Mering, O. V. (1996). *The future of long-term care.* Baltimore: Johns Hopkins University Press. A thorough analysis of the public policy issues concerning long-term care. Moderately difficult reading.

Dixon, R. A., & Bäckman, L. (Eds.). (1995). *Compensating for psychological deficits and declines: Managing losses and promoting gains.* Mahwah, NJ: Erlbaum. An excellent source for scholarly discussions of competence. Moderate to difficult reading.

Kidder, T. (1994). *Old friends.* Boston: Houghton Mifflin. A moving story of two older men adjusting to life in a nursing home. Easy reading.

Rowe, J. W., & Kahn, R. L. (1998). *Successful aging.* New York: Pantheon. Controversial report based on the MacArthur Foundation Study of older adults that serves as a guide to healthy aging. Easy reading.

Shephard, R. J. (1997). *Aging, physical activity, and health.* Champaign, IL: Human Kinetics. Presents a summary of research findings related to physical activity and exercise. Easy reading.

WEB SITES

The Medicare home page includes links to several important sites, including information about Medicare and selecting a nursing home. This site provides several very helpful guides in various formats, which can be found at http://www.medicare.gov/.

The National Institute on Aging and the National Aeronautics and Space Administration copublished a very useful booklet on exercise and aging. The foreword is written by John Glenn. The booklet is part of the Web of Life site maintained by NASA. The booklet can be found at http://weboflife.arc.nasa.gov/exerciseandaging/.

SEARCH ONLINE WITH
INFOTRAC COLLEGE EDITION

For more information on the topics in this chapter, explore InfoTrac College Edition, your online library. Go to http://www.infotrac-college.com/wadsworth and use the passcode that came on the card with your book. Try these search terms: nursing home, long-term care, health promotion.

ATTENTION AND PERCEPTUAL PROCESSING

© AP / Wide World Photos

A key question facing the Minnesota Vikings football team was who their starting quarterback would be in 2000. Randall Cunningham, who was a contender for the starting quarterback slot, is now old, in football standards, at the ripe old age of 37. However, given the fast reaction times needed to quarterback and the ability to selectively attend to players and position changes expeditiously under the onslaught of a defensive line, quarterbacks typically slow down around this age.

However, Cunningham argues, "It's just about going out and playing. I still have the same abilities. I work hard." Indeed, he had one of his best seasons in 1998, elected to his fourth Pro Bowl game and named All-Pro by the Associated Press, *Sports Illustrated,* and more. And for the 2000 season, he is the backup quarterback for the Dallas Cowboys. Of particular interest in this chapter is how one determines when attentional capacity declines to a point at which a football quarterback such as Cunningham is no longer effective in processing in a fast and expeditious manner the deluge of information encountered in quarterbacking a football game.

These are the kinds of questions we face in this chapter. This chapter begins a three-chapter sequence on cognition. In general, we examine how people process information from the world around them and make sense out of it. Although this material can be approached in several different ways, we adopt the one that builds upward from basic processes, such as attention, through more complex ones, such as memory, to higher-order thought. This approach should be viewed in context, though. Cognition is highly dynamic; lower-order processes such as attention help create higher-order thought, and higher-order thought helps determine where we focus our lower-order processes. We need to notice things to build our knowledge, but what we know shapes what we notice.

In this chapter, we explore how people pay attention to things and what constitutes paying attention. We consider researchers' studies of how fast people process information and react to events, such as a car pulling into their lane on the highway. We will see how attention and other aspects of information processing are extremely important in understanding how accidents occur. Finally, we consider some basic aspects of language processing. The remaining two chapters in the cognitive section cover many aspects of memory (Chapter 7) and intelligence (Chapter 8). Together, these three chapters provide a broad view of cognition.

Research on how people process, store, and remember information, as well as how they think, tends to involve highly technical research methods and concepts. This means that we must consider research studies in more detail to understand and appreciate the findings. Another problem is that although we begin our consideration of cognition with a prominent theoretical model, much of the research in the field makes only indirect contact with it. That is, much research on cognition and aging is conducted without an explicit connection to a specific theoretical framework. Nevertheless, a great deal of evidence has been amassed, some of it apparently contradictory but all of it providing insight into how cognition works. Once all the pieces have been considered, we will have a fairly detailed picture of how adults acquire, process, remember, and think.

Throughout this chapter, we consider results from experiments in which people made responses on computers. Although there is much evidence of age differences in some of the ways young and older adults process information, part of the difference may be caused by cohort effects. Specifically, older adults in general are much less used to working on computers than are younger adults, making the task unfamiliar to older adults. Consequently, they may not perform at their best. Whether this experiential difference accounts for a large or small amount of the age differences researchers have uncovered remains to be seen; however, because the research is cross-sectional, meaning that age and cohort effects are confounded, this explanation remains a possibility.

THE INFORMATION-PROCESSING MODEL

LEARNING OBJECTIVES

- What are the primary aspects of the information-processing model?
- What evidence exists for age differences in sensory memory?

*B*randon strolled into a Lamborghini dealership and convinced the salesperson to let him take a Countach for a spin around the block. When he climbed behind the wheel of the most expensive sports car, his excitement almost got the better of him. But as he started it up and eased into first gear, he was filled with terror. He suddenly realized that he must pay complete attention to what he was doing. After all, he wouldn't want to have an accident. Now he was faced with the need to filter out everything: people's conversations, the radio, and the sound of the wind whipping through his hair.

How can Brandon filter everything out? More importantly, what abilities can he use to avoid an accident? If something happened on the road, how quickly could he respond? Would these abilities be any different in a younger adult than in an older adult? And, by the way, did you know that a Lamborghini Countach was a sports car before you read this? If so, how did you access this knowledge? If not, how did you incorporate this new knowledge?

How do we learn, remember, and think about things? Psychologists do not know for sure. About the best they can do is create models or analogues of how they believe our cognitive processes work. In this section, we consider the most popular model: the information-processing model.

Overview of the Model

The information-processing model uses a computer metaphor to explain how people process stimuli. Just as with a computer, information enters the system (people's brains) and is transformed, coded, and stored in various ways. Information enters storage temporarily, as in a computer's buffer, until it is stored more permanently, as on a computer disk. At a later time, information can be retrieved in response to some cue, such as a command to retrieve a file. Let's see how this works more formally.

The **information-processing approach** *is based on three assumptions (Neisser, 1976): People are active participants in the process, both quantitative (how much information is remembered) and qualitative (what kinds of information are remembered) aspects of performance can be examined, and information is processed through a series of hypothetical stages, or stores.* First, incoming information is transformed based on such things as what a person already knows about it. The more one knows, the more easily the information is incorporated. Second, researchers look for age differences in how much information is processed and what types of information are remembered best under various conditions. Finally, researchers in adult development and aging focus on several specific aspects of information processing: early aspects, which include a very brief sensory memory; attention; speed of processing; a limited-capacity primary memory (Poon, 1985); active processing of information in working memory (Hultsch & Dixon, 1990); a somewhat longer-term but limited-capacity secondary memory; and a more permanent and very large-capacity long-term memory (Poon, 1985).

The information-processing model poses three fundamental questions for adult development and aging: Is there evidence of age differences in the storage aspects of information processing (e.g., early stages of processing, secondary memory, long-term memory)? What evidence is there for age differences in the process aspects of information processing (e.g., attention)? Can the age differences in the storage aspects be explained through process aspects?

It will take us two chapters to answer these questions. In this chapter, we focus on early aspects of processing, on attention, and on perceptual speed and language processing. In Chapter 7, we consider working memory, secondary memory, and long-term memory and address the reasons for age differences later in the system. By the end of these chapters, we will have a complete picture of how we acquire, process, store, and remember the information in these chapters. Before we begin, we can see that information processing incorporates the four basic forces in development (see Forces in Action feature).

Sensory Memory

All memories start as sensory stimuli: a song heard, a person seen, a hand felt. We need to experience these things for only a small fraction of a second to process the information. *This ability results from the earliest step in information processing:* **sensory memory,** *where new, incoming information is first registered.* Sensory memory takes in very large amounts of information very rapidly. It does not appear to have the limits that other processes do when attentional focus is applied. It is more like a very brief and almost identical representation of the stimuli that exist in the observable environment. The representation exists in your mind in the absence of the stimuli. However, unless we pay attention to this information very quickly, the representation is lost. For example, try drawing either side of a U.S. penny in detail. (Those who are not from the United States can try drawing a common coin in their own country.) Most of us find this task difficult although we see the coins every day. Much detailed information about pennies has passed through our sensory memory repeatedly, but because we failed to pay attention it was never processed to a longer lasting store. It should be noted that age differences in sensory memory are not common. In fact, older adults can efficiently retrieve information briefly represented in sensory memory (Poon & Fozard, 1980; Smith, 1975). However, when attentional processes are applied to sensory memory, age differences begin to appear.

In Chapter 1, we saw that one of the four types of developmental forces was psychological forces, including sensory and perceptual functioning, motor functioning, and intellectual functioning. The information-processing model provides a fuller description of these forces and specifies the ways in which they operate. The information-processing model emphasizes the complexity of human thinking and the need to be aware of a vast array of influences on performance. We must place all these influences into larger contexts; biological forces such as changes in the brain, for example, could dramatically alter the effects of any particular influence. Life-cycle factors, such as why adults of different ages interpret instances of forgetting differently, may also influence how well people remember.

Among other important considerations for information processing are normative and disease-related biological, physiological, and lifestyle issues. For example, underlying neural changes, cardiovascular disease, Alzheimer's disease, and severe depression can all affect information-processing abilities as we age. We must keep these in mind as we examine the evidence for age differences in information processing. Although most of the research we consider was conducted on apparently healthy people, our knowledge of the relation between normative changes in the brain and performance on information-processing tasks is limited.

Attentional Processes

As McDowd and Shaw (2000) maintain in a recent review, attention and perceptual processing are best conceived from a functional perspective. Attention, for example, is composed of separable dimensions serving different functions. They note that the complex tasks we engage in when processing information usually use more than one attentional function. For example, Brandon must selectively attend to or focus on the road and its obstacles while filtering out distracting information.

In addition, attentional processes are influenced by the capacity to direct and sustain attention and the speed with which information is processed. As we will see, such capacities are affected by age-related limitations that permit most cognitive processes to be performed (McDowd & Shaw, 2000). Finally, there are consequences of age-related decline in attentional and perceptual capacities for other cognitive functions such as processing language and processing information during driving. We explore these consequences later in the chapter.

CONCEPT CHECKS

1. What three assumptions underlie the information-processing approach?
2. What is the pattern of age differences in sensory memory?

ATTENTION

LEARNING OBJECTIVES

- How is selective attention tested? What age differences are found?
- What is divided attention? Under what conditions are age differences observed?
- How is sustained attention assessed? When are age differences found?
- What are automatic processes? In what situations are age differences present?
- What cognitive resources underlie attentional processes?

*C*hloe was gazing out the window during her history class. The teacher sternly told her to pay attention. As the teacher came to the question-and-answer period of class, she immediately called on Chloe. Of course, Chloe did not know the answer. "I expect you to pay better attention in class!" was the teacher's next remark.

All of us probably have had similar experiences. Someone asks us a question and we continue to stare off into space. We are driving along a long, boring stretch of interstate highway and suddenly realize that we have gone 20 miles with no awareness of anything we saw along the way. The examples are quite varied but the outcome is the same: Somehow we come to realize that a lot of information was available to us that we never processed. In short, we simply did not pay attention.

These everyday experiences are so vivid to us that we would expect psychologists to have a clear handle on what attention is. After all, it is one of the most important ways in which information continues to get processed beyond the sensory memory stage. James's (1890) view that we all know what attention is reflects this belief. It turns out that vivid experiences can be misleading. Attention is actually difficult to pin down. However, researchers have described three interdependent aspects of it (McDowd & Shaw, 2000): selective attention, divided attention, and sustained attention.

Selective attention *is the way in which we choose the information we will process further.* As the term implies, selectivity in attention means that our ability to process information is limited. As we saw earlier during Brandon's spin in the Lamborghini, a great deal of information bombards sensory memory: telephone poles zipping past, other cars on the highway, dashboard information, passengers' conversations, and scenery outside the car. However, this information remains there for only a very brief time. The next stop, working memory, can handle only a small amount of information at a time (see Chapter 7). This creates a problem: How can we move information from a large-capacity store to a very small-capacity store? This situation is similar to the problem created when a large-capacity freeway (say, eight lanes in one direction) must use a small-capacity tunnel (two lanes in one direction). The potential traffic jam could be enormous, with many drivers simply opting to exit the freeway. The problem in the information-processing system is similar: We are trying to move a great deal of information from sensory memory to working memory. Much of it simply exits the system and is lost before it can be passed along.

Several hypotheses have been proposed to explain where and how the bottleneck in information flow occurs. All agree that somehow information is selected out for further processing and that this selection is part of attention. Although no one knows for sure how selectivity happens, several possibilities have been suggested. For example, some information is simply processed automatically, whereas other in-

Dividing one's attention between driving and talking on the phone may be done better by young adults, but may also not be the safest thing to do.

formation takes effort. Also, we are more likely to process novel or unexpected information than information we have encountered many times before.

Divided attention *is the degree to which information competes for our attention at any given time.* Craik (1977) wrote that one of the clearest findings in cognitive aging research is that older adults are more penalized when they must divide their attention between sources of information and responding. This type of research looks at how well people perform multiple tasks simultaneously. For example, paying attention to a lecture in class while simultaneously taking notes requires us to monitor two things (lecture content and what we are writing) simultaneously.

Vigilance *or* **sustained attention** *is the ability to maintain attention or focus in performing a task over a long period of time.* In general, these tasks involve monitoring a display (such as a radar screen) for the appearance of targets (such as airplane blips). Fewer studies of age differences in sustained attention have been conducted than for selectivity or divided attention.

Finally, when studying attentional capacity as a pool of resources available to support information-processing activity, we must consider automatic and effortful processing. In other words, a key assumption to information processing is that some processing occurs automatically, whereas other processing requires effort. **Automatic processing** *places minimal demands on attentional capacity.* Some automatic processes appear to be "prewired" in the sense that they use no attentional capacity and do not benefit from practice; others are learned through experience and practice (Smith & Earles, 1996). In either case, information that is processed automatically gets into the system largely without our knowledge. For example, those who have been driving a car for many years usually are unaware of how hard they are pressing the accelerator pedal to make the car go forward from a stop.

In contrast, **effortful processing** *uses all available attentional capacity.* Most of the tasks involving deliberate memory, such as learning the words on a list, use effortful processing. In most such cases, we are aware of what we are doing. For example, when we are first learning how to drive a car with a clutch, we are very aware of the information we are processing (e.g., how much to let up on the clutch and how hard to press the accelerator pedal). Researchers who study aging and cognition investigate both automatic processing and effortful processing and often look at differences in performance between the two categories.

Our examination of age differences in selective attention, divided attention, and sustained attention focuses on visual information processing for several reasons (McDowd & Shaw, 2000; Plude & Doussard-Roosevelt, 1990). First, most of the research has examined visual processing. Second, the potential loss of vision is of great concern to older adults. Third, age differences in visual processing are believed to generalize to other sensory modalities. Let's see what the findings indicate.

Selective Attention

As we have seen, a small proportion of information in sensory memory is selected for further processing. In this section we consider evidence of age differences in selective attention by examining research on visual search, attention switching, and filtering out irrelevant information. Age-related decrements are consistently found in visual search, but spatial cuing sometimes eliminates age differences (Plude & Doussard-Roosevelt, 1990). Age differences in the ability to shift attention appear to depend on the sensory modality being tested (McDowd & Birren, 1990).

How do researchers studying aging and cognition investigate selective attention? Most do so by creating tasks in which multiple sources of information are available for processing but only a subset of the information is relevant to the primary task. The rest of the information is considered distractors. Then performance on a task without distractors is compared with performance in the presence of distractors. If people demonstrate a decrease in speed or accuracy in the presence of distractors, it is suggested that there is difficulty in filtering out the distractors.

For example, researchers have found that older adults' reading times are slowed down by the presence of distracting information (Connelly et al., 1991; Earles et al., 1997). However, when the target and distractors occupy different and predictable locations, the age differences are substantially smaller (Carlson et al., 1995). In other words, advance knowledge about the target location reduces the negative impact of distractors for older adults.

VISUAL SEARCH. Imagine yourself sitting at a computer terminal. You are told to push a key as fast as you can every time you see a red *X*, the target stimulus. "So far, so good," you say. To make things difficult, sometimes you see other letters or colors (green *X*s, green *O*s, and red *O*s): the nontarget stimuli or distractors. The problem is that you have no idea where in the display the target will appear, so you must search for it among the nontargets.

This procedure is typical of visual search tasks (Humphrey & Kramer, 1997; Plude & Doussard-Roosevelt, 1989). Visual search tasks always involve responding to a specific stimulus, the target, and ignoring everything else, the nontargets. Such tasks measure selective attention because the main data involve nontarget interference effects (i.e., the degree to which the nontargets interfere with the ability to respond only to targets). Usually, nontarget interference effects are a matter of display size (i.e., how many nontargets are presented with the target). For example, it would be harder to find 1 red *X* among 50 red *O*s than among 5 red *O*s.

Performance or attentional filtering on visual search tasks is measured in terms of *how quickly people respond, called* **reaction time,** or the number and kinds of errors they make (accuracy). The ability to use attentional processes to filter nontargets on visual search tasks with small display sizes is comparable for young and older adults (Allen et al., 1994). However, older adults are slower and more prone to errors than young adults when the amounts of distractor information (e.g., nontargets) are increased and when the location of the target presented in the display is unpredictable (Allen et al., 1992; Kotary & Hoyer, 1995; Madden & Plude, 1993).

Let's make things a bit easier. Imagine sitting at the same computer terminal as before. You are now told to watch for an asterisk that will show up somewhere on the screen; shortly after it appears, the target or a nontarget stimulus will be displayed in exactly the same spot.

This procedure, in which the location of a future stimulus is shown on a screen, is known as **spatial cuing.** The idea behind using spatial cuing is to rule out certain other explanations for age differences in visual search tasks. For example, older adults may decline in their ability to find the location of a target embedded among many nontargets. If this is true, telling them ahead of time where it will appear solves this problem. Any remaining age differences would result from factors other than the person's ability to find the target.

When the spatial cue signals that a target will appear in that location, age differences disappear (Plude & Doussard-Roosevelt, 1990). As the actual locations of the targets move away from the locations of the cues, age differences reappear (Madden, 1990). In other words, when people know where to look, older and younger adults are equally able to identify targets. However, there are important qualifications to the advantages of spatial cuing. Age differences are eliminated only when the spatial cue provides unambiguous information about the target's subsequent position. When the cue is ambiguous (e.g., several as-

terisks appear and only one provides accurate information), age differences remain. This may suggest that other processes, such as generalized cognitive slowing (discussed later in this chapter), are also important for understanding age decrements in visual search. Additionally, experience and practice may play a role in eliminating age differences.

ATTENTION SWITCHING. Once again, you are back at your computer terminal. This time, however, you are asked to do two different things. Some of the time you are told to focus your attention on the center character in a five-character string, which is the target. Let's call this the narrow attention condition. At other times, you are told to widen your attention to include all five characters. In this case, the target is one of the peripheral characters. Let's call this the broad attention condition. Thus, you must switch your attention from one character to five characters. A number of researchers use this type of task to demonstrate that under some circumstances older and young adults focus and switch their attentional focus similarly (Hartley & McKenzie, 1991; Madden & Gottlob, 1997).

Interestingly, research on adults' ability to switch attention between different sensory modalities reveals age differences in the speed in which adults switch attention from an auditory to a visual task (Hawkins et al., 1992). Several factors may account for these discrepancies, such as possible differences in the rates of change in vision and hearing or different types of changes in visual and auditory sensory memory.

Hawkins et al. (1992) examined the possibility that increased aerobic fitness might improve older adults' performance on the attention-switching task. They compared a group of older adults who participated in an aquatic exercise program of three weekly exercise sessions across 10 weeks with an age-matched group that did not participate in the exercise activities. They found that the exercise group's performance in the switching task improved significantly after the exercise program. The comparison group's performance did not change. In this case, the improved cerebrovascular sufficiency may have led to

Recent research suggests that the more adults exercise and increase their aerobic fitness, the better they are able to focus and sustain attention.

the improvement in attentional capacity in the exercise group (Hawkins et al., 1992). At this point, more research investigating the importance of exercise on cognitive functioning is needed.

SELECTIVE ATTENTION AND IRRELEVANT INFORMATION. Thus far we have reached two major conclusions. Age decrements in selectivity appear to be greatest when tasks are complex (e.g., greater display size) and little information is available to assist performance. With advance information (such as spatial cuing), age differences are lessened. Why?

One popular hypothesis is that older adults have fewer **processing resources,** *or available attention,* be-

cause of greater difficulty inhibiting the processing of irrelevant information (Hasher & Zacks, 1988). That is, older adults have more task-irrelevant thoughts during processing and have trouble keeping them out of their minds. This difference could explain why older people tend to be less accurate at finding targets: They have to process information about nontargets as well.

The inhibition idea has much support (Kane et al., 1994). For example, McDowd and colleagues (1991) showed that when relevant and irrelevant information are both presented in the same modality (e.g., visually), older adults distribute their attention more equally between the two types of information than younger adults. However, when relevant information was presented in one modality (e.g., visually) and irrelevant information in another (e.g., aurally), older and younger adults both showed similar patterns of attention allocation. Thus, older adults apparently have more trouble selectively attending to relevant information when the irrelevant information is presented in the same modality. One practical implication of this concerns driving, where both relevant and irrelevant information are presented visually. Given these research findings, we would expect that older adults would have more difficulty in this situation, which could result in accidents. We check our prediction a bit later in this chapter.

Additional research shows that the problem with inhibition is not universal across all aspects of stimuli (Connelly & Hasher, 1993). Adults were presented with letter pairs. They were asked to name the target letter, which always appeared in red, and ignore the distractor letter, which always appeared in green. The letter pairs were also presented in one of four locations. Young adults demonstrated appropriate inhibition because their response time was longer when a previous target in red (e.g., the letter *K*) became a distractor in green on a subsequent trial. Older adults did not. Such age-related inhibitory deficits may be limited to an item's identity. When inhibition was assessed by examining location (i.e., the target stimulus appeared in the same location as the distractor was on an earlier trial), there were no age differences. Moreover, attempts to get older adults to inhibit processing of key aspects of a distractor by increasing the time the target and distractor are displayed do not appear to work (Kane et al., 1994). Such data support Hasher and Zacks's (1988) inhibition hypothesis but mean that inhibitory deficits probably are limited to specific aspects of stimuli.

However, it is important to note that much research is needed to validate age-related deficits in inhibitory processing. A number of studies evaluating the inhibitory deficit hypothesis had mixed results (Burke, 1997; McDowd, 1997). For example, no age differences were found in mind wandering (Einstein & McDaniel, 1997), in inhibition in an auditory information task (Rouleau & Belleville, 1996), and in speech recognition (Stine & Wingfield, 1994).

Divided Attention

Given that some evidence exists for age differences in what information is processed, do age differences also exist in how much information is processed? This question is answered by studying **attentional capacity,** *the amount of information that can be processed at a time.* This is usually done by testing divided attention, which is the ability to successfully perform more than one task at the same time.

Life is full of situations in which we need to do at least two things at once. Two common examples are listening to a lecture while writing in a notebook and driving a car while conversing with a passenger. Each of these situations entails monitoring what is going on in at least two different domains. How well we are able to perform these multiple tasks simultaneously depends on how much attentional capacity we have available for each. To the extent that any one task uses a great deal of our capacity, our ability to do other things may be impaired.

Older adults report that dividing attention between most combinations of activities becomes more difficult with increasing age, and, compared with young adults, they rate most combinations of activities as more difficult (Tun & Wingfield, 1995). However, ratings of one's ability to perform various types of activities vary a great deal across tasks. Keeping track of novel information in combinations of tasks

is perceived as more difficult than performing routine tasks or speech processing. These findings reflect the importance of self-evaluations of how well people think they can (or did) perform, which may have important implications for performance.

These self-reports about the difficulty of divided-attention activities are consistent with other findings that old adults perform divided-attention tasks more poorly than young adults do (McDowd & Shaw, 2000). Experimental research on divided attention is a good example of how conclusions about age differences can change in the face of new evidence. At one time, researchers were convinced that age-related decrements in divided attention were inevitable (Craik, 1977). But Somberg and Salthouse's research in 1982 changed all that. By equalizing the amount of attention allocated to two tasks, Somberg and Salthouse were able to eliminate age differences on the divided-attention task. Other researchers corroborated Somberg and Salthouse's findings (e.g., Wickens et al., 1987). Researchers had to go back to the lab to try to account for these new data.

Subsequent studies clarified things. It turns out that age differences are found on some divided-attention tasks and not others. The explanation involves task complexity and practice. When the divided-attention tasks are easy, age differences usually are absent. However, when the tasks become more complicated, we observe age differences (Kramer & Larish, 1996; Salthouse et al., 1995). In other words, adults of all ages can perform multiple easy tasks simultaneously, but older adults do not do as well as young adults when they must perform multiple difficult tasks at the same time.

Age differences on divided-attention tasks can also be minimized if older adults are given extensive practice in performing the tasks and reducing the demands on attention (Kramer et al., 1995; Tsang & Shaner, 1998). For example, when very large numbers of practice trials (from roughly 500 to more than 11,000) are provided, age differences may disappear; with fewer practice trials (less than 300), age differences often are found (Kramer et al., 1995, in press; Rogers et al., 1994). These results imply that older adults may be able to learn through experience how to divide their attention effectively between tasks. Check out this idea by completing the Discovering Development feature.

In sum, divided-attention ability per se does not change with age. Rather, task complexity is a primary determinant of age-related decrements; older adults are at a disadvantage when they must perform two or more complex tasks simultaneously (McDowd & Shaw, 2000; Plude & Doussard-Roosevelt, 1990). Moreover, age differences on divided-attention tasks may actually reflect the fact that each task involves different component processes that are separately affected by aging (Hartley, 1992; Salthouse et al., 1995).

Sustained Attention

Did you ever think about the job air traffic controllers have? They must sit in front of radar screens for hours keeping track of blips on the screen. Each blip represents an airplane, many of which have hundreds of people aboard. Air traffic controllers must sustain high levels of attention over long periods of time because even the slightest error could have disastrous consequences.

Watching a radar screen is an excellent example of vigilance: the ability to sustain attention on a task for long periods of time. Researchers interested in studying age differences in vigilance use tasks very much like those performed by air traffic controllers. Investigators obtain two different measures of sustained attention: the number of targets correctly detected (vigilance performance) and the decrease in detection accuracy over time (vigilance decrement).

Compared with work on other aspects of attention, little research has focused on vigilance. What little there is suggests age-related decrements in vigilance performance but not in vigilance decrement (Bunce et al., 1996; Giambra, 1993; McDowd & Shaw, 2000). This means that although older adults are not as accurate as younger adults in detecting targets, performance deteriorates at the same rate in both age groups.

What influences age differences in detection? One possible source of decrements in vigilance performance is that fitness level may affect sustained atten-

tion, particularly for older adults. In several studies Bunce and colleagues (1993, 1996) demonstrated that aerobic fitness level (measured by body mass, body fat, and lung function) was positively related to sustained attention in older adults but not young adults. Bunce and colleagues suggest that there may be an age-related vulnerability to inhibitory failures that affect concentration and sustained attention in less fit people.

A second way of identifying sources of age differences in vigilance is by manipulating the predictability of how often or where a target will occur. In other words, expectations of how often and when a target will appear and the ability to adapt to these expectations may account for age differences in vigilance. First let's consider manipulation frequency of targets in a vigilance study involving monitoring a computer screen. The target is programmed to appear on the screen 10% of the time; the other 90% of the stimuli that appear are nontargets. Before beginning, participants are told one of two things: the true probability of a target appearing (10%) or an incorrect probability (50%). If a similar situation were presented to older and younger adults, would age differences emerge? Although vigilance decrements were greater for the incorrect probability condition, older and younger adults were affected equally. Thus, both groups were able to adapt their performance to reflect how often they expected to see a target. However, this is true only up to a point. At very high rates of target presentations in tasks that last a long time, older adults' performance is poorer than younger adults' performance (Mouloua & Parasuraman, 1995; Parasuraman & Giambra, 1991).

Another way to manipulate predictability is to vary the information given to people about where the target is likely to appear on the screen and to vary the context in which the target is presented. Mouloua and Parasuraman (1995) did this by creating three uncertainty conditions (low, medium, and high) in which the target was a lowercase letter: presenting letters one at a time in the center of the screen, presenting a lowercase letter in the middle of a string of uppercase letters in the middle of the screen, and presenting a lowercase letter in a string of uppercase

At the beginning of this section we encountered several examples of divided-attention tasks. You are very familiar with one of them: writing notes while listening to a lecture. An interesting developmental question is whether the ability to take good notes differs with age. One way to find out informally is to compare the notes taken in the same class by young adult and older adult students. If there are no older adults in your class, there may be in other courses. Ask them whether you can compare their notes with those of someone much younger. What predictions would you make based on the research evidence you have read thus far? What role would practice play in these differences? Whose notes are better? Why do you think this is?

letters randomly in one of the four corners of the screen. The researchers found no age differences for the low uncertainty condition (when single letters were presented at the center of the screen), but younger adults had significantly higher hit rates than did the older adults in both of the other conditions.

Taken together, these results show a clear pattern. As long as vigilance tasks involve a low presentation rate of targets and the spatial location of targets is predictable, age differences typically are absent. However, when the presentation rate is increased or the spatial predictability is decreased, older adults' performance begins to decline relative to younger adults' performance.

Attentional Resources

During our discussion of attention, a number of sources were identified that could account for age differences in attentional functioning. One of the major explanatory factors for age differences is a limited supply of attentional resources. In particular, age-related performance differences in situations that demand attention, such as divided attention or sustained attention, may reflect an age-related reduction in processing resources. However, as we noted in Chapter 1, because these studies are based on cross-sectional data, we must be careful in interpreting findings as demonstrating age-related change. We now examine this explanatory construct in more detail.

THE PROCESSING RESOURCES HYPOTHESIS. Even though task complexity and high levels of practice can reveal or minimize age differences in divided-attention and sustained-attention tasks, an important question remains: Why do older adults have more problems performing more difficult tasks, or tasks on which they have little practice, simultaneously? Many researchers believe that with increasing age comes a decline in the amount of available processing resources, the amount of attention one has to apply to a particular situation. The idea of declining processing resources was appealing because it could account for poorer performance on attention tasks (Plude & Hoyer, 1985) and on a host of others (Salthouse, 1991).

On the surface the notion of age-related decrements in processing resources offers a concise explanation of a wide range of age-related performance differences. But there is a nagging problem about the processing resource construct: It has never been defined clearly (McDowd & Shaw, 2000; Neumann, 1996; Salthouse, 1991). In a carefully designed series of investigations, Salthouse and colleagues (Salthouse, 1988; Salthouse et al., 1988) set out to provide an empirical test of the processing resource explanation of age-related performance differences. Their results demonstrate that complete reliance on this idea probably is a mistake. Salthouse was able to show that although a processing resource difference is a parsimonious explanation, the strong version of the resource decline idea that marks much current research has little empirical support. In other words, something besides a decline in processing resources is responsible for performance decrements with age.

Identifying a physiological index of resources could provide one possible answer. For example, researchers have identified neural efficiency as a characteristic of the central nervous system that could correspond to attentional resources (Stankov & Dunn, 1993) or the amplitude of brain activity. Lorist et al. (1995) demonstrated that caffeine seemed to improve selective attention in both young and older adults by changing the availability of energy resources. However, although psychophysiological indices of resources are enticing explanations, the underlying mechanisms remain to be identified.

AUTOMATIC PROCESSES. Another way to study processing resources involves investigating how responses become automatic. Because attention tasks (sustained attention in particular) tend to be highly repetitive (i.e., people make the same kinds of responses over and over, such as driving a car with a clutch every day for years), people's performance on them tends to improve for a while and then plateau. If this plateau is accompanied by a high rate of accuracy that is maintained over time, then the response is considered to have become automatic. In general, **automatic processes** *are those that are fast, reliable, and insensitive to increased cognitive demands* (e.g., performing other tasks).

An interesting developmental question is whether age differences exist in the rates at which responses on vigilance tasks become automatic. This is often investigated by manipulating characteristics of new tasks and observing whether older and younger adults are equally adept at achieving a high level of performance with a great deal of practice. Most of these studies involve search tasks with two conditions (e.g., Rogers et al., 1994). In the consistent mapping (CM) practice condition, people are told to press one key if a target letter that is drawn from one set of letters appears and another key when the letters from a separate, nonoverlapping distractor set appear. A trial consists of a letter, the target, appearing on a screen followed by another display that either has or does not have the target in it. For example, the screen may show the target letter "N" followed by the display "B D F N P T." With practice, people learn which letters make up the target set and which letters make up the distractor set, so eventually the search becomes automatic. In the varied mapping (VM) practice condition, target and

distractor letters are chosen from the same set, meaning that people cannot learn to ignore any of the letters, as they eventually do for the distractor letters in the CM practice condition. Thus, the VM practice condition is more difficult than the CM practice condition, and only the CM practice condition results in the development of automatic processing.

The search tasks used to study automatic processing can involve memory search or visual search. Memory search entails the presentation of a target in the center of a screen, followed by a letter at the center surrounded by a set of placeholders, which are squares the same size as letters. The person must determine whether the letter in the second screen was the target letter. In visual search, a target letter is presented followed by a test consisting of a string of letters that may contain the target letter; the person must search the string to see whether the target is among the distractors.

Using these search paradigms, numerous investigators have examined the development of automatic processes in older and younger adults. The general conclusion from these studies is that whether older adults develop automatic processing depends on two major factors (Rogers et al., 1994). First, a sufficient amount of practice must be provided. This practice sometimes consists of thousands of trials of consistent mapping (CM) over several sessions. Second, the type of search task matters. Automatic processing in older adults occurs with extensive CM practice on memory search tasks but not on visual search tasks (Fisk, Cooper, Hertzog, Anderson-Garlach, & Lee, 1995; Fisk & Rogers, 1991). However, if the memory search task is difficult, age differences may emerge (Strayer & Kramer, 1994).

Why do these task differences occur? How do people learn automatic processing? One possibility is that *the processing of a specific and well-trained stimulus, such as a target letter, can automatically capture attention, making it an* **automatic attention response.** In this case, the process attracts attention even though attention was not required initially; an everyday example of this is when people respond to hearing their name being called by looking up even though they were engaged in another activity. In the context of a divided-attention paradigm, Rogers and colleagues (1994) found that older adults do not develop an automatic attention response in visual search situations; instead, older adults searched each display in looking for a target instead of responding only when a target was present.

Closer examination of how processes become automatic reveals a second set of possibilities. By varying the type of CM task, Fisk, Cooper, Hertzog, and Anderson-Garlach (1995) discovered that it is the components of tasks, not the tasks themselves, that become automatic. For a task to appear automatic, all its component processes must be automatic. Whether this happens depends on age and the learning processes involved. Thus, age and task differences may be the result of differences in the ease with which task components become automatic in people of different ages.

Research on age-related differences in attention point to two main conclusions. First, age differences are greatest when older adults have to perform complex tasks, especially more than one at a time. Second, these decrements appear to be localized where the various pieces of information picked up from a visual display are put together to figure out what the display is.

However, these conclusions do not answer an intriguing question: Why do these age-related decrements occur? At present, the leading possibility is generalized cognitive slowing. It is to this possibility that we now turn.

CONCEPT CHECKS

1. Under what conditions do age differences disappear in selective attention tasks?
2. What are processing resources?
3. What are the effects of manipulating predictability in vigilance tasks?
4. What are automatic processes?

SPEED OF PROCESSING

LEARNING OBJECTIVES

- How is reaction time measured?
- What is processing speed? What age differences are observed in processing speed?
- Why do people slow with age?
- How can age-related slowing be moderated?
- What do age differences in reaction time mean?

*E*ugene was driving home from a friend's house and all seemed to be going well. Suddenly, a car pulled out of a driveway right into his path. He had to hit the brakes as fast as he could. Fortunately, he was able to quickly move his foot from the accelerator to the brakes and avoid the oncoming car.

This situation is a real-life example of psychomotor speed: making a quick motor movement in response to information that has been processed. In this case, the motor movement is switching Eugene's foot from one pedal to another, and the information is the visual stimulus of a car in Eugene's path.

To what extent are there age differences in cognitive slowing? One of the most replicated findings in the literature is that as people age their response time in cognitive tasks slows down (Ratcliff et al., 2000; Salthouse, 1996). In fact, the slowing-with-age phenomenon is so well documented that many gerontologists accept it as the only universal behavioral change yet discovered. In this section we examine some of the evidence for slowing of cognitive processes, or perceptual speed.

Speed of processing *reflects the outcomes of sensory memory and attention.* In fact, we have already encountered some of the ways in which speed is measured, such as reaction time tasks, as indices of sensory memory functioning. Thus, speed of processing can be viewed as a reflection of how quickly and efficiently these early steps in information processing are completed.

Basic Psychomotor Speed: Reaction Time Tasks

We have already encountered several situations in which rapid responding is essential. How is speed measured in a laboratory? Researchers use three types of reaction time tasks to study rapid responses to events: simple reaction time tasks, choice reaction time tasks, and complex reaction time tasks. In each task, the key measurement is the amount of time it takes to respond under the appropriate conditions. We will consider each briefly.

Simple reaction time *involves responding to one stimulus, such as pressing a button as fast as possible every time a light comes on.* Consistent age differences in overall simple reaction time have been reported (Salthouse, 1991). Interestingly, the most noticeable difference between young and old is in the time needed to decide to push the button rather than the motoric time needed to push the button itself.

Tasks involving choice reaction time *offer more than one stimulus and require a response to each in a different way.* An example would be presenting a person with two lights, one red and one blue. That person is to press the left button every time the red light comes on and the right button when the blue light comes on. To perform well on such tasks the person must identify correctly the stimulus, decide which response goes with it, and make the response; moreover, he or she must do all of this as quickly as possible (Fozard, 1981). Researchers typically find that older adults are significantly slower on choice reaction tasks than younger adults (Plude et al., 1996; Salthouse, 1991).

The most difficult reaction time task involves complex reaction time, *which entails making many decisions about when and how to respond.* A good example of a complex reaction time task is driving a car: The number of stimuli is extremely large, and the range of possible responses is huge. For instance, suppose you are driving along the freeway when the car next to you begins to swerve into your lane right in front of you. Do you hit the brakes? (Or is there someone right behind you?) Swerve around it? (Or is there no place to go?) Blow your horn? (The other driver may not hear you.) Hit the car? Researchers try to recreate these complex situations in the laboratory using computer tasks. When they do, the results are very consistent: Older adults become increasingly disadvantaged as situations demanding rapid response become more complex (McDowd & Shaw, 2000).

Finally, age changes in slowing must be demonstrated using longitudinal designs (see Chapter 1). In fact, data from the Baltimore Longitudinal Study of Aging indicate that the degree to which reaction time changes with age depends on gender and the type of task (Fozard et al., 1994). In fact, evidence suggests that people with higher abilities may actually decline

in reaction time more slowly than others with less initial ability (Schaie, 1996). Overall, reaction time declines significantly when examined within the same participants over time. However, men are consistently faster than women across the adult life span, a difference that is not explained by such demographic characteristics as education or health. Although practice may be a factor, more research is needed to provide an answer.

Processing Speed

Because there is much evidence that we slow down as we grow older, an important question to ask is how this affects the cognitive processing ability of older adults. Mental processing speed, as measured by reaction time, is sensitive to aging and may be one of the most important contributors to age-related decline in memory and attention (Bashore et al., 1997; Kail & Salthouse, 1994). In the case of attention, slower processing speed may compromise older adults' ability to attend to and select critical elements from the deluge of information presented to them.

The pressing issue in the current literature is whether declines in processing speed with age are fundamental to deficits in memory and attention. In other words, do all components of mental processing slow equivalently? If so, then cognitive decline can be reduced to one basic change: slowing. However, an alternative perspective to this global view suggests that age-related slowing is specific to particular levels of processing (e.g., response selection) and that the level in which slowing affects processing may vary from one task to another (Allen et al., 1995; Fisher et al., 1995). We explore these conflicting views in the Current Controversies feature.

Overall it appears that with advancing age there are multiple influences on the speed of mental processing (Bashore et al., 1997). The type of strategy an older adult is more likely to use (e.g., cautiously examining and reexamining information) could affect processing speed (Hertzog et al., 1993; Rogers et al., 2000). Slowing is also process specific: How fast a person responds is more vulnerable to advancing age than how fast the person encodes (e.g., detects and

DECLINE IN PROCESSING SPEED: GENERAL SLOWING OR PROCESS-SPECIFIC SLOWING?

Many researchers maintain that the speed of all components of processing (from selective attention to responding) declines as we grow older. For example, the complexity hypothesis posits that slowing in older adults is fundamental in that it affects the central nervous system. It becomes even more apparent as the complexity of the processing demands increases (Birren et al., 1980; Cerella & Hale 1994). The bottom line is that slowing occurs in all components of processing for all tasks. As Bashore et al. (1997) point out, a general slowing model would simplify the task of identifying structural changes in the brain that produce cognitive decline in older adults.

Support for general slowing or processing speed theory is well articulated by Salthouse (1996). In a series of studies he has shown that measures of processing speed largely account for age deficits across a wide variety of cognitive tasks (Salthouse et al., 1998). However, as McDowd

and Shaw (2000) point out, studies that explicitly ask whether slowing is the cause of other cognitive deficits in older adults or the consequence of some more basic age-related change (e.g., neuronal loss) are far and few between.

There have been a number of interesting challenges to this notion of a single, general slowing factor accounting for cognitive aging deficits. Bashore et al.'s (1997) findings suggest that speed of processing differs between young and older adults because they have adopted different performance strategies. Thus, all age groups may not perform speeded information-processing tasks in the same ways. Similarly, Ratcliff et al. (2000) proposed a diffusion model of slowing. In this model, they jointly considered response time, accuracy of responding, and individual differences in responding within age groups, among other variables. One of the outcomes of this model was that they were able to discriminate older from

young adults in their decision criteria. For example, older adults tend to be more conservative in their decision criteria (preferring accuracy to speed). Furthermore, the interesting questions do involve not only identifying differences between older and young adults but also examining the consistency of processing components within and across age groups. In this way, we can obtain a deeper understanding of the effects of aging on response time or speed.

Search Online with InfoTrac College Edition For more information on these controversies, explore InfoTrac College Edition, your online library. Go to http://www.infotrac-college.com/wadsworth and use the passcode that came on the card with your book. Try these search terms: processing speed, cognitive slowing, response time, speed-accuracy trade-off.

---

processes) the stimulus (Bashore et al., 1997). Thus, it is very important to consider a variety of measures of processing speed to more accurately examine the relationship between speed of processing and cognitive functioning (Bashore et al., 1997). Whether it is global or process specific, slowing does occur. In the next section, we examine some of the hypotheses underlying age-related slowing.

What Causes Age-Related Slowing?

Although there is still debate about the nature of age-related slowing, the evidence documenting a normative decline with age in speed of processing

is still overwhelming, representing one of the most robust findings in gerontological research. What causes people to slow down? After many years of debate and several different ideas, researchers are zeroing in on an intriguing answer. Several researchers (Cerella, 1990; Myerson et al., 1990; Raz, 2000; Salthouse, 1996) argue that the reason people slow down has to do with age changes in neurons in the brain. More specifically, studies using neuroimaging (see Chapter 2) suggest that age-related slowing may reflect the need of older brains to recruit additional resources to manage the accumulation of numerous simple and automatic tasks (Raz, 2000). Researchers have observed a localized neural deficit in resource managing brain circuits, which may relate to a generalized cognitive impairment. Although there is disagreement about exactly what is happening, most researchers believe that physiological changes in the brain, rather than changes in higher-level cognitive processes, are responsible for age-related slowing. We consider two variations on this theme: neural networks and information loss.

NEURAL NETWORKS. One way to conceptualize thinking is to consider it as a computational process occurring in a neural network (McClelland et al., 1986). In this approach, thinking involves making connections between many neurons. Efficient thinking means making the fewest of necessary connections between the point at which information comes in and the point at which an answer (or thought) comes out. Each connection takes a certain amount of time, so how quickly one thinks depends on the number of connections one needs to use.

For simplicity's sake, let's consider a simple reaction time task from this view of a neural network. The original neural network of Figure 6.1 shows that, hypothetically, eight links are the minimum number needed to get the information from the input side to the output side. Using only eight links would therefore be the most efficient (i.e., the fastest) way to process the information. Suppose that one of the neurons dies. The revised route of Figure 6.1 shows what happens. Notice that an extra (or a new) link is needed to bypass the break, bringing the minimum number up to nine links. Reaction time is faster in the first case (using only eight links) than in the second (using nine).

Cerella (1990) argues that reaction times in older adults are slower because they must build many such bypasses. Based on sophisticated analyses of reaction time data, he constructed a set of mathematical equations that fit a neural network model and account for the research findings. His analyses show that reaction time data are very consistent with what would be expected in a brain undergoing systematic changes in how its neurons are interconnected.

Additional support for a neural network approach comes from simulation research on visual processing (Hannon & Hoyer, 1994). In a series of computer simulations, a specific model of age-related differences in figure completion performance was identified. Such simulations may provide insights into why older adults slow down with age.

INFORMATION LOSS. Myerson and colleagues (1990) took a slightly different approach. They focused not so much on the links between neurons but on what happens during processing at each line. Their model is based on four assumptions:

Information processing occurs in discrete steps, and overall processing speed is the total of how long it takes to accomplish each step. This assumption is based on the same neural network model as Cerella used.

How long each step takes depends on how much information is available at the beginning of the step. For example, if the task being done entails identifying particular letters, and if the quality of the printing is very poor, insufficient information may be available to make a rapid response. Additionally, as the task gets more complicated and more information is needed, processing speed slows down.

Information is lost during processing. This point is illustrated by thinking about photocopying a document. Each time the document is copied, there is a slight loss of quality. If the copy is then used to make a copy, more quality is lost. Continuing this process several times nicely demonstrates Myerson's theory of how information is lost during information processing.

The most important effect of aging is an age-related increase in the rate at which information is lost. To continue our example, age differences in information loss would be analogous to the quality of the copy deteriorating faster in an old photocopy machine.

Like Cerella's neural network model, Myerson's information loss model accounts for a wide range of data. Myerson and colleagues are able to predict with a high degree of accuracy older adults' reaction times

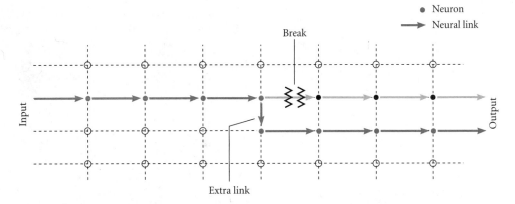

FIGURE 6.1 Schematic neural network. The network transmits signals from left to right. One link in the original, intact route is broken, forcing the signal to detour and adding one more link to the path for a total of nine.

Source: Cerella, J. (1990). Aging and information-processing rate. In J. E. Birren & K. W. Schaie (Eds.), Handbook of the psychology of aging (3rd ed., p. 203). San Diego: Academic Press. With permission from the *Annual Review of Psychology,* volume 50 © 1999 by Annual Reviews. www.AnnualReviews.org.

from young adults' performance, irrespective of task. As a result, they view age-related slowing as a global process that is not localized in specific age-sensitive components.

Together, these models provide powerful explanations of age-related slowing. They also provide strong support for working within the four basic developmental forces by explicitly connecting a psychological process (making quick responses) with underlying physiological processes. As noted in Chapter 2, rapid advances are being made in understanding how the brain works. These advances clearly advance our understanding of psychomotor speed and aging. However, the question remains: Is there a way to slow these age-related decrements in speed?

Slowing Down How Much We Slow Down

Consider for a moment what it takes to be a successful race car driver: a fast car, lots of driving knowledge, and lightning-fast reactions. On the face of it, auto racing sounds tailor-made for young adults. But few drivers in their 20s win major races such as the Indianapolis 500. Many of the best drivers (e.g., Al Unser, Jr.) reach the peak of their careers in their 30s. Or consider Paul Newman, the famous movie star

and race car driver. He was racing successfully even in his late 50s. The data indicate that people in their 20s are faster than middle-aged adults, so how can older drivers still succeed?

An important reason that middle-aged race car drivers are able to win is experience. They have driven in many races and have accumulated a wealth of information about driving in these events. Veteran drivers know that younger drivers have quicker reflexes to get themselves out of trouble. But because of their experience, veterans often are able to avoid getting into trouble in the first place; they can anticipate what is likely to happen in front of them. This experience compensates for slower psychomotor speed.

Researchers have studied real-world tasks to learn about the effects of experience on reaction time. Salthouse (1984) examined performance in adults aged 19–72 on transcription typing. The typists in his study ranged in speed from 17 to 104 words per minute, with ability and age being unrelated. Salthouse examined several components of reaction time, including choice reaction time, speed of repetitive tapping, and the rate at which people can substitute specific digits for letters (for example, *3* for *d*). Results are shown in Figure 6.2.

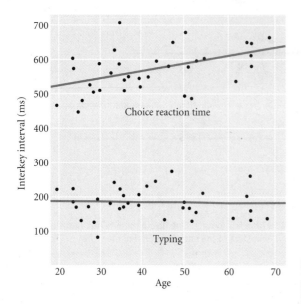

FIGURE 6.2 Comparison of speed (in milliseconds) of responding in a choice reaction time task and typing as a function of age. Notice how choice reaction time responses slow down with age, whereas typing speed does not.

Source: Salthouse, T. A. (1984). Effects of age and skill in typing. *Journal of Experimental Psychology: General, 113,* 345–371. Copyright © 1984 by the American Psychological Association. Reprinted with permission of the author.

Although younger secretaries may type more characters within a specific time span than older secretaries, such differences are greatly reduced or eliminated when accuracy is taken into account.

As you can see in the graph, age-related slowing occurred on the choice reaction time task. Interestingly, however, no age effect occurred for typing. Why? Both tasks involved pressing keys, so what was the difference? One measure revealed a difference favoring older adults: span of anticipation. This measure was derived by manipulating the number of simultaneously visible to-be-typed characters, and it was interpreted as an indication of how far ahead of the currently typed character the typist was focusing his or her attention. Because a greater span of anticipation minimizes the importance of the speed of psychomotor processes as a major factor in skilled typing, the larger span on the part of the older typists is an extremely effective compensatory mechanism. Thus, in some cases experience may allow older adults to compensate for psychomotor slowing.

CONCEPT CHECKS

1. What are the three types of reaction time tasks?
2. Contrast general slowing with process-specific slowing. What age differences are observed in each?
3. What are the two major explanations of why people slow with age?
4. What effects do practice and experience have on reaction time?

DRIVING AND ACCIDENT PREVENTION

LEARNING OBJECTIVES

- What age-related differences are there in driving?
- What information-processing abilities are critical to driving?
- How can home accidents be prevented?

Michael is 83 years old, and he has noticed that none of his friends will allow him to drive to the weekly poker game. He begins to question his driving ability. He also finds that it is difficult for him to navigate the busy freeways, so he uses only side streets when he drives somewhere. When he renewed his driver's license he found out that he must take a driving test in addition to a written test each time he goes in for a renewal. In addition, the renewal period is shorter. He has to renew his license every year instead of every 3 years. Michael begins to fear that he will lose his license and thus a major component of his independence.

Up to this point, we have concentrated on age differences in basic aspects of the information-processing system, attention in particular, as found in laboratory settings. We have seen that in several areas older adults are at a disadvantage compared with younger (and often middle-aged) adults. However, most of the research we considered was based on esoteric tasks, such as finding the letter *X* in a visual display or pressing different keys for different light colors. If you are wondering what this work has to do with real life, you are not alone; many researchers wonder the same thing. Consider the problem facing Michael.

In this section and the next section we look at the functional consequences of age-related changes in attentional processes. First we examine the consequences of attentional deficits on an important part of daily living: driving. Next, we examine the cognitive consequences of attentional deficits in another important aspect of daily living: language.

Early steps in information processing have many important connections with everyday life, as we have noted throughout the chapter. For example, driving a car involves bombarding sensory memory with vast amounts of information, directing attention to some of it, and, when necessary, having excellent psychomotor speed. Thus, we must consider these connections between basic information-processing skills and everyday situations. Doing so will help us anticipate whether Michael will be allowed to keep his driver's license.

Making connections between laboratory research findings and everyday life is one aspect of human factors research. **Human factors** *is the field of study concerned with designing living and working environments* (Bosman & Charness, 1996; Rogers & Fisk, 2000). Human factors professionals deal with interesting problems in just about every conceivable area. For example, they may be asked to design an easy-to-use computer keyboard, the layout of a cockpit for a jumbo jet, or a safe environment for nursing home residents. Although most human factors work focuses on designing work environments, increased interest is being paid to everyday situations. For example, many of the safety features built into modern appliances (such as irons that automatically shut off) and automobiles (brake lights mounted in the rear window, for example) are the result of human factors research.

To make the most effective designs, planners must know as much as possible about their clients. This entails integrating information about people's basic sensory and information-processing abilities. In designs meant for older adults, planners must understand changes in sensory abilities and those in basic information-processing abilities. Recently, human factors researchers have focused specifically on the needs of older adults (Rogers & Fisk, 2000). Most work has involved driving and other highway safety issues and safety in the home.

Driving and Highway Safety as Information Processing

Most older adults live independently. Thus, access to workplaces, community services, leisure activities, and the like is an important consideration. Because roughly 80% of all trips made by older adults are in private automobiles (U.S. Department of Transportation, 1994), driving and highway safety are major issues for human factors research. In fact, according to the U.S. Department of Transportation, in 1994 15.7 million older adults over age 70 were licensed drivers (a 45% increase over 1984). In addition, older adults account for 13% of all traffic fatalities and 18% of all pedestrian fatalities.

What causes older adults' problems with driving? We have already noted that certain changes in vision,

Given the significant proportion of older adults driving private automobiles, it is important for human factor researchers to design vehicle interfaces better suited to age-related changes in visual, attention, and perceptual functioning.

hearing, and information processing could cause problems for older drivers. For example, changes in light and dark adaptation and sensitivity to glare and changes in psychomotor speed present challenges to older adult drivers. Older drivers themselves report several difficulties (Gallo et al., 1999), from trouble reading highway signs and the instrument panel to difficulty seeing the road to problems reaching the seatbelt. Difficulty with inhibiting irrelevant information could mean trouble sorting out benign situations from potentially dangerous ones. Observational and other objective data suggest additional problems: trouble with backing up, changing lanes, noting signs and warnings, turning properly, and yielding the right of way (National Highway Traffic Safety Administration, 1998).

Redesigning vehicles with older adults in mind could solve many of these problems. For example, researchers have attempted to develop smart vehicle technologies that use communication devices and displays within the vehicle to transmit information about roadway and traffic conditions (Lerner, 1994). Other technologies focus on perceptual enhancements such as navigational aids (Walker et al., 1997; Rogers & Fisk, 2000) and infrared images to improve night vision. However, Yanik (1994) argues that three barriers remain in designing automobiles for older

drivers. First, the designers tend to be young adults who lack experiential knowledge of the aging process. Second, young designers' notions of aging tend to be based on social stereotypes rather than on research. Finally, there is little applied research on how older adults interact with their cars. Removing these barriers would entail education (which would address the first two) and a systematic effort to conduct the appropriate research.

One area in which applied research has been conducted relates to visual attention in older drivers (Ball & Owsley, 1991; Ball et al., 1993; Ball & Rebok, 1994). One particularly important variable predictive of driving success is the useful field of view (UFOV). The UFOV is the extent of the visual field available to a person at a brief glance. Research by Ball and colleagues has demonstrated that the UFOV varies across people and across situations and decreases when the person is faced with competing attentional demands (Ball & Owsley, 1991). This is particularly evident in older adults. Aging can dramatically restrict a person's UFOV, so that for some older adult drivers it may be like looking through a peephole while driving (Rogers & Fisk, 2000).

Whereas visual acuity tests typically predict less than 5% of accidents, UFOV assessments predict 13% of accidents in a sample of older drivers and 21% of intersection accidents (Rogers & Fisk, 2000). Figure 6.3 illustrates the association between UFOV and crashes. It is interesting to note that the association is strong within each of the three age groups evaluated, although UFOV reduction and crashes are more prevalent with increasing age. We examine a study that investigated the joint contribution of sensory and cognitive variables in predicting the frequency of crashes among older adults in the How Do We Know? feature. Finally, the good news is that attentional processes assessed by UFOV can be improved with training (Ball et al., 1988).

Another important driving problem that could be affected by vision and information-processing changes is identifying signs, especially at dusk (Kline, 1994). For example, Lambert and Fleury (1994) found that older drivers needed to be much closer to text signs at night to read them, despite the fact that

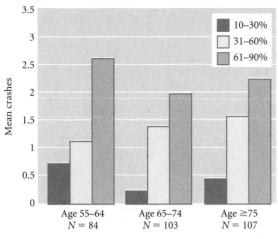

FIGURE 6.3 Mean crash frequency as a function of UFOV reduction for drivers subdivided into three age groups.

Source: Ball, K., & Rebok, G. W. (1994). Evaluating the driving ability of older adults. *Journal of Applied Gerontology, 13,* p. 29.

they had been matched with younger drivers for daytime vision.

Kline and colleagues (1990) examined how well younger, middle-aged, and older drivers could read text and icon highway signs. Text signs have various messages printed on them, such as "Men Working" and "Divided Highway." Icon signs are picture versions of text signs following international conventions; for example, a "Men Working" icon sign depicts a man using a shovel. Kline and colleagues showed that all age groups identified icon signs at greater distances than text signs. This effect was especially true at dusk. Most important, no age differences were found; older adults identified signs as well as younger adults. This finding is important, especially in view of the well-documented changes in vision and in visual information processing. Additionally, the distance at which older adults were able to identify the signs allowed enough time for them to prepare for any decisions, such as the need to exit or slow down.

Research on the visibility of signs indicates that when the visual abilities of older adults are used to guide the design of signs, their visibility is greatly enhanced (Kline, 1994). Moreover, optical simulation and image-processing filters also appear promising in designing signs and displays that are more effective for older drivers.

HIGHWAY ACCIDENTS. Many people believe that older drivers are unsafe. However, testing that theory is difficult, primarily because older adults have very different driving habits than younger and middle-aged adults. Older adults drive fewer total miles, less at night, less in bad weather, less in rush hour traffic, and less on freeways and the open highway (Smith, 1990). The consensus among researchers is that if older adults have a higher accident risk, it is compensated for by changes in driving habits, at least until late life (National Highway Traffic Safety Administration, 1998; Williams & Carsten, 1989).

Psychologists approach the study of age and highway accidents by focusing on the role of skills known to be relevant to driving. As we observed with the UFOV research, age per se does not lead to accidents; rather, it is decreased skills that can cause them (Rogers & Fisk, 2000). A number of information-processing variables are especially important in understanding automobile accidents, such as perceptual strategies, selective attention, divided attention, and reaction time (Carr & Rebok, 2000; Holland & Rabbitt, 1994; Lambert & Fleury, 1994; Lerner, 1994).

Several researchers have studied the relationship between measures of attentional skills and on-the-road behavior. Crook and colleagues (1993) used a driving simulation task. Young and older adults had to press an accelerator pedal on a computer touchscreen when a traffic light was green and press a brake pedal when the light was red. They had to switch back and forth at a rapid rate with the changing light. They measured lift time, which was the time from the onset of the light to the release of the current pedal, and travel time, which was the time it took to release one pedal and press the other pedal. Lift time corresponds to attention and concentration, whereas travel time corresponds to psychomotor speed. When the task had no distractions, both lift and travel time increased with age. When the participants had to listen to a

Who were the investigators, and what was the aim of the study? Driving is the preferred mode of travel among older adults. In addition, driving provides the mobility that older adults rely on to maintain their independence. Yet many older adults experience changes that make driving more difficult for them. Ball and Rebok (1994) were interested in isolating risk factors within the older driver population that contribute to frequency of automobile accidents.

How did the investigators measure the topic of interest? Ball and Rebok measured several variables, including a battery of visual sensory function measures, a battery of mental status measures, UFOV assessment, a driving habit questionnaire, and an eye health examination. These measures focused on participants' visual and cognitive skills.

Who were the participants in the studies? A total of 294 adults ranging in age from 56 to 90 were studied. All participants lived independently in the community.

What was the design of the study? This study was correlational in nature and assessed the ability of the various measures to predict the frequency of crashes in which the participant was involved. Recruitment of participants was aimed at equal representation across the age span and in three categories of crash involvement (0, 1–3, and more than 4 crashes).

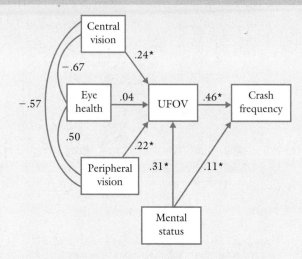

FIGURE 6.4   **Model for predicting crash frequency in older drivers.**

Source: Ball, K., & Rebok, G. W. (1994). Evaluating the driving ability of older adults. *Journal of Applied Gerontology, 13*, p. 32.

Were there ethical concerns with the study? Participants gave informed consent, so there were no ethical concerns.

What were the results? As can be seen in Figure 6.4, only two variables, UFOV and mental status, had direct effects on crash frequency. Central and peripheral vision affect UFOV but do not directly affect crash frequency. Thus, visual attention skills such as UFOV depend on how well information enters through the sensory channel.

What did the investigators conclude? Ball and Rebok conclude that visual

attention, or the size of the useful field of view, is a critical predictor of which older drivers are at risk for crash involvement. Current visual screening techniques such as visual acuity that are typically used at driver licensing sites are not adequate in identifying which older drivers are likely to be involved in crashes. Finally, age alone does not successfully distinguish between older adults who were or were not involved in crashes. Thus, basing driving privileges solely on age is not scientifically well founded.

weather report and traffic report while they were performing the driving simulation, older adults performed more poorly than young adults did on lift time only. Thus, the attention-demanding part of the task was more vulnerable to aging. Problems in atten-

tion are evident in accident victims' statements; "I never saw the other car" is a common example of a failure to detect important information. Moreover, older drivers have difficulty judging the speed of oncoming vehicles (Scialfa et al., 1991).

An additional problem facing older drivers is that older adults tend to be taking more prescription and nonprescription medications than young adults are. Because many medications have side effects that could impair sensory, perceptual, and reaction time processes, all adults, but especially older adults, need to be aware of these effects (Carr & Rebok, 2000).

Given the number of potential problems facing older drivers, some researchers have emphasized a need for specialized training programs. A good example of this approach is a study conducted by Ashman and colleagues (1994). They evaluated a driver's education training program based on the sensory, perceptual, physical, and reaction time processes involved in driving. Intensive retraining on perceptual processes and a general driver education course improved driving in older adults the most. It should be noted that there were 2 years of training. Importantly, short-term training was not effective.

In sum, many sensory and information-processing changes affect driving. However, human factors research shows that icons signs and training programs based on information-processing interventions help older drivers compensate for these changes.

Home Safety and Accident Prevention

By far, the most important home safety issue is falls. Changes in the vestibular system and combinations of changes in the muscular and skeletal systems place older adults at much greater risk of falling down. Additional risk factors include information-processing changes involving attention and focusing on relevant information such as cracks in the sidewalk. Much human factors research on falls has focused on the role of stair construction (Pauls, 1985). This research has resulted in the incorporation of several safety standards into U.S. building codes concerning such things as handrails, ramps, and grab bars.

Most recently human factors research has been conducted on home safety issues involving warning labels. Cognitive aging may pose problems for the warning process. For example, evidence suggests that older adults' comprehension of symbols typically used to convey warnings is impaired (Hancock et al., 1998; Rogers & Fisk, 2000). Rousseau and colleagues

© Lara Hartley

Age-related changes in sensory, motor, and physiological systems increase the likelihood that this woman may have an accident getting on or off the train.

(1998) provide recommendations for user-friendly warning designs for older adults. These include cues to aid memory for warning information, simple sentences, interactive warnings, and using older adults in the evaluation samples for symbol development.

ACCIDENT PREVENTION. We are exposed to environmental risks every day; at any moment we could slip on a throw rug, trip on the stairs, or run a stop sign. We cannot eliminate risk entirely. Rather, we must be take a balanced approach to minimizing risk wherever possible by developing better designs, instituting better assessment of cognitive abilities involved, and educating people about hazards (Rogers & Fisk, 2000).

The key to addressing the problem of safety is to remember that age alone does not cause accidents. Rather, the decline in sensory and information-processing skills are responsible for age-related increases in some types of accidents. However, large differences exist across (and even within) individuals in the rate and extent of such changes. Consequently, accident prevention strategies must be sensitive to individual differences rather than simply focusing on age. Incorporating this knowledge is desirable, but it may be difficult to accomplish this goal.

CONCEPT CHECKS

1. What age-related differences are observed in highway accidents?
2. What is the primary cause of older adults' accidents in the home?
3. How can we prevent accidents by older adults?

LANGUAGE PROCESSING

LEARNING OBJECTIVES

- What age differences are observed in understanding speech?
- What is the relation between language processing and information processing?

Robin and her grandmother are having dinner in a restaurant to talk about Robin's upcoming wedding. The noise level is high. Robin is amazed that her grandmother can even understand her, given her hearing problems. However, they are able to hold an intelligent conversation, although stressful at times. After dinner, however, Robin's grandmother suggests that they have dinner at home when they have important things to talk about.

In everyday life another important consequence of information-processing abilities in general and attentional deficits in particular is understanding and using language. Understanding what is said in a conversation, being able to read a note from a friend, and being able to respond allow us to interact with others and maintain social ties, as in the case of Robin and her grandmother.

Once information has been registered in sensory memory and noticed by attentional processes, it is transformed again based on its meaning. In language information, such as words or speech, this meaning is based on our ability to make a basic linguistic decision about it: Is the information being presented a word? Do we know what the information means? Thus, simple linguistic decisions are the next step in information processing. If the information has linguistic meaning, is it processed automatically, or do we have to exert effort every time? These are the fundamental issues we consider in this section. These basic language-processing steps set the stage for research on the subsequent steps of working memory and other aspects of memory, which we consider in Chapter 7.

Clearly, language processing is an important area of research in information processing. Like human factors, it is based on interactions between sensory systems and basic information-processing abilities. Language-processing researchers distinguish between language comprehension and language production. Language comprehension involves handling words coming into the information-processing system and figuring out what they mean. Knowing the definition of words or knowing that the person sitting across the table just asked you to pass the salt are two examples of language comprehension. In contrast, language production means being able to come up with an appropriate word or phrase when you are trying to say, write, or think about something. A common example of language production is coming up with a person's name when you encounter him or her in a store.

Researchers have studied many aspects of language comprehension and language production. Much of this work has been done in the context of memory or intelligence research. For example, having people learn and remember word lists or text passages is commonly examined in memory research, and testing people's vocabulary knowledge is typical in intelligence research. Both areas rely heavily on language production because people's scores are based on how often and how well they produce correct responses. In this section, we focus on the basic processes of language comprehension.

Language Comprehension and Sensory Systems

Let's reflect a moment on some connections between language processing and what we know about age-related differences in information processing. Language comprehension is based initially on visual or auditory input. Many important changes in each of these sensory systems could influence how well or how easily we understand language. In vision, changes in light transmission and accommodation could affect how clearly we see letters or words. In hearing, changes in pitch perception may alter how well we hear certain sounds. Earlier in this chapter we examined several changes in visual information processing that could also affect language comprehension. Most important, the data suggested that older adults have difficulty integrating different visual features. This could present problems when older adults read. One area we have not yet considered is understanding speech.

UNDERSTANDING SPEECH. Have you ever tried to have a serious conversation at a noisy party or restaurant as the case of Robin and her grandmother? You may have had trouble understanding what the other person was saying. Or perhaps you have been in a quieter environment such as an art museum and couldn't quite pick up what the tour director was saying about the Monet masterpiece. Both situations can be annoying and embarrassing. Constantly saying, "I can't hear you; would you repeat what you said?" is no fun.

Obviously, being able to hear plays an important role in understanding speech. Given the normative decline in hearing caused by presbycusis, does people's ability to understand speech decline as well? Fortunately, presbycusis normally does not affect the pitches used in most speech sounds until around age 80. As a result, speech understanding usually is not seriously impaired until late in life. This was illustrated in Robin's grandmother and her ability to hold a conversation in a noisy restaurant given hearing problems. However, a few sounds in English, such as *s*, *ch*, and *sh* involve pitches that are affected earlier.

Consequently, middle-aged and young-old adults (ages 60–75) may have trouble understanding these sounds (Brant & Fozard, 1990).

How well people understand speech is tested in two ways. Speech recognition is measured by presenting the listener with a list of spondee words: Spondaic two-syllable words are pronounced with equal emphasis on both syllables (some English examples are *airplane, baseball, birthday,* and *headlight*). Speech discrimination is tested with monosyllabic words that include the various sounds in English.

Several studies have documented an age-related decrement in both speech recognition and speech discrimination abilities (Tun & Wingfield, 1993; Wingfield & Stine-Morrow, 2000). Typical results are shown in Figure 6.5. Notice that age differences become especially pronounced when the listening situation is made more difficult, such as when other voices are in the background or when speech is interrupted. Older adults also have difficulty understanding speech that is embedded in noise (Schneider & Pichora-Fuller, 2000).

How well people understand speech is also affected by how fast it is presented and whether the words are presented alone or in the context of regular speech. Stine-Morrow, Wingfield, and colleagues examined these issues in a series of studies (Stine et al., 1986; Wingfield, 1996; Wingfield & Stine-Morrow, 2000). They looked for age differences in speech understanding by using compressed speech, which allowed them to use presentation rates between 200 and 400 words per minute. In addition, they manipulated whether words were presented in sentences, with normal voice inflections, in meaningless but grammatically correct strings, or in random order. Results demonstrated the power of context. When words were presented normally in sentences, older adults performed at more than 90% accuracy even at 400 or more words per minute. However, when words were presented in random strings or without normal vocal cues, older adults performed poorly even at slower rates (around 250 words per minute).

Stine-Morrow and Wingfield's work clearly shows how context affects older adults' understanding of

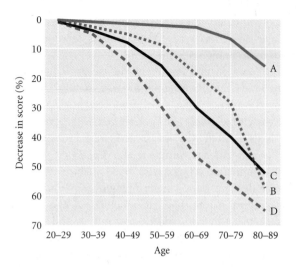

Figure 6.5 Decrease in percentage of intelligibility for speech as a function of age. **A,** Unaltered speech; **B,** reverberated speech; **C,** overlapping speech with spondaic words; **D,** interrupted speech. For each curve, normal subjects 20–29 years served as zero reference.

Source: Bergman, M. (1971). Hearing and aging: Implications of recent research findings. *Audiology, 10,* 164–171. Copyright © 1971 S. Karger AG. Reprinted with permission.

speech. On one hand, context allows older adults to understand what is said even at very fast presentation rates. This finding is similar to the results from Salthouse's work on typing that we considered earlier. On the other hand, Stine-Morrow and Wingfield's research also demonstrates how much older adults depend on context; their understanding of speech drops dramatically when contextual cues are not present. These effects get us into the realm of the role of information processing in language, to which we now turn.

Language Comprehension and Information Processing

How do we process words beyond basic sensory systems so that we understand what they mean? This question has intrigued researchers for many years and continues to be one of the most active areas in cognitive psychology. Some argue that language pro-cessing is the key to understanding a host of other processes, including understanding memory. If this is true, then age-related changes in language processing may underlie the age-related differences in memory we discuss in Chapter 7. For example, Craik and Byrd (1982) claim that age-related differences in language processing result in less richly encoded information that makes information less memorable. Their claim is based on the belief that older adults' information-processing abilities are compromised by less attentional capacity, drops in processing speed, and changes in working memory.

Numerous investigators have examined aspects of Craik and Byrd's claim (Light, 1990). We consider this research under two general headings: richness and extensiveness of encoding and encoding deficits.

RICHNESS AND EXTENSIVENESS OF ENCODING. Suppose you and a friend hear the name *Martin Luther King, Jr.,* as part of a lecture in history class. Suppose further that you are very familiar with him but your friend is not. You will have a distinct advantage over your friend in remembering him. Why?

When linguistic information comes in, you look for ways to connect it to other information you already know. The more connections you can make, the better off you are later when you need to remember the name. Because your friend can make only a few connections, getting the name to stick in memory is more difficult.

The number of different connections created between incoming information and information already in a knowledge base is what is meant by rich and extensive encoding. If age differences in encoding occur, they could be manifested in two ways. First, how knowledge is structured could change across adulthood, making it harder to keep connections intact (Wingfield & Stine-Morrow, 2000). Second, the processes by which connections are made could change with age. However, neither appears to change substantially with age (Light, 1996).

ENCODING DEFICITS. One school of thought is that extensive encoding underlies the ability to retrieve information. That is, information that is richly encoded is more easily retrieved. One way to test this is to ask people to judge whether a particular letter string is a word (called a lexical decision task). One variant of a lexical decision task, called priming, involves showing people related words before the letter string (for example, show the word *nurse* and ask people to judge whether the letter string "d-o-c-t-o-r" is a word). Researchers then focus on how quickly people make these decisions as the major variable of interest.

Performing well on lexical decision tasks requires a fairly rich knowledge base. Adults of all ages are equally adept at lexical decision tasks. For example, in a review of the literature, Wingfield and Stine-Morrow (2000) concluded that older and younger adults had equal automatic lexical access. But what if people are then given a test to see whether they can remember the words they saw? In this case, older adults do worse than younger adults do. This performance pattern of equivalent lexical access but poorer memory does not support the idea that poor encoding of lexical information underlies memory problems. Why? If encoding were the problem, people would not be able to make the lexical decisions because they would not have processed the necessary information to make the judgment. Because adults of all ages perform this part very well, we know that the necessary information has been processed. Thus, the age differences that emerge in the memory task cannot be caused by significant age differences in encoding of the basic lexical information.

A second issue concerning encoding deficits is that older adults do not take advantage of contextual cues when they encode information. Specifically, Rabinowitz and colleagues (1982) believe that older adults do not tend to create distinctive context-specific encoding but rather have a tendency to use the same approach each time. Although there is some support for this position, several investigators disagree. We have already seen that older adults use sentence context to process rapid speech. Additionally, researchers have shown that older adults often use context-specific information at encoding (Pichora-Fuller et al., 1995) and in naming words (Laver & Burke, 1993).

In sum, there is no support for the contention that basic linguistic processing is the basis for age-related differences in memory. Knowledge is organized similarly in younger and older adults, and tests of immediate comprehension as measured by word naming and lexical decision tasks show no age differences. What accounts for memory problems? As we see in Chapter 7, the answer to this question is complex and involves the interaction of several factors.

CONCEPT CHECKS

1. What is the effect of the rate of speech on older adults?
2. What evidence is there that linguistic processing underlies age differences in memory?

PUTTING IT ALL TOGETHER

There is substantial evidence in the literature that attentional capacities and speed of processing decline with age. Randall Cunningham experienced this as a quarterback trying to maintain his career in his late 30s. When speeding in a Lamborghini, Brandon taxed his attentional capacities and ability to focus. This is why we do not typically see older adults in sports cars. Attention is an elusive quality; we can slip out of attention without awareness. Chloe experienced this while gazing out of a window and not paying attention in class. And because we are slowing down as we age, our driving and information processing become more and more taxed, as Eugene experienced when he had to brake quickly to avoid an accident. The degree to which driving taxes our attentional resources was brought home when Michael tried to renew his driver's license. His decreasing capacity prevented him from driving the way he used to, and he was evaluated much more regularly. Finally, Robin's conversation with her grandmother illustrated the interaction between sensory decline and information processing. We have automatic skills that compensate for our sensory losses. The ability to hold a conversation despite stressful surroundings demonstrates this.

Summary

THE INFORMATION-PROCESSING MODEL

Overview of the Model

- The information-processing model assumes an active participant, both quantitative and qualitative aspects of performance, and information processing through a series of hypothetical stages.

Sensory Memory

- Sensory memory is the first level of processing incoming information from the environment. Sensory memory has a large capacity, but information stays there only a very short time.

ATTENTION

- Three aspects of attention, selectivity, divided attention, and sustained attention, involve how we choose information to process, how we delegate our attention to different pieces of information, and how we maintain our attention while performing a task.

Selective Attention

- Age-related decrements are found in visual search. Cuing spatial locations sharply reduces age differences when the cue provides unambiguous information. No age differences are found on visual attention switching tasks, but they are found on auditory tasks. Older adults have more difficulty filtering out or inhibiting irrelevant information than younger adults, but this may be limited to the item's identity.

Divided Attention

- Divided attention is the degree to which information competes for our attention at a given time. Age differences in divided attention depend on the degree of task complexity and practice.

Sustained Attention

- Older adults are not as good as younger adults at detecting targets on vigilance tasks, but there are no age differences in the rate at which performance declines over time. As task complexity increases or predictability of the target decreases, age differences on vigilance tasks increase.

Attentional Resources

- Some researchers claim that older adults have fewer processing resources than young adults do. However, this conclusion is suspect because processing resources are ill defined.

- In general, age differences are not observed in consistent mapping practice because of automatic processing, but differences are found on variable mapping practice tasks.

SPEED OF PROCESSING

- A major explanation of age-related decline in cognitive performance speed is cognitive slowing.

Basic Psychomotor Speed: Reaction Time Tasks

- Simple reaction time involves responding as quickly as possible to a stimulus.

- Choice reaction time involves making separate responses to separate stimuli as quickly as possible.

- Complex reaction time involves making complicated decisions about how to respond based on the stimulus observed.

Processing Speed

- An important issue is whether processing speed represents a general phenomenon that affects all mental processing. Evidence shows that age-related slowing is specific to particular levels of processing and particular tasks.

What Causes Age-Related Slowing?

- One explanation of age differences, based on neural networks, is that older people need more neuronal connections to make a response. A second possibility, called the information loss model, is that older adults lose more information at each step of processing.

Slowing Down How Much We Slow Down

- Although practice improves performance, age differences are not eliminated. However, experience allows older adults to compensate for loss of speed by anticipating what is likely to happen. The span of anticipation appears to be the reason that experience helps.

DRIVING AND ACCIDENT PREVENTION

- Much recent work in the human factors literature has examined vehicle design and assessed driving ability in relation to driving accidents by older adults.

Driving and Highway Safety as Information Processing

- Human factors research is intended to optimize the design of living and working environments. Older drivers have several problems, including reading highway signs, seeing at night, noting warnings, and performing various operating skills. Changes in information-processing abilities could make older adults more susceptible to accidents, although documenting the actual risk is difficult.

Home Safety and Accident Prevention

- Older adults are more likely to hurt themselves by falling at home than younger adults. Age alone does not cause such accidents; rather, declines in physiological and sensory functioning are responsible.

LANGUAGE PROCESSING

Language Comprehension and Sensory Systems

- Language comprehension involves attaching meaning to incoming words. Language production involves coming up with an appropriate word or phrase. Speech comprehension usually is not affected by presbycusis until age 80. Speech recognition and speech discrimination show age-related decline. The faster speech is presented, the greater the age differences in understanding it.

Language Comprehension and Information Processing

- Age differences usually are not found in lexical decision tasks or in the number of connections people make to incoming information. Basic language processing deficits do not appear to cause age differences in memory. Older adults do not take advantage of contextual cues when they encode information.

Review Questions

THE INFORMATION-PROCESSING MODEL

- What assumptions does the information-processing model make?
- What are the early steps in sensory memory? What age differences have been noted?

ATTENTION

- What aspects of attention have been studied? Define each of them.
- What age differences have been reported in visual search? How can these age differences be reduced or eliminated?
- What age differences have been noted in divided-attention tasks? Why do these differences occur?
- What age differences occur in vigilance tasks? What variables affect the magnitude of age differences?

SPEED OF PROCESSING

- What different types of reaction time tasks are used to study psychomotor speed? What age differences have been found in each?
- How does task complexity affect age differences in reaction time tasks?
- How do interpretations of age differences in slowing differ when comparing global and process-specific processing speeds?
- Describe the neural network approach to accounting for age differences in reaction time.
- How do practice and experience affect age differences in reaction time?

DRIVING AND ACCIDENT PREVENTION

- What is human factors?
- What problems do older drivers have, and what interventions can be applied to help them?
- What is the UFOV, and how does it relate to driving accidents?
- What accident risks do older adults face in their homes?
- How is research on warning labels used in accident prevention for older adults?

Language Processing

- What is the difference between language comprehension and language production?
- How do speech comprehension, speech recognition, and speech discrimination differ with age?
- What role do basic language-processing deficits play in age differences in memory?

Integrating Concepts in Development

- How are changes in the sensory systems (discussed in Chapter 2) related to age differences in information processing?
- Besides driving, what practical implications are there for slowing down with age?
- How could a car's instrument panel be designed to help older drivers?
- What connections are there between lifestyle factors in health and information processing?

Key Terms

attentional capacity The amount of information that can be processed at a time.

automatic attention response Processing of a specific and well-trained stimulus, such as a target letter, that automatically captures attention.

automatic processes Processes that are fast, reliable, and insensitive to increased cognitive demands.

automatic processing Processing that places minimal demands on attentional capacity.

choice reaction time The time it takes to make separate responses to separate stimuli.

complex reaction time The time it takes to make separate responses to separate stimuli as quickly as possible.

divided attention The ability to pay attention and successfully perform more than one task at a time.

effortful processing Processing that uses all the available attentional capacity.

human factors The study of how people interact with machines and other objects in their environment.

information-processing approach The study of how people take in stimuli from their environment and transform them into memories; the approach is based on a computer metaphor.

processing resources The amount of attention one has to apply to a particular situation.

reaction time The speed with which one makes a response.

selective attention The process by which information is chosen for further processing in attention.

sensory memory The earliest step in information processing in which new, incoming information is first registered.

simple reaction time The time it takes to respond to a stimulus.

spatial cuing A technique in visual processing research in which subjects are given a hint about where the next target will appear.

speed of processing The speed and efficiency with which early steps in information processing are completed.

vigilance or sustained attention The ability to maintain attention to the same task over an extended period of time.

Resources

Readings

Cerella, J. (1990). Aging and information-processing rate. In J. E. Birren & K. W. Schaie (Eds.), *Handbook of the psychology of aging* (3rd ed., pp. 201–221). San Diego: Academic Press. Provides an overview of theories and data about processing resources and speed. Moderate to difficult reading.

Cerella, J., Rybash, J. M., Hoyer, W., & Commons, M. L. (Eds.). (1993). *Adult information processing: Limits on loss.* San Diego: Academic Press. One of the best single-volume accounts of age differences in information processing. Moderately difficult reading.

Light, L. L., & Burke, D. M. (Eds.). (1988). *Language, memory, and aging.* New York: Cambridge University

Press. A good introduction to the issues in this area. Moderately difficult reading.

McDowd, J. & Shaw, R. (2000). Attention and aging: A functional perspective. In F. I. M. Craik & T. A. Salthouse (Eds.), *The handbook of aging and cognition* (pp. 221–291). Hillsdale, NJ: Erlbaum. Good review of research on attention. Moderately difficult reading.

Search Online with

InfoTrac College Edition

For more information on the topics in this chapter, explore InfoTrac College Edition, your online library. Go to http://www.infotrac-college.com/ wadsworth and use the passcode that came on the card with your book. Try these search terms: elderly attention; driving, elderly; cognitive slowing, elderly.

7

MEMORY

© AP / Wide World Photos

Jerry Lucas has been known as many things, including a top basketball player in college at Ohio State University and in the pros (New York Knicks), telecommunication professional, and the world's leading authority in memory training, which has earned him the name *Dr. Memory*. In fact, he is touted as having written more material on memory training than anyone else. He has intense dedication to improving education. What can he do? In front of millions of people on television he has memorized the names of up to 700 people in a television audience and memorized an entire 100-page magazine.

What is particularly relevant to this chapter is that he has developed a business using the Lucas Learning System techniques. These techniques are teachable and transferable to everyone, including older adults. He says that people can discover "learning that lasts." This brings hope to a growing segment of our population: older adults, who are known for memory decline.

Memory is such a pervasive aspect of our daily lives that we take it for granted. From remembering where we keep our toothbrush to tying our shoes to timing soft-boiled eggs, memory is always with us. It gives us a sense of identity. Imagine how frightening it would be to wake up and have no memory whatsoever—no recollection of your name, address, parents, or anything else.

Perhaps that is why we put so much value on maintaining good memory in old age and why memory training becomes so important. Memory is the yardstick with which society judges whether a person's mind is intact. Older adults are stereotyped as people whose memory is on the decline, people for whom forgetting is not to be taken lightly. Many people think that forgetting to buy a loaf of bread when one is 25 is all right, but forgetting it when one is 65 is cause for concern ("Do I have Alzheimer's disease?"). We will see that this belief is wrong. However, there is more at stake here than just another cognitive process: Memory intimately involves our sense of self (Cavanaugh, 1996).

Most of the research described in this chapter views memory as an end in itself. That is, the goal is simply to learn and remember some material. Doing well on a memory test is the name of the game. Indeed, many situations in life present similar demands. We may need to have a lot of information at our fingertips to do well at game shows such as *Who Wants to Be a Millionaire?*

But many other situations in everyday life call for memory to serve some other function. That is, we use memory as a means to an end. For example, we use memory when we summarize the most recent episode of our favorite soap opera, tell other people about ourselves, or reminisce about our high school days. In these situations we are using memory, but the point is not just how much we remember. More often, the idea is to facilitate social exchange, to allow other people to get to know us, or to give ourselves a shared past with others.

These different uses of memory raise some intriguing questions about adult development and aging. Are there differences in the ways in which adults of different ages use memory? How would these differences affect performance on traditional memory tests? What should our criteria be for good memory? Think about these questions as we explore what has been discovered about aging and memory. We attempt to answer them by looking at memory from different vantage points. First, we continue applying the information-processing model introduced in Chapter 6 and see what happens to the various memory systems. Second, we focus specifically on how we keep information stored in memory and how we get it back out. An important aspect here is how adults use different types of strategies to help themselves remember. Third, we look at memory for discourse and see how

people vary in the kinds of information they remember from such things as prose passages and television. Fourth, we consider several ways in which adults remember things in everyday life and the differences between these settings and laboratory research. Fifth, we examine how we use memory as a yardstick by which to judge our competence. In particular, we consider the processes by which we evaluate our memory. Finally, we explore how memory problems are assessed and how some problems can be treated.

Memory researchers have long focused on three general steps in memory processing as potential sources of age differences: encoding, storage, and retrieval (Smith, 1996). **Encoding** *is the process of getting information into the memory system.* **Storage** *is the manner in which information is represented and kept in memory. Getting information back out of memory is called* **retrieval.** Because there is no evidence of age differences in how information is organized in storage, most research has examined encoding and retrieval as sources of age differences (Light, 1996; Zacks et al., 2000).

Researchers have looked at research on working memory capacity, speed of processing, and impaired inhibition to gain insights into why age differences in memory occur. As we will see, these mechanisms involve information that is being actively processed, and they show clear age differences. More recently, researchers have examined contextual features and social contextual factors that could account for age-related differences in memory. We will see that these approaches offer alternative explanations for memory decline.

INFORMATION PROCESSING REVISITED

Susan is a 75-year-old widow who feels that she does not remember recent events, such as whether she took her medicine, as well as she used to. She also occasionally forgets to turn off the gas on her stove and sometimes does not recognize her friend's voice on the phone. However, she has no trouble remembering things from her 20s. Susan wonders if this is normal or whether she should be worried.

Chapter 6 introduced us to the most widely used model of cognitive processes: the information-processing model. Recall that the information-processing model is based on a computer metaphor and that different aspects of the model have different jobs to perform. We focused on early steps in processing, speed of processing, attention, and language processing. Our focus in this section is on two other main components: short-term memory, including both short-term capacity and working memory, and multiple systems of long-term memory. The multiple systems of long-term memory are what Susan is most worried about. As we shall see, it is very common to have trouble remembering more recent episodes and events as opposed to more remote memories from the past.

Working Memory

When we left off in Chapter 6, we had followed the flow of information from its initial reception in sensory memory, through attention, to the initial steps of linguistic processing. We are now ready to consider how information is kept in one's mind for additional processing into long-term memory systems or is held temporarily during retrieval. How this happens involves working memory.

Originally, this type of immediate memory process was conceptualized as passive short-term storage or short-term memory. The idea is that people have a limited capacity for remembering information (about seven chunks of information; Miller, 1956). The question is whether older adults maintain this capacity. A typical short-term memory task measures the longest span of digits a person can recall immediately after presentation. Studies typically report little or no age difference in these simple and passive span measures (Zacks et al., 2000).

However, some researchers have found evidence that, depending on the stimuli presented, older adults perform more poorly on simple span tasks than young adults (Zacks et al., 2000). However, this age difference can be accounted for by more active information processing variables involved in short-term memory (Verhaeghen et al., 1993). One such variable is working memory, an age-sensitive factor that affects long-term memory processing, such as encoding information into long-term memory (Zacks et al., 2000). **Working memory** *is the active processes and structures involved in holding information in mind and simultaneously using that information, sometimes in conjunction with incoming information, to solve a problem, make a decision, or learn new information* (Zacks et al., 2000). Although some authors regard working memory as a specific store (Stine, 1990), others consider it an umbrella term for many similar short-term holding and computational processes relating to a wide range of cognitive skills and knowledge domains (Zacks et al., 2000). This places working memory right in the thick of things: It plays an active, critical, and central role in encoding, storage, and retrieval.

Recall that sensory memory has a very large capacity to deal with incoming information. In contrast, researchers generally agree that working memory has a small capacity. This capacity limitation of working memory operates like a juggler who can keep only a small number of items in the air simultaneously. Because working memory deals with information being processed right at this moment, it also acts as a kind of mental scratchpad. This means that unless we take direct action to keep the information active, the page we are using will be used up quickly and tossed away. For this reason, we need to have some way to keep information in working memory.

Most evidence indicates that there is greater age-related decline in working memory than in the passive short-term memory storage just described (Salthouse, 1991; Zacks et al., 2000), although the extent of the decline is still in doubt. Foos (1995) found that both young and middle-aged adults can perform more than one memory task with equal success, but when older adults are presented with multiple tasks,

Activities such as spinning involve retrieving elaborate memory representation for each aspect of the activity as well as accurately monitoring what one is doing.

they performed more poorly. This finding is consistent with the notion that the ability to allocate capacity in working memory to more than one task declines with age.

Salthouse and colleagues (1991; Verhaeghen & Salthouse, 1997) believe that working memory is the key to understanding age differences in memory. They argue that the loss of some of the ability to hold items in working memory may limit older adults' overall cognitive functioning. For example, many researchers propose working memory as the basis for understanding language processing and production difficulties encountered in later life (Kemtes & Kemper, 1997; Light et al., 1994; Stine, 1990) as well as reasoning (Salthouse, 1994) and memory (Park et al., 1996). This idea is based on the extremely important role working memory is believed to play in information processing. For example, working memory is where all the action is during processing: It is where information obtains meaning and is transformed for

longer storage. As a result, age differences here would have profound implications for almost all aspects of memory. If information becomes degraded or is only partially integrated into one's knowledge base, it is very difficult to remember it.

Moreover, Salthouse points out that many of the apparent differences in working memory may be related to processing speed. That is, older adults' reduced working memory capacity may result from their overall slower rate of processing. In an effort to understand the role of speed in working memory, Salthouse and Babcock (1991) conducted a large-scale study of 400 adults. They were able to separate working memory performance into storage, processing, and executive functions (which involve the coordination of storage and processing). Their results indicated that age differences in working memory were caused mostly by the processing component of tasks, which in turn was mediated by reductions in simple speed of processing. Similarly, other studies have found that age-related decline in language processing could be completely accounted for by working memory, which in turn is accounted for by speed (Van der Linden et al., 1999).

However, some evidence suggests that age differences in working memory are not universal. For example, working memory appears to depend on the type of information being used and may even vary across different tasks (Hale et al., 1996; Logie, 1995). Such differences complicate matters. Myerson and colleagues (1999) found that age-related decline in spatial working memory is much greater than that in verbal working memory, although there is decline in both types of working memory. In other words, age differences were more pronounced when subjects were asked to remember locations than when they were asked to remember digits.

To complicate matters further, a study of university professors provides evidence that professors have fewer declines in working memory than most people do, probably because of their jobs, which require more efficient planning, organizational, and retrieval strategies (Shimamura et al., 1995). For example, giving a lecture places great demands on working memory, which, when practiced over many years, results in better efficiency in later life.

Overall, the evidence of age-related decline in working memory is not entirely clear, but there is compelling evidence for how age-differences in working memory relate to performance on more complex cognitive tasks. Yet a great deal more must be done. Salthouse and colleagues' attempt to link age differences in working memory with age differences in processing speed will open up new and exciting avenues for research. Differential magnitude of decline in different domains of working memory suggest that it may not be a matter of overall general decline but a much more specific decline in certain areas. There is little doubt that working memory is a critical concept for understanding age-related differences in memory performance. For example, researchers have begun to show that working memory may be key to understanding the age differences in recall performance (discussed in the next section), especially in situations in which few cues for remembering exist (Park et al., 1994).

Long-Term Memory

When most people think about memory, they think about having to remember something over time, whether a few minutes or many days. Everyday life is full of examples: remembering routines, performing on an exam, summarizing a book or movie, and remembering an appointment. These types of situations constitute what memory researchers call long-term memory (Smith, 1996; Zacks et al., 2000). **Long-term memory** *is the ability to remember extensive amounts of information from a few seconds to a few hours to decades.* Memory researchers have created a wide variety of tasks requiring subjects to remember all sorts of information for varying lengths of time. More than a century of research has indicated that long-term memory represents a large-capacity store in which information can be kept for long periods. More recently, mounting research in cognitive neuropsychology suggests that long-term memory is not a unitary construct but consists of distinct multiple systems (Gabrieli, 1998) that are functionally different and are served by different brain structures (Zacks et al., 2000).

These functionally different systems can be divided into memory systems that involve **explicit memory,** *which is deliberate and conscious remembering of information that is learned and remembered at a specific time,* and memory systems that involve information retrieval without conscious recollection (e.g., implicit memory, procedural memory). We return to this nonconscious type of memory later. Let us focus first on the more deliberate and effortful systems of long-term memory. Two important types of long-term memory are episodic and semantic memory. **Episodic memory** *is the general class of memory having to do with the conscious recollection of information from a specific event or time.* Examples of episodic memory include learning the material in this course so that you will be able to reproduce it on an examination in the future, remembering what you did on your summer vacation last year, and memorizing a speech for a play.

Semantic memory *concerns learning and remembering the meaning of words and concepts that are not* *tied to specific occurrences of events in time.* Examples of semantic memory include recalling the definitions of words to complete crossword puzzles, translating this paragraph from English into French, and understanding what the instructor is saying in a lecture. The distinction between episodic and semantic memory is important in understanding age differences in memory. For example, people with Alzheimer's disease show extreme deficits in episodic memory, compared with older adults who do not have this disease, but these groups are more comparable on semantic memory performance (Cavanaugh & Nocera, 1994).

AGE DIFFERENCES IN EPISODIC MEMORY. Because episodic memory includes so many of the day-to-day activities adults perform, it has been the focus of more research than any other topic in memory development (Zacks et al., 2000). Typically, researchers study episodic memory by having people learn information, such as a list of words, and then asking them to recall or recognize the items. **Recall** *involves remembering information without hints or cues.* Everyday examples of recall include telling everything that you can remember about a movie or taking an essay exam. **Recognition,** *on the other hand, involves selecting previously learned information from among several items.* Everyday examples of recognition include taking multiple-choice tests and picking out the names of your high school friends from a complete list of your classmates.

Memory researchers use several techniques to study the variables that influence episodic memory performance. For example, they may vary the way in which the information to be learned is presented (such as in organized groups, with cues, or randomly), the speed at which it is presented, the familiarity of the material, and the conditions for remembering the items (e.g., giving recall cues or making a recognition test easy or hard).

The results from hundreds of studies point to several conclusions. Overall, older adults perform worse than younger adults on tests of episodic memory recall in that they omit more information, include more intrusions, and repeat more previously recalled items

(Spencer & Raz, 1995; LaVoie & Light, 1994; Zacks et al., 2000). These age differences are large; for example, more than 80% of a sample of adults in their 20s will do better than adults in their 70s (Verhaeghen et al., 1993; Verhaeghen & Salthouse, 1997). These differences are not reliably lowered by providing slower presentation or by giving cues or reminders during recall. On recognition tests, differences between older and younger adults are smaller. However, in comparison with young adults, older adults are more likely to accept never-represented items as having occurred on the test, especially if they share a conceptual meaning or perceptual resemblance to the previously presented items (Zacks et al., 2000).

Older adults also tend to be less efficient at spontaneously using internal study strategies, such as using imagery or putting items into categories in one's mind to organize information during study. When older adults are instructed to use internal organizational strategies such as categorization, however, they not only can do so but also perform significantly better. However, these improvements generally are not sufficient to substantially reduce age differences in recall performance (Verhaeghen et al., 1993). Additionally, the failure to use strategies such as association and repetition may be the result of age changes in speed of processing and associative memory (Verhaeghen & Marcoen, 1994). These findings suggest that older adults are not as successful in situations requiring them to devise an efficient way to acquire disorganized information, especially when they will be expected to recall it later.

Age differences between older and younger adults can be reduced in several ways. First, allowing older adults to practice or to perform a similar task before learning a new list improves performance. Knowing what one is expected to do usually makes it easier to perform well. Interestingly, better memory performance after practice parallels similar improvements after practice on tests of skills related to fluid intelligence (discussed in Chapter 8). Second, using material that is more familiar to older adults also improves their performance. For example, older adults do not remember words such as *byte* and *Walkman* as well as words such as *jitterbug* and *bobbysox.* Third, older adults can use compensatory strategies to help themselves remember, and their beliefs about memory can affect performance.

What can we conclude about episodic memory? Older adults apparently are disadvantaged when left on their own to face rapid-paced, disorganized information. However, memory performance appears to be somewhat flexible and can be manipulated, with improvements coming from a variety of sources. Later we consider some attempts to explain why age differences occur and several ways in which memory problems can be corrected. Let us now explore memory systems that do not show dramatic age differences.

AGE DIFFERENCES IN SEMANTIC MEMORY. As indicated earlier, semantic memory is spared with age in the absence of a disease state. Evidence suggests that there are no deficits in semantic memory processes such as language comprehension, knowledge structure, and general knowledge activation (Light, 1996). Semantic memory retrieval typically does not tax working memory, so older adults can draw upon experience in word meanings or general world knowledge. In addition, whereas retrieval of episodic memories is based on cues to the original experience, semantic memories are retrieved conceptually as part of our world knowledge. The fact that semantic memory emphasizes the retrieval of general knowledge is coextensive with a major component of intelligence, acquired knowledge, which is discussed in Chapter 8. As we shall see, intelligence as acquired knowledge remains stable throughout most of older adulthood.

The major area in which age-related decline in semantic memory can be observed is in its accessibility. This is illustrated in word-finding deficits. Older adults typically have more trouble retrieving a target word when presented with a definition of the word, and they tend to have more tip-of-the-tongue (TOT) experiences (MacKay & Abrams, 1996; Smith & Earles, 1996). A TOT experience occurs when you try to retrieve a name or word and you feel you know the word, but it is not quite accessible. For example, you are at a party and you see someone very familiar and you know that you know that person's name but you

cannot retrieve it. Another aspect of this TOT experience is that you can retrieve partial information, such as the number of syllables in that person's name, the initial sounds or letters, and where to stress each syllable (stress pattern). Older adults not only experience more TOTs but also report less partial information about the target, both in the laboratory and in everyday life (MacKay & Abrams, 1996). TOT problems indicate that even highly familiar information can become more difficult to retrieve as we grow older.

Let's now examine a memory process that entails both semantic and episodic memory but is spared with age: autobiographical memory.

Remote Memory, or Autobiographical Memory

Information that must be kept for a very long time (from a few hours to many years) is housed in **remote memory,** traditionally called tertiary memory (Hess & Pullen, 1996; Poon, 1985). Such information includes facts learned earlier, the meaning of words, past life experiences, and the like. Very little research has been conducted on age differences in remote memory, for a variety of reasons. For one thing, designing an adequate test of very long-term memory so that we know how to interpret performance is difficult. For example, we often cannot know whether an incident that someone recalls from the past is what actually happened because we cannot verify the facts. Additionally, if a person does not remember a fact from years past, it may be because of an inability to retrieve the information or a failure to learn the information in the first place. This latter issue is especially important when older and younger adults are compared; we must make certain that both groups had the opportunity and learned the information. Some ingenious researchers have managed to circumvent these problems and have studied a particular aspect of very long-term memory: autobiographical memory.

Autobiographical memory *involves remembering information and events from one's own life.* These recollections provide each of us with a personal history and help define who we are. As important as autobiographical memory is, very few studies have looked at how well people remember things over the course of their lives.

One kind of personal information we remember is the names of our high school classmates. Bahrick and colleagues (1975) tested high school graduates aged 17 to 74 for recall of their classmates' names and recognition of their faces in yearbook pictures. Recognition of faces was consistently over 90% up to 15 years after graduation. Amazingly, adults in their 70s could still recognize 70% of their classmates' names 48 years after graduation. Clearly, autobiographical memory remains fairly good. The study also demonstrates that in some areas we can assess the accuracy of very long-term memory. Being able to verify what people remember using a record of the true event is extremely important in evaluating our ability to remember over long periods of time.

The issue of verification is crucial in testing people's recollections of personally experienced events. Only in cases where records have been kept for many years is this usually possible. Coleman and colleagues (1991) examined records that were available from the Harvard Longitudinal Studies of Child Health and Development on people from birth to age 50. Detailed information was collected over the years on such things as which childhood diseases the participants had, whether they smoked cigarettes, and what kinds and how much food they ate. At age 50, participants completed a lengthy questionnaire about these issues, and their responses were compared with similar reports made 10 and 20 years earlier, as well as with the official records. Coleman and colleagues found amazing accuracy for information such as whether a person had ever been a smoker or had a particular disease such as chicken pox. In fact, half of the memories elicited at age 50 were more accurate than the memories of the same information elicited at age 40. However, information about amounts of food consumed or about individual episodes was not remembered very well. Apparently, these events tend to get blended together and are not stored as separate incidents.

What distinguishes events that are memorable from those that are not? What makes a moment we will remember the rest of our lives? Many people

Memory for faces from the past can be maintained for long periods of time, as people have experienced at high school reunions as far back as 50 years.

think that highly traumatic events are ones that are indelibly etched in our memories. If so, then people who survived Nazi concentration camps should have vivid memories of their experiences. Wagenaar and Groeneweg (1990) examined the testimony of 78 survivors of Camp Erika, a Nazi concentration camp in the Netherlands during World War II. Dutch police initially interviewed the survivors about their experiences between 1943 and 1948. In 1984, during a war crimes trial for an accused Nazi collaborator, these witnesses gave sworn depositions about their experiences at Camp Erika.

The camp survivors' recollections were a mix of accurate and inaccurate information. In many cases memory was quite good; even 40 years later about half of the survivors remembered the exact date of their arrival at the camp and their entire identification number. They were able to recall the general conditions of the camp, overall treatment, and the like. However, they had forgotten many important details, including in some cases their own brutal treatment. Wagenaar and Groeneweg point out that these forgotten details mean that even extreme trauma is no guarantee that an event will be remembered. Perhaps forgetting the horrors of being brutalized is even a type of self-protection.

Events do not always have to be personally traumatic to be highly memorable, however. Some historical events that have great personal relevance, very unusual or novel events, and other events that are highly emotional are also remembered very well. Such memories are called flashbulb memories because they are so vivid that it seems as if we have a photograph of the event (Fitzgerald, 1999; Rubin & Kozin, 1984). Although many events tend to be of major historical significance, such as the assassinations of John F. Kennedy and Martin Luther King, Jr., or the death of major movie or music stars, flashbulb memories may also involve personal autobiographical events (Rubin & Kozin, 1984). Such events tend to impress the circumstances in which the person first heard the news about the event and include information about the place, other people present at the time, what activities were occurring, and the source of the information (Cohen et al., 1994).

An interesting phenomenon arises when you examine the distribution of flashbulb memories as well as vivid autobiographical events across people's life spans. As can be seen in Figure 7.1, for both younger and older adults vivid memories experienced earlier in life (between 10 and 30 years of age) are reported more often than those occurring during middle adulthood (between 30 and 50 years of age; Fitzgerald & Lawrence, 1984; Fitzgerald, 1999; Rubin & Schulkind, 1997). In addition, on a factual memory test of Academy Award winners, news stories, and teams that played in the World Series, events that occurred earlier rather than later in life were remembered better (Rubin et al., 1998). It may be the case that this earlier period of life has importance in defining oneself and thus helps organize personal memories (Fitzgerald, 1999).

Implicit Memory

As we discussed earlier, there is a type of long-term memory that is nonconscious and effortless: implicit memory. **Implicit memory** *is a facilitation or change in task performance that is attributable to having been exposed to information at some earlier time but does not involve active, explicit memory.* A good example of implicit memory is a language task such as stem completion. In a stem completion task, you would be

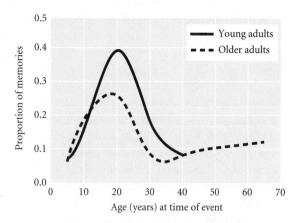

FIGURE 7.1 **The distribution of flashbulb memories produced by younger and older adults.**

Source: Fitzgerald, J. (1999). Autobiographical memory and social cognition. In T. M. Hess & F. Blanchard-Fields (Eds.), *Social cognition and aging* (p. 161). San Diego: Academic Press.

required to complete a word stem with the first word that comes to mind (for instance, "con____"). Previously, you may have been shown a list of words that contained a valid completion of the stem (such as "contact"). If you have seen valid completions of the stems, you are more likely to use them later to complete the stems than you are to make up a different one ("contest"). This facilitation is called priming (Zacks et al., 2000). The memory aspect of the task is remembering the stem completion you were shown; the implicit part is remembering it without being told to do so.

Early research on implicit memory focused on demonstrating that it was a separate process from explicit memory. For example, whereas explicit memory performance is affected by having people think about the meaning of the items, implicit memory is not (Graf & Mandler, 1984), and people with amnesia show severe problems on explicit memory tests but often perform similarly to normal people on implicit memory tests (Shimamura, 1986). These findings suggested that implicit memory may be an exception to the general finding of age-related decline in long-term memory for new information (Fleischman & Gabrieli, 1998; Zacks et al., 2000).

More recent research reveals that age differences on implicit memory tests are either not there or are notably smaller than age effects on more explicit memory tasks (Fleischman & Gabrieli, 1998; LaVoie & Light, 1994). When age differences do appear, it is almost always in favor of young adults, although the age difference is smaller than for explicit memory tests (LaVoie & Light, 1994). In addition, there are some differences between various types of implicit memory tests. The most important distinction has been between perceptually based and conceptually based tests (Roediger & McDermott, 1993). Perceptually based implicit memory tasks rely on processing the physical features of a stimulus; an example would be processing whether a word appears in lowercase or uppercase letters. Conceptually based implicit memory tasks rely on the semantic meaning of the items, such as whether the word is a verb. Depending on what people are asked to process (i.e., physical features or semantic meaning), performance on the tests differs (Small et al., 1995).

The difference between the types of tests has important implications for age differences (Small et al., 1995). Results from several studies reveal a mixed pattern of age differences in implicit memory; some studies find no differences on conceptual tasks and age differences on perceptual tasks (Small et al., 1995), whereas others find the reverse pattern (Jelicic et al., 1996). Furthermore, others find that older adults show greater conceptual priming, whereas young adults do not (Multhaup et al., 1998). However, overall evidence suggests equal age effects in the two types of priming (Fleischman & Gabrieli, 1998).

What accounts for the sparing of implicit memory with age? Recent research in cognitive neuropsychology suggests that there is differential age-related deterioration in the brain underlying more explicit forms of memory (e.g., frontal–striatal system) as opposed to those underlying implicit memory (e.g., cerebral neocortex; Prull et al., 2000; Tulving & Schacter, 1990). However, more behaviorally oriented researchers point out that some age-related decline is evident in implicit memory tasks, so this biological distinction warrants further research (La Voie & Light, 1994; Zacks et al., 2000).

CONCEPT CHECKS

1. Why is working memory important in understanding age differences in performance?
2. What major differences are there between older and younger adults' working memory?
3. How do age differences in episodic and semantic memory compare?
4. What differences have been observed between older and younger adults in aspects of autobiographical memory?
5. What are the age-related differences between implicit and explicit memory?

SOURCES OF AGE DIFFERENCES IN MEMORY

LEARNING OBJECTIVES

- What evidence is there for age differences in encoding?
- What age differences have been observed in retrieval?
- What are the relative contributions of encoding and retrieval in explaining age differences in performance?
- How does automatic retrieval affect age differences in memory?
- What age differences have been observed in processing misinformation as true?

Cynthia is an older woman sitting on a jury for the first time. The crime is a burglary. An eyewitness speculates about whether the defendant had a crowbar, given that someone told him that there was a crowbar at the crime scene. The judge announces to the jury to disregard that statement; it is from an unreliable source. Back in deliberation, Cynthia has trouble remembering whether evidence of a crowbar in the hands of the defendant was to be disregarded or believed.

We have seen that older and younger adults differ in how well they perform on some memory tasks. Why do these age differences exist? Are older adults poorer at getting information into memory? Or do they get the information in just as well but have more difficulty getting it back out? Is it related to how efficiently they manipulate information in working memory? Or do they forget the source of the information, as Cynthia did?

For many years, researchers examining age differences in memory performance have tried to implicate encoding or retrieval as the source of the problem. However, such attempts have met with mixed results (Zacks et al., 2000). More recent work based on brain metabolism, automaticity in retrieval, and the social context of memory raises some interesting questions about the source of memory deficits. Before we do, let's examine the evidence for the relative contribution of encoding and retrieval deficits to poorer memory performance in older adults.

Age Differences in Encoding and Retrieval

Results from years of research suggest an age-related decrement in encoding processes (Craik & Byrd, 1982; Kausler, 1982; Poon, 1985; Smith, 1996). An example of an encoding process that affects memory is elaborative rehearsal. Elaborative **rehearsal** *involves making connections between incoming information and information already known.* For example, a person presented with the word *emu* and told that this is a bird that does not fly may try to think of other flightless birds. With some thought, *ostrich* may come to mind. Linking *emu* and *ostrich* would be an example of this type of rehearsal.

Research in support of an age-related decrement in elaborative rehearsal finds that older adults have more difficulty making such connections than younger adults do (Light, 1996; Smith, 1996). Interestingly, however, once these connections have been made, older and younger adults maintain them equivalently (which supports the conclusion that whereas encoding differences exist, storage differences do not). For example, older adults would be slower than younger adults at making the emu–ostrich connection, but once it is made both groups would remember it just as well.

However, studies testing the hypothesis that older adults are slower at making connections with incoming information are confusing. Some find that increased elaboration at encoding disproportionately benefits older adults (Park et al., 1990), whereas others find either no difference (Park et al., 1986) or greater benefits for younger adults (Puglisi & Park,

1987). These findings point to a complex relation between elaboration at encoding and age (Zacks et al., 2000). Some suggest that these discrepancies can be accounted for by the type of retrieval process (e.g., recall or recognition) used (Baddeley, 1990; Zacks et al., 2000). However, it is difficult to draw a distinction between encoding and retrieval. In fact, a growing perspective is that older adults are less likely to engage in effective ways of processing information both at encoding and at retrieval (Craik et al., 1995; Hasher et al., 1999).

This is exemplified in studies that examine task variables that could affect encoding or retrieval. One such variable is divided attention (discussed in Chapter 6). In this type of experiment, participants perform an extra task such as a reaction time task (see Chapter 6) under one of two conditions: while they are studying a list of words (i.e., during encoding) or while they are recalling the words (i.e., during retrieval; Anderson et al., 1998). First, it should be noted that divided attention disrupts memory performance for both younger and older adults, just more so for older adults. Second, using this type of design, some studies find costs in performance for older adults when the divided attention occurs at retrieval (Whiting & Smith, 1997). However, a majority of others find that memory is significantly more compromised when the divided attention task occurs at encoding (Anderson et al., 1998; Nyberg et al., 1997).

For example, Anderson and colleagues (1998) conclude that attentional resources are consumed to a greater extent at encoding, whereas at retrieval processes operate outside attentional control. If you are trying to study for a test while trying to tune out a conversation going on in the same room, you will place a lot of effort into using strategies to focus on the information to be studied. However, if you were told that the conversation was about you, you would probably exert more effort listening to the conversation. You would perform better on the test in the first case than in the second case. Attentional control was necessary while you encoded the information you needed to succeed on the test. However, the distracting conversation would not hurt you when you were taking the test in either condition.

One important aspect of maintaining attentional control and expending attentional resources is that when we are confronted with large amounts of information we need to remember, we tend to use various techniques, called **strategies,** that make the task easier and increase the efficiency of storage. Let us examine strategy differences in older adults.

USE OF STRATEGIES

A critical issue is whether older adults behave strategically when trying to study information to be remembered. Two effective strategies for learning new information are to organize it and to establish links to help you remember the information. For example, consider a student's efforts to learn the information in college courses. Learning the necessary facts of chemistry, psychology, literature, and so forth is much easier if separate notebooks are kept for each class. Imagine the potential for confusion if all the class notes were mixed together. Keeping them separate is an example of an organizational strategy. Evidence suggests that older adults do not spontaneously organize incoming information or establish meaningful links to aid in recall as often or as well as younger adults, which could account for poorer memory performance (Kausler, 1994; Smith, 1996). For example, older adults are less likely to take advantage of similarities in meaning between words (such as the link between *river* and *lake*) presented randomly in a list as a way to organize the items. Because the number of items remembered from such a list is highly related to the use of organization, younger adults outperform older adults on such tasks. However, the available evidence suggests that the spontaneous production of effective strategies does not fully account for age differences in memory performance (Hertzog & Hultsch, 2000; Light, 1996; Salthouse, 1991).

In fact Hertzog and colleagues (1998) found that only 35% of older adults, compared with 49% of younger adults, used optimal strategies for encoding such as placing related items into meaningful categories. However, as Figure 7.2 shows, there were large age differences in recall irrespective of strategy methods used. Finally, they found that strategy production

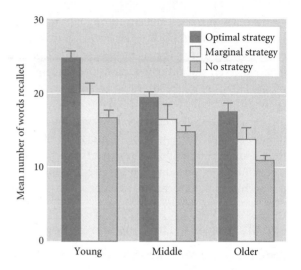

FIGURE 7.2 Mean recall for young, middle-aged, and older adults as a function of strategy groups.

From Herzog, C. et al. (1998), *Aging, Neuropsychology, and Cognition,* pp. 85–106, © Swets & Zeitlinger. Used with permission.

had a very modest effect on age differences in recall. To support this finding, Dunlosky and Hertzog (1998) also found that large age differences in recall remained even when older adults were instructed to use effective strategies. However, as Hertzog and Hultsch (2000) point out, producing a strategy does not necessarily imply that one can use the strategy effectively. We need more research to differentiate the quality of strategy implementation from their production. Current thinking suggests that this is an important avenue for future research on adaptive behavior in learning new information (Hertzog & Hultsch, 2000). We explore this avenue more when we discuss remediation of memory deficits later.

With respect to retrieval, one of the clearest findings concerns the TOT phenomenon we discussed earlier. Older adults show greater frequency of TOT and feeling-of-knowing (feeling you know something yet you are not sure what it is) states after failure to retrieve information (Burke & Harrold, 1988; MacKay & Abrams, 1996; Maylor, 1990). This is probably because of a temporary inaccessibility. In fact, older adults are as likely as young adults to recognize the material they cannot recall when in the TOT state.

Based on the available evidence, we can conclude that memory functioning in the aging adult is influenced by deficits in both encoding and retrieval (Zacks et al., 2000). Recent evidence also indicates that encoding difficulties may be especially important (Anderson et al., 1998; Grady et al., 1995).

The positron emission tomography (PET) brain imaging can be used to help understand changes in memory. Grady and her research team (1995) examined cerebral blood flow in younger and older adults during encoding and recognition of faces. Both age groups showed similar patterns of increased blood flow in specific areas of the brain during recognition but differed significantly during encoding. Compared with older adults, younger adults showed significantly greater increases in blood flow to the left prefrontal and temporal areas of the brain. Grady and colleagues interpreted these differences as evidence that age-related memory differences may be caused by older adults' failure to encode information adequately. Inadequate encoding could result in information not getting into memory at all or being less elaborately encoded, making retrieval more difficult.

The research on encoding and retrieval processes is important for three reasons. First, it emphasizes that age-related decrements in memory are complex; they are not caused by changes in a single process. Second, intervention or training programs must consider both encoding and retrieval. Training people to use encoding strategies without also training them how to use retrieval strategies will not work. To the extent that only partial information is encoded, retrieval strategies must focus on helping people find whatever aspects are available. Third, theories of how memory changes with age must take individual differences into account, especially differential rates of change in component processes. Overall, finding the sources of memory decline demonstrates the importance of considering multiple levels of influence. We illustrate this principle further in the Forces in Action feature.

Theories of memory development must consider the components of processes that change and those that do not. However, not all aspects of retrieval are effortful and do not necessarily demand resources that overburden older adults' processing. We next examine a recent area of research that centers on automatic retrieval processes that tend to be equivalent for older and younger adults.

The Emerging Role of Automatic Retrieval

Jacoby and colleagues (Hay & Jacoby, 1999; Jacoby, 1991; Jacoby et al., 1997) have found that memory situations involve both automatic and deliberate processes. They used a clever procedure called the process dissociation paradigm to separate the different contributions of each of these two types of processes in a memory task. To illustrate, Jacoby and colleagues conducted a series of studies examining the false fame effect (Dywan & Jacoby, 1990; Jennings & Jacoby, 1993). In a typical study, older and younger adults are asked to read a list of nonfamous names. Then they are given a new list consisting of three types of names: names from the first list, additional nonfamous names, and moderately famous names. Participants are asked to indicate which of the names presented are famous. They are also told that the names on the original list were nonfamous. If they recognize any names from that list, they are to exclude them from further consideration.

The false fame effect results when a previously observed nonfamous name (on the original list) is mistakenly identified as a famous name at testing. Studying the original nonfamous names increases their familiarity. When they see this name again and they do not consciously remember that it was on the original list, they mistake familiarity for fame. Dywan and Jacoby (1990) found that older adults produce a larger false fame effect than young adults do. In a subsequent study, Jennings and Jacoby (1993) added another condition: Adults were told that the names from the original list were obscure famous names, so if it looked familiar at testing, it would be appropriate to label it as famous whether or not you consciously recollected it. The first experiment assesses how conscious recollection affects memory, and the second study assesses how familiarity affects memory.'

Why does memory decline with age? This question lends itself nicely to understanding the role of the four developmental forces. First, at the biological level, a number of factors influencing memory decline have been identified. From a neuropsychological perspective, for example, deterioration of the frontal lobe areas has been implicated in the decline of working memory. The hippocampal region has been related to current memory functioning and the rate of further memory decline over time (Prull et al., 2000).

Psychological factors are apparent in memory functioning. For example, the degree to which a person believes he or she has control over his or her memory functioning and can maintain good memory influences actual memory functioning. Sociocultural forces are somewhat related to people's beliefs about their memory. Stereotypes about aging espouse negative competencies in the memory domain. This can have negative consequences because we are socialized to believe that our memory will decline as we grow older. Finally,

life-cycle forces influence memory performance. As we grow older, our environment changes as a function of retirement, loss of spouse, and other events. These life events influence the amount of stimulation in our lives. As indicated later in this chapter, exercising one's memory is important to maintain one's memory potential.

Thus, multiple levels of forces influence memory and aging. All must be considered in an integrated manner to obtain a more complete picture of the changes that take place in memory over the life span.

Overall, the assessment of conscious recollection was lower for older adults than for young adults, but the assessment for automatic retrieval (in this case familiarity testing) in the second study did not differ across age groups. Thus, although conscious recollection is impaired, as mentioned earlier in this chapter, automatic retrieval of familiar information is spared.

Misinformation and Memory

The fact that older adults exhibit the false fame effect to a greater degree than young adults suggests that although familiarity is intact, conscious recollection is not, thus allowing familiarity to misinform the older adult's performance. Two other recent areas of research further explore older adults' susceptibility to misinformation caused by memory deficits: source memory and false memory.

SOURCE MEMORY. One perspective on the false fame effect considers it a function of deficient source monitoring. **Source memory** *is the ability to remember the source of a familiar event and the ability to determine whether an event was imagined or experienced* (Johnson et al., 1993; Schacter et al., 1998). For example, it

is important for an older adult to be able to discriminate whether she actually remembered to take her medication or only thought to do it. The ability to discriminate between these two events entails retrieving information about the context in which the event in question originally occurred. By reconstructing the original event accurately, the older adult will remember whether she took the medication.

Research on age differences in source memory reveals that older adults are less accurate at a number of source memory tasks, including recalling and recognizing the contextual features of events (Spencer & Raz, 1995), remembering whether something was actually said versus imagining it was said (Hashtroudi et al., 1994), determining whether the speaker of information was female or male (Bayen & Murnane, 1996), and determining whether items were presented in video or photo format (Schacter et al., 1997).

FALSE MEMORY. Another line of research that examines misinformation effects in older adults is false memory. **False memory** *is memory of items or events that did not occur.* It is typically studied by presenting participants with a list of words that are all associated with a specific word that was not presented. For ex-

Larry Jacoby (1999) asks, What causes the "I-told-you claim" effect? Does it create a false memory? From this perspective, exposure to misleading questions about an event can result in a permanent loss from memory of details of the actual experience (Loftus, 1975). In other words, the experience was overwritten by the misleading information. A blocking account suggests that exposure to misinformation impairs accessibility to the correct information but does not overwrite it (Ayers & Reder, 1998). A source memory account suggests that memory of the original experience coexists with the misleading information. However, confusion arises about the source of the information (Lindsay & Johnson,

1989). Jacoby (1999) suggests that it is improbable that the false I-told-you claim is a function of memory alterations such as those suggested here. He maintains that it is probably a function of bias or guessing. In other words, a false claim might occur only if people are unable to remember the original experience and thus resort to guessing. Acceptance of the false claim might rely on a person's forgetting the original experience (the initial phone call) and willingness to guess that the claim is valid. Thus, it may be the case that apparent memory impairment produces misinformation effects through forgetting and guessing rather than real changes in the memory itself. Jacoby (1999) conducted a number of

studies demonstrating this last alternative. He calls this phenomenon the accessibility bias, which influences guessing (e.g., that the older adult did send in a $1,200 check) and is a basis of responding independent of remembering (sending the con artist a check for $900).

ample, the experimenter presents the words *nurse, hospital, patient,* and *surgery* for the participant to study. At recall, she adds words (such as *doctor*) that did not appear on the original list yet are semantically related to the list of words. People tend to falsely recall and incorrectly recognize such a target word and feel very confident about it (Roediger & McDermott, 1995). Older adults tend to show an even greater degree of false memories under such conditions (Norman & Schacter, 1997; Tun et al., 1998). This type of effect usually is explained in terms of a retrieval strategy called plausibility (if it is consistent with the other words, it seems more likely to have been in the original list; Reder, Wible, & Martin, 1986; Wingfield et al., 1995).

From a practical, everyday perspective, the misinformation effects we've reviewed (including the false fame effect, source memory deficits, and false memories in older adults) could render older adults more susceptible to deceptions such as consumer scams.

In fact, Jacoby (1999) suggests that older adults are targets for fraudulent practices because of misinformation effects and aging. For example, Jacoby (1999) describes a typical scam perpetrated by con artists who telephone older adults to talk with them and surreptitiously gather as much personal information on them as possible. In a later callback, the con artist asks questions based on the previously gathered personal information and determines whether the older adult fails to remember the previous conversation. If so, the memory deficit is exploited with a false claim: "We received a check from you for $1,200, but it should have only been $950. Please send us another check for $950 and we will send the original check back to you." Of course, no check was sent earlier. Jacoby calls this the "I-told-you" claim. How do we explain this memory deficit? Is it a false memory, faulty source monitoring, or faulty accessibility? This is discussed in the Current Controversies feature.

The importance of this area of research is in its implications for helping older adults form a counter-attack for deceptions. For example, older adults can be trained to counter deception by refusing to respond unless they are certain that they can recollect what happened (Jacoby, 1999). Another strategy is to generate an alternative response to the first response that comes to mind, such as asking the con artist to return the earlier check before you send a new one (Jacoby, 1999).

CONCEPT CHECKS

1. What are the relative age differences in encoding and retrieval?
2. What age differences have been found in the use of memory strategies?
3. How has recent evidence from brain scans affected our understanding of the relative importance of encoding and retrieval?
4. How do age differences compare in automatic and deliberate retrieval?
5. How does processing of misinformation differ in older and younger adults?

DISCOURSE MEMORY

LEARNING OBJECTIVES

- What age differences are observed in text-based levels of discourse memory?
- What age differences are observed in situation models of discourse memory?
- What social factors and characteristics of individuals influence discourse memory?
- What aspects of text materials affect memory?
- How does discourse memory relate to episodic memory?

An older woman, Dorothy, loves the movies. In fact, her adult children go to her for advice for good movies to see. She is able to recount in elaborative strokes what the movie was all about, what the moral of the story was, and how it relates to life in general. At the same time, she can never remember the specific details such as the type of car the heroine drove or the names of the actors and actresses. But her children love her re-counting of the movies and are not dismayed by her lack of detail.

Typically, memory of structured materials that relate to prior knowledge is better than memory of information that is unfamiliar or unstructured (Zacks et al., 2000). The question is whether there are age differences in memory of structured information that relates to prior knowledge. This is most evident in memory of text or discourse.

Like Dorothy, adults of all ages spend a great deal of time reading books, magazines, and newspapers and watching television programs and movies. Collectively, such material is called discourse. Indeed, how well adults remember prose, or text passages, is one of the fastest growing areas in memory research. In part, this rapid growth reflects the realization that prose (such as a newspaper story) is something people need to remember in everyday life; word lists typically are not.

In this section we focus mainly on adults' ability to remember information they have read. We examine the types of situations and conditions that put older adults at a disadvantage or advantage in remembering text. To do this, researchers examine memory in terms of the different levels of linguistic structure of the text. At a basic level, there are specific propositions, or basic ideas represented in a text. In addition, propositions can be central to the story or less important to the story. For example, in a story about a burglary, the fact that the neighbor stole the woman's purse is central to the story, and the fact that the purse was purple is less important. These propositions are considered text-based levels for processing (e.g., central or main ideas versus less important details).

A higher level of text representation is called a situation model. Unlike the propositions, which are text-based, *at the **situation model** level people use their world knowledge to construct a more global understanding of what the text is about* (Wingfield & Stine-Morrow, 2000; Zwaan & Radvansky, 1998). For example, comprehending the story about the burglary involves elaborating on the story with several kinds of knowledge relevant to the situation (e.g., damage done by the break-in, anger felt from this violation, and loss of priceless mementos). Let's look at age differences in remembering text at both of these levels.

Text-Based Levels

Most of the work conducted in aging and discourse processing has examined memory at text-based levels. Because texts are constructed with information at these different hierarchical levels of importance, a key question is whether there are age differences in memory at these different levels. Answering this question amounts to looking for age differences between memory of main ideas and memory of details. The literature on this issue is large and complex (Wingfield & Stine-Morrow, 2000). In general, the data indicate two important points. First, when text is clearly organized, with emphasis on structure and the main ideas, older adults are similar to younger adults in recalling more main ideas than less important details.

However, in addition to these competencies in text processing, there are observed deficits under specific conditions. Studies show that older adults are adversely affected by rapid presentation, highly unpredictable or unorganized material, and material that is dense in propositions (Hartley et al., 1994; Stine et al., 1986; Wingfield & Lindfield, 1995). Older adults may be at a disadvantage when presented with text at speeds geared to younger adults. Indeed, when the speed-of-presentation variable is removed and participants can pace themselves, age differences are eliminated (Wingfield & Lindfield, 1995; Wingfield & Stine, 1986). In addition, the more predictable and meaningful the text, the better the older adults perform even at rapid rates (Gordon-Salant & Fitzgibbons, 1997; Wingfield, 1996). Finally, high verbal ability reduces age differences in overall recall during rapid presentation (Wingfield & Stine-Morrow, 2000).

Another area of difficulty for older adults appears when the text becomes propositionally dense (an increase in the number of propositions) and less familiar. In this case, older adults have more difficulty than young adults do in identifying or inhibiting less important details (Hartley, 1993; Wingfield & Stine-Morrow, 2000). These difficulties on the part of older

© Jeff Greenberg / PhotoEdit

Older and younger adults alike remember gist information from text, but younger adults tend to remember more low-level details.

adults can be related to reduced working memory capacity, which constrains the number of propositions to be considered at one time, or lack of inhibitory control (discussed in Chapter 6), which allows less relevant propositions to interfere with processing of main ideas (Wingfield & Stine-Morrow, 2000).

Situation Models

Sometime in your educational career you probably had to read a long novel for a literature class. If you opted for the book rather than the video or abridged version, you probably were surprised at how different your recollections of the story were from your classmates'. Many of these differences result from differences in the ways in which each of us constructs a situation model of the text. Situation models of the text include other features besides text-based information such as characters' emotional states, goals, and personality characteristics as well as spatial relations between the people, objects, and events described (Morrow et al., 1997; Zwaan & Radvansky, 1998). In addition, the reader's characteristics such as personal biases, the social context in which you are recalling a text, and personal motivations for remembering certain bits of information while forgetting others influence the model.

Overall, both younger and older adults construct and update situation models similarly (Zacks et al., 2000). For example, Morrow and colleagues (1997) had older and younger adults memorize a map of a building in which there were several rooms with different objects in each of the rooms. They then read a narrative about a character who was moving from one room to another. The situation model consists of a spatial organization centered on the main character and her location. When they interrupted the participants' reading of the narratives and asked them whether certain objects were near or far from the main character's current location, both younger and older adults' answers were more accurate and faster when the object was close to the main character. However, older adults took longer to memorize the maps and were slower overall in their reading times. Morrow and colleagues (1997) conclude that although older and younger adults use similar strategies to update their situation models, the updating process is more effortful for older adults.

How adults decide to retell a story also is important. Adams and colleagues (1990) presented fables and nonfables to younger and older adults and examined their story recall styles. They found that older adults used a more integrative or interpretive style for nonfable passages, whereas younger adults used a more literal or text-based style. Age differences were not found for the fable passages. These findings mean that younger adults may spontaneously shift their recall style depending on the type of passage, whereas older adults may use a more consistently integrative style regardless of passage type.

Another variable that affects performance is amount of prior knowledge or expertise. Morrow and colleagues (1992) compared memory of narrative text concerning aviation or nonaviation themes in young and older pilots and young and older novices. Irrespective of age, higher expertise (in the pilots) was associated with better memory for aviation narratives. However, both pilots and nonpilots showed similar age deficits in memory in both types of narratives. Thus, although prior knowledge and expertise have similar effects on memory performance in young and older adults, they do not completely reduce age differences in memory.

Finally, another variable affecting both higher and lower levels of text is the social context of remembering. Retelling information more typically occurs in a social context in everyday life. After we see a movie we retell its contents to our friends, or we recount a story we have just read to a friend over the telephone. An interesting question posed by Cynthia Adams and colleagues (in press) is whether some contexts are better for remembering for older adults than are others. In essence she found that the social context matters, and older adults' retelling of stories varies depending on who the listener is. We examine this finding in more detail in the How Do We Know? feature.

Text Variables

All text material is not created equal. Some books or passages are very easy to read, comprehend, and remember, and others are not. Texts differ widely in how the information they contain is organized. One way to think about text organization is to compare it to the outline form that is taught in composition classes. Some information is basic and is given prominence in the outline; other information simply expands the main points and is embedded in the outline. In a well-organized text the main ideas are interrelated, and the passage is like a tightly woven tapestry. Such texts are more memorable, especially if one follows the built-in organizational structure.

An important aspect of text variables is that they may interact with personal characteristics to create differences in discourse memory. An example of this interaction involves situations in which people hold opinions or have knowledge about a topic and then read additional information. In terms of people's ability to remember this new information, does it matter whether the new information agrees or disagrees with what people already know?

Who were the investigators, and what was the aim of the study? How do younger and older adults adapt their story retellings to two different types of listeners: a young child and an adult experimenter? One hypothesis is that the child as listener is more relevant to the social roles of aging. Therefore in this social context younger adults should recall information better than older adults in the adult listener context. Cynthia Adams and colleagues (in press) tested this hypothesis.

How did the investigators measure the topic of interest? Adams and colleagues assessed story recall performance by asking women to learn one of two stories to retell from memory to an adult experimenter or a young child.

Who were the participants in the study? A sample of 48 older women and 47 younger women participated.

What was the design of the study? Adams and colleagues studied story recall using a cross-sectional research design with the two listener conditions just described.

Were there ethical concerns with the study? There were no concerns in this study; the topics were not controversial, nor were they likely to cause strongly negative feelings.

What were the results? As illustrated in Figure 7.3, Adams and colleagues found that when the child was the listener, older but not younger story retellers recalled more text-based content. In addition, both older and younger story retellers generated more elaborations on the text. Finally, both older and younger storytellers tended to reduce the complexity of the more complicated stories. In all, older story retellers were better able to adapt the complexity of the retellings of the stories to the needs of the listener.

What did the investigators conclude? An important implication of Adams and colleagues' findings is that it is important to consider the social and collaborative interaction between person and context in memory aging research to gain a more complete picture of memory changes as we grow older.

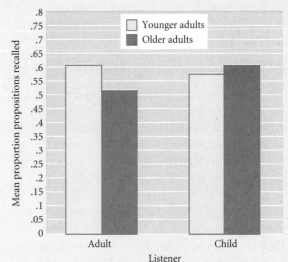

FIGURE 7.3 **Mean number of propositions recalled as a function of age group and type of listener.**

Source: Adams, C., Smith, M. C., Pasupathi, M., & Vitolo. L. (in press). Story recall and aging: Does the listener make a difference? *Journal of Gerontology: Psychological Sciences.*

To answer this question, Rice and Okun (1994) tested older adults' memory for accurate information about osteoarthritis that either contradicted their previously held false beliefs or affirmed their previously held accurate beliefs. All participants reported having osteoarthritis for at least 2 years. Rice and Okun found that older adults recall and recognize information that contradicts their previously held beliefs less accurately than they recall and recognize information that affirms their initial beliefs. The findings point out that people who educate older adults must be careful to identify misconceptions they bring into the situation.

However, Rice and Okun also found that if the disconfirming material was stated explicitly, older adults were better at remembering the information later. Thus, explicitly stating that certain information often is misunderstood, then stating the correct information, may help older adults remember the accurate information.

Text Memory and Episodic Memory

The research we have considered in this section is actually another way to examine episodic memory because it involves learning large amounts of information and remembering it over time. Thus, drawing parallels between the two literatures and comparing the important influences on memory for word lists and memory for text can be useful.

The most striking aspect about this comparison is that both are affected by a similar set of variables. Pacing, prior knowledge or familiarity, and organization of materials influence performance on word list tasks and text memory tasks. Note that age is not one of these influential variables. Being old does not necessarily mean that one cannot remember, especially if the situation provides an optimal opportunity to do so.

CONCEPT CHECKS

1. How do age differences vary as a function of text-based and situation model levels of discourse processing?

2. How does pacing or reading speed influence discourse memory?

3. How do social factors influence discourse memory?

4. How does the organization of text influence memory?

5. What similarities exist between discourse memory and episodic memory performance?

MEMORY IN EVERYDAY LIFE

LEARNING OBJECTIVES

- What age differences have been found in memory of location, landmarks, and routes?
- What age differences are found in memory of activities, especially in prospective memory?
- How does memory of pictures compare with list learning?

Tyler, an older man, has to go to a new HMO for his annual exam. This building is complex, and all the hallways look the same. He has a terrible time finding his way to the department of internal medicine. Although there are signs pointing the direction, he still is confused as to whether he had been that way before and has simply missed the signs. By the time he arrives at internal medicine, he is distressed and in need of comforting.

As we noted at the beginning of this chapter, memory is so integral to our everyday life that we take it for granted. For Tyler, using spatial processing capacities is extremely important in conducting the everyday business of going to the doctor. This concern is evidenced by the growing research focusing on age differences in memory in everyday life (Hertzog & Dunlosky, 1996; West, 1992). This research is extremely important for three reasons. First, it may shed some light on the generalizability of findings based on laboratory tasks such as word list recall. Second, new or alternative variables that affect performance could be uncovered. Third, research on everyday memory may force us to reconceptualize memory itself. In this section we focus on two aspects of everyday memory that have received the most attention: spatial memory and memory of activities.

Spatial Memory

Every time we remember where we left our keys, find our way by locating a prominent building, successfully return home from the grocery store, and remember where our car is parked after coming out a different door, we are using spatial memory. We consider the developmental trends in each of these abilities.

MEMORY OF LOCATION. Researchers test people's memory of location in three ways (Kirasic & Allen, 1985). One way is based on the psychometric approach to intelligence described in Chapter 8, in which relevant primary mental abilities such as spatial ability are tested. Results from this approach indicate that performance peaks by midlife and decreases steadily thereafter.

The second and most common way to test people's memory of location is to present them with an array of objects, remove the objects, and ask the participants to reconstruct the array. Older adults do not perform this task as well as younger adults, regardless of whether the objects are household items or building locations on a map (Denney et al., 1992; Zelinski & Light, 1988; Waddell & Rogoff, 1981). Charness (1981; Bosman & Charness, 1996) found that younger chess players could reconstruct chessboards more accurately than older players, even though the two groups were matched for chess-playing ability.

In contrast to this consistent picture of age-related deficits, some studies found no decline when they interviewed young and old participants about the exact location in their home of common personal items such as keys (West, 1992). Some argue that the lack of age differences in spatial memory under these circumstances is caused by familiarity of the setting and the fact that household locations are more predictable and stable. The familiarity effect may result from the additional contextual information available in home settings. Indeed, in a series of studies, Cherry (Cherry & Park, 1993; Cherry et al., 1993) found that providing contextual cues in laboratory-based studies of spatial memory clarified the issue. In these studies, the contextual cues consisted of locating objects in a three-dimensional array (rather than representing them in a three-dimensional drawing). Cherry found that contextual cues improve performance in both younger and older adults. The reason for the contextual enhancement effect may be related to working memory capacity (Dobson et al., 1995). That is, contextual cues may reduce the demand on working memory, thereby helping people remember locations.

The third way to test spatial memory consists of actually carrying out tasks in real physical space. For example, Kirasic (1991) had older and younger adults plan the most efficient route possible in picking up items on a designated shopping list and then actually go get them. The manipulation was the shopper's familiarity with the supermarket; some shoppers were tested in their usual supermarket, and others were tested in a different one. Younger adults performed equivalently in the two settings, whereas older adults performed better in the familiar environment.

RECALL OF LANDMARKS. Most studies of landmark recall involve the ability to place landmarks correctly on a map or other representation of a large-scale space. Young adults are more likely to organize their recall of a familiar downtown area based on spatial cues, which gives them an advantage in recalling correct location (Evans et al., 1984). In contrast, older adults' recall is influenced by frequency of usage, symbolic significance, natural landscaping, ease of finding the landmark, and uniqueness of architectural style (Lipman, 1991). Similarly, evidence suggests that older adults are less accurate at locating environmental features in pictures on which an assessment of potential landmark value could be based (Kirasic et al., 1992). These results suggest that older and younger adults use different strategies to learn and remember landmarks. Older adults may be more likely to use experiential or personal relevance as a way to remember location, whereas young adults may use physical space cues.

ROUTE LEARNING. Only a handful of studies have considered how people remember the way from one place to another. Findings are not consistent. Lipman (1991) found that older adults were more likely to recall nonspatial associations to routes and to regard salient landmarks rather than turns as critical route-maintaining events. Landmark saliency may relate to route learning more for older adults, influencing both encoding organization and evaluation of environmental events. Lipman concluded that sequential processing of route information is constrained by limits on cognitive capacity with advancing age.

On the positive side, Sinnott (1992) asked participants to describe routes to and around the hospital where they were undergoing a battery of tests and to recognize specific pathways that occurred en route from one area of the hospital to another. She found no differences with age on any of these tasks. Wilkniss and colleagues (1997) report that although older adults have greater difficulty ordering landmarks on a route, they are as good as young adults at recognizing landmarks occurring on the route. Finally, Titus and Everett (1996) found age differences in consumer in-store search behavior. Young adults performed more product searches and committed

In familiar environments, older adults may do as well as younger adults in remembering locations. But when older adults like these women find themselves in unfamiliar places, they may have more difficulty remembering where they are going.

more search errors than did older adults. Perhaps older adults gain an advantage in this situation from familiarity of this type of environment.

The research on learning and remembering routes raises a very practical question: What if people were provided with maps? Would they help people learn and remember the routes more effectively? Are some maps better than others? These are the questions Caplan and Lipman (1995) addressed. They had younger and older adults learn a route through a neighborhood from a series of slides. The experiment had three main conditions: no learning aid, a sketch of the route labeled "map," or the same sketch labeled "diagram." The "map" and the "diagram" either did or did not have landmarks indicated on them. The findings were intriguing. Older men's performance was poorer than younger men's only when they had no learning aid. Including landmarks eliminated age-related decrements in scene memory. However, age differences for women were found only when the learning aid was labeled a "map." Moreover, including landmarks increased the age differences.

Caplan and Lipman (1995) interpreted this pattern of differences in terms of people's history with spatial learning aids. They suggest that the findings reflect a cohort effect in that older women may not have had successful past experiences with using maps effectively. The fact that the same aid when labeled a "diagram" did not produce similar effects argues in favor of this conclusion. Presumably, older women who have had successful past experiences with maps will not show such effects. As we have seen throughout this chapter, age differences in memory are complex; here we see that one's personal experience may affect performance. It also points out the importance of labels for memory aids in assessing their utility.

Memory of Activities

How many times have you been asked, "What did you do today?" or "What have you been up to lately?" To answer these questions, you must use a second major type of everyday memory: memory of activities. Researchers test activity memory with a wide variety of tasks, including following instructions, recalling activities performed in a research laboratory, and remembering to perform actions.

Research on age differences in memory of activities shows that young adults remember more about both the activities and their order in time than do older adults (Kausler et al., 1985). One major factor influencing age differences in activity memory is the degree to which people must expend cognitive effort, or whether remembering what we do happens automatically. Kausler (1985) attacked this problem by separating activity memory into two parts. First, he argued that storing activities and actions performed in a laboratory probably is automatic, using no cognitive effort or resources. His view is supported by evidence that rehearsing the names of activities that participants perform does not help performance (Kausler et al., 1986). Second, he argued that remembering the activities one has performed involves cognitive effort because reliable age decrements are observed. Indeed, organization, which entails cognitive effort, facilitates recall of activities (Bäckman, 1985; Bäckman & Nilsson, 1984, 1985).

Other researchers have also tried to explain why age differences in memory of activities occur. One view is that effort is needed to retrieve the actions from memory and that older adults are less efficient at retrieval (Kausler & Lichty, 1988). To test this notion, researchers measure processing efficiency, which can be done by measuring processing speed in perceptual speed tests (Salthouse, 1992). Earles and Coon (1994) found that such measures of processing speed were an important predictor of adults' memory of activities they had performed in an experiment 2 to 182 days later. Indeed, the amount of variance associated with age was reduced by 70% when processing speed was considered. However, processing speed could not account for all the variance in adults' performance, meaning that other factors responsible for it remain to be discovered.

In essence, Kausler contends that the recall of activities performed in a laboratory is a direct analogue to everyday life. Many everyday memory situations involve the intentional, effortful retrieval of information learned by doing things (for example, we learn how to get around campus by walking around). In fact, activity memory may form the basis for acquiring much of our spatial memory.

Prospective Memory

One area related to activity memory research that has received increasing attention is prospective memory. **Prospective memory** *involves remembering to perform a planned action in the future* (Zacks et al., 2000), such as remembering to take your medication. The study of prospective memory is a good illustration of how performance on everyday memory tests stacks up to performance on traditional laboratory tests. For example, everyday memory assessments outside the laboratory find that when younger and older adults are asked to call a researcher at particular times, older adults are consistently better at remembering to do so (Moscovitch, 1982; Patton & Meit, 1993). Their secret is simple: They write down the number and message to be given. Younger adults rely on their own internal remembering strategies, which turns out to be less successful.

More recently, prospective memory has been examined in a more naturalistic context, remembering to take one's medication, which has produced counterintuitive findings: Older adults with rheumatoid arthritis were better at remembering to take their medications than middle-aged patients (ages 34 to 54; Park, Hertzog, et al., 1999). In fact, despite strong evidence of age-related cognitive decline in older adults on traditional psychometric measures, older adults had the cognitive ability to manage medications. What about the middle-aged adults? It turns out that a busy lifestyle in middle age was the major determinant of who forgot to take their medications. As Park et al. suggest, physicians should not assume that older adults do not have the cognitive capacity to manage medications. In fact, very busy middle-aged adults appear to be more at risk for managing medications improperly.

The success of prospective memory in naturalistic settings motivated researchers to more systematically examine the phenomenon in laboratory studies. In doing so, Einstein and McDaniel (1990) introduced a distinction between event-based and time-based prospective memory tasks. In event-based tasks, an action is to be performed when a certain external event happens, such as giving a certain person a message. A time-based task involves performing an action after a fixed amount of time, such as pressing a key every 8 minutes, or at a fixed point in time, such as remembering an appointment at 1 P.M. Einstein and colleagues (1995) found that time-based tasks showed more age differences as long as people use self-generated strategies to remember because these tend to decline with age; the cues in event-based tasks helped reduce age differences.

Age differences may also depend on the difficulty of the task. If the task is complex and places high cognitive demands on people, older adults do not perform as well as younger adults when self-initiated retrieval was required (Mäntylä, 1994). These findings imply that like remembering events from the past, prospective memory involves a complex interaction of aspects of information processing. Additionally, the effects of task complexity fit well with data concerning similar effects in various types of attention tasks. They also account for success in naturalistic settings: Older adults compensate for complexity by using and generating external cues such as notes to themselves.

Thus, whether there are age differences in prospective memory is a complex issue. It appears to depend on the type of task, the cues used, and what is being measured.

Memory of Pictures

Another area in which performance on a traditional laboratory task, list learning, can be compared with tasks closer to everyday life is memory of pictures. Researchers use a variety of things to study picture memory: faces, abstract drawings, line drawings, and complex scenes. Overall, studies show that older adults perform worse than younger adults in remembering many types of pictorial stimuli (Smith & Park, 1990). For example, older adults do not remember faces (Mason, 1986) or where objects are placed in a colored three-dimensional array or on a distinctive map (Park et al., 1990) as well as younger adults.

Still, we must not be too hasty in concluding that age differences found in the laboratory automatically generalize to the real world. Park and colleagues examined many of the traditional issues in laboratory research, including context effects, retention inter-

vals, and stimulus complexity (Park et al., 1983, 1984, 1986, 1988). Whereas older adults were clearly worse at remembering words, their immediate memory of pictures was about as good as young adults'. Age differences were observed only when delayed tests were given, and then only at certain time delay intervals. This research shows that we need to be cautious even in generalizing the findings from laboratory list-learning tasks using words to list-learning tasks using pictures.

Many factors influence what people remember from pictures. One of the most important of these concerns is the influence of schemas or what people expect to see. For example, people who are told that they will be shown a picture of a kitchen immediately anticipate seeing a stove, refrigerator, sink, and other things commonly associated with a kitchen. Collectively, these items form a kitchen schema. Now suppose that these people are shown a picture of a kitchen for a brief time and asked to name the objects they saw. After recalling a few, they might realize that there were more objects there than they named. So they might begin to guess what the others were, based on their kitchen schema.

Hess and Slaughter (1990) showed that older adults are more likely to use their schemas to fill in the blanks than younger adults do. This appears especially likely when the scenes are not well organized, such as when a picture of a kitchen has the sink over the stove as opposed to beside it. These results fit with a wide body of literature suggesting that we tend to rely more on experience as we grow older to compensate for decrements in specific aspects of information processing (recall Salthouse's study of typing from Chapter 6) and memory. As we will see in Chapter 8, our knowledge base continues to improve into old age, giving us a good basis for using schemas.

Despite these innovative studies, the direct comparison between everyday memory and list learning is hampered by the lack of data establishing equivalent everyday tasks and list-learning tasks. We need a comprehensive analysis in which the memory demands of many everyday tasks and list-learning tasks are described. This analysis would provide a way to address the reasons for the presence or absence of age differences across different task domains.

1. Under what conditions does a learning aid help people learn a route?

2. Why is task complexity important in prospective memory?

3. How are expectations related to memory for pictures?

SELF-EVALUATIONS OF MEMORY ABILITIES

LEARNING OBJECTIVES

* What are the major types of memory self-evaluations?
* What age differences have been found in metamemory?
* How do younger and older adults compare on memory-monitoring tasks? How is task experience important?

Jonathan has just reached his 70th birthday. However, he is greatly concerned. He has believed since he was very young that this is the age when your memory really goes downhill. He has great fears of losing his memory completely. He has taken to asking people to repeat things to him over and over for fear that he will forget them. It has taken a toll on his self-concept. He doesn't feel that he has as much control over his life as he used to.

How good is your memory? Are you absent-minded? Or are you like the proverbial elephant who never forgets anything? Like most people, you probably tend to be your own harshest critic when it comes to evaluating your memory performance. We analyze, scrutinize, nitpick, and castigate ourselves for the times we forget; we rarely praise ourselves for all the things we do remember, and we continue to be on guard for more memory slips. The self-evaluations we make about memory may affect our daily life in ways that traditionally were unrecognized. This is exactly what is happening to Jonathan. His negative evaluations of his memory ability are creating undue stress in his life.

Our self-evaluations about memory are complex (Cavanaugh, 1996; Hertzog & Hultsch, 2000). They are based not only on memory and performance per se but also on how we view ourselves in general, our ideas about how memory works, what we remember from past evaluations, and our attributions and judgments of our effectiveness.

Aspects of Memory Self-Evaluations

Interest in what people know about or are aware of concerning memory and how they evaluate it is an old topic in both philosophy and psychology (Cavanaugh, 1996). Psychologists have grappled with the topic for a century, studying everything from reports of children's awareness of problem-solving skills (Binet, 1903) to computer simulation of self-monitoring systems (Bobrow & Collins, 1975). In recent decades work on memory awareness has taken on a more developmental flavor. Researchers have focused primarily on two types of awareness about memory. The first type involves **metamemory,** or *knowledge about how memory works and what we believe to be true about it.* For instance, we may know that recall typically is harder than recognition, that memory strategies often are helpful, and that working memory is not limitless. We may also believe that memory declines with age, that appointments are easier to remember than names, and that anxiety impairs performance. Metamemory is assessed most often with questionnaires that ask about these various facts and beliefs.

The second type of self-evaluation, called **memory monitoring,** is *the awareness of what we are doing with our memory right now.* We can be aware of the process of remembering in many ways. At times we know how we are studying, how we are searching for some particular fact, or how we are keeping track of time for an appointment. At other times we ask ourselves questions while doing a memory task. For example, when faced with having to remember an important appointment later in the day, we may consciously ask ourselves whether the steps we have taken (writing a note) are sufficient.

Age Differences in Metamemory

Researchers have explored age differences in metamemory mainly by using questionnaires (see Berry, 1999; Hertzog & Hultsch, 2000, for reviews). Many questionnaires have been developed over the years.

Some of them, such as the Metamemory in Adulthood questionnaire (Dixon et al., 1989) and the Cognitive Failures Questionnaire (Gilewski et al., 1990), tap several different areas of knowledge about memory, including knowledge about strategies, tasks, change with age, and capacity. Other questionnaires, such as the Memory Self-Efficacy Questionnaire (Berry et al., 1989) and the Memory Controllability Inventory (Cavanaugh & Baskind, 1996; Lachman et al., 1995), assess specific aspects of memory beliefs.

The pattern of age differences in metamemory is interesting. Older adults seem to know less than younger adults about the internal workings of memory and its capacity, view memory as less stable, expect that memory will deteriorate with age, and perceive that they have less control over memory (Cavanaugh, 1996; Dixon et al., 1989; Soderberg Miller & Lachman, 1999; Lineweaver & Hertzog, 1998; McDonald-Miszczak et al., 1995; Ryan & Kwong See, 1993).

The belief in inevitable decline with age is potentially damaging. For example, people who think memory inevitably declines may also believe that strategy training is useless and that there is little point in exerting effort to remember something that does not come to mind immediately (Cavanaugh, 1996; Cavanaugh & Green, 1990). We take a closer look at these negative views a bit later.

Interestingly, the belief in inevitable decline does not apply equally to all aspects of memory. Older adults view memory of names as declining more rapidly than memory of things that happened long ago (Lineweaver & Hertzog, 1998). Similarly, adults report that different kinds of information pose different likelihoods of being troublesome. For example, remembering names is universally problematic, but especially for older adults (Cohen, 1993; Leirer et al., 1990). In contrast, remembering to pay bills, meet appointments, and take medications appears to remain unchanged with age (Cohen, 1993). You may find this to be the case yourself when you complete the exercise in the Discovering Development feature.

Although questionnaire studies of metamemory provide important information, they must be interpreted carefully (Berry, 1999; Hertzog & Hultsch,

2000). For example, Cavanaugh (1987, 1996) discovered that how questions are worded makes a difference in how older adults respond. For example, when questions request a general overall rating of memory, older adults give more negative ratings than younger adults do. But when the question pertains to a specific aspect of memory, such as memory of dates or errands, older adults' ratings are equivalent to those of younger adults.

Related work by Hertzog and his colleagues shows that the way in which metamemory is organized may change across adulthood (Hertzog et al., 1989, 1990). The facts people know about memory tend to form groups, or domains, of knowledge. As we age, the makeup of these domains may be a bit different. For example, for older adults an important aspect of metamemory is how the self responds emotionally to memory tasks. Because forgetting sometimes evokes strong emotional reactions in older adults, their memory knowledge may incorporate some of these feelings.

The Role of Memory Self-Efficacy

Belief in one's ability to accomplish things is a pervasive theme in literature, religion, psychotherapy, and many other diverse arenas (Berry, 1999; Cavanaugh & Green, 1990). As it applies to memory, belief in oneself is called **memory self-efficacy:** *the belief that one will be able to perform a specific task,* an important construct in understanding how memory changes with age (Berry, 1999; Cavanaugh, 1996). Memory self-efficacy is an important type of memory belief that is distinct from general knowledge about memory because, for example, one could know a great deal about how memory works but believe that one's ability to perform in a specific situation is poor.

Since the late 1980s, memory self-efficacy has emerged as one of the key aspects of metamemory because of its importance in accounting for performance in several different types of situations and in helping to explain how people make performance predictions in the absence of direct experience with tasks (a topic considered in the next section; Berry, 1999; Cavanaugh, 1996). Additionally, memory self-

We have seen that metamemory is what people know and believe to be true about their memory. Recall that in Chapter 1 we discussed various stereotypes about older adults, one of which is the stereotype that all aspects of memory decline with age. Of course, we know that this stereotype is false; although some aspects of memory differ with age, some do not.

Obtain a copy of one of the memory questionnaires described in the text. Examine it carefully and try to discern the different aspects of memory that are being assessed. Get your questionnaire approved by your human subjects research board and administer it to a broad range of adults of all ages. Gather your results and examine them for age

differences relating to the different kinds of memory and types of questions.

The data you obtain will give you insight into the various ways in which people view memory. Compare your findings to the results reported in the text. Do they agree? Why or why not?

---

efficacy has been shown to be reliably distinct from general memory knowledge as assessed through questionnaires (Hertzog et al., 1989).

Welch and West (1995) propose that memory self-efficacy is also a key to understanding a broader array of phenomena, such as mastering the environment. Briefly, they propose that some older adults assume that memory inevitably declines with age and have experienced some age-related decreases in performance themselves. As people experience tasks or situations across adulthood that they complete successfully, their memory self-efficacy should remain strong; those who experience failure should show decrements in memory self-efficacy. These experiences should influence subsequent behavior: People who experience success may be more likely to seek out more challenging cognitive environments, whereas people experiencing failure may seek less cognitively demanding environments.

Age Differences in Memory Monitoring

Memory monitoring involves knowing what you are doing mentally right now. The most popular way researchers usually study memory monitoring is by having people predict how well they will do on a memory task. One variation of this technique requires that people predict how well they will do before they get a chance to see the task. For example, participants are asked to predict how many words

they think they could remember from a 20-item list before they see the list. The second variation requires people to make performance predictions after they have seen the task. This time, they get to see the list first and then are asked to predict how many words they will remember.

PREDICTIONS WITHOUT EXPERIENCE. Estimating our performance without having a chance to see what we are up against is hard. For example, guessing how well we will do on the first exam in a course is tough if we do not know anything about the exam style of the instructor. How well we think we will do depends on test-related variables such as item difficulty and the numbers of fact and concept questions.

When older adults are asked to estimate performance without seeing the task, past research suggests that they tend to overestimate how well they will do (Bruce et al., 1982). For example, older adults typically predict that they will be able to remember more items than they actually can. Younger adults tend to be more accurate. However, more recent research suggests that this finding depends on the level of recall (Hertzog et al., 1994; Connor et al., 1997). In other words, older adults who had low levels of recall were more overconfident in their predictions.

PREDICTIONS AFTER EXPERIENCE. A very different picture of age differences emerges when participants have a chance to see the task before making a performance prediction. One way this is done is by asking people to rate their confidence that they will be able to remember each item on the list of words that will be learned. Results from several studies using this approach suggest strongly that older adults are just as accurate in predicting their recall and recognition performances as younger adults (Connor et al., 1997; Devolder et al., 1990; Hertzog et al., 1994). The usual finding is that regardless of age, adults overestimate performance on recall tasks but underestimate performance on recognition tasks.

COMPARING PREDICTION TYPES. Based on the research we have reviewed, older adults are at a disadvantage when asked to predict performance if they are given no information about the task. But when this information is available, from direct experience, instructions pertaining to important things to think about, or a request for predictions on familiar everyday tasks, older adults do as well as younger adults. However, these studies do not address a very important question: What happens if people are given multiple trials with a task and are asked to predict performance on each trial?

Hertzog and colleagues (1990) found that older and younger adults adjust their predictions across trials on a list-learning task. On the first trial, performance predictions tend to be inaccurate, and predictions are influenced by scores on memory questionnaires. On subsequent trials, though, predictions are more heavily influenced by actual performance on the preceding trial. Going one step further, Bieman-Copland and Charness (1994) had younger and older adults make predictions over trials on list-learning tasks in which they were given letter, rhyme, or meaning cues. Age differences were found in the ways younger and older adults adjusted their predictions from Trial 1 to Trial 2. Whereas younger adults raised or lowered their predictions across cue types based on their previous performance, older adults based their changed predictions on global differences between their previous prediction and performance.

These results indicate that the presence or absence of age differences on the first trial of a task, determined by whether people have experience before doing the task, may be caused by factors different from those responsible for age differences in how people change predictions over trials. Metamemory may be more important in understanding how people formulate initial predictions; analyzing one's previous performance may be more important for subsequent predictions. The good news is that evidence suggests that in older adulthood, the ability to monitor multiple aspects of memory functioning is spared (Hertzog & Hultsch, 2000).

CONCEPT CHECKS

1. What is metamemory?
2. What is the difference between memory knowledge and memory self-efficacy?
3. What age differences are found in memory monitoring when predictions are made without any experience with the task?

CLINICAL ISSUES AND MEMORY TESTING

LEARNING OBJECTIVES

- What is the difference between normal and abnormal memory aging?
- What is the connection between memory and mental health?
- What are the major ways in which clinicians assess memory?
- How is memory affected by nutrition and drugs?

*M*artha's children are concerned. Martha is 80 and is becoming more and more forgetful. With the scare of Alzheimer's disease so salient in our society, they are concerned that their mother is its next victim. What should they do? A friend tells them that memory decline is normal with aging. But to ease their concerns they make an appointment for a clinical screening for their mother. This could reassure them that normal aging is causing her forgetfulness, not Alzheimer's disease.

To this point we have been trying to understand the changes that occur in normal memory with aging. But what about people who have serious memory problems that interfere with their daily lives? How do we tell the difference between normal and abnormal memory changes? These are but two of the issues clinicians face. Clinicians often are confronted with relatives of clients who complain of serious memory difficulties. Clinicians must somehow differentiate the patients who have no real reason for concern from those with a disease. What criteria should be used to make this distinction? What diagnostic tests would be appropriate to evaluate adults of various ages?

Unfortunately, there are no easy answers to these questions. As we have seen, the exact nature of normative changes in memory with aging is not understood completely. This means that we have few standards by which to compare people who may have problems. Second, there are few comprehensive batteries of memory tests that are specifically designed to tap a wide variety of memory functions (Mayes, 1995). Too often, clinicians are left with hit-or-miss approaches and often have little choice but to piece together their own assessment battery (Edelstein & Kalish, 1999).

Fortunately, the situation is changing. Since the mid-1980s researchers and clinicians have begun to work together to devise better assessments (Mayes, 1995). This collaboration is producing results that will help address the key questions in memory assessment: Has something gone wrong with memory? Is the loss normal? What is the prognosis? What can be done to help the client compensate or recover?

In this section we consider some of the efforts being made to bridge the gap between laboratory and clinic. We begin with a brief look at the distinction between normal and abnormal memory changes. Because abnormal memory changes can be the result of some other psychological or physical condition, we consider links between memory and mental health. After that, we consider some of the ways in which memory can be assessed in the clinical setting. Finally, we discuss how memory is affected by nutrition and drugs.

Normal and Abnormal Memory Aging

As we have seen, many normative changes in memory occur as people grow old, such as changes in working memory and secondary memory. Still, many aspects of memory functioning do not change, such as the ability to remember the gist of a story. Increasingly forgetting names or what one needs at the supermarket, though annoying, appears to be part of aging. However, we also know that some people experience far greater changes, such as forgetting where they live or their spouse's name. Where is the line dividing normative memory changes from abnormal ones?

From a functional perspective, one way to distinguish normal and abnormal changes is to ask whether the changes disrupt a person's ability to perform daily living tasks. The normative changes we have encountered in this chapter usually do not interfere with a person's ability to function in everyday life. When problems appear, however, it is appropriate to find out what is the matter. For example, a person who repeatedly forgets to turn off the stove or forgets how to get home is clearly experiencing changes that affect personal safety and interfere with his or her daily life. Such changes should be brought to the attention of a physician or psychologist.

Recent advances in neuroscience, especially the study of brain–behavior relations, have led to an explosion in our knowledge of specific diseases or brain changes that can create abnormal memory performance. For example, researchers can test for specific problems in visual and verbal memory through neuroimaging by examining glucose metabolism with positron emission tomography (PET) scans and functional magnetic resonance imaging (fMRI; Prull et al., 2000). Such brain imaging techniques also allow researchers to find tumors, strokes, or other types of damage or disease that could account for poorer-than-expected memory performance. Certain changes in brain wave patterns in the medial–temporal lobe of the brain indicate decrements during encoding and retrieval of verbal information (Gabrieli et al., 1997; Tulving et al., 1994). Finally, significantly poorer-than-normal performance on neuropsychological tests of memory is also useful in establishing that the memory changes observed are indeed abnormal (Tuokko et al., 1990; Prull et al., 2000).

Some diseases, especially the dementias, are marked by drastic changes in memory. For example, Alzheimer's disease involves the progressive destruction of memory beginning with recent memory and eventually including the most personal: self-identity. Wernicke–Korsakoff syndrome involves major loss of recent memory and sometimes a total inability to form new memories after a certain point in time.

The most important point to keep in mind is that distinguishing between normal and abnormal memory aging, and in turn between memory and other cognitive problems, often is very difficult (Lezak, 1995; Prull et al., 2000). There is no magic number of times someone must forget something before getting concerned. Because serious memory problems can also be caused by underlying mental or physical health problems, these must be thoroughly checked out in conjunction with a complete memory assessment.

Memory and Mental Health

Several psychological disorders involve distorted thought processes, which sometimes result in serious memory problems. The two disorders that have been the main focus of research are depression (Watts, 1995) and the dementias (Brandt & Rich, 1995), but other disorders, such as amnesia caused by a head injury or brain disease, are also important (O'Connor et al., 1995). Depression is characterized by feelings of helplessness and hopelessness (American Psychiatric Association, 1994). Dementia, such as Alzheimer's disease, involves substantial declines in cognitive performance that may be irreversible and untreatable (American Psychiatric Association, 1994). Much of the research on clinical memory testing is on differentiating the changes in memory caused by depression from those involved in Alzheimer's disease.

Serious depression impairs memory (Bäckman, Small, Wahlin, & Larson, 2000; Gotlib et al., 1996; Watts, 1995). For example, severely depressed people show a decreased ability to learn and recall new information (Cohen et al., 1982), a tendency to leave out important information (McAllister, 1981), a decreased ability to organize (Bäckman & Forsell, 1994), less effective memory strategies (Weingartner et al., 1982), an increased sensitivity to sad memories (Kelley, 1986), and decreased psychomotor speed (La Rue et al., 1995).

An interesting finding emerges from the literature when age-related differences in the effects of depression on memory are considered. Two recent studies found that the negative effects of depression on memory are greater in young and middle-aged adults than in older adults (Burt et al., 1995; Kindermann & Brown, 1997). This suggests that the effect of depression on memory may decrease gradually as we grow older, especially in very old age (Bäckman et al., 1996). It may be the case that once normative age differences in episodic memory are eliminated statistically, few differences between depressed and nondepressed older adults remain. Thus, at this point the memory impairments that accompany severe depression appear to be equivalent across adulthood. However, much more research must be done before we have a clear answer. Additionally, we need to know more about the possible effects of mild and moderate levels of depression.

Alzheimer's disease is characterized by severe and pervasive memory impairment that is progressive and irreversible (Cavanaugh & Nocera, 1994). The memory decrements in Alzheimer's disease involve the entire memory system, from sensory to long-term to remote memory. The changes that occur early in Alzheimer's disease are very similar to those that occur in depression. However, because depression is treatable and Alzheimer's disease is not, clinicians must differentiate the two. This differentiation is the underlying reason for the major effort to develop sensitive and comprehensive batteries of memory tests.

Clinical Memory Tests

Over the years, researchers and clinicians have devised several different ways to test memory to determine whether a person is experiencing abnormal memory problems. We consider three major types of tests: neuropsychological tests, behavioral and self-report measures, and rating scales.

NEUROPSYCHOLOGICAL TESTS. The traditional way to assess a person's degree of memory impairment is to use all or part of large batteries of tests that were designed to assess several aspects of cognitive functioning, including attention, memory, and problem solving. Because these batteries of tests assess broad aspects of cognitive functioning and are used to assess possible psychological impairments caused by abnormal brain (neurological) functioning, they are typically called neuropsychological tests.

Ferris and Crook (1983) propose nine criteria for a comprehensive neuropsychological test, including that it samples a variety of cognitive functions, is sensitive to deficits, takes less than 1 hour to administer, has high reliability and validity, and is of appropriate difficulty for the population being studied. They recommend that all aspects of memory (primary, working, secondary, and tertiary) and attention and perceptual–motor speed be included in this battery. These suggestions have been supported and adopted by many of the leading clinicians involved in research on abnormal memory changes (Corkin et al., 1986; Mohs et al., 1986).

The tests clinicians use to evaluate memory are one aspect of neuropsychological tests. These tests are designed to assess specific brain–behavior relations in a wide variety of domains, from general intelligence to particular aspects of memory. Although most comprehensive neuropsychological tests include several memory tests, some are designed to focus primarily on memory functioning. For example, the Wechsler Memory Scale–Revised is a fairly comprehensive test that examines many different aspects of verbal memory. It includes a variety of tasks, such as serial learning, paired associates, and short prose passages. Others, such as the Memory for Designs test, focus on visual memory. In these tests, people typically are shown a picture (such as an octagon) and asked to draw it from memory.

A neuropsychological assessment should always be coupled with complete health screening. A key aspect of the basic developmental forces is the interaction between physiology and behavior; memory performance is no exception. In any case, a systematic comprehensive approach is essential to sort out potentially treatable causes of memory problems from those that are untreatable. If real problems are suspected, one should search for a clinic specializing in comprehensive assessment. Having someone simply administer a short questionnaire or a mental status exam is not enough.

BEHAVIORAL AND SELF-REPORT ASSESSMENTS OF MEMORY PROBLEMS. People often complain or express concerns about their memory. Perhaps you have complained that you do not remember names or dates very well or often lose your keys. Rather than administering a battery of memory tests from a general neuropsychological test, many researchers and clinicians recommend using behavioral assessments to diagnose memory problems (Knight & Godfrey, 1995). These tests involve having people perform everyday memory tasks using realistic material such as grocery lists or simulated situations in which they meet new people whose names they must remember (Crook & Larrabee, 1992). Such tests show great promise in assessing memory functioning and are much closer to the types of situations people actually face than are traditional memory batteries. However, such questionnaires must be used cautiously because they tend to measure global decline. They do not necessarily differentiate decline that occurs within various domains of functioning (Jorm, 1996; Waite et al., 1998).

Another way to assess memory complaints is to use self-report scales. There are about a dozen questionnaires that assess memory complaints (Dixon, 1989; Gilewski & Zelinski, 1986). These questionnaires assess a variety of memory situations, such as remembering people's names or remembering what time of year it is. Memory complaints assessed via questionnaires correlate moderately with performance on memory tasks and with standardized clinical memory tests (Hertzog & Hultsch, 2000; Zelinski et al., 1990). However, memory complaints show a stronger relation with depressed mood (Niederehe & Yoder, 1989). These findings indicate that although memory complaints should not be considered an accurate account of a person's current memory ability, they may provide important information about performance problems related to how the person is feeling emotionally.

A recent study sheds more light on the relation between typical memory complaint questionnaires and memory performance. Hertzog and colleagues (2000) had patients with rheumatoid arthritis, ranging in age from 35 to 84 years, complete memory tasks, assessments of depressive affect, and memory complaint questionnaires. In addition, they reported whether they were having problems remembering to take their medications. The interesting finding was that memory complaints were related to cognitive tasks but not to whether they had problems remembering to take their medication. Conversely, problems with remembering to take their medications during an interview were very predictive of later medication adherence problems but not of performance on memory tasks. They interpret this finding as evidence that adults' self-reports of memory problems are valid when they focus specifically on memory behaviors in an everyday context.

RATING SCALES. *Instruments designed to assess memory from the viewpoint of an observer, usually a mental health professional, are called* **rating scales** (Edelstein & Kalish, 1999; McDonald, 1986). This information is important in evaluating the clinical significance of memory impairment (Knight & Godfrey, 1995). The most common behavior rating scales that tap memory are structured interviews and checklists.

Structured interviews vary in length from very short to extensive, which means that they also vary in how sensitive they are at detecting abnormal memory performance. Most structured interviews were developed with an eye toward diagnosing dementia. The most common of these are the various mental status examinations (Blessed et al., 1968; Folstein et al., 1975; Kiernan et al., 1987; Mattis, 1988). Mental status exams are used to screen people for serious problems. That is, mental status exams provide a very crude estimate of memory functioning, not nearly as good as one would get from an extensive battery of tests. However, mental status exams are very quick and easy to administer. Items on these scales focus on orientation to time and place and contain simple memory tests such as spelling words backward. Mattis (1976) developed a more extensive mental status exam that provides a more complete view of cognitive processes. Mattis's scale examines primary memory and secondary memory more thoroughly than the other mental status exams.

Checklists are an easy way to obtain information from observers about the severity of memory impairment. One very important source of diagnostic information is a person who is close to the client. Spouses or adult children can provide different perspectives than health care professionals and usually can complete a checklist easily. Caregivers have known the person being assessed for a much longer time and may be in a better position to assess subtle changes in performance over time. They also provide important information about the severity of the problem that can be compared with information provided by the person being assessed. For example, the diagnosis of Alzheimer's disease often is furthered by examining the discrepancy between the client's assessment of memory functioning and the caregiver's assessment of the client's memory functioning (Reisberg et al., 1986). In the middle stages of the disease, the client's reports of memory problems drop, but the caregiver's reports continue to increase.

Memory, Nutrition, and Drugs

Researchers and clinicians often overlook nutrition as a cause of memory failures in later life (Perlmutter et al., 1987). Unfortunately, we know very little about how specific nutrient deficiencies relate to specific aspects of memory. The available evidence links thiamine deficiency to memory problems in humans (Cherkin, 1984), and it links niacin and vitamin B_{12} deficiencies to diseases in which memory failure is a major symptom (Rosenthal & Goodwin, 1985).

Likewise, many drugs have been associated with memory problems. The most widely known of these is alcohol, which if abused over a long period is associated with severe memory loss. Less well known are the effects of other prescription and over-the-counter medications. For example, sedatives and tranquilizers have been found to impair memory performance (Block et al., 1985).

These data indicate that it is important to consider older adults' diets and medications when assessing their memory performance. Serious decrements in functioning may be caused by poor nutrition or specific medications. Too often, researchers and clinicians fail to inquire about eating habits and the medications people take. Adequate assessment is essential to avoid diagnostic errors.

CONCEPT CHECKS

1. From a functional perspective, how does one tell the difference between normal and abnormal memory aging?
2. How does severe depression affect memory?
3. What are the major characteristics of neuropsychological tests, behavioral and self-report measures, and rating scales?
4. How does alcohol affect memory?

REMEDIATING MEMORY PROBLEMS

LEARNING OBJECTIVES

• What are the major ways in which memory skills are trained? How effective are these methods?
• What are the key individual difference variables in memory training?

After retirement, John and Amy noticed that they were having more trouble remembering things than they used to. They were worried that given their advanced age there was nothing they could do about it. However, they saw an advertisement on television suggesting that we have control over our memory fitness. The next day, a flyer was posted in their condominium recreation room for a memory training class to help older adults overcome memory failures. They immediately signed up.

Imagine that you have problems remembering where you left your keys. Or suppose that someone you love has gone through a comprehensive diagnostic process like that advocated in the previous section, and a memory problem was discovered. Can anything be done to help people remember? In most cases, yes. Researchers have developed several different types of memory training programs, many of which are effective even with people with severe memory impairments (Camp, 1998; West, 1995). In this section we examine some of the attempts at remediating memory problems and some of the individual differences that affect the success of these programs.

Training Memory Skills

The notion that memory can be improved through acquiring skills and practicing them is very old, dating back to prehistory (Yates, 1966). For example, the story of the *Iliad* was told for generations through the use of mnemonic strategies before it was finally written down. Books that teach readers how to improve their own memory have also been around for a very long time (Grey, 1756). Interestingly, these old how-to books teach techniques that are almost identical to those advocated in more contemporary books such as those by Jerry Lucas (Green, 1999; Lorayne & Lucas, 1996).

Learning how to remember information more effectively can be useful not only for people with identifiable disorders but also for people whose memory performance has declined as a result of normal, age-related changes (Camp, 1998; West, 1995). As you may have realized in our earlier discussion about memory strategies, most of them share several things in common. First, they entail paying attention to the incoming information. Second, they rely on stored information to facilitate making new connections with the new material. Finally, the best strategies are those that, in the process of encoding, provide the basis for future retrieval cues. In short, the best memory strategies are the ones that practically guarantee that the appropriate cue will be available to access the stored information when it must be retrieved (West, 1995).

Memory aids or strategies can be organized into meaningful groups. Among the most useful of these classifications is Camp and colleagues' (1993) E-I-E-I-O framework. The E-I-E-I-O framework combines two types of memory (explicit and implicit) with two types of memory aids (external and internal). Explicit memory involves the conscious and intentional recollection of information; remembering this definition on an exam is one example. Implicit memory involves effortless and unconscious recollection of information; knowing that stop signs are red octagons usually is not something that people need to exert effort to remember when they see one on the road. **External aids** *are memory aids that rely on environmental resources such as notebooks or calendars.* **Internal aids** *are memory aids that rely on mental processes, such as* *imagery.* The Aha! or O! experience in the framework is the one that comes with suddenly remembering something. As you can see in Table 7.1, the E-I-E-I-O framework helps organize how the two types of memory can be combined with the two types of memory aids to provide a broad range of intervention options to help people remember.

We can use Camp and colleagues' approach to examine research on external and internal memory aids. In addition, we briefly review two alternatives: memory exercises and medications.

EXTERNAL MEMORY AIDS. External memory aids are objects such as diaries, address books, calendars, notepads, microcomputers, and other devices commonly used to support memory in everyday situations such as taking notes during a visit to the physician (McGuire & Codding, 1998). Some external aids involve using an external device to store information (such as computers and date books), whereas others involve the use of external aids to cue action (for instance, setting a book out so you won't forget it).

In general, explicit external interventions are the most common, probably because they are easy to use and widely available (Cavanaugh et al., 1983). For example, almost everyone owns an address book, and small notepads are sold in hundreds of stores. But explicit external interventions have other important applications, too. The problem of remembering one's medication schedule is best solved with an explicit external intervention: a pillbox that is divided into compartments corresponding to days of the week and different times of the day. Research shows that this type of pillbox is the easiest to load and results in the fewest errors (Park et al., 1991; Park et al., 1999). Along these lines, Morrow and colleagues (1998) trained older adults with external aids such as icons representing time of day and the number of pills to take. This also helps older adults remember their medication. Memory interventions like this can help older adults maintain their independence. Nursing homes also use explicit external interventions, such as bulletin boards with the date and weather conditions, to help residents keep in touch with current events.

TABLE 7.1	The E-I-E-I-O Framework	
Type of Memory	Type of Memory Aid	
	External	*Internal*
Explicit	Appointment book	Mental imagery
	Grocery list	Rote rehearsal
Implicit	Color-coded maps	Spaced retrieval
	Sandpaper letters	Conditioning

Advocating the use of external aids in memory rehabilitation is becoming increasingly popular. Camp (1998) recommends external aids in working with patients with Alzheimer's disease. For example, caregivers may label their kitchen cabinets to make it easier for the person with Alzheimer's disease to remember what is in them. Harris (1984) suggests that for external cues to be most effective, they should be given close to the time at which action is needed, be active rather than passive, be specific to the particular action, be portable, fit a wide range of situations, store many cues for long periods, be easy to use, and not involve a pen or pencil.

Countering this trend toward greater use of external strategies, West (1995) cautions that overreliance on external aids can be a problem. She argues that memory is much like a muscle, which needs to be exercised to stay in shape, an approach we consider a bit later.

External implicit combinations, more widely used with children, nevertheless are useful for older adults in some situations. For example, many nursing homes use different color schemes to designate different wings or sections of the building. Because people process the color-coded aspects of the building automatically, the implicit nature of this external cue makes it ideal for people who may otherwise have difficulty learning and remembering new information.

INTERNAL MEMORY AIDS. Looking at Camp and colleagues' examples of internal memory aids may have triggered some personal experiences. For example, most people use rote rehearsal in preparing for an examination (repeating "Camp E-I-E-I-O" over and over) or use mental imagery in remembering the location of their car in a parking lot (we're parked near the giraffe on the lightpost). Most research on memory training concerns improving people's use of these and other internal strategies that supply meaning and help organize incoming information (Bäckman & Larsson, 1992; Willis, 1996a). Classic examples of formal internal strategies include the method of loci (remembering items by mentally placing them in locations in a familiar environment), mental retracing (thinking about all the places you may have left your keys), turning letters into numbers, and forming acronyms out of initial letters (such as *NASA* from *National Aeronautics and Space Administration*).

Most memory improvement courses train people to become proficient at using one of these internal strategies. For example, Yesavage (1983) trained older adults to use images to help themselves remember people's names. As shown in Figure 7.4, this training was effective. Interestingly, certain personality traits may be associated with who benefits most from training. Gratzinger and colleagues (1990) found that people who scored high on openness to experience (a dimension of personality) performed better with imagery than other people. In particular, the fantasy subfactor of the openness dimension (i.e., the tendency to engage in internal fantasizing) was related to greater improvement as a result of imagery training. It may be that people who find it easy to fantasize may be better at coming up with the imagery that helps them remember people's names.

Similar research has shown that training on most internal strategies improves memory significantly. For example, older adults have been successfully trained to use the method of loci as a way to help them remember items to be purchased at the grocery store (Anschutz et al., 1985). Unfortunately, these training programs have rarely been assessed over long intervals, so the degree of improvement after the course ends and how long this improvement lasts is largely unknown. One of the few exceptions was a 3-year follow-up to the grocery shopping study (Anschutz et al., 1987). Although Anschutz and her colleagues found that loci were readily available, older adults had abandoned their use of the

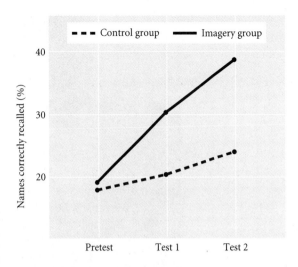

FIGURE 7.4 Proportion of names recalled at three points in the study. Pretest occurred in the first session before training. Test 1 was completed after imagery training in the imagery group and after attitude training in the control group. Test 2 was completed after both groups had received training in the face–name mnemonic.

Source: Yesavage, J. A. (1983). Imagery pretraining and memory training in the elderly. *Gerontology, 29,* 273. Copyright 1983 by S. Karger. Reprinted with permission.

locus method as a memory aid. Clearly, more research must be conducted to understand why adults stop using internal memory strategies that are effective in improving recall.

The internal strategies we have examined so far fall into the explicit internal category in Camp and colleagues' system. However, as we noted earlier, explicit strategies entail effortful processing and are more taxing on older adults. Thus, explicit memory intervention would be most likely to boost memory performance for older adults who are least likely to suffer failures or for young adults (Rybash, 1996). In fact, healthy older adults are less willing to use effortful internal strategies. In addition, older adults with dementia are unlikely to benefit from these types of strategies (Camp, 1998). Thus, Camp argues that older adults would benefit more from preserved implicit memory abilities. One implicit internal memory aid that has proven quite powerful is based on a technique called spaced retrieval. Camp (1998) re-

A cookbook can be an effective and helpful memory aid, no matter how often one has made black bean soup.

lates that even in Alzheimer's disease people can learn new things with this technique. He was able to teach people with Alzheimer's disease the names of the staff who worked with them even though they had no idea when or where they acquired this information.

EXERCISING MEMORY. Another approach to memory training is based on viewing memory as a mental muscle. This approach uses repetitive practice, which involves using specific memory exercises. Exercising memory on one type of task strengthens it, setting the stage for better memory in a variety of other tasks (Harris & Sunderland, 1981). For example, practicing how to organize a grocery list over and over will help one learn to organize other kinds of lists as well.

Exercising memory may have important benefits during rehabilitation after an accident or stroke. For one thing, the person knows that something is being done about his or her memory problems. This may result in the belief that improvement is possible and that it is worth the effort. Second, evidence from both animal research (Wall, 1975) and human research (Black,

Markowitz, & Cianci, 1975) indicates that early intervention with physical exercise promotes recovery after damage to the motor cortex. Harris and Sunderland (1981) suggest that the same benefit may accrue if memory practice is begun at the first sign of loss.

MEMORY DRUGS. Although much research has focused on the underlying neurological mechanisms in memory, little definitive information is available that can be translated easily into treatment approaches. For example, we still are not sure which neurotransmitters are primarily involved with memory. This is not for lack of trying, however. Many attempts to enhance memory by using drugs that affect the neurotransmitter acetylcholine, for example, have been made. However, attempts to improve memory by administering drugs that act on certain neurotransmitters produce only modest, short-term improvements with no long-term changes, and much of the work aimed at improving specific types of memory is disappointing (Lombardi & Weingartner, 1995). This research is especially important for Alzheimer's disease and related disorders.

COMBINING STRATEGIES. Which memory strategy is best clearly depends on the situation. For example, remembering names probably demands an internal strategy, whereas remembering appointments could most easily be helped by external strategies. For optimal improvement, the best approach is to tailor specific strategies to specific situations.

This is exactly what McEvoy and Moon (1988) did. They designed a comprehensive multiple strategy training program for improving older adults' memory in everyday situations. To remember names, older adults were taught an internal strategy emphasizing the need to associate new names with known information. In contrast, external aids were used for remembering appointments such as occasional physician visits. McEvoy and Moon found that after training, participants had fewer complaints about their memory of names and faces, appointments, routine tasks, and spatial orientation.

McEvoy and Moon's study points out the importance of tailoring an intervention to fit the problem. What works best for one kind of information may not help us remember another. Moreover, their work also emphasizes the need for broad-based comprehensive intervention programs. Training people to remember only one kind of information is not helpful when their daily lives are filled with far more complicated demands.

Individual Difference Variables in Memory Training

As we have seen throughout this chapter, adults are a very heterogeneous group when it comes to memory performance. For example, research reviewed earlier shows that verbal ability, prior knowledge, and familiarity influence how well one performs on memory tasks. Herrmann (1993) argues that individual difference variables should be considered when designing memory training programs. Moreover, training may be more effective when changes in emotional status (Herrmann, 1993) and feelings of self-efficacy (Berry, 1999; Cavanaugh et al., 1989) are major goals of the program. Research finds that the benefits of memory training depend on the specific needs of the client (Bendiksen & Bendiksen, 1996; Yesavage et al., 1988). For example, older adults who were highly verbal benefited most from a training program emphasizing ways to connect incoming information with information they already knew. In contrast, older adults who were highly anxious benefited most from training that included a relaxation component (Yesavage et al., 1988).

An approach to memory training that includes training on specific strategies with such relevant factors as relaxation (Stigsdotter Neely & Bäckman, 1993a, 1993b, 1995) and social support (Flynn & Storandt, 1990) has typically resulted in performance gains. However, whether the gains from the combined approach are greater than those from traditional strategy training is unclear (Stigsdotter Neely & Bäckman, 1993a, 1993b, 1995). Moreover, although providing memory strategies improves performance for adults of all ages, surprisingly little research has been done to identify how broadly the effects of training generalize across tasks and individuals.

To examine these issues, Stigsdotter Neely and Bäckman (1995) compared performance in a control group and a group given composite training involving encoding operations, attentional functions, and relaxation. The training task involved learning a list of concrete words, and generalization of the strategy was tested on tasks involving recall of objects, recall of participant-performed tasks, and recall of abstract words. People who were trained on the combined strategy still outperformed the control group 6 months after training but generalized their strategy only to the recall of objects task.

Additionally, age, education level, and level of general cognitive functioning did not predict performance after training; only performance on the pretraining task predicted future performance. These findings indicate that performance gains remain several months after strategy training on a specific task but that people tend not to use the strategy in other situations very much.

In sum, the memory training literature is emerging as an important area for addressing questions about how memory performance differs with age. Although much more work on the issues of generalization and individual differences in the effectiveness of training remains to be done, the available research demonstrates that training may need to include not only a memory technique but also memory-related components such as self-efficacy and relaxation. Also remaining to be answered are the questions of how to predict who will benefit from memory training and why people differ in the degree to which they benefit from training.

CONCEPT CHECKS

1. What is the E-I-E-I-O framework, and how does it help organize memory training?
2. What effect does combining approaches have on performance in memory training?

PUTTING IT ALL TOGETHER

Memory change with age is a multidimensional and complex process. Susan was experiencing memory failure in some domains and not in others. Cynthia had difficulty remembering whether information she heard in the past came from a reliable or nonreliable source. She reflects the problems older adults have in remembering when and how they acquired information. However, Dorothy exemplifies an area of memory that remains intact: memory of naturalistic prose and story information. Although she cannot remember details, she remembers the general gist of the movie and its relevance to everyday life. Memory failures can also interfere with our daily functioning, as when Tyler tried to make his way through an unfamiliar building. In fact, these changes in our memory can result in poor self-evaluations of our memory functioning, as was the case for Jonathan. In other words, our self-esteem can be placed in jeopardy. That is why it is sometimes important to rule out dementia by obtaining a clinical assessment, as Martha did. Finally, as John and Amy found, an increasing number of memory training interventions are available to help older adults maintain the integrity of their memory functioning.

Summary

INFORMATION PROCESSING REVISITED

Working Memory

- Working memory is the processes and structures involved in holding information in mind and using that information, sometimes in conjunction with incoming information, to solve a problem, make a decision, or learn.

- Information is kept active through rehearsal. In general, working memory capacity and rehearsal decline with age, although the extent of the decline is still in doubt. There is some evidence that age differences in working memory are not universal.

Long-Term Memory

- Long-term memory is the ability to remember extensive amounts of information over long periods. In episodic memory, age-related decrements typically are found on recall tests but not on recognition tests.

- Older adults tend not to use memory strategies spontaneously as often or as well as younger adults. Age differences can be reduced in several ways.

Remote Memory, or Autobiographical Memory

- Remote memory involves remembering information over very long periods of time. In remote memory, age differences typically are not found in tests of the knowledge base.

- Some aspects of autobiographical memory remain intact for many years whereas other aspects do not. Verification of autobiographical memories often is difficult. Older adults have fewer flashbulb memories.

Implicit Memory

- Implicit memory is the facilitation or change in task performance that is attributable to having been exposed to information at some earlier time but does not involve active, explicit memory.

- Older adults generally do slightly worse on implicit memory tasks than younger adults.

SOURCES OF AGE DIFFERENCES IN MEMORY

Age Differences in Encoding and Retrieval

- Age-related decrements in encoding may be caused by decrements in rehearsal in working memory and in the ability to make connections with incoming information. Older adults do not spontaneously organize incoming information as well as younger adults, but they can use organizational helps when told to do so. However, the benefits of this approach are short-lived.

- Although older adults tend not to use optimal encoding strategies, this does not account for poor memory performance.

- Age differences are greater for tip-of-the-tongue memory failures. Age differences are greater on recall than on recognition tests. Older adults benefit more than younger adults from retrieval cues, but age differences in performance are not eliminated.

- Changes in memory with age are caused by both encoding and retrieval problems. Research involving imaging studies of blood flow in the brain shows substantially less brain activity in older adults than in younger adults during encoding.

The Emerging Role of Automatic Retrieval

- Although conscious recollection shows decline with age, nonconscious, automatic retrieval of information does not reveal decline.

Misinformation and Memory

- The ability to remember the source of a familiar event or whether the event was imagined or experienced declines with age.

- Older adults are more susceptible to false memories in that they remember items or events that did not occur under specific conditions of plausibility.

DISCOURSE MEMORY

- Age differences are more pronounced for text-based levels of discourse such as lower-level detailed information.

- Age differences are less pronounced at higher levels of text, such as the situation, which can involve emotional information, goals, and personality characteristics of main characters.

- Age differences in performance are influenced by the use of effective reading strategies, how a story is retold, and prior knowledge. Older adults are especially likely to put pieces of prior knowledge in their recall of newly learned text.

- Higher presentation speeds may put older adults at a disadvantage; age differences decrease when self-pacing is used. Age differences in recall tend to increase as the length of reading time increases. Age-related slowing in cognitive processing explains much of this difference.

Text-Based Levels

- There are different hierarchical levels of importance in the information presented in text, including propositions that are central or peripheral.

- Age differences in discourse memory vary depending on the level one is assessing.

Situation Models

- In this case, individuals use their world knowledge to construct a more global understanding of what the text is about.

- Age differences are less pronounced at higher levels of text, such as the situation, which can involve emotional information, goals, and personality characteristics of main characters.

- Age differences in performance are influenced by the use of effective reading strategies, how a story is retold, and prior knowledge. Older adults are especially likely to put pieces of prior knowledge in their recall of newly learned text.

- Higher presentation speeds may put older adults at a disadvantage; age differences are reduced when self-pacing is used. Age differences in recall tend to increase as the length of reading time is increased. Age-related slowing in cognitive processing explains much of this difference.

Text Variables

- Age differences usually are not found for the major organizational elements of text, but performance is related to verbal ability. With well-organized text, which emphasizes the structure and main ideas, age differences typically are not found.

- Older adults may be more interested in learning general points than in learning the details. Prior beliefs also make it difficult to learn and remember elements of text.

Text Memory and Episodic Memory

- List learning and text memory are affected by similar variables, including pacing, prior knowledge, and verbal ability. Age per se is not a major cause of performance differences.

MEMORY IN EVERYDAY LIFE

Spatial Memory

- Older adults do not reconstruct objects in a spatial array as accurately as do younger adults. However, with familiar objects or locations, or when contextual cues are provided, older adults' performance improves, and they may perform as well as younger adults.

- Older and younger adults use different strategies to learn the locations of landmarks, which sometimes results in performance differences. Older and younger adults appear equally able to learn a route, but complex differences (including gender differences) emerge when people use maps as a learning aid.

Memory of Activities

- It is thought that processing activities is automatic. Actually performing activities aids memory for older adults, but older adults are more likely to claim that they performed actions they actually didn't. Some activities, such as problem-solving tasks, are remembered better than others, such as perceptual–motor tasks.

Prospective Memory

- Age differences are less likely on event-based prospective memory tasks than on time-based prospective memory tasks. How accurately prospective memory tasks are performed depends on the time of day. Processing speed may help explain these age differences.

Memory of Pictures

- Older adults are worse at remembering some types of pictures, including faces, but sometimes these differences are found only on delayed tests involving particular delays.

- Older adults are more likely to rely on their experience, or schematic knowledge, to help them remember scenes, especially when the scenes depicted are not well organized.

SELF-EVALUATIONS OF MEMORY ABILITIES

Aspects of Memory Self-Evaluations

- There are two general categories of memory self-evaluations. Metamemory is knowledge about how memory works and what one believes to be true about it. Memory monitoring is the awareness of what we are doing with our memory right now.

Age Differences in Metamemory

- Metamemory typically is assessed with questionnaires. Older adults seem to know less than younger adults about the workings of memory and its capacity, view memory as less stable, believe that their memory will decline with age, and feel that they have little control over these changes. However, the belief in inevitable decline does not apply equally to all aspects of memory. How metamemory is organized may differ across adulthood.

The Role of Memory Self-Efficacy

- Memory self-efficacy is one's beliefs about how well one will perform in a specific situation and is an important construct in understanding how people make judgments about performance before they have experience with a task.

Age Differences in Memory Monitoring

- Older adults often overestimate how well they will do when making predictions without knowledge of or experience with the task. With task knowledge or experience, age differences usually are absent. These changes in pattern of predictions appear to result from people's ability to use performance on earlier trials to adjust their predictions in subsequent trials.

Clinical Issues and Memory Testing

Normal and Abnormal Memory Aging

- Whether memory changes affect daily functioning is one way to separate normal from abnormal aging. Brain imaging techniques allow localization of problems with more precision. Some diseases also are marked by severe memory impairments. However, in many cases telling the difference between normal changes and those associated with disease or other abnormal events is difficult.

Memory and Mental Health

- Dementia (such as Alzheimer's disease) and severe depression both involve memory impairment. In depression, negative belief systems may underlie these memory problems. Researchers and clinicians must learn to differentiate the various types of mental health problems.

Clinical Memory Tests

- Neuropsychological tests assess broad aspects of cognitive functioning, including memory, attention, and problem solving. Such tests are designed to assess specific brain–behavior relations.

- Scores on memory self-evaluation questionnaires measuring memory complaints correlate with depression.

- Rating scales are completed by people other than the person with the memory problems and often are used to diagnose dementia. Two common types of rating scales are the mental status exam and checklists of specific memory problems.

Memory, Nutrition, and Drugs

- Research evidence links niacin and vitamin B_{12} deficiencies with memory impairment. Drugs such as alcohol and some prescription and over-the-counter medications also have deleterious effects on memory.

Remediating Memory Problems

Training Memory Skills

- The E-I-E-I-O framework, based on explicit and implicit aspects of memory and external and internal types of strategies, is a useful way to organize memory training techniques. Older adults can learn new internal memory strategies, but like all other adults they probably will abandon them over time. External explicit strategies (such as lists and calendars) are common, but internal implicit strategies are effective even for people who have Alzheimer's disease.

- Practicing remembering things helps to improve memory. Use of memory-enhancing drugs does not work in the long run. Combining types of strategies may be the best approach.

Individual Difference Variables in Memory Training

- Memory training may be more effective when individual difference factors, such as emotional issues, are taken into account. Combining memory strategy training with relaxation training, for example, has been shown to be effective. However, older adults appear not to generalize the strategies across a range of different tasks.

Review Questions

Information Processing Revisited

- What is working memory? What age differences have been found? What role does working memory play in understanding age differences in memory?

- What are episodic and semantic memory? How are they tested? What patterns of age differences have been found? What happens to the use of memory strategies with age?

- What is remote memory? How does remote memory differ with age in terms of the knowledge base and autobiographical memory?

- What age differences have been found on implicit memory tasks?

Sources of Age Differences in Memory

- What age differences have been found in encoding processes?

- What age differences have been found in retrieval processes?

- What is the relative contribution of encoding and retrieval in understanding age differences in memory?

- What is the emerging role of automatic retrieval in understanding age differences in memory?
- How do source memory and false memories change with age?

Discourse Memory
- What age differences have been uncovered related to text-based memory?
- What age differences are evident for situational information?
- How do the patterns of age differences for discourse and list learning compare?
- What text variables are most important?

Memory in Everyday Life
- What age differences are there in memory of location? What factors influence performance? When do older and younger adults perform equivalently? Why?
- What difference does it make in accuracy in whether older and younger people actually performed the actions they need to remember?
- What types of prospective memory have been distinguished? What age differences are there in prospective memory?
- How do younger and older adults compare at remembering pictures?

Self-Evaluations of Memory Abilities
- What major types of self-evaluations have been described?
- What age differences are there in memory knowledge and in beliefs about memory?
- What age differences have been found in making predictions about performance? What factors influence people's predictions?

Clinical Issues and Memory Testing
- What criteria are used to determine the difference between normal and abnormal changes in a person's memory?
- What major mental health conditions involve significant memory problems?
- What do neuropsychological tests assess? Of what use are self-report questionnaires?

- How are rating scales used to assess memory impairments?
- What effects do nutrition and drugs have on memory?

Remediating Memory Problems
- What is the E-I-E-I-O framework? How does it help organize memory training programs?
- How much do older adults benefit from each of the major types of memory training programs?
- What kinds of memory interventions work over time?

Integrating Concepts in Development

1. Based on material in Chapter 6 on attention and perceptual speed and the material in this chapter, what are the major factors involved in understanding age-related differences in memory?
2. What aspects of attention, as discussed in Chapter 6, would be important to consider in designing memory training programs?
3. How would you design an informational brochure for older adults to maximize their ability to remember it?

Key Terms

autobiographical memory Remembering information and events from your own life.

encoding The process of getting information into the memory system.

episodic memory The general class of memory having to do with the conscious recollection of information from a specific event or time.

explicit memory The conscious and intentional recollection of information.

external aids Memory aids that rely on environmental resources.

false memory Memory of items or events that did not occur.

implicit memory The effortless and unconscious recollection of information.

internal aids Memory aids that rely on mental processes.

long-term memory The aspects of memory involved in remembering extensive amounts of information over long periods of time.

memory monitoring The awareness of what we are doing in memory right now.

memory self-efficacy The belief in one's ability to perform a specific memory task.

metamemory Memory about how memory works and what one believes to be true about it.

prospective memory Process involving remembering to remember something in the future.

rating scales Instruments designed to assess memory from the viewpoint of an observer, usually a mental health professional.

recall Process of remembering information without the help of hints or cues.

recognition Process of remembering information by selecting previously learned information from among several items.

rehearsal Process by which information is held in working memory, either by repeating items over and over or by making meaningful connections between the information in working memory and information already known.

remote memory Aspect of memory involved with information kept over very long periods of time.

retrieval The process of getting information back out of memory.

semantic memory Learning and remembering the meaning of words and concepts that are not tied to specific occurrences of events in time.

situation model A level at which people use world knowledge to construct a more global understanding of what a text is about.

source memory The ability to remember the source of a familiar event and the ability to determine whether an event was imagined or actually experienced.

storage The manner in which information is represented and kept in memory.

strategies Various techniques that make learning or remembering easier and increase the efficiency of storage.

working memory The processes and structures involved in holding information in mind and simultaneously using that information, sometimes in conjunction with incoming information, to solve a problem, make a decision, or learn new information.

Resources

Readings

Blanchard-Fields, F., & Hess, T. M. (Eds.). (1996). *Perspectives on cognitive changes in adulthood and aging.* New York: McGraw-Hill. The best basic overview of age-related cognitive changes. Easy to moderate difficulty.

Craik, F. I. M., & Salthouse, T. A. (Eds.). (2000). *The handbook of aging and cognition.* Hillsdale, NJ: Erlbaum. One of the best overviews of memory and cognition in one volume. Moderate to difficult reading.

Sinnott, J. D. (Ed.). (1994). *Interdisciplinary handbook of adult lifespan learning.* Westport, CT: Greenwood. A broad discussion of many different aspects of cognition, including cross-cultural studies. Moderate difficulty.

West, R. L., & Sinnott, J. D. (Eds.). (1991). *Everyday memory and aging: Current research and methodology.* New York: Springer-Verlag. Good overview of memory in everyday life. Moderate difficulty.

Search Online with

InfoTrac College Edition

For more information on the topics in this chapter, explore InfoTrac College Edition, your online library. Go to http://www.infotrac-college.com/wadsworth and use the passcode that came on the card with your book. Try these search terms: self-efficiency, everyday memory, semantic memory, episodic memory, cognitive aging.

INTELLIGENCE

© AP / World Wide Photos

The Dalai Lama is the spiritual leader of the Tibetan people, recipient of the 1989 Nobel Peace Prize, and recognized as a leader in Buddhist philosophy, human rights, and global environmental problems. He has reached this stature as a simple Buddhist monk, "no more, no less," he claims. To the world, the Dalai Lama is recognized for his wisdom. A sample of this wisdom is in his plea for "a new way of thinking . . . for responsible living and acting. If we maintain obsolete values and beliefs, a fragmented consciousness and a self-centered spirit, we will continue to hold to outdated goals and behaviors. Such an attitude by a large number of people would block the entire transition to an interdependent yet peaceful and cooperative global society." He also states that as a Buddhist monk, he tries to develop compassion, not simply as religious practice but on a human level. To do so he "sometimes finds it helpful to imagine himself standing as a single individual on one side, facing a huge gathering of all other human beings on the other side. Then he asks himself, 'Whose interests are more important?' To him it is quite clear that however important he feels he is, he is just one individual while others are infinite in number and importance."*

The Dalai Lama drives home the point that wisdom has long been associated with age. Surprisingly, psychologists have only recently become interested in wisdom,

---

*From www.tibet.com/DL/biography.

perhaps because they have been busy studying a related topic: intelligence. Another reason for not researching wisdom was the widespread belief that it would be a waste of time. At one time researchers and theorists were convinced that all intellectual abilities inevitably declined as people aged because of biological deterioration. For instance, Wechsler (1958, p. 135) wrote that "nearly all studies have shown that most human abilities decline progressively after reaching a peak somewhere between ages 18 and 25."

In the decades since Wechsler's pessimistic view, many things changed. Researchers discovered that intellectual development is an extremely complex process. We cannot give a simple "yes" or "no" answer to the question "Does intelligence decline with age?" And we continue to move farther away, rather than closer to, a simple answer. The controversy intensified in the 1970s. Based on methodological comparisons between cross-sectional and longitudinal studies, Baltes and Schaie (1974, p. 35) concluded that "general intellectual decline is largely a myth." Botwinick (1977, p. 580) countered that "decline in intellectual ability is clearly a part of the aging picture."

Who is right? Where do we stand now? Does intelligence decline, or is that a myth? Does wisdom come with age? Answering these questions is our goal in this chapter. Such widely divergent conclusions about age-related changes in intelligence reflect different sets of assumptions about the nature of intelligence, which are then translated into different theoretical and methodological approaches. We examine three avenues of research on intelligence and age: the psychometric approach, the life-span approach, and the cognitive process approaches. Along the way we look at some attempts to modify intellectual abilities through training programs. But first we need to consider the question of what intelligence is.

DEFINING INTELLIGENCE

LEARNING OBJECTIVES

- How do people define intelligence in everyday life?
- What are the major components of the life-span approach?
- What are the major research approaches for studying intelligence?

After Beverly graduated high school she decided to start her own pet-sitting business. She started small but ultimately cornered the market in her city. She lives a comfortable and wealthy lifestyle. After high school Helene went to college and majored in math. She pursued her Ph.D. and now lives a comfortable and modest lifestyle as a university professor. If we compared Beverly and Helene on intellectual ability, who would come out on top?

In terms of intelligence, the distinction between Beverly and Helene's success points to an important question to ask: What is intelligence? Is it being able to learn new things very quickly? Is it knowing a great deal of information? Is it the ability to adapt to new situations or to create new things or ideas? Or is it the ability to make the most of what we have and to enjoy life? Intelligence is all of these abilities and more, as we can see in the different pathways Beverly and Helene took. It is all of them in the sense that people who stand out on these dimensions often are considered smart or intelligent. It is more than just these abilities because intelligence also involves the qualitative aspects of thinking style, or how one approaches and conceptualizes problems.

Intelligence in Everyday Life

Some intriguing work by Sternberg and his colleagues points out that intelligence involves more than just a particular fixed set of characteristics (Berg & Sternberg, 1992; Sternberg et al., 1981). They compiled a list of behaviors that laypeople at a train station, supermarket, or college library reported to be distinctly characteristic of exceptionally intelligent, academically intelligent, everyday intelligent, or unintelligent people. This list of behaviors was then given to experts in the field of intelligence and to a new set of laypeople, who were asked to rate either how distinctively characteristic each behavior was of an ideally intelligent, academically intelligent, or everyday intelligent person or how important each behavior was in defining these types of intelligent people. Ratings were analyzed separately for the experts and the laypeople.

Sternberg and his colleagues found very high agreement between experts and laypeople on ratings

Vocabulary ability, essential in solving crossword puzzles, is one example of an intellectual ability that shows improvement or stability across adulthood.

of the importance of particular behaviors in defining intelligence. The two groups agreed that intelligence consisted of three major clusters of related abilities: problem-solving ability, verbal ability, and social competence. Problem-solving ability consists of behaviors such as reasoning logically, identifying connections between ideas, seeing all aspects of a problem, and making good decisions. Verbal ability includes such things as speaking articulately, reading with high comprehension, and having a good vocabulary. Social competence includes behaviors such as accepting others for what they are, admitting mistakes, displaying interest in the world at large, and being on time for appointments.

Berg and Sternberg (1992) also wanted to know how these conceptions of intelligence differed across the adult life span. To find out, people aged 22 to 85 were asked to rate 55 behaviors that they viewed as characteristic of exceptionally intelligent 30-, 50-, or 70-year-olds. Behaviors such as motivation, intellectual effort, and reading were said to be important indicators of intelligence for people of all ages. But other behaviors were specific to particular points in the life span. For example, planning for the future and being open-minded were listed most often for a 30-year-old. The intelligent 50- and 70-year-olds were described as acting responsibly, adjusting to life situations, verbally fluent, and displaying wisdom.

The Big Picture: A Life-Span View

One thing is clear about the ways people view intelligence: Everyone considers it a complex construct. In the big picture, then, intelligence consists of many different types of skills. Theories of intelligence therefore are **multidimensional,** *specifying many domains of intellectual ability.* Although people disagree on the number of dimensions, they do agree that no single generic type of intelligence is responsible for all the different kinds of mental activities we perform.

Baltes and colleagues (Baltes, 1993; Baltes, Staudinger, & Lindenberger, 1999) take a broad view of intellectual development. The life-span concepts discussed in Chapter 1, including multidirectionality, plasticity, and interindividual variability, play an important role in this conceptualization of intellectual change. Overall, this perspective asserts that some intellectual decline may be seen with age but that stability and growth in mental functioning also can be seen across adulthood. It emphasizes the role of intelligence in human adaptation and daily activity.

The first concept, **multidirectionality,** *is the distinct patterns of change in abilities over the life span;* these patterns are different for different abilities. For example, developmental functions for specific abilities differ, meaning that the directional change in intelligence depends on the skills in question. As we shall see later on, everyday knowledge accumulates over time and thus increases with age. However, basic cognitive mechanisms show more declines, especially into older age.

Plasticity *is the range of functioning within a person and the conditions under which a person's abilities can be modified within a specific age range.* Plasticity implies that what may appear to be declines in some skills may in part represent a lack of practice in using them. The research on training cognitive abilities described later in this chapter supports this view in that older adults who show decline in cognitive functioning can be trained to perform at a higher level.

The last concept, **interindividual variability,** *acknowledges that adults differ in the direction of their intellectual development* (Schaie, 1996). Schaie's sequential research indicates that within a given cohort or generation some people show longitudinal decline in specific abilities, whereas some people show stability of functioning in those same abilities. Finally, others show increments in performance in those same abilities (Schaie, 1996). Consequently, a curve representing typical or average changes with age may not represent how the various individuals in a group function.

Using these four concepts of multidimensionality, plasticity, multidirectionality, and interindividual variability, Baltes and his colleagues proposed the dual-component model of intellectual functioning. Two interrelated types of developmental processes are postulated. The first component, called the mechanics of intelligence, concerns the neurophysiological architecture of the mind (P. B. Baltes et al., 1999). Cognitive abilities include basic forms of thinking associated with information processing and problem solving such as reasoning, spatial orientation, or perceptual speed. Intellectual change in this first component is greatest during childhood and adolescence, as we acquire the requisite skills to handle complex cognitive tasks, such as those encountered in school. The second component, pragmatic intelligence, concerns acquired bodies of knowledge available from and embedded within culture. In other words, it includes everyday cognitive performance and human adaptation. Such abilities include verbal knowledge, wisdom, and practical problem solving. Pragmatic intellectual growth dominates adulthood. Indeed, later in this chapter we will see that such knowledge continues to increase until very late in life. Both of these components are grounded in the four developmental forces, although in different degrees, as seen in the Forces in Action feature.

This broad view of intellectual development in adulthood provides the background for asking more specific questions about particular aspects of intelligence. As we will see, three primary research approaches have emerged.

Research Approaches to Intelligence

Sternberg's work points out that many different skills are involved in intelligence, depending on one's point of view. Interestingly, the behaviors listed by Sternberg's participants fit nicely with the more formal attempts to define intelligence that we encounter in this chapter. Researchers have studied these skills from many different perspectives, depending on their theoretical orientation. For example, some investigators approach these skills from a factor analysis approach and study them as separate pieces that can be added together to form intelligence. Others take a more holistic view and think of intelligence as a way or mode of thinking. These various theoretical orientations result in very different ways of studying intelligence.

Some investigators, such as Schaie and Horn, have concentrated on the **psychometric approach,** *measuring intelligence as performance on standardized tests.* For example, the problem-solving and verbal abilities in Sternberg and colleagues' study would be assessed by tests specifically designed to assess these skills. These tests focus on getting correct answers and tend

The two-component model of life-span intelligence (P. B. Baltes et al., 1998, 1999) is grounded in the dynamic interplay between biological, sociocultural, psychological, and life-cycle forces. However, as Baltes points out, these forces differentially influence the mechanics and pragmatics of intelligence. Whereas the mechanics of intelligence is more directly an expression of the neurophysiological architecture of the mind, the pragmatics of intelligence is associated more with the bodies of knowledge that are available from and mediated through one's culture (Baltes et al., 1998). This is illustrated in Figure 8.1. The mechanics of intelligence in later life is more associated with the fundamental organization of the central nervous system (i.e., biological forces). Thus, it is more closely linked with a gradual loss of brain efficiency with age (Horn & Hofer, 1992).

On the other hand, the pragmatics of intelligence is more closely associated with psychological and cultural forces. At the psychological level, knowledge structures change as a function of the accumulated acquisition of knowledge over time. At the sociocultural level, knowledge structures are also influenced by how we are socialized given the particular historical period in which we are raised. Overall, these knowledge structures influence the way we implement our professional skills, solve everyday problems, and conduct the business of life (Baltes et al., 1998; Berg & Klaczynski, 1996; Marsiske & Willis, 1995; Staudinger, 1999).

Finally, as the figure suggests, different weightings of the forces of intelligence lead to specific predictions about the developmental pathway they take across the adult life span. Given that biological and genetic forces govern the mechanics more, there is a downward trajectory with age. However, given that the pragmatics of intelligence is governed more by environmental and cultural factors, there is an upward trajectory that is maintained across the adult life span.

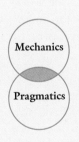

Mechanics

Basic information processing
Content-poor
Universal, biological
Genetically predisposed

Pragmatics

Acquired knowledge
Content-rich
Culture-dependent
Experience-based

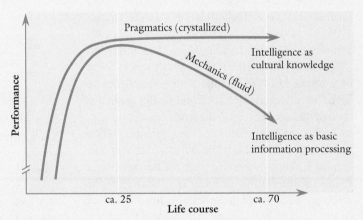

FIGURE 8.1   **Life-span conceptualization of fluid mechanics and crystallized pragmatics of intelligence.**

Source: Baltes, P. B., Staudinger, U. M., & Lindenberger, U. (1999). Lifespan psychology: Theory and application to intellectual functioning. *Annual Review of Psychology, 50,* 471–507. With permission from the *Annual Review of Psychology,* volume 50 © 1999 by Annual Reviews. www.AnnualReviews.org.

to put less emphasis on the thought processes used to arrive at them. Other researchers, such as Salthouse and Craik, focus on information-processing mechanisms reviewed in Chapters 6 and 7. This approach aims at a detailed analysis of aging-associated changes in components of cognitive mechanisms and their interactions. Finally, a number of researchers have focused their efforts on reconceptualizing the meaning

Earlier in this chapter, we encountered Sternberg and colleagues' research on people's implicit theories of intelligence. However, that study examined only broad categories of behavior that could be considered intelligent. Moreover, it was not conducted in such a way as to permit comparisons with research-based approaches to intelligence.

You and your classmates could address these shortcomings in the following way. Ask adults of different ages what they think constitutes intelligent behavior, much as Sternberg and colleagues did. However, make sure these people are specific about the abilities they list. Additionally, ask them about what makes adults' thinking different from adolescents' thinking and whether

they believe there might be different stages of adults' thinking. Again, try to get your respondents to be as specific as possible.

Collate all the data from the class. Look for common themes in specific abilities and in the qualitative aspects of thinking. As you read the rest of the chapter, see to what extent your data parallel that from more formal investigations.

---

and measurement of intelligence by taking a **cognitive structural approach,** *which addresses the ways in which people conceptualize and solve problems* rather than scores on tests. Such approaches to intelligence emphasize developmental changes in the modes and styles of thinking. These include a search for postformal operations (Labouvie-Vief, 1992; Sinnott, 1996), the assessment of wisdom (Baltes et al., 1995; Staudinger, 1999), and studies of practical intelligence (Marsiske & Willis, 1995). The age differences Sternberg found in which abilities their respondents believed were important correspond to the qualitative changes discussed by these theorists.

In this chapter we consider these theories and the research they stimulated. We will discover that each approach has its merits and that whether age-related changes in intelligence are found depends on how intelligence is defined and measured. But before you continue, complete the exercise in the Discovering Development feature. The information you uncover will be useful as you read the rest of the chapter.

CONCEPT CHECKS

1. What three clusters of ability did Sternberg and colleagues identify in their study of people's everyday conceptualizations of intelligence?

2. What are the four major aspects of intelligence emphasized by the life-span approach?

3. What are the three major approaches for researching intelligence?

DEVELOPMENTAL TRENDS IN PSYCHOMETRIC INTELLIGENCE

LEARNING OBJECTIVES

- What are primary mental abilities? How do they change across adulthood?

- What are secondary mental abilities? What are the developmental trends for fluid and crystallized intelligence?

- What are the primary moderators of intellectual change?

- How successful are attempts to train primary mental abilities?

*L*inda and Jerry retired recently. They are delighted with the prospect of engaging in activities they did not have time for in the past because of work and child-rearing responsibilities. They both enrolled in courses at the local community college to pursue their mutual interests in English literature. After the first day of class, they both revealed that they were worried about being able to keep up with the younger students and wondered whether they were smart enough. They both shrugged their shoulders and realized that they would find out soon enough.

Many older adults who are returning to a learning environment worry that they many not be "smart enough" to keep up with 18- or 19-year-olds. Are these fears realistic? An extensive amount of psychometric evidence describes how intellectual performance changes through the latter half of the life span.

One way to psychometrically measure intelligence is to focus on people's performances on various tests of intellectual abilities and on how these performances are interrelated. This approach to intelligence has a long history; the ancient Chinese and Greeks used this method to select people for certain jobs, such as master horseman (Doyle, 1974; DuBois, 1968). It also served as the basis for Binet's (1903) pioneering work in developing standardized intelligence tests and many modern theories of intelligence.

Because of this long history of research in psychometric intelligence, we probably know more about this area than any other area in cognitive aging except for episodic memory. Yet we still are not sure how intelligence changes with age. There is substantial agreement on descriptions of change in different intellectual abilities (as we discuss later) and agreement on the methodological issues that must be addressed in studying intellectual change. However, there is little convergence on the proper interpretation of the data. For example, what does it mean that changes in intellectual abilities are related to increasing age? Remember that in Chapter 1 we discussed the fact that age does not cause change. The fact that age is related to intellectual abilities is not the same thing as aging per se. As we shall see, age-graded intellectual change is also related to important variables such as health, activity level, and educational achievements. It is in these areas that much of the controversy is still brewing.

Measuring Intelligence

Because the psychometric approach focuses on the relations between intellectual abilities, the major goal is to describe the ways in which these relations are organized (Sternberg, 1985). This organization of interrelated intellectual abilities is called the structure of intelligence. The most common way to describe the structure of intelligence is to picture it as a hierarchy (Cunningham, 1987).

Each higher level of this hierarchy represents an attempt to organize components of the level below in a smaller number of groups. The lowest level consists of individual test questions, the specific items that people answer on an intelligence test. These items can be organized into tests at the second level. *The third level,* **primary mental abilities,** *reflects relations between performances on intelligence tests. Relations between the primary mental abilities produce the* **secondary mental abilities** at the fourth level. Third-order mental abilities in turn represent relations between the secondary mental abilities. Finally, general intelligence at the top refers to the relations between the third-order abilities.

Keep in mind that each time we move up the hierarchy we are moving away from people's actual performance. Each level above the first represents a theoretical description of how things fit together. Thus, there are no tests of primary abilities per se; primary abilities represent theoretical relations between tests, which in turn represent theoretical relations between actual performances.

So exactly how do researchers construct this theoretical hierarchy? The structure of intelligence is uncovered through sophisticated statistical detective work using factor analysis. First, researchers measure people's performances on many types of problems. Next, the results are examined to determine whether performance on one type of problem (e.g., filling in missing letters in a word) predicts performance on another type of problem (e.g., unscrambling letters to form a word). *If the performance on one test is highly related to the performance on another, the abilities measured by the two tests are interrelated and are called a* **factor.**

Most psychometric theorists believe that intelligence consists of several factors. However, although factor analysis is a sophisticated statistical technique, it is not an exact technique. Thus, estimates of the exact number of factors vary from a few to more than 100. Most researchers and theorists believe the number to be small. We examine two types of factors: primary mental abilities and secondary mental abilities.

PRIMARY MENTAL ABILITIES. Early in this century researchers discovered the existence of several independent intellectual abilities, each indicated by different combinations of intelligence tests (Thurstone, 1938). The abilities identified in this way led to the proposition that intelligence is composed of several independent abilities, called primary mental abilities. Thurstone initially examined seven primary mental abilities: number, word fluency, verbal meaning, associative memory, reasoning, spatial orientation, and perceptual speed. Over the years this list has been refined and expanded, resulting in a current list of 25 primary mental abilities that have been documented across many studies (Ekstrom et al., 1979). Because it is difficult to measure all 25 primary abilities in the same study, researchers following in Thurstone's tradition concentrate on measuring only a subset. Typically, this subset originally consisted of the following five primary mental abilities:

Numerical facility, or the basic skills underlying one's mathematical reasoning

Word fluency, or how easily one can produce verbal descriptions of things

Verbal meaning, or one's vocabulary ability

Inductive reasoning, or one's ability to extrapolate from particular facts to general concepts

Spatial orientation, or one's ability to reason in the three-dimensional world in which we live

However, two other important information-processing abilities were incorporated into the battery of measures in subsequent work (Schaie, 1994, 1996):

Perceptual speed, or one's ability to rapidly and accurately find visual details and make comparisons

Verbal memory, or the ability to store and recall meaningful language units

Note that tests of verbal memory typically include word fluency. In these analyses, word fluency is eliminated as a separate ability. How these abilities change with age is considered next.

Age-Related Changes in Primary Abilities

One of the most important research projects on adult intellectual development is the longitudinal study being conducted by K. Warner Schaie and his colleagues in Seattle, Washington, which began in 1956 as Schaie's dissertation (Schaie, 1996). This study not only has uncovered most of what we know about how primary mental abilities change across adulthood, but has also been the basis for creating new research methods such as the sequential designs discussed in Chapter 1. Over the course of the study, more than 5,000 people have been tested over six testing cycles (1956, 1963, 1970, 1977, 1984, 1991). All participants were recruited through a very large health maintenance organization in Seattle that is representative of the upper 75% of the socioeconomic spectrum. Like most longitudinal studies, though, Schaie's project has encountered selectivity effects; that is, people who return over the years for retesting tend to do better than those who fail to return. However, an advantage of Schaie's sequential design is that by bringing in new groups of participants, he has been able to estimate the importance of selection effects, a major improvement over previous research.

Schaie (1996) proposes a hierarchical relation in intellectual abilities. Information-processing abilities such as perceptual speed and verbal memory are considered the most basic and are tied to neuropsychological functioning (see also Salthouse, 1991). Mental abilities such as reasoning and number are products of acquired information. Finally, all mental abilities underlie all meaningful activities of a person's daily life (Willis et al., 1992). Thus, the developmental trends uncovered in the Seattle Longitudinal Study provide important insights into the course of intellectual changes that ultimately affect people's work and daily living routines.

Schaie (1996) summarizes the findings as follows. Based on analysis of the data collected through the fifth time of measurement, people tend to improve on the primary abilities tested until their late 30s or early 40s. Scores then tend to stabilize until people reach their mid-50s or early 60s. But by their late 60s, people tend to show consistent declines in each test. Although some people begin to show declines in their mid-50s, these decrements tend to be small until the mid-70s. Considering the modest improvements most people make between young adulthood and middle age, scores are significantly lower than they were in young adulthood (roughly age 25) only by the mid-70s. These changes are depicted in Figure 8.2.

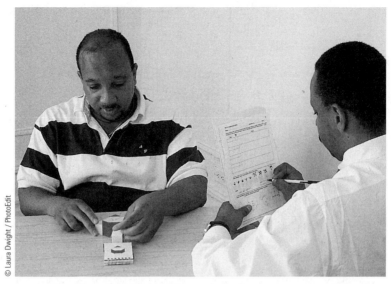

Formal intelligence testing typically assesses primary or secondary abilities in which an overall IQ score can be computed.

Do the general trends observed reflect global or specific changes in intelligence? That is, do people decline on all the primary abilities tested or only some of them? As you can see in Figure 8.3, even though by age 60 nearly everyone shows decline on one ability, very few people show decline on four or five abilities (Schaie, 1996). Even by age 88, only an extremely small number of people had declined significantly on all five abilities.

What happens when we consider both pragmatic and mechanic types of abilities related to Baltes' two-component theory of intelligence? Abilities that are typical of mechanics such as reasoning, verbal memory, spatial orientation, and perceptual speed typically show a pattern of decline during adulthood, with some acceleration in decline in very old age. However, more pragmatic abilities, such as verbal meaning or ability and numerical ability, tend to remain stable or even increase up to the 60s and 70s. Little or no age decrements occur before age 74. They start to show decline only in very old age. It appears that most of the loss occurs in highly challenging,

complex, and stressful situations that require activating cognitive reserves (Baltes et al., 1998).

These patterns may reflect a strategy of optimization of cognitive functioning in late life by selectively maintaining some abilities and not others (Baltes et al., 1998). Even so, the evidence is clear that significant decrements in both types of intellectual abilities occur by the time people are in their 80s. In addition, although the distinction between pragmatic and mechanic types of abilities still exists into very old age (over 80), they both show precipitous decline, just at different levels of functioning (Lindenberger & Baltes, 1997; Lindenberger & Reischies, 1999).

Secondary Mental Abilities

Because so many primary mental abilities have been identified, some researchers think it may be easier to understand intellectual development by looking at relations between them. Careful consideration of the relations between the primary mental abilities has resulted in the identification of secondary mental abil-

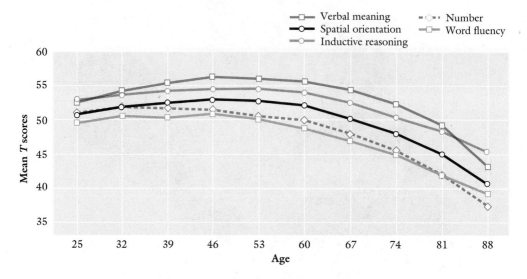

FIGURE 8.2 Longitudinal estimates of age changes on observed measures of five primary mental abilities.

Source: Schaie, K. W. (1994). The course of adult intellectual development. *American Psychologist, 49,* 304–313. Copyright © 1994, American Psychological Association. Reprinted with permission.

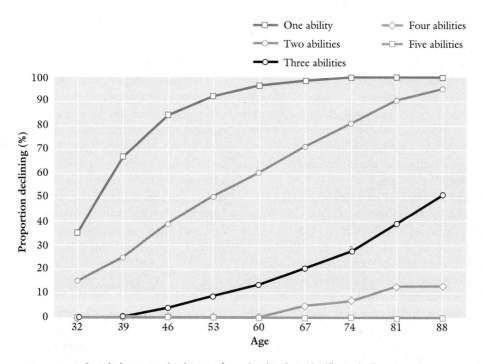

FIGURE 8.3 Cumulative proportion by age of people who show significant decline on one or more primary mental abilities.

Source: Schaie, K. W. (1989). The hazards of cognitive aging. *The Gerontologist, 29,* 490.

ities, which are broad-ranging skills, each composed of several primary abilities (Horn, 1982; Horn & Hofer, 1992). At present, at least six secondary abilities have been found; they are described in Table 8.1. Most developmental research and discussion of these abilities has focused on two: *fluid* intelligence and crystallized intelligence.

FLUID AND CRYSTALLIZED INTELLIGENCE. Crystallized and fluid intelligence include many of the basic abilities we associate with intelligence, such as verbal comprehension, reasoning, integration, and concept formation (Horn, 1982; Horn & Hofer, 1992). Interestingly, they are associated with age differently, are influenced by different underlying variables, and are measured in different ways.

Fluid intelligence *consists of the abilities that make you a flexible and adaptive thinker, allow you to draw inferences, and enable you to understand the relations between concepts independent of acquired knowledge and experience.* It reflects the abilities you need to understand and respond to any situation, but especially new ones, such as inductive reasoning, integration, and abstract thinking (Horn, 1982). An example of a question that taps fluid abilities is as follows:

What letter comes next in the series *d f i m r x e*?[1]

Other typical ways of testing fluid intelligence include mazes, puzzles, and relations between shapes. Most of the time, these tests are timed, and higher scores are associated with faster solutions.

Crystallized intelligence *is the knowledge you have acquired through life experience and education in a particular culture.* Crystallized intelligence includes your breadth of knowledge, comprehension of communication, judgment, and sophistication with information (Horn, 1982). Your ability to remember historical facts, definitions of words, knowledge of literature, and sports trivia information are some examples. Many popular television game shows (such as *Jeopardy* and *Wheel of Fortune*) are based on tests

of contestants' crystallized intelligence. However, even though crystallized intelligence involves cultural knowledge, it is based partly on the quality of a person's underlying fluid intelligence (Horn, 1982; Horn & Hofer, 1992). For example, the breadth of your vocabulary depends to some extent on how quickly you are able to make connections between new words you read and information already known, which is a component of fluid intelligence.

Any standardized intelligence test taps abilities underlying both fluid and crystallized intelligence. No single test of either ability exists because each represents a cluster of underlying primary abilities. As a general rule, tests that minimize the role of acquired, cultural knowledge involve mainly fluid intelligence; those that maximize the role of such knowledge involve mainly crystallized intelligence.

Developmentally, fluid and crystallized intelligence follow two very different paths, similar to the individual primary abilities characterized by the pragmatics and mechanics of intelligence. This pattern is depicted in Figure 8.4. Notice that fluid intelligence declines significantly throughout adulthood, whereas crystallized intelligence improves. Although we do not fully understand why fluid intelligence declines, it may be related to changes in the underlying changes in the brain from the accumulated effects of disease, injury, and aging or from lack of practice (Horn & Hofer, 1992). In contrast, the increase in crystallized intelligence (at least until late life) indicates that people continue adding knowledge every day.

What do these different developmental trends imply? First, they indicate that although learning continues across adulthood, it becomes more difficult the older one gets. Consider what happens when Michele, age 17, and Marion, age 70, try to learn a second language. Although Marion's verbal skills in her native language (a component of crystallized intelligence) probably are better than Michele's verbal skills, Michele's probable superiority in the fluid abilities necessary to learn another language probably will make it easier for her to do so.

Second, these developmental trends point out once again that intellectual development varies a great deal from one set of skills to another. Beyond

---

[1]The next letter is *m*. The rule is to increase the difference between adjacent letters in the series by one each time. Thus, *f* is two letters away from *d*, *i* is three letters away from *f*, and so on.

TABLE 8.1 Descriptions of Major Second-Order Mental Abilities

Crystallized intelligence (Gc)
This form of intelligence is indicated by a very large number of performances indicating breadth of knowledge and experience, sophistication, comprehension of communications, judgment, understanding of conventions, and reasonable thinking. The factor that provides evidence of Gc is defined by primary abilities such as verbal comprehension, concept formation, logical reasoning, and general reasoning. Tests used to measure the ability include vocabulary (What is a word near in meaning to *temerity*?), esoteric analogies (Socrates is to Aristotle as Sophocles is to _____?), remote associations (What word is associated with *bathtub, prizefighting*, and *wedding*?), and judgment (Determine why a foreman is not getting the best results from workers). As measured, the factor is a fallible representation of the extent to which a person has incorporated, through the systematic influences of acculturation, the knowledge and sophistication that constitutes the intelligence of a culture.

Fluid intelligence (Gf)
The broad set of abilities of this intelligence includes those of seeing relationships between stimulus patterns, drawing inferences from relationships, and comprehending implications. The primary abilities that best represent the factor, as identified in completed research, include induction, figural flexibility, integration, and, cooperatively with Gc, logical reasoning and general reasoning. Tasks that measure the factor include letter series (What letter comes next in the series *d f i m r x e*?), matrices (Discern the relationships between elements of 3-by-3 matrices), and topology (From among a set of figures in which circles, squares, and triangles overlap in different ways, select a figure that will enable one to put a dot within a circle and square but outside a triangle). The factor is a fallible representation of such fundamental features of mature human intelligence as reasoning, abstracting, and problem solving. In Gf these features are not imparted through the systematic influences of acculturation but instead are obtained through learning that is unique to an individual or is in other ways not organized by the culture.

Visual organization (Gv)
This dimension is indicated by primary mental abilities such as visualization, spatial orientation, speed of closure, and flexibility of closure, measured by tests such as gestalt closure (Identify a figure in which parts have been omitted), form board (Show how cutout parts fit together to depict a particular figure), and embedded figures (Find a geometric figure within a set of intersecting lines). To distinguish this factor from Gf, it is important that relationships between visual patterns be clearly manifest so performances reflect primarily fluency in perception of these patterns, not reasoning in inferring the patterns.

Auditory organization (Ga)
This factor has been identified on the basis of several studies in which primary mental abilities of temporal tracking, auditory cognition of relations, and speech perception under distraction or distortion were first defined among other primary abilities and then found to indicate a broad dimension at the second order. Tasks that measure Ga include repeated tones (Identify the first occurrence of a tone when it occurs several times), tonal series (Indicate which tone comes next in an orderly series of tones), and cafeteria noise (Identify a word amid a din of surrounding noise). Like Gv, this ability is best indicated when the relationships between stimuli are not such that one needs to reason for understanding but instead are such that one can fluently perceive patterns among the stimuli.

Short-term acquisition and retrieval
This ability comprises processes of becoming aware and processes of retaining information long enough to do something with it. Almost all tasks that involve short-term memory have variance in this factor. Span memory, associative memory, and meaningful memory primary abilities define the factor, but measures of primary and secondary memory can also be used to indicate the dimension.

Long-term storage and retrieval
Formerly this dimension was regarded as a broad factor among fluency tasks, such as those of the primary abilities called associational fluency, expressional fluency, and object flexibility. In recent work, however, these performances have been found to align with others indicating facility in storing information and retrieving information that was acquired in the distant past. It seems, therefore, that the dimension mainly represents processes for forming encoding associations for long-term storage and using these associations, or forming new ones, at the time of retrieval. These associations are not so much correct as they are possible and useful; to associate *teakettle* with *mother* is not to arrive at a truth so much as it is to regard both concepts as sharing common attributes (e.g., warmth).

Source: Horn, J. L. (1982). The aging of human abilities. In B.B. Wolman (Ed.), *Handbook developmental psychology* (pp. 847–870). Englewood Cliffs, NJ: Prentice Hall.

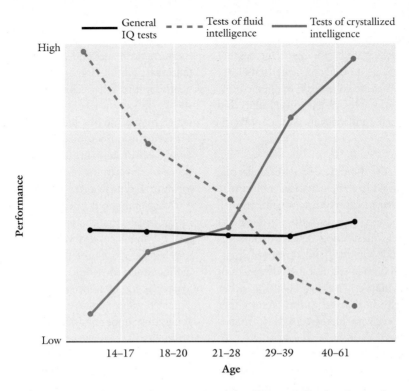

FIGURE 8.4 Performances on tests used to define fluid, crystallized, and general intelligence, as a function of age.

Source: Horn, J. L. (1970). Organization of data on life-span development of human abilities. In L. R. Goulet & P. B. Baltes (Eds.), *Life-span developmental psychology: Research and theory* (p. 463). Copyright © 1970 by Academic Press, reproduced by permission of the publisher.

the differences in overall trends, individual differences in fluid and crystallized intelligence also vary. Whereas individual differences in fluid intelligence remain nearly uniform over time, individual differences in crystallized intelligence increase with age, largely because maintaining one's crystallized intelligence depends on being in situations that require one to use it (Horn & Hofer, 1992). For example, few adults get much practice in solving complex letter series tasks like the one we encountered earlier. But because people can improve their vocabulary skills by reading and because people vary widely in how much they read, differences are likely to emerge. In short, crystallized intelligence provides a rich knowledge base to draw on when material is somewhat familiar, whereas fluid intelligence provides the power to deal with learning in novel situations.

Moderators of Intellectual Change

Based on the research we have considered thus far, two different developmental trends emerge: We see gains in experience-based processes but losses in information-processing abilities. The continued growth in some areas is viewed as a product of lifelong learning. The losses are viewed as an inevitable result of the decline of physiological processes with age.

A number of researchers emphasize individual differences in the rate of change in intellectual aging (Arbuckle et al., 1998; P. B. Baltes et al., 1999; Schaie, 1996). These researchers do not deny that some adults show intellectual decline. Based on large individual differences in intellectual performance over time, they simply suggest that these decrements may not happen to everyone to the same extent. They argue that there are many reasons besides age why performance differences occur. In this section we explore some of the social and physiological factors that have been proposed as modifiers of intellectual development. These include cohort differences, educational level, social variables, personality, health and lifestyle, mindlessness, and relevancy and appropriateness of tasks.

COHORT DIFFERENCES. Do the differences in intellectual performance obtained in some situations reflect true age-related change or mainly cohort, or generational, differences? This question gets right to the heart of the debate over interpreting developmental research on intelligence. On one hand, dozens of cross-sectional studies document significant differences in intellectual performance with age. On the other hand, several longitudinal investigations show either no decrement or even an increase in performance (Labouvie-Vief, 1985).

The way to resolve the discrepancy between the two approaches involves comparing data collected over long periods of time from several samples and analyzed simultaneously in both cross-sectional and longitudinal designs, as we discussed in Chapter 1. When this has been done, the results indicate that part of the apparent decline with age in performance on intelligence tests is caused by generational differences rather than age differences (Schaie, 1996).

Marked generational changes in performance on tests of primary abilities have been noted in the Seattle Longitudinal Study (Schaie, 1996). As you can see in Figure 8.5, more recent-born cohorts generally score better than earlier-born cohorts on verbal meaning, spatial orientation, and inductive reasoning. These trends reflect better educational opportunities (e.g., in the past compulsory education varied more widely by state than it does today), better lifestyles, better nutrition, and improved health care. Note that cohort differences on number ability show gradual declines over the mid-20th century and that word fluency is gradually increasing after showing declines earlier in this century.

The complex pattern of cohort differences indicates that interpreting data from cross-sectional studies is difficult. Recall from Chapter 1 that cross-sectional studies confound age and cohort; because there are both age- and cohort-related changes in intellectual abilities, drawing meaningful conclusions is nearly impossible. Schaie (1996) argues that the trends indicate a leveling off of cohort differences, which may come to a halt by the end of this century. This conclusion is supported by a study of 531 adult parent–offspring pairs that indicated that generational (cohort) improvements were becoming smaller for more recently born pairs (Schaie et al., 1992).

What is it about one's generation that affects the rate of intellectual change? The importance of education for intellectual development during adulthood may partially account for cohort differences. More highly educated people tend to adopt lifestyles that foster the maintenance of cognitive abilities. Highly educated older adults are also the exception in their generation; opportunities to go to college were not as prevalent 50 years ago as they are now.

Thus, one source of the cohort effect may be differences in the type and amount of education. The evidence points to the maintenance of intellectual abilities in well-educated adults at least into old age (Schaie, 1990, 1996). As more well-educated cohorts grow old, education may also explain why cohort differences on many measures are not increasing at the same rates as they did earlier in this century.

In sum, cohort differences provide important evidence about changes in intellectual abilities in adulthood. However, we must be careful not to read too much into these trends and recognize that they may not be sustained into the next century.

INFORMATION PROCESSING. A number of researchers suggest that general processing constraints that occur with aging may help identify mechanisms that underlie decline in mechanic and fluid intelligence abilities with age (P. B. Baltes et al., 1999; Kail & Salthouse, 1994; Salthouse, 1996). For example, evidence suggests that perceptual speed accounts for the lion's share of age-related decline in both fluid and crystallized mental abilities. Similarly, working memory decline with increasing age accounts for poor performance on the part of older adults when the tasks

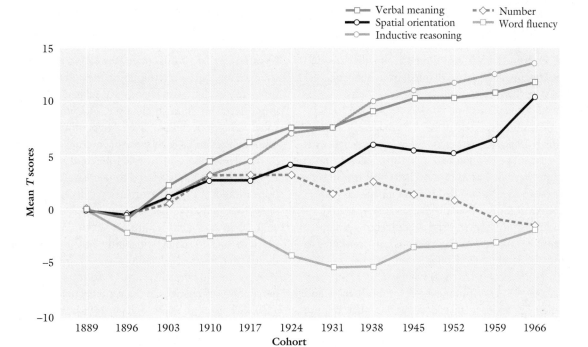

FIGURE 8.5 Cohort gradients showing cumulative cohort differences on five primary mental abilities for cohorts born from 1889 to 1966.

Source: Schaie, K. W. (1994). The course of adult intellectual development. *American Psychologist, 49,* 304–313. Copyright © 1994, American Psychological Society. Reprinted with permission.

involve coordinating new incoming information and stored information such as that found in the fluid or mechanic component of intelligence (Mayr et al., 1996; Salthouse, 1991). Finally, recent evidence suggests that the inability to inhibit actions and thoughts or to avoid interference typically found in older adults may also account for efficient functioning in fluid or mechanic abilities (Brainerd, 1995; Stoltzfus et al., in press).

Overall, processing rate, working memory, and ability to inhibit tend to show decline during later adulthood and old age and are linked to physiological decline. However, studies in this area still are inconclusive in that it is difficult to make a clear-cut distinction between these three information-processing mechanisms. For example, proneness to interference when performing a task is highly correlated with perceptual speed (Salthouse & Meinz, 1995). It may be

the case that future developments in cognitive neuroscience are likely to shed more light on the determinants of mental abilities involved in intellectual functioning (P. B. Baltes et al., 1999; Gazzaniga, 1995).

SOCIAL AND LIFESTYLE VARIABLES. Numerous social demographic variables have been identified as important correlates of intellectual functioning. Think for a minute about the kind of job you currently have or would like to get. What kinds of intellectual skills does it demand? What similarities or differences are there between your chosen job (for example, school counselor) and a different one (say, accountant)? An interesting line of research concerns how the differences in cognitive skills needed in different occupations make a difference in intellectual development (Schooler, 1990; Schooler et al., 1999). To the extent that a job requires you to use certain cognitive abilities a great deal, you may be less likely to show declines in them as you age.

Support for this hypothesis comes from a study that examined both psychometric intelligence and practical intelligence as defined by Sternberg, discussed earlier. Practical intelligence, in this case, is tacit knowledge (generic knowledge about a particular area) and expertise in bank managers (Colonia-Willner, 1998). As expected, age was associated with decreases in psychometric test performance. However decline was not found in more practical intelligence areas such as tacit knowledge and managerial skills.

Support for this hypothesis also comes from a longitudinal study showing that as adults grow older, the level of complexity of their occupation continues to affect the level of their intellectual functioning as it did when they were 20 to 30 years younger (Schooler et al., 1999). This finding held for both men and women. It appears that occupations that require complex thought and independent judgment raise the level of people's intellectual functioning, whereas occupations that do not require such complex processes decrease their level of intellectual functioning. Interestingly, the positive effect of job complexity is greater for older than for younger workers (Schooler et al., 1999).

Other social demographic variables implicated in slower rates of intellectual decline include a lengthy marriage to a well-educated and intelligent spouse (Schaie et al., 1992), exposure to stimulating environments, and the use of cultural and educational resources throughout adulthood (Schaie, 1984).

Finally, although some researchers suggest that a cognitively engaging lifestyle is a predictor of intellectual functioning (Arbuckle et al., 1998), it is still a matter of debate (Hertzog et al., 1999; Pushkar et al., 1999). We examine this debate in the Current Controversies feature.

PERSONALITY. Several aspects of personality have been proposed as important for understanding intellectual change. Like the research we examined in Chapter 7 on memory, one of these aspects concerns self-efficacy (Grover & Hertzog, 1991; Lachman & Leff, 1989). Lachman (1983) examined the causal relation between perceptions of one's own cognitive abilities and performance on several measures of intelligence based on data collected on two occasions about 2 years apart. Most important, she found that people changed in their perceptions of their abilities over time. Interestingly, this change was related to people's initial levels of fluid intelligence and sense of personal control over their lives. High initial levels of fluid abilities and a high sense of internal control led to positive changes in people's perceptions of their abilities; low initial levels led to decreases in perceptions of ability. Thus, Lachman's results support the view that initial levels of cognitive ability affect changes in how abilities are perceived. How people perceive their abilities apparently has no effect on their actual intellectual abilities.

A related personality aspect concerns people's perceptions of changes in their intellectual performance (Schaie et al., 1994; Schaie, 1996). By comparing people's perceptions with actual test performance, Schaie and colleagues classified people as realists (people who accurately estimated changes in performance), optimists (people who overestimated positive change), and pessimists (people who overestimated negative change). Most people were classified as realists, although women were more likely than men to be pessimists on spatial abilities, and older people were more likely than younger people to be pessimists on verbal meaning and inductive reasoning.

Research also indicates that people who have flexible attitudes at midlife tend to experience less decline in intellectual competence than people who were more rigid in middle age (Schaie, 1996; Schooler et al., 1999). Similarly, motor cognitive flexibility in one's 60s is highly predictive of one's numerical and verbal abilities in late life (O'Hanlon, 1993).

Hayslip (1988) investigated relations between personality and ability from an ego development perspective (see Chapter 10). He was interested in establishing connections between how people view themselves and their level of intellectual ability. He found that anxiety over the adequacy of one's ideational ability and feelings about bodily integrity were related to crystallized intelligence, whereas

In an interesting debate in the literature, researchers from two major longitudinal studies on intellectual change in older adulthood (the Victoria Longitudinal Study and Canadian War Veterans Study) found conflicting results regarding the effects of an active lifestyle on intellectual functioning. On one hand, Pushkar and colleagues (1999) claim to have evidence that engaged lifestyles have significant but small causal effects on verbal performance across the adult life span. In other words, an engaging and intellectually active adult lifestyle is associated with a more complex social environment in which intellectual abilities can flourish. However, Hertzog and colleagues (1999) did not find this relation in their study. They argue that the verdict is still out given conflicting findings in the literature and underdeveloped methods of assessing engaging lifestyles. Neither of these research teams would discourage older adults to actively engage in intellectual activities such as crossword puzzles, reading, and adult education. Instead, Hertzog et al. (1999) argue that whether such activities are the same thing as aerobic exercise for the brain is still a matter of debate.

using cognitive resources to deal with reality and organizational ability related to fluid intelligence. These relations suggest that individual differences in the maintenance of higher levels of intellectual functioning in later life may be motivated by the desire to protect oneself from feelings of worthlessness and loss of control over one's abilities.

HEALTH. One of the most difficult problems in any study of aging is the separation of normal processes from abnormal ones. So far our discussion of intellectual development has ignored this distinction; we have been concerned only with normal changes. However, not everyone is healthy, experiencing only normal cognitive aging. Moreover, disease is a hit-or-miss proposition, affecting some people primarily physically, as in arthritis, and others primarily cognitively, as in the early stages of dementia. Thus, we need to consider how specific aspects of health influence intellectual ability.

The most obvious relation between health and intelligence concerns the functioning of the brain itself. We noted in Chapter 2 that several normative changes in brain structure with age affect functioning. Disorders such as Alzheimer's disease and head injuries may damage the brain and interfere with its functioning. In some cases these problems get worse as the person ages. Obviously, the more extensive the damage, the more significant the impairment of intellectual ability.

The connection between disease and intelligence has been established fairly well in cardiovascular disease (Schaie, 1996). Schaie (1990) reports that people in the Seattle Longitudinal Study who declined in inductive reasoning ability (one aspect of fluid intelligence) had significantly more illness diagnoses and visits to physicians for cardiovascular disease. However, results concerning hypertension are more complex. Whereas severe hypertension has been associated with earlier-than-usual declines, mild hypertension may actually have positive effects on intellectual functioning (Sands & Meredith, 1992).

Finally, other research indicates that health-related factors are related to very specific types of intellectual functioning. For example, in a longitudinal study the absence of an APOE genotype (associated with Alzheimer's disease, discussed in Chapter 4) and self-reported sensory functioning were associated with spatial functioning, whereas reports of current health symptoms, depression, and anxiety were associated with perceptual speed (Christiansen et al., 1999). Similarly, Lindenberger and Baltes (Baltes &

Lindenberger, 1997; Lindenberger & Baltes, 1994) found that visual and auditory acuity (measures of sensory functioning) were related to fluid intelligence, which may explain why we see age-related decline in these intellectual abilities. In fact, they suggest that sensory functioning is a better predictor of intellectual ability than variables such as educational level or occupational success. Given these findings, it appears that a variety of variables including health, sensory functioning, lifestyle, and education predict the variability in individual trajectories of intellectual change in adulthood (Christiansen et al., 1999).

Typical IQ testing doesn't necessarily tap into everyday decision making such as the decision to purchase a new product.

RELEVANCY AND APPROPRIATENESS OF TASKS. All the psychometric tests used today trace their origin to Binet's (1903) original attempt to measure academic performance. Some researchers argue that the academic settings and skills that led to the development of these tests may not be equally important or relevant to adults. Consequently, they argue that we need new tests that are based on the problems adults typically face.

To build new tests, one must understand what types of skills adults use in everyday situations. Given that a major concern of older adults is to maintain independent living, Willis and colleagues have been conducting a program of research examining the relation between mental abilities and older adults' competence in everyday situations (Diehl et al., 1995; Willis & Schaie, 1993). They drew on the seven domains of daily living outlined by the Instrumental Activities of Daily Living (IADL) scale (Fillenbaum, 1985): taking medications, managing finances, shopping for necessities, using the telephone, managing transportation, preparing meals, and housekeeping. These domains provide a very different starting point for developing tasks for an intelligence test than trying to figure out how to measure classroom learning potential.

Willis and colleagues (Diehl et al., 1995; Diehl, 1998; Marsiske & Willis, 1995; Willis & Schaie, 1993) examined the relations between seven primary mental abilities, measured by traditional tests, and eight categories of everyday tasks, measured by the ETS Basic Skills Test. The categories of everyday tasks included understanding labels on medical or household articles, reading street maps, understanding charts or schedules, comprehending paragraphs, filling out forms, reading newspaper and phone directory ads, understanding technical documents, and comprehending news text. Three scores on the skills test were calculated; two scores reflected different levels of comprehension and information processing (literal and inference) and the third was the total score. Correlations between the scores for primary abilities and basic skills were very high for the older adults, indicating that the two tests were measuring similar things.

When Willis and colleagues examined their data to see which of the primary abilities best predicted each of the eight categories of everyday tasks, some interesting findings emerged. They had expected their measures of crystallized intelligence to be the best predictors, on the basis that these everyday skills reflect cultural knowledge and should not decline with age. Much to their surprise, the measures of fluid intelligence, especially figural relations, were the best predictors most of the time. Moreover, older adults did not always perform as well as the younger adults on the everyday skills test. In fact, the younger adults obtained near-perfect scores, whereas the older adults were significantly below ceiling, on average. Finally, a longitudinal analysis indicated that crystallized and fluid measures of intelligence predicted everyday functioning 7 years from the first time of measurement.

The Willis study is important for two reasons. First, it shows that traditional tests of primary mental abilities may predict performance on everyday tasks. For supporters of the psychometric approach, these data show that a total rejection of traditional tests on the ground that they are inadequate may be unwarranted. Second, the findings also show that tests consisting of what appear to be more relevant tasks may tap some of the same components of intelligence that the traditional tests are thought to measure. This suggests that we might develop new tests that consist of familiar tasks, but those skills still tap the components of intelligence identified in psychometric research. We return to this point when we discuss everyday problem solving.

The issue of task relevancy is still far from being settled, however. As we will see later, many researchers and theorists argue strongly that only by abandoning a purely psychometric approach and moving to a focus on everyday uses of intelligence will we advance our understanding of intellectual aging. As with most controversies, there is something to be said for both sides.

Modifying Primary Abilities

As we have seen, older adults do not perform as well on tests of some primary abilities as younger adults, even after taking the moderators of performance into account (Schaie, 1995). In considering these results, investigators began asking whether there was a way to slow down or even reverse the declines. Are the age-related differences that remain after cohort and other effects are removed permanent? Or might these differences be reduced or even eliminated if older adults were given appropriate training? Can we modify adults' intelligence? This addresses the important issue of plasticity in intellectual functioning, one of the life-span tenets discussed in Chapter 1.

Attempts to answer these questions have appeared with increasing frequency since the mid-1970s. Several types of tasks have been examined, ranging from tests of skills underlying primary mental abilities

(Willis & Schaie, 1999) to the information-processing skills necessary to drive a car (Sterns & Sanders, 1980). Of these, perhaps the most interesting and important research area is the attempt to modify primary abilities that show early and substantial declines.

Primary abilities that are known to begin to decline early in adulthood, such as inductive reasoning, spatial orientation, memory abilities, and figural abilities, have been examined most closely in intervention research (Baltes & Lindenberger, 1998; Willis & Schaie, 1999). In a prototypical study, performance on a fluid ability is measured on the training task (e.g., inductive reasoning) and on a new transfer task that participants had not seen during training (e.g., a different measure of inductive reasoning). Training is given to three groups. Members of the first group are told to give themselves self-directional statements and feedback. The second group combines these with additional statements that are designed to help them cope with anxiety and to emphasize self-approval and success. Members of the third group receive unspecific training; they simply practice taking the test with no instructions or feedback. Typical findings demonstrate that inductive reasoning can be increased through training (Willis & Schaie, 1999; Willis, 1996a; Baltes et al., 1999). There is also evidence of transfer of the training effects because the performance of the trained groups was also better on the new measure of fluid skill.

In addition to primary mental abilities, significant training effects have been found for other areas of cognitive functioning, including memory, problem solving, and perceptual speed (Kliegl et al., 1990; Yesavage et al., 1989).

PROJECT ADEPT. A much more comprehensive training study, involving a series of short longitudinal studies, was Pennsylvania State University's Adult Development and Enrichment Project (ADEPT) (Baltes & Willis, 1982). The training studies conducted as part of ADEPT included two levels of intervention in addition to a no-training control group. All groups were equivalent at the outset.

The first level of intervention involved minimal direct training and had test familiarity as its goal.

Participants were given the same tests on several occasions to familiarize them with test taking so that the researchers could learn about the effects of repeated testing alone.

The second type of training involved interventions tailored specifically to each of the primary abilities tested. Each training package was based on a thorough task analysis of the thinking processes involved in each ability. The resulting training programs varied a little in specific details, but in general they focused on teaching the relational rules associated with each test problem over five sessions. Training on figural relations, for instance, involved practice with paper-and-pencil tests, oral feedback by the experimenter, group discussion, and review of the kinds of problems involving figural relations ability.

Overall, the ability-specific training resulted in improvements in primary abilities. But the ability to maintain and to transfer the training effects varied. Evidence of long-term and broad transfer effects was strongest for figural relations. Training effects were found for inductive reasoning, attention, and memory, but these effects did not transfer as well to new tasks.

These findings from the training studies are impressive when we consider their implications. Baltes and Willis's improvements in fluid abilities were equivalent to the average 21-year longitudinal decline in these abilities reported by Schaie (1983). The implication of this comparison is that the decline in primary abilities can be slowed or even reversed by proper intervention strategies. The results are even more exciting given that the training packages in ADEPT were fairly short: an average of five 1-hour sessions. Although the reversal of age-related declines in all primary abilities and the duration of the effects of training remain to be seen, clearly we need to revise our view of pervasive, universal decline in primary abilities.

OTHER ATTEMPTS TO TRAIN FLUID ABILITIES. Schaie and Willis have extended the findings from Project ADEPT (Willis, 1990; Willis & Schaie, 1992, 1999). This research involves the participants in Schaie's longitudinal study in Seattle. In one study (Schaie & Willis, 1986), participants were assigned to one of two groups based on their performance over a 14-year period (1970–1984). One group showed significant decline on spatial ability or reasoning ability, and the other group remained stable on these measures. Schaie and Willis then provided a 5-hour training session on spatial ability and a similar session on reasoning ability for those who had declined. To examine the effects of training as a function of amount of decline, training was also provided to the people who had remained stable.

Schaie and Willis found that the cognitive training techniques could reverse declines that had been reliably documented over the 14-year period. However, the effects of cognitive training were largely ability specific. That is, gains were largest when the training matched the ability being tested; only modest gains in abilities were found that were not trained.

Most exciting, the improvements for both spatial and reasoning abilities essentially returned people who had declined to their earlier levels of functioning. In addition, the training procedures even enhanced the performance of many older people who had remained stable. This finding demonstrates that training is effective not only in raising the performance of decliners but also in improving functioning in nondecliners beyond their initial levels (Willis, 1990).

Rather than simply training older adults on particular fluid abilities, Hayslip (1989) tried something different. He randomly assigned 358 community-dwelling older adults to one of four groups: inductive reasoning training (from Project ADEPT), stress inoculation training (to reduce people's feelings of anxiety), no training at all (a control group), or posttest only (a control group to examine the effects of just taking the final test). Several measures of inductive reasoning and other measures of intellectual abilities were given before training, 1 week after, and 1 month after training. Hayslip found that both training groups improved their performance, the effects of the stress inoculation training varied with the difficulty of the task and participants' willingness to apply the anxiety-reducing techniques they had learned to use with the tasks, and the degree to which training generalized to other tasks was limited. He concluded that at least part of the gain in performance resulted from reductions in people's level of anxiety in taking tests of intellectual ability.

Considered together, the results from Project ADEPT, the data from Schaie and Willis's research, and Hayslip's work allow us to conclude that declines in fluid abilities may be reversible. But how long do the improvements last?

LONG-TERM EFFECTS OF TRAINING. Getting older adults to do better on skills underlying fluid intelligence is impressive. Having those benefits last over time would be even better because it would provide a powerful argument in favor of providing intervention programs to more people.

Willis and Nesselroade (1990) report results from a 7-year follow-up to the original ADEPT study. Participants were initially trained in 1979 and received booster training sessions in 1981 and 1986. Significant training effects were found at each point, indicating that people continue to benefit from cognitive intervention as they move from young-old to old-old age. Even people in their late 70s and early 80s continued to perform at levels better than they had 7 years earlier, before training. In fact, 64% of the training group's performance was above their pretraining baseline, compared with only 33% of the control group.

Similarly positive results were reported by Willis and Schaie (1994), who examined members of the Seattle Longitudinal Study 7 years after they received training on inductive reasoning or spatial orientation. The effects of training were substantial and were most impressive for people who had shown declines in the skills trained over the previous 14 years. However, the effects of booster sessions diminished as people grew older.

Hayslip and colleagues (1995) conducted a 3-year follow-up of Hayslip's (1989) original study involving training on inductive reasoning and stress inoculation. Their findings provide strong support for the importance of booster sessions, especially for induc-

tive reasoning training. Without subsequent retraining, performance levels approached levels 3 years earlier, before the original training.

What can we conclude from these findings? First, there is strong evidence that in the normal course of development no one is too old to benefit from training and that training slows down the rates of decline for the fluid abilities examined. However, unless people are somehow reminded of the training through booster sessions, gains demonstrated during training may be lost. Second, transfer is limited to similar tests of the same ability. Third, training gains are durable and last up to several years (Neely & Bäckman, 1993).

Overall, these studies suggest that there is cognitive plasticity in fluid skills well into old age that can be activated in intervention techniques. However, the question still remains whether these training gains apply to related abilities in everyday functioning (P. B. Baltes et al., 1999). In addition, what is the scope of plasticity during adulthood? Are there limits? This question is addressed in studies designed to uncover age differences in the upper limits of mental abilities (Baltes & Kliegl, 1992; Lindenberger & Baltes, 1995). In these studies, training of a mental ability continues until younger and older adults reach their maximum level of performance. Two findings are important. First, both young and older adults improve their performance. Second, performance at maximum levels indicates that sizeable age differences remain. Young adults outperform older adults. In other words, not a single older adult reached the level of performance of young adults. This is a good reminder that genuine age decline does occur. But it is also important to remember that within the older adult herself or himself, there is always room for improvement.

CONCEPT CHECKS

1. What primary mental abilities have been studied most?
2. How do the developmental trajectories of fluid and crystallized intelligence differ?
3. What are the main moderators of intellectual change, and what influences do they have?
4. How effective are programs aimed at training primary mental abilities?

QUALITATIVE DIFFERENCES IN ADULTS' THINKING

LEARNING OBJECTIVES

- What are the main points in Piaget's theory of cognitive development?
- What evidence is there for continued cognitive development beyond formal operations?
- What is the role of emotion and cognition in cognitive maturity?

John, a student at a local university, thought the test he had just taken in his math course was unfair because the instructors simply marked the answers to complex problems right or wrong. He complained that he deserved partial credit for knowing how to set up the problem and being able to figure out some of the steps.

Although John did not know it, his argument parallels one in the intelligence literature: the debate on whether we should pay attention mainly to whether an answer is right or wrong or to how the person reasons the problem through. The psychometric approach we considered earlier does not focus on the thinking processes that underlie intelligence; rather, psychometrics concentrates on relations between answers to test questions. In contrast, cognitive structural approaches focus on the ways in which people think; whether a particular answer is right or wrong is not very important.

We consider two theories that represent cognitive structural approaches. First, we examine Piaget's theory as a foundation for this approach. Second, we explore the recent discussions of possible extensions of it: postformal theory. Both approaches postulate that intellectual changes are mainly qualitative, even though they differ on many points.

Piaget's Theory

According to Piaget (1970, 1980), intellectual development is adaptation through activity. We create the very ways in which our knowledge is organized and, ultimately, how we think. Piaget believed that the development of intelligence stems from the emergence of increasingly complex cognitive structures. He organized his ideas into a theory of cognitive development that changed the way psychologists conceptualize intellectual development.

BASIC CONCEPTS. For Piaget, thought is governed by the principles of adaptation and organization. Adaptation is the process of adjusting thinking to the environment. Just as animals living in a forest feed differently than animals living in a desert, how we think changes from one developmental context to another.

Because all biological systems adapt, the principle of adaptation is fundamental to Piaget's theory. Adaptation occurs through organization, which is how the organism is put together. Each component has its own specialized function, which is coordinated into the whole. In Piaget's theory the organization of thought is reflected in cognitive structures that change over the life span. Cognitive structures determine how we think. It is the change in cognitive structures, the change in the fundamental ways in which we think, that Piaget tried to describe.

What processes underlie intellectual adaptation? Piaget defined two: assimilation and accommodation. **Assimilation** *is the use of currently available knowledge to make sense out of incoming information.* It is the application of cognitive structures to the world of experience that makes the world understandable. For example, a child who knows only the word *dog* may use it for every animal she encounters. So when the child sees a cat and calls it a dog, she is using available knowledge (the word *dog*) to make sense out of the world, in this case the cat that is walking across the living room. The process of assimilation sometimes distorts incoming information because we may have to force-fit it into our knowledge base. This is apparent in our tendency to forget information about a person that violates a stereotype.

Accommodation *involves changing one's thought to make it a better approximation of the world of experience.* The child in our example who thinks that cats are dogs eventually learns that cats are cats. When this happens, she has accommodated her knowledge to incorporate a new category of animal.

The processes of assimilation and accommodation link the structure of thought to observable behavior. Piaget believed that most changes during development involve cognitive structures. His research led him to conclude that there are four structures (that is, four stages) in the development of mature thought: sensorimotor, preoperational, concrete operational, and formal operational. We consider the major characteristics of each stage briefly. Because we are most interested in Piaget's description of adult thought, we emphasize it.

SENSORIMOTOR PERIOD. In this first stage of cognitive development, intelligence is seen in infants' actions. Babies and infants gain knowledge by using their sensory and motor skills, beginning with basic reflexes (sucking and grasping) and eventually moving to purposeful, planned sequences of behavior (such as looking for a hidden toy). The most important thing infants learn during the sensorimotor period is that objects continue to exist even when they are out of sight; this ability is called object permanence.

PREOPERATIONAL PERIOD. Young children's thinking is best described as egocentric. This means that young children believe that all people and all inanimate objects experience the world just as they do. For example, young children believe that dolls feel pain. Although young children can sometimes reason through situations, their thinking is not based on logic. For example, a young child may believe that his father's shaving causes the tap water to be turned on because the two events always happen together.

CONCRETE OPERATIONAL PERIOD. Logical reasoning emerges in the concrete operational period. Children become capable of classifying objects into groups based on a logical principle, such as fruits or vegetables; mentally reversing a series of events; realizing that when changes occur in one perceptual dimension and they are compensated for in another, no net change occurs (called conservation); and understanding the concept of transitivity (for instance, if A is greater than B and B is greater than C, then A is greater than C). However, children are still unable to deal with abstract concepts such as love; for example, love to children is a set of concrete actions, not an abstract, ill-defined concept.

FORMAL OPERATIONAL PERIOD. For Piaget, the acquisition of formal operational thought during adolescence marks the end of cognitive development. Because he argues that formal operational thinking characterizes adult thought, we consider this level in some detail. Several theorists have commented on the characteristics of formal operational thought (Basseches, 1984; Kramer, 1989; Labouvie-Vief, 1980, 1981, 1984; Sinnott, 1984b). We use these commentaries to focus on four aspects of formal operational thought: It takes a hypothesis-testing approach (called hypotheticodeductive) to problem solving, thinking is done in one framework at a time, the goal is to arrive at one correct solution, and it is unconstrained by reality.

Piaget describes the essence of formal operational thought as a way of conceiving abstract concepts and thinking about them in a very systematic, step-by-step way. Formal operational thought is governed by a generalized logical structure that provides solutions to problems that people have never seen and may never encounter. Hypotheticodeductive thought is similar to scientific methods in that it involves forming a hypothesis and testing it until it is either confirmed or rejected. Just as scientists are very systematic in testing experimental hypotheses, formal operational thinking allows people to approach problem solving in a logical, methodical way.

For example, when your car breaks down and you take it for repairs, the mechanic forms hypotheses about what may be wrong, based on a description of the trouble. The mechanic then begins to test each hypothesis systematically. For example, the compression of each cylinder can be checked, one cylinder at a time. This ability to hold other factors constant while testing a particular component is one of the hallmarks of formal operational thought. By isolating potential causes of the problem, the mechanic arrives at a correct solution very efficiently.

When we use hypotheticodeductive thought, we do so to arrive at one unambiguous solution to the problem (Kramer & Woodruff, 1986; Labouvie-Vief,

1980, 1984, 1992). Formal operational thought is aimed at resolving ambiguity; one and only one answer is the goal. When more than one solution occurs, there is a feeling of uneasiness, and people begin a search for clarification. This situation can be observed in high school classes when students press their teacher to identify the right theory (from among several equally good ones) or the right way to view a social issue (such as abortion). Moreover, when people arrive at an answer, they are quite certain about it because they arrived at it through the use of logic. When answers are checked, the same logic and assumptions typically are used, which sometimes means that the same mistake is made several times in a row. For example, a person may repeat a simple subtraction error time after time when trying to figure out why his or her checkbook failed to balance.

Formal operational thinking knows no constraints (Labouvie-Vief, 1984; Piaget, 1970, 1980). It can be applied just as easily to real or to imaginary situations. It is not bound by the limits of reality (Labouvie-Vief, 1980). Whether one can implement a solution is irrelevant; what matters is that one can think about it. For example, this is how people arrive at solutions to disarmament such as getting rid of all nuclear warheads tomorrow. To the formal operational thinker, the fact that this solution is logistically impossible is no excuse. The lack of reality constraints is not all bad, however. Reasoning from a "why not?" perspective may lead to the discovery of completely new ways to approach a problem or even to the invention of new solutions.

DEVELOPMENTAL TRENDS IN PIAGETIAN THOUGHT. Much research has been conducted examining the developmental course of Piagetian abilities (Blackburn & Papalia, 1992). Overall, the results are mixed and difficult to interpret, largely because the majority of studies are cross sectional, the procedures used have strayed widely from those described by Piaget, and the scoring criteria for performance are not systematized (Blackburn & Papalia, 1992). Nevertheless, some general conclusions can be drawn (Papalia & Bielby, 1974; Reese & Rodeheaver, 1985). We consider the findings from research on formal operations and concrete operations.

One serious problem of Piaget's theory is that many adults apparently do not attain formal operations. Several studies report that only 60% to 75% of American adolescents can solve any formal operational problems (Neimark, 1975), and some estimate that no more than 30% of adults ever complete the transition to the highest levels of formal operational thought (Kuhn, 1992). Piaget (1972) himself admitted that formal operations probably were not universal but rather tended to appear only in areas in which people were highly trained or specialized.

Extreme pessimism may not be warranted, however. Kuhn and her colleagues showed that as many as 94% of the adolescents in her research demonstrated formal operational thought after being given appropriate background and practice (Kuhn, 1992; Kuhn et al., 1979). Chandler (1980, p. 82) notes that the lack of evidence for formal operations in older adults may be more indicative of their lack of interest in doing formal operational problems than a lack of ability; older adults "generally dislike bookish, abstract, or childish tasks of low meaningfulness." Tomlinson-Keasey (1972) points out that attainment of the highest levels of formal operations may depend on preference as well as personal experience and the cognitive structures that are available. These results imply that the estimates of how many people attain formal operations may be misleading, that formal operational thought is used only in specialized situations, and that adults' thinking is not described very well by Piaget. We develop the last alternative in more detail later.

Does the ability to use formal reasoning differ with age in people who achieve this level of thinking? The results are mixed. Some studies find that older adults do not perform as well as younger adults on formal operational tasks (Clayton & Overton, 1973). Clayton and Overton also found that performance on the formal operations tasks was correlated with measures of fluid intelligence, thereby linking formal operational abilities to normative decline. However, other research does not show evidence of age-related differences, at least not on all types of formal reasoning tasks. For example, no age differences were found in younger and older adults' use of deductive or formal reasoning unless the task involved emotional aspects, in which case younger adults' performance was better than that of older adults (Pollack et al., 1995).

Because some cross-sectional studies of formal operations showed a lack of these abilities in some adults, researchers have also focused on the development of concrete operations. Two types of tasks have been used most frequently: classification tasks and conservation tasks. In general, the results from these investigations support Papalia and Bielby's (1974) conclusion that cognitive operations decline in the reverse order of their acquisition. That is, the highest, most complex abilities are the last to be acquired but the first to be lost. However, investigations of concrete operations are all cross-sectional and involve highly specialized tasks. Thus, conclusions about age differences must be made with caution.

Some studies document significant age differences between older adults and middle-aged adults in performance on classification tasks, with older adults' performance being worse (Denney & Cornelius, 1975; Storck et al., 1972).

A much larger number of investigators have examined conservation abilities. Conservation tasks involve judgments about whether the amount of a substance has been changed after a particular manipulation. For example, an investigator might show two clay balls of equal size, flatten one of them, and ask whether the lumps are still the same size. Papalia (1972) found that conservation of substance, weight, and volume increased during childhood and declined in old age in the reverse order that they were acquired in childhood. Although some researchers confirmed her findings (Papalia et al., 1973; Storck et al., 1972), other researchers found little evidence of loss of conservation abilities (Chance et al., 1978; Eisner, 1973; Papalia-Finlay et al., 1980). Still other researchers have obtained very inconsistent results, with age differences not showing any particular pattern (Hornblum & Overton, 1976; Hughston & Protinsky, 1978; Protinsky & Hughston, 1978).

Clearly, whether conservation abilities change across adulthood remains an open question. At-tempts to explain the results by gender differences, educational level, intelligence, and even institutionalization have not succeeded (Reese & Rodeheaver, 1985). It may be that traditional concrete operational tasks, like traditional formal operational tasks, may not be interesting or challenging to older adults (Chandler, 1980).

Going Beyond Piaget: Postformal Thought

Consider the following problem:

> John is known to be a heavy drinker, especially when he goes to parties. Mary, John's wife, warns him that if he gets drunk one more time, she will leave him and take the children. Tonight John is out late at an office party. John comes home drunk. Does Mary leave John? How certain are you of your answer? (Adams et al., 1988, p. 13)

When this and similar problems are presented to people of different ages, interesting differences emerge. Formal operational adolescents' responses clearly showed the ambiguity of the situation but also clearly reflected the need to search for the right answer. The ambiguity was considered a problem rather than an acceptable state of affairs. This is evident in the following answer:

> It's a good chance that she would leave him because she warns him that she will leave him and take the children, but warning isn't an absolute thing. . . . And, I'd be absolutely sure that, well let's see. . . . I'm trying to go all the way. I'm trying to think of putting everything [together] so I can be absolutely certain of an answer. . . . It's hard to be absolutely certain. "If he gets drunk, then she'll leave and take the children." I want to say yes 'cause everything's in that favor, in that direction, but I don't know how I can conclude that she does leave John. (Adams et al., 1988, pp. 17–18)

When adults were given the same problem, they handled it differently, for the most part. Their responses showed a combination of logic, emotion,

Many adults are reluctant to draw conclusions based on limited information when multiple perspectives are involved.

and tolerance for ambiguity, as can be seen in the following example:

> There was no right or wrong answer. You could get logically to both answers [yes or no]. . . . It depends on the steps they take to their answer. If they base it on what they feel, what they know, and they have certain steps to get an answer, it can be logical. (Adams et al., 1988, p. 41)

Based on a strict interpretation of formal operational thought, the adults who made responses like the second example showed little evidence of formal operational thinking. Thus, it could be argued that Adams and colleagues' research supports the data described earlier that point to declines in formal operational thought across adulthood. But not everyone agrees that the research examining formal operational thinking across adulthood points to loss. Rather than concluding that differences in performance reflect declines in ability, the results are seen as indicative of another, qualitatively different style of thinking. This latter interpretation implies that Piaget's theory may need modification. Specifically, some researchers propose that these performance differences on Piagetian tasks reflect cognitive development beyond formal operations.

DEVELOPMENTAL PROGRESSIONS IN ADULT THOUGHT. By the 1970s, it was clear that Piaget's contention that formal operations was the endpoint of cognitive development had serious problems. One of the first to formally propose an alternative model was Riegel (1973, 1976), who argued that formal operations was quite limited in its applicability. By the mid-1980s many other authors agreed (Basseches, 1984; Cavanaugh et al., 1985; Commons et al., 1982; Labouvie-Vief, 1980, 1992; Sinnott, 1984b).

Riegel and other writers point out that Piaget is concerned with describing logical, hypotheticode-ductive thinking in his stage of formal operations but that this is not the only kind of thinking adults do. In addition, they argue that Piaget's stage of formal operations is limited primarily to explaining how people arrive at one correct solution. How adults discover or generate new problems and how they sometimes appear to accept several possible solutions are not explained. Finally, the fact that adults often limit their thinking in response to social or other realistic constraints appears to be in conflict with the unconstrained generation of ideas characteristic of formal operations.

For these reasons some researchers propose that there is continued cognitive growth beyond formal operations (Commons et al., 1984, 1989; Sinnott, 1996). **Postformal thought** *is characterized by a recognition that truth (the correct answer) varies from situation to situation, that solutions must be realistic to be reasonable, that ambiguity and contradiction are the rule rather than the exception, and that emotion and subjective factors usually play a role in thinking.*

In one of the first investigations of cognitive growth beyond adolescence, Perry (1970) traced the development of thinking across the undergraduate years. He found that adolescents relied heavily on the expertise of authorities to determine what was right and wrong. At this point thinking is tightly bound by the rules of logic, and the only legitimate conclusions are those that are logically derived. For Perry, the continued development of thinking involves the development of increased cognitive flexibility. The first step in the process is a shift toward relativism. Relativism in thought is the realization that more than one explanation of a set of facts could be right, depending on one's point of view. Although relativism frees the person from the constraints of a single framework, it also leads to skepticism. Because one can never be sure whether one is right or wrong, the skeptic may not try to develop knowledge further, which may lead him or her to feel confused or adrift. Perry points out that the price of freeing oneself from the influence of authority is the loss of the certainty that came from relying on logic for all the answers.

To develop beyond skepticism, Perry showed, adults develop commitments to particular viewpoints. In Perry's later stages adults recognize that they are their own source of authority, that they must make a commitment to a position, and that others may hold different positions to which they are equally committed. In other words, mature thinkers are able to understand many perspectives on an issue, choose one, and still allow others the right to hold differing viewpoints. Thinking in this mature way is different from thinking in formal operational terms.

REFLECTIVE JUDGMENT. Perry's landmark research opened the door to documenting systematic changes in thinking beyond formal operations. One of the best to emerge is King and Kitchener's (1994) refined descriptions of the development of reasoning in young adults. On the basis of nearly two decades of research, they mapped the development of **reflective judgment:** *reasoning through problems involving current affairs, religion, science, and the like.* On the basis of well-designed longitudinal studies of young adults, they identified a systematic progression of thinking, which is described in Table 8.2.

The first three stages in the model represent prereflective thought. People do not acknowledge and may not even perceive that knowledge is uncertain. Consequently, they do not understand that some problems exist for which there is not a clearly and absolutely correct answer. Stages 4 and 5 represent quasireflective thinking in which people recognize that some problems contain an element of uncertainty. However, although they use evidence, they are not adept at using evidence to draw conclusions. Stages 6 and 7 represent true reflective judgment. People realize that knowledge must be constructed and that claims about knowledge must be evaluated within the context in which they were generated, and that conclusions, though based on data, are open to reevaluation.

How does a person move from prereflective judgment to reflective judgment? Is the progression a gradual one or one involving qualitative shifts? Kitchener and Fischer (1990) argue that the progression involves both, depending on which aspect of development one emphasizes. Their view is based on the distinction between optimal level and skill acquisition aspects of development. The **optimal level** *of development is the highest level of information-processing capacity that a person is capable of doing.* The optimal level increases with age and is marked by abrupt changes ("growth spurts") followed by periods of stability. Each spurt represents the emergence of a new developmental level (stage) of thinking; the

| TABLE 8.2 | Description of the Stages of Reflective Judgment |

Stage 1

View of knowledge   Knowledge is assumed to exist absolutely and concretely. It can be obtained with absolute certainty through direct observation.

Concept of justification   Beliefs need no justification because there is assumed to be an absolute correspondence between what is believed and what is true. There are no alternatives.

Stage 2

View of knowledge   Knowledge is absolutely certain, or certain but not immediately available. Knowledge can be obtained via direct observation or via authorities.

Concept of justification   Beliefs are justified via authority, such as a teacher or parent, or are unexamined and unjustified. Most issues are assumed to have a right answer, so there is little or no conflict in making decisions about disputed issues.

Stage 3

View of knowledge   Knowledge is assumed to be absolutely certain or temporarily uncertain. In areas of temporary uncertainty, we can know only via intuition and bias until absolute knowledge is obtained.

Concept of justification   In areas in which answers exist, beliefs are justified via authorities. In areas in which answers do not exist, because there is no rational way to justify beliefs, they are justified arationally or intuitively.

Stage 4

View of knowledge   Knowledge is uncertain and idiosyncratic because situational variables (for example, incorrect reporting of data, data lost over time) dictate that we cannot know with certainty. Therefore, we can only know our own beliefs about the world.

Concept of justification   Beliefs often are justified by reference to evidence but still are based on idiosyncratic reasons, such as choosing evidence that fits an established belief.

Stage 5

View of knowledge   Knowledge is contextual and subjective. Because what is known is known via perceptual filters, we cannot know directly. We may know only interpretations of the material world.

Concept of justification   Beliefs are justified within a particular context via the rules of inquiry for that context. Justifications are assumed to be context-specific or are balanced against each other, delaying conclusions.

Stage 6

View of knowledge   Knowledge is personally constructed via evaluations of evidence, opinions of others, and so forth across contexts. Thus we may know our own and other's personal constructions of issues.

Concept of justification   Beliefs are justified by comparing evidence and opinion on different sides of an issue or across contexts and by constructing solutions that are evaluated by personal criteria, such as one's personal values or the pragmatic need for action.

Stage 7

View of knowledge   Knowledge is constructed via the process of reasonable inquiry into generalizable conjectures about the material world or solutions for the problem at hand, such as what is most probable based on the current evidence or how far it is along the continuum of how things seem to be.

Concept of justification   Beliefs are justified probabilistically via evidence and argument or as the most complete or compelling understanding of an issue.

Source: Adapted from King P. M., & Kitchener, K. S. (1994). *Developing reflective judgment: Understanding and promoting intellectual growth and critical thinking in adolescents and adults.* Copyright © 1994. Reprinted by permission of Jossey-Bass, Inc., a subsidiary of John Wiley & Sons, Inc.

period of stability reflects the time needed to become proficient at using the newly acquired skills. **Skill acquisition** *is the gradual, somewhat haphazard process by which people learn new abilities.* People progress through many small steps in acquiring skills before they are ready for the next growth spurt.

One's optimal level indicates the highest stage a person has achieved in cognitive development but probably does not indicate the level he or she will use most of the time (King & Kitchener, 1994). Why is this the case? Mostly it is because the environment does not provide the supports necessary for high-level performance, especially for issues concerning knowledge. Consequently, if pushed and if given the necessary supports, people demonstrate a level of thinking and performance far higher than they typically show on a daily basis. This discrepancy may explain why fewer people are found at each more complex level of thinking who consistently use it.

ABSOLUTIST, RELATIVISTIC, AND DIALECTICAL THINKING. A growth in reflective judgment is not the only aspect of postformal thought that researchers have examined. For example, Kramer and colleagues (1992) identified three distinct styles of thinking: absolutist, relativistic, and dialectical. Absolutist thinking involves firmly believing that there is only one correct solution to problems and that personal experience provides truth. Adolescents and young adults typically think this way. Relativistic thinking involves realizing that there are many sides to any issue and that the right answer depends on the circumstances. Young and early middle-aged adults often think relativistically. One potential danger here is that relativistic thinking can lead to cynicism or an "I'll do my thing and you do yours" approach to life. Because relativistic thinkers reason things out on a case-by-case basis based on the situation, they are not likely to be strongly committed to any one position. The final step, dialectical thinking, clears up this problem. Dialectical thinkers see the merits in the different viewpoints but are able to synthesize them into a workable solution. This synthesis often produces strong commitment and a definite plan of action.

Notice that there is much agreement between the first two styles in Kramer's model and the progression described in the reflective judgment model. Both talk about moving from an "I'm right because I've experienced it" position to an "I'm not so sure because your experience is different from mine" position. Both also provide insight into how young adults are likely to approach life problems. For example, Kramer (1989) shows how different thinking styles have major implications on how couples resolve conflict. She demonstrates that only couples who think dialectically truly resolve conflict; other thinking styles tend to result in resentment, drifting apart, or even breaking up.

The absolutist, relativistic, and dialectical framework has been adopted widely in the study of postformal thought. For example, Kramer and Kahlbaugh (1994) show that what people remember from prose passages differs as a function of the kind of thinking people use. Sinnott (1994a, 1994b) applied this framework to understanding how adults learn and how they should be taught. In this regard, teachers need to recognize that relativistic thought marks the point at which learning processes become inherently social.

INTEGRATING EMOTION AND LOGIC. A theme in descriptions of the first set of qualitative changes in postformal thinking is a movement from "I'm right because I've experienced it" to an "I'm not so sure who's right because your experience is different from mine" position discussed previously (Kramer, 1989). How can people avoid conflicts and deal with life problems more effectively?

Labouvie-Vief proposes that the answer lies in adults' gaining the ability to integrate emotion with logic in their thinking (Labouvie-Vief, 1992, 1997). She sees the main goal of adult thought as effectiveness in handling everyday life rather than as the generation of all possible solutions. To her, adults make choices not so much on logical grounds but on pragmatic, emotional, and social grounds. Mature thinkers realize that thinking is a social phenomenon that demands making compromises and tolerating ambiguity and contradiction.

Consider the evidence that despite the possibility of pregnancy and sexually transmitted diseases, adolescents still tend not to use contraceptives or safer-sex practices when they have sexual relations. Why?

Labouvie-Vief would argue that sexuality is too emotionally charged for adolescents to deal with intellectually. But is this a reasonable interpretation?

It may be. In a very provocative study, Blanchard-Fields (1986) asked high school students, college students, and middle-aged adults to resolve three dilemmas. One dilemma had low emotional involvement: conflicting accounts of a war between two fictitious countries, North and South Livia, each written by a supporter of one country. The other two dilemmas had high emotional involvement: a visit to the grandparents in which the parents and their adolescent son disagreed about going (the son did not want to go) and a pregnancy dilemma in which a man and a woman had to resolve an unintentional pregnancy (the man was antiabortion, the woman was prochoice).

Results are shown in Figure 8.6. Two important findings emerged. First, there were clear developmental trends in reasoning level, with the middle-aged adults scoring highest. Second, the high school and college students were equivalent on the fictitious war dilemma, but the high school students scored significantly lower on the grandparents and the pregnancy dilemmas. These findings suggest that high school students tend to think at a lower developmental level when confronted with problems that are especially emotionally salient to them. Although more evidence certainly is needed, Blanchard-Fields's findings support the idea that emotion and logic are brought together in adulthood.

Whether the findings from research examining relativistic or other forms of postformal thought document qualitative cognitive growth has been a topic of debate. Overall, Cavanaugh and Stafford (1989) point out that because the roles of experience and education are not understood and because the measures of postformal thought vary widely from study to study, firm conclusions on the nature of adult cognitive development may be premature.

GENDER ISSUES AND POSTFORMAL THOUGHT. The evidence of differences between adolescents' and adults' thinking is substantial. However, the research that produced this evidence typically is grounded in the as-

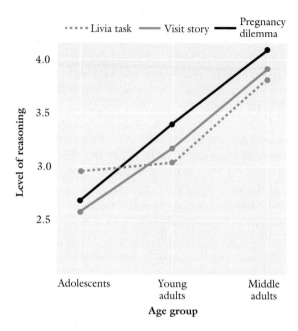

FIGURE 8.6 Level of reasoning as a function of age group and socioemotional task.

Source: Blanchard-Fields, F. (1986). Reasoning on social dilemmas varying in emotional saliency: An adult developmental study. *Psychology and Aging, 1,* 325–333. Copyright © 1986 by the American Psychological Association. Reprinted with permission.

sumption that men and women think in essentially similar ways. Is this a reasonable assumption?

Some researchers do not think so; they argue that men and women use different thinking styles. Within this critique, researchers argue that the styles of thinking we have discussed so far reflect a male bias and do not describe how women know the world. The most prominent of these critiques is Belenky and colleagues' (1986) identification of five ways of knowing in women: silent, received, subjective, procedural, and constructed. Silent knowing reflects the passive acceptance of others' knowledge and one's own incompetence. Received knowing involves accepting from authorities ideas that are concrete, absolute, and dualistic (i.e., representing dichotomies such as good versus bad, with no gray areas). Subjective knowing involves using personal and private intuitions as the major source of understanding and authority. Procedural knowing involves adopting the dominant viewpoint and using a systematic and deliberate process of analysis in two ways. One way of accomplishing procedural knowing is using impersonal strategies based on the criteria of justice and fairness to establish what is "right." The second way is using interdependence and caring as the basis for establishing truth. Finally, constructed knowing includes being articulate about the self, reflecting one's own point of view, while tolerating contradiction and ambiguity.

These descriptions certainly are reminiscent of the styles of thinking considered earlier. For example, relativistic thinking has much in common with constructed knowing. Moreover, Belenky and colleagues' description has an implicit developmental progression in that each way of knowing appears to reflect a higher level of complexity. Thus, important questions are whether the proposed women's ways of knowing reflect a developmental progression, are more typical of women, and are related to other descriptions of postformal thinking.

Orr and Luszcz (1994) decided to address these issues by assessing the ways of knowing and relativistic thinking in a sample of male and female undergraduate and graduate students. They found that education, but not age, predicted relativistic thinking but not constructed knowing. Women used subjective knowing more than men, but men used procedural knowing more than women. No gender differences were observed for constructed knowing or relativistic thinking, but the degree to which traditional notions of femininity were endorsed was positively related to both. Finally, procedural knowing decreased, whereas constructed knowing increased, with increasing evidence of relativistic thinking. Overall, these results point to minimal differences between men's and women's thinking; Belenky and colleagues' (1986) ways of knowing do not appear to be unique to women. However, the ways of knowing do appear to reflect a developmental progression of increasingly complex thought. Still, differences exist between constructed knowing and relativistic thinking that must be pursued in additional studies.

The possibility of stages of cognitive development beyond formal operations is intriguing and has focused our attention on the existence of different styles of thinking across adulthood. It has certainly presented an alternative to the stereotype of inevitable decline. The evidence supporting a separate stage of cognitive development beyond formal operations is growing, and its applicability has extended to solving practical problems, which we explore a little later in this chapter. At this point, the existence of different styles of thinking in adulthood may help us understand why people sometimes have difficulty understanding each other.

CONCEPT CHECKS

1. What are the four stages of cognitive development and their respective characteristics in Piaget's theory?
2. What major styles of thinking have been identified beyond formal operations?
3. What role does emotion play in postformal thinking?

EVERYDAY REASONING AND PROBLEM SOLVING

LEARNING OBJECTIVES

- What are the characteristics of older adults' decision making?
- What are optimally exercised abilities and unexercised abilities?
- What age differences have been found in practical problem solving?
- What is encapsulation, and how does it relate to expertise? What is the role of experience in expertise?
- What is wisdom, and how does it relate to age and life experience?

Lillie is a 75-year-old grandmother visiting her 14-year-old grandson. When he asks her to help with his algebra homework she declines, stating that she did not have enough schooling to understand it. However, when he had trouble communicating with his parents, Lillie was able to give him excellent advice on how to understand things from their perspective. He ended up getting what he wanted and was delighted to know that he could always go to his grandma for advice.

So far, our consideration of intellectual abilities has included examinations of how people's performance on standardized tests and their modes of thinking differ with age. But what we have not considered in detail yet is how people use their intellectual abilities and demonstrate characteristics we associate with intelligent people: solving problems, making decisions, gaining expertise, and becoming wise. This contrast in intellectual abilities is illustrated in Lillie's lack of algebraic skills and her wisdom in interpersonal skills and the conduct of life. What we have discovered in this chapter to this point is that people's crystallized intelligence, reflecting life experience, continues to grow (or at least not decline) until later in life and that one hallmark of adults' thinking is the integration of emotion and logic. One might expect, then, that the ability to make decisions and solve real-life problems would not decline until late adulthood, that expertise would increase, and that wisdom would be related to age. Are these expectations correct? Let's find out.

As we have discussed in Chapters 6 and 7 and earlier in this chapter, there are many declines in basic cognitive and sensory mechanisms. We have also learned that there are age-related increases in experience and the pragmatics of knowledge (illustrated by wisdom and expertise, discussed later). Given these two perspectives on aging, an important distinction must be made. Although there are distinct age-related declines in the structure and processes of cognitive functioning, it is also important to consider the functional architecture of everyday behavior that is cognitively demanding. Although older adults may experience decline in memory, for example, they may have appropriate skills and knowledge adequate for tasks in their daily lives. In other words, we cannot necessarily take information we learn in laboratory experiments on cognitive and intellectual aging and easily apply it to everyday life. Let's explore this distinction first in the area of everyday decision making.

Decision Making

Older adults demonstrate less effective decision making when the decision-making situation is novel and unfamiliar to them (Chasseigne et al., 1997; Mutter & Pliske, 1994; Hastie, 1999). For example, older adults have difficulty in determining how water temperature corresponds to different settings (Chasseigne et al., 1997). Older adults also have difficulty making decisions under time pressure (Johnson, 1990). When decision making involves a high degree of working memory capacity (e.g., a lot of information must be held in memory simultaneously to make quick decisions), older adults do not perform as well (Hastie, 1999). However, everyday decision making is not necessarily characterized by firm time constraints. Let's examine these types of situations.

Many different types of everyday decision-making situations have been examined across the adult life span. These include assessing automobiles for future purchase (Johnson, 1990), making treatment decisions for breast cancer (Meyer et al., 1994), to planning for retirement (Walsh & Hershey, 1993). Findings are quite comparable. Younger adults are much quicker at coming to a decision. Older adults search for less information to arrive at a decision, need less information to arrive at a decision, and rely on easily accessible information. However, the important point here is that despite these age-related characteristics, the literature suggests no age differences in the quality of the decision made in such everyday contexts.

These findings suggest some interesting directions for future research. Do older adults try to conserve diminishing resources when making decisions and thus search for less information? Are there cohort differences in the belief in powerful others or in trust of authority (and therefore less need for deliberation)? For example, older cohorts are socialized to believe in the ultimate word of the physician and not question his or her opinion. Or do older adults draw on a rich and elaborate knowledge system that makes them experts in particular areas of decision making? In this case, experts do not exhaustively search for information given their sophisticated knowledge base. All these possible explanations must be explored to yield a better understanding of everyday decision making in older adults.

The quality of older adults' decisions in making major purchases does not appear to differ significantly from those of younger adults.

Problem Solving

One of the most important ways in which people use their intellectual abilities is to solve problems. Think for a minute about everyday life and the number of problem-solving situations one encounters in school, on the job, in relationships, driving a car, and so forth. In each of these settings one must analyze complex situations quickly, apply knowledge, and create solutions, sometimes in a matter of seconds.

Some people tend to be better at dealing with certain problems than with others. Why is that? One possible explanation has to do with the kinds of abilities we use regularly versus the abilities we use only occasionally. Denney proposes a more formal version of this explanation, which we consider next.

DENNEY'S MODEL OF UNEXERCISED AND OPTIMALLY EXERCISED ABILITIES. Denney developed a model of problem solving that is based on using intellectual abilities in everyday life. Denney (1984) postulates that intellectual abilities related to problem solving follow two types of developmental functions. One of these functions represents unexercised, or unpracticed, ability, and the other represents optimally trained, or optimally exercised, ability. **Unexercised ability** *is the ability a normal, healthy adult would exhibit without practice or training.* Fluid intelligence is thought to be an example of untrained ability, because, by definition, it does not depend on experience and is unlikely to be formally trained (Horn & Hofer, 1992). **Optimally exercised ability** *is the ability a normal, healthy adult would demonstrate under the best conditions of training or practice.* Crystallized intelligence is an example of optimally exercised ability because the component skills (such as vocabulary ability) are used daily.

Denney argues that the overall developmental course of both abilities is the same: They tend to increase until late adolescence or early adulthood and slowly decline thereafter. At all age levels there is a difference in favor of optimally exercised ability, although this difference is less in early childhood and old age. As the developmental trends move away from the hypothetical ideal, Denney argues, the gains seen in training programs increase. As we noted earlier in our discussion of attempts to train fluid intelligence, it appears that this increase occurs.

PRACTICAL PROBLEM SOLVING. Denney's model spurred interest in how people solve practical problems. Based on the model, adults should perform better on practical problems than on abstract ones such as those typically used on standardized intelligence tests. Tests of practical problem solving would use situations such as the following:

> Let's say that a middle-aged woman is frying chicken in her home when, all of a sudden, a grease fire breaks out on top of the stove. Flames begin to shoot up. What should she do? (Denney, Pearce, & Palmer, 1982, p. 116)

Findings from studies examining how well adults solve problems like this are mixed (Cornelius, 1990; Denney, 1990). Although most researchers find better performance on practical problems, how this performance differs with age is unclear. Some investigators (such as Denney & Pearce, 1989) find that performance peaks during midlife and decreases after that, as predicted by Denney's model. Other researchers (such as Cornelius & Caspi, 1987) find continued improvement at least until around age 70.

What is clear is that performance on practical problems increases from early adulthood to middle age. Differences between studies occur in the age at which maximal performance is attained and in the direction and degree of change beyond midlife. However, some important differences between these studies could explain the differences in findings. One key difference is that several different measures are used in assessing practical problem-solving ability. Marsiske and Willis (1995) addressed this issue by using three separate measures of practical problem solving and seeing whether they converged on a single set of abilities. Their results were enlightening. Each measure proved to be reliable and apparently valid, but they were not strongly interrelated, and their relation to age varied. Thus, competence in solving practical problems is a multidimensional construct, much like intelligence itself, calling into question whether a global construct of practical problem solving exists.

One way to assess practical problem solving in more focused terms is to create measures with clearly identifiable dimensions that relate to specific types of problems. This is what Diehl and colleagues (1995) did by creating the Observed Tasks of Daily Living (OTDL) measure. The OTDL consists of three dimensions, which reflect three specific problems in everyday life: food preparation, medication intake, and telephone use. Each of these dimensions also reflects important aspects of assessing whether people can live independently, a topic we explored in Chapter 5. Diehl and colleagues showed that performance on the OTDL is directly influenced by age, fluid intelligence, and crystallized intelligence and indirectly by perceptual speed, memory, and several aspects of health. These results provide important links between practical problem solving and basic elements of psychometric intelligence and information processing. However, more recent study findings indicate that basic measures of inductive reasoning, domain-specific knowledge, memory, and working memory were related to everyday assessments of each of these abilities (Allaire & Marsiske, 1999). Allaire and Marsiske (1999) conclude that everyday problems reflecting well-structured challenges from activities of daily living show a strong relation to traditional psychometric abilities.

Other research into the relation between practical problem solving and intellectual abilities provides more insight. Heidrich and Denney (1994) showed that different measures of problem solving relate differently to traditional measures of intelligence. Specifically, the ability to solve social problems (such as how an arguing couple might reconcile) and practical problems were related to each other and to measures of crystallized intelligence (vocabulary ability), whereas traditional problem-solving ability (scores on a Twenty Questions test) were related to measures of fluid intelligence (solving mazes). Thus, practical problem solving is a multidimensional construct, and which psychometric intellectual abilities are most influential depends on the type of problems to be solved.

The search for relations between psychometric intelligence and practical problem-solving abilities is only one way to examine the broader linkages with intellectual functioning. Recall that postformal thinking is grounded in the ways in which people conceptualize situations. Indeed, much of the research that led to the discovery of postformal thought involved presenting adults with lifelike problems; Blanchard-Fields's (1986) study, which we considered earlier, is an excellent example.

This close linkage between postformal thinking and practical problem solving also involves the role of emotionality. Remember that one of the key aspects of postformal thinking is the integration of emotion and logic. Blanchard-Fields and colleagues (1995) took this as a starting point and carefully manipulated the emotionality of problems. As described in more detail in the How Do We Know? feature, they found important age differences in problem-solving styles that were highly dependent on whether the problem situation was emotionally salient.

Another important factor that influences the way we solve everyday problems is the context in which the problem occurs. Do we use the same strategies when solving a conflict between two siblings as we do when solving a conflict over the leading role in a project at work? No. Interestingly, however, young adults are more likely to use a similar strategy across

Who were the investigators, and what was the aim of the study? Fredda Blanchard-Fields, Heather Jahnke, and Cameron Camp (1995) were interested in the link between practical problem solving and postformal thinking. This relationship becomes particularly important when problems that have an emotional aspect are examined. As the investigators point out, most research on practical problem solving uses problems that have little emotional content in them. This may stack the deck against older adults because of the connection between higher emotional intensity and dialectical thinking (Kramer, 1990) and because they make more relativistic causal attributions in problem situations that are high in emotional salience (Blanchard-Fields & Norris, 1994). Age differences in problem-solving styles tend to be absent on problems low in emotional salience; however, on problems high in emotional salience, older adults show more awareness of when to avoid or passively accept a situation within interpersonal, emotional domains, whereas younger adults tend to use a cognitive analytic approach to all problems (Blanchard-Fields & Camp, 1990). What would happen if the emotional salience of problems were carefully manipulated? Would it influence people's preferred mode of problem solving?

How did the investigators measure the topic of interest? Participants were given 15 problem situations, with 5 rated in each of three categories as high (such as caring for an ill or aging parent), medium (such as moving to a new town), or low (such as returning defective merchandise) in emotional salience. Each solution was rated as reflecting one of four problem-solving styles: problem-focused action, involving overt behaviors that deal directly with the problem; cognitive problem analysis, involving cognitive efforts to solve the problem by thinking it through; passive–dependent behavior, involving attempts to withdraw from the situation in some way; and avoidant thinking and denial, involving attempts to manage the meaning of the problem.

Who were the participants in this study? Blanchard-Fields and colleagues studied 70 adolescents (aged 14 to 17), 69 young adults (aged 25 to 35), 74 middle-aged adults (aged 45 to 55), and 74 older adults (aged 65 to 75).

What was the design of the study? The study was a cross-sectional examination of age differences in adults' problem-solving strategies.

Were there ethical concerns with the study? Because the study used volunteers and received parental permission for adolescents and the tasks contained no questions about sensitive topics, there were no ethical concerns.

What were the results? Results showed that emotional salience has a clear effect on the problem-solving approaches people of different ages adopt. No age differences were found in relation to problem-focused strategies; they were found in all age groups with all types of problems. However, these strategies decrease as the emotional salience of the problem increases. In fact, passive–dependent and cognitive analysis strategies increase with greater emotional salience of the problems. Young adults preferred cognitive analysis strategies more than any other age group, which fits with their tendency to adopt formal operational or absolutist thinking. Although all age groups adopted avoidant denial strategies as their second most preferred choice, older adults were especially likely to adopt this approach. Similarly, older adults used passive–dependent strategies more than younger adults in situations with high emotional saliency.

The tendencies of younger adults to use cognitive analysis strategies and for older adults to use more avoidant denial and passive–dependent strategies may reflect a combination of cognitive level and life experience.

In sum, the degree to which emotionality is part of a problem, in conjunction with life experience and preferred modes of thinking, appears to influence the way one attempts to deal with the problem. One limitation of Blanchard-Fields and colleagues' study was that the problems they used represented hypothetical situations. Future research should examine problems that participants actually face to get a more accurate picture of how people solve emotional problems in everyday life.

problem-solving contexts: self-action to fix the problem. However, older adults are more likely to vary their strategy given the problem-solving context. For example, in interpersonal conflicts (e.g., family conflict) they use more emotion regulation strategies (i.e., managing their emotions), whereas in more instrumental situations (e.g., dealing with defective merchandise) they use self-action strategies (return the product; Blanchard-Fields et al., 1997). Blanchard-Fields et al. (1997) argue that as we grow older and accumulate more everyday experience, we become more sensitive to the problem context and use strategies accordingly.

There are also individual differences in the way the same problem situation is interpreted. In other words, how people represent problems differs and could vary across the life span as developmental life goals change (Berg et al., 1998). Berg and colleagues (Berg et al., 1998; Strough et al., 1996) found age differences in how people define their own everyday problems. Overall, middle-aged older adults defined problems more in terms of interpersonal goals (e.g., getting along with a person or spending more time with an person), whereas adolescents and young adults focused more on competence goals (e.g., lose weight or study for an exam). Furthermore, problem-solving strategies fit the problem definitions. For example, older adults defined problems more in terms of interpersonal concerns and subsequently reported strategies such as regulating others or including others, whereas competency goals resulted in strategies that involved more self-action.

What can we conclude from the research on practical problem solving? First, practical problem-solving abilities are multidimensional and may not even relate strongly with each other. Second, the developmental functions of these abilities are complex and may differ somewhat across abilities. Third, the relations between practical problem-solving abilities and psychometric intelligence are equally complex. Finally, the close connection between solving practical problems and postformal thinking may prove fruitful in furthering our understanding of individual differences in abilities. In short, solving practical problems offers an excellent way to discover how all the topics we have considered in this chapter come together to produce behavior in everyday life.

Expertise

On many basic information-processing tasks, younger adults clearly outperform older adults. Yet many people in their 60s and some in their 70s hold jobs that demand complex decision making, abstract reasoning, and memory of a lot of information. How do they do it?

The most popular answer is that older adults compensate for poorer performance through their expertise. That is, through years of experience and practice, adults build up a wealth of knowledge about alternative ways to solve problems or make decisions that enables them to bypass steps needed by younger adults (Ericsson & Charness, 1994). In a way, this represents "the triumph of knowledge over reasoning" (Bosman & Charness, 1996); experience and age can defeat skill and youth. In research terms, older people sometimes are able to compensate for declines in some basic intellectual abilities (for example, the information-processing skills underlying fluid abilities).

Figuring out exactly what expertise is turns out to be difficult. Charness and Bosman (1990) point out that experts are identified at times because they use novel approaches to solve difficult problems, because they have extensive knowledge about a particular topic, or because they are highly practiced. For example, expert physicians diagnose diseases differently than novice physicians (Patel & Groen, 1986), chess masters quickly evaluate very complex board positions (Charness & Bosman, 1990), and typists look ahead to help avoid mistakes (see Chapter 6).

What research has been conducted on age differences in expertise? Within a specified domain expert performance tends to hold up as we grow older, with only slight declines in older age groups (Charness & Bosman, 1990). The important issue here is whether this increase in expertise makes up for losses in fluid intelligence. The results are encouraging in that acquired knowledge (i.e., expertise) helps the aging adult compensate for losses in other skills such as those strongly related to fluid intelligence (Bosman & Charness, 1996; Dixon & Bäckman, 1995; Morrow et al., 1994). In other words, older adults may be compensating for underlying decline by relying more on their experience.

Notice that the difference in developmental trajectories for expertise and basic information-processing abilities apparently means that the two are not strongly related. How can this be? Rybash and colleagues (1986) propose a process called encapsulation as the answer. **Encapsulation** *is the way in which the processes of thinking (such as attention, memory, and logical reasoning) become connected to the products of thinking (such as knowledge about world history).* This process of encapsulation allows expertise to compensate for decrements in underlying processing ability, perhaps by making thinking in the particular domain more efficient.

Encapsulation reflects the fact that in adulthood knowledge becomes more and more specialized based on experience, which in turn reflects a lesser role of age-related neurological development and social demands for increased specialization of knowledge and expertise (Hoyer & Rybash, 1994). The emergence of encapsulated knowledge, unique to adulthood, becomes increasingly complex and resistant to change. Because it is experientially based, the development of cognition in adulthood is directed toward mastery and adaptive competency in specific domains, making it very different from cognitive development during childhood, which is more genetically driven and uniform across content domains (Hoyer & Rybash, 1994). Knowledge encapsulation also implies that the notion of a general slowing of processing underlying cognitive changes in later life may be wrong. Research examining processing in different domains indicates that speed of processing differs across knowledge domains (Clancy & Hoyer, 1993). These findings indicate that the efficiency of the underlying mechanics (e.g., neural pathways), procedures, or computations needed to carry out cognitive tasks depends on the amount of experientially acquired knowledge a person has in that domain.

Knowledge encapsulation has important implications for studying intellectual development in adulthood. Encapsulated knowledge cannot be decomposed to study its constituent parts, meaning that mechanistic approaches (such as the one used in the psychometric research we examined earlier in this chapter) or ones predicating across-the-board declines are inappropriate. Rather, approaches that take a more holistic view and stress developing formal models of computational processes with a specific domain in particular contexts are more appropriate (Hoyer & Rybash, 1994).

In the next section, we will see how the role of experience in cognitive development is changing the way we conceptualize wisdom. Wisdom is more closely associated with having certain types of experiences than it is with age per se.

Wisdom

We began this chapter with a description of the wisdom of the Dalai Lama. Similarly, many folktales recount the wisdom of older characters. For example, caught in a no-win situation with his son-in-law, an old alchemist comes up with an insightful and clever solution on how to turn base elements (dirt) into gold. Chinen (1989) points out that folktales highlight several aspects of wisdom: It involves practical knowledge, it is given altruistically, it involves psychological insights, and it is based on life experience.

A growing body of research has been examining these aspects of wisdom. Baltes and Staudinger (2000) conclude that implicit conceptions of wisdom are widely shared within a culture and include exceptional levels of functioning, a dynamic balance between intellect, emotion, and motivation, a high degree of personal and interpersonal competence, and good intentions. Drawing from this cultural, historical, and philosophical analysis of wisdom, psychologists have attempted to operationalize wisdom to study it scientifically. One attempt to operationalize wisdom can be seen in the postformal literature we reviewed earlier. In this case wisdom-related behavior is characterized by dialectical and relativistic thinking (Labouvie-Vief, 1990).

One of the best-known programs of research on wisdom and aging is the Berlin wisdom paradigm (Baltes & Staudinger, 2000; Staudinger & Baltes, 1994). In this line of research, wisdom is conceptualized as an expert system dealing with the meaning and conduct of life (Baltes & Smith, 1990; Staudinger & Baltes, 1994). Similarly, Sternberg (1998) studies wisdom as the application of tacit knowledge toward the achievement of the common good.

To define wisdom as expertise, Baltes and colleagues specified the content of wisdom in terms of the fundamental pragmatics of life. This includes knowledge and judgment about the human condition and ways to plan, manage, and understand a good life. Based on years of research using in-depth think-aloud interviews with young, middle-aged, and older adults about normal and unusual problems people face, Baltes and Staudinger (2000) studied the nature of wisdom and how it relates to age and other psychosocial factors. To study wisdom scientifically, Baltes and Staudinger used their general framework to develop five specific criteria for determining whether a person demonstrates wisdom. These are described in Table 8.3.

One important issue with Baltes and Staudinger's approach to wisdom is whether it has a psychological bias. That is, the framework and criteria may not capture the true essence of wisdom if one were to examine the characteristics of what people in everyday life define as wise behavior. To examine this possibility, Baltes and colleagues (1995) compared people who were nominated as wise with groups of clinical psychologists and highly educated older and younger groups. Their results indicated that the wise nominees performed as well on the five criteria of wisdom as did the clinical psychologists, who in other studies had outperformed other groups. The wisdom nominees also scored extremely well in tasks involving life management and on the criterion

of recognizing that the "right thing to do" varies across people. Based on these findings, Baltes and colleagues concluded that their framework and criteria are not biased in such a way as to differentially favor psychologists.

Two important aspects of wisdom have been demonstrated fairly clearly. First, wisdom is not the same thing as creativity; wisdom is the growth of expertise and insight, whereas creativity is the generation of a new solution to a problem (Simonton, 1990).

Second, the relation between age and wisdom is complex. Certainly, wisdom has long been characterized as the province of older adults. For example, studies of people's implicit theories of wisdom, in which people are asked to nominate the wisest person they know, indicate that people of all ages tend to nominate someone who is older than they are (Denney et al., 1995). However, when the criteria for wisdom discussed earlier are applied to people's knowledge and actions, a different picture emerges. The typical way in which wisdom is assessed is to have adults respond to hypothetical life-planning problems, such as whether to accept a promotion or whether to retire (Staudinger & Baltes, 1996). The problems were presented as dilemmas facing fictitious people, and participants had to reason out a solution. For example, one study had people respond to life-planning problems such as this: A 15-year-old girl wants to get married right away. What should she consider and do? Answers were then analyzed in terms of the degree to which they reflect the five wisdom-related criteria listed earlier. High and low wisdom-related responses are shown in Table 8.4.

Contrary to our stereotypes about wisdom and aging, in a number of studies using this method, Baltes and colleagues (Baltes & Staudinger, 2000; Smith & Baltes, 1990; Staudinger, 1999) found no association between age and wise answers. Instead, they found evidence of wisdom in adults of all ages. The key variable appears to be having extensive life experience with the type of problem given, not just life experience in general. Thus, given the right circumstances, a 35-year-old and a

TABLE 8.3 Five Criteria for Wisdom-Related Performance

Basic criteria

Factual knowledge	To what extent does this performance show general (*conditio humana*) and specific (e.g., life events, variations, institutions) knowledge about life matters and demonstrate scope and depth in the coverage of issues?
Procedural knowledge	To what extent does this performance consider strategies of decision making (e.g., cost–benefit analysis), self-regulation, life interpretation, life planning (e.g., means–ends analysis), and advice giving (e.g., timing, withholding)?

Metalevel criteria

Life-span contextualism	To what extent does this performance consider the past, current, and possible future contexts of life and the many circumstances (e.g., culturally graded, age-graded, idiosyncratic) in which a life is embedded and how they relate to each other?
Value relativism	To what extent does this performance consider variations in values and life priorities and the importance of viewing each person within his or her own framework of values and life goals, despite a small set of universal values such as the orientation toward the well-being of oneself and others?
Awareness and management of uncertainty	To what extent does this performance consider the inherent uncertainty of life (in terms of interpreting the past, predicting the future, managing the present) and effective strategies for dealing with uncertainty (e.g., backup solutions, optimizing gain–loss ratio)?

Copyright 1999 from "Older and wiser? Integrating results on the relationship between age and wisdom-related performance" by U. M. Staudinger, *International Journal of Behavioral Development*, 23. Reproduced by permission of Taylor & Francis, Inc., http://www.routledge-ny.com.

TABLE 8.4 Illustration of a Wisdom-Related Task with Examples of Extreme Responses

A 15-year-old girl wants to get married right away.
What should she consider and do?

Low wisdom-related score:
"A 15-year-old girl wants to get married? No, no way, marrying at age 15 would be utterly wrong. One has to tell the girl that marriage is not possible." (After further probing) "It would be irresponsible to support such an idea. No, this is just a crazy idea."

High wisdom-related score:
"Well, on the surface, this seems like an easy problem. On average, marriage for 15-year-old girls is not a good thing. But there are situations where the average case does not fit. Perhaps in this instance, special life circumstances are involved, such that the girl has a terminal illness. Or the girl has just lost her parents. And also, this girl may live in another culture or historical period. Perhaps she was raised with a value system different from ours. In addition, one has to think about adequate ways of talking with the girl and to consider her emotional state."

Source: Baltes, P. B., & Staudinger, U. M. (2000). Wisdom: A metaheuristic (pragmatic) to orchestrate mind and virtue toward excellence. *American Psychologist, 55,* 136.

75-year-old could give equally wise solutions to a life problem.

Research based on cognitive developmental changes in adulthood such as those discussed earlier in the context of postformal thinking has uncovered other aspects in the growth of wisdom. Several investigators point out that a wise person is one who is able to integrate thinking, feeling, and acting into a coherent approach to a problem (Labouvie-Vief, 1990; Orwoll & Perlmutter, 1990). This research implies that empathy or compassion is an important characteristic of wise people, enabling them to overcome automatic responses to show concern for core human experiences and values (Pascual-Leone, 1990). Thus, wise people are able to see through situations and get to the heart of the matter rather than be caught in the superficial aspects of the situation.

So what specific factors help one become wise? Baltes and Staudinger (2000) identified three factors: general personal characteristics, such as mental ability; specific expertise conditions, such as mentoring or practice; and facilitative life contexts, such as education or leadership experience. First, the most important personal characteristics related to wisdom are cognitive style (evaluation of issues, moving beyond existing rules, and tolerance for ambiguity) and creativity (Staudinger et al., 1997). Second, people with expertise in the form of professional clinical psychology show higher levels of wisdom-related performance than other groups (Smith et al., 1994; Staudinger et al., 1992). Finally, social collaboration facilitates wisdom-related performance, and older adults profit more from this collaboration than young ones (Staudinger & Baltes, 1996).

Other researchers point to additional criteria. For example, Labouvie-Vief (1990) argues that the integration of affect and cognition that occurs during adulthood results in the ability to act wisely. Personal growth across adulthood, reflecting Erikson's concepts of generativity and integrity (see Chapter 10), helps foster the process as well. All of these factors

take time. Thus, although growing old is no guarantee that wisdom will develop, it provides one with the time that, if used well, will provide a supportive context for it.

The picture of wisdom that is emerging appears to support the tale that opened this section. Just as the old alchemist's response was based on his own specific experience with trying to make gold, our own wisdom comes from becoming experts at dealing with particular kinds of problems.

CONCEPT CHECKS

1. What differentiates an older decision maker from a younger one?

2. What are optimally exercised abilities and unexercised abilities?

3. How does encapsulation occur?

4. What five criteria determine whether someone is wise according to Baltes and colleagues?

PUTTING IT ALL TOGETHER

Intellectual change as we grow older is complex. There are multiple dimensions of intellectual functioning, as we observed in the career trajectories of Beverly and Helene. Both women were successful and exhibited different forms of intelligence integral to their success. At retirement, Linda and Jerry were concerned about their performance when they returned to college to study literature. It is in this area of intellectual functioning that older adults experience declines in basic mental abilities. However, change in academic abilities does not reflect change in qualitatively different forms of intelligence. John's concern about his test performance and his underlying reasoning illustrate these different forms. As we grow older, the qualitative nature of our thinking changes and matures. For example, although Lillie did not have the skills to solve algebra problems, she did have the wisdom to give advice to solve interpersonal conflicts. Overall, there are different trajectories of intellectual change for different types of abilities. The key is not to underestimate the functioning of an older adult by observing change on only one dimension, such as fluid intelligence. To gain a more complete picture of intellectual functioning, we need to place it in the context of everyday living.

Summary

DEFINING INTELLIGENCE

Intelligence in Everyday Life

Experts and laypeople agree that intelligence consists of problem-solving ability, verbal ability, and social competence. Motivation, exertion of effort, and reading are important behaviors for people of all ages; however, some age-related behaviors also are apparent.

The Big Picture: A Life-Span View

The life-span view emphasizes that there is some intellectual decline with age, primarily in the mechanics, but there is also stability and growth, primarily in the pragmatics.

Four points are central. Plasticity is the range within which one's abilities are modifiable. *Multidimensionality* refers to the many abilities that underlie intelligence. *Multidirectionality* refers to the many possible ways people may develop. Interindividual variability is the degree to which people differ from each other.

Research Approaches to Intelligence

Three main approaches are used to study intelligence. The psychometric approach focuses on performance on standardized tests. The cognitive structural approach emphasizes the quality and style of thought. The information-processing approach emphasis basic cognitive mechanisms.

DEVELOPMENTAL TRENDS IN PSYCHOMETRIC INTELLIGENCE

Measuring Intelligence

Primary abilities comprise the several independent abilities that form factors on standardized intelligence tests. Five have been studied most: number, word fluency, verbal meaning, inductive reasoning, and spatial orientation.

Age-Related Changes in Primary Mental Abilities

Primary mental abilities show normative declines with age that may affect performance in everyday life after around age 60, although declines tend to be small until the mid-70s. However, within-individual differences show that very few people decline equally in all areas.

Secondary Mental Abilities

Fluid intelligence is the innate abilities that make people flexible and adaptive thinkers and that underlie the acquisition of knowledge and experience. Fluid intelligence normally declines with age.

Crystallized intelligence is knowledge acquired through life experience and education. Crystallized intelligence does not normally decline with age until very late life. As age increases, individual differences remain stable with fluid intelligence but increase with crystallized intelligence.

Moderators of Intellectual Change

Age-related declines in fluid abilities have been shown to be moderated by cohort, education, social variables, personality, health, lifestyle, and task familiarity. Cohort effects and familiarity have been studied most. Cohort differences are complex and depend on the specific ability. Age differences in performance on familiar tasks are similar to those on standardized tests. Although taking both into account reduces age differences, it does not eliminate them.

Modifying Primary Abilities

Several studies show that fluid intelligence abilities improve after direct training and after anxiety reduction. Improvements in performance match or exceed levels of decline. Training effects appear to last for several years regardless of the nature of the training, but generalization of training to new tasks is rare.

QUALITATIVE DIFFERENCES IN ADULTS' THINKING

Piaget's Theory

Key concepts in Piaget's theory include adaptation to the environment, organization of thought, and the structure of thought. The processes of thought are assimilation (using previously learned knowledge to make sense of incoming information) and accommodation (making the knowledge base conform to the environment).

According to Piaget, thought develops through four stages: sensorimotor, preoperations, concrete operations, and formal operations. Older adults do not perform as well on tests of formal operations as younger adults, but results on tests of concrete operations are mixed.

Going Beyond Piaget: Postformal Thought

Evidence shows that the style of thinking changes across adulthood. The development of reflective judgment in young adulthood occurs as a result of seven stages. Other research has identified a progression from absolutist thinking to relativistic thinking to dialectical thinking.

A key characteristic of postformal thought is the integration of emotion and logic. Much of this research is based on people's solutions to real-world problems. Although there have been suggestions that women's ways of knowing differ from men's, research evidence does not provide strong support for this view.

EVERYDAY REASONING AND PROBLEM SOLVING

Decision Making

Older adults make decisions differently than younger adults. They tend to search for less information, need less information, and rely on preexisting knowledge structures in making everyday decisions.

Older adults perform more poorly when asked to create or invent new decision rules, when they are in unfamiliar situations, and when the decision task entails high cognitive load.

Problem Solving

In Denney's model, both unexercised and optimally exercised abilities increase through early adulthood and slowly decline thereafter. Performance on practical problem solving increases through middle age.

Research indicates that sound measures of practical problem solving can be constructed, but these measures do not tend to relate to each other, indicating that problem solving is multidimensional. The emotional salience of problems is an important feature that influences problem-solving style.

Expertise

Older adults often compensate for declines in some abilities by becoming experts, which allows them to anticipate what a task will entail.

Knowledge encapsulation occurs with age, in which the processes of thinking become connected with the products of thinking. Encapsulated knowledge cannot be decomposed and studied in a componential fashion.

Wisdom

Wisdom has four general characteristics: It deals with important matters of life; it consists of superior knowledge, judgment, and advice; it is knowledge of exceptional depth; and it is well intentioned.

Five specific behavioral criteria are used to judge wisdom: expertise, broad abilities, understanding how life problems change, fitting the response with the problem, and realizing that life problems often are ambiguous. Wisdom also entails integrating thought and emotion to show empathy or compassion. Wisdom may be more strongly related to experience than to age.

Review Questions

DEFINING INTELLIGENCE

• How do laypeople and researchers define intelligence?

• What are the two main ways in which intelligence has been studied? Define each.

DEVELOPMENTAL TRENDS IN PSYCHOMETRIC INTELLIGENCE

• What are primary mental abilities? Which ones have been studied most? How do they change with age?

• Define *fluid* and *crystallized intelligence*. How does each change with age?

• What factors moderate age changes in fluid intelligence? What role does cohort play? What roles do health and lifestyle play?

• What benefits do older people get from intervention programs aimed at improving fluid abilities? What training approaches have been used? How well do trained skills generalize?

• Are there any limitations on the extent to which older adults can improve their cognitive performance?

QUALITATIVE DIFFERENCES IN ADULTS' THINKING

• What are the key concepts in Piaget's theory?

• What stages of cognitive development did Piaget identify? What age differences have been found in them? Do adults use formal operations?

• What is reflective judgment? What are the stages in its development? What are absolutist, relativistic, and dialectical thinking?

• How do emotion and logic become integrated?

• What evidence is there for gender differences in postformal thinking?

EVERYDAY REASONING AND PROBLEM SOLVING

• How do older adults differ from younger adults in everyday decision making?

• What are unexercised and optimally exercised abilities? How do their developmental paths differ from each other?

• What are the developmental trends in solving practical problems? How does emotional salience of problems influence problem-solving style?

• What is an expert? How is expertise related to age?

• What is knowledge encapsulation?

• What criteria are used to define wisdom? How is wisdom related to age?

Integrating Concepts in Development

1. How are the primary and secondary mental abilities related to the aspects of information processing considered in Chapters 6 and 7?

2. What do you think an integrated theory linking postformal thinking, practical problem solving, expertise, and wisdom would look like?

3. What aspects of secondary mental abilities do you think would be most closely linked to expertise? Why?

4. How does effective social cognitive functioning (considered in Chapter 9) relate to wisdom-related behaviors?

Key Terms

accommodation Changing one's thought to make it a better approximation of the world of experience.

assimilation Using currently available knowledge to make sense out of incoming information.

cognitive structural approach An approach to intelligence that emphasizes the ways in which people conceptualize problems and focuses on modes or styles of thinking.

crystallized intelligence Knowledge that is acquired through life experience and education in a particular culture.

encapsulation The idea that the processes of thinking become connected to the products of thinking.

factor The relations between performances on similar tests of psychometric intelligence.

fluid intelligence Abilities that make one a flexible and adaptive thinker, allow one to draw inferences, and allow one to understand the relations between concepts independent of acquired knowledge and experience.

interindividual variability An acknowledgment that adults differ in the direction of their intellectual development.

multidimensional The notion that intelligence consists of many dimensions.

multidirectionality The distinct patterns of change in abilities over the life span, with these patterns being different for different abilities.

optimal level In the reflective judgment framework, the highest level of information-processing capacity that a person is capable of doing.

optimally exercised ability The ability a normal, healthy adult would demonstrate under the best conditions of training or practice.

plasticity The range of functioning within a person and the conditions under which a person's abilities can be modified within a specific age range.

postformal thought Thinking characterized by a recognition that truth varies across situations, that solutions must be realistic to be reasonable, that ambiguity and contradiction are the rule rather than the exception, and that emotion and subjective factors play a role in thinking.

primary mental abilities Independent abilities within psychometric intelligence based on different combinations of standardized intelligence tests.

psychometric approach An approach in which intelligence is defined as performance on standardized tests.

reflective judgment Thinking that involves how people reason through problems involving current affairs, religion, science, and the like.

secondary mental abilities Broad-ranging skills composed of several primary mental abilities.

skill acquisition In the reflective judgment framework, the gradual, somewhat haphazard process by which people learn new abilities.

unexercised ability The ability a normal, healthy adult would exhibit without practice or training.

Resources

Readings

Commons, M. L., Richards, F. A., & Armon, C. (Eds.). (1984). *Beyond formal operations: Late adolescent and adult cognitive development.* New York: Praeger. One of the best collections of research and theory on postformal thinking. Easy to difficult reading.

Commons, M. L., Sinnott, J. D., Richards, F. A., & Armon, C. (Eds.). (1989). *Adult development: Vol. 1. Comparisons and applications of adolescent and adult developmental models.* New York: Praeger. One of the best collections of research and theory on postformal thinking. Easy to difficult reading.

King, P. M., & Kitchener, K. S. (1994). *Developing reflective judgment: Understanding and promoting intellectual growth and critical thinking in adolescents and adults.* San Francisco: Jossey-Bass. The most thorough description of the reflective judgment framework, including excellent discussions on the longitudinal data on which it is based. Easy reading.

Labouvie-Vief, G. (1994). *Psyche and Eros.* Cambridge, England: Cambridge University Press. A thorough examination of the adult developmental pathway to the reintegration of emotion and logic. It draws from multiple areas, including psychological research, mythology, religion, and literature. Moderate reading.

Schaie, K. W. (1996). *Intellectual development in adulthood: The Seattle Longitudinal Study.* New York: Cambridge University Press. The most complete review of the Seattle Longitudinal

Study in a single volume. A must read not only for the information about psychometric intelligence but also for the information on research methods. Moderately difficult reading.

Sinnott, J. D. (Ed.). (1994). *Interdisciplinary handbook of adult lifespan learning.* Westport, CT: Greenwood. An excellent, eclectic collection of chapters on various topics pertaining to intellectual development in adulthood. Easy to moderately difficult reading.

Sternberg, R. J. (Ed.). (1990). *Wisdom: Its nature, origins, and development* (pp. 279–313). Cambridge, England: Cambridge University Press. One of the few collections of articles on wisdom that provides a broad survey of the topic. Moderately difficult reading.

Search Online with

InfoTrac College Edition

For more information on the topics in this chapter, explore InfoTrac College Edition, your online library. Go to http://www.infotrac-college.com/wadsworth and use the passcode that came on the card with your book. Try these search terms: wisdom, fluid intelligence, crystallized intelligence.

SOCIAL COGNITION

© Alex Wong / Newsmakers / Liaison Agency

When a prominent Democrat marries a prominent Republican, as occurred when the top consultants to the competing presidential candidates of 1992 tied the knot, people try to make sense of it. Many thought the marriage of Mary Matalin (Bush's political director) and James Carville (Clinton's campaign strategist) was doomed because they were political opposites. In contrast, the newlyweds saw their passion for politics as a core similarity.

The public speculation about the Matalin–Carville relationship illustrates how people try to make sense of other people's behavior. As we will see, this is the essence of social cognitive functioning. In this chapter we first consider how the social context is involved in our cognitive processes. Next we take a closer look at how our basic cognitive abilities influence our social cognitive processing. We examine how our past experiences influence our social cognitive processing. Finally, we examine four aspects of social cognition: how social beliefs affect how we judge older adults' behavior, how people explain behavior (causal attributions), how much personal control people feel they have, and how cognition is affected when we communicate with others in a social context.

As discussed in the last three chapters, traditional cognitive aging research has focused on the basic architecture of human information processing and how it is tied to physiological decline. In pursuit of this goal, painstaking efforts have been made to try to create tasks and stimuli that are not familiar to the participants in the study and devoid of social implications. Although these traditional approaches to cognition and aging are important to identify basic cognitive processes and how they change over time, they do not address how social knowledge (e.g., beliefs about aging) and social goals (e.g., what is important for one to remember in a given task) affect cognition.

A new wave of social cognition research has raised some important issues for aging research such as how our life experiences and changes in our pragmatic knowledge, social expertise, and values influence how we think. To address these issues, we must consider both the basic cognitive architecture of the aging adult (identified in Chapters 6 and 7) and the functional architecture of everyday cognition in a social context (discussed in Chapter 8). Even if certain basic cognitive mechanisms decline (such as memory recall or speed of processing), older adults may still possess the social knowledge and skills that allow them to function effectively. The basic goal of the social cognitive approach is to understand how people make sense of themselves, others, and events in everyday life (Fiske, 1993).

BASIC COGNITIVE ABILITIES AND SOCIAL COGNITION

LEARNING OBJECTIVES

- To what extent do processing capacity limitations influence social judgments in older adults?
- What is the negativity bias, and how does it influence older adults' thinking?
- Are there age differences in accessibility of social information?
- How does processing context influence social judgments?

*M*aria and Emanuel are taking care of their grandchildren for the weekend. They took them to the zoo for an outing. When they passed the gift shop the children would not stop whining that they wanted a present. This frustrated Maria and Emanuel, and they both tried to explain this distressing behavior. At first, they were worried because it seemed that the behavior of their grandchildren indicated that they were selfish children. But on further reflection, they considered other factors. The children's parents always bought them a gift at the zoo, so they naturally expected it to happen again. They felt better about the situation after considering the parents' role in it and bought the gifts for the children.

In this situation, Maria and Emanuel carefully analyzed the situation by focusing on all factors involved in it. But what would have happened if they did not have the time to think about it and instead had multiple distractions such as dealing with the emotional outbursts of their grandchildren and their own emotional reaction? In this section we consider how cognitive capacity, or having enough time and effort to reflect on a situation, influences the social judgments we make.

A wealth of laboratory studies have examined abstract cognitive skills and how they change as we get older (see Chapters 6 and 7). Like the everyday cognition research discussed in Chapter 8, an important question in social cognition research is the extent to which the findings from the lab translate into understanding behavior in everyday context as people grow older. The social cognitive perspective provides a way to place basic cognitive abilities into the context of social situations.

Processing Capacity

Social cognitive researchers use information-processing models to describe how people make social judgments (Gilbert & Malone, 1995). For example, Gilbert and his colleagues have shown that the ability to make nonbiased social judgments depends on the cognitive demand accompanying those judgments. In other words, all of us make snap judgments, but then we reconsider and evaluate possible extenuating circumstances to revise those initial judgments. This takes processing resources, and if we are busy thinking about something else we might not be able to revise our initial judgment. Because older adults typically display lower levels of cognitive processing resources (see Salthouse, 1996), it is possible that this decline in resource capacity might affect this type of social judgment process.

As we consider in more depth in the section on causal attributions later in this chapter, Blanchard-Fields (1999) found that older adults consistently hold onto their initial judgments or conclusions about why negative events occur more often than do younger adults. They appear not to adjust their initial judgments by considering other factors, as Maria and Emanuel were able to do when they revised their interpretation of their grandchildren's behavior. Remember that older adults typically display lower levels of cognitive processing resources. This point is further illustrated later in this chapter. For now it is important to remember that this effect was demonstrated only when events reflected negative interpersonal content. If processing resource capacity is the major factor explaining social judgment biases, then it should affect all types of situations older people encounter. We examine the implications of this when we consider how social knowledge and motivation affect these types of social judgment bias.

Impression Formation

In an intriguing set of studies, Hess and colleagues (Hess, 1999; Hess & Pullen, 1994) demonstrated how cognitive resources influence social judgments by examining **impression formation,** *or the way people form and revise first impressions.* They examined how people use diagnostic trait information in making initial impressions of a person and how this process varies with age. One group of adults was presented with positive information about a person, such as evidence of honesty. They were then presented with negative information, including incidents of dishonest behavior. Another group of adults was presented the information in reverse: First, they were given a

Older adults tend to hold on to first impressions longer when meeting new persons.

negative portrayal (dishonesty) followed by incidents of positive behavior (e.g., honest behavior).

As you can see in Figure 9.1, Hess and Pullen (1994) found that all study participants modified their impressions. However, for older adults, when new negative information was presented after the initial positive portrayal of the target, they were willing to modify their impression of the target from positive to negative. However, they were less willing to modify their first impression when the negative portrayal was followed by positive information. Younger adults did not show this pattern. Instead, they were more concerned with making sure the new information was consistent with their impressions. To do so, they modified their impressions to correspond with the new information regardless of whether it was positive or negative. Hess and Pullen suggest that older adults may rely more on life experiences and social rules of behavior when making their interpretations, whereas young adults were more concerned with situational consistency of the new information presented. Also, given older adults' experience in life, they suggest that *older adults do not correct their initial impressions because negative information is more striking to them and thus affects them more strongly, called a* **negativity bias.** This bias corresponds well with other studies demonstrating that older adults pay attention to and seek out emotional information more so than

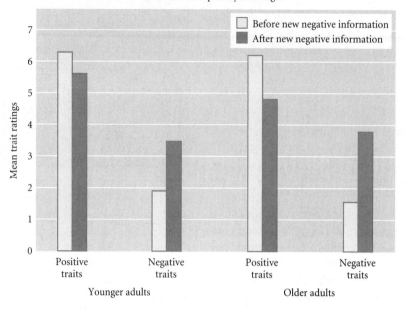

Positive initial portrayal of target

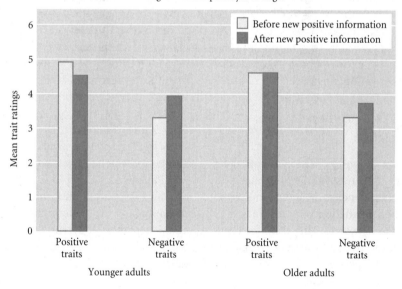

Negative initial portrayal of target

FIGURE 9.1 Mean trait ratings before and after presentation of new negative or positive information.

Source: Hess, T. M., & Pullen, S. M. (1994). Adult age differences in informational biases during impression formation. *Psychology and Aging, 9,* 239.

younger age groups (Carstensen, 1995). We will discuss this further later on in the chapter. This bias suggests that decline in cognitive functioning limits the ability of older adults to override the impact of their initial impressions.

More support for this perspective is found in a subsequent study (Hess et al., 1998). Young and older adults were asked to form impressions of a target person based on a set of six positive behaviors (e.g., considers others' feelings) and three negative behaviors (e.g., is rude to others). In this case, the first impression would be more positive because the person demonstrated more positive than negative behaviors. The participants in the experiment were then presented with a list of descriptive traits and asked to judge the extent to which each of the traits characterized the target person. The traits were either positive (sensitive, friendly) or negative (dishonest, unfriendly). Age differences occurred in that young adults were more likely to distinguish between traits that referred to the initial behavior and those that did not. Hess and colleagues suggest that older adults are less likely than young adults to use detailed, specific information in forming impressions. This is because use of such information overworks processing resources. Thus, the conclusion drawn here is that these age differences imply deficiencies in working memory resources. However, as with Blanchard-Fields' work, Hess also suggests that the use of such information appears to be related to age differences in social experience and knowledge.

In the next section we examine processes involved in accessing knowledge used to make social judgments.

Knowledge Accessibility

When we are faced with new situations, we draw on our previous experiences stored in memory, or our **social knowledge.** The content of that experience and knowledge and how easily we can retrieve it affect how we behave in social situations. For example, if you are attending your first day of class, you draw on social knowledge that tells you how to behave in a classroom. This process includes having stored representations of the social world or memories of past

events, knowing how to apply those memories to various situations, and having easy access to the memories. For example, we draw on implicit theories of personality (our personal theories of how personality works) on how a professor should act in a classroom. If the professor is inconsistent with your implicit theory of how he or she should act, this affects the impression you form of the professor. For example, if the professor dresses in shorts and makes casual references to the party he attended last night, this may violate your implicit theory that professors are reserved and work all of the time. Research supports this in that implicit personality theories we have about people, in general, influence the impressions we form about specific people (Epstein et al., 1992; Skowronski & Carlston, 1989).

However, availability of information in memory does not necessarily imply easy access to that social information. The degree to which information in memory is easily accessible determines the extent to which that information guides social judgments or behavior. Easy access to information is influenced by a number of variables. First, accessibility depends on the strength of the information stored in memory. For example, if you have extensive past experience retrieving and applying a particular construct, such as a personality trait (aggressive), you will have a highly accessible social knowledge structure representing features of this particular personality trait (e.g., dominant in social situations, highly competitive). Thus, you would judge a person as aggressive by interpreting dominant behaviors as clearly diagnostic of aggressiveness. The personality trait construct would not be easily accessible for other people who do not have experience with aggressive people and thus have not retrieved the trait of aggressiveness very often. These people would be likely to interpret the behavior very differently (Bargh, 1997; Higgins et al., 1977). For example, they may see the dominant or aggressive person as an expert in the area in question.

Accessibility of social knowledge can explain age-related differences in social judgments. First, as we saw in the case of impression formation, older adults rely on easily accessible social knowledge structures such as the initial impression made about a person. This may be a function of limited cognitive resources to process detailed information presented after the initial impression is formed.

Second, age differences in accessibility are also illustrated when one examines the framing effect (Schwarz et al., 1999). *A framing effect occurs when information you just processed influences subsequent social judgments.* Empirical demonstrations of the influence of the framing effect often involve experimental manipulation of the sequence of exposure or the context of presented information preceding a social judgment. For example, before judging a person's behavior in a social situation you are told that the event occurred on a very sunny, pleasant day. Thus, the situation is framed positively. Processing this contextual information can influence your subsequent social judgments in that you will make more positive ones than if you were told that the situation occurred on a dark and gloomy day. Accordingly, Schwarz and his colleagues (1998) found that manipulating this kind of information and thus making it more accessible can modify social judgments in both young and older adults. However, in some circumstances, older adults' judgments show smaller effects than young adults' judgments. Instead of processing the contextual information presented (e.g., details about a sunny day), it may be that reduced processing resources prevent older adults from accessing it.

Based on this research and the research on **processing capacity,** *or the degree to which processing resources are available during a cognitive task,* it appears that processing resource limitations play an important role in how older adults process and access social information. However, it is also the case that the extent to which social information is accessible may operate independently of a processing resource limitation to influence social judgments. Before we can entertain the notion that knowledge influences social cognitive processing, we must first explore how social knowledge develops and changes as we grow older.

CONCEPT CHECKS

1. How is impression formation affected by processing resource capacity?
2. How does knowledge accessibility explain age-related differences in social judgments?

SOCIAL KNOWLEDGE STRUCTURES AND SOCIAL BELIEFS

LEARNING OBJECTIVES

- What are social knowledge structures and social beliefs?
- How does the content of stereotypes about aging differ across adulthood?
- How do young and older adults perceive the competence of older adults?
- How do negative stereotypes about aging unconsciously guide our behavior?
- What are implicit social beliefs, and how do they change with age?

Alison is going on her first date since the death of her husband a year ago. She is 62 years old and was married for 30 years, so she is extremely nervous about what to do and how to act. When her date, Gray, picks her up he announces that he has made reservations at a nice Italian restaurant, and that afterward they will go to a late movie. Although Alison is nervous, she makes it through the date with very few problems. To her delight, how to act and what to do seemed to come flooding back to her without a bit of effort.

On her date Alison was experiencing the easy accessibility of a well-learned social script or social knowledge on how to behave on a date. Social cognitive research has paid much attention to how social knowledge structures and social beliefs guide behavior. What are social knowledge structures and social beliefs? They are defined in terms of how we represent and interpret the behavior of others in a social situation (Fiske, 1993). They come in many different forms. For example, we have scripted knowledge structures regarding everyday activities such as what people should do when they go to the doctor's office or a restaurant. We also have stereotypes of groups of people and how we feel they will act in certain situations, such as "Older adults are more rigid in their point of view" or "Older adults talk on and on about their past." Finally, we have been socialized to adhere to and believe in social rules, or how to behave in specific social situations such as how a husband should act toward his wife.

Two interesting developmental questions arise with respect to social knowledge structures. First, does the content of our social knowledge and beliefs change as we grow older? Second, how do our knowledge structures and beliefs affect our social judgments, memory, problem solving, and more? For each type of social knowledge structure we explore, we address both of these questions.

Stereotypes

Negative stereotypes of aging are pervasive in our culture. Just peruse your local greeting card store and you will find humorous birthday cards capitalizing on our negative expectations about aging, with jokes about the older adult who loses her or his memory. For a notorious example, a cartoon features an aging Superman ready to leap out the window. His lapse in memory captures our negative stereotypes about memory and aging. Fortunately, positive expectations about aging coexist with the negative ones (Hummert, 1999). On one hand, older adults are seen as grouchy and forgetful, losing physical stamina and sexual abilities. On the other hand, older adults are seen as wise, generous, and responsible. The important question is what effect stereotypes have on our social judgments and our behavior toward others.

CONTENT OF STEREOTYPES. **Stereotypes** *are a special type of social knowledge structure or social belief that represent organized prior knowledge about a group of people that affects how we interpret new information* (Hilton & von Hippel, 1996). In other words, they help us process information when we are engaged in social interactions. We use our stereotypes to size up people when we first meet them. They help us understand why people behave the way they do and guide us in our behavior toward other people. Remember that stereotypes are not inherently negative in their effect. But too many times they are applied in ways that underestimate the potential of the person we are observing. This will become more evident as we explore age-related stereotypes.

There has been much research examining adult developmental changes in the content and structure of stereotypes (Hummert, 1999). From a developmental perspective, we would ask whether the nature and

Superman in his later years.

Many cartoons and greeting cards depict our fear of memory loss as we grow older.

strength of our stereotypes change as we grow older. However, as described in Table 9.1, Hummert (1999) found that older and younger adults hold quite similar age stereotypes. Such stereotypes include clusters of cognitive, personality, and general physical traits. When asked to generate and sort a list of traits associated with the category *older person,* young, middle-aged, and older adults shared the same categories of aging including golden ager, John Wayne conservative, perfect grandparent, shrew or curmudgeon, recluse, despondent, and severely impaired (Hummert et al., 1994, 1995; Schmidt & Boland, 1986). Recent research also shows that African Americans have similar stereotypes (Adams & Hummert, in preparation).

Yet there are also developmental differences in how we perceive older adults. The consensus on stereotype categories across age groups is accompanied by developmental changes in the complexity of

TABLE 9.1   Traits Associated with Stereotypes of Older Adults

Stereotype	Traits
Negative	
Severely impaired	Slow-thinking, incompetent, feeble, inarticulate, incoherent, senile
Despondent	Depressed, sad, hopeless, afraid, neglected, lonely
Shrew or curmudgeon	Complaining, ill-tempered, demanding, stubborn, bitter, prejudiced
Recluse	Quiet, timid, naive
Positive	
Golden ager	Active, capable, sociable, independent, happy, interesting
Perfect grandparent	Loving, supportive, understanding, wise, generous, kind
John Wayne conservative	Patriotic, conservative, determined, proud, religious, nostalgic

age stereotype beliefs. For example, Heckhausen and colleagues (1989) found that older adults identified a greater number of desirable and undesirable traits that characterize people as they develop across the life span. They also found that older adults perceive a greater potential for change in these characteristics in older age. Other studies show that older adults identify more categories that fit under the superordinate category *older adult* than do younger and middle-aged adults (Brewer & Lui, 1984; Heckhausen et al., 1989; Hummert et al., 1994). For example, as can be seen in Table 9.1, *golden ager* came up as a category only when older adults were included in the study (Hummert et al., 1994). Overall, these findings suggest that as we grow older, our ideas and age stereotypes become more elaborated and rich as we integrate our life experiences into our beliefs about aging (P. B. Baltes et al., 1999; Whitbourne, 1986).

AGE STEREOTYPES AND PERCEIVED COMPETENCE. Stereotypes are not simply reflected in our perceptions of what we think are representative personality traits or characteristics of older adults. We also make appraisals or attributions of older adults' competence when we observe them perform tasks, and we assess whether we can count on them to perform important tasks. No area is more susceptible to negative stereotyped attributions of aging than memory competence. As you may recall from Chapter 7, people of all ages believe that memory decreases with age and that we have less and less control over current and future memory functioning as we grow older (Lineweaver & Hertzog, 1998).

The interesting question is how this strong belief in age-related loss of memory affects our attributions (explanations) about older adults' competencies. In an elegant series of studies, Erber and Prager (1999) found that there is an age-based double standard in judging the competence of old and young adults. *The* **age-based double standard** *is operating when a person attributes an older person's failure in memory as more serious than a memory failure observed in a young adult.* For example, if an older adult cannot find her keys, this is seen as a much more serious memory problem (e.g., possibly attributed to senility) than if a young adult cannot find her keys. This is most evident when young people are judging the memory failure. In contrast, when older people observe the memory failure, they tend to judge both young and old targets of the story more equally. In fact, most of the time older adults were more lenient toward memory failures in older adults. However, in other types of competence judgments older adults also display the age-based double standard. For example, when assessing the cause of a memory failure, both younger and older people felt that it was caused by greater mental difficulty in older adults, whereas it was attributed to a lack of effort or attention in younger adults (Erber et al., 1990).

These findings involve global attributions of memory failures in young and older adults. However, what happens when you are asked to decide whether an older adult should get a job or perform a task that demands memory capabilities? In several studies Erber and colleagues presented younger and older participants with an audiotaped interview of people applying for various volunteer positions such as in a museum (Erber et al., 1996; Erber & Prager, 1997). The applicant was either old or young and either forgetful or not forgetful. They found that despite the age-based double standard in judging older adults' memory failures found in earlier studies, people (both young and old) had more confidence in and would assign tasks or jobs to nonforgetful people irrespective of their age.

What accounts for this apparent discrepancy in findings? It may be the case that when we form an impression about someone's capability, we take other factors into consideration. For example, traits such as responsibility could come into play. Remember that stereotypes about older adults included many positive ones, including responsibility. In fact, in another study young adults were asked whom they would choose to be a neighbor they could rely on. Despite forgetfulness ratings, they consistently chose older neighbors over younger ones (Erber et al., 1993). They also judged older neighbors to be more responsible, reliable, dependable, and helpful than younger ones. Thus, these positive traits may have compensated for older neighbors' forgetfulness.

What can we conclude from the trait studies of stereotypes and the attribution studies of stereotypes? First, when more individualized information (e.g., an audiotaped interview of the person) is provided and the person is placed in a social setting (e.g., a volunteer position interview, a neighborly interaction), we consider more than just negative trait-based stereotypes in making our social judgments. As in the neighborly interaction, we consider additional and

more positive trait information such as reliability or dependability. The volunteer position may be perceived as a context in which older adults would be effective regardless of their memory competence. In fact, research is drawing on these findings to identify what types of social environments will be most conducive to older adults' social competence. We examine research about this later.

ACTIVATION OF STEREOTYPES. From this research we know that stereotypes of older adults exist in the form of personality traits and perceptions of competence. They also influence our judgments about how capable older adults will be in memory-demanding situations. However, it is not enough to know that the stereotypes exist; we need to know under what conditions they are activated and, if activated, how they affect our behavior and social judgments. For example, why do negative stereotypes of older adults tend to influence our behaviors (e.g., talking down to older adults as if they were children) and attitudes (Hummert, 1999)? Much work has focused on stereotype activation as a nonconscious and automatic process that guides our behavior and social judgments (Bargh, 1997; Devine, 1989; Greenwald & Banaji, 1995).

Social psychologists suggest that stereotypes are automatically activated because they become overlearned and thus spontaneously activated when you encounter a member or members of a stereotyped group, such as African Americans (Devine, 1989; Greenwald et al., 1998). *The activation of strong stereotypes is not only automatic but also nonconscious, making it more likely that they will influence your behavior without you being aware of it, an effect called* **implicit stereotyping.** The effects of such implicit stereotyping are illustrated in a clever study conducted by Bargh and colleagues (Bargh et al., 1996). They demonstrated that if you subliminally (out of conscious awareness) prime young people with the image of an older adult, the young people's behavior is influenced in an age-related manner. In this case, the implicitly primed young adults walked down the hall more slowly after the experiment than young adults who were not primed with the older adult image. This is a powerful demonstration of how our unconscious stereotypes of aging can guide our behavior.

In another study, Perdue and Gurtman (1990) also presented stimuli subliminally to participants. They found that the subliminal presentation of the word *old* increased the speed of a subsequent decision that a word presented on a computer screen (such as *ugly*) was a negative word. When these participants were subliminally presented with the word *young*, their decision time to indicate that a word such as *pretty* was a positive word was much quicker. In other words, when we are unconsciously presented with the word *old* it activates a negative evaluation and makes it easier and quicker to evaluate a negative word, such as *ugly*. Both the Bargh et al. and Perdue and Gurtman experiments demonstrate that the activation of our negative stereotypes about aging affects our behavior without us being aware of it.

Implicit stereotyping is illustrated in many different domains of our behavior toward others. For example, in many situations nursing staff or younger adults in general are trying to instruct or communicate with older adults. There is much evidence that young people engage in patronizing talk toward older adults in these situations (Hummert, 1999). **Patronizing talk** *includes slow speech, simple vocabulary, careful enunciation, a demeaning emotional tone (e.g., overbearing or overly familiar), and superficial conversation.* It is very similar to the way adults engage in baby talk to very young children. Research shows that negative age stereotypes are a primary cause of this behavior (Hummert et al., 1998; Kemper et al., 1998). It creates social alienation and has damaging effects on older adults' self esteem (Hummert, 1999). Interestingly, people who are likely to engage in patronizing talk to older adults evaluate this type of talk to older adults as disrespectful and demeaning (Ryan et al., 1994).

Why is this so? Again, implicit stereotyping may be the answer. When communicating to others, we try to accommodate so that they will understand what we are saying. In this case, negative stereotypes of older adults as less competent, with poor hearing and memory, may be activated and unconsciously and inadvertently result in an inaccurate assessment

Nursing home staff must be careful not to communicate with older adult residents as if they were childlike.

of how to accommodate our speech (Hummert, 1999; Ryan et al., 1994).

Another important question to ask is whether implicit negative stereotypes of aging influence the cognitive functioning of older adults. This possibility is raised in the context of widely cited social psychological research on stereotype threat. Steele and colleagues conducted a number of studies suggesting that stigmatized groups such as African Americans and women are vulnerable to stereotype threat (Spencer et al., 1999; Steele, 1997; Steele & Aronson, 1995). **Stereotype threat** *is an evoked fear of being judged in accordance with a negative stereotype about a group to which you belong.* For example, if you are

African American, you may be vulnerable to cues in your environment that activate stereotype threat about academic ability. In turn, you may perform more poorly on a task associated with that stereotype regardless of high competence in academic settings.

In a seminal study, African Americans at Stanford University were divided into two groups. Both groups scored very high on their SAT verbal scores. However, one group was told that they were going to take a test that was highly diagnostic of their verbal ability. The other group did not receive this highly evaluative instruction. When scores were compared on verbal tests for both groups, despite the fact that all participants were highly verbal, the group that received the diagnostic instructions performed more poorly. Caucasians in the diagnostic evaluation did not differ from Caucasians in the nondiagnostic group. However, they outperformed African Americans in the diagnostic condition. Importantly, there were no differences between African Americans and Caucasians in the nondiagnostic group. Why? Steele argues that the performance of African Americans in the diagnostic condition suffered because they felt threatened by the negative stereotype that African Americans perform poorly on academic ability tests. This same type of effect was found when women were told that a test evaluated their mathematical competence. In this case, women are the stigmatized group because of negative stereotypes suggesting that women are less capable at math than men.

Do older adults belong to a stigmatized group that is vulnerable to stereotype threat? Recently researchers have suggested that negative stereotypes adversely affect older adults' cognitive functioning and may account for the fact that we see age-related decline in cognitive functioning (see Chapters 6 and 7). This issue is examined in the Current Controversies feature.

Implicit Social Beliefs

We have just discussed stereotypes as an important type of social belief that guides our behavior. However, there are many other types of belief systems that differ in content across age groups and also influence behavior. There are three important considerations in understanding age differences in social belief systems (Blanchard-Fields & Hertzog, 2000). First, we must examine the specific content of social beliefs (i.e., the particular beliefs and knowledge people have about rules, norms, and patterns of social behavior). Second, we must consider the strength of these beliefs to know under what conditions they may influence behavior. Third, we need to know the likelihood that these beliefs will be activated automatically when they are violated or questioned. If these three aspects of the belief system are understood, it is possible to explain when and why age differences occur in social judgments. In other words, older adults may hold different beliefs than other age groups (e.g., different rules for appropriate social behavior during dating, as in the case of Alison). Furthermore, how strongly people hold these beliefs may vary as a function of how particular generations were socialized. For example, although younger and older people may both believe that couples should not live together before marriage, the oldest generation may be more adamant and rigid about this belief.

A good portion of the research literature focuses on age differences in the content of attitudes, beliefs, and values. However, evidence of age differences in the content of social beliefs does not completely account for age differences in how and when such beliefs are activated and how they influence behavior.

Social cognition researchers argue that individual differences in the strength of social representations of rules, beliefs, and attitudes are linked to specific situations (Mischel & Shoda, 1995). Such representations can be both cognitive (how we conceptualize the situation) and emotional (how we react to the situation). When one encounters a specific situation, the person's belief system triggers an emotional reaction and related goals tied to the content of that situation. This in turn drives social judgments. Consider the belief that couples should not live together before marriage. If you were socialized from childhood to believe in this rule, you would evaluate anyone violating that rule negatively. For example, suppose you were told about a man named Allen who put pressure on Joan to live with him before they were married,

A major controversial issue in the cognitive aging literature is whether living in a society that equates old age with memory decline, senility, and dependency produces what Langer (1989) calls a "premature cognitive commitment" early in life. As children we acquire ideas of what it means to be old, usually negative, and these stereotypes guide and influence our behavior later in life. To what degree do negative societal beliefs, attitudes, and expectations determine the cognitive decline we observe in older adults?

When Levy and Langer (1994) compared memory performance and attitudes about aging of Chinese older adults, hearing American older adults, and deaf American older adults, they found that the Chinese older adults outperformed both groups of American older adults on several memory tasks. In addition, the deaf American older adults outperformed their hearing counterparts. Attitudes on aging held by the different cultures were related to memory performance

(Chinese had more positive attitudes than Americans). Levy and Langer conclude that negative stereotypes in American culture accounted for this difference.

However, the results are not definitive because this is a correlational study. In other words, does enhanced memory performance lead to more positive attitudes, or do positive attitudes lead to enhanced memory performance? Are there educational differences between the two cultural groups? Are the memory tests really the same given that they had to be translated into Chinese?

To further test this notion, Levy (1996) subliminally primed young and older adults with negative stereotypes of an older adult (e.g., the word *senile*) or positive stereotypes (e.g., the word *wise*). She found that when older adults were primed with negative aging stereotypes, their performance was worse on memory tests than that of older adults primed with positive stereotypes. However, this study has not been replicated in

other labs. In fact, Stein (1999) tried to replicate this finding and failed to do so.

It seems likely that there is a self-fulfilling prophecy operating with respect to older adults' memory performance. If society portrays older adults as declining in cognitive capacity and you are socialized to believe so at a very young age, then it makes sense that this will influence your memory performance as an older adult. However, as we observed in Chapters 6 and 7, other processes related to physiological decline (e.g., speed of processing) account for many declines in memory performance. Negative stereotypes of aging may indeed have some effect on cognitive performance without accounting for all of it. Thus, although we may not be able to eliminate decline in performance, interventions in improving one's attitudes and outlook on aging could improve one's cognitive performance.

and they subsequently broke up. You may have a negative emotional response and blame Allen for the breakup of the relationship because he was lobbying for cohabitation.

A study exploring social beliefs found age differences in the types of social rules and evaluations evoked in different types of situations (Blanchard-Fields, 1996, 1999). For example, when subjects considered a husband who chooses to work long hours instead of spending more time with his wife and children, the social evaluation "marriage is more important than a career" tended to increase in importance

with age. As can be seen in Figure 9.2, this was particularly evident from age 24 to age 65. Figure 9.2 also shows that the social rule "the marriage was already in trouble" was also produced and has an inverted U-shaped relationship. In other words, adults around age 35 to 55 years produced this social evaluation the most.

These findings may relate to how the oldest generation was socialized with respect to the social rules of marriage. Your grandparents' generation probably was socialized very differently from your generation in terms of appropriate behavior by husbands and wives.

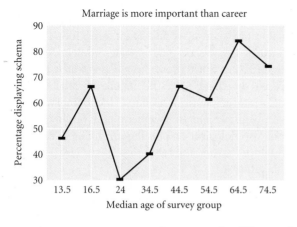

Marriage is more important than career

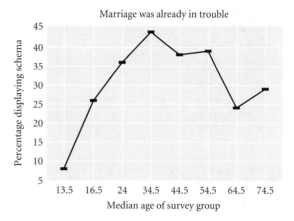

Marriage was already in trouble

FIGURE 9.2 Age differences in social rules and relationships.

Thus, these findings may reflect such cohort differences. Alternatively, viewing marriage as more important than one's career may relate to the particular life stage and life circumstances different age groups confront. During midcareer and mid–child-rearing stages, making a living and proving oneself in a career may take precedence (Schaie, 1977–1978). In contrast, during the retirement and empty nest phase, the importance of a marital relationship may reemerge. On the other hand, the middle-aged group may not have relied on social rules to guide their thinking about the problem situation and focused more on the marital conflict itself. This could possibly reflect the 1960s focus on communicating feelings. These are only a few examples of sociocultural experiential factors that may influence different social beliefs.

For a situation involving a youthful couple who eloped despite the objections of their parents, the social rules "parents should have talked, not provoked the young couple" and "they were too young" also showed an inverted *U*-shaped relationship with age. In other words, middle-aged people endorsed these rules, whereas younger and older people did not. On the other hand, the social rule "you can't stop true love" showed a *U*-shaped relationship with age. In other words, younger and older age groups endorsed this rule, whereas people in middle adulthood did

not. It may be that in middle adulthood, between ages 30 and 45, people are not focusing on issues of true love. This makes sense because they are in the stage of life where the pragmatics of building a career are important. They also emphasized the pragmatics of age (e.g., being too young) as an important factor in marriage decisions.

One possible explanation for these findings is that cohort effects or generational differences (as we discussed in Chapter 1) influenced whether strong family social rules would be activated. For example, older women adopted the social rule "marriage is more important than career" much more than men of their same generation and more than women and men of younger generations. The fact that older women endorsed this social rule more strongly than the other age groups is a good example of how emotionally laden values are evoked in these situations. The next interesting question is whether these age differences in social beliefs influence social judgments, which we explore in the next section.

CONCEPT CHECKS

1. Describe positive and negative age-related stereotypes.
2. What is implicit stereotyping?
3. What is stereotype threat?
4. How do social beliefs differ with age?

CAUSAL ATTRIBUTIONS

LEARNING OBJECTIVES

- What are causal attributions?
- What is the correspondence bias?
- How does the nature of our causal attributions change with age?
- What alternative explanations are there for the dispositional bias found in older adults?

Katie is cleaning up after her son, who spilled his dinner all over the table and floor. At the same time, she is listening to her co-worker, Carolyn, on the phone describing how anxious she was when she gave the marketing presentation in front of their new clients that day. Carolyn also describes how the boss told her that the company depended on this presentation to obtain a contract from new clients. After the phone call, Katie reflects on Carolyn's situation. She decides that Carolyn is an anxious person and should work on reducing her anxiety in these types of situations.

Katie was interested in what caused Carolyn's anxiety when presenting information at work. Was it something about Carolyn, such as being an anxious person? Or was it some other reason, such as luck or chance? Or was it the pressure placed on Carolyn by her boss? *Answers to these questions provide insights into the explanations people construct to explain their behavior, called* **causal attributions**. *Causal attributions can be behavioral explanations that reside within the actor (such as "Carolyn is an anxious person"), called* **dispositional attributions**. *Or they can be behavioral explanations that reside outside the actor (such as "Carolyn is succumbing to pressures from her boss"), called* **situational attributions**. In this case, Katie made a dispositional attribution about Carolyn. In this section we explore whether there are age differences in the tendency to rely more on dispositional or situational attributions or a combination of both when making causal attributions.

Historically, the study of attributions and aging has been confined to studying attributional judgments made about the aging population, usually involving competence in memory or cognition. This is reminiscent of Erber's work on stereotypes and attributions about older adults' mental competence. In this case, attributions about older adults' successes and failures are compared with similar successes and failures of younger adults. These attributions are related to the stereotyping of older adults. However, more recent attribution and aging research has focused on changes in the nature of attributional processes per se from an adult developmental context. Thus, we can ask whether typical findings in social psychological attribution theory and research hold true beyond the college age (Blanchard-Fields & Abeles, 1996).

For many years, we have known that college students typically produce informational distortions when making causal attributions about problem solving (Gilbert & Malone, 1995). *In this* **correspondence bias,** *youth rely more on dispositional information in explaining behavior and ignore compelling situational information such as extenuating circumstances.* For example, you may have tried to approach your psychology professor the other day. He did not even acknowledge that you were there and kept walking with his face buried in a manuscript. You might decide that because your professor ignored your question, he is arrogant (a dispositional attribution). At the same time, you may have ignored important situational information such as the fact that he is overwhelmed by upcoming deadlines. Thus, you did not consider all the pertinent information to make a more accurate judgment. This type of finding has been documented primarily in college students. However, the life experience accumulated by middle-aged and older adults may cause them to reach different conclusions such as considering equally both types of information in explaining why things happen the way they do.

In a series of creative investigations, Blanchard-Fields (1994, 1996, 1999; Blanchard-Fields & Norris, 1994; Blanchard-Fields et al., 1998, 1999) studied the differences in causal attributions across the adult life span. In a number of studies, Blanchard-Fields presented participants with different situations with positive or negative outcomes and asked them to decide whether something about the main character in the story (dispositional attributions), the situation (situational attributions), or a combination of both (interactive attributions) was responsible for the event. For example, a vignette may present the situation described earlier in which Allen pressured Joan to live with him before marriage. Joan protested, but Allen continued to pressure her. The relationship fell apart.

When the target events were ambiguous as to the specific cause of the outcome, as in the case of Allen and Joan, all adults tended to make interactive attributions, but older adults did so at a higher rate. However, as can be seen in Figure 9.3, older adults also blamed the main character more (dispositional attributions) than younger groups, especially in negative relationship situations.

In another study, Blanchard-Fields and Norris (1994) examined the connection between cognitive level and attributions. They found that middle-aged adults scored higher on dialectical attributional reasoning (ability to consider multiple explanations such as dispositional and situational factors and how these factors can be incorporated into a workable explanation of behavior) than adolescents, young adults, or older adults. Also, older adults made stronger dispositional attributions. Blanchard-Fields and Norris took a sociocultural perspective in explaining why older adults were more predisposed to making dispositional attributions and engaged in less dialectical reasoning in negative relationship situations. First, it is interesting to note that the correspondence bias in older adults occurred only in negative relationship situations. In this case, older adults appeared to apply specific social rules about relationships in making their attributional judgments, apparently because of their stage in life and the beliefs of the cohort in which they were socialized. In these situations, strong beliefs about how one should act in relationships appeared to be violated for the older adults, particularly older women. Therefore, these women made snap judgments about the main character who violated their strong beliefs and did not feel that it was necessary to engage in conscious, deliberate analyses. They *knew* the character was wrong.

The question arises whether these attributional biases in older adults are caused by activated belief systems that strongly affect their judgments or by deficiencies in conducting causal analyses. This deficiency could take the form of limited cognitive resources that may prevent them from processing all

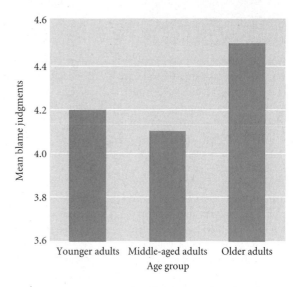

FIGURE 9.3 Dispositional attributions as a function of age.

the details of the situation (e.g., extenuating situational circumstances). Remember, earlier we questioned whether a processing resource hypothesis was the best explanation of social judgment biases, given that the dispositional bias was found for older adults only when they were presented with negative relationship situations. This issue was addressed in a study by Chen and Blanchard-Fields (1997) described in the "How Do We Know?" feature.

These findings indicate that the explanations people create to account for behavior vary depending on the type of situation (e.g., relationship or achievement situations), the age of the person, and whether strong social beliefs have been violated. This research also indicates the importance of the sociocultural context in which people are socialized, which appears to create different social rules that are then used to make causal attributions. More research is needed to shed additional light on how these age differences are created and under what circumstances they appear.

CONCEPT CHECKS

1. What is the correspondence bias?
2. What are dispositional and situational attributions?

Social Cognition

Who were the investigators, and what was the aim of the study? Yiwei Chen and Fredda Blanchard-Fields (1997) tested the idea that processing resource limitations accounted for the dispositional bias typically observed in older adults. Does older adults' limited resource capacity prevent them from adjusting initial dispositional biases? In addition, would older adults engage in an adjustment procedure if they were given more time, which would reduce cognitive processing demands? Alternatively, do strong social beliefs and social rules better explain older adults' dispositional biases?

How did the investigators measure the topic of interest? Chen and Blanchard-Fields presented 12 social dilemmas to participants. Within each situation a character violated a social rule about appropriate social behavior in the specific type of situation. On a computer screen, participants had to rate the degree to which the character

was to blame for the situation either immediately after the story or 30 seconds later.

Who were the participants in the study? Chen and Blanchard-Fields selected a random sample of older adults and young adults from the Southeast. Because the young adults were college students and the older adults were from the community, the sample was not representative of the population at large.

Were there ethical concerns with the study? Because the study used volunteers who performed the computerized task and there were no questions about sensitive topics, there were no ethical concerns.

What were the results? As you can see in Figure 9.4, older adults made higher dispositional ratings than young adults did in the immediate-rating condition only. Older adults made lower dispositional attribution ratings (i.e., adjusted more) if they were forced to take more time to think

about the situations than in the immediate rating condition.

The age differences in immediate and delayed conditions defined processing limitations in terms of time constraints. Given more time, older adults adjust their attributions. However, we can only infer this given that the manipulation of processing constraints was not directly compared within participants. Also, adjustment does not always work in the same way. For example, young adults had a slight tendency to increase their dispositional attributions given more time.

However, Chen and Blanchard-Fields also asked participants to complete brief written essays explaining their attributional judgments. The content of their statements was used to identify each person's social rules about appropriate behaviors in the social situations portrayed in the vignettes. They found that older adults made more evaluative rule statements

MOTIVATION AND SOCIAL PROCESSING GOALS

LEARNING OBJECTIVES

- How do emotions influence the way we process information, and how does it change with age?
- How does a need for closure influence the way we process information, and how does it change with age?

*R*enee and Scott are visiting their children and grandchildren on Cape Cod. They all are having a good time until their son, Chris, brings up the hot topic of the upcoming presidential election. The debate between family members about whom they should vote for becomes heated. Renee and Scott are very concerned

about the negative feelings generated in the debate and try to encourage everyone to change the topic. However, the brothers and sisters are more interested in settling the issue. Renee and Scott cannot handle the negative energy and go to bed early.

Why did Renee and Scott focus on the emotional side of the problem (the increase in negative feelings) and the siblings focus on the more instrumental side of the problem (e.g., whom to vote for)? A growing area of research suggests that change in the relative importance of social goals across the life span profoundly influences how we interpret and use social information or direct attention and effort to certain aspects of problems (Hess, 1999). The idea is that goals change with age as a function of experience and

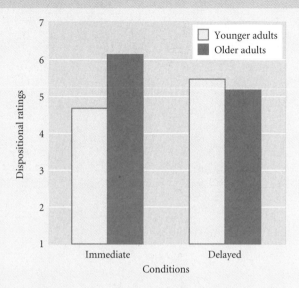

FIGURE 9.4 Dispositional ratings as a function of age group and rating condition.

Source: Chen, Y., & Blanchard-Fields, F. (1997). Age differences in stages of attributional processing. *Psychology and Aging, 12,* 698.

about the main character in the immediate rating condition (e.g., "You shouldn't take friendship for granted"). In addition, high dispositional attributional ratings were correlated with such evaluative rule statements about the main character. Finally, the degree to which participants produced evaluative rule statements about the main character accounted for the relationship between age and dispositional ratings about the main character in the immediate rating condition.

What did the investigators conclude? Chen and Blanchard-Fields provide evidence against a resource limitation explanation for older adults' dispositional bias and provide evidence that the degree to which a person endorses social rules leads to a dispositional bias. In this case, older adults felt that more social rules had been violated in these vignettes and thus displayed more dispositional bias than younger adults.

time left in the life span. This can influence the degree to which we observe age differences in social cognitive functioning, such as the desire to focus on eliminating negative affect in problem situations. Let's explore this further.

Emotion as a Processing Goal

We examine the idea of socioemotional selectivity with aging in Chapter 11. For now, you need to know that this theory maintains that emotional goals become increasingly important and salient as we grow older (Carstensen, 1993, 1995). It is primarily a motivational model that posits that the degree to which a person construes time as limited or ex-

pansive causes him or her to assign priority to emotional or knowledge-seeking goals, respectively. Thus, given limited time left in the life span, older adults may be more motivated to emphasize emotional goals and aspects of life. We examine this motivational factor in the context of maintaining and choosing intimate relationships in Chapter 11. However, it also can be applied in the context of social information processing.

For example, Carstensen and Turk-Charles (1994) predicted that given the heightened salience of emotion in later life, emotional information should be better remembered by older adults. They conducted a memory experiment in which participants 20 to 83 years of age were asked to recall a passage from a popular novel. The passage contained both emotional and nonemotional text. Although young adults remembered more of the passage than older adults did, it was confined mainly to neutral material. The finding most relevant to their argument can be seen in Figure 9.5. The figure reveals that the proportion of emotional material recalled increased with age. Carstensen and Turk-Charles argue that the success in older adults' recall of emotional material could be accounted for by processing goals: heightened attention paid to emotional information.

We could also reinterpret the findings in the Hess and Pullen (1994) study on impression formation discussed earlier. The negativity bias (older adults being more influenced by negative information) could very well result from a processing goal. In this case negative emotional material became more salient to older adults (Isaacowitz et al., 2000).

Cognitive Style as a Processing Goal

Another type of motivational goal that can influence our thinking comes from our **cognitive style,** *or how we attempt to solve problems.* Examples include a need for closure and the inability to tolerate ambiguous situations. People with a high need for closure prefer order and predictability, are uncomfortable with ambiguity, are close-minded, and prefer quick and decisive answers (Kruglanski et al., 1997; Neuberg et al., 1997). Empirical research on this construct has resulted in the development of well-validated questionnaires such as the Need for Closure Scale (Webster & Kruglanski, 1994) and the Personal Need for Structure scale (Thompson et al., 1992).

The question is whether cognitive resources or need for closure are implicated in biased judgments. In the social cognition literature it is maintained that situations that demand substantial cognitive resources (i.e., those that demand a lot of effort in cognitive processing, such as processing information under time pressure) result in an increase in inaccuracies and biases in how we represent social information (Kruglanski & Webster, 1996). However, biased judgments can also be caused by motivational differences such as an increase in need for closure. In fact,

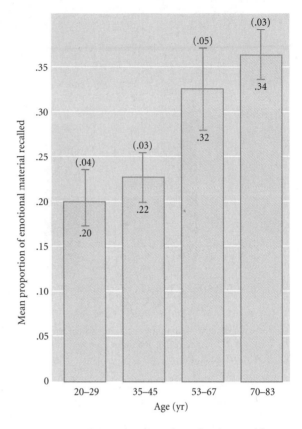

FIGURE 9.5 **Mean proportions of emotional propositions recalled by age group.**

Source: Carstensen, L. L., & Turk-Charles, S. (1994). The salience of emotion across the adult life span. *Psychology and Aging, 9,* 262. Copyright © 1994 by the American Psychological Association. Adapted with permission.

research measuring need for closure suggests that high need for closure or structure is related to attributional biases, the tendency to make stereotyped judgments, the formation of spontaneous trait inferences, and the tendency to assimilate judgments to primed constructs (Schaller et al., 1995).

It may also be the case that limited cognitive resources and motivational differences are age-related and influence social judgments in interaction with each other. Hess and colleagues (1998) argue that changes in resources with aging (such as the declines we observed in working memory in Chapter 7) may lead to an increase in a need for closure with age. This can lead to biases in the way older adults process social information. In a recent study, Hess and colleagues (1998) found that a high need for closure did not influence susceptibility to emotional priming influences on neutral stimuli of young and middle-aged adults. However, priming effects increased with higher need for structure in older adults. In other words, older adults with a high need for closure were unable to inhibit the effects of an emotional prime (e.g., a subliminally presented negative word) on their subsequent behavior (e.g., whether they liked or disliked an abstract figure). Because of age-related changes in personal resources (social and cognitive), motivational factors such as coming to quick and decisive answers to conserve resources become important to the older adult.

CONCEPT CHECKS

1. What is socioemotional selectivity with respect to processing goals?
2. What is need for closure?

PERSONAL CONTROL

LEARNING OBJECTIVES

- What are the internal and external locus of control?
- What is the multidimensionality of personal control?
- How do assimilation and accommodation influence behavior?
- What are primary and secondary control?
- What is the primacy of primary control over secondary control?

*D*aniel did not perform as well as he thought he would on his psychology exam. He now has to try to determine why he did so poorly on the exam. Was it his fault? Was the exam too picky? To add insult to injury, Daniel has to pick his grades up to maintain his scholarship. He decides that the exam was too picky. This helps Daniel motivate himself to study for his next exam.

Daniel's behavior sheds light on how we tend to explain, or attribute, our behavior. One of the most important ways in which we analyze the cause of events is in terms of who or what is in control in a specific situation. **Personal control** *is the degree to which one believes that one's performance in a situation depends on something that one personally does.* A high sense of personal control implies a belief that performance is up to you, whereas a low sense of personal control implies that your performance is under the influence of forces other than your own.

Personal control has become an extremely important idea in a wide variety of settings because of the way in which it guides behavior (Baltes & Baltes, 1990; Brändstadter, 1997; Soederberg Miller & Lachman, 1999; Rowe & Kahn, 1997; Skinner, 1995). For example, it is thought to play a role in memory performance (see Chapter 7), intelligence (see Chapter 8), depression (see Chapter 4), and adjustment to and survival in institutions (see Chapter 5). Despite this range of research, however, we do not have a clear picture of developmental trends in people's sense of personal control.

Locus of Control

Most of the research on personal control has been conducted using a locus-of-control framework. *Locus of control* refers to who or what one thinks is responsible for performance. Traditionally, researchers have used the label *internal* to describe people who take personal responsibility for their behavior and *external* to describe people who believe that others (or chance) are responsible for their behavior. Evidence from cross-sectional studies and longitudinal studies (Kogan, 1990; Lachman, 1986; Welch & West, 1995) is contradictory. Some find that older adults are more likely to be internal than younger adults, whereas others find older adults more likely to be external than younger adults. Adding to the confusion, other studies find no changes in control perceptions across the life span (Brändstadter & Rothermund, 1994; Reker et al., 1987).

Multidimensionality of Personal Control

There are a number of reasons why this discrepancy in the literature exists. First, the conflicting findings may result from the multidimensionality of per-

As you progress through college, you are concerned about your grade point average, how much you will learn, and how you will score on exams. The more control you believe you have over the situation, the more confident you feel. You can make two types of control attributions. You can make an entity attribution about your performance in school, which means that you attribute control to your innate ability to perform, or you can hold a skill perspective, in which you attribute control over your performance in terms of the effort you exert, such as how much you study for an exam.

Are there age differences in these control beliefs? To find out, talk to students at your university in all grade levels and age groups. A lot of older students are coming back to school.

Find out what they believe is the major cause of the successes and failures in school. Bring your results to class and pool them. See whether there are grade level differences or age differences in perceptions of control over academic performance. Compare your findings with the age differences reported in the text.

sonal control (Soederberg Miller & Lachman, 1999). Specifically, one's sense of control depends on which domain, such as intelligence or health, is being assessed. Moreover, older adults often acknowledge the importance of outside influences on their behavior but still believe that what they do matters. In fact, Soederberg Miller and Lachman (1999) find lower levels of perceived control with increasing age in the intellectual domain.

Given that you are in an academic context, college, attributions of control are particularly important in determining the causes of your success and failure in school. It would be interesting to explore the notion of control over class performance among older and younger students. The exercise in the Discovering Development feature will help you examine this question.

Indeed, Brändtstadter (1999) clearly showed that the developmental patterns of personal control vary widely from one domain to another. For example, perceived control over one's development shows an overall age-related decrease. However, perceived marital support shows an age-related increase. Brändtstadter and Rothermund (1994) found a high degree of stability over 8 years in middle-aged adults' general sense of control. They also examined the effects of perceptions of control within 17 specific life goal domains (e.g., family security, emotional stability, and self-development) on general perceptions of control. The degree to which self-perceptions of control within a particular goal domain affect a general sense of control depends on the personal importance of that domain. Additionally, losses of control within a goal domain affects general perceptions of control to a lesser degree if the importance of the goal declines over time.

Grob and colleagues (1999) also found variable change in perceived control over the life span depending on the particular life domain assessed. As can be seen in Figure 9.6, they found an increase in perceived control for social (harmony within a close relationship) and personal (personal appearance) issues up to early middle age (e.g., middle 30s), and thereafter there was a general decline into old age. On the other hand, perceived control over societal issues (e.g., a natural environmental problem such as the demise of forests due to pollution) was low across the adult life span, with a slight decrease in older adulthood.

Control Strategies

A second reason for the discrepancy in the literature is in the different conceptualizations of control. The research just discussed examined primarily control-

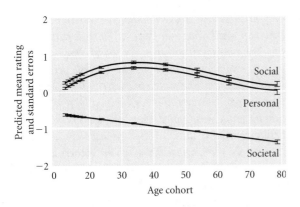

FIGURE 9.6 Developmental trajectories of control expectancy across three life domains.

Source: Grob, A., Little, T. D., & Wanner, B. (1999). Control judgements across the lifespan. *International Journal of Behavioral Decisions, 23,* 844.

related beliefs such as locus of control. However, a number of theoretical approaches and much empirical work examine control-related strategies. For example, Brändtstadter (1999) proposes that the preservation and stabilization of a positive view of the self and personal development in later life involve three interdependent processes. First, people engage in assimilative activities that prevent or alleviate losses in domains that are personally relevant for self-esteem and identity. For example, people might use memory aids more if having a good memory is an important aspect of self-esteem and identity. Second, people make accommodative changes and readjust their goals and aspirations to lessen or neutralize the effects of negative self-evaluations in key domains. For instance, if a person notices that the time it takes to walk a mile at a brisk pace has increased, he or she could increase the target time to help lessen the impact of feelings of failure. Third, people use immunizing mechanisms that alter the effects of self-discrepant evidence. In this case, a person who is confronted with evidence that his or her memory performance has declined could look for alternative explanations or simply deny the evidence.

Taking a similar approach, Heckhausen and Schulz (1995, 1999) view control (i.e., people's abilities to

control important outcomes) as a motivational system that regulates human behavior over the life span. They define control-related strategies in terms of primary control and secondary control. Much like Brändstadter's assimilative activities, primary control involves bringing the environment into line with one's desires and goals. Action is directed toward changing the external world. Much like Brändstadter's accommodative activities, secondary control involves bringing oneself in line with the environment. It typically involves cognitive activities directed at the self. For example, if you lost your job and thus your income, primary control strategies would include searching actively for another job (changing the environment so you once again have a steady income). Secondary control could involve asserting that you really did not enjoy that particular job.

An important part of this theoretical perspective is that primary control has functional primacy over secondary control. In other words, primary control allows people to shape their environment to fit their goals and developmental potential. Thus, primary control has more adaptive value. The major function of secondary control is to minimize losses or expand levels of primary control.

Heckhausen and Schulz (1995, 1999) believe that this has important implications for aging. In childhood they find that much of development is directed at expanding the child's primary control potential. However, they predict that there will be stability in primary control striving through most of one's adult life. However, as we enter old age, maintaining primary control increasingly depends on secondary control processes because threats to primary control increase as a function of biological decline that occurs as we grow older. Thus, secondary control increases with age. Research shows that secondary control does indeed increase with age (Grob et al., 1999; Heckhausen & Schulz, 1995).

However, the notion of increases in accommodative strategies (Brändtstadter, 1999) and secondary strategies (Heckhausen & Schulz, 1995, 1999) is not without its criticisms. For example, Carstensen and Freund (1994) question whether losses people experience, though real, actually threaten the self. Additionally, these authors argue that age-related changes in goals could also be the result of natural movement through the life cycle, not simply coping with blocked goals.

In addition, from a sociocultural perspective (e.g., cross-cultural research), much criticism points to a bias toward Western cultures in the development of theories such as primary and secondary control and, in particular, the primacy of primary control over secondary control. In a fascinating rebuke of the Heckhausen and Schulz theory, Gould (1999) suggests that in collectivist societies such as those found in Asia, the emphasis is not on individualistic strategies such as those found in primary control. Instead, the goal is to establish interdependence with others, to be connected to them and bound to a larger social institution. He cites studies that show that throughout adulthood, Asian cultures exceed Western cultures in levels of secondary control and emotion-focused coping (Gould, 1999; Seginer et al., 1993).

Thus, one's sense of personal control is a complex, multidimensional aspect of personality. Consequently, general normative age-related trends might not be found. Rather, changes in personal control may depend on one's experiences in different domains and the culture one grows up in and may differ widely from one domain to another.

CONCEPT CHECKS

1. What is locus of control?
2. What control strategies are related to preserving a positive perspective?

SOCIAL SITUATIONS AND SOCIAL COMPETENCE

LEARNING OBJECTIVES

- What is the social facilitation of cognitive functioning?
- What is collaborative cognition, and does it facilitate memory in older adults?
- How does the social context influence memory performance in older adults?

Christie and Frank's granddaughter asked them what happened when they first met. Christie recalled that they met at a social gathering for World War II soldiers, but she couldn't remember the name of the person who introduced them. She could only describe him as tall and dark-haired. However, this cued Frank; he remembered that his name was George. This back-and-forth remembering continued until, to their amazement, they had successfully reconstructed the whole gathering. Their granddaughter was delighted and complimented them on what good memories they had.

When we typically think about the memories of older adults, we don't usually think of these kinds of successes. However, there is a growing interest in how the social context can compensate memory loss and facilitate memory performance. In this section we examine two approaches to this issue: collaborative cognition and facilitative social contexts.

The social cognition perspective offers us an enriched understanding of social competence in older adulthood. We are interested in how changes in social cognitive functioning reflect the changing life context and affect adaptation to these changing contexts. In the previous sections we have focused primarily on how developmental changes in representations of self or other (such as social beliefs and self-beliefs) influence social cognitive processes such as making attributional judgments. In this section we focus on social cognition as it relates to the dynamic interplay between self, others, and context. For example, a less researched but extremely important domain of social cognition and aging is how the particular types of social settings in which we communicate with others influences our cognitive processing. This relates to a different aspect of social cognition and aging research: the social facilitation of cognitive functioning.

Collaborative Cognition

There has been a recent focus in the social cognition and aging literature on examining cognition in social contexts or studying how cognition works when we are interacting with others. This can be seen in work on the benefits and costs of collaborative cognition on cognitive performance (e.g., memory, problem

Older adults tend to use compensatory strategies for failing memories by jointly remembering events.

solving) conducted by Dixon (1999) and colleagues as well as Staudinger and Baltes (Baltes & Staudinger, 1996). These researchers argue that collaborative cognition is one aspect of social competence. **Collaborative cognition** *occurs when two or more people work together to solve a cognitive task* (Dixon, 1999).

Staudinger and Baltes (1996) demonstrated the influence of an interactive, social context on the promotion of wisdom-related behavior (see Chapter 8). They found that wisdom-related potential could be activated when the performance setting involved the discussion of a wisdom task with a natural partner (such as a husband or wife). In addition, they found that one could engage in "virtual dialogues" with an imagined natural partner to promote wisdom-related performance. Strategy enhancement was underscored in an interactive setting when researchers examined coping with everyday problems (Berg et al., 1998).

In Dixon's work, collaborative cognition may serve an important adaptive function in older adults' cognitive performance. Given the age-old saying that "two heads are better than one," the interest here is in whether this type of collaborative context could mitigate deficits in memory that we typically see when assessing older adults in the laboratory (see Chapter 7). Dixon and colleagues (Dixon, 1999; Dixon & Gould, 1998) found that older adults can collaborate on story

recall as well as problem-solving performance, and their performance is better than the average performance of older adults in individual settings. In other words, cognitive performance improves in a collaborative context.

However, there is another way to look at the benefits of collaborative cognition. How do groups accomplish what they want to accomplish? What processes do older adults use to effectively remember an event, as Christie and Frank did? By examining the Forces in Action feature, we can see how people of different ages divide up the cognitive work when they cooperate on a task. Overall, findings indicate that well-acquainted older couples develop an adaptive pattern of recalling information, which includes both social support issues and strategic efforts.

Social Context and Memory

Another approach to identifying conditions under which social facilitation of cognition in older adults occurs is in examining contextual variables that influence memory performance. For example, Adams and colleagues (in press) argue that memory performance is influenced when the task approximates a real-world learning and social memory experience. In this case, what happens to memory performance when the assessment situation approximates the kinds of memory demands that naturally occur in a real-life situation?

For example, a typical and relevant cognitive task for older adults is to transmit sociocultural information to younger generations (Adams et al., 1994; Chinen, 1989). In this context, the older adult would be motivated to communicate effectively. A storytelling situation is a good example. This kind of context is very different from the traditional laboratory context, in which the demand is to reproduce as much of the content of a text as possible. Adams and colleagues (1994) found that when they placed older adults in a storytelling situation in which they were asked to learn and retell a story from memory to a young child, their retellings of the story contained more detail and were more fluent than those of young adults. Perhaps their motivation was greater in

It is suggested that when older adults collaborate with someone to recall an event or a movie or how to get from one place to another, it compensates for declines in performance you would observe if they tried to do it alone. If this is so, then this should be even more evident in marriage partners. Thus, although biological factors of aging result in memory decline, psychological and social forces hold a key that could ameliorate these negative outcomes.

In fact, at a psychological level, when older adults work with their spouses to remember something, they use a cognitive style together that minimizes working memory demands. In fact Dixon and Gould

(1998) found that older married couples performed just as well as younger couples on a recall task. It is rare that you find older adults equal to younger adults' cognitive performance.

However, at the social level, interesting effects of marriage in the collaborative context are found when we examine how memory tasks are shared. In a story retelling study, older married couples produced more statements resulting from a shared discussion (Gould et al., 1994). Unacquainted pairs produced more sociability or support statements. Sociability statements were about agreeing with the partner's recall or comparing the story with events in

their own lives. Thus, older married couples know each other well and get right down to business. Older unacquainted couples are more concerned with being sociable to the other member of the dyad. Older married couples were experienced enough with one another to bypass the sociability concern and concentrate on better strategies to improve their performance.

In sum, by looking at the interaction between the biological, psychological, and social level of functioning in a collaborative memory context, we get a more complete picture of how memory operates in an everyday social environment.

---

a social context where their concerns were directed at producing an interesting and coherent account of the story for the child. This is a demonstration of how the social communicative context or experience can enhance what is most salient to the person. It illustrates the importance of considering the social context of a task situation when examining change in cognitive functioning as we grow older.

The research on collaborative cognition and social context effects further highlights the importance of considering social factors in explaining social cognitive functioning. Such factors as the social context in which we communicate influence social information processing in important ways. Thus, it is important not to limit our explanations of social cognitive change to cognitive processing variables even though they can be seasoned with a social flavor. Important social factors influence how and when a person will attend to specific information and when this information will influence social cognitive functioning. These factors include those we have discussed earlier:

motivational goals, cognitive style, attitudes, and values, among others. We can be very optimistic about the future promise of research on aging and social cognition in identifying and probing important social components of information processing.

CONCEPT CHECKS

1. What is collaborative cognition?
2. What is a social communicative context?

PUTTING IT ALL TOGETHER

As humans, we are constantly trying to make sense out of others' behavior. As we grow older, our extensive experience in the social world changes these types of perceptions. Maria and Emanuel show how we can correct our initial assessments of others if we take the time to reflect on the extenuating circumstances. Alison shows how we can rely on our experience as older adults to guide us through uncomfortable situations. And Katie shows how a reduction in our capacity can prevent us from considering all relevant information to make an accurate judgment about another person's behavior. Renee and Scott's need to focus on emotional issues in a problem-solving situation and the children's need to analyze the situation further resulted in very different problem-solving strategies. Taken together, these people demonstrate the many factors that influence the way we make social judgments about others and events. Finally, Daniel's assessment that his poor performance was a problem inherent in the exam and Christie and Frank's reliance on each other to remember a past event show how our social cognitive processes serve adaptive functions.

Summary

BASIC COGNITIVE ABILITIES AND SOCIAL COGNITION

Processing Capacity

Since older adults typically display lower levels of cognitive processing resources, it is possible that this decline in resource capacity might impact this type of social judgment process. Age-related changes in processing capacity influences make older adults more vulnerable to social judgment biases.

Stages of processing suggest that we make initial snap judgments and later correct or adjust them based on more reflective thinking.

Older adults tend to make more snap judgments because of their processing resource limitations.

Impression Formation

When forming an initial impression, older adults rely heavily on preexisting social structures. They also use less detailed information in forming impressions than young adults do. This may be because they have deficiencies in working memory capacity.

Older adults weigh negative information more heavily in their social judgments than young adults do. This may be related to age differences in social experience and knowledge.

Knowledge Accessibility

Social knowledge structures must be available to guide behavior. In addition, social information must also be easily accessible to guide behavior. It is important to distinguish between the two because accessibility depends on the strength of the information available in memory. Thus, although older adults have social knowledge available to them, the question is how easily they can access this knowledge.

How a situation is framed influences what types of social knowledge a person will access. Older adults are more susceptible to this type of an effect, possibly because they cannot access the information.

SOCIAL KNOWLEDGE STRUCTURES AND SOCIAL BELIEFS

Stereotypes

The content of stereotypes varies by the age of the individual. Whereas younger adults primarily adhere to negative stereotypes of aging, older adults include more positive stereotypes along with negative ones.

An age-based double standard operates when people judge older adults' failures in memory. In this case, younger adults judge older adults who are forgetful more harshly than older adults do.

Although young adults rate older adults more harshly about the seriousness of their memory failures, they also make positive judgments about them as being more responsible despite such failures.

Automatically activated negative stereotypes about aging guide behavior beyond our awareness. If a negative stereotype is activated in an older adult, it can negatively influence performance of ability tasks. This could partially account for why older adults perform more poorly than younger adults on cognitive tasks.

Implicit stereotyping influences the way we patronize older adults in our communications. Young and middle-aged adults have the tendency to engage in elder speak when addressing an older person. This can have negative side effects on the older adults' well being and cognitive performance.

Implicit Social Beliefs

To understand age differences in social beliefs, we must first examine content differences. For example, what are the differences in social beliefs and values advocated by different generations? Age differences in social beliefs can be attributed to generational differences and life stage differences.

Second, we must assess the strength of the beliefs. Even though an individual may hold a particular belief, the degree to which it will drive behavior depends on how strong the belief is.

Third, we need to know how likely beliefs are to affect behavior. Given that an individual holds a particular belief and it is a strongly held belief, this increases the likelihood that social judgements will be harsh on individuals who violate those beliefs.

CAUSAL ATTRIBUTIONS

When confronted with negative relationship situations, older adults tend to display a dispositional bias. In other words, they tend to blame the primary character more for causing the negative outcome and do not consider other extenuating and external circumstances.

Paradoxically, older adults also display more interactive attributions in negative relationship situations. In other words, they are more likely to consider both situational and dispositional characteristics of the situation in making their social judgments.

The dispositional bias or the tendency to blame the primary characters in negative relationship situations on the part of older adults can be attributed to both processing resource limitations and differences in social knowledge that influence their attributional judgments. If the primary character violates a strongly held value

or belief held by the rater, she or he will be more likely to blame the character for the negative outcome.

MOTIVATION AND SOCIAL PROCESSING GOALS

Emotion as a Processing Goal

Older adults regard emotional information as more important and salient than young adults do. They are more likely to pay attention to emotional information and hold emotion-related goals when processing information.

Cognitive Style as a Processing Goal

The need for closure is a need for a quick and decisive answer with little tolerance for ambiguity. Older adults' social judgment biases are predicted by the degree to which they need quick and decisive closure. This is not so for younger age groups.

PERSONAL CONTROL

Personal control is the degree to which one believes that performance depends on something one does. Age differences in the degree of personal control depend on the domain being studied. Some evidence suggests that people develop several personal control strategies to protect a positive self-image.

Locus of Control

There is conflicting evidence as to whether older adults are more internal or external in the perceived control over different aspects of life. When examining an overall sense of control, evidence suggests that older adults are more external (i.e., see their aging process as out of their control).

Multidimensionality of Personal Control

Older adults perceive less control over specific domains of functioning such as intellectual changes with aging.

Older adults perceived less control over social issues and personal appearance.

Control Strategies

Assimilative strategies are used when one must prevent losses important to self-esteem. In this case, people use aids and assistance more if performing a particular task is an important aspect of self-esteem and identity.

Accommodative strategies involve readjusting one's goals and aspirations. This involves lowering one's target goals when faced with the loss or diminution of the capacity to perform certain behaviors.

Immunizing mechanisms alter the effects of self-discrepant information. When a person is confronted with evidence of a decline in memory performance, she or he might look for alternative explanations or simply deny the evidence.

Primary control helps change the environment to match one's goals. It involves bringing the environment into line with one's desires and goals. Action is directed toward changing the external world.

Secondary control reappraises the environment in light of one's decline in functioning. Thus, the individual turns inward toward the self and assesses the situation. Secondary control could involve appraising the situation in terms of enjoyment of the situation. Primary control is said to have functional primacy over secondary control. Therefore, primary control would be a more adaptive value to the individual, whereas secondary control simply minimizes losses or expands levels of primary control.

Cross-cultural perspectives challenge the notion of primacy of primary control. In collectivist societies, the emphasis is not on individualistic strategies such as those found in primary control, but to establish interdependence with others, to be connected to them, and bound to a larger social institution.

Social Situations and Social Competence

Collaborative Cognition

Collaborating with others in recollection helps facilitate memory in older adults. Findings indicate that well-acquainted older couples demonstrate an expertise to develop an adaptive pattern of recalling information, which includes both social support issues and strategic efforts.

Social Context and Memory

The social context can serve a facilitative function in older adults' memory performance. The social context in which we communicate, among others, influence social information processing in important ways. Thus, it is important not to limit our explanations of social cognitive change simply to cognitive processing variables.

Review Questions

BASIC COGNITIVE ABILITIES AND SOCIAL COGNITION

- How does processing capacity affect social cognitive processing?
- What are stages in attributional processing?
- What is the negativity bias, and what are age differences in its impact?
- Describe age differences in the extent to which trait information is used in forming an impression.
- What influences the accessibility of social information?
- What are framing effects?
- What is the status of processing resource limitations as an explanation for social judgment biases?

SOCIAL KNOWLEDGE STRUCTURES AND SOCIAL BELIEFS

- What are stereotypes?
- How is the content of stereotypes similar across age groups?
- How does the content of stereotypes differ across age groups?
- What is the age-based double standard of perceived competence in young and older adults?
- What do older and young adults perceive as the cause of memory failure in older adults?
- How does perceived competence influence the way tasks are assigned to older and younger targets?
- What other factors besides competence are taken into consideration when people judge older adults' future performance?

- Under what conditions are stereotypes activated?
- How do negative stereotypes of aging influence young adults' behavior?
- What evidence supports the notion that stereotypes can be automatically activated out of conscious awareness?
- What is implicit stereotyping?
- What three important factors must be considered to understand implicit social beliefs?
- Describe evidence for age differences in the content of social beliefs.

Causal Attributions

What are causal attributions?

What is a correspondence bias?

Are there age differences in the correspondence bias? If so, under what conditions?

What accounts for the age differences in the correspondence bias?

Motivation and Social Processing Goals

To what extent are there age differences in emotion as a processing goal in social cognitive functioning?

What is need for closure?

How does need for closure influence the processing of social information?

Are there age differences in the degree to which need for closure influences social information processing?

Personal Control

What evidence is there on age differences in personal control beliefs?

In what domains do older adults exhibit low levels of perceived control and in what domains do they exhibit high levels of perceived control?

How are assimilative and accommodative strategies adaptive in older adults' functioning?

Why is primary control viewed as having more functional primacy than secondary control?

What cross-cultural evidence challenges the notion of primary control as functionally more important?

Social Situations and Social Competence

What is collaborative cognition?

What evidence suggests that collaborative cognition compensates for memory failures in older adults?

How does collaborative cognition facilitate wisdom-related behavior?

How do marital relationships influence collaborative cognition?

How does a storytelling context influence age differences in memory of stories?

What does it mean to say that the social context facilitates cognitive performance?

Integrating Concepts in Development

1. To what degree are the declines in processing resource capacity discussed in Chapters 6 and 7 ubiquitous in their effects on social cognitive processes?

2. What relations can be found between dispositional traits, personal concerns, and life narratives?

3. How does emotion as a processing goal relate to socioemotional selectivity theory?

4. How does social cognition relate to postformal thought?

5. How does personal control relate to concepts such as memory self-efficacy?

Key Terms

age-based double standard Attributing an older person's failure in memory as more serious than a memory failure observed in a young adult.

causal attributions Explanations people construct to explain their behavior, which can be situational, dispositional, or interactive.

cognitive style A pattern of behavior one uses when solving a problem.

collaborative cognition Cognitive performance that results from the interaction of two or more people.

control strategies Behavior patterns used to obtain a sense of control over how an outcome or desired goal will be achieved.

correspondence bias Relying more on dispositional information in explaining behavior and ignoring compelling situational information such as extenuating circumstances.

dispositional attribution An explanation for someone's behavior that resides within the actor.

framing effect The influence of information just processed on subsequent social judgments.

implicit stereotyping Stereotype beliefs that affect one's judgments of others without one's knowledge.

impression formation The way in which people combine the components of another person's personality and come up with an integrated perception of the person.

negativity bias Bias that occurs when negative information is weighed more heavily in a social judgment than positive information.

patronizing talk Superficial conversation, slow speech, simple vocabulary, careful enunciation, and a demeaning emotional tone.

personal control The belief that what one does influences the outcome of an event.

processing capacity The degree to which processing resources are available to a person during a cognitive task.

situational attribution An explanation for someone's behavior that is external to the actor.

social knowledge A cognitive structure that represents one's general knowledge about a given social concept or domain.

stereotype threat An evoked fear of being judged in accordance with a negative stereotype about a group to which one belongs.

stereotypes Beliefs about characteristics, attributes, and behaviors of members of certain groups.

Resources

READINGS

Baltes, P. B., & Staudinger, U. (1996). *Interactive minds.* Cambridge, England: Cambridge University Press. A collection of chapters focusing on the area of collaborative cognition. Moderate to difficult reading.

Fiske, S., & Taylor, S. (1991). *Social cognition.* New York: McGraw-Hill. A comprehensive book covering all aspects of social cognition research. Easy to moderate reading.

Hess, T. M., & Blanchard-Fields, F. (1999). *Social cognition and aging.* San Diego: Academic Press. An excellent collection of chapters covering all aspects of social cognition covered in this chapter. Moderate to difficult level of reading.

SEARCH ONLINE WITH
INFOTRAC COLLEGE EDITION

For more information on the topics in this chapter, explore InfoTrac College Edition, your online library. Go to http://www.infotrac-college.com/wadsworth and use the passcode that came on the card with your book. Try these search terms: social cognition, person perception, stereotyping.

PERSONALITY

© AP / Wide World Photo

Maya Angelou maintains that "There is no agony like bearing an untold story inside of you." True to her conviction, she has spent a lifetime writing her story in numerous books, poems, and other literary works. She describes an incredible developmental path of oppression, hatred, and hurt that she ultimately transformed into self-awareness, understanding, and compassion. For example, in her later years she realized that in confronting the atrocities of the world, if she accepts the fact of evil, she must accept the fact of good, easing her fear of death. Another example involves integrating spirituality into her self-perception. When asked how spirituality fits into a way of life, she answered, "There is something more, the spirit, or the soul. I think that that quality encourages our courtesy, and care, and our minds. And mercy, and identity."

Maya Angelou's writings reflect some of the key issues involved in personality development that we examine in this chapter. First, we consider whether personality changes or remains stable across adulthood. We examine this from a trait perspective as well as personal concerns that change across the life cycle. This leads us to the study of people's life narratives and changes in identity and self.

One of the oldest debates in psychology concerns whether personality development continues across the life span. From the earliest days, prominent people argued both sides. William James and Sigmund Freud, for example, believed that personality was set before adulthood. Indeed, Freud thought that development was essentially complete in childhood. On the other hand, Carl Jung asserted that personality was shaped throughout our lives. Aspects of personality come and go as people's experiences and life issues change.

A century of research has done little to clarify the issue. We still have two main theoretical camps, one arguing for stability and the other for change. There is far less agreement on the developmental course of personality than for any other topic in adult development and aging. Hypotheses and concepts abound. Data are contradictory, and results often depend on which specific measures researchers use.

Why should the area of personality be so controversial? The answer lies in the paradoxical beliefs we hold about personality. At one level we all believe that people have complex personalities that remain constant over time. A person with a stable personality is easier to deal with in different situations; when a person behaves in ways that violate our expectations, we are surprised. Imagine the chaos that would result if every week or so everyone woke up with a brand new personality: The once easygoing husband is now a tyrant, trusted friends are now completely unpredictable, and our patterns of social interaction are in shambles. Clearly, we must rely on consistency of personality to survive in day-to-day life.

Still, we like to believe that we can change undesirable aspects of our personalities. Imagine what it would be like, for example, if we could never overcome shyness; if anxiety were a lifelong, incurable curse; or if our idiosyncratic tendencies that cause others to tear their hair out could not be eliminated. Our assumption of the modifiability of personality is very strong indeed. The field of psychotherapy is a formal verification of that.

Levels of Analysis and Personality Research

The debate over the degree to which personality in adulthood remains stable or changes has generated numerous studies and theoretical perspectives. Sorting out the various approaches helps us understand what aspects of personality the various researchers are describing. Drawing on the work of several theorists and researchers, McAdams (1994) describes three parallel levels of personality structure and function. Each level contains a wide range of personality constructs. McAdams refers to the levels with generic names: dispositional traits, personal concerns, and life narrative.

Dispositional traits *are aspects of personality that are consistent across different contexts and can be compared across a group along a continuum.* This is the level of personality most people think of first, and it includes commonly used descriptors such as *shy, talkative,* and *authoritarian.* **Personal concerns** *consist of things that are important to people, their goals, and their major concerns in life.* Personal concerns usually are described in motivational, developmental, or strategic terms; they reflect the stage of life a person is in at the time. **Life narrative** *consists of the aspects of personality that pull everything together, the integrative aspects that give a person an identity or sense of self.* The creation of an identity is the goal of this level.

McAdams (1994) points out that as one moves from dispositional traits to personal concerns to life narrative, the more likely it is that change will be observed. In a sense, the level of dispositional traits can be viewed as the raw ingredients of personality, whereas each successive level is constructed to a greater extent. In the following sections, we use McAdams's levels to organize our discussion of personality in adulthood. Let's begin with the raw ingredients and see how dispositional traits are structured in adulthood.

DISPOSITIONAL TRAITS ACROSS ADULTHOOD

LEARNING OBJECTIVES

- What is the five-factor model of dispositional traits?
- What evidence is there for long-term stability in dispositional traits?
- What criticisms have been leveled at the five-factor model?
- What can we conclude from theory and research on dispositional traits?

*J*oyce was attending her high school reunion. She hadn't seen her friend Michelle in 20 years. In high school Joyce remembered that Michelle was always surrounded by a group of people. She always walked up to people and initiated conversations, was at ease with strangers, was pleasant, and was often described as the life of the party. Joyce wondered whether Michelle would be the same outgoing person she was in high school.

Most of us will eventually attend a high school reunion. It can be amusing to see how our classmates have changed over the years. In addition to noticing gray or missing hair and a few wrinkles, we should pay attention to personality characteristics. The questions that arose for Joyce are similar to the ones we generate ourselves. For example, will Jackie be the same outgoing person she was as captain of the debate team? Will Shawn still be as concerned about social issues at 48 as he was at 18? To learn as much about our friends as possible, we could make careful observations of our classmates' personalities over the course of several reunions. Then, at the gathering marking 60 years since graduation, we could examine the trends we observed. Did our classmates' personalities change substantially? Or did they remain essentially the same as they were 60 years earlier?

How we think these questions will be answered provides clues to our biases about personality stability or change across adulthood. As we will see, biases about continuity and discontinuity are more obvious in personality research than in any other area of adult development.

In addition to considering the age-old debate of whether Michelle's personality characteristics will remain stable or change, Joyce's description of Michelle suggests that she is an outgoing, or extroverted, person. How did she arrive at this judgment? She probably combined several aspects of Michelle's behavior into a concept that describes her concisely. What we have done is to use the notion of a personality trait. Extending this same reasoning to many areas of behavior is the basis for trait theories of personality. More formally, people's characteristic behaviors can be understood through attributes that reflect underlying dispositional traits, which are enduring aspects of personality. We use the basic tenets of trait theory when we describe ourselves and others with such terms as *calm, aggressive, independent,* and *friendly.*

Three assumptions are made about traits (Costa & McCrae, 1998). First, traits are based on comparisons of people because there are no absolute quantitative standards for concepts such as friendliness. Second, the qualities or behaviors making up a particular trait must be distinctive enough to avoid confusion. Imagine the chaos that would result if friendliness and aggressiveness had many behaviors in common. Finally, the traits attributed to a specific person are assumed to be stable characteristics. We normally assume that people who are friendly in several situations are going to be friendly the next time we see them. These three assumptions are all captured in the definition of a trait: A trait is any distinguishable, enduring way in which one person differs from others (Guilford, 1959, p. 6). Based on this definition, trait theories assume that little change in personality occurs across adulthood. The primary interest here is when trait stability peaks and when traits stop changing.

Most trait theories have several guiding principles in common. An important one for our present discussion concerns the structure of traits. Structure is the way in which traits are organized within a person. This organization usually is inferred from the pattern of related and unrelated traits and is generally expressed in terms of dimensions. Personality structures can be examined over time to see whether they change with age.

The Case for Stability: The Five-Factor Model

Although many different trait theories of personality have been proposed over the years, few have been concerned with or have been based on adults of different ages. A major exception to this is the five-factor model proposed by Costa and McCrae (1994; McCrae & Costa, 1990). Their model is strongly grounded in cross-sectional, longitudinal, and sequential research. *The* **five-factor** model *consists of five independent dimensions of personality: neuroticism, extroversion, openness to experience, agreeableness, and conscientiousness.*

The first three dimensions of Costa and McCrae's model—neuroticism, extroversion, and openness to experience—have been the most heavily researched. Each of these dimensions is represented by six facets that reflect the main characteristics associated with it. The remaining two dimensions were added to the original three in the late 1980s to account for more data and to bring the theory closer to other trait theories. In the following sections we consider each of the five dimensions briefly.

NEUROTICISM. The six facets of neuroticism are anxiety, hostility, self-consciousness, depression, impulsiveness, and vulnerability. Anxiety and hostility form underlying traits for two fundamental emotions: fear and anger. Although we all experience these emotions at times, the frequency and intensity with which they are felt vary from one person to another. People who are high in trait anxiety are nervous, high-strung, tense, worried, and pessimistic. Besides being prone to anger, hostile people are irritable and tend to be hard to get along with.

The traits of self-consciousness and depression relate to the emotions shame and sorrow. Being high in self-consciousness is associated with being sensitive to criticism and teasing and to feelings of inferiority. Trait depression refers to feelings of sadness, hopelessness, loneliness, guilt, and low self-worth.

The final two facets of neuroticism—impulsiveness and vulnerability—are most often manifested as behaviors rather than emotions. Impulsiveness is the tendency to give in to temptation and desires because of a lack of willpower and self-control. Consequently, impulsive people often do things in excess, such as overeating and overspending, and they are more likely to smoke, gamble, and use drugs. Vulnerability is a lowered ability to deal effectively with stress. Vulnerable people tend to panic in a crisis or emergency and to be highly dependent on others for help.

Costa and McCrae (1998) note that, in general, people who are high in neuroticism tend to be high in each of the traits. High neuroticism typically results in violent and negative emotions that interfere with people's ability to handle problems or get along with other people. We can see how this cluster of traits would operate. A person gets anxious and embarrassed in a social situation such as a class reunion, and the frustration in dealing with others makes the person hostile, which may lead to excessive drinking at the party, which may result in subsequent depression for making a fool of oneself, and so on.

EXTROVERSION. The six facets of extroversion can be grouped into three interpersonal traits (warmth, gregariousness, and assertiveness) and three temperamental traits (activity, excitement-seeking, and positive emotions). Warmth, or attachment, is a friendly, compassionate, intimately involved style of interacting with other people. Warmth and gregariousness (a desire to be with other people) make up what is sometimes called sociability. Gregarious people thrive on crowds; the more social interaction, the better. Assertive people make natural leaders, take charge easily, make up their own minds, and readily express their thoughts and feelings.

Temperamentally, extroverts like to keep busy; they are the people who seem to have endless energy, talk fast, and want to be on the go. They prefer to be in stimulating, exciting environments and often go searching for challenging situations. This active, exciting lifestyle is evident in the extrovert's positive emotion; these people are walking examples of zest, delight, and fun.

An interesting aspect of extroversion is that this dimension relates well to occupational interests and values. People high in extroversion tend to have people-oriented jobs, such as social work, business administration, and sales. They value humanitarian goals and a person-oriented use of power. People low in extroversion tend to prefer task-oriented jobs, such as architecture or accounting.

OPENNESS TO EXPERIENCE. The six facets of openness to experience represent six different areas. In the area of fantasy, openness includes having a vivid imagination and active dream life. In aesthetics, openness is seen in the appreciation of art and beauty, sensitivity to pure experience for its own sake. Openness to action is a willingness to try something new, whether it is a new kind of cuisine, a new movie, or a new travel destination. People who are open to ideas and values are curious and value knowledge for the sake of knowing. Open people also tend to be open-minded in their values, often admitting that what may be right for one person may not be right for everyone. This outlook is a direct outgrowth of open people's willingness to think of different possibilities and their tendency to empathize with others in different circumstances. Open people also experience their own feelings strongly and see them as a major source of meaning in life.

Not surprisingly, openness to experience is also related to occupational choice. Open people are likely to be found in occupations that place a high value on thinking theoretically or philosophically and less emphasis on economic values. They are typically intelligent and tend to subject themselves to stressful situations. Occupations such as psychologist or minister, for example, appeal to open people.

AGREEABLENESS. The easiest way to understand the agreeableness dimension is to consider the traits that characterize antagonism. Antagonistic people tend to set themselves against others; they are skeptical, mistrustful, callous, unsympathetic, stubborn, and rude; and they have a defective sense of attachment. Antagonism may be manifested in ways other than overt hostility. For example, some antagonistic people are skillful manipulators or aggressive go-getters with little patience.

Scoring high on agreeableness, the opposite of antagonism, may not always be adaptive either, however. These people may tend to be overly dependent and self-effacing, traits that often prove annoying to others.

CONSCIENTIOUSNESS. Scoring high on conscientiousness indicates that one is hard working, ambitious, energetic, scrupulous, and persevering. Such people have a strong desire to make something of themselves. People at the opposite end of this scale tend to be negligent, lazy, disorganized, late, aimless, and nonpersistent.

WHAT IS THE EVIDENCE FOR TRAIT STABILITY?. Costa and McCrae have investigated whether the traits that make up their model remain stable across adulthood (Costa & McCrae, 1988, 1997; McCrae & Costa, 1994). In fact, they suggest that personality traits stop changing by age 30 and appear to be "set in plaster" (McCrae & Costa, 1994, p. 21). The data from the Costa, McCrae, and colleagues' studies came from the Baltimore Longitudinal Study of Aging for the 114 men who took the Guilford–Zimmerman Temperament Survey (GZTS) on three occasions, with each of the two follow-up testings about 6 years apart.

What Costa and colleagues found was surprising. Even over a 12-year period, the 10 traits measured by the GZTS remained highly stable; the correlations ranged from .68 to .85. In much of personality research we might expect to find this degree of stability over a week or two, but to see it over 12 years is noteworthy.

We would normally be skeptical of such consistency over a long period. But similar findings were obtained in other studies conducted over a 8-year span by Siegler and colleagues (1979) at Duke University, a 30-year span by Leon and colleagues (1979) in Minnesota, and in other longitudinal studies (Schaie & Willis, 1995; Schmitz-Scherzer & Thomae, 1983). Even more amazing was the finding that personality ratings by spouses of each other showed no systematic changes over a 6-year period (Costa & McCrae, 1988). Thus, it appears that people change very little in self-reported personality traits over periods of up to 30 years and over the age range of 20 to 90 years.

This is a truly exciting and important conclusion. Clearly, lots of things change in people's lives over 30 years. They marry, divorce, have children, change jobs, face stressful situations, move, and maybe even retire. Social networks and friendships come and go. Society changes, and economic ups and downs have important effects. Personal changes in appearance and health occur. People read volumes, see dozens of movies, and watch thousands of hours of television. But their underlying personality dispositions hardly change at all. Or do they?

Critiques of the Five-Factor Model

Despite the impressive collection of research findings based on it, the five-factor model has its share of critics. First, data indicate that certain personality traits (self-confidence, cognitive commitment, outgoingness, and dependability) show some change over a 30- to 40-year period (Jones & Meredith, 1996). Second, Alwin (1994) points out that the evidence for stability reported by Costa and McCrae could result from several different statistical functions other than an essentially flat line across adulthood that would allow change in parts of the life span not studied by trait researchers. Third, in a major review of the literature, Block (1995) raises several concerns with Costa and McCrae's approach. Most of Block's criticisms are based on perceived methodological problems, such as the way the dimensions were identified statistically and the way the questionnaire assessment was developed and used. This critique is based on the view that the statistical and empirical grounds on which the five-factor model is built are shaky. For example, Block argues that using laypeople to specify personality descriptors, the approach used to create the terms used in the five-factor model, is fraught with risk, chiefly because of the lack of compelling scientific data to support such labeling. Thus, Block argues that the wide acceptance of the five-factor model is premature and that much more research is needed. Block argues in favor of personality research that takes into consideration the sociocultural context in which personality development occurs and the variability across the life course (Labouvie-Vief & Diehl, 1999).

McAdams (1992, 1995) raises additional limitations of the five-factor model. First, he points out that any model of dispositional traits says nothing about the core or essential aspects of human nature. In contrast, theorists we consider later, such as Erikson and Loevinger, discuss such core aspects, which cannot be translated into the language of dispositional traits. Second, dispositional traits rarely provide enough information about people so that accurate predictions can be made about how they will behave in a particular situation. Third, the assessment of dispositional traits generally fails to provide

compelling explanations of why people behave the way they do. Fourth, dispositional traits are seen as independent of the context in which the person operates. In other words, the five-factor model approach ignores the sociocultural context of human development. Fifth, the assessment of dispositional traits reduces a person to a set of scores on a series of linear continua anchored by terms that are assumed to be both meaningful and opposite. Sixth, the assessment of dispositional traits through questionnaires assumes that the respondent is able to take an objective, evaluative stance about his or her personal characteristics. McAdams's criticisms nevertheless reflect the view that assessing dispositional traits has its place in personality research; his point is simply that dispositional traits should not be viewed as reflecting one's entire personality.

As we might expect, the critiques themselves are controversial. For example, Costa and McCrae (1995, 1998) and Goldberg and Saucier (1995) point to flaws in Block's argument, such as his overlooking of research favorable to the five-factor model. Arguments about the place for assessing dispositional traits within the study of personality reflect the biases of the authors. The controversy surrounding Costa and McCrae's basic claim that dispositional traits typically remain stable in adulthood will continue, and it is likely to result in more and better research.

In fact, one of the most recent and exciting approaches to this controversy is to take an intraindividual perspective (Mroczek & Spiro, in press). Mroczek and colleagues challenge the conclusions drawn from the typical longitudinal studies on stability and change in personality by examining personality across the adult life span at the level of the individual. We describe this challenge in more detail in the feature Current Controversies.

Additional Longitudinal Studies of Dispositional Traits

THE BERKELEY STUDIES. Researchers in Berkeley, California, conducted one of the largest longitudinal studies on personality development. In this investigation the parents of participants being studied in research on

Whether personality remains stable across the life span or whether it changes remains controversial. Because personality traits have been shown to be important predictors of mental and physical health and psychological well-being, potential changes in personality can have important implications for gains and declines in such life outcomes. However, as this chapter indicates, there is no clear-cut evidence for one position or the other. An important aspect to consider in this controversy is the level of analysis at which stability and change are assessed. Typically, stability and change are examined through mean level comparisons over time. In other words, does an age group's mean level on a particular personality trait such as extroversion remain stable from one time to another (say 10 years apart), or does it change?

Mroczek and Spiro (in press) suggest that examining change in mean levels of a personality trait does not adequately address stability and change at the level of the individual. In other words, a group mean hides the extent to which individual people change. In their recent work they examined the extent to which each person in their longitudinal study changed or remained the same over time. This allowed them to ask the questions "Do some people remain stable whereas others change?" and, if there are people who change, "Do some people change more than others?" They examined individual patterns of change for 1,366 men over a 6-year period. They assessed personality change and stability by examining each man's change pattern, called an individual growth curve. They then grouped each man into categories of no change in the personality trait, increases in the personality trait, and decreases in the personality trait. Preliminary findings indicate that over a 6-year period, a large proportion of older men remained stable with respect to extroversion, whereas a smaller but substantial proportion of men changed. In addition, among those who changed, equal numbers of men increased in extroversion and decreased. They found similar results for neuroticism. These findings indicate important individual differences in the extent to which people change.

This approach allows a more detailed answer to questions of stability and change. When we rely on the major longitudinal approaches such as McCrae and Costa's (1994), we see that at the group level there is primarily stability. However, when we examine individuals' growth curves we see a more complete picture of personality development. A large proportion of people may remain stable, but there is a substantial number of people whose personality traits increase or decrease over time. Perhaps we can resolve this debate in the future as more intraindividual studies on personality development emerge.

Search Online with
InfoTrac College Edition
For more information on these controversies, explore InfoTrac College Edition, your online library. Go to http://www.infotrac-college.com/ wadsworth and use the passcode that came on the card with your book. Try these search terms: personality traits, stability in personality, longitudinal studies of personality.

intellectual development were followed for roughly 30 years between ages 40 and 70 (Maas, 1985; Maas & Kuypers, 1974; Mussen, 1985). From the enormous amount of data gathered over the years, researchers were able to categorize men and women into sub-groups based on their lifestyles (for instance, whether mothers were employed) and personality type. Based on the longitudinal follow-up data, gender differences were identified in terms of the best predictors of life satisfaction in old age. The data suggest that lifestyle during young adulthood is the better predictor of life satisfaction in old age for women but that personality is the better predictor for men (Mussen, 1985).

Additional analyses of the Berkeley data provide other insights into personality development. For example, when examining whether stability was always the case within different time periods and time intervals over 50 years, they found that consistency in personality was found mainly for adjacent age periods (Haan et al., 1986). There was less consistency across time when personality was examined across the entire time span. For example, the transition to parenthood in young adulthood and family and work-related transitions (e.g., retirement) in later adulthood showed much more variability than stability. In this case, the sociocultural context was important in determining when we see change and when we do not.

In follow-up assessments, both stability and change characterized personality development in advanced old age (Field & Millsap, 1991). Field and Millsap found moderate stability for traits such as satisfaction, extroversion, agreeableness, and intellect but also found changes in some of these traits as the participants moved into advanced age. In this case agreeableness increased significantly into old age, and the oldest participants declined significantly in extroversion. They concluded that these results do not necessarily support rigidified personality in old age (Field & Millsap, 1991; Labouvie-Vief & Diehl, 1999).

Finally, in another study examining multiple dimensions of personality and lifestyles, Haan and colleagues (1986) found that orderly, positive progressions over time were observed for all the personality components except assertiveness and submissiveness. When Haan tried to explain these developmental patterns, however, she ran into difficulty. Accounts based on theories that examine other aspects of personality, such as those discussed later in this chapter, could not account for the results. Personality did not change in all areas simultaneously, nor was there evidence of change only during times of transitions. The observation of several gender differences, the nonlinear trends over time, and the lack of equal change in all components indicate that personality development is a complicated process. Haan and colleagues argue that changes in personality probably stem from life-cycle experiences that may force a person to change. We consider a stronger version of this view later in the chapter.

WOMEN'S PERSONALITY DEVELOPMENT DURING ADULTHOOD. Several longitudinal studies of women's personality development have adopted a process approach in which they examine the interplay between social context and personality development (Helson & Moane, 1987; Helson et al., 1995). Helson and colleagues followed the lives of women who chose a typically feminine social clock (i.e., get married, have children, etc.) and observed how they adapted to the roles of wife and mother. This adaptation process typically was accompanied by a withdrawal from social life, the suppression of impulse and spontaneity, a negative self-image, and decreased feelings of competence. Twenty percent of the women who adhered to the social clock were divorced between ages 28 and 35. However, of these women, those who also had careers by the age of 28 were less respectful of norms and more rebellious toward what they experienced. Note that these women were not lower on femininity or on well-being; they were simply more independent and self assertive than those who followed the social clock (Helson & Moane, 1987). Follow-ups showed that these independent women remained so and showed greater confidence, initiative, and forcefulness than women who did not. Overall Helson and her colleagues showed that women's personality change was systematic in early and middle adulthood, yet changes were evident in the context of specific changes in social roles and transitions in social contexts (Labouvie-Vief & Diehl, 1999; Van Manen & Whitbourne, 1997).

Conclusions about Dispositional Traits

What can we conclude from the research on the development of personality traits across adulthood? From both conceptual and empirical perspectives it seems that the idea that personality traits stop changing at age 30 does not have uniform support. On one hand, we have a definition of traits that requires stability. Costa and McCrae, among others, argue strongly for this position; they report that there is little evidence (and perhaps possibility) of change. On the other hand, the Berkeley group and Helson and colleagues argue for both change and stability. They say that at least some traits change, opening the door to personality development in adulthood. One partial resolution can be found if we consider how the research was done. Clearly, the overwhelming evidence supports the view that personality traits remain stable throughout adulthood when data are averaged across many different kinds of people. However, if we ask about specific aspects of personality in very specific kinds of people, we are more likely to find some evidence of both change and stability.

The recent critiques of the five-factor model have created a climate in which more careful scrutiny of research on dispositional traits is likely to occur. More sophisticated statistical techniques are now being applied, as we saw in the Current Controversies feature, which should help address many of the criticisms.

In addition, the idea that trait stability may not be fixed at age 30 invites the question of whether periods beyond age 30 may be associated with greater trait stability (Roberts & Del Vecchio, 2000). In fact, Roberts and Del Vecchio found that trait stability peaks in middle age when identity certainty (achieving a strong sense of identity, ability to choose environments that fit well with one's identity, and the ability to assimilate more experience into one's identity) is more likely to be achieved (Stewart & Ostrove, 1998). Future research must examine the extent to which many factors that may be linked to increased stability, such as a stable environment or identity integration, account for age and trait stability (Roberts & Del Vecchio, 2000).

Another important issue for future research is the role of life experiences. If a person experiences few events that induce him or her to change, then change is unlikely. In this view a person at 60 will be the same as he or she was at 30, all other factors being held constant. As we will see later, this idea has been incorporated formally into other theories of personality. On the basis of dispositional traits, then, we should have little difficulty knowing our high school classmates many years later.

CONCEPT CHECKS

1. What are the five dimensions of the five-factor model?
2. What criticisms have been aimed at the five-factor model?
3. What were the main findings from the Berkeley studies and women's personality development studies?
4. Are dispositional traits stable over time?

PERSONAL CONCERNS AND QUALITATIVE STAGES IN ADULTHOOD

LEARNING OBJECTIVES

- What are personal concerns?
- What are the main elements of Jung's theory?
- What are the stages in Erikson's theory? What types of clarifications and extensions have been offered? What research evidence is there to support his stages?
- What are the stages in Loevinger's theory? What evidence is there to support her stages?
- What are the main points and problems with theories based on life transitions?
- How is midlife best described?
- What can we conclude about personal concerns?

*J*im showed all the signs. He divorced his wife of nearly 20 years to start a relationship with a woman 15 years younger, traded in his ordinary-looking midsize sedan for a red sportscar, and began working out regularly at the health club after years of being a couch potato. Jim claims he hasn't felt this good in years; he is happy to be making this change in middle age. All Jim's friends agree: This is a clear case of midlife crisis. Or is it?

Many people believe strongly that middle age brings with it a normative crisis called the midlife crisis. There appears to be a lot of evidence to support this view, based on case studies like Jim's. But is everything as it seems? We'll find out in this section. First we consider the evidence that people's priorities and personal concerns change throughout adulthood, requiring adults to reassess themselves from time to time. This alternative position to the five-factor model discussed earlier claims that change is the rule during adulthood.

What does it mean to know another person well? McAdams (1994) believes that to know another person well takes more than just knowing where he or she falls on the dimensions of dispositional traits. It also means knowing what issues are important to a person, what the person wants, how the person tries to get what he or she wants, what the person's plans for the future are, how the person interacts with others who provide key personal relationships, and so forth. In short, we need to know something about a person's personal concerns. Personal concerns reflect what people want during particular times of their lives and within specific domains; they are the strategies, plans, and defenses people use to get what they want and avoid getting what they don't want.

What's Different about Personal Concerns?

Recently, many researchers have begun analyzing personality in ways that are explicitly contextual, in contrast to work on dispositional traits, which ignores context. This recent work emphasizes the importance of sociocultural influences on development that shape people's wants and behaviors. For example, Thorne (1989; Thorne & Klohnen, 1993) showed that when people talk about themselves, they go well beyond speaking in dispositional trait terms. Rather, people provide more narrative descriptions that rely heavily on their life circumstances, that is, the sociocultural experiences they have had that shape their lives. Moreover, people are highly likely to describe developmentally linked concerns that change over time. Cantor (1990; Cantor & Harlow, 1994) highlights this aspect of self-descriptions in differentiating between having traits and doing everyday behaviors that address the strivings, tasks, and goals that are important in everyday life. The latter aspect of personality emphasizes the importance of understanding culturally mandated, developmentally linked life tasks that reflect these changing concerns.

Although little research has been conducted on the personal concerns level of personality, a few things are clear (McAdams, 1994). Personality constructs at this level are not reducible to traits. Rather, such constructs must be viewed as conscious descriptions of what a person is trying to accomplish during a given period of life and what goals and goal-based concerns the person has. As Cantor (1990) notes, these constructs speak directly to the question of what people do in life. Moreover, we would expect that much change would be seen at this level of personality, given the importance of sociocultural influences and the changing nature of life tasks as people mature.

In contrast to the limited empirical data on the development of personal concerns, the theoretical base is arguably the richest. For the better part of a century, the notion that personality changes throughout the life span has been described in numerous ways, typically in theories that postulate qualitative stages that reflect the central concern of that period of life. In this section, we consider several of these theories and evaluate the available evidence for each. Let's begin with the theory that got people thinking about personality change in midlife: Carl Jung's theory.

Jung's Theory

Jung represents a turning point in the history of psychoanalytic thought. Initially allied with Freud, he soon severed the tie and developed his own ideas, which have elements of both Freudian theory and humanistic psychology. He was one of the very first theorists to believe in personality development in adulthood; this marked a major break with Freudian thought, which argued that personality development ended in adolescence.

Jung's theory emphasizes that each aspect of a person's personality must be in balance with all others. This means that each part of the personality is expressed in some way, whether through normal means or through neurotic symptoms or in dreams. Jung asserts that the parts of the personality are organized in such a way as to produce two basic orientations of the ego. One of these orientations is concerned with the external world; Jung labels it extroversion. The opposite orientation, toward the inner world of subjective experiences, is labeled introversion. To be psychologically healthy, both orientations must be present, and they must be balanced. People must be able to deal with the external world effectively and be able to evaluate their inner feelings and values. It is when people emphasize one orientation over another that they are classified as extroverts or introverts.

Jung advocates two important age-related trends in personality development. The first relates to the introversion–extroversion distinction. Young adults are more extroverted than older adults, perhaps because of younger people's needs to find a mate, have a career, and so forth. With increasing age, however, the need for balance creates a need to focus inward and explore personal feelings about aging and mortality. Thus, Jung argued that with age comes an increase in introversion.

The second age-related trend in Jung's theory involves the feminine and masculine aspects of our personalities. Each of us has elements of both masculinity and femininity. In young adulthood, however, most of us express only one of them while usually working hard to suppress the other. In other words, young adults most often act in accordance with gender role stereotypes appropriate to their culture. As they grow older, people begin to allow the suppressed parts of their personality out. This means that men begin to behave in ways that earlier in life they would have considered feminine, and women behave in ways that they formerly would have thought masculine. These changes achieve a better balance that allows men and women to deal more effectively with their individual needs rather than being driven by socially defined stereotypes. However, this balance does not mean a reversal of sex roles. On the contrary, it represents the expression of aspects of ourselves that have been there all along but that we have simply not allowed to be shown. We return to this issue at the end of the chapter when we consider gender role development.

More recently, Jung's ideas that self and personality are organized by symbols and stories and the notion that we transcend the dualities of femininity–masculinity, conscious–unconscious, and so on, have become active areas of research (Labouvie-Vief & Diehl, 1999; McAdams, 1995). However, as Labouvie-Vief and Diehl (1999) point out, most empirical evidence suggests that the reorganizations proposed by Jung are more indicative of advanced or exceptional development (Labouvie-Vief et al., 1995).

Jung stretched traditional psychoanalytic theory to new limits by postulating continued development across adulthood. Other theorists took Jung's lead and argued not only that personality development occurred in adulthood but also that it did so in an orderly sequential fashion. We consider the sequences

developed by two theorists, Erik Erikson and Jane Loevinger.

Erikson's Stages of Psychosocial Development

The best-known life-span theorist is Erik Erikson (1982), who called attention to cultural mechanisms involved in personality development. According to him, personality is determined by the interaction between an inner maturational plan and external societal demands. He proposes that the life cycle comprises eight stages of development, summarized in Table 10-1. Erikson believed that the sequence of stages is biologically fixed.

Each stage in Erikson's theory is marked by a struggle between two opposing tendencies, both of which are experienced by the person. The names of the stages reflect the issues that form the struggles. The struggles are resolved through an interactive process involving both the inner psychological and the outer social influences. Successful resolutions establish the basic areas of psychosocial strength; unsuccessful resolutions impair ego development in a particular area and adversely affect the resolution of future struggles. Thus, each stage in Erikson's theory represents a kind of crisis.

The sequence of stages in Erikson's theory is based on the **epigenetic principle,** *which means that each psychosocial strength has its own special time of ascendancy, or period of particular importance.* The eight stages represent the order of this ascendancy. Because the stages extend across the whole life span, it takes a lifetime to acquire all the psychosocial strengths. Moreover, Erikson argues that present and future behavior must have their roots in the past because later stages build on the foundation laid in previous ones.

Erikson argues that the basic aspect of a healthy personality is a sense of trust toward oneself and others. Thus, the first stage in his theory involves trust versus mistrust, representing the conflict an infant faces in developing trust in a world it knows little about. With trust come feelings of security and comfort.

The second stage, autonomy versus shame and doubt, reflects children's budding understanding that

TABLE 10.1 Summary of Erikson's Theory of Psychosocial Development, with Important Relationships and Psychosocial Strengths Acquired at Each Stage

Stage	Psychosocial Crisis	Significant Relations	Basic Strengths
1 Infancy	Basic trust versus basic mistrust	Maternal person	Hope
2 Early childhood	Autonomy versus shame and doubt	Paternal people	Will
3 Play age	Initiative versus guilt	Basic family	Purpose
4 School age	Industry versus inferiority	"Neighborhood," school	Competence
5 Adolescence	Identity versus identity confusion	Peer groups and outgroups; models of leadership	Fidelity
6 Young adulthood	Intimacy versus isolation	Partners in friendship, sex, competition, cooperation	Love
7 Adulthood	Generativity versus stagnation	Divided labor and shared household	Care
8 Old age	Integrity versus despair	Humankind, "my kind"	Wisdom

From *The life cycle completed: A review* by Erik H. Erikson. Copyright © 1982 by Rikan Enterprises, Ltd. Used by permission of W. W. Norton & Company, Inc.

they are in charge of their own actions. This understanding changes them from reactive beings to ones who can act on the world intentionally. Their autonomy is threatened by their inclinations to avoid responsibility for their actions and to go back to the security of the first stage.

The third stage of the conflict is initiative versus guilt. Once children realize that they can act on the world and are somebody, they begin to discover who they are. They take advantage of wider experience to explore the environment on their own, to ask many questions about the world, and to imagine possibilities about themselves.

The fourth stage is marked by children's increasing interests in interacting with peers, their need for acceptance, and their need to develop competencies. Erikson views these needs as representing industry versus inferiority, which is manifested behaviorally in children's desire to accomplish tasks by working hard. Failure to succeed in developing self-perceived competencies results in feelings of inferiority.

During adolescence, Erikson believes, we deal with the issue of identity versus identity confusion. The choice we make, that is, the identity we form, is not so much who we are but whom we can become. The struggle in adolescence is choosing from among a multitude of possible selves the one we will become. Identity confusion results when we are torn over the possibilities. The struggle involves trying to balance our need to choose a possible self and the desire to try out many possible selves.

During young adulthood the major developmental task, intimacy versus isolation, involves establishing a fully intimate relationship with another. Erikson (1968) argues that intimacy means the sharing all aspects of oneself without fearing the loss of identity. If intimacy is not achieved, isolation results. One way to assist the development of intimacy is to choose a mate who represents the ideal of all one's past experiences. The psychosocial strength that emerges from the intimacy–isolation struggle is love.

With the advent of middle age the focus shifts from intimacy to concern for the next generation, expressed as generativity versus stagnation. The struggle occurs between a sense of generativity (the feeling that people must maintain and perpetuate society) and a sense of stagnation (the feeling of self-absorption). Generativity is seen in such things as parenthood, teaching, or providing goods and services for the benefit of society. If the challenge of generativity is accepted, the development of trust in the next generation is facilitated, and the psychosocial strength of care is obtained.

Many men, like the man in the photograph, report that priorities change during middle age.

In old age people must resolve the struggle between ego integrity and despair. This last stage begins with a growing awareness of the nearness of the end of life, but it is actually completed by only a small number of people (Erikson, 1982). The task is to examine and evaluate one's life and accomplishments to make sense of them. This process often involves reminiscing with others and actively seeking reassurance that one has accomplished something in life. People who have progressed successfully through earlier stages of life face old age enthusiastically and feel that their lives have been full. Those who feel a sense of meaninglessness do not anticipate old age, and they experience despair. The psychosocial strength achieved from a successful resolution of this struggle is wisdom. Integrity is not the only issue facing older adults; Erikson points out that they have many opportunities for generativity as well. Older people often play an active role as grandparents, for example, and many maintain part-time jobs.

CLARIFICATIONS AND EXPANSIONS OF ERIKSON'S THEORY. Erikson's theory has had a major impact on thinking about life-span development. However, some aspects of his theory are unclear, poorly defined, or unspecified. Traditionally, these problems have led critics to dismiss the theory as untestable and incomplete. The situation is changing, however. Other theorists have tried to address these problems by identifying common themes, specifying underlying mental processes, and reinterpreting and integrating the theory with other ideas. These ideas are leading researchers to reassess the utility of Erikson's theory as a guide for research on adult personality development.

Logan (1986) points out that Erikson's theory can be considered a cycle that repeats: from basic trust to identity and from identity to integrity. In this approach the developmental progression is trust → achievement → wholeness. Throughout life we first establish that we can trust other people and ourselves. Initially, trust involves learning about ourselves and others, represented by the first two stages (trust versus mistrust and autonomy versus shame and doubt). The recapitulation of this idea in the second cycle is seen in our struggle to find a person with whom we can form a very close relationship yet not lose our own sense of self (intimacy versus isolation). Additionally, Logan shows how achievement—our need to accomplish and to be recognized for it—is a theme throughout Erikson's theory. During childhood this idea is reflected in the two stages initiative versus guilt and industry versus inferiority, whereas in adulthood it is represented by generativity versus stagnation. Finally, Logan points out that the issue of understanding ourselves as worthwhile and whole is first encountered during adolescence (identity versus identity confusion) and is reexperienced during old age (integrity versus despair). Logan's analysis emphasizes that psychosocial development, although complicated on the surface, may actually reflect only a small number of issues. Moreover, he points out that we do not come to a single resolution of these issues of trust, achievement, and wholeness. Rather, we struggle with them throughout our lives.

One aspect of Erikson's theory that is not specified is the rules that govern the sequence in which issues are faced. That is, Erikson does not make clear why certain issues are dealt with early in development and others are delayed. Moreover, how transitions from one stage to the next happen is not fully explained. Van Geert (1987) proposes a set of rules that fills in these gaps. He argues that the sequence of stages is guided by three developmental trends. First, an inward orientation to the self gradually replaces an outward orientation to the world. This trend is similar to Jung's increase in introversion with age. Second, we move from using very general categories in understanding the world to using more specific ones. This trend is reflected in cognitive development in that our earliest categories do not allow the separation of individual differences (for example, we use *dog* to mean all sorts of animals). Third, we move from operating with limited ideas of social and emotional experiences to more inclusive ideas. During childhood we may love only the people we believe are deserving, for example, whereas in adulthood we may love all people as representatives of humanity. By combining these three developmental trends, Van Geert constructs rules for moving from one stage to another.

Although Van Geert's approach has not been tested completely, his ideas fit with Erikson's theory and with other related data. For example, Neugarten (1977) points to an increase in interiority with age across adulthood, an idea very similar to Van Geert's inward orientation. Cognitive developmental research (see Chapter 8) supports the development of more refined conceptual categories. Thus, Van Geert's approach may be useful in understanding psychosocial development and in providing a way to identify the cyclic progression described by Logan.

Viney (1987) shows how other approaches to human development can add to Erikson's theory. As an example, she points to the sociophenomenological approach, which emphasizes that people change in how they interpret and reinterpret events. That is, the meaning of major life events changes from earlier to later in the life span. In a study that examined people between ages 6 and 86, she documented that the positive and negative descriptors people used to characterize their lives changed considerably. Interestingly, these shifts in descriptors appear to parallel Erikson's stages. For example, adults over age 65 are more likely to talk about trying to get their lives in order or feeling completely alone than are adults under age 65. Although Viney's research was not intended to be a direct test of Erikson's theory, her results indicate that we may be able to document his stages in research based on different approaches to development. Additionally, Viney's research may indicate that the themes Erikson identified are applicable to many situations, including the way in which we view events.

Some critics argue that Erikson's stage of generativity is much too broad to capture the essence of adulthood. For example, Kotre (1984) contends that adults experience many opportunities to express generativity that are not equivalent and do not lead to a general state. Rather, he sees generativity more as a set of impulses felt at different times in different settings, such as at work or in grandparenting. More formally, Kotre describes five types of generativity: biological and parental generativity, which concerns raising children; technical generativity, the passing of specific skills from one generation to another; cultural generativity, or being a mentor (as discussed in more detail in Chapter 12); agentic generativity, the desire to be or to do something that transcends death; and communal generativity, a person's participation in a mutual, interpersonal reality. Only rarely, Kotre contends, is there a continuous state of generativity in adulthood. He asserts that the struggles Erikson identified are not fought constantly; rather, they probably come and go. We examine this idea in more detail a bit later in the next section.

Finally, Hamachek (1990) provides behavioral and attitudinal descriptors of Erikson's last three stages. These descriptors are meant to create a series of continua of possibilities for individual development. This reflects the fact that few people have an exclusive orientation to either intimacy or isolation, for example, but more commonly show some combination of the two. These behavioral and attitudinal descriptors provide a framework for researchers who need to operationalize Erikson's concepts.

RESEARCH ON GENERATIVITY. Perhaps the central period in adulthood from an Eriksonian perspective is the stage of generativity versus stagnation. One of the best empirically based efforts to describe generativity is McAdams's model (McAdams, 1995; McAdams et al., 1998) shown in Figure 10-1. This multidimensional model shows how generativity results from the complex interconnections between societal and inner forces, which create a concern for the next generation and a belief in the goodness of the human enterprise, leading to generative commitment, which produces generative actions. A person derives personal meaning from being generative by constructing a life story or narration, which helps create the person's identity (Whitbourne, 1996c, 1999).

The components of McAdams's model relate differently to personality traits. For example, generative concern is a general personality tendency of interest in caring for younger people, and generative action is the behaviors that promote the well-being of the next generation. Generative concern relates to life satisfaction and overall happiness, whereas generative action does not (de St. Aubin & McAdams, 1995). New grandparents may derive much satisfaction from

their grandchildren and are greatly concerned with their well-being but have little desire to engage in the daily hassles of caring for them regularly. These results have led to the creation of positive and negative generativity indices that reliably identify differences between generative and nongenerative people (Himsel et al., 1997).

Although they can be expressed by adults of all ages, certain types of generativity are more common at some ages than others. For example, middle-aged and older adults show a greater preoccupation with generativity themes than do younger adults in their accounts of personally meaningful life experiences. Middle-aged adults have made more generative commitments (e.g., "save enough money for my daughter to go to medical school"), reflecting a major difference in the inner and outer worlds of middle-aged and older adults as opposed to younger adults (McAdams et al., 1993).

Similar research focusing specifically on middle-aged women yields comparable results. Peterson and Klohnen (1995) examined generativity from the viewpoint of personality characteristics, work productivity, parental involvement, health concerns, and political interests in separate samples of Mills College and Radcliffe College alumnae who were in their early to mid-40s. They found that women who exhibit high generativity tend to have prosocial personality traits, are personally invested in being parents, express generative attitudes at work, and exhibit caring behaviors toward others outside their immediate families (Peterson & Klohnen, 1995); they also show high well-being in their role as a spouse (MacDermid et al., 1996).

These data demonstrate that the personal concerns of middle-aged adults are fundamentally different from those of younger adults. Moreover, these concerns are not consistently or uniformly related to dispositional traits. Considered together, these findings provide much support for Erikson's contention that the central concerns for adults change with age. However, the data also indicate that generativity is much more complex than Erikson originally proposed and may not diminish in late life.

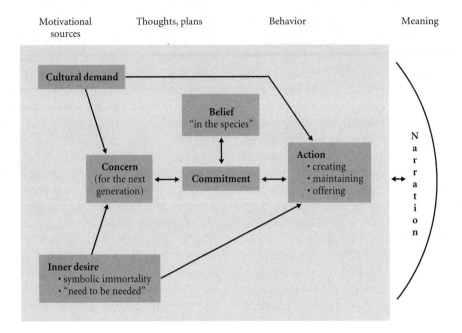

| Motivational sources | Thoughts, plans | Behavior | Meaning |

FIGURE 10.1   McAdams's model of generativity.

Source: McAdams, D. P., H. M. Hart, & S. Mzrnna, "The Anatomy of Generativity," 1998, p. 7. In D. P. McAdams & E. de St. Aubin (eds.), *Generativity & adult development: How and why we care for the next generation.* Copyright © 1998 by the American Psychological Association. Adapted by permission.

Loevinger's Theory

Loevinger (1976) saw a need to extend the groundwork laid by Erikson both theoretically and empirically. For her, the ego is the chief organizer: the integrator of our morals, values, goals, and thought processes. Because this integration performed by the ego is so complex and is influenced by personal experiences, it is the primary source of individual differences at all ages beyond infancy. **Ego development** *is the result of dynamic interaction between the person and the environment.* Consequently, it consists of fundamental changes in the ways in which our thoughts, values, morals, and goals are organized. Transitions from one stage to another depend on both internal biological changes and external social changes to which the person must adapt.

Although Loevinger proposes eight stages of ego development, beginning in infancy, we focus on the six that are observed in adults (Table 10-2). An important aspect of her theory is that most people never

go through all of them; indeed, the last level is achieved by only a handful of people. There is growing cross-sectional and longitudinal evidence that these stages are age related (Cook-Greuter, 1990; Loevinger, 1997; Redmore & Loevinger, 1979). At each stage Loevinger identifies four areas that she considers important to the developmental progression: character development (reflecting a person's standards and goals), interpersonal style (representing the person's pattern of relations with others), conscious preoccupations (reflecting the most important things on the person's mind), and cognitive style (reflecting the characteristic way in which the person thinks). As we consider the ego levels important for adults, we examine them in terms of these four areas.

A few adults operate at the conformist level. Character development at this stage is marked by absolute conformity to social rules. If these rules are broken, feelings of shame and guilt result. Interpersonally, conformists need to belong and show a superficial

TABLE 10.2   Summary of Loevinger's Stages of Ego Development in Adulthood

Stage	Description
Conformist	Obedience to external social rules
Conscientious–conformist	Separation of norms and goals; realization that acts affect others
Conscientious	Beginning of self-evaluated standards
Individualistic	Recognition that the process of acting is more important than the outcome
Autonomous	Respect for each person's individuality, tolerance for ambiguity
Integrated	Resolution of inner conflicts

niceness. Of central importance is appearance and social acceptability. Conformists see the world only in terms of external tangibles, such as how one looks and whether one behaves according to group standards. Thinking is dominated by stereotypes and clichés and is simplistic.

Most adults in American society operate at the conscientious–conformist level. At this stage character development is marked by a differentiation of norms and goals; in other words, people learn to separate what they want for themselves from what social norms may dictate. People deal with others by recognizing that they have an impact on them and on the group as a whole. People at this level begin to be concerned with issues of personal adjustment and coping with problems; they need reasons for actions and recognize that life presents many opportunities from which they may choose. They are still concerned with group standards, and the desire for personal adjustment may be suppressed if it conflicts with the needs of the group.

The next level, the conscientious stage, is marked by a cognitive style in which people begin to understand the true complexity of the world. People at this stage focus on understanding the role of the self; character development involves self-evaluated standards, self-critical thinking, self-determined ideals, and self-set goals. This level represents a shift away from letting other people or society set their goals and standards for them. Intensity, responsibility, and mutual sharing characterize interpersonal relations. People evaluate behavior using internalized standards developed over the years. They come to realize

that they control their own future. Although more complex, conscientious people still think in terms of polarities, such as love versus lust or inner life versus outer appearance. But they recognize responsibility and obligation in addition to rights and privileges.

Loevinger postulates that the individualistic level builds on the previous (conscientious) level. A major acquisition at the individualistic level is a respect for individuality. Immature dependency is seen as an emotional problem rather than as something to be expected. Concern for broad social problems and differentiating one's inner life from one's outer life become the main preoccupations. People begin to differentiate process (the way things are done) from outcome (the answer); for example, people realize that sometimes the solution to a problem is right but the way of getting there involves hurting someone. The flavor of the individualistic person is an increased tolerance for oneself and others. Key conflicts are recognized as complex problems: dependence as constraining versus dependence as emotionally rewarding and morality and responsibility versus achievement for oneself. However, resolving these conflicts usually involves projecting the cause onto the environment rather than acknowledging their internal sources.

At Loevinger's autonomous level comes a high tolerance for ambiguity with conflicting needs within oneself and others. An autonomous person's interpersonal style is characterized by a respect for each person's independence but also by an understanding that people are interdependent. The preoccupations at this level are vividly conveyed feelings, self-fulfillment, and understanding of the self in a social context. Autonomous people have the courage to acknowledge and face conflict head-on rather than projecting it onto the environment. They see reality as complex and multifaceted and no longer view it in the polarities of the conscientious stage. Autonomous people recognize that problems can be viewed in multiple ways and are comfortable with the fact that other people's viewpoints may differ from their own. They recognize the need for others' self-sufficiency and take a broad view of life.

The final level in Loevinger's theory is the integrated stage. Inner conflicts are not only faced but also reconciled and laid to rest. Goals that are recognized to be unattainable are renounced. People at the integrated level cherish an individuality that comes from a consolidated sense of identity. They are very much like Maslow's (1968) self-actualized person; that is, they are at peace with themselves and have realized their maximum potential. They recognize that they could have chosen other paths in life but are content with and make the most out of the one that they picked. Such people are always open to further growth-enhancing opportunities and make the most out of integrating new experiences into their lives.

Loevinger has spent decades developing the Sentence Completion Test, which provides a measure of ego development. The measure consists of sentence fragments that respondents complete. Responses are then scored in terms of the ego developmental level they represent. Although it is a difficult instrument to learn how to use, the Sentence Completion Test has very good reliability. Trained coders have high rates of agreement in rating responses, often more than 90% of the time.

Loevinger's theory is having an increasing impact on adult developmental research. One of its advantages is that because of the Sentence Completion Test it is more empirically based than Erikson's theory, so researchers can document the stages more precisely. Loevinger's theory is the major framework for research examining relationships between cognitive development and ego development (King et al., 1989). For example, Blanchard-Fields and Norris (1994) found that ego level was the best predictor of social

judgments by adolescents and young, middle-aged, and older adults about negative outcomes in personal relationships. Likewise, Labouvie-Vief, Hakim-Larson, and Hobart (1987) reported that ego level was a strong predictor of the coping strategies used across the life span from childhood to old age. Both studies documented age-related increases in ego level that were associated with higher levels of social reasoning or with more mature coping styles.

Theories Based on Life Transitions

Jung's belief in a midlife crisis, Erikson's belief that personality development proceeds in stages, and Loevinger's notion that cognitive and ego development are mutually interactive laid the foundation for other theorists' efforts. To get a flavor of what these theorists did, take a moment to think about your own life, as suggested in Forces in Action.

For many laypeople, the idea that adults go through an orderly sequence of stages that includes both crises and stability reflects their own experience. This is probably why books such as Sheehy's *Passages* (1976), *Pathfinders* (1981), and *New Passages* (1995) are met with instant acceptance or why Levinson's and colleagues' (1978) and Vaillant's work (Vaillant, 1977; Vaillant & Vaillant, 1990) have been applied to everything from basic personality development to understanding how men's careers change. A universal assumption of these theories is that people go through predictable, age-related crises. Some life transition theories (e.g., Levinson's) also propose that these crises are followed by periods of relative stability. The overall view is that adulthood consists of a series of alternating periods of stability and change.

Compared with the theories we have considered to this point, however, theories based on life transitions are built on shakier ground. For example, some are based on small, highly selective samples (such as men who attended Harvard) or surveys completed by readers of particular magazines. This is in contrast, for example, to the large databases used to test the five-factor model or Loevinger's theory. These theories are associated with psychometrically sound measures and are well researched. Thus, the research

Studying stage theories generally makes us wonder how we stand and how we ended up that way. Evaluating our own ego development and other aspects of personality can be both fun and humbling. It can be fun in the sense that learning something about oneself is enjoyable and enlightening; it can be humbling in the sense that we may have overestimated how advanced we are. But there is another side to this personal evaluation that is equally important.

Take a few moments and think back perhaps 5 or 10 years. What things were important to you? How well did you know yourself? What were your priorities? What did you see yourself becoming in the future? What were your relationships with other people based on? Now answer these questions from your perspective today.

If you are like most people, answering these questions will make you see the ways in which you have changed. Many times we are in the worst position to see this change because we are embedded in it. We also find ourselves reinterpreting the past based on the experiences we have had in the meantime.

The focus of the stage theories we have considered is the change in the ways in which we see ourselves. We look at the world differently as we grow older. Our priorities change. Take a few moments now and jot down how you have changed over the years since high school. Then write down what you think were the causes of these changes. For example, was it biological, such as the advent of puberty? Was it psychological, such as the ability to reason more complexly? Was it social, in that peer pressure was important? Finally, was it the historical time that influenced such changes?

Thinking about personality from the perspective of the basic developmental forces provides a very helpful way to understand the arguments in personality theory and research. As pointed out throughout this book, the forces emphasize the complexity of influences on any specific issue; personality is no exception. Genetic factors and physical health exert important influences on personality and how it is expressed. Socialization influences which aspects of personality may be learned as we grow up and age. Life-course factors are especially important for theorists who emphasize the fact that issues people face change over time. Although few attempts have been made to integrate these influences in personality research, we need to keep them in mind when drawing our own conclusions on the matter.

Finally, write down how you see yourself now and how you would like your life to be in the future. These ideas will give you something to think about now and again later when we consider Whitbourne's ideas about scenarios and life stories.

---

methods used in studies of life transitions lead one to question the validity of their findings.

An important question about life transition theories is the extent to which they are real and actually occur to everyone. Life transition theories typically present stages as if everyone universally experiences them. Moreover, many have specific ages tied to specific stages (such as age 30 or age 50 transitions). As we know from cognitive developmental research in Chapter 8, however, this is a very tenuous assumption. Individual variation is the rule, not the exception. What actually happens may be a combination of expectations and socialization. For example, Dunn and Merriam (1995) examined data from a large, diverse national sample and found that less than 20% of people in their early 30s experienced the Age Thirty Transition (which encompasses the midlife crisis) that forms a cornerstone of Levinson and colleagues' (1978) theory. The experience of a midlife crisis, discussed next, is an excellent case in point.

IN SEARCH OF THE MIDLIFE CRISIS. One of the most important ideas in theories that consider the importance of life transitions (after periods of stability) is that middle-aged adults experience a personal crisis that results in major changes in how they view themselves. During a midlife crisis, people are supposed to take a good hard look at themselves and, they hope, attain a much better understanding of who they are. Difficult issues such as one's own mortality and inevitable aging are supposed to be faced. Behavioral changes are supposed to occur; we even have stereotypic images of the middle-aged man, like Jim, running off with a much younger woman as a result of his midlife crisis. In support of this notion, Levinson and his colleagues (1978; Levinson & Levinson, 1996) write that middle-aged men in his study reported intense internal struggles that were much like depression.

However, far more research fails to document the existence and more importantly the universality of a particularly difficult time in midlife. In fact, it may be the case that those who do experience a crisis may be those who are suffering from general problems of psychopathology (Labouvie-Vief & Diehl, 1999; Rosenberg et al., 1999). Baruch (1984) summarizes a series of retrospective interview studies of American women between ages 35 and 55. The results showed that women in their 20s were more likely to be uncertain and dissatisfied than were women at midlife. Middle-aged women rarely mentioned normative developmental milestones such as marriage, childbirth, or menopause as major turning points in their lives. Rather, unexpected events such as divorce and job transfers were more likely to cause crises. Studies extending Levinson's theory to women have not found strong evidence of a traumatic midlife crisis either (Harris et al., 1986; Reinke et al., 1985; Roberts & Newton, 1987).

The midlife crisis was also missing in data obtained as part of the Berkeley studies of personality traits. Most middle-aged men said that their careers were satisfying (Clausen, 1981), and both men and women appeared more self-confident, insightful, introspective, open, and better equipped to handle stressful situations (Haan, 1985; Haan et al., 1986). Even direct attempts to find the midlife crisis failed. In two studies Costa and McCrae (1978) could identify only a handful of men who fit the profile, and even then the crisis came anytime between 30 and 60. A replication and extension of this work, conducted by Farrell and colleagues (Farrell et al., 1993; Rosenberg et al., 1992, 1999; Rosenberg, 1991), confirmed the initial results.

Middle-age women struggle to reconcile physical aging and self-development.

McCrae and Costa (1990) point out that the idea of a midlife crisis became widely accepted as fact because of the mass media. People take it for granted that they will go through a period of intense psychological turmoil in their 40s. The problem is that there is little hard scientific evidence of it. The data suggest that midlife is no more or no less traumatic for most people than any other period in life. Perhaps the most convincing support for this conclusion comes from research conducted by Farrell and Rosenberg (Rosenberg et al., 1999). These investigators initially set out to prove the existence of a midlife crisis because they were firm believers in it. After extensive testing and interviewing, however, they emerged as nonbelievers.

However, Labouvie-Vief and Diehl (1999) offer some good evidence that there is a reorganization of self and values across the adult life span. They suggest that the major dynamic driving such changes may not be age dependent but may follow general cognitive changes. As discussed in Chapter 8, people around middle adulthood show the most complex understanding of self, emotions, and motivations. Cognitive complexity also is shown to be the strongest predictor of higher levels of complexity in general. Thus a midlife crisis may be the result of general gains in cognitive complexity from early to middle adulthood (Labouvie-Vief & Diehl, 1999).

Stewart (1996) found that well-educated women who reported regrets about adopting a traditional feminine role in life (i.e., they wished they pursued an education or a career) and subsequently made adjustments in midlife were better off than those who did not make adjustments or had no role regrets at all. Stewart suggests that rather than a midlife crisis, it may be more appropriate to think about a **midlife correction,** *reevaluating ones' roles and dreams and making the necessary corrections.*

Perhaps the best way to view midlife is as a time of both gains and losses (Lachman et al., 1994). That is, the changes people perceive in midlife can be viewed as representing both gains and losses. Competence, ability to handle stress, sense of personal control, purpose in life, and social responsibility are all at their peak, whereas physical abilities, women's ability to bear children, and physical appearance are examples of changes many view as negative. This gain–loss view emphasizes two things. First, the exact timing of change is not fixed but occurs over an extended period of time. Second, change can be both positive and negative at the same time. Thus, rather than seeing midlife as a time of crisis, one may want to view it as a period during which several aspects of one's life acquire new meanings.

Conclusions about Personal Concerns

Based on the theories and research evidence we have considered, substantive change in adults' personal concerns definitely occurs as people age. This conclusion is in sharp contrast to the stability observed in dispositional traits, but it supports McAdams's (1994) contention that this middle level of personality should show some change. What is also clear, however, is that a tight connection between such change and specific ages is not supported by the bulk of the data. Rather, change appears to occur in wide windows of time depending on many factors, including one's sociocultural context. Finally, more research is needed in this area, especially investigations that provide longitudinal evidence of change within people.

CONCEPT CHECKS

1. What are personal concerns?
2. What happens in midlife according to Jung?
3. What are Erikson's eight stages?
4. What are the main points in Loevinger's theory?
5. What is the principal problem with theories based on life transitions?
6. Do personal concerns change across adulthood?

LIFE NARRATIVES, IDENTITY, AND THE SELF

LEARNING OBJECTIVES

- What are the main aspects of McAdams' life-story model?
- What are the main points of Whitbourne's identity theory?
- How does self-concept come to take adult form? What is its development during adulthood?
- What are possible selves? Do they show differences during adulthood?
- What role does religion play in adult life?
- How does gender role identity develop in adulthood?
- What conclusions can be drawn from research using life narratives?

*F*elicia is a 19-year-old sophomore at a community college. She expects her study of early childhood education to be difficult but rewarding. She figures that along the way she will meet a great guy, whom she will marry soon after graduation. They will have two children before she turns 30. Felicia sees herself getting a good job teaching preschool children and some day owning her own day care center.

Who are you? What kind of person are you trying to become? These are the kinds of questions Felicia is trying to answer. Answering these questions involves concepts of personality that go beyond dispositional traits and personal concerns. The aspects of personality we have discussed thus far are important, but they lack integration, unity, coherence, and overall purpose (McAdams, 1994). For example, understanding a person's goals (from the level of personal concerns) does not reveal who a person is trying to be or what kind of person the person is trying to create. What is lacking in other levels of analysis is a sense of the person's identity or sense of self.

In contrast to Erikson's (1982) proposition that identity formation is the central task of adolescence, many researchers are now coming to understand the important ways in which identity and the creation of the self continue to develop throughout adulthood (Labouvie-Vief et al., 1995; Whitbourne & Connolly, 1999). This emerging field of how adults continue constructing identity and the self relies on life narratives, or the internalized and evolving story that integrates a person's reconstructed past, perceived present, and anticipated future into a coherent and vitalizing life myth (McAdams, 1994). Careful analysis of people's life narratives provides insight into their identity.

In this section, we consider two evolving theories of identity. McAdams is concerned with understanding how people see themselves and how they fit into the adult world. Whitbourne investigated people's own conceptions of the life course and how they differ from age norms and the expectations for society as a whole. To round out our understanding of identity and the self, we also examine related constructs. Before reading this section, take time to complete the exercise in the Discovering Development feature. It will give you a sense of what a life narrative is and how it might be used to gain insight into identity and the sense of self.

McAdams's Life-Story Model

McAdams (1993, 1994, 1995) argues that a person's sense of identity cannot be understood using the language of dispositional traits or personal concerns. It is not just a collection of traits, nor is it a collection of plans, strategies, or goals. Instead, it is based on a story of how the person came into being, where the person has been, where he or she is going, and who he or she will become, much like Felicia's story.

McAdams argues that people create a life story that is an internalized narrative with a beginning, a middle, and an anticipated ending. The life story is created and revised throughout adulthood as people change and the changing environment places different demands on them.

McAdams's (1993) research indicates that people in Western society begin forming their life story in late adolescence and early adulthood, but it has its roots in the development of one's earliest attachments in infancy. According to McAdams, each life story contains seven essential features: narrative tone, image, theme, ideological setting, nuclear episodes, character, and ending.

The narrative tone of a person's identity is the emotional feel of the story, ranging from bleak pessimism, conveyed through tragedy and irony, to blithe optimism, conveyed through comic and romantic descriptions. A life story's unique imagery consists of the characteristic sights, sounds, emotionally charged pictures, symbols, metaphors, and the like that a person incorporates. The themes are recurrent patterns of motivational content, reflected in terms of the person repeatedly trying to attain his or her goals over time. The two most common themes are agency (reflecting power, achievement, and autonomy) and communion (reflecting love, intimacy, and belongingness). The life story's ideological setting is the backdrop of beliefs and values, or the ideology a person uses to set the context for his or her actions.

Every life story contains certain nuclear episodes of key scenes involving symbolic high points, low points, and turning points. These episodes provide insight into scenes involving perceived change and continuity in life. People prove to themselves and others that they have either changed or remained the same by pointing to specific events that support the appropriate claim. The main characters in people's lives represent idealizations of the self, such as "the dutiful mother" or "the reliable worker." Integrating these various aspects of the self is a major challenge of midlife and later adulthood. Finally, all life stories need an ending through which the self is able to leave a legacy that creates new beginnings. Life stories in

From the time you were a child, people have posed this question to you. In childhood, you probably answered by indicating some specific career, such as firefighter or teacher. But now that you are an adult, the question takes on new meaning. Rather than simply a matter of picking a profession, the question goes much deeper to the kinds of values and the essence of the person you would like to become.

Take a few minutes and think about who you would like to be in another decade or two (or maybe even 50 years hence). What things will matter to you? What will you be doing? What experiences will you have had? What lies ahead?

This exercise will give you a sense of the way in which researchers try to understand people's sense of identity and self through the use of personal narrative. You might even keep what you have written and check it when the appropriate number of years have elapsed.

---

middle-aged and older adults have a clear quality of giving birth to a new generation, a notion essentially identical to generativity.

McAdams (1994) believes that the model for change in identity over time is a process of fashioning and refashioning one's life story. This process appears to be strongly influenced by culture. At times, the reformulation may be at a conscious level, as when people make explicit decisions about changing careers. At other times, the revision process is unconscious and implicit, growing out of everyday activities. The goal is to create a life story that is coherent, credible, open to new possibilities, richly differentiated, reconciling of opposite aspects of oneself, and integrated within one's sociocultural context (McAdams, 1993, 1994, 1995).

Whitbourne's Identity Theory

A second and related approach to understanding identity formation in adulthood is Whitbourne's (1987, 1996c) idea that people build their own conceptions of how their lives should proceed. The result of this process is the **life-span construct,** *the person's unified sense of the past, present, and future.*

There are many influences on the development of a life-span construct: identity, values, and social context are a few. Together, they shape the life-span construct and the ways in which it is manifested. The life-span construct has two structural components, which in turn are the ways in which it is manifested. The first of these components is the scenario, which consists of expectations about the future. The scenario translates aspects of our identity that are particularly important at a specific point into a plan for the future. The scenario is strongly influenced by age norms that define key transition points; for example, graduating from college is a transition normally associated with the early 20s. In short, a scenario is a game plan for how we want our lives to go.

Joan, a typical college sophomore, may have the following scenario: She expects that her course of study in nursing will be difficult but that she will finish on time. She hopes to meet a nice guy along the way whom she will marry shortly after graduation. She imagines that she will get a good job at a major medical center that will offer her good opportunities for advancement. She and her husband probably will have a child, but she expects to keep working. Because she feels that she will want to advance, she assumes that at some point she will obtain a master's degree. In the more distant future she hopes to be a department head and to be well-respected for her administrative skills.

Tagging certain expected events with a particular age or time by which we expect to complete them creates a social clock (see Chapter 1). Joan will use her scenario to evaluate her progress toward her goals. With each major transition she will check how she is doing against where her scenario says she should be. If it turns out that she has achieved her goals earlier than she expected, she will be proud of being ahead of the game. If things work out more slowly than she planned, she may chastise herself for being slow. If she begins to criticize herself a great deal, she may end up changing her scenario altogether; for example, if she does not get a good job and makes no progress, she may change her scenario to one that says she should stay home with her child.

As Joan starts moving into the positions laid out in her scenario, she begins to create the second component of her life-span construct: her life story. The life story is a personal narrative history that organizes past events into a coherent sequence. The life story gives events personal meaning and a sense of continuity; it becomes our autobiography. Because the life story is what we tell others when they ask about our past, it eventually becomes overrehearsed and stylized. An interesting aspect of the life story, and autobiographical memory in general, is that distortions occur with time and retelling (Fitzgerald, 1999). In life stories, distortions allow the person to feel that he or she was on time, rather than off time, in terms of past events in the scenario. In this way people feel better about their plans and goals and are less likely to feel a sense of failure.

Whitbourne (1986) conducted a fascinating cross-sectional study of 94 adults ranging in age from 24 to 61. They came from all walks of life and represented a wide range of occupations and life situations. Using data from very detailed interviews, Whitbourne was able to identify what she believes is the process of adult identity development based on equilibrium between identity and experience. Her model is presented in Figure 10-2. As the figure shows, there is continuous feedback between identity and experience; this explains why we may evaluate ourselves positively at one point in time yet appear defensive and self-protective at another.

As can be seen, the processes of equilibrium are based on Piaget's concepts of assimilation and accommodation (see Chapter 8). Whitbourne has explicitly attempted to integrate concepts from cognitive development with identity development to understand how identity is formed and revised across

adulthood. The assimilation process involves using existing aspects of identity to handle present situations. Overreliance on assimilation makes the person resistant to change. Accommodation, on the other hand, reflects the person's willingness to let the situation determine what he or she will do. This often occurs when the person does not have a well-developed identity around a certain issue.

Not surprisingly, Whitbourne (1986) found that most adults listed family as the most important aspect of their lives. Clearly, adults' identity as loving constitutes the major part of the answer to the question "Who am I?" Consequently, a major theme in adults' identity development is trying to refine their belief that "I am a loving person." Much of this development is in acquiring and refining deep, emotional relationships.

A second major source of identity for Whitbourne's participants was work. In this case the key seemed to be keeping work interesting. As long as people had an interesting occupation that enabled them to become personally invested, their work identity was more central to their overall personal identity. This is a topic we pursue in Chapter 12.

Although Whitbourne found evidence of life transitions, she found no evidence that these transitions occurred in a stagelike fashion or were tied to specific ages. Rather, she found that people tended to experience transitions when they felt they needed to and to do so on their own time line. More recently, Whitbourne (1996a) has developed the Identity and Experiences Scale–General to measure identity processes in adults. Her model has been expanded to incorporate how people adapt more generally to middle age and the aging process (Whitbourne, 1996b; Whitbourne & Connolly, 1999). This scale assesses a person's use of assimilation and accommodation in forming identity in a general sense and is based on her earlier work (Whitbourne, 1986). Results thus far are promising in that the scale reliably differentiates people with an assimilative style from those with an accommodative style. Additionally, identity style appears to be different from one's coping style, indicating that both are necessary to understand how adults deal with events in their lives. Inter-

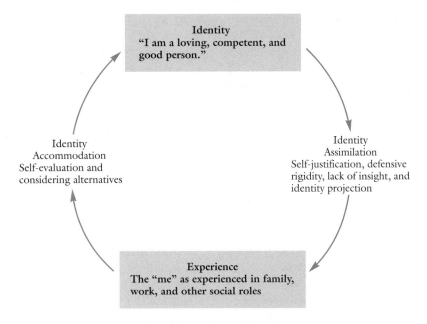

FIGURE 10.2 **Whitbourne's model of adult identity processes.**

Source: Whitbourne, S. K. (1986). The psychological construction of the life span. In J. E. Birren & K. W. Schaie (Eds.), *Handbook of the psychology of aging* (pp. 594–618). New York: Van Nostrand Reinhold.

estingly, Whitbourne and Collins (1999) found that there is a relationship between identity and changes in physical functioning over the adult years. Most adults, especially in the area of cognitive functioning, used identity assimilation. Identity assimilation was also positively related to self-esteem. This suggests that people may make behavioral adjustments to promote health adaptation to aging (see Chapter 3).

Self-Concept

As we have seen, an important aspect of identity in adulthood is how one integrates various aspects of the self. Self-perceptions and how they differ with age have been examined in a wide variety of studies and are related to many behaviors. Changes in self-perceptions often are manifested in changed beliefs, concerns, and expectations. **Self-concept** *is the organized, coherent, integrated pattern of self-perceptions.* It includes the notions of self-esteem and self-image.

Kegan (1982) attempted to integrate the development of self-concept and cognitive development. He postulated six stages of the development of self, corresponding to stages of cognitive development described in Chapter 8. Kegan's first three stages, which he calls incorporative, impulsive, and imperial, correspond to Piaget's sensorimotor, preoperational, and concrete operational stages (see Chapter 8). During this time, he believes children move from knowing themselves on the basis of reflexes to knowing themselves through needs and interests. At the beginning of formal operational thought during early adolescence (see Chapter 8), he argues, a sense of interpersonal mutuality begins to develop; he calls this period the interpersonal stage. By late adolescence or young adulthood, people move to a mature sense of identity based on taking control of their own lives and developing ideologies; Kegan calls this period the institutional stage. Finally, with the acquisition of postformal thought (see Chapter 8) comes an understanding that the self is a very complex system that takes into account other people; Kegan calls this period the interindividual stage. Kegan's (1982) work emphasizes the fact that personality development does not occur in a vacuum. Rather, we must not forget that the person is a complex integrated whole. Consequently, an understanding of the development of self-concept or any other aspect of personality is enhanced by an understanding of how it relates to other dimensions of development.

This point was clearly demonstrated by Labouvie-Vief and colleagues (1995). Working within a cognitive–developmental framework, they documented age differences in self-representation in people ranging in age from 11 to 85 years. Specifically, they found that mature adults move from representations of the self in young adulthood that are poorly differentiated from others or from social conventions and expectations to representations in middle age that are highly differentiated to representations in old age that are less differentiated. An important finding was that the degree of differentiation in self-representation was related to the level of cognitive development, providing support for Kegan's position.

In one of the few longitudinal studies of self-concept, Mortimer and colleagues (1982) followed a group of men for 14 years, beginning when in the first year of college. They found that self-image consisted of four dimensions: well-being, interpersonal qualities, activity, and unconventionality. Well-being included self-perceptions of happiness, lack of tension, and confidence. Interpersonal qualities were self-perceptions of sociability, interest in others, openness, and warmth. The activity component consisted of self-perceptions of strength, competence, success, and activity. The unconventionality dimension indicated that men saw themselves as impulsive, unconventional, and dreamy. Clearly, what Mortimer and colleagues found about self-image is very closely related to Costa and McCrae's model of personality, described earlier in this chapter.

Over the 14-year period the men in the Mortimer study showed little change as a group. The structure of self-concept remained stable. Some fluctuation at the level of self-image was noted, however. Both well-being and competence declined during college but rebounded after graduation. Self-perceptions of unconventionality declined after college. Sociability showed a steady decline across the entire study.

At the intraindividual level, the data indicated that self-perceptions of confidence were related to life events. The course of a man's career, his satisfaction with career and marriage, his relationship with his parents, and his overall life satisfaction followed patterns that could be predicted by competence. For example, an employee whose competence scores remain above the group average will report fewer job problems and higher marital and life satisfaction than men whose competence scores are below the group average.

Interestingly, a man's degree of confidence as a college senior influenced his later evaluation of life events, and it may have even set the stage for a self-fulfilling prophecy. Mortimer and colleagues suggest that these men may actively seek and create experiences that fit their personality structure. This hypothesis is supported by longitudinal research on gifted women, whose high self-confidence in early adulthood becomes manifested as a high life satisfaction during their 60s (Sears & Barbee, 1978).

The results from the Mortimer and colleagues (1982) study are strikingly similar to the data from the Berkeley studies described earlier in this chapter. Recall that data from these studies also support the idea that life events are important influences on personality development. In the present case, life events clearly influence one's self-concept. In the next section we consider how adults explain why certain things or certain events happen to them.

Possible Selves

Another important aspect of self-concept and creating a scenario about ourselves is the ability to project ourselves into the future and to speculate about what we might be like (Markus & Nurius, 1986). How do we do this? *Projecting ourselves into the future involves creating* **possible selves** *that represent what we could become, what we would like to become, and what we are afraid of becoming.* What we could or would like

Employees who remain above average in their competency report fewer job problems and higher marital and life satisfaction.

to become often reflects personal goals; we may see ourselves as leaders, as rich and famous, or as in shape. What we are afraid of becoming may show up in our fear of being undervalued, overweight, or lonely. Our possible selves are very powerful motivators; indeed, much of our behavior can be viewed as efforts to approach or avoid these various possible selves and to protect the current view of self (Markus & Nurius, 1986).

The topic of possible selves offers a way to understand how both stability and change operate in adults' personality. On one hand, possible selves tend to remain stable for at least some period of time and are measurable with psychometrically sound scales (Hooker, 1999; Ryff, 1991). On the other hand, possible selves may change in response to efforts at personal growth (Cross & Markus, 1991; Hooker, 1991), which would be expected from ego development theory. In particular, possible selves facilitate adaptation to new roles across the life span. For example, a full-time mother who pictures herself as an executive

once her child goes to school may begin to take evening courses to acquire new skills. Thus, possible selves offer a way to bridge the experience of the current self and our imagined future self.

Researchers have begun studying age differences in the construction of possible selves (Cross & Markus, 1991; Hooker, 1999). In a set of similar studies conducted by Cross and Markus (1991) and Hooker and colleagues (Hooker, 1999; Hooker et al., 1996; Hooker & Kaus, 1994), people across the adult life span were asked to describe their hoped-for and feared possible selves. Responses are grouped into categories (such as *family, personal, material, relationships,* and *occupation*). Several interesting age differences emerged. In terms of hoped-for selves, young adults listed as most important family concerns (Cross & Markus, 1991), such as marrying the right person, whereas Hooker et al. (1996) also found that getting started in an occupation was important in this age group. In contrast, middle adults (ages 25 to 39) listed family concerns last; their main issues concerned personal things (such as being a more loving and caring person; Cross & Markus, 1991). By ages 40 to 59, Cross and Markus found that family issues again became most common (such as being a parent who can let go of his or her children). Hooker and Kaus (1994) also found that reaching and maintaining satisfactory performance in one's occupational career and accepting and adjusting to the physiological changes of middle age were also important to this age group. For adults over 60, Cross and Markus found that personal issues were most prominent (for example, being able to be active and healthy for another decade at least). In addition, Hooker (1992) replicated this finding and found that establishing satisfactory living arrangements and adjusting to retirement also were well represented in their possible self repertoires.

Both sets of studies found that all age groups listed physical issues as their most common feared self. For the two younger groups, being overweight and, for women, becoming wrinkled and unattractive when old were commonly mentioned. For middle-aged and older adults, fear of having Alzheimer's disease or being unable to care for oneself were common responses.

Overall, adolescents and young adults are far more likely to have multiple possible selves and to believe more strongly that they can actually become the hoped-for self and successfully avoid the feared self. By old age, though, both the number of possible selves and the strength of belief decrease. Older adults are more likely to believe that neither the hoped-for nor the feared self is under their personal control. These findings may reflect differences with age in personal motivation, beliefs in personal control, and the need to explore new options.

Other researchers have examined possible selves in a different way by asking adults to describe their present, past, future, and ideal selves (Ryff, 1991; Keyes & Ryff, 1999). Instead of examining categories of possible selves, this approach focuses on people's perceptions of change over time. The data indicate that young and middle-aged adults see themselves as improving with age and expecting to continue getting better in the future. In contrast, older adults see themselves as having remained stable over time, but they foresee decline in their future. These findings may indicate that the older group has internalized negative stereotypes about aging, especially in view of the fact that they are currently healthy and well educated (see Chapter 9).

This general look at the issues that most influence possible selves indicates that the most important ones differ with age. But how are these issues reflected in aspects of personal well-being? Do the age differences in possible selves depend on whether one is projecting into the future or into the past? Such questions warrant a more complex approach.

This is exactly what Ryff (1991) did. In a fascinating series of studies, she adopted the notion of possible selves as a way to redefine the meaning of well-being in adulthood and showed how adults' views of themselves differ at various points in adulthood. Based on the responses of hundreds of adults, Ryff (1989, 1991) identified six dimensions of psychological well-being for adults and discovered many important age and gender differences in well-being based on these components:

Self-acceptance: having a positive view of oneself, acknowledging and accepting the multiple parts of oneself, and feeling positive about one's past.

Positive relationships with others: having warm, satisfying relationships with people; being concerned with their welfare; being empathic, affectionate, and intimate with them; and understanding the reciprocity of relationships.

Autonomy: being independent and determining one's own life, being able to resist social pressures to think or behave in a particular way, and evaluating one's life by internal standards.

Environmental mastery: being able to manipulate, control, and effectively use resources and opportunities.

Purpose in life: having goals in life and a sense of direction in one's life, feeling that one's present and past life has meaning, and having a reason for living.

Personal growth: feeling a need for continued personal improvement, seeing oneself as getting better and being open to new experiences, and growing in self-knowledge and personal effectiveness.

Like Linus in the Peanuts cartoon, young and middle-aged adults
see themselves as improving with age.

PEANUTS reprinted by permission of United Feature Syndicate, Inc.

How do these aspects of well-being change in adulthood? The How Do We Know? feature has one answer.

Taken together, the research on possible selves opens up new and exciting avenues for personality research. Possible selves are a way to examine the importance of personal perception in determining motivation to achieve and change as well as a way to study personality systematically with sound research methods. For example, possible selves research enables us to examine the creation of scenarios and life stories systematically. Because it provides an interesting bridge between different approaches to personality theory, it probably will be the focus of much research in the future.

Religiosity and Spiritual Support

For many adults, their relationship with God is a key aspect of their identity. In addition, when faced with the daily problems of living, older adults use their religious faith more than anything else, including family or friends, as a coping mechanism (McFadden, 1996). When asked to describe their most common ways of dealing with problems in life, nearly half of the people surveyed in one study listed coping strategies associated with religion (Koenig et al., 1988). Of these, the most common were placing trust in God, praying, and getting strength and help from God. These strategies can also be used to augment other ways of coping. Spouses caring for partners with Alzheimer's disease also report using religion as a primary coping mechanism (Ishler et al., 1998).

Researchers are increasingly focusing on **spiritual support,** *which includes seeking pastoral care, participating in organized and nonorganized religious activities, and expressing faith in a God who cares for people as a key factor in understanding how older adults cope.* McFadden (1996) points out that even when under high levels of stress, people such as Buddhist monks who rely on spiritual support report better personal well-being. Krause (1995) reports that feelings of self-worth are lowest for older adults with very little religious commitment, a finding supported by cross-cultural research with Muslims, Hindus, and Sikhs (Mehta, 1997). However, Pargament and colleagues (1995) also note the importance of individual differences in the effectiveness of spiritual support: Some people are helped more than others, some problems are more amenable to religious coping, and certain types of religious coping may be more effective than others.

Reliance on religion in times of stress appears especially important for many African Americans, who as a group are intensely involved in religious activities (Levin et al., 1994). Churches offer much social support for the African American community and serve an important function in advocating social justice (Roberts, 1980). For example, Dr. Martin Luther King, Jr., a Baptist minister, led the civil rights movement in the 1950s and 1960s, and contemporary congregations champion equal rights. The role of the church in African Americans' lives is central; indeed, one of the key predictors of life satisfaction among African Americans is regular church attendance (Coke, 1992).

Who was the investigator, and what was the aim of the study? How people see themselves is an important part of their sense of well-being. However, previous research on well-being in late life has been conducted without theoretical guidance (Ryff, 1989). Consequently, many researchers approached well-being from the perspective of loss; that is, researchers assumed that well-being, like physical prowess, was something that declined as people age. Ryff (1989; Ryff & Keyes, 1998) disagreed with this loss perspective and set out to demonstrate her point. She thought that well-being is a more complex issue and that it can improve in late life.

How did the investigator measure the topic of interest? In preliminary studies, Ryff administered numerous self-report scales that measured many aspects of personality and well-being. Her method in this investigation represented a new approach, one aimed at describing the complex developmental patterns she wanted to uncover. This new approach drew from life-span developmental theories (such as those presented in this text), clinical theories of personal growth

adapted from successful techniques in psychotherapy, and various definitions of mental health, yielding the most complete description yet of well-being in adulthood. On the basis of her research and thinking, Ryff (1989, 1991) developed a new measure of well-being that reflects the six-dimension model discussed earlier in this chapter. This new measure allowed her to obtain people's ratings of how they view themselves right now, what they were like in the past, what they think they might be like in the future, and what they would most like to be like.

Who were the participants in this study? A total of 308 young, middle-aged, and older men and women participated. The middle-aged and older adults were contacted through community and civic organizations. All participants were well educated.

What was the design of the study? Ryff used a cross-sectional design that compared young, middle-aged, and older adult groups.

Were there ethical concerns with this study? There were no serious concerns; each participant was informed about the purpose of the study, and participation was voluntary.

What were the results? The most important discovery from Ryff's research is that young, middle-aged, and older adults have very different views of themselves, depending on whether they are describing their present, past, future, or ideal self-perceptions. The left graph in Figure 10-3 shows that young and middle-aged adults are much more accepting of their ideal and future selves than they are of their present and past selves. For older adults, differences are much smaller. The right graph shows a similar pattern for autonomy, the feelings of being independent and determining one's own life.

Perhaps the most interesting findings of Ryff's research concern the difference between people's ideal vision of themselves and what they thought they were really like. If you carefully look at the graphs, you will notice that the differences between the ideal self ratings and the present self ratings diminish with age. When combined with similar findings in other aspects of well-being, this implies that older adults see themselves as closer to really being the person they wanted to become than do people of any other age

Within the African American community, religion is especially important to many women. The greater importance of the church in the lives of older African American women is supported by results from four national surveys of African American adults (Levin et al., 1994). The women reported that they are more active in church groups and attend services more frequently than African American men or European American men or women. However, the gender dif-

ferences diminish in people over age 70, when religion becomes equally important for African American men. Religion and spiritual support also serve as more important resources for many African American caregivers than for European American caregivers (Picot et al., 1997).

Many older adults of Mexican heritage adopt a different approach. Research indicates that they use *la fe de la gente* ("the faith of the people") as a coping

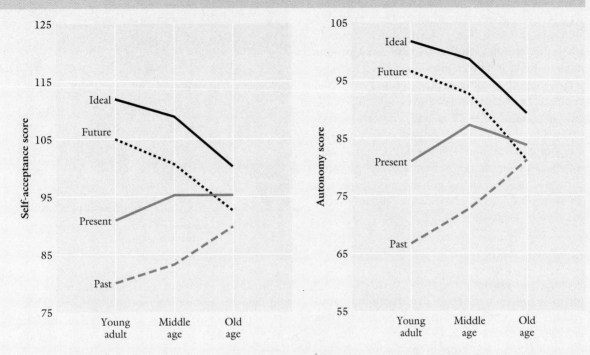

FIGURE 10.3 Age differences in self-acceptance scores and autonomy scores in young, middle-aged, and older adults.

Source: Ryff, C. D. (1991). Possible selves in adulthood and old age: A tale of shifting horizons. *Psychology and Aging, 6,* 286–295.

group. Ryff's data fit well with Erikson's (1982) idea of integrity. As people achieve integrity, they view their past less critically and become content with how they have lived their lives.

What did the investigator conclude? As Ryff (1991; Keyes & Ryff, 1999) notes, only by including all of these self-ratings will we understand people's sense of personal progress or decline over time from their goal of ideal functioning. Clearly, people judge themselves by many standards, and these change with age.

strategy (Villa & Jaime, 1993). The notion of *fe* incorporates varying degrees of faith, spirituality, hope, cultural values, and beliefs. *Fe* does not necessarily imply that people identify with a specific religious community. Rather, they identify with a cultural value or ideology.

Among many Native Americans, the spiritual elders are the wisdom-keepers, the repositories of the scared ways and natural world philosophies that ex-

tend indefinitely back in time (Wall & Arden, 1990). The wisdom-keepers also share dreams and visions, perform healing ceremonies, and may make apocalyptic prophecies. The place of the wisdom-keepers in the tribe is much more central than that of religious leaders in Western society.

Service providers would be well advised to keep in mind the self-reported importance of religion in the lives of many older adults when designing interventions to help them adapt to life stressors. For example, older adults may be more willing to talk with their minister about a personal problem than they would be to talk with a psychotherapist. However, when they seek help from a professional, it is more often with their family physician. When working with people of Mexican heritage, providers need to realize that a major source of distress for this group is lack of familial interaction and support. Overall, many churches offer a wide range of programs to assist poor or homebound older adults in the community. Such programs may be more palatable to recipients than programs based in social service agencies. To be successful, service providers should try to view life as their clients see it.

What happens to the gender identity of the man and woman in the photograph?

Gender Role Identity

People's beliefs about the appropriate characteristics for men and women reflect shared cultural beliefs and stereotypes of masculinity and femininity (Best & Williams, 1993; Huyck, 1999). Across a wide age range in U.S. society, women are traditionally described as weaker, less active, more concerned with affiliation, and more nurturing and deferential. Men are regarded as stronger, more active, and higher in autonomy, achievement, and aggression (Huyck, 1999). Collectively, such descriptions help form one's gender role identity.

In addition, some gender stereotypes are sensitive to age (Gutmann, 1994). Old men are seen as less stereotypically masculine or warriorlike and more as powerful older men striving for peace. Older women are noted for their greater assertiveness and control; stereotypes include matriarchs overseeing extended families or dangerous witches who use power malevolently. Some cultures view older adults as genderless, having lost the need for differentiated gender role identity after they concluded their child-rearing duties (Gailey, 1987).

As we know, the five-factor model makes a strong case for the stability of personality traits through adulthood. In contrast, we have seen that people's priorities and personal concerns change during adulthood.

Beginning with Jung (1933), several researchers and theorists argue for a crossover effect of gender identity during middle age. As we noted earlier, Jung (1933) proposed that in adolescence women initially suppress their masculine aspects and men initially suppress their feminine aspects. Each discovers these suppressed aspects and develops them in midlife, with the goal of achieving a balance between one's masculine and feminine characteristics. For example, during midlife women may place increased emphasis on achievement and accomplishment, and men may place more emphasis on familial and nurturing concerns (Parker & Aldwin, 1997).

Overall, the data on actual changes in people's gender role identity are mixed. Some studies find a tendency for middle-aged and older adults to endorse similar self-descriptions concerning gender role identity. For example, data from the Berkeley studies document a move toward greater similarity between older men and older women. Haan (1985; Haan et al., 1986) and Livson (1981) found that both men and women described themselves as more nurturant, intimate, and tender with increasing age, trends that are related to generativity. Gutmann (1987), Sinnott (1986), and Turner (1982) report similar findings. Huyck (1996) found evidence of **androgyny**, *the greater acceptance of both gender roles,* in midlife. Other studies show decreasing endorsement of traditional feminine traits in both men and women but stable endorsements of masculine traits (Parker & Aldwin, 1997). Collectively, the data indicate that men and women are most different in their gender role identities in late adolescence and young adulthood but become increasingly similar in midlife and old age (Huyck, 1999).

Longitudinal data on individual development are lacking. What evidence is available suggests that a majority (54%) of people remain in the same gender role category over a 10-year period (Hyde et al., 1991). However, this still means that a substantial number of people demonstrate change. As Hyde and colleagues (1991) note, however, we currently have no way of predicting who will change and who will not.

Increasing similarity in self-descriptions does not guarantee increased similarity in the way men and women behave. For example, older men often indicate a greater willingness to develop close relationships but few actually have the skills to do so (Turner, 1982). Thus, the change may happen more internally than behaviorally (Parker & Aldwin, 1997; Troll & Bengtson, 1982). Moreover, much of the change may be caused by the failing health of older men. Because older women tend to be healthier than their husbands, the balance of power may shift out of necessity to women, and men may be forced to accept a more dependent role.

Does gender role identity converge with increasing age? It is still debatable. The lack of consistent behavioral evidence and the statistically small differences in some of the self-assessment data lead some authors to argue that no changes in personality occur (McCrae & Costa, 1994). In contrast, others see the convergence in self-assessments as evidence that older men and women transcend stereotypes to become essentially gender free (Sinnott, 1986). Still others view any change in self-assessment, no matter how small, as at least personally relevant (Gutmann, 1987).

It will be interesting to see whether the trend toward similarity continues over the next few generations. Changes in how younger men and women view themselves as a result of women's new roles in society may shift the trend downward in age or may make it disappear altogether. As noted in Chapter 1, gender is one way in which societies stratify themselves. Whether changes in self-report have any bearing on true behavioral change is something that only time will tell.

Conclusions about Narratives, Identity, and the Self

We have seen that to fully understand a person, we must consider how the person integrates his or her life into a coherent structure. The life narrative approach provides a way to learn how people accomplish this integration. The theoretical frameworks developed by McAdams and Whitbourne offer excellent avenues for research. One of the most promising new areas of inquiry, possible selves, is already providing major insights into how people construct future elements of their life stories.

When combined with the data from the dispositional trait and personal concerns literatures, research findings on identity and the self provide the capstone knowledge needed to understand what people are like. The complexity of personality is clear from this discussion; perhaps that is why it takes a lifetime to complete.

CONCEPT CHECKS

1. What is a life story, as defined in McAdams's theory?
2. What connection is there between Whitbourne's theory of identity and Piaget's theory of cognitive development?
3. What are possible selves?
4. How does religiosity factor into identity?
5. How does gender role identity develop in adulthood?
6. Does the sense of identity and self change in adulthood?

PUTTING IT ALL TOGETHER

We have considered the importance of examining the extent to which our personality changes and remains stable across the adult life cycle. Joyce's high school reunion experience is reminiscent of how we expect our friends to remain the same throughout our lives and how these expectations are typically borne out. However, Jim reminds us that stability is not always the rule. Instead, given life transitions, we move through transformations of our own, changing the nature of what is meaningful to us. Felicia exemplifies the process we go through in planning our lives, dreams, and goals that factor into who we are to become. Taken together, these people reflect both change and stability in our personalities. The fact that we both change and remain stable is not a contradiction in terms but reflects the complexities in our personality makeup.

Summary

DISPOSITIONAL TRAITS ACROSS ADULTHOOD

The Case for Stability: The Five-Factor Model

The five-factor model posits five dimensions of personality: neuroticism, extroversion, openness to experience, agreeableness, and conscientiousness. Each of these dimensions has several descriptors.

Several longitudinal studies indicate that personality traits show long-term stability.

Critiques of the Five-Factor Model

Several criticisms of the five-factor model have been made: several different statistical functions could account for the stability observed, the research may have methodological problems, dispositional traits do not describe the core aspects of human nature and do not provide good predictors of behavior, and dispositional traits do not consider the contextual aspects of development.

An intraindividual perspective challenges stability by examining personality at the individual level.

Additional Longitudinal Studies of Dispositional Traits

Evidence from the Berkeley studies shows that lifestyle is a better predictor of life satisfaction for women, but personality is a better predictor for men.

Both stability and change characterize personality development in advanced old age.

Women's personality change is systematic in early and middle adulthood and is a function of changes in social roles and social contexts.

Conclusions about Dispositional Traits

The bulk of the evidence suggests that dispositional traits are stable across adulthood, but there may be a few exceptions. Criticisms of the research point to the need for better statistical analyses and a determination of the role of life experiences.

Stability in personality traits may be more evident later in the life span.

PERSONAL CONCERNS AND QUALITATIVE STAGES IN ADULTHOOD

What's Different about Personal Concerns?

Personal concerns take into account a person's developmental context and distinguish between having traits and doing everyday behaviors. Personal concerns are descriptions of what people are trying to accomplish and the goals they create.

Jung's Theory

Jung emphasizes various dimensions of personality (e.g., masculinity–femininity; extroversion–introversion). Jung argues that people move toward integrating these dimensions as they age, with midlife being an especially important period.

Erikson's Stages of Psychosocial Development

The sequence of Erikson's stages is trust versus mistrust, autonomy versus shame and doubt, initiative versus guilt, industry versus inferiority, identity versus identity confusion, intimacy versus isolation, generativity versus stagnation, and ego integrity versus despair. Erikson's theory can be seen as a trust–achievement–wholeness cycle repeating twice, although the exact transition mechanisms have not been clearly defined.

Generativity has received more attention than other adult stages. Research indicates that generative concern and generative action can be found in all age groups of adults, but they are particularly apparent among middle-aged adults.

Loevinger's Theory

Loevinger proposes eight stages of ego development, six of which can occur in adulthood: conformist, conscientious–conformist, conscientious, individualistic, autonomous, and integrated. Most adults are at the conscientious–conformist level. Linkages to cognitive development are apparent.

Theories Based on Life Transitions

In general, life transition theories postulate periods of transition that alternate with periods of stability. These theories tend to overestimate the commonality of age-linked transitions.

Research evidence suggests that crises tied to age 30, or the midlife crisis, do not occur for most people. However, most middle-aged people do point to both gains and losses, which could be viewed as change. This transition may be better characterized as a midlife correction.

Conclusions about Personal Concerns

Theory and research provide support for change in the personal concerns people report at various times in adulthood.

LIFE NARRATIVES, IDENTITY, AND THE SELF

McAdams's Life-Story Model

McAdams argues that people create a life story that is an internalized narrative with a beginning, middle, and anticipated ending. He also describes seven essential features of a life story: narrative tone, image, theme, ideological setting, nuclear episodes, character, and ending. Adults reformulate their life stories throughout adulthood.

Whitbourne's Identity Theory

Whitbourne believes that people have a life-span construct: a unified sense of their past, present, and future. The components of the life-span construct are the scenario (expectations of the future) and the life story (a personal narrative history). She integrates the concepts of assimilation and accommodation from Piaget's theory to explain how people's identity changes over time. Family and work are two major sources of identity.

Self-Concept

Self-concept is the organized, coherent, integrated pattern of self-perception. The events people experience help shape their self-concept. Self-presentation across adulthood is related to cognitive developmental level. Self-concept tends to stay stable at the group mean level.

Possible Selves

People create possible selves by projecting themselves into the future and thinking about what they would like to become, what they could become, and what they are afraid of becoming.

Age differences in these projections depend on the dimension examined. In hoped-for selves, young adults and middle-aged adults report family issues as most important, whereas 25- to 39-year-olds and older adults consider personal issues to be most important. However, all groups include physical aspects as part of their most feared selves.

Whereas younger and middle-aged adults view themselves as improving, older adults view themselves as declining. The standards by which people judge themselves change over time.

Ryff identified six aspects of well-being: self-acceptance, positive relationships with others, autonomy, environmental mastery, purpose in life, and personal growth. Older adults view their past more positively than younger or middle-aged adults, and they see themselves as closer to their ideal selves.

Religiosity and Spiritual Support

Older adults use religion and spiritual support more often than any other strategy to help them cope with problems in life. This provides a strong influence on identity. This is especially true for African American women, who are more active in their church groups and attend services more frequently. Other ethnic groups also gain important aspects of identity from religion.

Gender Role Identity

There is some evidence that gender role identity converges in middle age, to the extent that men and women are more likely to endorse similar self-descriptions. However, these similar descriptions do not necessarily translate into similar behavior.

Conclusions about Narratives, Identity, and the Self

The life narrative approach provides a way to learn how people integrate the various aspects of their personality. Possible selves, religiosity, and gender role identity are important areas that warrant additional research.

Review Questions

Dispositional Traits across Adulthood

- What is a dispositional trait?

- Describe Costa and McCrae's five-factor model of personality. What are the descriptors in each dimension? How do these dimensions change across adulthood?

- What evidence is there in other longitudinal research for change in personality traits in adulthood? Under what conditions is there stability or change?

- What specific criticisms have been raised about the five-factor model?

- What does most of the evidence say about the stability of dispositional traits across adulthood?

Personal Concerns and Qualitative Stages in Adulthood

- What is a personal concern? How does it differ from a dispositional trait?

- Describe Jung's theory. What important developmental changes does he describe?

- Describe Erikson's eight stages of psychosocial development. What cycles have been identified? How has his theory been clarified and expanded? What types of generativity have been proposed? What evidence is there for generativity? What modifications to Erikson's theory has this research suggested?

- Describe Loevinger's theory of ego development, with particular emphasis on the stages seen in adults.

- What are the major assumptions of theories based on life transitions? What evidence is there that a midlife crisis really exists? How can midlife be viewed from a gain–loss perspective?

- Overall, what evidence is there for change in personal concerns across adulthood?

Life Narratives, Identity, and the Self

- What are the basic tenets of McAdams's life-story theory? What are the seven elements of a life story?

- What is Whitbourne's life-span construct? How does it relate to a scenario and a life story? How did Whitbourne incorporate Piagetian concepts into her theory of identity?

- What is self-concept? What shapes it?

- What are possible selves? What developmental trends have been found in possible selves?

- How are religiosity and spiritual support important aspects of identity in older adults?

- How does gender role identity develop across adulthood?

Integrating Concepts in Development

1. What relations can be found between dispositional traits, personal concerns, and life narratives?

2. How does personality development reflect the four basic forces of development discussed in Chapter 1?

3. How does cognitive development relate to personality change?

4. How does personality change relate to stages in occupational transition?

Key Terms

androgyny Gender role reflecting the most adaptive aspects of the traditional masculine and feminine roles.

dispositional trait A stable, enduring aspect of personality.

ego development The fundamental changes in the ways in which our thoughts, values, morals, and goals are organized. Transitions from one stage to another depend on both internal biological changes and external social changes to which the person must adapt.

epigenetic principle In Erikson's theory, the notion that development is guided by an underlying plan in which certain issues have their own particular times of importance.

five-factor model A model of dispositional traits with the dimensions of neuroticism, extroversion, openness to experience, agreeableness, and conscientiousness.

life narrative The aspects of personality that pull everything together, the integrative aspects that give a person an identity or sense of self.

life-span construct In Whitbourne's theory of identity, the way in which people build a view of who they are.

midlife correction Reevaluating ones' roles and dreams and making the necessary corrections.

personal concerns Things that are important to people, their goals, and their major concerns in life.

possible selves Aspects of the self-concept involving oneself in the future in both positive and negative ways.

self-concept The organized, coherent, integrated pattern of self-perceptions.

spiritual support The value of seeking pastoral care, participating in organized and nonorganized religious activities, and expressing faith in a God who cares for people as a key coping strategy.

Resources

READINGS

Erikson, E. H. (1982). *The life cycle completed: Review.* New York: Norton. Erikson's own summary of his theory that highlights adulthood. Moderately difficult reading.

Funder, D. C., Parke, R. D., Tomlinson-Keasey, C., & Widaman, K. (Eds.). (1993). *Studying lives through time: Personality and development.* Washington, D.C.: American Psychological Association. Examines the different pathways individuals take across the life span and how this affects growth and development of their personality. Moderate reading.

Labouvie-Vief, G. (1994). *Psyche and Eros: Mind and gender in the life course.* New York: Cambridge University Press. An exploration of gender differences in the development of thinking across the life span. Moderately difficult.

McAdams, D. P. (1993). *The stories we live by: Personal myths and the making of the self.* New York: William Morrow. Fascinating reading that lays the groundwork for McAdams's theory of life narratives. Easy to moderate reading.

Pervin, L. A. (1996). *The science of personality.* New York: Wiley. General overviews of personality research and theories in adulthood. Moderate reading.

Whitbourne, S. K. (1996). *The aging individual: Physical and psychological perspectives.* New York: Springer-Verlag. The general overview of Whitbourne's theory of identity from a cognitive perspective. Interesting reading that is easy to moderately difficult.

SEARCH ONLINE WITH
INFOTRAC COLLEGE EDITION

For more information on the topics in this chapter, explore InfoTrac College Edition, your online library. Go to http://www.infotrac-college.com/wadsworth and use the passcode that came on the card with your book. Try these search terms: neurotocism, extroversion, androgyny, self-identity.

RELATIONSHIPS

© AP/Wide World Photos

By all accounts, Gloria Estefan is enormously successful. You've undoubtedly heard her music, and you may have seen her in concert in person or on TV or video. But you may not know that Gloria provides an excellent example of relationships. For example, Gloria cared for her father, who had multiple sclerosis, and her younger sister while her mother worked and attended evening classes. As an aspiring psychologist at the University of Miami, she attended a wedding in 1975 where she met Emilio Estefan, leader of a small band. Three years later, Gloria and Emilio married, forging a very strong personal and professional partnership.

Gloria's experiences reflect some of the key relationships we examine in this chapter. First, we consider friendships and love relationships and how they change across adulthood. Because love relationships usually involve a couple, we will explore how two people find each other and marry and how marriages develop. We also consider singlehood, divorce, remarriage, and widowhood. Finally, we take up some of the important roles associated with personal relationships, including parenting, family roles, and grandparenting.

RELATIONSHIP TYPES AND ISSUES

LEARNING OBJECTIVES

- What role do friends play across the adult life span?
- How are siblings important, especially in late life?
- What characterizes love relationships? How do they vary across cultures?
- What are abusive relationships? What are elder abuse and neglect?

Jamal and Kahlid have known each other all their lives. They grew up together in New York, attended the same schools, and even married sisters. Their business careers took them in different directions, but they always got together on major holidays. Now as older men, they feel a special bond; many of their other friends have died.

Jamal and Kahlid remind us that some of the most important people in our lives are our friends. Indeed, a popular television show, *Friends,* was based on the relationships between young adults and the need to have people around who really care about you. Sometimes, friendships turn into something more. Love blossoms, and relationships become more intimate and intense. In this section, we examine friendships and love relationships in adulthood and see why and how they are central to our lives.

Friendships

What is a friend? Someone who is there when you need to share? Someone not afraid to tell you the truth? Someone to have fun with? Friends are all these and more.

Friends are very different from family and represent a point of contrast (de Vries, 1996). Friendships are based predominantly on feelings and grounded in reciprocity and choice. Our friends help us develop self-esteem, self-awareness, and self-respect. They also help us become socialized into new roles throughout adulthood.

Friendships are important throughout adulthood, in part because a person's life satisfaction is strongly related to the quantity and quality of contacts with friends (Antonucci, 1985). The importance of main-

Friendships are a very important aspect of older adults' lives.

taining contacts with friends cuts across ethnic lines as well. For example, African Americans who have many friends are happier than those with only a few friends (Ellison, 1990). Thus, regardless of one's background, friendships play a major role in determining how much we enjoy life.

Researchers have uncovered three broad themes that underlie adult friendships (de Vries, 1996):

The most frequently mentioned dimension is the affective or emotional basis of friendship. This dimension includes self-disclosure and expressions of intimacy, appreciation, affection, and support, all of which are based on trust, loyalty, and commitment.

A second theme is the shared or communal nature of friendship, in which friends participate in or support activities of mutual interest.

The third dimension is sociability and compatibility: Our friends keep us entertained and are sources of amusement, fun, and recreation.

These three dimensions are found in friendships among adults of all ages (de Vries, 1996).

DEVELOPMENTAL ASPECTS OF FRIENDSHIPS. People tend to have more friends and acquaintances during young adulthood than at any later period (Antonucci, 1985). Although their numbers decline, friendships are still important in later life. Even when faced with constraints on maintaining friendships such as increased disability, most people over age 85 still actively maintain friendships (Johnson & Troll, 1994).

Surprisingly, older adults' life satisfaction is largely unrelated to the quantity or quality of contact with the younger members of their own family but is strongly related to the quantity and quality of contacts with friends (Fehr, 1996).

Why are friends so important to older adults? Some researchers believe that one reason may be older adults' concerns about becoming burdens to their families (Roberto & Scott, 1986). As a result, they help their friends foster independence. This reciprocity is a crucial aspect of friendship in later life because it allows the paying back of indebtedness over time. Also important is that friends are fun for people of all ages (Cavanaugh, 1999b).

Older adults tend to have fewer relationships with people in general and to develop fewer new relationships than people do in midlife and particularly in young adulthood (Carstensen, 1995). For many years, researchers tended to view this phenomenon as merely a reflection of the loss of relationships in late life through death and other means. However, Carstensen (1993, 1995) has shown that the changes in social behavior seen in late life reflect a much more complicated and important process. She proposes a life-span theory of **socioemotional selectivity**, *which argues that social contact is motivated by a variety of goals, including information seeking, self-concept, and emotional regulation.*

Each of these goals is differentially salient at different points of the adult life span and results in very different social behaviors. For example, when information seeking is the goal, such as when a person is exploring the world, trying to figure out how he or she fits, what others are like, and so forth, meeting many new people is an essential part of the process. However, when emotional regulation is the goal, people tend to become highly selective in their choice of social partners and nearly always prefer people who are familiar to them.

Carstensen (1993, 1995) believes that information seeking is the predominant goal for young adults, that emotional regulation is the major goal for older people, and that the three goals are in balance in midlife. Her research supports this view; people become increasingly selective in whom they choose to have contact with. Carstensen's theory provides a more complete explanation of why older adults tend not to replace the relationships they lose to any great extent: Older adults are more selective and have fewer opportunities to make new friends.

With time, older adults begin to lose members of their friendship network, usually through death. Rook (2000) proposes that older adults compensate for this loss through three strategies: forming new ties, redefining the need for friends, or developing alternative nonsocial activities. Although not always successful, these strategies reflect the need to address an important loss in people's lives.

GENDER DIFFERENCES IN FRIENDSHIPS. Men's and women's friendships tend to differ in adulthood, reflecting continuity in the learned behaviors from childhood (Fehr, 1996; Rawlins, 1992; Tannen, 1990). Women tend to base their friendships on more intimate and emotional sharing and use friendship as a means to confide in others. For women, getting together with friends often takes the form of getting together to discuss personal matters. Confiding in others is a basis of women's friendships. In contrast, men tend to base friendships on shared activities or interests. They are more likely to go bowling or fishing or to talk sports with their friends. For men, confiding in others is inconsistent with the need to compete; this may be one reason men are reluctant to do so (Cutrona, 1996). Rather, competition often is a part of men's friendships, as evidenced in basketball games with friends. However, the competition usually is set up so that the social interaction is the most important element, not who wins or loses (Rawlins, 1992). Men's friendships usually are less intimate than women's, no matter how one defines intimacy (Fehr, 1996).

Women tend to have more close relationships than do men. Although you may think that this puts women at an advantage, research shows that this is not always the case. Sometimes, friends can get on people's nerves or make high demands. When these things happen, women tend to be less happy even when they have lots of friends (Antonucci et al., 1998).

Sibling Relationships

For many adults, especially older adults, relationships with siblings are among the closest. This closeness dates to childhood and adolescence and is based on shared family experiences. Besides closeness, other dimensions of sibling friendships include involvement with each other, frequency of contact, envy, and resentment. Based on these dimensions, Gold and colleagues (1990) identified five different types of sibling interactions:

Congenial sibling relationships, characterized by high levels of closeness and involvement, average levels of contact, and low levels of envy and resentment

Loyal sibling relationships, characterized by average levels of closeness, involvement, and contact and low levels of envy and resentment

Intimate sibling relationships, characterized by high levels of closeness and involvement and low levels of envy and resentment

Apathetic sibling relationships, characterized by low levels on all dimensions

Hostile sibling relationships, characterized by high levels of involvement and resentment and low levels on all other dimensions

When combined across different possible sibling pairs, the frequencies of these five types of sibling relationships differ. Loyal and congenial relationships describe nearly two-thirds of all older sibling pairs. Additionally, older African American siblings have apathetic or hostile relationships with their siblings about one fifth as often as older European Americans do (4.5% for African Americans versus 22% for European Americans; Gold, 1990). Sometimes, hostile sibling relationships in late life date back to sibling rivalries that began in childhood (Greer, 1992).

When different combinations of sibling pairs are considered separately, ties between sisters typically are the strongest, most common, and most intimate (Lee et al., 1990). In contrast, brothers tend to maintain less frequent contact (Connidis, 1988). Developmentally, though, sibling ties tend to be strongest in adolescence and late life, as shown in Figure 11.1 (Schmeeckle et al., 1998). These shifts in importance

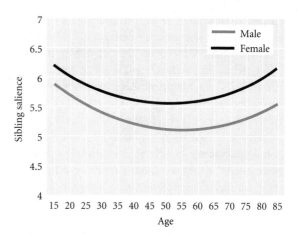

FIGURE 11.1 **Strength of sibling ties across the lifespan.**

Source: Schmeeckle, M., Giarusso, R., & Wang, Q. (1998, November). *When being a brother or sister is important to one's identity: Life stage and gender differences.* Paper presented at the annual meeting of the Gerontological Society, Philadelphia.

may result from people acquiring, and subsequently losing, other key roles and relationships. Jamal and Kahlid's relationship is a good example of how brothers may get closer with age.

Some older adults end up providing care for or living with one of their siblings, especially when one sibling has no other family members to provide care. Research indicates that siblings who receive help from their brothers or sisters tend to be younger, live alone (never-married, divorced, or single), have few children, and live in small cities (Cicirelli et al., 1992). Most people with two or more siblings believe that their brothers or sisters would provide help in a crisis and would share their home if necessary (Connidis, 1994).

Clearly, there are major gaps in our understanding of sibling relationships. This is unfortunate because our brothers and sisters play an important and meaningful role throughout our lives.

Love Relationships

Love is one of those things that everybody can feel but nobody can define adequately or completely. (Test yourself: How would you explain what you mean when you look at someone and say, "I love you"?) Despite the difficulty in defining it, love underlies our most important relationships in life.

There is little consensus about the nature of love. Sternberg (1986) conducted a series of detailed studies on people's conceptions of love and how love is manifested in different ways. Based on this research, Sternberg developed a theory of love based on three components: passion, an intense physiological desire for someone; intimacy, the feeling that one can share all one's thoughts and actions with another; and commitment, the willingness to stay with a person through good and bad times. Ideally, a true love relationship such as marriage has all three, although the balance shifts as time passes.

Everybody wants to be loved by somebody, but actually having it happen is fraught with difficulties. In his book *The Prophet* (1923), Kahlil Gibran points out that love is a two-sided issue: Just as it can give one the greatest ecstasy, it can cause one the greatest pain. Yet most of us are willing to take the risk.

As you may have experienced, taking the risk is fun (at times) and trying (at other times). Making a connection can be ritualized, as when people use pickup lines in a bar, or can happen almost by accident, as when two people run into each other in a crowded corridor. Because nearly all the research that has examined the process by which people meet and fall in love has been done with heterosexual couples, we focus on them. How do men and women fall in love?

The theory that does the best job explaining the process is the theory of **assortative** *mating, which states that people find partners based on their similarity to each other.* Assortative mating occurs along many dimensions, such as religious beliefs, physical traits, age, socioeconomic status, intelligence, and political ideology (Sher, 1996). Such nonrandom mating occurs most often in Western societies, which allow people to have more control over their own dating and pairing behaviors.

How do these dimensions based on U.S. samples compare with cross-cultural evidence? In an extraordinary study grounded in sociobiological theory, Buss and a large team of researchers (1990) identified the effects of culture and gender on mate preferences in 37 cultures worldwide. They had people rate and rank each of 18 characteristics (such as mutual attraction, chastity, dependable character, good health) on how important or desirable it would be in choosing a mate. These characteristics were based on ones used in U.S. research since the 1940s.

Buss found strong cultural effects, with each culture producing somewhat different preferences. Chastity proved to be the characteristic showing the most variability across cultures; in some cultures it is highly desired, whereas in others it matters little. Interestingly, consistent gender differences emerged across cultures on the characteristics of earning potential (endorsed consistently more often by women) and physical attractiveness (endorsed consistently more often by men). Buss and colleagues argue that the consistency of these gender differences across cultures supports evolution-based speculation about the importance of resources and reproductive value in mates. That is, in their respective search for mates, men around the world value physical attractiveness in women whereas women around the world look for men who will be good providers.

Violence in Relationships

Up to this point, we have been considering relationships that are healthy and positive. Sadly, this is not always the case. *Sometimes relationships become violent; one person becomes aggressive toward the partner, creating an* **abusive relationship.** Such relationships have received increasing attention over the past few decades. Indeed, some authors believe, as does the U.S. criminal justice system under some circumstances, that abusive relationships can be used as an explanation for one's behavior (Walker, 1984). *For example,* **battered woman syndrome** *occurs when a woman believes that she cannot leave the abusive situation and may even go so far as to kill her abuser.*

What kind of aggressive behaviors occur in abusive relationships? What causes such abuse? Researchers are beginning to find answers to these and related questions. Based on a decade of research on abusive partners, O'Leary (1993) argues that there is a continuum of aggressive behaviors toward a spouse, which progresses as follows: verbally aggressive behaviors, physically aggressive behaviors, severe physically aggressive behaviors, and murder of the partner. The causes of the abuse also vary with the type of abusive behavior being expressed. O'Leary's continuum is shown in Figure 11.2.

Two points about the continuum are interesting. First, there may be fundamental differences in the types of aggression that go beyond level of severity. Lower levels of physically aggressive behavior, such as pushing or slapping, are common; 25% to 40% of men and women who are in committed relationships display such behaviors on occasion (Riggs & O'Leary, 1992). In contrast, some men are extremely abusive from the outset of the relationship; they are thought to comprise the subset of batterers who seriously physically injure their partners and exert coercive control over their lives (Stark, 1992).

The second interesting point, depicted in the figure, is that the suspected underlying causes of aggressive behaviors differ as the type of aggressive behaviors change (O'Leary, 1993). As can be seen, the number of suspected causes of aggressive behavior increases as the level of aggression increases. Thus, the causes of aggressive behavior become more complex as the level of aggression worsens. Such differences in cause imply that the approaches to treating abusers should vary with the nature of the aggressive behavior (O'Leary, 1993). Situational factors that contribute to all levels of aggression are alcoholism, job stressors, and unemployment; the presence of these factors increases the likelihood that violence will occur in the relationship (O'Leary, 1993).

Gender differences in some of the underlying causes of aggressive behavior in relationships have been reported (O'Leary, 1993). Most important, the triad of need to control, misuse of power, and jealousy are more pertinent causes for men than for women. For example, men are more likely than women to act aggressively because they want to make sure their partner knows "who the boss is" and who makes the rules.

ELDER ABUSE AND NEGLECT. In addition to the types of abuse that occur in couple relationships, abuse is a part of some relationships involving older parents and their adult children. In this section, we consider what elder abuse and neglect are, how often they happen, and what victims and abusers are like.

Elder abuse is difficult to define precisely in practice. In general, researchers and public policy advocates describe several different categories of elder abuse (National Center on Elder Abuse [NCEA], 1999): physical (such as beating or withholding care), psychological and emotional (such as verbal assaults and social isolation), sexual, material or financial exploitation (such as illegal or improper use of funds), and the violation of rights (such as forcing one out of one's house or denying privacy).

In addition to abuse, neglect of older adults is also a growing problem (NCEA, 1999). Neglecting older adults can be either intended, such as refusing to fulfill basic caregiving obligations with the intention of inflicting harm, or unintended, such as not providing adequate medical care because of a lack of knowledge on the caregiver's part (Wolf et al., 1986).

Part of the problem in agreeing on a common definition of elder abuse and neglect is that perceptions differ across ethnic groups. For example, African American, Korean American, and European American older women used different criteria in deciding whether scenarios they read represented abuse (Moon & Williams, 1993). Specifically, older Korean American women were much less likely to judge a particular scenario as abusive and to indicate that help should be sought than older women in either of the other groups. These ethnic differences may result in conflicts between social service workers, who may be using one set of definitions, and clients, who may be using another, in deciding who should receive protective services. Perhaps the only firm conclusion that can be drawn is that the perception of elder abuse is relativistic and depends on characteristics of both the perceiver and the victim (Childs et al., 2000).

Estimates are that nearly 500,000 older Americans experience abuse or neglect, with another 150,000 suffering self-neglect (NCEA, 1998). Although the number of cases has increased over the years, it is unclear whether this is caused by actual increases in the rate of abuse and neglect or by better reporting

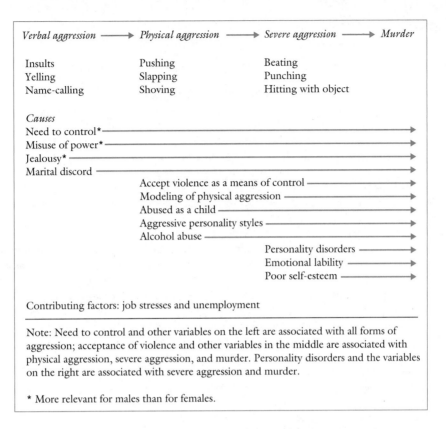

Verbal aggression ⟶ Physical aggression ⟶ Severe aggression ⟶ Murder

Insults	Pushing	Beating
Yelling	Slapping	Punching
Name-calling	Shoving	Hitting with object

Causes
Need to control* ───────────────────────────────────────⟶
Misuse of power* ──────────────────────────────────────⟶
Jealousy* ───⟶
Marital discord ───────────────────────────────────────⟶

Accept violence as a means of control ──────⟶
Modeling of physical aggression ──────────⟶
Abused as a child ───────────────────────⟶
Aggressive personality styles ────────────⟶
Alcohol abuse ───────────────────────────⟶

Personality disorders ────⟶
Emotional lability ───────⟶
Poor self-esteem ────────⟶

Contributing factors: job stresses and unemployment

Note: Need to control and other variables on the left are associated with all forms of aggression; acceptance of violence and other variables in the middle are associated with physical aggression, severe aggression, and murder. Personality disorders and the variables on the right are associated with severe aggression and murder.

* More relevant for males than for females.

FIGURE 11.2   Continuum of progressive behaviors in abusive relationships.

From K. D. O'Leary, Through a psychological lens: Personality traits, personality disorders, and levels of violence, R. J. Gelles & D. R. Loseke (eds.), *Current Controversies on Family Violence*, pp. 7–30, copyright © 1993 by Sage Publications, Inc. Reprinted by permission of the publisher.

(Schick & Schick, 1994). One of the most hotly contested issues in adulthood and aging is trying to understand which older adults are at greatest risk for abuse and neglect. This issue must be sorted out to provide the most appropriate services to victims and to develop effective prevention strategies. At present there are two competing views of who is at risk. At the heart of the debate is a deceptively simple question: Are abuse victims dependent on perpetrators, or are perpetrators dependent on abuse victims? These positions are discussed in the Current Controversies feature. Research evidence supports both views (Pillemer, 1993; Steinmetz, 1993).

Much more attention has been paid to identifying characteristics of abusers. Adult children generally are more likely to abuse older adults than are other people (NCEA, 1999). In general, people who abuse or neglect older adults show higher rates of substance abuse and mental health problems, are inexperienced caregivers, have more economic problems, receive little help from other family members for caregiving, are hypercritical and insensitive to others, and are more likely to have been abused themselves (NCEA, 1999; Pillemer, 1993).

We need to learn much more about abusive relationships across adulthood. Little is known

One of the most controversial issues in aging is which older adults are at greatest risk for abuse and neglect. Sorting out this issue is important in providing the most appropriate services to victims and developing effective prevention strategies. There are two competing views of who is at risk. At the heart of the debate is a deceptively simple question: Are abuse victims dependent on perpetrators, or are perpetrators dependent on abuse victims?

Most researchers and policymakers assume that abuse victims are dependent. Indeed, the typical picture is one of a victim who has been abused by his or her caregiver, who in turn is under great stress from having to provide care (Steinmetz, 1993). Such victims usually are over age 80, female, excessively loyal to their caregiver, involved in frequent intergenerational conflict, burdened with a history of abuse, socially isolated, and characterized by the abusers as unpleasant or demanding. The stress, frustration, and burden caregivers experience are too much for

some to take; they lash out and turn their emotions into abusive behavior. For example, there is evidence that the onset of new cognitive impairments in a care recipient increases the likelihood of abuse (Lachs et al., 1997). In this view, abuse and neglect of older adults have much in common with child abuse and neglect; both involve victims who are highly dependent on their perpetrators for basic care. This view is easy for people to understand, which is probably why most prevention programs are based on a dependent victim model.

Other researchers strongly disagree. Rather than the victims being dependent on caregiver–perpetrators, they see the perpetrators as being dependent on the victims (Pillemer, 1993). These perpetrators are not merely acting out their frustration; they are seen as deviant and suffering from mental disorders. In this approach, perpetrators depend on their victims in four areas: housing, financial assistance, household repair, and transportation. Perpetrators also tend to be more violent in general, to have

been arrested for other crimes, and to have been hospitalized for psychiatric disorders (Pillemer, 1993).

Which of these views is correct? Based on the research to date, both positions have support. This has profound implications for prevention and treatment. If victims are dependent, then programs are needed to provide basic services to caregivers to lower their stress. If perpetrators are deviant and have mental disorders, then programs must identify people who are at risk for abusing older adults. Clearly, additional research is needed to provide the appropriate direction for policymakers and to settle the controversy.

Search Online with **InfoTrac College Edition** For more information on these controversies, explore InfoTrac College Edition, your online library. Go to http://www.infotrac-college.com/wadsworth and use the passcode that came on the card with your book. Try this search term: aged—abuse of.

---

about developmental differences in types of abuse, characteristics of abuse victims, and abusers. Such knowledge would provide key insights into identifying those at risk and preventing abuse from occurring.

CONCEPT CHECKS

1. What are the key characteristics of adults' friendships?
2. What are the key aspects of sibling relationships across adulthood?
3. What are the three fundamental components of love relationships?
4. What are the types of violent behavior in abusive relationships and their associated causes?

LIFESTYLES AND LOVE RELATIONSHIPS

LEARNING OBJECTIVES

- What are the challenges and advantages of being single?
- What are gay male and lesbian relationships like?
- What is marriage like across adulthood?
- Why do people divorce and remarry?
- What are the experiences of widows and widowers?

*B*obbie *and Jack were high school sweethearts who married a few years after World War II. Despite many trials in their relationship, they have remained* *firmly committed to each other for over 50 years. Not only are they still in love, but they are best friends. In looking back, they note that once their children moved away they grew closer again. Bobbie and Jack wonder whether this is typical.*

Bobbie and Jack show us that forging relationships is only part of the picture in understanding how adults live their lives with other people. For most, one relationship becomes special and results in commitment, typically through marriage. Putting relationships in context is the goal of this section as we explore the major lifestyles of adults. First, we consider people who never get married. Next, we look at those who cohabitate and those who are in same-sex relationships. We also consider those who get married and those who divorce and remarry. Finally, we discuss people who are widowed.

Singlehood

When Susan graduated from college with a degree in accounting, she took a job at a consulting firm. For the first several years in her job, she spent more time traveling than she did at home. During this time, she had a series of love relationships, but none resulted in commitment even though she had marriage as a goal. By the time she was in her mid-30s, Susan had decided that she no longer wanted to get married. "I'm now a partner in my firm, I enjoy traveling, and I'm pretty flexible in terms of moving if something better comes along," she stated to her friend Michele. "But I do miss being with someone to share my day or to just hang around with."

During early adulthood, most people are single, like Susan, defined as not living with an intimate partner. Estimates are that approximately 75% of men and 60% of women between ages 20 and 25 are unmarried, with increasing numbers deciding to stay that way. These percentages have been rising over the past few decades, and they are fairly similar in all industrialized countries (Burns, 1992).

Susan's experience is common among women who ultimately decide not to marry (Dalton, 1992). Many women focus on career goals rather than marriage or relationships. Others report that they simply did not meet "the right person" or prefer singlehood to the disappointment they experienced with men. However, the pressure to marry is especially strong for women; frequent questions such as "Any good prospects yet?" may leave women feeling conspicuous or left out as many of their friends marry. Research indicates that single women have unresolved or unrecognized ambivalences about being single (Lewis & Moon, 1997). Such feelings result from being aware of the advantages and disadvantages of being single and ambivalence about the reasons they are single.

Men tend to remain single longer in young adulthood because they tend to marry at a later age than women (U.S. Bureau of the Census, 1999). Fewer men than women remain unmarried throughout adulthood, largely because men find partners more easily as they select from a larger age range of unmarried women. Because men also tend to "marry down" in social status, women with higher levels of education are overrepresented among unmarried adults compared with men with similar levels of education.

Ethnic differences in singlehood reflect both differences in age at marriage and social factors. For example, nearly twice as many African Americans are single during young adulthood as European Americans; however, the high unemployment rate among young African American men has a strong influence on marriage rates (Cherlin, 1992; U.S. Bureau of the Census, 1999). However, by the time African and European Americans are in their 40s, marriage rates are comparable between the groups (U.S. Bureau of the Census, 1999).

In general, singles recognize the pluses and minuses in their lifestyles. They enjoy the freedom and flexibility but also feel loneliness, dissatisfaction with dating, limited social life in a couple-oriented society, and less sense of security (Chasteen, 1994). Interestingly, being single has negative health and longevity effects on men but not on women (Whitbourne, 1996a). In the end, most singles come to terms with their lifestyles and may even become parents.

Gay Male and Lesbian Couples

Less is known about the developmental course of gay male and lesbian relationships than about any other type. Perhaps this is because these relationships are not widely viewed as an acceptable alternative to traditional marriage. Besides the usual problems of instability and guilt that sometimes accompany other forms of cohabitation, gay male and lesbian couples experience several additional problems resulting from the disapproval of much of society for such relationships. For example, the loss of one's mate cannot be mourned as easily because in many situations revealing one's gay or lesbian relationship may create difficulties in one's life (Kimmel, 1995; Kimmel & Sang, 1995). However, older lesbian and gay adults find support in their friendship networks, especially from those who know of their sexual orientation (Grossman et al., 2000).

Gay male and lesbian relationships are similar to traditional marriages in many ways; financial problems and decisions, household chores, and power differentials are issues for all couples. Gay and lesbian couples overall are more egalitarian than heterosexual couples, with lesbian couples most egalitarian of all (Peplau, 1991). Moreover, gay male and lesbian parents do not differ substantially on these dimensions from heterosexual parents (Kimmel & Sang, 1995; Kurdek, 1995b). Like heterosexual couples, at midlife gay male and lesbian partners must deal with developing their careers, creating social networks as a couple and as individuals, planning for retirement, and the like (Kimmel & Sang, 1995).

Few longitudinal studies of gay male and lesbian couples have been conducted. Kurdek (1995a, 1995b) summarizes his own work, which focused on specific relationship issues that are important over time. In interpersonal intimacy, Kurdek found that compared with gay male couples, lesbian partners attributed greater importance to equality in their notion of an ideal relationship. Additionally, the value attributed to attachment (i.e., doing things together as a couple) in the ideal relationship declined for both types of relationships, reflecting increased feelings of trust and security. This pattern is essentially the same for heterosexual couples. The balance between changes in current levels of equality and attachment predicted the degree of commitment in the relationship for both gay male and lesbian couples.

Despite the general lack of research on gay male and lesbian relationships, several general conclusions can be drawn (Kurdek, 1995b). At the most basic level, gay men and lesbians see themselves as part of a couple. However, lesbian couples are more likely to view themselves as sexually exclusive. Compared with heterosexual couples, gay couples and especially lesbian partners are more likely to practice an ethic of equality. Gay male and lesbian couples show much the same types of changes over time, general patterns of satisfaction with the relationship, and similar predictors of relationship success as do heterosexual couples.

Marriage

Most adults want their love relationships to result in marriage. However, U.S. residents are in less of a hurry to achieve this goal; the median age at first marriage for adults in the United States has been rising for several decades. As you can see in Figure 11.3, the median age for men is about 26, and the median age for women is roughly 24 (U.S. Bureau of the Census, 1999). This trend is not bad; women under age 20 at the time they are first married are three times more likely to end up divorced than women who first marry in their 20s and six times more likely than those who first marry in their 30s (U.S. Bureau of the Census, 1999). Let's explore age and other factors that keep marriages going strong over time.

Being married has benefits besides providing companionship. For example, being married encourages healthy behaviors for couples of all ages (Schone & Weinick, 1998), and married people tend to have greater average longevity (U.S. Bureau of the Census, 1999).

FACTORS INFLUENCING MARITAL SUCCESS. Although marriages, like other relationships, differ from one another, some important predictors of future success can be identified. One key factor in enduring marriages is the relative maturity of the two partners at the time they are married. In general, the younger the partners are, the lower the odds that the marriage will last, especially when the people are in their teens or

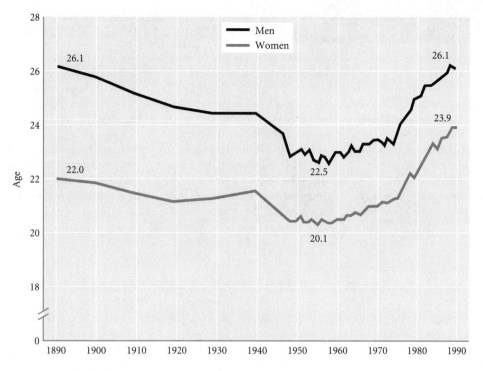

FIGURE 11.3 Average age at first marriage in United States

Source: U.S. Bureau of the Census, 1999. Online document at http://www.cdc.gov/nchs/fastats/marriage.htm.

early 20s (U.S. Bureau of the Census, 1999). In part, the age issue relates to Erikson's (1982) belief that intimacy cannot be achieved until after one's identity is established (see Chapter 10). Other reasons that determine whether marriages last include low financial security and pregnancy at the time of the marriage.

A second important predictor of successful marriage is **homogamy,** *or similarity of values and interests.* To the extent that the couple shares similar values, goals, attitudes, socioeconomic status, ethnic background, and religious beliefs, their relationship is more likely to succeed. Homogamy is an important predictor across a wide variety of cultures and societies, as diverse as Americans in Michigan and Africans in Chad (Diamond, 1986).

A third factor in predicting marital success is a feeling that the relationship is equal. *According to* **exchange theory,** *marriage is based on each partner con-*

tributing something to the relationship that the other would be hard pressed to provide. Satisfying and happy marriages result when both partners perceive a fair exchange across all the dimensions of the relationship. Couples often experience problems achieving equity because of competing demands between work and family, an issue we take up again in Chapter 12.

The Developmental Course of Marital Satisfaction. Much research has been conducted on marital satisfaction across adulthood. Research shows that for most couples overall marital satisfaction is highest at the beginning of the marriage, falls until the children begin leaving home, and rises again in later life (Miller et al., 1997). Thus, Bobbie and Jack's experience is typical of most couples. However, for some couples, satisfaction never rebounds and remains low; in essence, they have become emotionally divorced.

Most newspapers have a section devoted to weddings and anniversaries. Each week or so, papers publish the names (and often the pictures) of couples celebrating their golden (50th) or higher anniversary. Occasionally, there may even be a couple celebrating their diamond (75th) anniversary.

Most of us marvel at the longevity such couples demonstrate, not just in years lived but in the fact that they managed to keep a relationship together for so long. How do they do it? To find out, talk to couples who have been married at least 40 years. Ask them what initially got them together, how their relationship changed (and perhaps remained the same) over the years. Find out what things are most different now, what happened that they least expected, and what their happiest and most difficult times were. Make sure you get their advice for young couples on how to ensure a long and happy marriage.

Bring your interview results to class and pool them. See whether you can create a prescription for marital success. Compare your findings with those reported in the text.

Overall, marital satisfaction ebbs and flows over time. The pattern of a particular marriage over the years is determined by the nature of the dependence of each spouse on the other. When dependence is mutual and about equal, the marriage is strong and close. When the dependence of one partner is much higher than that of the other, however, the marriage is likely to be characterized by stress and conflict. Changes in individual lives over adulthood shift the balance of dependence from one partner to the other; for example, one partner may go back to school, become ill, or lose status. Learning how to deal with these changes is the secret to long and happy marriages.

The fact that marital satisfaction has a general downward trend but varies widely across couples led Karney and Bradbury (1995) to propose a vulnerability–stress–adaptation model of marriage. This model sees marital quality as a dynamic process resulting from the couples' ability to handle stressful events in the context of their particular vulnerabilities and resources. For example, as couples' ability to adapt to stressful situations gets better over time, the quality of the marriage probably will improve.

WHAT ARE LONG-TERM MARRIAGES LIKE? You probably know couples who have celebrated their golden wedding anniversary. Perhaps you have even participated in such a celebration for your parents or grandparents. You may have wondered how these couples managed to stay together for so long. If so, you would probably find the exercise in the Discovering Development feature an interesting one.

In a classic study, Weishaus and Field (1988) conducted a longitudinal study of 17 couples married between 50 and 69 years that included measures of relationship quality over almost the entire length of the couples' years together. The results of their research show that long-term marriages vary in their developmental trajectories. Moreover, couples show a real ability to roll with the punches and adapt to changing circumstances. For example, a serious illness to one spouse may not be detrimental to the relationship and may even make the bond stronger. Likewise, couples' expectations about marriage change over time, gradually becoming more congruent.

What specific characteristics differentiate middle-aged and older married couples? To answer this question, Levenson and colleagues (1993, 1994; Carstensen et al., 1995) conducted a series of studies. They found that compared with middle-aged married couples, older married couples showed less potential for conflict and more potential for pleasure in several areas (including interacting with their children), equivalent levels of overall physical and mental health, fewer gender differences in sources of pleasure, and more positive emotions. When discussing a problem, older couples were less emotionally negative and more positive.

Middle-Aged Couples		Older Couples	
Rank	*Topic*	*Rank*	*Topic*
	Sources of Conflict		
1	Children	1	Communication
2	Money	2	Recreation
3	Communication	3	Money
4	Recreation	4	Children
5	Sex	5	Sex
6	In-laws	6	In-laws
7	Friends	7	Friends
8	Religion	8	Religion
9	Alcohol and drugs	9	Jealousy
10	Jealousy	10	Alcohol and drugs
	Sources of Pleasure		
1	Good times in the past	1	Children or grandchildren
2	Other people	2	Good times in the past
3	Children or grandchildren	3	Vacations taken
4	Vacations taken	4	Things done together recently
5	Things done together recently	5	Other people
6	Silly and fun things	6	Plans for the future
7	Plans for the future	7	Television, radio, and reading
8	Television, radio, and reading	8	Casual and informal things
9	Casual and informal things	9	Silly and fun things
10	Accomplishments	10	Accomplishments

Source: Levenson, R. W., Carstenson, L. L., & Gottman, J. M. (1993). Long-term marriage: Age, gender, and satisfaction. *Psychology and Aging, 8,* 307.

When discussing a problem, older couples were less emotionally negative and more affectionate than middle-aged couples. Not surprisingly, older unhappy couples acted like unhappy couples of all ages; they showed more negative emotions, and when discussing a problem they engaged in more negative exchanges with their spouse. As you can see in Table 11.1, the specific topics creating stress and pleasure also differed between the two groups.

In sum, people who have been happily married for a long time act much like Bobbie and Jack, a couple married more than 50 years, who point to open and honest communication with each other, a desire to support each other no matter what, and an undying commitment to each other. Their advice to couples on how to help ensure their own golden anniversary? "Never go to sleep angry at your partner." Excellent advice.

CARING FOR A SPOUSE. When most couples pledge their love to each other "in sickness and in health," most envision the sickness part to be no worse than an illness lasting a few weeks. For most couples that may be the case. But for some couples, this pledge may be severely tested.

Caring for a chronically ill spouse presents different challenges than caring for a chronically ill parent (a topic we consider later in this chapter). Spousal caregivers assume their role usually after decades of shared responsibilities in the marriage. Without warning, the division of labor that worked for years must be readjusted. Such change inevitably stresses the relationship. This is especially true in cases involving Alzheimer's disease or other dementias because of the cognitive and behavioral consequences of the disease (see Chapter 4).

Studies of spousal caregivers of people with Alzheimer's disease typically show that marital satisfaction is much lower than for healthy couples (Cavanaugh & Kinney, 1994). Spousal caregivers report a loss of companionship and intimacy over the course of caregiving (Williamson & Schulz, 1990; Wright, 1991). Marital satisfaction is also an important predictor of spousal caregivers' reports of depressive symptoms; the better the perceived quality of the marriage, the fewer symptoms caregivers report (Cavanaugh & Kinney, 1994). Partners caring for a spouse who has had a stroke are similar; for example, communication patterns reveal the difficulty couples have in adjusting to a spouse with a serious health problem (Stephens & Clark, 1997).

Most spousal caregivers are forced to respond to an environmental challenge they did not choose, their partner's illness, and adopt the caregiver role out of necessity. Once they adopt the role, though, caregivers assess their ability to carry out the necessary duties. Longitudinal research indicates that how caregivers perceive their ability to provide care at the outset of caregiving may be key (Kinney & Cavanaugh, 1993). Caregivers who perceive themselves as competent try to rise to the occasion; data indicate that they report fewer and less intense caregiving hassles than spousal caregivers who see themselves as less competent (Kinney & Cavanaugh, 1993). In addition to trying at times to tackle problems head-on and dealing with one's feelings about caregiving, spousal caregivers also use religion as a means of coping with their situation (Ishler et al., 1995).

All things considered, though, providing full-time care for a spouse is very stressful (Aneshensel et al., 1995; Cavanaugh, 1999a). Coping with a spouse who may not remember your name, who may act aggressively toward you, and who has a chronic and fatal disease presents serious challenges even to the happiest couples.

Divorce and Remarriage

Through separation, divorce, and desertion, many adults make the transition from being married back to being single each year. (Later we consider people who return to singlehood as the result of the death of their spouse.) The difficult and stressful transition from being married to being single again brings with it important changes in status and role expectations. Let's explore these issues.

DIVORCE. Most adults enter marriage with the idea that the relationship will be permanent. Unfortunately, this permanence is becoming less attainable for more and more couples. Their early intimacy fails to grow. Rather than growing together, they grow apart.

As shown in Figure 11.4, the rate of divorce in the United States rose rapidly from 1940 to 1980, when the divorce rate slowed. Currently, at least one in every three households is affected by divorce. Based on current trends, couples who have recently married have about a 50–50 chance of remaining married for life (U.S. Bureau of the Census, 1999). In contrast to the United States, the divorce rates in Canada, Great Britain, Australia, and Sweden are about 1 in 3, and they are only 1 in 10 in Japan, Italy, Israel, and Spain. Even these rates represent increases (Lester, 1996).

Statistics worldwide and from different periods indicate that marriages fail quickly. Internationally, the peak time for divorce is 3 or 4 years after the wedding, or when the couple are in their late 20s. The United States reflects that trend, with half of all divorces occurring within the first 7 years of marriage (U.S. Bureau of the Census, 1999).

One consistent factor related to divorce is ethnicity. African Americans are more likely than European Americans to divorce or separate (U.S. Bureau of the Census, 1999). Hispanic groups show great variability: Mexican Americans and Cuban Americans have divorce rates similar to those of European Americans; the rate for Puerto Ricans is much higher (Bean & Tienda, 1987). Ethnically mixed marriages are at

FIGURE 11.4 **Divorce rates in United States.**

Source: U.S. Bureau of the Census, 1999.

greater risk of divorce than ethnically homogenous ones (Jones, 1996).

Two reasons given for the increase in divorce is that it is not perceived as negatively as it once was (perhaps because of the liberalization of divorce laws), and people have much higher expectations for marriage (Rogers & Amato, 1997). Couples now expect to find partners who will help them grow personally and provide much more than just financial support, a sexual partner, and children. Such expectations have paradoxically lowered the quality of marriages in recent generations. In other cultures, such expectations are rare or contrary to traditional values, providing a partial explanation of different divorce rates around the world.

The effects of divorce change over time. Shortly after the breakup, ex-partners often become angrier and more bitter toward each other than they were beforehand. Many underestimate their attachment to each other and may be overly sensitive to criticism from the ex-spouse. Increased hostility often is accompanied by periods of depression and disequilibrium (Kelly, 1982). Indeed, ex-spouses who are preoccupied with thoughts of their former partner and who have high feelings of hostility toward him or her have significantly poorer emotional well-being than ex-spouses who are not preoccupied or who have feelings of friendship toward the former partner (Masheter, 1997). It appears that low preoccupation

is the key to healthy postdivorce relationships and may be an indicator of the extent to which ex-spouses are moving on with their lives.

Gender differences also are found. Men report being shocked by the breakup, especially if the wife filed for divorce (Kelly, 1982). Men are more likely to be blamed for the problems that led to the divorce, to accept the blame, to move out, and thereby to find their social life disrupted (Kitson & Sussman, 1982). Women are affected differently. They tend to file for divorce more often. Socially, they have fewer prospects for potential remarriage, and they find it more difficult to establish new relationships if they have custody of the children (Maccoby et al., 1990; Masheter, 1991). Women are at a serious financial disadvantage, largely because they usually have custody of the children, typically are paid less than men, and are likely to have inadequate child support from their ex-husbands (Gallagher, 1996; Kurz, 1995).

Divorce in middle age or late life has some special characteristics. In general, the trauma is greater for these people because of the long period of investment in each other's emotional and practical lives (Uhlenberg et al., 1990). Longtime friends may turn away or take sides, causing additional disruption to the social network. Middle-aged and older women are at a significant disadvantage for remarriage, an especially traumatic situation for women who obtained much of their identity from their roles as wife and mother. Even if the divorce occurred many years earlier, children may still blame their parents for breaking the family apart (Hennon, 1983).

We must not overlook the financial problems faced by middle-aged divorced women (Gallagher, 1996; Kurz, 1995). These problems are especially keen for the middle-aged divorced woman who has spent years as a homemaker and has few marketable job skills. For her, divorce presents an especially difficult financial hardship.

REMARRIAGE. Although divorce is a traumatic event, it does not seem to deter people from beginning new relationships that typically lead into another marriage. Nearly 80% of divorced people remarry within the first 3 years (U.S. Bureau of the Census, 1999).

However, rates vary across ethnic groups. African Americans remarry more slowly than European Americans, and Hispanics remarry more slowly than either of these other groups (Coleman & Ganong, 1990). Remarriage is much more likely if the divorced people are young, mainly because there are more partners available. Partner availability favors men at all ages because men tend to marry women younger than themselves. For this reason, the probability that a divorced woman will remarry declines with increasing age. Although women are more likely to initiate a divorce, they are less likely to remarry (Buckle et al., 1996). Divorced men without children tend to marry women who have never been married before; divorced men with children tend to marry divorced women without children.

Very little research has been conducted on second (or third or more) marriages. Remarried people report that they experience their second marriage differently. They claim to enjoy much better communication, to resolve disagreements with greater goodwill, to arrive at decisions more equitably, and to divide chores more fairly (Furstenberg, 1982). Indeed, most couples believe that they will be more likely to succeed the second time around (Furstenberg, 1982). For African Americans, this appears to be true; divorce rates for remarriages are lower than for first marriages (Teachman, 1986). However, second marriages in general have a slightly higher risk of dissolution than first marriages if one spouse has custody of children from a previous marriage. Perhaps this optimism is the only way people can overcome the feelings of vulnerability that usually accompany the breakup of the first marriage.

Adapting to new relationships in remarriage can be difficult. Hobart (1988) reports differences between remarried men and women in this regard. For remarried men, the preeminent relationship is with his new wife; other relationships, especially those with his children from his first marriage, take a back seat. For remarried women, the relationship with their new husband remains more marginal than their relationship with their children from the first marriage. Thus, the higher failure rate for second marriages involving stepchildren may stem from differ-

Many older men who are divorced or widowed tend to remarry; many older women do not.

ences in the centrality of particular relationships between husbands and wives.

Perhaps one key to understanding remarriage is the lack of a socializing mechanism for becoming a stepparent. No consensus exists for how stepparents are supposed to behave, how stepparenting is to be similar to or different from biological parenting, or how one's duties, obligations, and rights should be meshed with those of the absent biological parent. In many cases stepparents adopt their partner's children to surmount some of these problems. However, emotionally charged issues remain. Much more remains to be learned about the experience of stepparenting, and the status, rights, and obligations of stepparents must be clarified.

Widowhood

Traditional marriage vows proclaim that the union will last "until death us do part." Experiencing the death of a spouse certainly is a traumatic event (see Chapter 13), and it is experienced by couples of all ages. Widowhood is more common for women; more than half of all women over age 65 are widows, but only 15% of the same-aged men are widowers. The reasons for this discrepancy are related to biological and social forces: Women have longer life ex-

© Walter Hodges / CORBIS

pectancies and typically marry men older than themselves. Consequently, the average American married woman can expect to live 10 to 12 years as a widow.

The impact of widowhood goes far beyond the ending of a long-term partnership (Matthews, 1996; Pearson, 1996). Widowed people often are left alone by family and friends who do not know how to deal with a bereaved person. As a result, widows and widowers often lose not only a spouse but also the friends and family who feel uncomfortable including a single person rather than a couple in social functions (Matthews, 1996). Additionally, widowed people may feel awkward as the third party or may even view themselves as a threat to married friends (Field & Minkler, 1988). Going to a movie or a restaurant by oneself may be unpleasant or unsatisfying to widows or widowers, so they may just stay home. Unfortunately, others may assume that they want or need to be alone.

For both widows and widowers, the first few months alone can be very difficult. Both are at risk for increased physical illness and report more symptoms of depression, lost status, economic hardship, and lower social support (Stroebe & Stroebe, 1983). But feelings of loss do not dissipate quickly. As we will see in Chapter 13, feeling sad on important dates is a common experience, even many years after a loved one has died.

Unlike some other cultures, U.S. society does not have well-defined social roles for widowed people. We tend to show disapproval toward those who continue to grieve for too long. Because widowhood is most often associated with older women, the few social supports are organized primarily for them.

Men and women react differently to widowhood. Widowers are at higher risk of dying themselves soon after their spouse, either by suicide or natural causes (Osgood, 1992; Smith & Zick, 1996). Some people believe that the loss of a wife is a more serious problem for a man than the loss of a husband for a woman. Perhaps this is because a wife often is a man's only close friend and confidant or because men usually are unprepared to live their lives alone. Older men often are ill equipped to handle such routine and necessary tasks as cooking, shopping, and keeping house, and they become emotionally isolated from other family members.

Although both widows and widowers suffer financial losses, widows often suffer more because survivor's benefits usually are only half of their husband's pensions (Smith & Zick, 1996). For many women, widowhood results in poverty (Pearson, 1996).

Men usually are older than women when they become widowed. To some extent, the difficulties reported by widowers may result from this age difference. If age is held constant, data over many years indicate that widows report higher anxiety than widowers (Pearson, 1996; Smith & Zick, 1996). Regardless of age, men have a clear advantage over women in the opportunity to form new heterosexual relationships and to remarry because there are fewer social restrictions on relationships between older men and younger women (Matthews, 1996). However, older widowers actually are less likely to form new, close friendships than are widows. Perhaps this is simply a continuation of men's lifelong tendency to have few close friendships. Also, widows are more likely to join support groups, which foster the formation of new friendships.

For many reasons, including the need for companionship and financial security, some widowed people remarry. One study examined remarriage as a coping response by older widows by interviewing 39 widows who had remarried, 192 who had considered remarriage, and 420 who had not considered it (Gentry & Schulman, 1988). Women who had remarried reported significantly fewer concerns than either of the other groups. Interestingly, the remarried widows also were the ones who recalled the most concerns about being alone and reported higher levels of emotional distress immediately after the death of their spouses. Apparently, remarriage helped these widows deal with the loss of their husbands by providing companionship and comfort.

CONCEPT CHECKS

1. What are the two most difficult issues for single people?
2. What differences are there between gay male and lesbian couples and heterosexual couples?
3. How does marital satisfaction change across the length of the marriage?

4. What are the main reasons people get divorced?

5. What gender differences have been reported among people who are widowed?

FAMILY DYNAMICS AND THE LIFE COURSE

LEARNING OBJECTIVES

- What are family life stages? How are intergenerational relations conceptualized?
- What is it like to be a parent? How do the key issues change over time?
- How do grandparents interact with their grandchildren? What key issues are involved?
- How do middle-aged adults get along with their children? How do they deal with the possibility of providing care to aging parents?

Susan is a 42-year-old married woman with two preadolescent children. She is an only child. Her mother, Esther, is a 67-year-old widow and has been showing signs of dementia. Esther has little money, and Susan's family is barely making ends meet. Susan knows that her mother cannot live alone much longer, and she feels that she should have her move in with their family. Susan feels that she has an obligation to provide care but also feels torn between her mother and her family and job. Susan wonders what to do.

Increasingly, families are facing the dilemma confronting Susan. As more people live long lives, the need for families to deal with health problems in their older members is on the rise. Most people understand the issues involved with raising children, but few of us are socialized for parental care.

In this section, we examine several issues relating to family dynamics. First, we consider conceptual frameworks of the family life cycle and intergenerational relationships. Next, we examine the parental role, especially concerning critical times in the process. An important role for many middle-aged and older adults is grandparenting, a role over which they have no direct control. We also examine the stress of caring for aging parents and see what Susan is facing. We conclude with a discussion of families in later life.

Family Life Cycle and Intergenerational Relationships

To understand the dynamics of families, it helps to have a conceptual framework that describes the family over time. *From a developmental perspective, families experience a series of predictable changes, which constitute the* **family life cycle.** One model describes eight sequential stages, based on the age of the oldest child and the kinds of tasks families confront (Duvall, 1977).

Family life-cycle models help us understand the changes families go through as children mature, but they also have limitations. They are based on traditional, first-time marriages with children; child-free relationships are ignored, as are the effects of occupational factors, friends, family, and spouse. Only the issues pertaining to raising the oldest child are used to define a family's current stage, and ethnic differences in parenting are overlooked (Vinovskis, 1988). Nevertheless, because the majority of families fit the basic assumptions, the family life-cycle model serves as a useful tool.

Equally important are conceptual models of intergenerational relationships. In this case, we are trying to conceptualize the ways in which people in different generations interact with each other. Riley and Riley (1996) present three basic ways of structuring such kinship ties. The simple type focuses only on two generations, typically parents and children. Such models are common in the child development area and represent power differential in favor of the parents. The expanded type of kinship involves three generations, but in formal connections with each other that are mediated by the middle generation. This model can be used to describe the long period in which the middle generation has lived independently while their parents are aging. Power differentials tend to diminish as the generations become more equal. The latent type of kinship differs from the previous two by a lack of formal boundaries and includes many diverse relationships, such as several degrees of step-kin and in-laws who are not bonded through blood relationships. In the latent model, generational links continually shift to provide dynamic relationships as they are needed.

Riley and Riley (1996) argue that the latent model is the best framework for contemporary American society based on several changes in the nature of kin relationships:

Parents and their children are living much longer, so they now achieve a point of being status equals.

Property transfer no longer constitutes the primary reason for formal intergenerational ties.

Most older adults are reasonably healthy and self-sufficient.

Contemporary families are increasingly diverse in age because of divorce and remarriage, reducing traditional generation gaps.

Many forms of relationships provide alternatives to traditional parent–child interactions.

These changes create a more fluid context for forging intergenerational relationships. As we will see, many of these new relationship possibilities exist already.

The Parental Role

The birth of a child transforms a couple (or a single parent) into a family. *Although the most common form of family in Western societies is the* **nuclear family,** *consisting only of parents and children, the most common form around the world is the* **extended family,** *in which grandparents and other relatives live with parents and children.* As noted in the Forces in Action feature, becoming a parent is a good example of how the developmental forces operate. Let's consider what this transformation brings in more detail.

One of the biggest decisions couples have to make is whether to have children. (Of course, in some cases pregnancies are unintended.) This decision is more complicated than most people think because a couple must weigh the many benefits of childrearing, such as personal satisfaction, fulfilling personal needs, continuing the family line, and companionship, with the many drawbacks, including expense and lifestyle changes. What influences the decision process? Psychological and marital factors are always

important, and career and lifestyle factors matter when the prospective mother works outside the home (Wilk, 1986). These four factors are all interconnected. They raise many important matters for consideration, such as relationships with one's own parents, marital stability, career satisfaction, and financial issues.

For many reasons, such as personal choice, financial instability, and infertility, an increasing number of couples are remaining child-free. These couples have several advantages over those who choose to have children: happier marriages, more freedom, and higher standards of living. But the larger society does not view being child-free as something positive, providing that being child-free was by choice and not due to infertility (Lampman & Dowling-Guyer, 1995). Child-free couples must also face social criticism from the larger child-oriented society and may run the risk of feeling more lonely in old age.

Today, couples have fewer children and have their first child later than in the past. Indeed, until 1993 the number of couples in which mothers were over 30 when they had their first child was increasing. The slight decline since then has resulted mainly from the lower numbers of women of childbearing age in cohorts after the baby boomers. Delaying first children has important benefits. Traditionally, mothers have been thought to be crucial for the normal development of the child (Fields & Widmayer, 1982). Older mothers are more at ease being parents, spend more time with their babies, and are more affectionate and sensitive to them (Ragozin et al., 1982).

Timing of fatherhood also makes a difference in the ways in which fathers interact with their children. Compared with men who become fathers in their 20s, men who become fathers in their 30s generally are more invested in their paternal role and spend up to three times as much time in caring for preschool children as younger fathers (Cooney et al., 1993). However, men who become fathers in their 30s also are more likely to feel ambivalent and resentful about time lost to their careers (Cooney et al., 1993).

In general, parents deal with the many challenges of childrearing reasonably well. They learn when to compromise and when to apply firm but fair disci-

Parenthood is an excellent context for understanding the role of the four developmental forces. At one level, biological forces are quite apparent; without biology, one could not become a parent. Beyond the obvious lie many genetic influences that shape everything from eye color to whether we are susceptible to certain types of cancer. Most important, some adults must think carefully about having children because they are carriers of certain genetically linked disorders.

Psychological factors also are evident in parenting. From coping with children's behaviors to negotiating with partners about childrearing practices, psychological aspects are key. Parents' personalities play a major role in socializing their children. Parents' cognitive abilities also come into play, especially when children need help with homework.

Sociocultural forces exert their influence through social and cultural norms of childrearing. For example, whether mothers breast feed their infants is heavily influenced by social norms. Likewise, how parents decide to discipline their children and what skills they emphasize are influenced by cultural expectations.

Finally, life-cycle forces influence all others. Having children very early or late in life affects biology; the risk of certain birth defects increases in very young or old mothers. As discussed in the text, older parents tend to be more settled in other aspects of their lives, which influences how they interact with their children.

In sum, by keeping the influences of the four developmental forces in mind, we get a more complete picture of how parents interact with their children.

---

pline. And if given the choice, most parents do not regret their decision to have children.

ALTERNATIVE FORMS OF PARENTING. An increasing number of families are not the traditional, two-parent type in which the parents are in their first (and only) marriage. One of the fastest-growing groups of adults is single parents, most of whom are women. The increasing divorce rate, the large number of women who keep children born out of wedlock, and the desire of many single adults to have or adopt children are all contributing factors to this phenomenon. Being a single parent raises important questions: What happens when only one adult is responsible for child care? How do single parents meet their own needs for emotional support and intimacy? Certainly, how one feels about being single also has important effects. Single parents, regardless of gender, face great obstacles. Financially, they are usually much less well-off than their married counterparts. Integrating the roles of work and parenthood is difficult enough for two people; for the single parent the hardships are compounded. Financially, single mothers are hardest hit. Emotionally, single fathers may have the worst of it.

Not all parents raise their own biological children. In fact, roughly one third of North American couples become stepparents, foster parents, or adoptive parents sometime during their lives. To be sure, the parenting issues we have discussed thus far are just as important in these situations as when people raise their own biological children. However, some special problems arise as well.

A big issue for foster, adoptive, and stepparents is how strongly the child bonds with his or her new parent. Although infants less than 1 year old usually bond well, children who are old enough to have formed attachments with their biological parents may have competing loyalties. For example, some stepchildren remain strongly attached to the noncustodial parent, actively resist attempts to integrate them into a new family ("My real mother wouldn't make me do that"), or exhibit behavioral problems such as drinking or continually invading the stepparent's privacy (Pasley & Ihinger-Tallman, 1987). Children in blended families also tend not to be as mentally healthy as children in nondivorced families (Cherlin & Furstenberg, 1994). Stepparents often must deal with continued visitation by the noncustodial parent, which may exacerbate difficulties. These problems are a major reason why second marriages are at high risk for dissolution, as discussed earlier in this chapter. Still, many stepparents and stepchildren ultimately develop good relationships with each other. Stepparents must be sensitive to and understanding of the relationship between the stepchild and his or her biological, noncustodial parent. Allowing stepchildren to develop the relationship with the stepparent at their own pace also helps.

Adoptive parents also contend with attachment to birth parents, but in different ways. In addition to attachments that may predate the adoption, adopted children may want to locate and meet their birth parents. Wanting to know one's origins is understandable, but such searches can strain the relationships between these children and their adoptive parents, who may interpret these actions as a form of rejection (Rosenberg, 1992). In general, though, recent research indicates that, compared with nonadopted children, adopted children are more confident, have a more positive view of the world, feel more in control of their lives, and view their adoptive parents as more nurturing (Marquis & Detweiler, 1985). They also show few effects of being adopted in their adult adjustment (Smyer et al., 1998).

Foster parents tend to have the most tenuous relationship with their children because the bond can be broken for many reasons having nothing to do with the quality of the care being provided, such as courts awarding custody back to birth parents or another couple legally adopting the child. Dealing with attachment is difficult; parents want to provide secure homes but may not have children long enough to establish continuity. Furthermore, because many children in foster care have been unable to form attachments at all, they may not be willing or able to form ones that inevitably will be broken. As a result, foster parents must be willing to tolerate ambiguity in the relationship and have few expectations about the future.

Finally, many gay men and lesbian women also want to be parents. Some have biological children themselves, whereas others choose adoption or foster parenting. Although gay men and lesbian women make good parents, they often experience resistance to having children. Actually, research indicates that children reared by gay or lesbian parents do not experience any more problems than children reared by heterosexual parents. Substantial evidence exists that children raised by gay or lesbian parents do not develop sexual identity or any other problems any more than children raised by heterosexual parents (Flaks et al., 1995; Patterson, 1995). In fact, evidence suggests that children raised by gay and lesbian parents may have some advantages over children raised by heterosexual parents. Gay men often are especially concerned about being good and nurturing fathers and try hard to raise their children with nonsexist, egalitarian attitudes (Bozett, 1988). And lesbian mothers exhibit more parenting awareness skills than do heterosexual parents (Flaks et al., 1995).

LAUNCHING CHILDREN: EMPTY NEST AND BECOMING FRIENDS. Being a parent has a strange side, when you think about it. After creating children out of love, parents spend much of their time, effort, and money preparing them to become independent and leave. For most parents, the leaving (and sometimes returning) occurs during midlife.

Sometime during middle age, most parents experience two positive developments with regard to their children. Suddenly their children see them in a new light, and the children leave home.

After the strain of raising adolescents, parents appreciate the transformation that occurs when their children head into young adulthood. In general, parent–child relationships improve when children become young adults (Troll & Fingerman, 1996). The difference can be dramatic, as in the case of Deb, a middle-aged mother. "When Sacha was 15, she acted as if I was the dumbest person on the planet. But now that she's 21, she acts as if I got smart all of a sudden. I like being around her. She's a great kid, and we're really becoming friends."

Who were the investigators, and what was the aim of the study? Ryff and colleagues (1994) believed that parents' assessment of their children's accomplishments is an important part of the parents' midlife evaluation of themselves. Moreover, because parents are the major influence on children, the stakes for this self-evaluation are high; how one's child turns out is a powerful statement about one's success or failure as a parent (Ryff et al., 1994). Ryff and colleagues decided to see how these issues play out in parents' and children's lives.

How did the investigators measure the topic of interest? Ryff and colleagues asked the parents to rate their child's adjustment and educational and occupational attainment, to compare the child with others of that age, and to rate their own psychological well-being.

Who were the participants in the study? Ryff and colleagues selected a random sample of 114 middle-aged mothers and 101 middle-aged fathers, all from different middle-class families in the Midwest, who had at least one child aged 21 or over. With these characteristics, the sample was not representative of the population at large.

What was the design of the study? The study was a cross-sectional examination of parents' ratings of their children's achievements.

Were there ethical concerns with the study? Because the study used volunteers who completed surveys containing no questions about sensitive topics, there were no ethical concerns.

What were the results? As you can see in Figure 11.5, mothers and fathers have many hopes and dreams for their children. Happiness and educational success were the most common responses, followed by career success. There were no statistically significant differences between mothers' and fathers' responses.

The data also showed that the parents' views of their children's personal and social adjustment correlated closely with measures of parents' own well-being. Parents' sense of self-acceptance, purpose in life, and environmental mastery were strongly related to how well they thought their children were adjusted. Similar but somewhat weaker relations were found between children's accomplishments and parental well-being. Again, no differences between mothers and fathers were found.

Parents were also asked how well they thought their children were doing compared with themselves when they were the same age. These data were intriguing. Parents who thought their children were better adjusted (that is, more self-confident, happy, and interpersonally skilled) than they themselves were in early adulthood reported low levels of well-being. Why? Shouldn't parents be pleased that their children are well adjusted? Ryff and colleagues suggest that this finding, though seemingly counterintuitive, is understandable in terms of social comparison. That is, people suffer negative consequences (such as having lower self-esteem) when they perceive other people as doing better than they are (Suls & Wills, 1991). Even though parents want their children to be happy, they may have difficulty accepting it if they turn out to be *too* happy.

A key factor in making this transition as smooth as possible is the extent to which parents foster and ap-prove of their children's attempts to be independent. Most parents manage the transition to an empty nest successfully (Lewis & Lin, 1996). That's not to say that parents are heartless. When children leave home, emotional bonds are disrupted. Both mothers and fa-thers feel the change. It's just that only about 25% of mothers and fathers report being very unhappy when the last child leaves home (Lewis & Lin, 1996).

Still, parents provide financial help (such as pay-ing college tuition) when possible. Most help in other ways, ranging from the mundane (such as making the washer and dryer available to their college-age children) to the extraordinary (providing the down-payment for their child's house). Young adults and their middle-aged parents generally believe that they have strong, positive relationships and that they can count on each other for help when necessary (Troll & Bengtson, 1982).

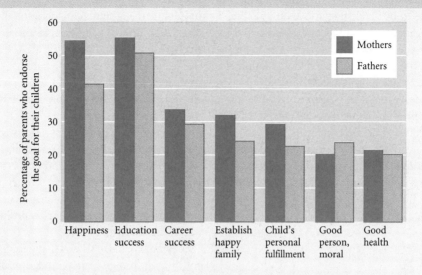

FIGURE 11.5 **Mothers' and fathers' dreams for their children.**

Source: Ryff, C. D., Lee, Y. H., Essex, M. J., & Schmutte, P. S. (1994). My children and me: Mid-life evaluations of grown children and self. *Psychology and Aging, 9,* 197.

In contrast, parents who rated their children as having attained better educational and occupational levels felt more positive about themselves than parents who rated their children lower on these dimensions. In this case, parents may feel that they have fulfilled the American dream, helping the next generation do better than they did.

What did the investigators conclude? Ryff and colleagues showed that midlife parents' self-evaluations of their own well-being are clearly related to their perceptions of how their children turned out. Thus, their supposition that how children turn out is strongly connected with middle-aged parents' sense of self was supported.

Of course, all this help doesn't mean that everything is perfect. Conflicts still arise. One study found that about one third of middle-class fathers surveyed complained about their sons' lack of achievement or their daughters' poor choice of husbands (Nydegger, 1986). This study highlights the importance parents place on how their children turn out. As discussed in the How Do We Know? feature, this issue is complex.

Parents' satisfaction with the empty nest sometimes is short-lived. Roughly half of all middle-aged parents who have adult children have at least one child, typically unmarried, living with them. Interestingly, this living arrangement is more common if the parents are in good health, and parents continue to do most of the housework (Ward et al., 1992). Moreover, adult children do not move back home primarily to help their parents. For example, college graduates are more likely to move back in with their parents if they are male, had low college GPAs, or do not have a job (Steen & Peterson, 2000).

Although middle-aged parents rarely turn their backs on their children, most do not plan on children returning home to live once they move out. Neither generation is thrilled with living together again. Both tend to handle the situation better if the returning children are in their early 20s and if the situation is clearly temporary (Clemons & Axelson, 1985). Still, conflict can arise. About 4 in 10 parents report serious conflicts, and arguments over lifestyle, friends, and personal care habits are common (Clemons & Axelson, 1985). Unless parents and adult children both choose to live together, parents' marriages are negatively affected when such conflicts arise. When times are hard, though, adult children may not have much choice but to live with their parents.

Becoming a Grandparent

Becoming a grandparent is an exciting time for most people and represents the acquisition of new roles (Somary & Stricker, 1998; Szinovacz, 1998). These days, becoming a grandparent usually happens while one is middle-aged rather than older, and it is frequently occurring as early as the 30s (Szinovacz, 1998). Moreover, many younger and middle-aged grandparents have living parents themselves, making for truly multigenerational families.

Overall, surprisingly little research has been conducted on grandparents and their relationships with their grandchildren. We know that grandparents differ widely in how they interact with grandchildren and in the meanings they derive from these interactions (Somary & Stricker, 1998). We also know a little about how each group perceives the other and about the benefits of these relationships.

STYLES AND MEANINGS OF GRANDPARENTING. One of the earliest topics of research about grandparenting concerned how grandparents and grandchildren interact. *Because grandparents, like all other groups, are diverse, how they interact with their grandchildren, called their* **grandparenting** style, *differs* (Neugarten & Weinstein, 1964). In a classic study, Neugarten and Weinstein (1964) identified five primary styles. The most common style, characterizing about one third

of grandparents, is called formal. These grandparents see their role in fairly traditional terms, occasionally indulging the grandchild, occasionally babysitting, expressing a strong interest in the grandchild, but maintaining a hands-off attitude toward childrearing, leaving that aspect to the parents. A second common style is used by the fun seeker, whose relationship is characterized by informal playfulness. The distant grandparent appears mainly on holidays, birthdays, or other formal occasions with ritual gifts for the grandchild but otherwise has little contact with him or her. A few grandmothers are surrogate parents, filling in for working mothers. Finally, a few grandparents play the role of dispenser of family wisdom, assuming an authoritarian position and offering information and advice.

Research has also shown that people derive several positive meanings from grandparenthood. Kivnick (1982) conducted the first definitive study of the meanings people derive from grandparenting, in which she administered a lengthy questionnaire to 286 grandparents. Kivnick identified five meanings of grandparenting: centrality, or the degree to which grandparenting is a primary role in one's life; value as an elder, or being perceived as a wise, helpful person; immortality through clan, in that the grandparent leaves behind not one but two generations; reinvolvement with one's personal past, recalling relationships with one's own grandparents; and indulgence, or getting satisfaction from having fun with and spoiling one's grandchildren.

Is there any connection between the styles of grandparenting and the meaning grandparents derive? Comparing the meanings derived by grandparents with the styles of grandparenting reveals several similarities. For example, the notion that grandparents tend to spoil or indulge their grandchildren appears as both a style and a meaning. Because of these apparent similarities, Miller and Cavanaugh (1990) decided to investigate whether there were any systematic relationships. They reported two major findings. First, most grandparents find several sources of meaning in being a grandparent. Second, there are few consistent relationships between the style of grandparenting and the various sources of meaning.

What role grandparents play in their grandchildren's lives tends to vary somewhat across cultures.

Thomas and colleagues (1988) also found that the symbolic meaning of grandparenthood was of little importance to the satisfaction derived from being a grandparent.

What these results imply is that we may not be able to describe specific standardized styles or meanings of grandparenthood. This is not that surprising because grandparents are so diverse. Additionally, it is less likely that grandparents will live near their grandchildren than in past decades (Szinovacz, 1998). Distance changes grandparenting. Detachment rather than involvement seems increasingly to characterize grandparent–grandchild relations, except for African American women, who tend to be more highly involved (Szinovacz, 1998). There are many complex reasons for a more detached style. Increased geographic mobility often means that grandparents live far away from their grandchildren, making visits less frequent and the relationship less intimate. Grandparents today are more likely to live independent lives apart from their children and grandchildren and to be involved in several other roles. Grandmothers are more likely to be employed themselves, thereby having less time to devote to caring for their grandchildren. Because of the rising di-

vorce rate, some grandparents rarely see grandchildren who are living with a former son- or daughter-in-law. Finally, grandparents are not seen as the dispensers of childrearing advice that they once were, so they tend to take a background role to maintain family harmony.

Most grandparents are comfortable with their reduced role and are quite happy to leave childrearing to the parents unless they have no other choice (Szinovacz, 1998). In fact, those who feel responsible for advising their grandchildren tend to be less satisfied with the grandparenting role than those who feel that their role is mainly to enjoy their grandchildren (Thomas, 1986).

But what if we asked grandparents how they expect to interact with their grandchildren before they become grandparents? What would the results look like then?

That's exactly what Somary and Stricker (1998) did. While their first grandchild was still in utero, the researchers asked the grandparents-to-be what they expected being a grandparent would be like and then reassessed them 1 to 2 years after their grandchild was born. Somary and Stricker found that expectations and experiences of grandparenting differed by both gender and lineage. In terms of gender, grandmothers reported greater overall satisfaction and meaning than grandfathers, but grandfathers felt more able to give childrearing advice to the parents. In terms of lineage, maternal grandparents were more satisfied with grandparenthood than they expected to be, whereas paternal grandparents were not.

Clearly, the differences between grandparents in how they interact with grandchildren, and the meanings they derive, differ a great deal across grandparents. Even grandparents of the same grandchild differ with gender and lineage. Thus, few generalizations can be made about how grandparents feel about their grandchildren.

GRANDPARENTS, GRANDCHILDREN, AND DIVORCE. A growing concern among grandparents is maintaining contact with grandchildren after a divorce of the parents (Drew & Smith, 1999). Because the law relating to grandparents' visitation rights is still evolving, grandparents do not always have legal recourse in seeing their grandchildren. In some cases the former in-laws break contact. In other cases paternal grandmothers actually expand their family network by maintaining contact with their grandchildren from their sons' first marriage as well as subsequent ones (Drew & Smith, 1999). Overall, maternal grandmothers whose daughters have custody have more contact with grandchildren after their daughters' divorces, and paternal grandmothers have less contact after their sons' divorces if their son does not have custody of the grandchildren (Cherlin & Furstenberg, 1986). Many grandparents who have had contact with their grandchildren broken report emotional and physical health problems related to the loss of contact (Drew & Smith, 1999).

Step-grandparenthood is another increasingly common experience in the United States, given the high divorce rates, and represents the majority of African American grandparents (Szinovacz, 1998). Family patterns become extremely complex when multiple divorces are involved. Unfortunately, very little research has been conducted examining the psychological impact on grandchildren and grandparents of step-grandparenthood or the forging and loss of multiple grandparental relationships through multiple divorces of the parents.

ETHNIC DIFFERENCES. Grandparenting styles and interaction patterns differ somewhat between ethnic groups. In the United States, for example, African Americans, Asian Americans, Italian Americans, and Hispanic Americans are more likely to be involved in the lives of their grandchildren than are members of other groups. Differences within these ethnic groups also are apparent. For example, family is a core value in Hispanic cultures, making grandparents more likely to participate in childrearing (Burnette, 1999). Italian American grandmothers tend to be much more satisfied and involved with grandparenting than Italian American grandfathers, who tend to be more distant. Among Hispanic groups, Cuban Americans are least likely and Mexican Americans most likely to be involved with the daily lives of their descendants (Bengtson, 1985). African American grandmothers under age 40 feel pressured to provide care for a grandchild that they were not eager for, whereas those over age 60 tend to feel that they are fulfilling an important role. However, African American men perceive grandparenthood as a central role and do so more strongly than European American grandfathers (Kivett, 1991).

Kornhaber (1985) notes that styles of grandparenting vary with ethnic background. This fact is highlighted by the case of an 18-month-old girl who had grandparents from two very different ethnic backgrounds: one pair Latino and one pair Nordic. Her Latino grandparents tickled, frolicked with, and doted over her. Her Nordic grandparents let her be but loved her no less. Her Latino mother thought the Nordic grandparents were "cold and hard," and her Nordic father thought his in-laws were "driving her crazy." However, the child was perfectly content with both sets of grandparents.

Weibel-Orlando (1990) also reports variations between Native Americans and other groups. Among Native Americans, grandmothers tend to take a more active role than grandfathers. She also identified four main styles: distant, custodial, fictive, and cultural conservator. The first two parallel styles found in other ethnic groups, whereas the latter two are particularly Native American. Fictive grandparents are ones who fill in for missing or dead biological grandparents; cultural conservator grandparents actively solicit their children to allow the grandchildren to live with them to expose them to the Native American way of life.

GRANDPARENTS RAISING THEIR GRANDCHILDREN. Roughly 800,000 U.S. households include a grandparent raising a grandchild under age 18 when neither of the child's parents is present (U.S. Bureau of the Census, 1999). The exponential growth in such households since 1980 is another facet of the changing nature of families. Nearly half of these households are European American (47%), 36% are African American, and 15% are Hispanic. Most European American custodial grandmothers are married, whereas most African American custodial grandmothers are not.

Grandparents who raise their grandchildren face many special problems (Fuller-Thompson et al., 1997). Few grandparents have legal custody of their grandchildren, making it difficult for them to deal with schools, health care organizations, and other formal service providers. When the parents are incarcerated or are substance abusers, grandparents face the additional burden of explaining these situations to young grandchildren. Why do children live with their grandparents? Table 11.2 lists several of the most common reasons. As you can see, most often grandparents become caregivers of their grandchildren because of substance abuse by one or both parents, which often results in child maltreatment. Note that the frequency of some reasons differs significantly between European American and African American groups.

Having childrearing responsibility for a grandchild is not easy. Comparisons between traditional, noncustodial grandparents, custodial grandparents who report low problem frequency, and custodial grandparents who report their grandchild to be a problem differ in the type and frequency of problem behaviors reported in the grandchild. Although alcohol use rates are comparable, rates of oppositional behavior, hyperactivity, and learning problems are not. Such problems negatively affect the relationship between grandparents and grandchildren (Hayslip et al., 1998). Even custodial grandparents raising apparently normal grandchildren experience more stress and disruption of roles than traditional grandparents (Emick & Hayslip, 1999).

Caring for grandchildren has other effects (Pruchno, 1999). Grandmothers indicated that the responsibilities of caregiving took a very high toll on their work lives, with 40% of employed custodial grandmothers reporting that they arrived late to work, missed work, left work suddenly, or left because of a grandchild's medical appointment. Surprisingly, few married custodial grandmothers report negative effects on their marriage; on the contrary, they report that their spouses are supportive.

GREAT-GRANDPARENTHOOD. With increasing numbers of people, especially women, living to a very old age, the number of great-grandparents is rising rapidly. However, cohort trends in age at first marriage and age at parenthood also play a role. When these factors are combined, we find that most great-grandparents are women who married young and had children and grandchildren who also married and had children early.

The little research that has been conducted on this group indicates that their sources of satisfaction and meaning differ somewhat from those of grandparents (Doka & Mertz, 1988; Wentkowski, 1985). Three aspects of great-grandparenthood appear to be most important (Doka & Mertz, 1988).

First, being a great-grandparent provides a sense of personal and family renewal. Their grandchildren have produced new life, renewing their own excitement for life and reaffirming the continuance of their lineage. Seeing their families stretch across four generations may also provide psychological support through feelings of symbolic immortality that help them face death. That is, they know that their families will live many years beyond their own lifetime. Second, great-grandchildren provide diversion in great-grandparents' lives. There are now new things to do, places to go, and new people to share them with. Third, becoming a great-grandparent is a mile-

TABLE 11.2   Reasons Why Children Live with Their Grandparents

	Total	European American (SD)		African American (SD)	
		% Giving Reason			
Child's mother					
Dead	10.5	9.8	(.30)	11.3	(.32)
In jail	6.2	4.8	(.21)	7.9	(.27)
Mentally ill	6.2	8.3	(.28)	3.5	(.18)
Pregnant teenager	7.6	8.1	(.27)	6.9	(.25)
Addicted to drugs	46.4	40.1	(.49)	54.2	(.50)
Addicted to alcohol	21.9	23.7	(.43)	19.7	(.40)
Whereabouts unknown	2.5	2.8	(.16)	2.2	(.15)
Financially unable to care for child	7.9	8.3	(.28)	7.3	(.26)
Physically abusive	11.5	12.9	(.34)	9.7	(.30)
Emotionally abusive	21.3	25.5	(.44)	16.0	(.37)
Physically neglectful	35.1	40.9	(.49)	27.9	(.45)
Emotionally neglectful	37.6	42.4	(.49)	31.7	(.47)
Abandoned child	7.7	8.3	(.28)	6.9	(.25)
Child's father					
Dead	4.8	5.3	(.22)	4.1	(.20)
In jail	9.4	8.1	(.27)	11.1	(.31)
Mentally ill	1.7	2.5	(.16)	.6	(.08)
Teenage father	3.2	3.3	(.18)	3.2	(.18)
Addicted to drugs	30.4	32.2	(.47)	28.1	(.45)
Addicted to alcohol	22.1	26.7	(.44)	16.4	(.37)
Financially unable to care for child	4.6	4.3	(.20)	5.1	(.22)
Whereabouts unknown	21.3	17.6	(.38)	25.8	(.44)
Physically abusive	6.8	9.3	(.29)	3.8	(.19)
Emotionally abusive	11.6	16.6	(.37)	5.3	(.22)
Physically neglectful	16.9	22.9	(.42)	9.4	(.29)
Emotionally neglectful	16.1	21.9	(.41)	8.8	(.28)
Abandoned child	3.5	4.0	(.20)	2.8	(.17)

Source: Pruchno, R. (1999). Raising grandchildren: The experiences of black and white grandmothers. *The Gerontologist, 39,* 214.

stone, a mark of longevity. The sense that one has lived long enough to see the fourth generation is perceived very positively.

For many reasons, such as geographic distance and health, most great-grandparents maintain a distant relationship with their great-grandchildren. Still, the vast majority (more than 90%) are proud of their new status (Wentkowski, 1985). As we enter the 21st century and the number of older people increases, four-generation families may become the norm.

Middle-Aged Adults and Their Aging Parents

Family ties across generations provide the basis for socialization and continuity in the family's identity. These ties are particularly salient for members of the middle-aged generation precisely because they are the link between their aging parents and their young adult children. The pressure on this generation is great; in fact, middle-age adults often are called the sandwich generation to reflect their position between two generations that put demands and pressures on them.

Being a middle-aged parent also affords the opportunity to assume new roles (Hareven & Adams, 1996). Mothers (more so than fathers) tend to take on the role of kinkeepers, the people who gather the family together for celebrations and keep family members in touch with each other. Studies of African American families, for example, show that kinship ties provide a wide variety of support, from financial aid and role models for young parents to caregiving for the older generation (Jackson et al., 1996). Kinkeeping becomes especially important once grandchildren arrive, which we discussed in more detail earlier in this chapter. Mothers may also go to college or begin new careers because their children encourage them. Unfortunately, much less is known about new roles for middle-aged fathers.

Being caught between two generations presents some interesting paradoxes. Looking downward in terms of generations, one is still a parent, yet one does not (nor should) have the same degree of control over an adult child's behavior that was the case years earlier. Nevertheless, a parent still cares and loves an adult child very much. Nearly all middle-aged parents understand the paradox of feeling parental but recognizing that one's child is now an independent adult.

A second and even more complex paradox involves caring for one's aging parent. This problem especially affects women, who end up doing most of the family caregiving. Caring for a parent involves several paradoxes (Bengston et al., 1995): between the degrees to which one is truly sandwiched, between the burdens and benefits of providing care, and between objective and subjective realities.

Without question, having to care for a parent adds a role to one's life. However, emerging evidence suggests that people who have a number of roles they must fulfill may have more opportunities for greater social support, better access to resources, and greater personal competence (Lopata, 1993).

Some people believe that caring for a parent always brings more burdens than benefits. Such beliefs belie a bias that caring is a one-directional flow of help. Actually, most adult child–older parent interactions are highly reciprocal. Only when a parent is in extremely poor health does the relationship become more burdensome for the adult child.

This latter point is related to the third paradox. Any relationship may be perceived as burdensome, rewarding, or both. Thus, we must take a careful look at each person's situation to understand how the relationship is being perceived. We must look not only at what adult children give but also what they get back in the form of satisfaction, meaning, and feelings of continuity (Marshall et al., 1993).

Most middle-aged adults have parents who are in reasonably good health. For a growing number of people, however, being a middle-aged child of aging parents involves providing some level of care. More often than not the job of caring for older parents falls to a daughter or daughter-in-law. This gender difference is striking. Even after ruling out all other demographic characteristics of adult child caregivers and their care recipients, daughters are more than three times more likely to provide care than are sons (Dwyer & Coward, 1991; Kriseman & Claes, 1997). This gender difference is also found in other cultures. For example, even though in Japanese culture the oldest son is responsible for parental care, his wife actually does the day-to-day caregiving (Morioka, 1996).

In some situations, older parents must move in with one of their children. Such moves usually occur after decades of both generations living independently. This pattern holds for most cultures around the world (Hareven & Adams, 1996; Knodel et al., 1996; Morioka, 1996). This history of independent living sets the stage for adjustment difficulties after the move because both parties must accommodate their lifestyles. Most of the time, adult children provide care for their mothers, who may in turn have provided care for their husbands before they died.

Caring for one's parent presents a dilemma: feeling obligated to care versus focusing on one's family and career (Aneshensel et al., 1995; Stephens & Franks, 1999). *Most adult children feel a sense of responsibility, called **filial obligation**, to care for their parents if necessary.* For example, adult child caregivers sometimes express the feeling that they "owe it to mom or dad" to care for them; after all, their parents provided for them for many years and now the adult child has the chance to give something back.

Much research over the past few decades clearly documents that middle-aged adults expend a great deal of energy, time, and money helping their older parents (Hareven & Adams, 1996; Stephens & Franks, 1999). In fact, nearly 90% of the daily help older people receive comes from adult children and other relatives. These efforts pay off. Family care helps prevent or at least delay institutionalization (Brody, 1981).

But caring for an older parent has its price (Aneshensel et al., 1995). Living with one's parent after decades on one's own usually is not done by choice; both parties would just as soon live apart. The potential for conflict over daily routines and lifestyles is high. Adult children may have trouble coping with declines in their parents' functioning, especially when the declines involve cognitive abilities. If caregivers do not know why their parents are declining, such lack of knowledge may result in feelings of ambivalence and antagonism toward their parents. When the caregiving situation is perceived as confining or seriously infringes on the adult child's other responsibilities (such as spouse, parent, employee, and so forth), the situation is likely to be perceived negatively. Such interrole conflict may be especially stressful for women, and it may lower well-being (Stephens et al., 2001). This is likely to lead to mixed feelings of anger and guilt.

Caring for one's parent can have psychological costs. Even the most devoted adult child caregiver feels depressed, resentful, angry, and guilty at times (Cavanaugh, 1999a). To the extent that caregivers have to deal with high levels of behavior problems in care recipients, feel trapped in their role as caregiver, and feel overloaded, they are at risk for long-term depression (Alspaugh et al., 1999). Caregivers who appraise stressors as benign, use appropriate coping skills, and have good social support have better psychological outcomes and report better mental health (Goode et al., 1998). Similarly, caregivers who take advantage of adult day care facilities for their care recipient report lower levels of stress and better psychological well-being (Zarit et al., 1998). Over the long run, daughters and daughters-in-law who care for older parents can show considerable resilience and adapt to their situation (Lawton et al., 2000).

Many middle-aged caregivers are pressed financially; they may still be paying child care or college tuition expenses and may not be able to save adequately for retirement. Financial pressures are especially serious for those caring for parents with chronic conditions, such as Alzheimer's disease, that necessitate services not covered by medical insurance. In some cases, adult children may even need to quit their jobs to provide care because adequate alternatives, such as adult day care, are unavailable. Although caring for parents is stressful for all adult children, adult daughters' level of stress is especially affected (Mui, 1995; Stephens & Franks, 1999).

Although caregiving often is viewed only as stressful, many caregivers also report experiencing rewards. Stephens and Franks (1999) point out that both perspectives must be considered to fully understand caregivers' experiences. Examples of stressors and rewards are presented in Table 11.3. Note that many of the stressors involve problem behavior or cognitive impairment, whereas several rewards concern feelings of filial obligation.

From the parent's perspective, things are not always rosy, either. Independence and autonomy are important traditional values in American culture, and their loss is not taken lightly. Older adults are more likely than their children to express the desire to pay a professional for assistance rather than ask a family member for help, and they are more likely to find it demeaning to live with their children (Hamon & Blieszner, 1990). Most move in only as a last resort. As many as two thirds of older adults who receive help with daily activities feel negatively about the help they receive (Newsom, 1999).

Stressor	Percentage Endorsing
Parent criticized or complained	71.6
Parent was unresponsive	67.4
Parent was uncooperative or demanding	67.4
Helped parent with personal care needs	67.3
Parent asked repetitive questions	67.3
Parent was agitated	66.4
Managed legal or financial affairs of parent	66.4
Parent's health declined	66.3
Supervised parent	63.1
Did not receive help with caregiving from friends or family	61.1
Had extra caregiving expenses	54.7
Parent was forgetful	53.6

Reward	Percentage Endorsing
Knew parent was well cared for	100.0
Fulfilled family obligation	93.7
Spent time in the company of parent	92.6
Gave care because wanted to not because had to	89.5
Saw parent enjoy small things	84.2
Parent showed affection or appreciation	81.1
Helped parent with personal care	81.0
Parent was cooperative or not demanding	77.8
Parent's good side came through despite the illness	73.7
Parent was calm or content	70.5
Relationship with parent became closer	64.2
Parent's health improved	47.3

Source: Stephens, M. A. P., & Franks, M. M. (1999). Intergenerational relationships in later-life families: Adult daughters and sons as caregivers to aging parents. In J. C. Cavanaugh & S. K. Whitbourne (Eds.), *Gerontology: An interdisciplinary perspective* (pp. 329–354). New York: Oxford University Press.

Determining whether older parents are satisfied with the help their children provide is a complex issue (Newsom, 1999). Based on a critical review of the research, Newsom (1999) proposes a model of how certain aspects of care can produce negative perceptions of care directly or by affecting the interactions between caregiver and care recipient. This model is shown in Figure 11.6. The important thing to conclude from the model is that even under the best circumstances there is no guarantee that the help adult children provide their parents will be well received. Misunderstandings can occur, and the frustration caregivers feel can be translated directly into negative interactions.

In sum, taking care of one's aging parents is a difficult task. Despite the numerous challenges and risks of negative psychological and financial outcomes, many caregivers nevertheless experience positive outcomes.

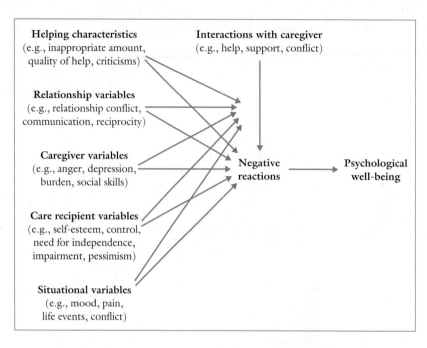

FIGURE 11.6 Model showing how perceptions of care can result directly or be mediated by the caregiver–care recipient relationship.

Source: Newsom, J. T. (1999). Another side to caregiving: Negative reactions to being helped. *Current Directions in Psychological Science, 8,* 185.

Concept Checks

1. What are the major issues in the family life cycle and intergenerational relationships?
2. What are the key aspects in the parental role?
3. What are the major styles and meaning of grandparenthood?
4. What happens to parent–child relationships as children and parents age? What are the key considerations in taking care of aging parents?

Putting It All Together

Relationships with others are a key aspect of adulthood and aging. Jamal and Kahlid remind us that friendships can sustain us over our entire lives and take on special meaning in late life. Bobbie and Jack show how couples can endure the ups and downs of relationships and forge strong bonds that last decades. Susan exemplifies the growing number of adult children, especially daughters and daughters-in-law, who find themselves providing care to parents. Taken together, these people reflect the importance others have in our lives. They also show how relationships can last a very long time and be recast time and time again. The parent–child bond in particular takes on different forms across adulthood. But most of us couldn't imagine what it would be like to live our adult lives without relationships, trying as they may be sometimes.

Summary

RELATIONSHIP TYPES AND ISSUES

Friendships

People tend to have more friendships during young adulthood than during any other period. Friendships in old age are especially important for maintaining life satisfaction.

Men tend to have fewer close friends and base them on shared activities. Women tend to have more close friends and base them on emotional sharing. Cross-gender friendships tend to be difficult.

Sibling Relationships

Sibling relationships are important, especially in late life. Five types of sibling relationships have been identified: congenial, loyal, intimate, apathetic, and hostile. Ties tend to be strongest between sisters.

Love Relationships

Passion, intimacy, and commitment are the key components of love.

The theory that does the best job explaining the process of forming love relationships is the theory of assortative mating.

Selecting a mate works best when there are shared values, goals, and interests. There are cross-cultural differences in which specific aspects of these are most important.

Violence in Relationships

Levels of aggressive behavior range from verbal aggression to physical aggression to murdering one's partner. The causes of aggression become more complex as the level of aggression increases. People remain in abusive relationships for many reasons, including low self-esteem and the belief that they cannot leave.

Abuse and neglect of older adults is an increasing problem. Most perpetrators are adult children. It is unclear whether older victims are dependent on their caregivers or the caregivers are dependent on the victims.

LIFESTYLES AND LOVE RELATIONSHIPS

Singlehood

Most adults in their 20s are single. People remain single for many reasons; gender differences exist. Ethnic differences reflect differences in age at marriage and social factors.

Singles recognize the pluses and minuses in the lifestyle. There are health and longevity consequences from remaining single for men but not for women.

Gay Male and Lesbian Couples

Gay male and lesbian couples are similar to married heterosexual couples in terms of relationship issues. Lesbian couples tend to be more egalitarian.

Marriage

The most important factors in creating stable marriages are maturity, similarity (called homogamy), and conflict resolution skills. Exchange theory is an important explanation of how people contribute to their relationships.

For couples with children, marital satisfaction tends to decline until the children leave home, although individual differences are apparent, especially in long-term marriages.

Most long-term marriages tend to be happy, and partners in them express fewer negative emotions.

Caring for a spouse presents challenges. How well it works depends on the quality of the marriage. Most caregiving spouses provide care based on love.

Divorce and Remarriage

Currently, half of all new marriages end in divorce. Reasons for divorce include a lack of the qualities that make a strong marriage. Also, societal attitudes against divorce have eased, and expectations about marriage have increased.

Recovery from divorce is different for men and women. Men tend to have a tougher time in the short run. Women clearly have a harder time in the long run, often for financial reasons.

Difficulties between divorced partners usually involve visitation and child support.

Most divorced couples remarry. Second marriages are especially vulnerable to stress if stepchildren are involved. Remarriage in later life tends to be very happy.

Widowhood

Widowhood is more common among women because they tend to marry men older than they are. Widowed men typically are older.

Reactions to widowhood depend on the quality of the marriage. Men generally have problems in social relationships and in household tasks; women tend to have more financial problems.

FAMILY DYNAMICS AND THE LIFE COURSE

Family Life Cycle and Intergenerational Relationships

Families experience a series of fairly predictable changes that constitute the family life cycle. One model describes eight stages.

Three ways of conceptualizing kinship ties are used: simple (involving two generations), expanded (involving three generations), and latent (involving in-laws and other relatives). Such kin relationships are changing.

The Parental Role

The most common form of family in Western societies is the nuclear family, consisting only of parents and children; the most common form around the world is the extended family, in which grandparents and other relatives live with parents and children.

Most couples choose to have children, although for many different reasons. The timing of parenthood determines in part how involved parents are in their families as opposed to their careers.

Single parents face many problems, especially if they are women and are divorced. The main problem is reduced financial resources. A major issue for adoptive parents, foster parents, and stepparents is how strongly the child will bond with them. Each of these relationships has some special characteristics. Gay and lesbian parents also face numerous obstacles, but they usually are good parents.

Most parents do not report severe negative emotions when their children leave. Difficulties emerge to the extent that children were a major source of a parent's identity. However, parents typically report distress if adult children move back.

Becoming a Grandparent

Five major styles of grandparenting have been identified: formal, fun seeker, distant, surrogate parents, and dispenser of family wisdom. Additionally, five meanings have been identified: centrality, value as an elder, immortality through clan, reinvolvement with one's personal past, and indulgence. Individual differences are the rule in both style and meaning, with gender and ethnic differences apparent.

Grandparental rights concerning visitation of their grandchildren after their children get divorced are evolving. Although step-grandparenting is increasingly common, little is known about how people form relationships.

Ethnic differences in grandparenting are evident. Ethnic groups with strong family ties differ in style from groups who value individuality.

Grandparents are increasingly being put in the position of raising their grandchildren. Reasons include incarceration and substance abuse by the parents.

Great-grandparenthood is a role enjoyed by more people and reflects a sense of family renewal.

Middle-Aged Adults and Their Aging Parents

Middle-aged women often assume the role of kinkeeper to the family. Middle-aged parents may be squeezed by competing demands of their children, who want to gain independence, and their parents, who want to maintain independence; therefore, they are often called the sandwich generation.

Most caregiving by adult children is done by daughters and daughters-in-law. Filial obligation, the sense of responsibility to care for older parents, is a major factor.

Caring for aging parents is highly stressful. Symptoms of depression, anxiety, and other problems are widespread. Financial pressures also are felt by most. Parents often have a difficult time in accepting the care. However, many caregivers also report feeling rewarded for their efforts.

Review Questions

RELATIONSHIP TYPES AND ISSUES

- How does the number and importance of friendships vary across adulthood?

- What gender differences are there in the number and type of friends?

- What are the major types of sibling relationships?

- What are the components of love?

- What characteristics make the best matches between adults? How do these characteristics differ across cultures?

- What is the relation between type of abusive behavior and its cause?

- What characteristics of the victim and the abuser can lead to elder abuse?

LIFESTYLES AND LOVE RELATIONSHIPS

- How do adults who never marry deal with the need to have relationships?

- What are the relationship characteristics of gay male and lesbian couples?

- What are the most important factors in creating stable marriages?

- What developmental trends are occurring in marital satisfaction? How do these trends relate to having children?

- What factors are responsible for the success of long-term marriages?

- What are the major reasons people get divorced? How are these reasons related to societal expectations about marriage and attitudes about divorce?

- What characteristics about remarriage make it similar to and different from first marriage? How does satisfaction in remarriage vary as a function of age?

- What are the characteristics of widowed people? How do men and women differ in their experience of widowhood?

FAMILY DYNAMICS AND THE LIFE COURSE

- What are the major stages in the family life cycle?

- What is kinship?

- Why do couples decide to have children? What effects do children have on relationships?

- What are the important issues in being an adoptive parent, foster parent, or stepparent? What special challenges are there for gay and lesbian parents?

- What impact does children leaving home have on parents? Why do adult children return?

- What styles and meanings of grandparenting do people demonstrate?

- How do grandparents and grandchildren relate? How do these relationships change with the age of the grandchild?

- What effects does divorce have on grandparent–grandchild relationships?

- What ethnic differences have been noted in grandparenting?

- What are the important issues and meanings of being a great-grandparent?

- How do middle-aged parents relate to their children?

- What are the important issues facing middle-aged adults who care for their parents?

- How does independence relate to children, their middle-aged parents, and their grandparents?

Integrating Concepts in Development

1. What components would a theory of adult relationships need to have?

2. What are some examples of each of the four developmental forces as they influence adult relationships?

3. What role do the changes in sexual functioning discussed in Chapter 2 have on love relationships?

4. What key public policy issues are involved in the different types of adult relationships?

Key Terms

abusive relationship A relationship in which one partner displays aggressive behavior toward the other partner.

assortative mating A theory that states that people find partners based on their similarity to each other.

battered woman syndrome A situation in which a woman believes that she cannot leave an abusive relationship and may even go so far as to kill her abuser.

exchange theory A theory of relationships based on the idea that each partner contributes something to the relationship that the other would be hard pressed to provide.

extended family A family consisting of parents, children, grandparents, and other relatives all living together.

family life cycle A series of predictable changes that most families experience.

filial obligation The feeling that, as an adult child, one must care for one's parents.

grandparenting style The various ways in which grandparents interact with their grandchildren.

homogamy The notion that similar interests and values are important in forming strong, lasting interpersonal relationships.

nuclear family A family consisting of parents and children.

socioemotional selectivity A theory of relationships that argues that social contact is motivated by a variety of goals, including information seeking, self-concept, and emotional regulation.

Resources

Readings

Blieszner, R., & Bedford, V. H. (Eds.). (1995). *Handbook of aging and the family.* Westport, CT: Greenwood. An excellent collection of chapters covering all aspects of the aging family from basic characteristics to social policy issues. Easy to moderate reading.

Boss, P. G., Doherty, W. J., LaRossa, R., Schumm, W. R., & Steinmetz, S. K. (1993). *Sourcebook of family theories and methods.* New York: Plenum. A superb book that covers all the major theories and methods used in family research in one volume. Easy to moderate reading.

Brody, E. M. (1990). *Women in the middle: Their parent-care years.* New York: Springer. A solid, research-based description of women's experiences as middle-aged parents and caregivers. Easy to moderate reading.

Hareven, T. K. (1996). *Aging and generational relations: Life-course and cross-cultural perspectives.* New York: Aldine de Gruyter. One of the few books examining middle-aged adults and their aging parents that includes ethnic and cross-cultural perspectives. Moderate reading.

Lopata, H. Z. (1995). *Current widowhood: Myths and realities.* Thousand Oaks, CA: Sage. A good overview of research on widowhood by the leading scholar in the field. Easy reading.

Mace, N. L., & Rabins, P. V., & McHugh, P. R. (1999). *The 36-hour day* (3rd ed.). Baltimore: Johns Hopkins University Press. The first and still the best family guide to caregiving. Easy reading.

Web Sites

Research findings and professional materials about all aspects of families can be obtained through the National Council on Family Relations. Its home page can be found at http://www.ncfr.com.

The Family Violence Prevention Fund (FVPF) is a national nonprofit organization that focuses on domestic violence education, prevention, and public policy reform. Its home page can be found at http://www.fvpf.org.

The National Network for Family Resiliency maintains a good Web site for grandparents raising grandchildren. Topics include dealing with stress, financial matters, and legal issues. The site can be found at http://www.nnfr.org/igen/GRG.htm.

Information on all aspects of caring for older people who are frail or who have dementia can be found at ElderWeb. The site includes such topics as health care, living arrangements, spiritual support, financial and legal information, and regional resources. The home page can be found at http://www.elderweb.com.

The Family Caregiver Alliance provides a wealth of information about medical, policy, and resource issues concerning caregiving. It is intended for people caring for adults with Alzheimer's disease, stroke, brain injury, and related brain disorders. Its home page can be found at http://www.caregiver.org.

SEARCH ONLINE WITH

InfoTrac College Edition

For more information on the topics in this chapter, explore InfoTrac College Edition, your online library. Go to http://www.infotrac-college.com/wadsworth and use the passcode that came on the card with your book. Try these search terms: aged—abuse of, marriage, divorce, widowhood, grandparent.

WORK, LEISURE, AND RETIREMENT

© Reuters NewMedia Inc. / CORBIS

In 1996, U.S. Senator Strom Thurmond, the oldest person to serve in the Senate, won his eighth straight term in office. If he serves all 6 years of his term, he will be 100 when he leaves office. Is he too old to serve? Praises from his colleagues and his continuing accomplishments suggest not. For example, he is the senior member of the Judiciary Committee, he chairs the Senate Armed Services Committee, and he is the senior member of the Veterans Affairs Committee. After being dogged by questions about his age, Thurmond says that his opponents should stop digging at his age and start talking about the issues. When asked about retirement, he laughs and says he'd have to think about that.

Strom Thurmond's tenure as U.S. senator at such an advanced age reflects some of the key issues we examine in this chapter, especially in the section on retirement. First, we examine how people choose occupations and how they develop in their occupations. However, there are obstacles to occupational development. Thus, next we explore such obstacles, including discrimination and bias issues. Given the current fluctuations in occupational status, we explore how people make transitions within their occupation and to other occupations. Finally, we answer two important questions: How do people spend time when they are not working? What happens to them after they retire?

As will become clear, research addressing these questions about work has focused primarily on middle-class European American men; far less is known about women or about other ethnic groups. Although more research on women and on other ethnic groups is being conducted, we must be careful in applying existing research and theory to these groups until data have been compiled.

Occupational Choice and Development

Learning Objectives

- How do people view work? How do occupational priorities vary with age?
- How do people choose their occupations?
- What factors influence occupational development?
- What expectations do people have about occupations?
- What role do mentors play in occupational development?
- What factors influence job satisfaction? What causes alienation and burnout?

Angela, a 28-year-old senior communication major, wonders about careers. Should she enter the broadcast field as a behind-the-scenes producer, or would she be better suited as a public relations spokesperson? She thinks that her outgoing personality is a factor she should consider. Should she become a broadcast producer?

Choosing one's work is serious business. Like Angela, we try to select a field in which we are trained, and that is appealing. Work colors much of what we do in life. You may be taking this course as part of your preparation for work. People make friends at work and schedule personal activities around work schedules. Parents may choose child care centers on the basis of their proximity to their place of employment. In this section, we explore what work means to adults. We also examine issues pertaining to occupational selection and examine occupational development. Finally, we see how satisfaction with one's job changes during adulthood.

The Meaning of Work

In the 1960s the phrase "different strokes for different folks" was used to make the point that people's motives and needs differ. Thus, work has different meanings for different people. Studs Terkel, the author of the fascinating book *Working* (1974), writes that work is "a search for daily meaning as well as daily bread, for recognition as well as cash, for astonishment rather than torpor; in short, for a sort of life rather than a Monday through Friday sort of dying." (p. xiii). Kahil Gibran (1923), in his mystical book *The Prophet,* put it this way: "Work is love made visible."

For some of us, work is a source of prestige, social recognition, and a sense of worth. For others, the excitement of creativity and the opportunity to give something of themselves make work meaningful. But for most, the main purpose of work is to earn a living. This is not to imply that money is the only reward in a job; friendships, the chance to exercise power, and feeling useful also are important. The meaning most of us derive from working includes both the money we can exchange for life's necessities (and maybe a few luxuries, too) and the possibility of personal growth. These **occupational priorities,** *or what people want from their employment, reflect the culture and the times in which people live.*

Occupational priorities change over time because cultural values change. An excellent example of these influences is the longitudinal study conducted by American Telephone and Telegraph (AT&T), begun in the mid-1950s (Howard & Bray, 1988). Look carefully at Figure 12.1. Three key things are depicted. First, the vertical axis represents the rating of the importance of work in employees' lives. The horizontal axis reflects two things: length of time in the study at AT&T (which gives an idea of the length of employment) and relative age (in general, the less time in the study, the younger the employee).

Notice that the importance of work changed dramatically over time. The longer employees were in the study, the more differentiated the various levels of managers became in terms of the importance of work. Underlying these changes are key differences in

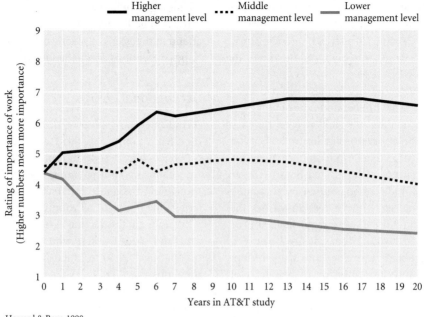

Higher management level ━━━ Middle management level •••• Lower management level ━━━

Howard & Bray, 1990.

FIGURE 12.1 Changes in the relative importance of work at different levels of management in the AT&T study.

Source: Howard, A., & Bray, D. W. (1980, August). *Career motivation in mid-life managers.* Paper presented at the meeting of the American Psychological Association, Montreal.

motivation for upward mobility, leadership, and desire for emotional support, depending on the age of the managers. For higher management levels, those who had been in the AT&T study briefly had much lower expectations of rewards from work than those who had been in the study 10 years or more; they did not see most of their major rewards or life satisfaction coming from work. Interestingly, the picture was reversed for lower-level managers; those who had been in the study longer gave a lower rating of the importance of work.

The findings at AT&T are not unique. Other research has also documented that younger workers in upper management are less interested in materialism, power seeking, upward mobility, and competition; instead, they consistently emphasize individual freedom, personal growth, and cooperation (Jones, 1980; Yankelovich, 1981).

Regardless of what occupational priorities people have, they view their occupation as a key element in their sense of identity (Whitbourne, 1996a). This feeling can be readily observed when people introduce themselves socially: "Hi, I'm Kevin. I'm an accountant. What do you do?" Occupation affects your life in a host of ways, often influencing where you live, what friends you make, and even what clothes you wear. In short, the impact of work cuts across all aspects of life. Work is a major social role and influence on adult life. Occupation is an important anchor that complements the other major role of adulthood: love relationships.

The Changing Nature of Work

The traditional view of work assumes that one's job consists of a certain set of tasks that must be performed (Cascio, 1995). But this view is rapidly becoming outmoded. Global competition means that workers in the United States are competing for jobs with workers in the same industries in France, Russia, Taiwan, China, Poland, Argentina, and the rest of the world (Avolio & Sosik, 1999).

The globalization of work has also resulted in extensive changes in the number and type of jobs available to U.S. workers and the skills needed for these jobs (Avolio & Sosik, 1999). For example, between 1987 and 1994, more than 7 million permanent layoffs were announced in the United States (Cascio, 1995). These layoffs were not caused by companies losing money; indeed, 81% of the companies that downsized during this period were profitable during that year. Rather, layoffs occur mostly because of competition, productivity, relocation of operations, mergers and acquisitions, infusion of new technology, or plant obsolescence. Even though many laid off workers find new jobs, the new positions can involve drastic pay cuts, resulting in downward mobility.

What do these changes mean? A fundamental redefinition of the nature of work is occurring. Whereas traditional organizational careers consisted of meeting the needs of the organization, now the emphasis is on occupational flexibility and learning (Hall & Mirvis, 1995; Sullivan, 1999). Organizations must respond rapidly to market conditions that change quickly. Managers must use flexible leadership styles depending on the situation, with an emphasis on bringing out employees' creativity and best efforts. Workers must assume more autonomy and decision-making authority and must have a variety of technical skills. There is an increasing need for training and development to maintain workers' competencies and fulfillment. Everyone must stay current with the latest technology and newest skills.

As the nature of work has changed, so has the nature of the work force. The median age of the work force has steadily increased and is expected to reach 40 years by the year 2010 (Capowski, 1994). We are witnessing the graying of the work force. With mandatory retirement becoming less common, workers 55 and over are fast becoming a predominant segment of the work force (Capowski, 1994). The aging work force and the increasingly complex,

technologically based workplace are here to stay. We must change the way we think about organizations, attend to the needs of older workers, and reassess our basic conceptions of what a job entails.

Occupational Choice

As indicated earlier, our work life is a major source of our identity, provides us with an official position, and influences our lifestyle and social interactions; therefore, choosing an occupation is a serious matter. Although most people think that occupational choice is largely the province of young adults, much of what we consider in this section also holds true for middle-aged and older workers who are looking to change occupations, either voluntarily or because they lost their jobs. As we will see later, more adults are changing occupations than ever before and have to rethink the kinds of jobs they want to hold. Moreover, as the downsizing trend in corporations continues, many adults may be forced to look for new employment in different fields.

From a developmental perspective, the decisions people make about occupations may change over time. As people face different life issues or achieve new insights about themselves, they may well decide that their best bet would be to change occupations. Additionally, occupational choices may reflect personal or social clocks (see Chapter 1); people of different ages may feel different degrees of pressure to make a certain occupational choice. Regardless of age, personality and interests are important factors in deciding on an occupation. Let's turn our attention to one of the theories explaining how and why people choose the occupations they do.

HOLLAND'S THEORY OF OCCUPATIONAL CHOICE. Although we tend to think of occupational choice as something done during adolescence or young adulthood, recent theories and research have increasingly adopted a life-course perspective (Sterns & Gray, 1999). However, the main theoretical frameworks for occupational choice have taken a trait factor approach, which focuses on aspects of one's personality (see Chapter 10).

TABLE 12.1	General Occupational Themes in Holland's Theory	
Theme	Description	Careers
Realistic	Individuals enjoy physical labor and working with their hands, and they like to solve concrete problems.	mechanic, truck driver, construction worker
Investigative	Individuals are task-oriented and enjoy thinking about abstract relations.	scientist, technical writer
Social	Individuals are skilled verbally and interpersonally, and they enjoy solving problems using these skills.	teacher, counselor, social worker
Conventional	Individuals have verbal and quantitative skills that they like to apply to structured, well-defined tasks assigned to them by others.	bank teller, payroll clerk, traffic manager
Enterprising	Individuals enjoy using their verbal skills in positions of power, status, and leadership.	business executive, television producer, real estate agent
Artistic	Individuals enjoy expressing themselves through unstructured tasks.	poet, musician, actor

Holland (1985, 1987, 1996) developed a theory based on the intuitively appealing idea that people choose occupations to optimize the fit between their individual traits—such as personality, intelligence, skills, and abilities—and their occupational interests. He categorizes occupations in two ways: by the interpersonal settings in which people must function and by their associated lifestyle. He identifies six work environments in which people can express their vocational personalities; they are summarized in Table 12.1. Each one is best suited to a specific set of occupations, as indicated in the right-hand column of Table 12.1. Remember that these are merely prototypes. Most people do not match any one personality type exactly. Instead, their work-related personalities are a blend of the six.

Holland's theory exists at the level of interest, not at the level of performance requirements per se. He predicts that people will choose the occupation that has the greatest similarity to their personality type. By doing this, they optimize their ability to express

themselves, apply their skills, and take on new roles. Having a good match between personality and occupation maximizes occupational satisfaction. This model is useful in describing the career preferences of African, Asian, European, Native, and Mexican American adults; it is also useful for both men and women (Day et al., 1998). Research also shows that when people have jobs that match their personality type, in the short run they are more productive employees, and, in the long run they have more stable career paths (Holland, 1996). Similarly, in a study of 171 African American nursing personnel, Day and Bedeian (1995) found that personality traits significantly predicted how well employees perform and how long they remain with the same organization.

Holland's theory does not mean that personality completely determines what occupation one chooses. The connection is that people who act or feel a certain way typically choose certain occupations. Most of us would rather do something that we like to do than something that we are forced to do. Thus, unless we have little choice because of financial or other constraints, we typically choose occupations on that basis. When mismatches occur, people usually adapt by changing jobs, changing interests, or adapting the job to provide a better match.

Although the relations between personality and occupational choice are important, we must also recognize the limits of the theory as it relates to adults' occupational choices. If we simply consider the gender distribution of Holland's personality types, adult men and women are represented differently (Costa et al., 1984). Regardless of age, women are more likely than men to have social, artistic, and conventional personality types. In part, gender differences reflect different experiences in growing up (e.g., hearing that girls grow up to be nurses whereas boys grow up to be firefighters), differences in personality (e.g., gender role identity), and differences in socialization (e.g., women being expected to be more outgoing and people-oriented than men). However, if we look within a specific occupational type, women and men are very similar to each other and closely correspond to the interests Holland describes (Betz et al., 1996).

We know very little about how Holland's types vary in different ethnic groups, mostly because such groups have not been included in the studies investigating the links between personality and occupation. Additionally, Holland's theory ignores the context in which occupational decisions are made. For example, he overlooks the fact that many people have little choice in the kind of job they can get because of external factors such as family, financial pressures, or ethnicity.

Holland's theory also ignores evidence of the dynamic quality of the match between personality type and occupation, or how it changes during adulthood (Adler & Aranya, 1984). Holland takes a static view of both personality and occupations, but it must be recognized that the occupation we choose is not dictated solely by what we are like. Equally important is the dynamic interplay between us and the sociocultural context in which we find ourselves—just as one would suspect, given the biopsychosocial model presented in Chapter 1. Occupational selection is a complex developmental process involving interactions between personal, ethnic, gender, and economic factors.

Occupational Development

For most of us, getting a job is not enough; we would also like to move up the ladder. Promotion is a measure of how well one is doing in one's career. How quickly occupational advancement occurs (or does not) may lead to such labels as fast-tracker or dead-ender (Kanter, 1976). Bill Clinton, inaugurated as president at age 46, is an example of a fast-tracker. People who want to advance learn quickly how long to stay at one level and how to seize opportunities as they occur; others soon learn the frustration of remaining in the same job, with no chance for promotion.

How a person advances in a career seems to depend on professional socialization, which includes several factors besides those that are that are important in choosing an occupation. Among these are expectations, support from co-workers, priorities, and job satisfaction. Before we consider these aspects, we look at a general scheme of occupational development.

SUPER'S THEORY. Over four decades, Super (1957, 1980) developed a theory of occupational development based on self-concept. He proposed a progression through five distinct stages during adulthood, resulting from changes in people's self-concept and adaptation to an occupational role: implementation, establishment, maintenance, deceleration, and retirement. *People are located along a continuum of* **vocational maturity** *through their working years; the more congruent their occupational behaviors are with what is expected of them at different ages, the more vocationally mature they are.*

Implementation → Establishment →
Deceleration → Retirement

The initial two phases of Super's theory, crystallization (identity development as a source of career ideas) and specification (focusing on and training in specific lines of work), occur primarily during adolescence, and the first adulthood phase has its origins

Bill Clinton is shown being inaugurated as U.S. President at age 46.

then as well. Each stage in adulthood has distinctive characteristics:

The implementation stage begins in late adolescence or the early 20s, when people take a series of temporary jobs to learn firsthand about work roles and to try out some possible career choices.

The establishment stage begins with selecting a specific occupation during young adulthood. It continues as the person advances up the career ladder in the same occupation.

The maintenance stage is a transition phase during middle age; as workers maximize their efficiency, they begin to reduce the amount of time they spend fulfilling work roles.

The deceleration stage begins as workers begin planning in earnest for their upcoming retirement and separating themselves from their work.

The retirement stage begins when people stop working full-time.

In Super's framework, people's occupations evolve in response to changes in their self-concept (Salomone, 1996). Consequently, this is a developmental process that reflects and explains important life changes. This process sheds a developmental light on Holland's ideas. Investigative and enterprising people are likely to come from more affluent families in which the parents tended not to be in investigative or enterprising occupations. Interestingly, initial occupational goals were not as important for social types as for the other two; social types appeared more flexible in eventual occupational choice.

However, a shortcoming of Super's theory is that the progression assumes that once people choose an occupation, they stay in it for the rest of their working lives. Although this may have been true for some employees in the past, it is not the case for most North American workers today (Cascio, 1995). The downsizing of public and private organizations since the late 1980s has all but eliminated the notion of lifetime job security with a particular employer. It remains to be seen whether new developmental stages will be found to adapt to the new occupational reality.

OCCUPATIONAL EXPECTATIONS. People have expectations about what they want to become and when they hope to get there. Levinson and colleagues (1978) built these expectations into their theory of adult male development, which was later extended to women (Levinson & Levinson, 1996). Based on findings from the original longitudinal study begun in the 1940s on men attending an elite private college, Levinson and colleagues (1978) found much similarity between the participants in terms of major life tasks during adulthood. Forming a dream, with one's career playing a prominent role, is one of the young adult's chief tasks.

Throughout adulthood, people continue to refine and update their occupational expectations. This usually involves trying to achieve the dream, monitoring progress toward it, and changing or even abandoning it as necessary. For some, modifying the dream comes as a result of realizing that interests have changed or that the dream was not a good fit. In other cases, failure leads to changing the dream, as when a student drops a business major because he or she is failing economics courses. Other causes are age, racial, or sexual discrimination, lack of opportunity, obsolescence of skills, and changing interests. In some cases, one's initial occupational choice may have been unrealistic. For example, nearly half of all young adults would like to become professionals (such as lawyers or physicians), but only one person in seven actually makes it (Cosby, 1974). Some goal modification is essential from time to time, but it usually surprises us to realize that we could have been wrong about what seemed to be a logical choice in the past. As Marie, a 38-year-old advertising manager, put it, "I really thought I wanted to be a pilot; the travel sounded really interesting. But it just wasn't what I expected."

Perhaps the rudest jolt for most of us first comes during the transition from school to the real world. **Reality shock,** *realizations about how the real world works,* sets in, and things never seem to happen the way we expect. Reality shock befalls everyone, from the young worker to the accountant who learns that the financial forecast that took days to prepare may simply end up in a file cabinet or, worse yet, in the wastebasket (Van Maanen & Schein, 1977). The visionary aspects of the dream may not disappear altogether, but a good dose of reality goes a long way toward bringing a person down to earth. Such feedback

comes to play an increasingly important role in a person's occupational development and self-concept. For example, the woman who thought that she would receive the same rewards as her male counterparts for comparable work is likely to become increasingly angry and disillusioned when her successes result in smaller raises and fewer promotions.

THE ROLE OF MENTORS. Imagine how hard it would be to figure out everything you needed to know in a new job with no support from the people around you. Entering an occupation involves more than the short formal training a person receives. Indeed, much of the most critical information is not taught in training seminars. Instead, most people are shown the ropes by co-workers. *In many cases, an older, more experienced person makes a specific effort to do this, taking on the role of a* **mentor.** Although mentors are not the only source of guidance in the workplace, they have been studied fairly closely.

A mentor is part teacher, part sponsor, part model, and part counselor (Heimann & Pittenger, 1996). The mentor helps a young worker avoid trouble ("Beware of what you say around Bentley"). He or she also provides invaluable information about the unwritten rules that govern day-to-day activities in the workplace, such as not working too fast on the assembly line, wearing the right clothes, and so on (Levinson et al., 1978; Levinson & Levinson, 1996). As part of the relationship, a mentor makes sure that his or her protégé is noticed and receives credit for good work from supervisors. Thus, occupational success often depends on the quality of the mentor–protégé relationship. The mentor fulfills two main functions: improving the protégé's chances for advancement and promoting his or her psychological and social well-being (Kram, 1980, 1985; Noe, 1987).

Playing the role of a mentor is also a developmental phase in one's occupation. Helping a younger employee learn the job fulfills aspects of Erikson's (1982) phase of generativity. In particular, the mentor makes sure that there is some continuity in the field by passing on the accumulated knowledge and experience he or she has gained by being in it for a while. This function of the mentor is part of middle-aged adults' attempts to ensure the continuity of society and to accomplish or produce something worthwhile (Erikson, 1982). In this sense, mentoring is clearly an example of intergenerational exchange in the workplace.

The mentor–protégé relationship develops over time. Based on her in-depth study, Kram (1985) proposes a four-stage sequence. The first stage, initiation, constitutes the 6- to 12-month period during which the protégé selects a mentor and they begin to develop their relationship. The second stage, cultivation, lasts from 2 to 5 years and is the most active phase of the mentoring relationship. This is the period when the mentor provides occupational assistance and serves as a confidant. The third stage, separation, is the most difficult. It begins when the protégé receives a promotion, often to the level of the mentor. The protégé must emerge from the protection of the mentor to demonstrate his or her own competence. Both parties experience feelings of loneliness and separation. The final period is redefinition. In this period the protégé and mentor reestablish their relationship but with a new set of rules based more on friendship between peers. Research supports this developmental process and the benefits of having a mentor (Chao, 1997; Seibert, 1999).

Some authors suggest that women have a greater need for a mentor than men do because they receive less socialization in the skills necessary to do well in the workplace (Busch, 1985). Women with mentors also have higher expectations about career advancement opportunities (Baugh et al., 1996). However, women seem to have a more difficult time finding adequate mentors; some evidence suggests that only one-third of young professional women find mentors (Kittrell, 1998). One reason is that there are few female role models who could serve a mentoring function, especially in upper-level management. This is unfortunate, especially in view of evidence that women who have female mentors are significantly more productive than women with male mentors (Goldstein, 1979). Although many young women report that they would feel comfortable with a male mentor (Olian et al., 1988), researchers note that male mentor–female protégé relationships may involve conflict and tension resulting from possible sexual

overtones, even when there has been no overtly sexual behavior on anyone's part (Kram, 1985).

Job Satisfaction

What does it mean to be satisfied with one's job or occupation? In a general sense **job satisfaction** *is the positive feeling that results from an appraisal of one's work*. In general, job satisfaction tends to increase gradually with age (Bernal et al., 1998; Sterns, Marsh, & McDaniel, 1994). The increased satisfaction has been linked to several factors.

First, self-selection factors suggest that people who truly like their jobs may tend to stay in them, whereas people who do not may tend to leave. To the extent that this is the case, age differences in job satisfaction may simply reflect the fact that with sufficient time, many people eventually find a job in which they are reasonably happy.

Second, the relationship between worker age and job satisfaction is complex. Satisfaction does not increase in all areas and job types with age. Older workers are more satisfied with the intrinsic personal aspects of their jobs than they are with the extrinsic aspects, such as pay (Morrow & McElroy, 1987). White-collar professionals show an increase in job satisfaction, whereas those in blue-collar positions do not (Sterns, Marsh, & McDaniel, 1994).

Third, increases in job satisfaction may not result from age alone but rather from the degree to which there is a good fit between the worker and the job (Holland, 1985). Older workers have had more time to find a job that they like or may have resigned themselves to the fact that things are unlikely to improve, resulting in a better congruence between worker desires and job attributes (White & Spector, 1987). Older workers also may have revised their expectations over the years to better reflect the actual state of affairs.

Fourth, as workers get older, they make work less of a focus in their lives, partly because they have achieved occupational success (Bray & Howard, 1983). Consequently, it takes less to keep them satisfied.

Fifth, the type of job and the degree of family responsibilities at different career stages may influence the relationship between age and job satisfaction (Engle et al., 1994). This suggests that the accumulation of experience, changing context, and the stage of one's career development may contribute to the increase in job satisfaction.

Finally, job satisfaction may be cyclical. That is, it may show periodic fluctuations that are not related to age per se but rather to changes people intentionally make in their occupations (Shirom & Mazeh, 1988). The idea is that job satisfaction increases over time because people change jobs or responsibilities on a regular basis, thereby keeping their occupation interesting and challenging. This provocative idea of periodicity in job satisfaction is explored further in How Do We Know?

ALIENATION AND BURNOUT. No job is perfect. There is always something about it that is not as good as it could be; perhaps the hours are not optimal, the pay is lower than one would like, or the boss does not have a pleasant personality. For most workers, these negatives are merely annoyances. But for others, such as air traffic controllers, they create extremely stressful situations that result in deeply rooted unhappiness with work: alienation and burnout.

When workers feel that what they are doing is meaningless and that their efforts are devalued, or when they do not see the connection between what they do and the final product, a sense of **alienation** *is likely to result.* Studs Terkel (1974) interviewed several alienated workers and found that all of them expressed feeling that they were merely nameless, faceless cogs in a large machine.

Employees are most likely to feel alienated when they perform routine, repetitive actions such as those on an assembly line (Terkel, 1974). Interestingly, many of these functions are being automated and performed by robots. But other workers can become alienated, too. Especially since the beginning of corporate downsizing in the 1980s, many middle-level managers do not feel that they have the same level of job security that they once had. Consequently, their feelings toward their employers have become more negative in many cases (Roth, 1991).

How can employers avoid creating alienated workers? Research indicates that it is helpful to in-

volve employees in the decision-making process, create flexible work schedules, and institute employee development and enhancement programs (Roth, 1991). Indeed, many organizations have instituted new practices such as total quality management (TQM), partly as a way to address worker alienation. TQM and related approaches are designed to get employees involved in the operation and administration of their plant or office. Such programs work; absenteeism drops and the quality of work improves in organizations that implement them (Offerman & Growing, 1990).

Sometimes the pace and pressure of one's occupation become more than a person can bear, resulting in **burnout,** *a depletion of a person's energy and motivation, the loss of occupational idealism, and the feeling that one is being exploited.* Burnout is a unique type of stress syndrome characterized by emotional exhaustion, depersonalization, and diminished personal accomplishment (Cordes & Dougherty, 1993). Burnout is most common among people in the helping professions, such as teaching, social work, and health care (Cordes & Dougherty, 1993). For example, nurses in intensive care units have high levels of burnout from stress (Iskra et al., 1996). People in these professions must constantly deal with other people's complex problems, usually under difficult time constraints. Dealing with these pressures every day, along with bureaucratic paperwork, may become too much for the worker to bear. Ideals are abandoned, frustration builds, and disillusionment and exhaustion set in. The situation is exacerbated when people must work long shifts in stressful jobs (Iskra et al., 1996). Finally, burnout tends to increase with increasing age and years on the job (Stanton-Rich et al., 1998).

The best defenses against burnout appear to be practicing stress reduction techniques, lowering workers' expectations of themselves, and enhancing communication within organizations. Providing longer rest periods between shifts in highly stressful jobs may help (Iskra et al., 1996). No one in the helping professions can resolve all problems perfectly; lowering expectations of what workers can realistically accomplish helps them deal with real-world constraints. Similarly, improving communication between different sections of organiza-

Who were the investigators, and what was the aim of the study? Why does job satisfaction tend to increase with age? One hypothesis is that job satisfaction has a complex relationship to the length of time one has been in a job, not to age per se. Satisfaction might be high in the beginning of a job, stabilize or drop during the middle phase, and rise again later. Each time a person changes jobs, the cycle might repeat. Arie Shirom and Tsevi Mazeh (1988) decided to test this hypothesis and see whether this cycle happens.

How did the investigators measure the topic of interest? Shirom and Mazeh administered questionnaires containing items measuring teachers' satisfaction with salary, working hours, social status, contacts with pupils, autonomy, opportunities for professional growth, and opportunities for carrying out educational goals.

Who were the participants in the study? A representative sample of 900 Israeli junior high school teachers with varying seniority participated.

What was the design of the study? Shirom and Mazeh studied the cyclical nature of job satisfaction using a cross-sectional research design. By using sophisticated data analysis techniques, they were able to identify year-to-year changes in job satisfaction.

Were there ethical concerns with the study? There were no concerns in this study; the topics were not controversial, nor were they likely to cause strongly negative feelings.

What were the results? Shirom and Mazeh found that teachers' job satisfaction followed systematic 5-year cycles that were strongly related to seniority but unrelated to age. That is, the cycles begin when the person starts a job, and the level of satisfaction is linked to how long the person has been on the job. Because the age at which people start new teaching jobs can vary a great deal, Shirom and Mazeh showed that the cycles had nothing to do with how old the teachers were; all ages showed the same basic pattern.

Most interesting, Shirom and Mazeh noted that a major work-related change, a sabbatical leave, or a change in school assignment seemed to occur approximately every 5 years. They concluded that such changes reinitiated the cycle with high job satisfaction. When tracked over long periods, the cycle appears to show a steady increase in overall job satisfaction. This long-term gradual increase in job satisfaction is consistent with the general finding of gradual increases in job satisfaction with age, even though the fundamental cyclic nature of job satisfaction is unrelated to age.

What did the investigators conclude? An important implication of Shirom and Mazeh's data is that change may be necessary for long-term job satisfaction. Although the teaching profession has change built into it (such as sabbatical leaves), many occupations do not (Latack, 1984). Based on Shirom and Mazeh's data, the option of periodic changes in job structure probably would benefit people in other occupations as well.

---

tions to keep workers informed of the outcome of their efforts gives them a sense that what they do matters in the long run. Finally, research also suggests that lack of support from one's co-workers may cause depersonalization; improving such support through teamwork or co-worker support can be an effective intervention (Corrigan et al., 1994; Greenglass et al., 1998).

In short, making sure workers feel that they are important to the organization by involving them in decisions, keeping expectations realistic, ensuring good communication, and promoting teamwork and co-worker support may help employees avoid alienation and burnout. Adopting different management styles can help organizations accomplish these goals.

CONCEPT CHECKS

1. What is Holland's theory?
2. Describe Super's stages of occupational development.
3. What is reality shock?
4. What are the stages in the development of the mentor–protégé relationship?
5. What factors are associated with job satisfaction in older workers?

GENDER, ETHNICITY, BIAS, AND DISCRIMINATION

LEARNING OBJECTIVES

- How do women's and men's occupational expectations differ? How are people viewed when they enter occupations that are not traditional for their gender?
- What factors are related to women's occupational development?
- What factors affect ethnic minority workers' occupational experiences and occupational development?
- What types of bias and discrimination hinder the occupational development of women and ethnic minority workers?
- What types of bias and discrimination hinder the occupational development of older workers?

Janice, a 35-year-old African American manager at a business consulting firm, is concerned because her career is not progressing as rapidly as she had hoped. Janice works hard and receives excellent performance ratings every year. But she has noticed that there are very few women in upper management positions in her company. Janice wonders whether she will ever be promoted.

Occupational choice and development are not equally available to all, as Janice is finding. Gender, ethnicity, and age may create barriers to achieving one's occupational goals. People of each group receive somewhat different socialization as children and adolescents, which makes it easier or harder for them to set their sights on particular careers. Bias and discrimination also create barriers to occupational success. In this section, we'll get a better appreciation for the personal and structural barriers that exist for many people.

Gender Differences in Occupational Choice

Traditionally, men have been groomed from birth for future employment. Boys learn at an early age that men are known by the work they do, and they are strongly encouraged to think about what occupation they would like to have. Occupational achievement is stressed as a core element of masculinity. Important social skills are taught through team games, in which they learn how to play by the rules, accept setbacks without taking defeat personally, follow the guidance of a leader, and move up the leadership hierarchy by demonstrating qualities that are valued by others.

Traditionally, women have not been trained in this manner. The skills they have learned are quite different: how to be accommodating, deferential, quiet, and supportive (Shainess, 1984). However, an increasing emphasis has been placed on the importance of teaching girls the necessary skills for occupations outside the home. The growth of women's athletic programs is giving more women the opportunity to learn key skills as well.

Given that more than 63% of women are employed outside the home (U.S. Department of Labor, 1996) and that this number probably will continue to increase, it is especially important that women be exposed to the same occupational socialization opportunities as men. However, major structural barriers to women's occupational selection remain (Schwartz & Zimmerman 1992; Shaiko, 1996; Yamagata et al., 1997). It is still the case that many occupational opportunities are more available to men than to women (Lyness & Thompson, 1997).

TRADITIONAL AND NONTRADITIONAL OCCUPATIONS. In the past, women who were employed tended to enter traditionally female-dominated occupations such as secretarial, teaching, and social work jobs, mainly because of their socialization into these occupational tracks. However, as more women enter the work force and as new opportunities are opened for women, a growing number of them work in occupations that have traditionally been male-dominated, such as construction and engineering. Research in this area has focused on three issues (Swanson, 1992): selection of nontraditional occupations, characteristics of women in nontraditional occupations, and perceptions of nontraditional occupations.

Why some women end up in nontraditional occupations appears to be related to personal feelings and experiences as well as expectations about the occupation (Brooks & Betz, 1990). Concerning personal experiences, women who attend single-sex high schools and who have both brothers and sisters end up in the least traditional occupations, apparently because they have been exposed to more options and fewer gender role stereotypes (Rubenfeld & Gilroy, 1991). Personal feelings are important; a study of Japanese students found that women had significantly lower confidence in their ability to perform in male-dominated occupations than in female-dominated occupations (Matsui et al., 1989).

The characteristics of women in nontraditional occupations have been studied as well. Betz and colleagues (1990) found that women who scored high on femininity, as defined by endorsing traditional feminine gender roles, and those in female-dominated occupations had the poorest match between their abilities and their occupational choices. These findings mean that women who score high on traditional measures of femininity have difficulty finding occupations that allow them to take advantage of their abilities. Additionally, women in female-dominated occupations generally find that their jobs do not allow them to use their abilities to the fullest. In sum, it appears that many women have difficulty finding occupations that match their skills.

Despite the efforts to counteract gender stereotyping of occupations, women who choose nontraditional occupations still are viewed with disapproval by their peers of either sex, even though they have high job satisfaction themselves (Brabeck & Weisgerber, 1989; Pfost & Fiore, 1990). This finding holds up in cross-cultural research as well. In a study conducted in India, both women and men gave higher "respectability" ratings to men than to women in the same occupation (Kanekar et al., 1989). People even make inferences about working conditions based on their perception of an occupation as traditionally masculine or feminine. Scozzaro and Subich (1990) report that occupations such as secretary are perceived as offering good pay and promotion potential. Worst of all, people are less likely to perceive incidents of sexual coercion as harassing when a woman is in a nontraditional occupation (Burgess & Borgida, 1997).

Taken together, these studies show that we still have a long way to go before people can choose any occupation they want without having to contend with gender-related stereotypes. Although differences in opportunities for women in traditional and nontraditional occupations are narrowing, key differences remain. Finally, almost no research has examined differences between men in traditional and nontraditional occupations (Swanson, 1992). This lack of data is troubling because it prevents our answering important questions such as why men choose traditional or nontraditional occupations and why some men still perpetuate gender stereotypes about particular occupations.

Women and Occupational Development

If you were to guess what a young woman who has just graduated from college will be doing occupationally 10 years from now, what would you say? Would you guess that she will be strongly committed to her occupation? Will she have abandoned it for other things? Betz (1984) wanted to know the answers, so she examined the occupational histories of 500 college women 10 years after graduation. Two-thirds of these women were highly committed to their occupations, which for 70% were traditionally female ones. Most had worked continuously since graduation. Only 1% had been full-time homemakers during the entire 10-year period; 79% reported that they had successfully combined occupations with homemaking. Women in traditional female occupations changed jobs less often. If they did change, they were more likely to move to a job with a lower rank and pay than were women in nontraditional occupations.

An intriguing question is why highly educated women leave what appear to be well-paid occupations. Studies of women with MBAs who have children identified a number of family and workplace issues (Rosin & Korabik, 1990, 1991). Family obligations, such as child care, appear to be most important for mothers working part-time. For these women, adequate child care arrangements or the flexibility to be at home when children get out of school often make the difference between being able to accept a job and remaining at home. In contrast, mothers

Researchers want to know what the young woman in the photograph will be doing occupationally 10 years from now.

who have decided to work full-time have resolved the problem of child care. The most important workplace issues for these women are gender-related. Unsupportive or insensitive work environments, organizational politics, and the lack of occupational development opportunities appear to be most important for women working full-time (Schwartz & Zimmerman, 1992). In this case, women are focusing on issues that could create barriers to their occupational development and are looking for ways around the barriers.

Such barriers are a major reason why women's careers do not show the developmental upward climb that is evident in men's career development. Because they cannot find affordable and dependable child care or they freely choose to take on this responsibility, many women stay home while their children are young. The lack of continuity in job participation makes it difficult to maintain an upward trajectory in one's career through promotion and to maintain skills. Some women make this choice willingly; however, many find they are forced into it.

Ethnicity and Occupational Development

What factors are related to occupational selection and development of people from ethnic minorities? Unfortunately, not much research has been conducted from a developmental perspective. Rather, most researchers have focused on the limited opportunities ethnic minorities have and structural barriers, such as discrimination, that they face. Three topics have received the most focus: nontraditional occupations, vocational identity, and issues pertaining to occupational aspirations.

African American women and European American women do not differ in terms of plans to enter nontraditional occupations (Murrell et al., 1991). However, African American women who choose nontraditional occupations tend to plan for more formal education than necessary to achieve their goal. This may make them overqualified for the jobs they get; for example, a woman with a college degree may be working in a job that does not require that level of education.

Vocational identity is the degree to which one views one's occupation as a key element of identity. Research shows that vocational identity varies with both ethnicity and gender. Compared with European American women and Hispanic men, African American and European American men have higher vocational identity when they graduate from college (Steward & Krieshok, 1991). Lower vocational identity means that people define themselves primarily in terms of things other than work.

A person's occupational aspiration is the kind of occupation he or she would like to have. In contrast, occupational expectation is the occupation the person believes he or she will get. Hispanics differ from European Americans in several ways with regard to these variables. They have high occupational aspirations but low expectations, and they differ in their educational attainment as a function of national origin, generational status, and social class (Arbona, 1990). However, Hispanics are similar to European Americans in occupational development and work values.

Research on occupational development of ethnic minority workers is clear on one point: Whether an organization is responsive to the needs of ethnic minorities makes a big difference for employees. Both European American and ethnic minority managers who perceive their organizations as responsive and positive for ethnic minority employees are more satisfied with and committed to the organizations (Burke, 1991a, 1991b). But much still remains to be accomplished. African American managers report less choice of jobs, less acceptance, more career dissatisfaction, lower performance evaluations and promotability ratings, and more rapid attainment of plateaus in their careers than European American managers (Greenhaus et al., 1990). More than 60% of African American protégés have European American mentors, which is problematic because same-ethnicity mentors provide more psychosocial support than cross-ethnicity mentors (Thomas, 1990). Nevertheless, having any mentor is more beneficial than having none (Bridges, 1996).

Bias and Discrimination

Since the 1960s, organizations in the United States have been sensitized to the issues of bias and discrimination in the workplace. Hiring, promotion, and termination procedures have come under close scrutiny in numerous court cases, resulting in a host of laws to govern these processes.

GENDER BIAS AND THE GLASS CEILING. Even though the majority of women work outside the home, women in high-status jobs are unusual (Morrison et al., 1992). Not until 1981 was a woman, Sandra Day O'Connor, appointed to the U.S. Supreme Court; it took another 12 years before a second woman, Ruth Bader Ginsburg, was appointed associate justice. As Janice noticed in the vignette, few women serve in the highest ranks of major corporations, and women are substantially outnumbered at the senior faculty level of most universities and colleges.

Why are there so few women in higher-status jobs? The explanation that has received much attention is **sex discrimination,** *denying a job to someone solely on the basis of whether the person is a man or a woman.* Baron and Bielby pull no punches in discussing sex discrimination. "Our analyses portray [sex] discrimination as pervasive, almost omnipresent, sustained by diverse organizational structures and processes. Moreover, this segregation drastically restricts women's career opportunities, by blocking access to internal labor markets and their benefits" (Baron & Bielby, 1985, p. 245). Despite some progress in the past two decades, sex discrimination is still common; women are being kept out of high-status jobs by the men at the top (Lyness & Thompson, 1997; Shaiko, 1996; Yamagata et al., 1997). However, we should also note that in the past there have been fewer women vying for these jobs. More recently we are seeing more and more competent women moving into academia and the business world and competing for positions.

Women themselves refer to a **glass ceiling,** *the level to which they may rise in a company but beyond which they may not go.* This problem is most obvious in companies that classify jobs at various levels (as does the civil service). The greatest barrier facing women is at the boundary between lower-tier and upper-tier job grades (Morrison et al., 1992). Women like Janice tend to move to the top of the lower tier and remain there, whereas men are more readily promoted to the upper tier, even when other factors, such as personal attributes and qualifications, are controlled (Diprete & Soule, 1988). Indeed, a longitudinal study of women in the high school class of 1972 showed that despite better academic records, women's achievement in the workplace is limited by structural barriers (Adelman, 1991). The U.S. Department of Labor (1991) admits that the glass ceiling pervades the workplace. Some surveys indicate that more than 90% of women believe that there is a glass ceiling in the workplace. Clear evidence of the glass ceiling has been found in private corporations (Lyness & Thompson, 1997), government agencies (Yamagata et al., 1997), and nonprofit organizations (Shaiko, 1996). Indeed, estimates are that if the present rate of advancement continues, it will take until the late 25th century for women to achieve equality with men in the executive suite (Feminist Majority Foundation, 1991). To add insult to injury, *certain occupations have a* **glass elevator** *in which men in traditionally female occupations such as nursing rise at a faster rate than their female counterparts.*

Besides discrimination in hiring and promotion, women are also subject to pay discrimination. According to the U.S. Department of Labor, in many occupations men are paid substantially more than women in the same positions; indeed, on the average, women are paid less than three-fourths of what men are paid annually (U.S. Department of Labor, 1997). The situation is much worse for women of color; African American women only earn roughly 63% and Hispanic women earn roughly 57% as much as white men (Castro, 1997). Even more distressing, the gender wage gap remains substantial even when educational backgrounds are equivalent (Castro, 1997).

Such averages conceal important developmental aspects of the gender difference: The wage gap widens over women's working years (Castro, 1997). As you can see in Figure 12.2, the wage gap begins widening rapidly in the 30s and remains substantial through age 65. These broadening differences reflect several factors: sex discrimination, the discontinuous participation of women in the work force, and the disproportionate number of women in low-paying jobs (Castro, 1997).

Several solutions to this problem have been promoted. One of these is **comparable worth:** *equalizing pay in occupations that are determined to be equivalent in importance but differ in the gender distribution of the people doing the jobs.* Determining which male-dominated occupations should be considered equivalent to which female-dominated occupations for pay purposes can be difficult and controversial. One way to do this is with gender-neutral job evaluations, which examine all positions within an organization to establish fair pay policies (Castro, 1997).

SEXUAL HARASSMENT. Although the sexual harassment of women in the workplace has been documented for centuries, only recently has it received much attention from researchers (Fitzgerald & Shullman, 1993). Interest among U.S. researchers increased dramatically terest among U.S. researchers increased dramatically after the 1991 Senate hearings involving Supreme Court nominee Clarence Thomas and Anita Hill, who accused him of sexual harassment; the scandals involving military personnel; and the impeachment of President Bill Clinton. By no means is sexual harassment a U.S.-only phenomenon; unfortunately, it occurs around the world (Luo, 1996).

Research on sexual harassment focuses on situations in which there is a power differential between two people, most often involving men with more power over women (Berdahl et al., 1996). Such situations exist in the workplace and in academic settings (Zappert, 1996). However, peer-to-peer harassment also occurs, such as that between classmates in academic settings (Ivy & Hamlet, 1996).

How many people have been sexually harassed? Evidence suggests that about 70% of women have "experienced or heard offensive slurs or jokes or remarks about women" (Piotrkowski, 1998). Interestingly, men report a similar level of such behavior. Reliable statistics on more serious forms of harassment, such as touching and sexual activity, are more difficult to obtain, in part because of the unwillingness of many victims to report harassment and because of differences in reporting procedures. Indeed, estimates are that less than 5% of victims report their experiences to anyone in authority (Fitzgerald et al., 1988). Even given these difficulties, several studies document that more than 40% of women report having been sexually harassed in the workplace at least once (Fitzgerald & Shullman, 1993). Victims are most often single or divorced women under age 35 (Tang & McCollum, 1996).

What effects does being sexually harassed have? Research evidence shows clear negative emotional, mental health, and job-related outcomes (Schneider et al., 1997). Establishing the degree of problems is difficult, though, because many women try to minimize or hide their reactions or feelings (Tang & McCollum, 1996). It is becoming evident, though, that one does not have to experience the worst kinds of sexual harassment to be affected. Even low-level but frequent experience of sexual harassment can have significant negative consequences for women (Schneider et al., 1997).

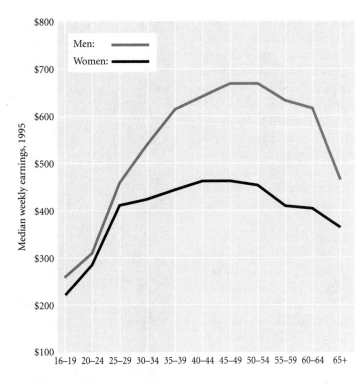

FIGURE 12.2 **The wage gap for weekly earnings between women and men.**

Source: Castro, I. L. (1997). Worth more than we earn: Fair pay as a step toward gender equity. *National Forum, 77*(2), 17–21.

Sexual harassment also has numerous ripple effects throughout a company (Piotrkowski, in progress, cited in Murray, 1998). For example, men of all ethnic backgrounds who work in companies that have cases of sexual harassment but who are not harassers themselves report less satisfaction with their jobs. Productivity at such companies also declines, as does general worker morale.

Of course, the crux of the matter is what constitutes harassment. What would have to be going on in a situation for you to say that it was harassment? In research on perceptions of what constitutes harassing behavior, people usually read vignettes of hypothetical incidents involving sexually suggestive touching, sexual remarks, and the like and then decide whether it was harassment. In general, women are more likely to view such behaviors as offensive than are men

(Berdahl et al., 1996; Fitzgerald & Ormerod, 1991). *Because of this gender gap in perceptions, a federal court, in the case of* Ellison v. Brady, *instituted the* **reasonable woman standard** *as the appropriate legal criterion for determining whether sexual harassment has occurred: If a reasonable woman would view a behavior as offensive, the court held, then it is offensive even if the man did not consider it to be so.* Even this standard is more likely to be understood by women than by men (Wiener et al., 1997).

Besides the gender of the perceiver, several other factors influence whether a behavior is considered offensive (Fitzgerald & Ormerod, 1991). These include the degree to which the behavior is explicit or extreme (for example, rape rather than a kiss), victim behavior (whether the victim was at all responsible for what happened), supervisory status (whether the perpetrator was a direct supervisor of the victim), harasser's intentions (whether the perpetrator knew that the victim found the behavior offensive), and frequency of occurrence (for example, a one-time occurrence as opposed to a regular event). Cultural differences also are important. For example, one study found that U.S. women judged specific interactions as more harassing than U.S. men; women and men from Australia, Brazil, and Germany did not differ (Pryor et al., 1997). Unfortunately, little research has been done to identify what aspects of organizations foster harassment or to determine the impact of educational programs aimed at addressing the problem.

In 1998, the U.S. Supreme Court (in *Oncale v. Sundowner Offshore Services*) ruled that sexual harassment is not limited to female victims but that the relevant laws also protect men. This case is also important for establishing that same-sex harassment is barred by the same laws that ban heterosexual harassment. Thus, the standard by which sexual harassment is judged could now be said to be a reasonable person standard.

What can be done to provide people with safe work and learning environments, free from sexual harassment? Training in gender awareness is a common approach that often works (Tang & McCollum, 1996). Clear, precise definitions that differentiate between what can be considered a workplace romance and what can be considered sexual harassment are another essential element (Pierce & Aguinis, 1997).

AGE DISCRIMINATION. *Another structural barrier to occupational development is* **age discrimination,** *which involves denying a job or promotion to someone solely on the basis of age.* In contrast to general older adult bias and discrimination, older worker biases affect younger ages and relate specifically to the work context. The U.S. Age Discrimination in Employment Act of 1986 protects workers over age 40. This law stipulates that people must be hired based on their ability, not their age. Under this law, employers are barred from refusing to hire and from discharging workers solely on the basis of age. Additionally, employers cannot segregate or classify workers or otherwise denote their status on the basis of age.

Employers are banned from firing workers like this man solely on the basis of age.

Employment prospects for middle-aged and older people around the world are lower than for their younger counterparts. For example, age discrimination toward those over age 45 is common in Germany (Frerichs & Naegele, 1997) and Britain (Ginn & Arber, 1996), resulting in long periods of unemployment and early retirement. Such practices may save companies money in the short run, but the loss of expertise and knowledge comes at a high price. Indeed, global corporations are beginning to realize that retraining and integrating middle-aged workers is a better strategy (Frerichs & Naegele, 1997).

Age discrimination occurs in several ways (Avolio & Sosik, 1999). For example, employers can make certain types of physical or mental performance a job requirement and argue that older work-

At some point in your life, you probably were told (and maybe believed) that choosing an occupation and enjoying occupational success were both simply a matter of working hard and performing well. As you've gotten older and experienced the world of work, you have probably seen firsthand (or you will) that there is more to it than that. The biopsychosocial model provides a good framework for understanding how people choose their occupations and develop in them.

Biological forces help shape job-related abilities and skills to the extent that the skills have a genetic component (some people are clearly natural athletes or chemists; others are not). Whether a person develops these innate abilities depends in part on psychological forces such as personality and behavior. These forces find expression in what people like to do, the choices they make about which courses to take, or the kinds of extracurricular activities they try. Holland's theory stresses the importance of psychological forces. But whether people have the opportunity to make these choices reflects the social forces that create or limit options. The powerful social forces of socioeconomic class, prejudice, and discrimination, among others, open doors for some and close doors for others. These social forces are a major factor in antidiscrimination, affirmative action, and related legislation in the United States. But reality also tells us that a person's position in the life cycle confers an advantage (or disadvantage) in a competitive job market. Two people with identical skills and experience may not be viewed as equivalent by an organization if one is 25 and the other is 55. So it matters a great deal when in our lives opportunity comes knocking.

---

ers cannot meet the standard. Or they can attempt to get rid of older workers by using retirement. Supervisors sometimes use age as a factor in performance evaluations for raises or promotions or in decisions about which employees are eligible for additional training.

Perceptions of age discrimination are widespread; nearly 1,600 suits were filed in 1993 alone, up from roughly 1,100 in 1990 (Cornish, 1994). Many of these cases stem from the corporate downsizing that began in the late 1980s. Winning an age discrimination case is difficult, however (Snyder & Barrett, 1988). Job performance information is crucial. However, most companies tend to report this information in terms of general differences between younger and older adults (such as differences in recent memory ability) rather than in specific terms of older and younger workers in a particular occupation (which rarely show any differences in productivity or performance). Surprisingly, many courts do not question inaccurate information or stereotypic views of aging presented by employers, despite the lack of scientific data documenting age differences in job performance. In fact, it may be the case that the court system is taking a more relaxed view of age discrimination. In a recent ruling by the Supreme Court, on January 11, 2000, the majority opinion held that people do not have a blanket protection from age discrimination under the 14th Amendment's rights to equal protection. In this case it suggests that age may serve as a useful proxy to determine qualifications for a job if it is related to a legitimate issue. The issue of age discrimination is still ambiguous, and we should witness interesting changes in the next century.

Discrimination practices are a negative social force operating in the work force. We examine other forces that contribute to occupational success in the Forces in Action feature.

CONCEPT CHECK

1. What factors lead some women to choose nontraditional occupations?

2. What is the primary reason women in full-time high-status jobs quit after having children?

3. How do ethnic groups differ in terms of choosing nontraditional occupations, vocational identity, occupational aspirations, and occupational development?

4. Define *glass ceiling, comparable worth, sexual harassment,* and *age discrimination.*

Work, Leisure, and Retirement

Occupational Transitions

- Why do people change occupations?
- Why is worker retraining necessary and important?
- How does the timing of job loss affect the amount of stress one experiences?

*F*red *has worked for an automobile manufacturer for 32 years. Over the years, more and more assembly-line jobs have been eliminated by robots and other technology, and manufacturing jobs have been exported to other countries. Although Fred has been assured by his boss that his job is safe, he isn't so sure. He worries that he could be laid off at any time.*

In the past, people commonly chose an occupation during young adulthood and stayed in it throughout their working years. Today, however, not many people take a job with the expectation that it will last a lifetime. Changing jobs is almost taken for granted; the average North American changes jobs multiple times during adulthood (Cascio, 1995). Some authors view occupational changes as positive; Havighurst (1982), for example, strongly advocates such flexibility. According to his view, building change into the occupational life cycle may help to avoid disillusionment with one's initial choice. Changing occupations may be one way to guarantee challenging and satisfying work, and it may be the best option for those in a position to exercise it (Shirom & Mazeh, 1988).

Several factors have been identified as important in determining who will remain in an occupation and who will change. Some factors, such as whether the person likes the occupation, lead to self-initiated occupation changes. For example, people who really like their occupation may seek additional training or accept overtime assignments in hopes of acquiring new skills that will enable them to get better jobs. Middle-aged workers often take advantage of these opportunities. However, other factors, such as obsolete skills and economic trends, cause forced occupational changes. For example, continued improvement of robots causes some auto industry workers to lose their jobs, corporations send jobs overseas to in-

crease profits, and economic recessions usually result in large-scale layoffs. But even forced occupational changes can have benefits. For instance, many adults go to college after being laid off. Some take advantage of educational benefits offered as part of a separation package. Others pursue educational opportunities to obtain new skills; still others look to advance in their careers elsewhere.

In this section, we explore the positive and negative aspects of occupational transitions. First we examine the retraining of midcareer and older workers. The increased use of technology, corporate downsizing, and an aging work force has focused attention on the need to keep older workers' skills current. Later, we examine occupational insecurity and the effects of job loss.

Retraining Workers

When you are hired into a specific job, you are selected because your employer believes that you offer the best fit between abilities you already have and those needed to perform the job. However, as noted earlier, the skills needed to perform a job typically change over time. Such changes may result from the introduction of new technology, additional responsibilities, or promotion.

Such rapid changes in the nature of work, as we discussed earlier, tend to result in the displacement of older workers. According to the U.S. Bureau of the Census (1993), 51.4% of displaced workers 55 to 64 years old do not find other employment, whereas 65–70% of workers under age 55 are reemployed. One approach to this problem is for midcareer and late career workers to be involved in continued development and retraining at work. If not, older workers are in jeopardy of cutting their careers short (Greller & Stroh, 1995). We discuss the implications of job loss later. Another outcome is career plateauing (Froman, 1994). **Career plateauing** *occurs when there is a lack of promotional opportunity in the organization or when a person decides not to seek advancement.*

What is critical here is that unless they keep their skills up-to-date, it may be very difficult for older workers to maintain their job or land new jobs when they are forced into retirement, displaced, or downsized (Froman, 1994; Simon, 1996). In cases of job loss or career plateauing, retraining may be an appropriate response. Nearly one third of the U.S. work force participates each year in courses aimed at improving job skills (American Council on Education, 1997). One objective of these courses is to improve technical skills, such as new computer skills. For midcareer or older employees, who make up the largest percentage of those who take courses (American Council on Education, 1997), retraining might focus on how to advance in one's occupation or how to find new career opportunities (e.g., through résumé preparation and career counseling).

Many corporations and community and technical colleges offer retraining programs in a variety of fields. Organizations that promote employee development typically offer in-house courses to improve one's skills or may offer tuition reimbursement programs for employees who successfully complete courses at colleges or universities.

The need to retrain midcareer and older workers points to the need for lifelong learning (Sinnott, 1994c). If corporations are to meet the challenges of a global economy, they must include retraining in their employee development programs. Such programs help improve people's chances of advancement in their chosen occupations, and they help people make successful transitions from one occupation to another.

Despite the benefits of and opportunities for retraining, some older workers may perceive fewer benefits in participating in such activities and have lower self-efficacy for skill development (Maurer, in press). Self-efficacy in this case is the belief that you have the ability to successfully learn, develop, and improve yourself at work. These beliefs have been found to be important predictors of effective training and development (Stajkovic & Luthans, 1998). Maurer & Tarulli, 1994). Older adults may have less self-confidence in developing career-relevant skills. Given the importance of training and development in the older worker's career, it is important to specify the ways in which organizations can be more sensitive to enhancing career development and self-efficacy of older workers.

Occupational Insecurity and Job Loss

Changing economic conditions in the United States over the past few decades (such as the move toward a global economy), as well as changing demographics, have forced many people out of their jobs. Heavy manufacturing and support businesses (such as the steel, oil, and automotive industries) and farming were the hardest hit during the 1970s and 1980s. But no one is immune. Indeed, the corporate takeover frenzy of the 1980s and the recession of the early 1990s put many middle- and upper-level corporate executives out of work in all kinds of businesses.

As a result of these trends, many people feel insecure about their jobs. Like Fred the auto worker, many worried workers have given numerous years of dedicated service to a corporation. Unfortunately, people who worry about their jobs tend to have poorer mental health, as discussed in Chapters 3 and 5 (Roskies & Louis-Guerin, 1990). For example, anxiety about one's job may result in negative attitudes about one's employer or even work in general, which in turn may result in diminished desire to be successful. Whether there is any basis for people's feelings of job insecurity may not matter; sometimes, what people think is true about their work situation is more important than what is actually the case. If people believe that they are at risk of losing their jobs, their mental health and behavior often are affected negatively, even when the actual risk of losing their jobs is very low (Roskies & Louis-Guerin, 1990). These effects vary with age. For example, whereas some middle-aged men are more susceptible to negative effects of losing one's job, others do not always report negative outcomes (Leana & Feldman, 1992). Some may have been planning to retire in the near future and see this as an opportunity to do so, others are hired back as consultants, and still others use their situation to try doing something new.

What happens to the mental health of people who remain unemployed for long periods of time? Wanberg (1995) assessed 129 people over a period of 9 months after the loss of a job. Only the people who were satisfied with their new jobs showed significant improvements in mental health; people who were unhappy in their new jobs and people who were still unemployed showed no change.

There is wide variability in people who are unemployed. For example, Wanberg and Marchese (1994) showed that four clusters of unemployed people could be identified, varying along the dimensions of financial concerns, employment commitment, job-seeking confidence level, degree of time structure, and adaptation to unemployment. These clusters can be identified as follows: confident but concerned about getting another job, distressed about being unemployed, unconcerned and indifferent about being unemployed, and optimistic about the future and coping with unemployment. Interventions for unemployed people must take these differences into account.

The effects of losing one's job emphasize the central role of occupations in forming a sense of identity in adulthood. How one perceives the loss of a job plays a major role in determining what the long-term effects will be.

CONCEPT CHECK

1. What major factors predict occupational transition?
2. What is career plateauing? How can it be avoided?
3. What effects do people experience when they lose their jobs?

DUAL-EARNER COUPLES

LEARNING OBJECTIVES

- What issues do employed people who care for dependents face?
- How do partners view the division of household chores?
- What is work–family conflict? How does it affect couples' lives?

Jennifer, a 38-year-old sales clerk at a department store, feels that her husband doesn't do his share of the housework or child care. Her husband says that real men don't do housework and that he's really tired when he comes home from work. Jennifer thinks that this isn't fair, especially because she works as many hours as her husband.

One of the most difficult challenges facing adults like Jennifer is trying to balance the demands of occupation with the demands of family. Over the past few decades, the rapid increase in the number of families in which both parents are employed has fundamentally changed how we view the relation between work and family. Parents may even have to bring a young child to work to deal with the pushes and pulls of being an employed parent. In nearly two thirds of two-parent households today, both adults work outside the home (U.S. Department of Labor, 1997). The main reason? Families need two incomes to pay the bills and maintain a moderate standard of living.

As we will see, dual-earner couples with children experience both benefits and costs from this arrangement. The stresses of living in this arrangement are substantial, and gender differences are clear, especially in the division of household chores.

The Dependent Care Dilemma

Many employed adults must also provide care for dependent children or parents. As we will see, the issues they face are complex.

EMPLOYED CAREGIVERS. Many mothers have no option but to return to work after the birth of a child. In fact, 56% of married mothers and nearly half of unmarried mothers with children under 1 year of age are in the work force (U.S. Department of Labor, 1997). The number of mothers in the work force with children of any age is even higher. As you can see in Figure 12.3, the overall number of women in the work force with children under age 18 has increased dramatically since the mid-1970s (U.S. Department of Labor, 1997).

Some women grapple with the decision of whether they want to return. Surveys of mothers with preschool children reveal that the motivation for returning to work tends to be related to how attached mothers are to their work. For example, in one survey of Australian mothers, those with high work attachment were more likely to cite intrinsic personal achievement reasons for returning. Those with low work attachment cited pressing financial

Work–family conflicts may result in mothers taking their young child to work as a way to deal with being an employed parent.

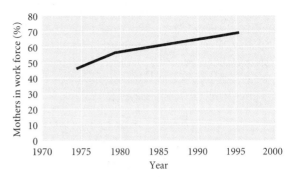

FIGURE 12.3 **Mothers in the work force.**

Source: U.S. Department of Labor. (1997). *Current population survey.* Washington, DC: Author.

needs. Those with moderate work attachment were divided between intrinsic and financial reasons (Cotton et al., 1989). Those who can afford to give up careers and stay home also must deal with changes in identity (Milford, 1997). Giving up a career means that the aspects of one's identity that came from work must be redefined to come from being a stay-at-home mother.

As discussed in Chapter 11, an increasing and often overlooked group of employed caregivers are those caring for a parent or partner. Of women in this situation, 60% work at least 35 hours per week outside the home (Jenkins, 1997). There is a higher level of interrole conflict and depression in these women (Stephens et al., 1997). **Interrole conflict** *results in a clash between competing sets of roles, in this case between work and family responsibilities.*

Whether care is needed for one's children or parent, key factors in selecting an appropriate care site are quality of care, price, and hours of availability (Metropolitan Area Agency on Aging, 1998; Vandell et al., 1997). Depending on one's economic situation, it may not be possible to find affordable high-quality care that is available when needed. In such cases, there may be no option but to drop out of the work force or enlist the help of friends and family.

DEPENDENT CARE AND EFFECTS ON WORKERS. Workers who care for dependents face tough choices. Especially when both partners are employed, dependent care is the central organizing aspect of couple's lives (Hertz, 1997).

Being responsible for dependent care has significant negative effects, especially for women. For example, when they are responsible for caring for an older parent, women report missing more meetings and being absent from work more often (Gignac et al., 1996). Such women also report higher levels of stress (Jenkins, 1997). Likewise, parents often have poor quality of life and report higher stress and trouble coping (Galinsky et al., 1996).

How can these negative effects be lessened? When women's partners provide good support and women have average or high control over their jobs, employed mothers are significantly less distressed than employed nonmothers (Roxburgh, 1997). When support and job controls are lacking, employed mothers are significantly more distressed than employed nonmothers. Clearly, having partner support and being in a job that allows one to have control over such things as one's schedule is key. What employers provide is also important, as we will see next.

DEPENDENT CARE AND EMPLOYER RESPONSE. Employed parents with small children are confronted with the difficult task of leaving their children in the care of others. In response to pressure from parents, most industrialized countries (but not the United States) provide government-supported child care centers for employees as one way to help ease this burden. Does providing a center make a difference in terms of an employee's feelings about work, absenteeism, or productivity?

The answer is that it's not as simple as opening a center. Just making a child care center available to employees does not necessarily reduce parents' work–family conflict or their absenteeism (Goff et al., 1990). A family-friendly company must also pay attention to attitudes of their employees and make sure that the company provides broad-based support. The key is how the supervisor acts. Irrespective of where the child care center is located, when supervisors are sympathetic and supportive regarding family issues and child care, parents report less work–family conflict and have lower absenteeism.

Research on specific working conditions and benefits that help caregivers perform optimally on the job points to several consistent conclusions. To the extent that employers provide better job security, autonomy, lower productivity demands, supervisor support, and flexible schedules, caregivers fare better (Aryee & Luk, 1996; Frone & Yardley, 1996; Galinsky et al., 1996).

It will be interesting to watch how these issues, especially flexible schedules, play out in the United States over the next several years. With the passage of the Family and Medical Leave Act in 1993, for the first time people will be able to take unpaid time off to care for their dependents, having the right to return to their jobs. Experience from other countries indicates that parental leave has different effects on each parent. For example, a large-scale study in Sweden showed that fathers who took parental leave were more likely to continue their involvement in child care and to reduce their work involvement. Regardless of fathers' participation, mothers still retained primary responsibility for child care and stayed less involved in and received fewer rewards in the labor market (Haas, 1990; Schwartz & Zimmerman, 1992).

Juggling Multiple Roles

When both members of a couple with dependents are employed, who cleans the house, cooks the meals, and takes care of the children when they are ill? This question gets to the heart of the core dilemma of modern, dual-earner couples: How are household chores divided? How are work and family role conflicts handled?

DIVIDING HOUSEHOLD CHORES. Despite much media attention and claims of increased sharing in the duties, women still perform the lion's share of housework regardless of employment status. Working mothers spend about twice as many hours per week as their husbands in family work and bear the greatest responsibility for household and child care tasks (Benin & Agostinelli, 1988; Etzion & Bailyn, 1994). This unequal division of labor creates most arguments and causes the most unhappiness for dual-earner couples. This is the case with Jennifer and Bill, the couple in the vignette; Jennifer does most of the housework.

A great deal of evidence indicates that women have decreased the amount of time they spend on housework since the 1970s, especially when they are employed, and that men have increased the amount of time they spend on such tasks (Swanson, 1992). The increased participation of men in these tasks is not all that it seems, however. Most of the increase is on weekends, with specific tasks that they agree to perform, and it is largely unrelated to women's employment status (Zick & McCullough, 1991). In short, this increase in men's participation has not done much to lower women's burdens around the house.

Women and men view the division of labor in very different terms. Men often are most satisfied with an equitable division of labor based on the number of hours spent, especially if the amount of time needed to perform household tasks was small. Women often are most satisfied when men are willing to perform women's traditional chores (Benin & Agostinelli, 1988). When ethnic minorities are studied, much the same is true. For example, in African American dual-earner couples, women were twice as likely as men to feel overburdened with housework and to be dissatisfied with their family life (Broman, 1988).

Ethnic differences in the division of household labor also are apparent. In a study of European American, African American, and Hispanic men, several interesting patterns emerged (Shelton & John, 1993). African American and Hispanic men tend to spend more time doing household tasks than do European American men. In the case of African American men, this finding supports the view that such households are more egalitarian than European American households. Moreover, the increased participation of African American men was primarily true of employed (as opposed to unemployed) men. There was greater participation in traditionally female tasks, such as washing dishes and cooking. Similarly, Hispanic men's participation also tended to reflect increased participation in these tasks. Overall, European American men spent the least time helping with traditionally female tasks. These data clearly indicate that the degree to which men and women divide household tasks varies not only with gender but also with ethnicity.

In sum, the available evidence from dual-earner couples indicates that women still perform more household tasks than men but that the difference varies between ethnic groups. The discrepancy is greatest when the man endorses traditional masculine gender roles and is less when the man endorses more feminine or androgynous gender roles (Gunter & Gunter, 1990; Napholz, 1995).

WORK–FAMILY CONFLICT. When people have both occupations and children, they must figure out how to balance the demands of each. People agonize over how to be at their daughter's ball game at the same time they have to be at an important business meeting. These competing demands cause **work–family conflict,** *the feeling of being pulled in multiple directions by incompatible demands from one's job and one's family.*

Research provides some evidence about how to deal with work–family conflict successfully. Women in one study were clear in their commitment to their careers, marriage, and children, and they successfully combined them without high levels of distress (Guelzow et al., 1991). How did they do it? Contrary to popular belief, the age of the children was not a factor in stress level. However, the number of children was important because stress increases greatly with each additional child, irrespective of their ages. Guilt also was not an issue for these women. In the same study, men reported sharing more of the child care tasks as a way to deal with multiple role pressures. Additionally, stress is lower for men who have a flexible work schedule that allows them to care for sick children and other family matters. Together, these findings are encouraging; they indicate that more heterosexual dual-earner couples are learning how to balance work and family adaptively.

This study also indicates the importance of taking a life-stage approach to work–family conflict. For example a number of studies find that the highest conflict between the competing demands of work and family occurs during the peak parenting years (the period in which there are two or more preschool children; Blanchard-Fields et al., 1997; Cournoyer & Mahalik, 1995; Shaw & Burns, 1993). By contrast, interrole conflict is reduced in later life stages, especially when the quality of their marriages are high (Blanchard-Fields et al., in preparation). Overall, it is important to note that perception of the quality of your roles is an important indicator of whether you will experience stress (Reid & Hardy, 1999).

Dual-earner couples often have difficulty finding time for each other, especially if both work long hours. The amount of time together is not necessarily the most important issue; as long as the time is spent in shared activities such as eating, playing, and conversing, couples tend to be happy (Kingston & Nock, 1987). Unfortunately, many couples find that

DIVISION OF LABOR AND ROLE CONFLICT IN DUAL-EARNER COUPLES

One of the largest issues still facing American society is how dual-earner couples can balance their occupational and family roles. With the majority of couples now consisting of two wage earners, issues such as who does the household chores and how child care is arranged will become increasingly important.

Many people believe that work and family roles mutually influence each other. That is, when things go bad at work, family suffers, and when problems occur at home, work suffers. As noted in the text, such role conflicts and mutual interaction appear not to be the case. It is more of a one-way street. For the most part, problems at home have little effect on job performance, whereas trouble at work could spill over to home life.

Negotiating agreeable arrangements of household and child care tasks is critical. But as noted in the text, truly equitable divisions of labor are the exception. Most American households with dual-earner couples still operate under a gender-segregated system: There are wives' chores and husbands' chores. Without question, all these tasks are important and must be performed to ensure domestic sanitation. However, these tasks take time. The important point for women is that it is not how much time they spend in performing household chores that matters but which tasks they perform. The research cited in the text indicates that what bothers wives the most is not that their husbands are lazy but that their husbands will not perform some "women's work." Men may mow the lawn, wash the car, and even cook, but they rarely run the vacuum, scrub the toilet, or change the baby's diaper.

Husbands would be viewed much more positively by their wives if they performed more of the traditionally female tasks. Marital satisfaction would be likely to improve as a result. Moreover, the role modeling provided to children in these households would be a major step in breaking the transmission of age-old stereotypes. It's something to think about.

Search Online with **InfoTrac College Edition** For more information on these controversies, explore InfoTrac College Edition, your online library. Go to http://www.infotrac-college.com/wadsworth and use the passcode that came on the card with your book. Try these search terms: dual-career families, family role conflict, child care.

---

by the time they have an opportunity to be alone together, they are too tired to make the most of it.

A number of studies suggest that stressors associated with work–family conflict may hold different meanings for women and men (Simon, 1996). Cross-cultural data show that burnout from work and parenting is more likely to affect women. A study of dual-earner married couples in Singapore showed that wives are more likely to suffer from burnout than husbands; wives' burnout resulted from both work and nonwork stress, whereas husbands' burnout resulted only from work stress (Aryee, 1993). This finding was also true of American men (Greenglass, 1991). Other studies find that women tend to experience more family demands than men do and spend more time on family work (Joshi &

Sastry, 1995). On the other hand, men are more vulnerable to work stress than family stress (Izraeli, 1993; Lai, 1995; Livingston & Burley, 1991). These findings suggest that the source of men's role stress involves conflict with work roles, and the source of women's role stress lies more in the conflict involving family roles.

Issues concerning balancing work and family are extremely important in couples' everyday lives. Learning how to deal with multiple roles is an important process in current industrial societies. We are creating patterns that provide the anticipatory socialization for our children. Even now, most dual-earner couples feel that the benefits, especially the extra income, are worth the costs. However, many dual-earner couples have no choice but to try to deal with the situation as best they can: Both partners must work simply to pay the bills.

As discussed in Current Controversies, this means that couples need to take seriously the job of deciding how to divide up tasks.

CONCEPT CHECK

1. What differences are there in how husbands and wives divide household tasks?

2. What is the most important thing an organization can do for employees with children?

3. What helps working fathers and mothers balance work and family obligations?

LEISURE ACTIVITIES

LEARNING OBJECTIVES

• What types of leisure activities do adults engage in?

• What developmental differences are there in leisure activities?

• What do people derive from leisure activities?

Claude is a 55-year-old electrician who has enjoyed outdoor activities his whole life. Since he was a boy, he has fished and water-skied in the calm inlets of coastal Florida. Although he doesn't compete in slalom races any more, Claude still skis regularly. He still participates in fishing competitions every chance he gets.

Adults do not work every waking moment of their lives. As each of us knows, we need to relax sometimes and engage in leisure activities. Intuitively, leisure consists of activities not associated with work. More formally, researchers define *leisure* as discretionary activity, which includes simple relaxation, activities for enjoyment, creative pursuits, and sensual transcendence (Gordon et al., 1976). However, men and women differ in their views of leisure, as do people in different ethnic groups (Henderson, 1990). For example, one study of African American women revealed that they view leisure as both freedom from the constraint of needing to work and as a form of self-expression (Allen & Chin-Sang, 1990).

Types of Leisure Activities

Leisure can include almost any activity. To help organize the options, researchers have classified leisure activities into four categories: cultural, such as attending sporting events, concerts, church services, and meetings; physical, such as basketball, hiking, aerobics, and gardening; social, such as visiting friends and going to parties; and solitary, including reading, listening to music, and watching television (Bossé & Ekerdt, 1981; Glamser & Hayslip, 1985). Leisure activities can also be considered in terms of the degree of cognitive, emotional, or physical involvement; skydivers would have high activity in all three areas. Examples of leisure activities organized along this dimension are listed in Table 12.2.

An alternative approach to classifying leisure activities involves the distinction between preoccupations and interests (Rapoport & Rapoport, 1975). Preoccupations are much like daydreaming. Sometimes, preoccupations become more focused and are converted to interests. Interests are ideas and feelings about things one would like to do, is curious about, or is attracted to. Jogging, surfing the Web, fishing, and painting are some examples of interests.

Rapoport and Rapoport's distinction draws attention to a key truth about leisure: Any specific activity has different meaning and value, depending on the person involved. For example, cooking a gourmet meal is an interest, or a leisure activity, for many people. For professional chefs, however, it is work and thus is not leisure at all.

Given the wide range of options, how do people pick their leisure activities? Apparently, each of us has a leisure repertoire, a personal library of intrinsically motivated activities that we do regularly (Mobily et al., 1991). The activities in our repertoire are determined by two things: perceived competence (how good we think we are at the activity compared with other people our age) and psychological comfort (how well we meet our personal goals for performance). Other factors are important as well: income, interest, health, abilities, transportation, education, and social characteristics. For example, some leisure activities, such as downhill skiing, are expensive and

TABLE 12.2	Forms of Leisure Activity and How They Vary in Intensity of Cognitive, Emotional, or Physical Involvement
Very high intensity	Sexual activity Highly competitive games or sports Dancing
Moderately high intensity	Creative activities (art, literature, music) Nurturance or teaching (children's arts and crafts) Serious discussion and analysis
Medium intensity	Attending cultural events Participating in clubs Sightseeing or travel
Moderately low intensity	Socializing Reading for pleasure Light conversation
Low intensity	Solitude Quiet resting Taking a nap

require transportation and reasonably good health and physical coordination for maximum enjoyment. In contrast, reading requires minimal finances (if one uses a public library) and is far less physically demanding. It is probable that how these factors influence leisure activities changes through adulthood (e.g., physical prowess typically declines somewhat). However, exactly how these factors result in changes in leisure activities is unknown (Burrus-Bammel & Bammel, 1985).

Developmental Changes in Leisure

Cross-sectional studies report age differences in leisure activities (Bray & Howard, 1983). Young adults participate in a greater range of activities than middle-aged adults do. Furthermore, young adults

tend to prefer intense leisure activities, such as scuba diving and hang gliding. In contrast, middle-aged adults focus more on home- and family-oriented activities. In later middle age, they spend less of their leisure time in strenuous physical activities and more in sedentary activities such as reading and watching television. Older adults narrow the range of activities and lower their intensity even further (Gordon et al., 1976). People of all ages report feelings of freedom during leisure activities (Larson et al., 1997).

Longitudinal studies of changes in people's leisure activities over time show stability over long periods (Cutler & Hendricks, 1990). Claude, who likes to fish and ski, is a good example of this overall trend. As Claude demonstrates, frequent participation in leisure activities during childhood tends to continue into adulthood. Similar findings hold for the preretirement and postretirement years. Apparently, one's preferences for certain types of leisure activities are established early in life; they tend to change over the life span primarily in terms of how physically intense they are.

Consequences of Leisure Activities

What do people gain from participating in leisure activities? Researchers agree that involvement in leisure activities is related to well-being (Guinn, 1999; Kelly, 1996; McGuire et al., 1996). The key aspect of this relation is not the level of participation. Instead, how much satisfaction you derive from your leisure activities is the important element in promoting well-being (Lawton et al., 1986–1987). Indeed, an Israeli study showed that satisfaction with leisure activities is the crucial variable (Lomranz et al., 1988). Whether leisure enhances one's well-being appears to depend on whether you like what you do for fun.

But what if leisure activities are pursued very seriously? In some cases, people create leisure–family conflict by engaging in leisure activities to extremes (Goff et al., 1997). Only when others support such extreme involvement are problems avoided (Goff et al., 1997). As in most things, moderation in leisure activities probably is best.

1. How can leisure activities be classified?
2. What age differences have been noted in leisure activities?
3. What benefits do people derive from leisure activities?

RETIREMENT

Learning Objectives

- What does being retired mean?
- Why do people retire?
- How should people prepare for retirement?
- How satisfied are retired people?
- What specific effects does retirement have on maintaining family and community ties?

*M*arcus is a 77-year-old retired construction *worker who labored hard all of his life. He managed to save a little money, but he and his wife live primarily off of his monthly Social Security checks. Though not rich, they have enough to pay the bills. Marcus is largely happy with retirement, and he stays in touch with his friends. He thinks maybe he's a little strange, though—he has heard that retirees are supposed to be isolated and lonely.*

You probably take it for granted that someday, after working for many productive years, you will retire. But did you know that until 1934, when a railroad union sponsored a bill promoting mandatory retirement, and 1935, when Social Security was inaugurated, retirement was rarely even considered by most Americans (Sterns & Gray, 1999)? Only since World War II have there been a substantial number of retired people in the United States. Today, the number is increasing rapidly, and the notion that people work a specified time and then retire is built into our expectations about work.

In this section, we consider what retirement is like for older adults. We consider people like Marcus as we examine how retirement is defined, why people retire, how people adjust to being retired, and how retirement affects interpersonal relationships.

What Does Being Retired Mean?

Like leisure, retirement is difficult to define. Retirement is more difficult to define than just guessing someone's age (Szinovacz & DeViney, 1999; Henretta, 1997). One way to look at retirement is to equate it with complete withdrawal from the work force. But this definition is inadequate; many retired people continue to work part time (Mutchler et al., 1997; Ruhm, 1990). Another possibility would be to define retirement as a self-described state. However, this definition does not work either because some African Americans define themselves with labels other than *retired* in order to qualify for certain social service programs (Gibson, 1991).

Part of the reason it is difficult to define retirement precisely is that the decision to retire involves the loss of occupational identity (discussed earlier). What people do for a living is a major part of their identity. Not doing those jobs anymore means that we either put that aspect of our lives in the past tense—"I used to work as a manager at the Hilton"—or say nothing at all. Loss of this aspect of us can be difficult to face, so some look for a label other than *retired* to describe themselves.

A useful way to view retirement is as a complex process by which people withdraw from full-time participation in an occupation (Henretta, 1997; Mutchler at al., 1997; Sterns & Gray, 1999). This withdrawal process can be described as crisp (making a clean break from employment by stopping work entirely) or blurred (repeatedly leaving and returning to work, with some unemployment periods; Mutchler et al., 1997). Bob is a good example of a crisp retirement. He retired from TWA at age 65; now in his late 80s, he has done nothing work-related in the interim.

Whereas many people think of retirement as a crisp transition, the evidence shows that less than half of older men who retire fit this pattern (Mutchler et al., 1997). Most men adopt a more gradual or blurred process involving part-time work in an effort to maintain economic status. Jack is one of these men. When he retired from DuPont at age 62, he and a friend began a small consulting company. For about

5 years, Jack worked when he wanted, gradually cutting back over time.

The lack of crisp retirement creates another complicating factor: the idea of a "normal" retirement age such as age 65 may no longer be appropriate (Cornman & Kingson, 1996; Mutchler et al., 1997). Instead, the notion of a typical retirement age changes to a range of ages, further blurring the meaning of *early* or *late retirement* (Cornman & Kingson, 1996).

We must acknowledge the complexity of the retirement process to understand what retirement means to people in different ethnic groups. For example, whereas middle-class European Americans often use a criterion of full-time employment to define themselves as retired or not, Mexican Americans use any of several different criteria depending on how the question is asked (Zsembik & Singer, 1990). For example, Mexican Americans are most likely to claim that they are retired when asked directly ("Are you retired?") than when asked indirectly ("What are you doing these days?"). It may be that people want to appear active, so they choose some other descriptor. In contrast, European Americans are just as likely to call themselves retired no matter how they are asked.

THE CHANGING NATURE OF RETIREMENT. Contributing to the complexity of the retirement process is that issues concerning retirement are changing rapidly. Just as there is fundamental change occurring in the definition of work, similar changes are occurring in the definition of retirement. More people in their postretirement years are working in part-time jobs, primarily to supplement their incomes but also to maintain adequate levels of activity. Many older adults also volunteer their time to many different organizations.

The need for some older adults to continue working is becoming more formally recognized. For example, one senior center in Wilmington, Delaware, offers job training programs for older workers. These programs prepare workers for a variety of jobs that enable them to earn a living. Some corporations, such as McDonald's, actively recruit older workers because of their reputation for reliability and responsibility. Indeed, roughly a third of recent retirees report being partially retired (or partially employed) at

some point, but their employment usually is in low-paying jobs taken out of economic necessity (Moen & Wethington, 1999).

As more people anticipate longer periods of retirement, and with the near removal of all mandatory retirement, one interesting research question will be whether more people will choose to continue working if possible. The numbers of employed older adults may also increase if people's financial status is insufficient to support them in retirement. Indeed, many debates occurred in the mid-1990s about the long-term viability of the Social Security system; if this system changes dramatically, it would have a major effect on decisions to retire. As the baby-boom generation approaches retirement age, examination of such programs will increase, as will debates about the proper time to retire. As you consider the issues in the following sections, you should recognize that new views on the role and nature of retirement are emerging that may force us to reconsider issues we previously thought were already settled. You can see this for yourself by doing the Discovering Development exercise.

Why Do People Retire?

The decision to retire is an intensely personal one that involves carefully weighing several factors. Overall, more workers retire by choice than for any other reason (Hayward et al., 1998; Henretta et al., 1992). People usually retire when they feel financially secure, considering projected income from Social Security, pension plans, and personal savings. Of course, some people are forced to retire because they lose their jobs (Henretta et al., 1992). As corporations downsized in the early and mid-1990s, some older workers were offered buyout packages involving supplemental payments if they retired. Others were permanently furloughed, laid off, or dismissed.

The complexity of the retirement decision is also influenced by one's occupational history (Hayward et al., 1998). The longest occupation held in the middle of one's career combines with occupational roles held in the last stages of the career to influence the decision to retire and the connection with health and disability. Feeling that retirement is a choice rather than a requirement is associated with an earlier planned retirement age and adjustment to retirement (Sterns & Gray, 1999). Let's examine these factors more closely.

HEALTH. One of the most important influences on retirement decisions is health, regardless of whether one is approaching mandatory retirement. Poor health is one of the main reasons people retire early (Feldman, 1994; Hansson et al., 1997; Mutchler et al., 1999). The importance of health cuts across ethnic group lines, especially in terms of early retirement. For example, health problems causing functional impairment are the main reason European Americans, African Americans, and Mexican Americans retire early (Burr et al., 1996; Stanford et al., 1991). However, it is not a simple relationship. For example, health has its greatest influence on the decision to retire early for people who find the idea of work unattractive because of family or economic factors (Mutchler et al., 1999). In other words, it appears that the impact of health on retirement is determined by trends in other work-related characteristics such as marital status.

GENDER DIFFERENCES. Most of what we know about retirement decisions is based on research on men (Sterns & Gray, 1999). However, women may enter the work force later, have more discontinuous work histories, and spend less time in the work force, and their financial resources may differ from men's, which may affect women's decisions to retire (Calasanti, 1996; Sterns & Gray, 1999). In fact, research indicates that men's and women's decisions to retire may be based on different factors. Talaga and Beehr (1995) found that women whose husbands were in poor health or who had more dependents were more likely to retire; the opposite was true for men. However, there were some similarities; having a retired spouse increased the likelihood that spouses would also retire.

As more women remain in the work force for much of their adult lives, more research will be needed to understand the extent to which gender differences matter in the decision to retire. At this point, it appears that the male model of retirement is insufficient to account for women's experiences (Sterns & Gray, 1999; Szinovacz & DeViney, 1999).

ETHNIC DIFFERENCES. Very little research has been conducted on retirement decisions as a function of ethnicity. A few investigators have examined the characteristics of retired African Americans (Gibson, 1986, 1987; Jackson & Gibson, 1985). These studies show that African Americans tend to label themselves as retired or not based on subjective disability, work history, and source of income rather than simply on whether they are currently employed. An important finding is that gender differences appear to be absent among African Americans; men and women base their self-labels on the same variables. Thus, findings based on European American samples must not be

Few studies have investigated the characteristics
of retired African Americans.

generalized to African Americans, and separate theoretical models for African Americans may be needed (Gibson, 1987). The same may be true for other ethnic groups as well.

Planning for Retirement

What do people need to do to plan for retirement? Is it just a matter of saving money? Or do people need to take psychological factors into account as well? Can prospective retirees anticipate and avoid some of the difficulties? For example, one common problem in adjusting to the retirement role is the abruptness of the transition from employment to unemployment. What processes might minimize the difficulties of this change?

One key element to successful retirement is preparation. People who plan for retirement tend to be more successful in adapting to this major life change (Lo & Brown, 1999; Sterns & Gray, 1999). Getting ready can take several forms: conscious or unconscious planning, informal or formal steps, and so on. *One formal way to prepare for retirement is to partici-*

*pate in a **preretirement education program,** which can cover a wide variety of topics, from financial planning to adjustment;* a typical content list is contained in Table 12.3. Potential benefits of such planning are more financial equity, the increased possibility of a healthier lifestyle, more positive attitudes toward retirement, exposure to new leisure activities, and ways to explore alternative housing (Atchley, 1996; Richardson, 1993; Sterns, Laier, & Dorsett, 1994).

Every comprehensive planning program for retirement focuses on a major obstacle to retirement: finances. Retirement typically involves a reduction in income. Obviously, if one is not prepared for this degree of income loss, financial pressures will be severe. Research shows that financial issues are strongly related to the decision to retire and adjustment to retirement (Davies et al., 1991; Feldman, 1994; Hansson et al., 1997). Surprisingly, many people do not adequately plan for the financial changes that accompany retirement (Ferraro & Su, 1999). Overall, older adults who are satisfied with their financial resources tend to make the decision to retire and adjust well to that decision. However, findings

TABLE 12.3	Topics in a Typical Preretirement Education Program

I. Deciding to retire: When is the right time?
II. Psychological aspects of aging
   A. Work roles and retirement
   B. Personal identity issues
   C. Retirement as a process, paradox, and change
   D. Effects on relationships with family and friends
III. Finances
   A. Social Security
   B. Pension
   C. Insurance
   D. Employment
IV. Legal aspects
   A. Wills
   B. Personal rights as senior citizens
V. Health
   A. Normal aging
   B. Medicare and Medicaid
   C. Health insurance issues
VI. Where to live: The pros and cons of moving
VII. Leisure activities
   A. Travel
   B. Hobbies
   C. Clubs and organizations
   D. Educational opportunities
   E. Volunteering

also indicate that financial issues influence retirement decisions and adjustment differently depending on the major reason for retirement (Henretta et al., 1996). When retirement is compulsory, financial security tends to increase the rate of retirement. However, when retirement was caused mainly by health limitations, financial security tends to decrease the rate of retirement. Finally, when job loss is the main reason for retirement, financial security does not influence retirement rate. However, despite any reason to retire, higher salaries overall tend to reduce the decision to retire.

Adjusting to Retirement

Researchers agree on one point about retirement: It is an important life transition. New patterns of involvement must be developed in the context of changing roles and lifestyles (Antonovsky & Sagy, 1990). Until the early 1990s, research focused on what was thought to be a sequence of predictable phases of retirement, such as honeymoon, disenchantment, reorientation, acceptance, and termination (Atchley, 1982). Because retirement is now viewed as a process, the "typical" age of retirement has lost its meaning, and gender differences are evident in the decision to retire, the idea that retirement proceeds in an orderly sequence has been abandoned (Sterns & Gray, 1999). Instead, researchers support the idea that people's adjustment to retirement evolves over time as a result of complex interactions of physical health, financial status, voluntary retirement status, and feelings of personal control (Gall et al., 1997).

How do most people fare? As long as people have financial security, health, and a supportive network of relatives and friends, they report feeling very good about being retired (Gall et al., 1997; Matthews & Brown, 1987). For men, being in good health, having enough income, and having retired voluntarily is associated with high satisfaction early in retirement; having an internal sense of personal control is correlated with well-being over the long run (Gall et al., 1997). For men, personal priorities also are important. Men who place more emphasis on family roles (e.g., as husband or grandfather) report being happier retirees. Interestingly, women's morale in retirement does not appear to be related to an emphasis on any specific roles (Matthews & Brown, 1987). For both men and women, high personal competence is associated with higher retirement satisfaction, probably because competent people are able to optimize their level of environmental press (as described in Chapter 5).

One stereotype of retirement is that health begins to decline as soon as people stop working. Research findings do not support this belief; in fact, there is no evidence that retirement has any immediate negative effects on health (Ekerdt, 1987). Moreover, well-being typically increases for men during the first year of retirement (Gall et al., 1997).

A second stereotype is that retirement dramatically reduces the number and quality of personal friendships. Again, there is no research support for this belief. In fact, several studies have shown that men like Marcus, from the vignette, are typical; neither the number nor the quality of friendships declines as a result of retiring (Bosse et al., 1993).

Finally, some people believe that retired people become much less active overall. This stereotype also is not supported by research. Although the number of hours in paid work decreases on average with age, older adults still are engaged for hundreds of hours per year in productive activities such as unpaid volunteer work and helping others (Herzog et al., 1989). We specifically consider volunteer activities in the next section.

Interpersonal Ties

Retirement rarely affects only a single person. No matter how personal the joys and sorrows of retirement are, interpersonal relationships shape retirees' reactions. Social ties help people deal with the stresses of retirement, as they do in other life transitions. In many cases, these ties involve friendships and other relationships formed earlier in adulthood.

Social relationships help cushion the effects of life stress throughout adulthood. This support takes many forms: letting people know that they are loved, offering help if needed, providing advice, taking care of others' needs, and just being there to listen. Retirees who have close and strong social ties have an advantage in adjusting to the life changes retirement brings (Henkens, 1999).

INTIMATE RELATIONSHIPS. In the past, much attention was focused on the role of intimate relationships in adjusting to retirement. Marriage has provided the framework for almost all of this research. Ideally, marital partners provide mutual support during the transition to retirement. Whether marriage actually serves this function is unclear. Marital status by itself has little effect on older women's satisfaction with retirement (Fox, 1979; Szinovacz, 1996). Never-married men are as satisfied as married retirees, whereas divorced, separated, or widowed retired men are much less happy (Barfield & Morgan, 1978). Perhaps never-married men prefer singlehood and become accustomed to it long before retirement. All in all, these findings point to the stabilizing effects of marriage for men.

Possible benefits aside, retirement undoubtedly has profound effects on intimate relationships such as marriage. It often disrupts long-established patterns of family interaction, forcing both partners (and others living in the house) to adjust (Pearson, 1996). Simply being together more may put strain on the relationship. Couples' daily routines may need rearrangement, which may be stressful. However, because marital satisfaction among older couples tends to be quite high, most couples are able to resolve these stresses.

One common change that confronts most retired married couples (in traditional households in which only the husband was employed) is the division of household chores. Although retired men tend to do more work around the home than they did before retirement, this situation does not always lead to desirable outcomes (Szinovacz, 1992, 1996). For example, an employed husband may compliment his wife on her domestic skills; after retirement, however, he may suddenly want to teach her to do things "correctly." Part of the problem may be that such men are not used to taking orders. One retired executive remarked that before he retired, when he said "Jump!" highly paid employees wanted to know how high. "Now, I go home, I walk in the door and my wife says, 'Milton, take out the garbage.' I never saw so much garbage" (Quigley, 1979, p. 9). Finally, part of the problem may be in the perception of one's turf; after retirement men feel that they are thrust into doing things that they and their partners may have traditionally thought of as "women's work" (Troll, 1971). As more dual-earner couples retire, it will be interesting to see how these issues are handled.

Intimate family relationships clearly are important sources of support for retirees. However, they are not the only ones; friendship networks also provide support that often complements family networks. Friends sometimes provide types of support that, because of the strong emotional ties, families may be less able to offer: a compassionate but objective listener, a companion for social and leisure activities, or a source of advice, transportation, and other assistance.

In general, neither the number nor the quality of friendships declines as a result of retirement (Bosse et al., 1993). When friendships change during retirement, it is usually for some other reason, such as very serious health problems, that interferes with people's ability to maintain friendships. However, we need to bear in mind the gender differences in friendships we discussed in Chapter 11. Older men have fewer close personal friends for support than older women. This difference may help explain the gender difference between marital status and satisfaction discussed earlier. Because of their fewer close relationships, men may be forced to rely more on their wives for support.

COMMUNITY TIES. Throughout adulthood, most people become and remain connected with their communities. Thus, an important consideration is whether the social environment aids retirees' ability to continue old ties and form new ones. The past few decades have witnessed the rapid growth of organizations devoted to providing such opportunities to retirees. National groups such as the American Association of Retired Persons (AARP) provide the chance to learn, through magazines, pamphlets, and Web sites, about what other retirees are doing and about services such as insurance and discounts. Numerous smaller groups exist at the community level; these include senior centers and clubs. Several trade unions also have programs for their retired members. These activities promote the notion of lifelong learning and help keep older adults cognitively fit.

A common way for retired adults to maintain community ties is by volunteering. Older adults report that they volunteer to help themselves deal with life transitions (Adlersberg & Thorne, 1990), to provide service to others (Hudson, 1996), to maintain social interactions, and to improve their communities (Morrow-Howell & Mui, 1989). There are many opportunities for retirees to help others. One federal agency, ACTION, administers four programs that have hundreds of local chapters: Foster Grandparents, Senior Companions, the Retired Senior Volunteer Program, and the Service Corps of Retired Executives (SCORE). Nearly half of older adults aged 65 to 74 volunteer their services in some way, with high participation rates even among people over age 80 (Chambre, 1993). These rates represent more than a 400% increase since the mid-1960s, when only about 1 in 10 older adults did volunteer work. What accounts for this tremendous increase?

Several factors are responsible (Chambre, 1993): improved public perception of the skills and wisdom older adults have to offer, a redefinition of the nature and merits of volunteer work, a more highly educated population of older adults, and greatly expanded opportunities for people to become involved in volunteer work that they enjoy. Given the demographic trends of increased numbers and educational levels of older adults discussed in Chapter 1, even higher rates of voluntarism are expected during the next few decades (Chambre, 1993). These opportunities may be a way for society to tap into the vast resources older adults offer and provide additional meaningful roles for older adults.

CONCEPT CHECK

1. What is the best way to conceptualize retirement?
2. What are the major predictors of the decision to retire?
3. What is included in a preretirement education program?
4. What factors contribute to adjustment to retirement?
5. How do retirees interact with their communities?

PUTTING IT ALL TOGETHER

Sigmund Freud once said that the two most important aspects of adulthood are love and work. In this chapter, we have seen how pervasive work is in our lives and how it is affected by many things. The occupation Angela ultimately chooses is partly influenced by talents or skills she inherited from her parents, the kind of environment in which she grew up, and the match between her personality style and her occupational skills.

We saw that occupational development is not an inevitable outcome of hard work. Unfortunately, the world of work also reflects the biases, prejudices, and discrimination people face in the world at large. Janice found that being a woman and a member of an ethnic minority may make it difficult to achieve the levels of advancement in her career that she truly deserves.

Work spills over into our personal lives, too. Fred and others like him worry about job security, and this sometimes affects home life. Although retraining may be an option, it may not alleviate all the concerns. Dual-earner couples are forced to think about how to divide household tasks to maintain balance. Jennifer and her husband are struggling with this issue; too often, women perform most of the chores at home.

But a life that is all work and no play is dull. Just as children need a certain amount of play for their development, adults like Claude find playful outlets through leisure activities. Such activities may be as quiet as reading a book or as daring as skydiving, but being able to do something besides work gives these activities value.

Finally, the match between people's competence and the environmental demands they face sets the stage for how well they adapt to changes in occupational status. How older people cope with retirement, for example, typically is a continuation of the ways they coped throughout their lives. Accordingly, we saw that the view of retirement as detrimental to health and as a cause of isolation is wrong; most people are like Marcus, who greatly enjoys retirement.

Summary

OCCUPATIONAL CHOICE AND DEVELOPMENT

The Meaning of Work

Although most people work for money, other reasons are highly variable. Occupational priorities have changed over time; younger workers' expectations from their occupations are lower, and their emphasis on personal growth potential is higher.

The Changing Nature of Work

Globalization of work has resulted in changes in the number and types of jobs available to workers in the U.S.

Occupational Choice

Holland's theory is based on the idea that people choose occupations to optimize the fit between their individual traits and their occupational interests. Six personality types that represent different combinations of these have been identified. They include investigative, social, realistic, artistic, conventional, and enterprising. Research supports the validity of this approach, although some gender differences have been found.

Occupational Development

Super's developmental view of occupations is based on self-concept and adaptation to an occupational role. Super describes five stages in adulthood: implementation, establishment, maintenance, deceleration, and retirement.

Reality shock is the realization that one's expectations about an occupation are different from the reality one experiences. Reality shock is common among young workers.

A mentor is a co-worker who teaches a new employee the unwritten rules and fosters occupational development. Mentor–protégé relationships develop over time, through stages, like other relationships.

Job Satisfaction

Older workers report higher job satisfaction than younger workers, but this may be partly because of self-selection; unhappy workers may quit. Other reasons include intrinsic satisfaction, good fit, lower importance of work, finding nonwork diversions, and life-cycle factors.

Alienation and burnout are important considerations in understanding job satisfaction. Both involve significant stress for workers.

GENDER, ETHNICITY, BIAS, AND DISCRIMINATION

Gender Differences in Occupational Choice

Men and women are socialized differently into occupational roles, and their occupational choices are affected as a result. Women choose nontraditional occupations for many reasons, including expectations and personal feelings. Women in such occupations still are viewed more negatively than men in the same occupations.

Women and Occupational Development

Women leave well-paid occupations for many reasons, including family obligations and workplace environment. Women who continue to work full-time have adequate child care and look for ways to further their occupational development.

Ethnicity and Occupational Development

Vocational identity and vocational goals vary in different ethnic groups. Whether an organization is sensitive to ethnicity issues is a strong predictor of satisfaction among ethnic minority employees.

Bias and Discrimination

Sex discrimination remains the chief barrier to women's occupational development. In many cases, discrimination operates as a glass ceiling. Pay inequity is also a problem; women often are paid a fraction of what men in similar jobs earn.

Sexual harassment is a problem in the workplace. Current criteria for judging harassment are based on the reasonable woman standard.

Denying employment to anyone over 40 because of age is age discrimination.

Age discrimination comes into play if a worker is denied promotion or employment because of her or his age. Age discrimination takes many forms, including differential layoff patterns and stereotypic views of the older worker. Several other labor market barriers also exist for older workers.

OCCUPATIONAL TRANSITIONS

Retraining Workers

To adapt to the effects of a global economy and an aging work force, many corporations provide retraining opportunities for workers. Retraining is especially important in cases of outdated skills and career plateauing.

The extent to which one believes that he or she has the ability to learn and develop (self-efficacy) also influences whether retraining will be effective.

Occupational Insecurity and Job Loss

Important reasons why people change occupations include personality, obsolescence, and economic trends. Occupational insecurity is a growing problem. Fear that one may lose one's job is a better predictor of anxiety than the actual likelihood of job loss.

Job loss is a traumatic event that can affect every aspect of a person's life. Degree of financial distress and the extent of attachment to the job are the best predictors of distress.

DUAL-EARNER COUPLES

The Dependent Care Dilemma

Whether a woman returns to work after having a child depends largely on how attached she is to her work. Simply providing child care on-site does not always result in higher job satisfaction. The more important factor is the degree to which supervisors are sympathetic.

Juggling Multiple Roles

Although women have reduced the amount of time they spend on household tasks over the past two decades, they still do most of the work. European American men are less likely than either African American or Hispanic American men to help with traditionally female household tasks.

Flexible work schedules and number of children are important factors in role conflict. Recent evidence shows that work stress has a much bigger impact on family life than family stress has on work performance. Some women pay a high personal price for having careers.

Work–family conflicts are influenced by the person's life stage and gender differences in the meaning attributed to the nature of the conflict.

LEISURE ACTIVITIES

Types of Leisure Activities

Preoccupations can become more focused as interests, which can lead to the selection of particular leisure activities. People develop a repertoire of preferred leisure activities.

Developmental Changes in Leisure

As people grow older, they tend to engage in leisure activities that are less strenuous and more family-oriented. Leisure preferences in adulthood reflect those in earlier life.

Consequences of Leisure Activities

Leisure activities promote well-being and can enhance all aspects of people's lives.

RETIREMENT

What Does Being Retired Mean?

Retirement is a complex process by which people withdraw from full-time employment. No single definition is adequate for all ethnic groups; self-definition involves several factors, including eligibility for certain social programs.

Why Do People Retire?

Most people retire because they choose to, although some people are forced to retire or do so because of financial status or serious health problems, such as cardiovascular disease or cancer. However, there are important gender and ethnic differences in why people retire and how they label themselves after retirement. Most of the research is based on European American men from traditional marriages.

Planning for Retirement

Preretirement education programs cover a variety of topics, including finances, attitudes, health, and expectations. Financial planning for retirement is essential. Realistic expectations for retirement are important predictors of future satisfaction.

Adjusting to Retirement

Retirement is an important life transition. Most people are satisfied with retirement. Most retired people maintain their health, friendship networks, and activity levels, at least in the years immediately after retirement. For men, personal life priorities are all important; little is known about women's retirement satisfaction. Most retired people stay busy in activities such as volunteer work and helping others.

INTERPERSONAL TIES

Retiring can disrupt long-held behavior patterns in marriages. Social relationships help buffer the stress of retirement. Readjusting to being home rather than at work is difficult for men in traditional marriages. Marriages sometimes are disrupted, but married men generally are happier in retirement than men who are not married. Participation in community organizations helps raise satisfaction. In particular, volunteer work can fill the void. Improved attitudes toward adults in society also help.

Review Questions

OCCUPATIONAL CHOICE AND DEVELOPMENT

- What are occupational priorities, and how do they change over time?

- How is work changing as a result of the global economy?

- Briefly describe Holland's theory linking personality and occupational choice. What personality types did Holland identify? How are they related to occupational fit?

- Briefly describe Super's theory of occupational development.

- What is a mentor? What role does a mentor play in occupational development?

- How does the mentor–protégé relationship change over time?

- What is the developmental course of job satisfaction? What factors influence job satisfaction?

- What are alienation and burnout? How are they related to job satisfaction?

GENDER, ETHNICITY, BIAS, AND DISCRIMINATION

- What gender differences have been identified that relate to occupational choice? How do the differences in men's and women's socialization influence occupational opportunities?

- How are women in nontraditional occupations perceived?
- What are the major barriers to women's occupational development?
- What are the major barriers to occupational development related to ethnicity?
- How are sex discrimination and the glass ceiling related?
- What structural barriers do ethnic minorities face in occupational settings?
- How is sexual harassment defined?
- What is age discrimination, and how does it operate?
- What are the main labor market barriers to older workers?

OCCUPATIONAL TRANSITIONS

- What are the major reasons that people change occupations?
- Why is retraining workers important?
- What effects do people report after losing their jobs?

DUAL-EARNER COUPLES

- What factors are important in dependent care for employees?
- How do dual-earner couples balance multiple roles and deal with role conflict?
- What important factors contribute to work–family conflict? What other occupational development effects occur?

LEISURE ACTIVITIES

- What are the major reasons people engage in leisure activities? What benefits do they derive?
- What kinds of leisure activities do people perform?
- How do leisure activities change over the life span?
- What gender differences are there in leisure activities?

RETIREMENT

- In what ways can retirement be viewed? What changes in the definition of retirement may occur in the next several years?
- What are the main predictors of the decision to retire?
- What steps should people take to prepare for retirement?
- How do people adjust to retirement?
- What effects does retirement have on relationships with family, friends, and community?

Integrating Concepts in Development

1. What role do personal relationships play in one's work, leisure, and retirement?
2. How do cognitive development and personality influence work roles?
3. What implications are there for the removal of mandatory retirement in terms of normal cognitive changes with age?

Key Terms

age discrimination Denying employment or promotion to someone on the basis of age. Age discrimination is illegal in the United States.

alienation The feeling that results when workers believe that what they are doing is worthless and that their efforts are devalued or when they do not see the connection between what they do and the final product.

burnout The feeling that results when the pace and the pressure of one's occupation becomes more than one can bear, depleting a person's energy and motivation.

career plateauing The lack of promotional opportunity from the organization or the person's decision not to seek advancement.

comparable worth The notion that people should be paid equally for similar work regardless of gender.

glass ceiling An invisible but real barrier to the occupational development of women and minorities that allows them to advance to a certain level in an organization and no higher.

glass elevator The means by which men in traditionally female occupations rise at a quicker rate than their female counterparts.

interrole conflict A clash between competing or incompatible sets of roles, most often seen in work and family settings.

job satisfaction How happy one is with one's job.

mentor A person who teaches a newer employee the informal rules of an organization.

occupational priorities The reasons why one works and how the worker views them.

preretirement education program A program aimed at educating workers about the broad range of issues they will face in retirement, including health, adjustment, and finances.

reality shock The realization of the complexities and difficulties of the real world.

reasonable woman standard The appropriate basis for defining sexual harassment; defined as the standard by which a reasonable woman would consider a behavior offensive.

sex discrimination Denying a person a position or a promotion solely on the basis of gender.

vocational maturity The more congruent occupational behaviors are with what is expected at different ages.

work–family conflict Competing demands between work and family.

Resources

READINGS

Bolles, R. N. (1997). *The 1998 what color is your parachute: A practical manual for job-hunters and career changers.* Berkeley, CA: Ten Speed Press. This popular reference is a valuable resource

for people in search of careers. It is updated regularly.

Crosby, F. (1991). *Juggling: If you'd like to learn more. The unexpected advantages of balancing career and home for women, their families and society.* New York: Free Press. Intriguing discussion of balancing multiple roles of work and family. Moderately difficult.

Feather, N. T. (1990). *The psychological impact of unemployment.* New York: Springer-Verlag. One of the best scholarly discussions of unemployment. Moderately difficult.

Gerson, K. (1993). *No man's land: Men's changing commitments to family and work.* New York: Basic Books. Based on a series of life history interviews, this book gives a male perspective on balancing work and family. Easy reading.

Keita, G. P., & Hurrell, J. J., Jr. (Eds.). (1994). *Job stress in a changing workforce.* Washington, DC: American Psychological Association. A wide-ranging discussion of issues including diversity, culture, ethnicity, age, and role conflict. Easy to moderately difficult depending on the chapter.

Schaie, K. W., & Schooler, C. (Eds.). (1998). *Impact of work on older adults.* New York: Springer. Edited book discussing work and nonwork factors influencing older adults' work performance and satisfaction.

WEB SITES

The U.S. Department of Labor provides many reports on various aspects of work force participation. Check out the many agencies within the department by clicking on the "DOL Agencies" button. The Women's Bureau on that list is especially good for statistics on women's employment status. The department's home page is at http://www.dol.gov.

A well-organized set of links to all aspects of employment, including career planning, law, unemployment, and women's issues can be found at http://www.yahoo.com/Business/Employment/.

Many Web sites are devoted to the issue of sexual harassment. An excellent and brief summary about myths and realities concerning sexual harassment and much additional information is available from the American Psychological Association at http://www.feminist.org/911/1_support.html.

The AARP provides a Web page that reports on major issues related to older adults, including community and volunteer programs, legislative issues on retirement benefits, financial and work issues, and leisure and fun at http://www.aarp.org/.

SEARCH ONLINE WITH
INFOTRAC COLLEGE EDITION
For more information on the topics in this chapter, explore InfoTrac College Edition, your online library. Go to http://www.infotrac-college.com/wadsworth and use the passcode that came on the card with your book. Try these search terms: retirement, sexual harrassment, dual-career families, retraining older workers, National Senior Service Corps.

DYING AND BEREAVEMENT

© AP / Wide World Photos

No family in the United States captured the imagination of more people during the latter half of the 20th century than the Kennedys. It seemed that few weeks could go by without one or more members of the family making headlines. Although many members across generations contributed to government and public service, many people remember the Kennedys through the grief they shared with them during times of loss. John F. Kennedy and his brothers Robert and Joseph, as well as John F. Kennedy, Jr., and other members of the family, all died at young ages under tragic circumstances. Also remembered for their stoic way of handling their grief, the Kennedy family is an excellent example of the ways in which death touches everyone, from the very rich to the very poor.

Americans have a paradoxical relationship with death. On one hand, we are fascinated by it, as evidenced by the popularity of news stories about murders or wars and the crowds of onlookers at accidents. Tourists often visit the places where famous people died or are buried. People around the world watch news broadcasts that show the horrors of war and genocide in which tens of thousands of people are killed. But when it comes to pondering our own death or that of people close to us, we have problems, as La Rochefoucauld wrote more than 300 years ago when he said that it is easier to look in to the sun than to contemplate death. When death is personal, we become uneasy. We may not be as willing to watch the news if we knew that the coverage would concern our own death. It is hard indeed to look at the sun.

For most people in the United States, death is no longer a personal experience until middle age. We typically do not experience death up close as children; indeed, many Americans believe it is important to shield children from death. But just a few generations ago in America, and still in most of the world, death is part of people's everyday life experience. Children are present when family members die. Viewings and wakes are held in the home, and children are active participants in funeral services. In our technological times, perhaps we should consider what these changes in personal experience with death mean for life-span development.

In this chapter we consider death from many perspectives. We examine some of the issues surrounding how it is defined legally and medically. We address several questions: Why do most of us avoid thinking about death? What is it like to die? How are dying people cared for? How do survivors grieve and cope with the loss of a loved one?

DEFINITIONS AND ETHICAL ISSUES

LEARNING OBJECTIVES

- How is death viewed in sociocultural terms?
- How is death defined legally and medically?
- What is euthanasia? How does one make decisions about medical care known to others?
- What are the costs of life-sustaining interventions?
- What are the major issues concerning suicide? Who is most likely to commit suicide?

Ernesto and Paulina had been married 48 years when Ernesto developed terminal pancreatic cancer. Ernesto was suffering terrible pain and begged Paulina to make it stop. Paulina had heard about "mercy killing" that involved administering high dosages of barbiturates, but she believed that this was the same as murder. Yet she could hardly bear to watch her beloved husband suffer. Paulina wondered what she should do.

The dictionary definition of death is very simple: It is the transition between being alive and being dead. Similarly, dying is the process of making this transition. It seems clear enough, doesn't it? Then you encounter situations like the one Paulina is in. The "right thing to do" becomes less clear, and the ethical and moral issues become complicated. What would you do if you were Paulina? What if you were Ernesto?

We will see that such tough issues and choices abound when we consider and confront death. The notions of death and dying are much like the notions of youth (or middle age or old age) and aging. We saw in Chapter 1 that it is extremely difficult to give precise definitions of these terms because age itself has many different meanings. Issues such as when middle age ends and old age begins have no easy answers. The same is true for death. What is death? When does death occur? The dictionary notwithstanding, it is very difficult in practice to give precise answers. As we will see, it depends on one's perspective.

Sociocultural Definitions of Death

What comes to mind when you hear the word *death*? Black clothing or a cemetery? A driver killed in a traffic accident? Old people in nursing homes? A gathering of family and friends? A transition to an eternal reward? A car battery that doesn't work anymore? An unknowable mystery? Each of these possibilities represents one of the ways in which death is considered in Western culture (Kalish, 1987). People in other cultures and traditions may view death differently. People around the world may use the same words or concepts that we do, but they may not mean the same things.

For example, Westerners tend to divide people into groups based on chronological age, even though we recognize the limitations of this concept (see Chapter 1). Although we would like to divide people along more functional lines, practicality dictates that chronological age has to do. However, other cultures divide people differently. Among the Melanesians the term *mate* includes the very sick, the very old, and the dead; the term *toa* refers to all other living people.

This distinction is the most important one, not the one between all the living and all the dead, as in our culture (Counts & Counts, 1985). Other South Pacific cultures believe that the life force may leave the body during sleep or illness, suggesting that sleep, illness, and death are considered together. In this way people "die" several times before experiencing "final death" (Counts & Counts, 1985). For example, among the Kaliai, "the people . . . are prepared to diagnose as potentially fatal any fever or internal pain or illness that does not respond readily to treatment" (p. 150). Mourning rituals and definitions of states of bereavement also vary across cultures (Simmons, 1945). Some cultures have formalized periods of time during which certain prayers or rituals are performed. For example, Orthodox Jews recite the Kaddish after the death of a close relative and cover the mirrors in the house, and the men slash their ties as a symbol of loss. Family members may be prohibited from doing certain things (such as social activities) for a specific period of time. Ancestor worship, a deep respectful feeling toward people from whom a family is descended or who are important to them, is an important part of Japanese culture and of Buddhism in Japan (Klass, 1996). Thus, in considering death, dying, and bereavement, we must keep in mind that the experiences of our culture may not generalize to others.

Death can be a truly cross-cultural experience. The international outpouring of grief over the death of Princess Diana in 1997 drew much attention to the ways in which the deaths of people one does not know personally can still affect us. At such times, we realize that death happens to us all and that death can be both personal and public.

Socioculturally, death can be viewed in many ways (Kastenbaum, 1999). Look at the list that follows and think about the examples of these different definitions. Then take another moment to think up some additional examples of your own.

Princess Diana's funeral was an excellent example of how death can be a very public event in which people from around the world experience grief.

Death as a Statistic
Mortality rates

Life expectancy tables

Number of patients with cancer who die

Murder rates

Death as an Event
Funeral

Memorial service

Cemetery service

Family gathering

Death as a State of Being
Time of waiting

Being with God

Nothingness

Transformation

Death as Fear and Anxiety
Will dying be painful?

I worry about my family.

Who will care for my children?

I'm afraid to die.

Death as an Image or Object
Flag at half staff

Sympathy card

Tombstone

Monument or memorial

Death as an Analogy
Dead as a door nail

Dead-end street

You're dead meat

In the dead of winter

Death as a Mystery

What is it like to die?

Will we meet family?

What happens after death?

Will I learn everything when I die?

Death as a Boundary

How many years do I have left?

What will happen to my family after I die?

What do I do now?

You can't come back.

Death as a Thief of Meaning

I feel cheated.

Why should I go on living?

Life doesn't mean much anymore.

I have much left to do.

Death as Reward and Punishment

Live long and prosper.

The wicked will go to hell.

Heaven awaits the just.

Purgatory prepares you for heaven.

The many ways of viewing death can be seen in various funeral customs. Perhaps you have experienced a range of different types of funeral customs, from very small, private services to very elaborate rituals. Variations in the customs surrounding death are reflected in some of the oldest monuments on earth, such as the pyramids in Egypt, and some of the most beautiful, such as the Taj Mahal in India. You may want to investigate some of the funeral customs in your area, in other parts of the country, and in other countries. Comparing these customs provides a much richer appreciation for how people around the world deal with death.

Legal and Medical Definitions

Sociocultural approaches help us understand the different ways in which people view death. But these views do not address a very fundamental question: How do we determine that someone has died? To answer this question, we must turn our attention to the medical and legal definitions of death.

Determining when death occurs has always been a judgment. Just as there is much debate over when life begins, so there is over when life ends. The solution typically has been for experts to propose a set of criteria, which are then adopted by society. *For thousands of years people accepted and applied the criteria known today as those defining* **clinical death,** *a lack of heartbeat and respiration. In the late 1970s, however, the health care profession agreed on the most widely accepted criteria, the eight listed here, which constitute* **brain death** (Jeffko, 1979):

No spontaneous movement in response to any stimuli

No spontaneous respirations for at least 1 hour

Lack of responsiveness to even the most painful stimuli

No eye movements, blinking, or pupil responses

No postural activity, swallowing, yawning, or vocalizing

No motor reflexes

A flat electroencephalogram (EEG) for at least 10 minutes

No change in any of these criteria when they are tested again 24 hours later

For a person to be declared brain dead, all eight criteria must be met. Moreover, other conditions that might mimic death—such as deep coma, hypothermia, or drug overdose—must be ruled out.

According to most hospitals, the lack of brain activity must be true of both the cortex (which involves higher processes such as thinking) and the brainstem (which involves vegetative functions such as heartbeat and respiration). *It is possible for a person's cortical functioning to cease while brainstem activity continues; this is a* **persistent vegetative state,** *from which the person does not recover.* This condition can result from a severe head injury or a drug overdose.

Because of conditions such as persistent vegetative state, family members sometimes face difficult ethical decisions about care. We consider these issues next.

Ethical Issues

Imagine the following situation. Betty is working in a health care facility when a woman who is not breathing and has no pulse is rushed into the facility. About

6 months ago, this woman was diagnosed as having ovarian cancer, a very aggressive form of the disease that typically is fatal in a short period of time. Should Betty attempt to revive her knowing that she is terminally ill and would be in a great deal of pain? Or should she let her die without any intervention?

This is an example of the kinds of problems faced in the field of **bioethics,** *the study of the interface between human values and technological advances in health and life sciences.* Bioethics grew from two bases: respect for individual freedom and the impossibility of establishing any single version of morality by rational argument or common sense (Cole & Holstein, 1996). In practice, bioethics emphasizes minimizing harm over maximizing good and the importance of individual choice.

In the arena of death and dying, the most important bioethical issue is **euthanasia:** *the practice of ending life for reasons of mercy.* The moral dilemma posed by euthanasia becomes apparent when we try to decide the circumstances under which a person's life should be ended. In our society this dilemma occurs most often when a person is being kept alive by machines or when someone is suffering from a terminal illness.

Euthanasia can be carried out in two different ways: active and passive. **Active euthanasia** *involves the deliberate ending of someone's life, which may be based on a clear statement of the person's wishes or a decision made by someone else who has the legal authority to do so.* Usually, this involves situations in which people are in a persistent vegetative state or the end stages of a terminal disease. Examples of active euthanasia include administering a drug overdose or disconnecting a life-support system.

The most controversial version of active euthanasia involves physician-assisted suicide. Dr. Jack Kevorkian, a physician in Michigan who was convicted of murder in 1999 for assisting in a patient's suicide broadcast on the TV news show *60 Minutes,* is a strong proponent of the right to die who created a suicide machine to help people end their lives. In an equally controversial move, voters in Oregon passed the Death with Dignity Act in 1994, the first physician-assisted suicide law in the United States. This law makes it legal for people to request a lethal dose of medication if they have a terminal disease and make the request voluntarily. Statistics indicate that about 15 people per year have used the law to take their own lives; the vast majority had cancer, and their average age was nearly 70 (McMahon & Koch, 1999). Although the U.S. Supreme Court ruled in two cases in 1997 (*Vacco v. Quill* and *Washington v. Glucksberg*) that there is no right to assisted suicide, the court decided in 1998 not to overturn the Oregon law. As discussed later in the Current Controversies feature, the issues concerning physician-assisted suicides will continue to be debated publicly and in the courts.

A second form of euthanasia, **passive euthanasia,** *involves allowing a person to die by withholding available treatment.* For example, chemotherapy might be withheld from a patient with cancer, a surgical procedure might not be performed, or food could be withdrawn. Again, these approaches are controversial. On the one hand, few would argue with a decision not to treat a newly discovered cancer in a person in the late stages of Alzheimer's disease if treatment would do nothing but prolong and make even more agonizing an already certain death. On the other hand, many people might argue against withholding nourishment from a terminally ill person; indeed, such cases often end up in court. For example, in 1990 the U.S. Supreme Court took up the case of Nancy Cruzan, whose family wanted to end her forced feeding. The court ruled that unless clear and incontrovertible evidence is presented that a person wants to have nourishment stopped, such as through a durable power of attorney or living will, a third party, such as a parent or partner, cannot decide to end it.

Euthanasia is a complex legal and ethical issue. In most jurisdictions, euthanasia is legal only when a person has made known his or her wishes about medical intervention. Unfortunately, many people fail to take this step, perhaps because it is difficult to think about such situations or because they do not know the options available to them. But without clear directions, medical personnel may be unable to take a patient's preferences into account.

Two ways exist to make such intentions known: living wills and durable power of attorney. The purpose of both is to make one's wishes about the use of life support known in the event one is unconscious or otherwise incapable of expressing them. A durable

California Medical Association
DURABLE POWER OF ATTORNEY FOR HEALTH CARE DECISIONS
(California Probate Code Sections 4600-4753)

WARNING TO PERSON EXECUTING THIS DOCUMENT

This is an important legal document. Before executing this document, you should know these important facts:

This document gives the person you designate as your agent (the attorney-in-fact) the power to make health care decisions for you. Your agent must act consistently with your desires as stated in this document or otherwise made known.

Except as you otherwise specify in this document, this document gives your agent power to consent to your doctor not giving treatment or stopping treatment necessary to keep you alive.

Notwithstanding this document, you have the right to make medical and other health care decisions for yourself so long as you can give informed consent with respect to the particular decision. In addition, no treatment may be given to you over your objection, and health care necessary to keep you alive may not be stopped or withheld if you object at the time.

This document gives your agent authority to consent, to refuse to consent, or to withdraw consent to any care, treatment, service, or procedure to maintain, diagnose, or treat a physical or mental condition. This power is subject to any statement of your desires and any limitations that you include in this document. You may

state in this document any types of treatment that you do not desire. In addition, a court can take away the power of your agent to make health care decisions for you if your agent (1) authorizes anything that is illegal, (2) acts contrary to your known desires or (3) where your desires are not known, does anything that is clearly contrary to your best interests.

This power will exist for an indefinite period of time unless you limit its duration in this document.

You have the right to revoke the authority of your agent by notifying your agent or your treating doctor, hospital, or other health care provider orally or in writing of the revocation.

Your agent has the right to examine your medical records and to consent to their disclosure unless you limit this right in this document.

Unless you otherwise specify in this document, this document gives your agent the power after you die to (1) authorize an autopsy, (2) donate your body or parts thereof for transplant or therapeutic or educational or scientific purposes, and (3) direct the disposition of your remains.

If there is anything in this document that you do not understand, you should ask a lawyer to explain it to you.

1. CREATION OF DURABLE POWER OF ATTORNEY FOR HEALTH CARE

By this document I intend to create a durable power of attorney by appointing the person designated below to make health care decisions for me as allowed by Sections 4600 to 4753, inclusive, of the California Probate Code. This power of attorney shall not be affected by my subsequent incapacity. I hereby revoke any prior durable power of attorney for health care. I am a California resident who is at least 18 years old, of sound mind, and acting of my own free will.

2. APPOINTMENT OF HEALTH CARE AGENT

(Fill in below the name, address and telephone number of the person you wish to make health care decisions for you if you become incapacitated. You should make sure that this person agrees to accept this responsibility. The following may not serve as your agent: (1) your treating health care provider; (2) an operator of a community care facility or residential care facility for the elderly; or (3) an employee of your treating health care provider, a community care facility, or a residential care facility for the elderly, unless that employee is related to you by blood, marriage or adoption, or unless you are also an employee of the same treating provider or facility. If you are a conservatee under the Lanterman-Petris-Short Act (the law governing involuntary commitment to a mental health facility) and you wish to appoint your conservator as your agent, you must consult a lawyer, who must sign and attach a special declaration for this document to be valid.)

I, _____, hereby appoint:
            (insert your name)

Name _____

Address _____

Work Telephone (_____) _____ Home Telephone (_____) _____

as my agent (attorney-in-fact) to make health care decisions for me as authorized in this document. I understand that this power of attorney will be effective for an indefinite period of time unless I revoke it or limit its duration below.

(Optional) This power of attorney shall expire on the following date: _____.

© California Medical Association 1996 (revised)

FIGURE 13.1 Example of a durable power of attorney for health care decisions.

power of attorney like the one in Figure 13.1 has an additional advantage: It names a specific person who has the legal authority to speak for another person if necessary. Although both of these documents have strong support (many states in the United States have laws concerning these documents), several problems exist as well. Foremost among these is that many people fail to inform their relatives about their living will, do not make their wishes known, or do not tell the person named in a durable power of attorney where the document is kept. Obviously, this puts relatives at a serious disadvantage if they need to make decisions about the use of life-support systems.

A living will or a durable power of attorney can be the basis for a Do Not Resuscitate (DNR) medical order. A DNR order applies only to cardiopulmonary resuscitation when one's heart and breathing stop. In the normal course of events, a medical team will immediately try to restore normal heartbeat and respiration. With a DNR order, this treatment is not done. As with living wills and durable powers of attorney, it is very important to let all appropriate medical personnel know that a DNR order is desired.

Public resistance to keeping terminally ill people alive on life-support equipment encouraged the U.S. Congress to pass the Patient Self-Determination Act

Should people have the right to obtain information that will help them end their lives soon, before enduring horrible pain that will ultimately end in death? Should physicians be permitted to give that information and provide assistance if the patient asks? What do you think?

Taking one's own life has never been popular in the United States because of religious and other prohibitions. In other cultures, such as Japan, suicide is viewed as an honorable way to die under certain circumstances. Some countries, like the Netherlands, allow physicians to assist people who want to commit suicide (Cutter, 1991). In 1984, the Dutch Supreme Court barred prosecution of physicians who assist in suicide if five criteria are met:

The patient's condition is intolerable with no hope for improvement.

No relief is available.

The patient is competent.

The patient makes a request repeatedly over time.

Two physicians agree with the patient's request.

As noted in the text, voters in Oregon passed the first physician-assisted suicide law in the United States so that a terminally ill person may obtain a prescription for medication for the purpose of ending his or her life. The Oregon law is similar to Dutch law. It requires that physicians inform the person that he or she is terminally ill and of alternative options (e.g., hospice care, pain control); the person must be mentally competent and make two oral requests and a written request, with at least 15 days between the oral requests. Such provisions are included to ensure that people making the request fully understand the issues and that they do not make the request hastily.

Although most Americans support a person's right to decide when to die, many people do not. The latter group often argues their position on religious grounds, stating that only God should decide when it is time for people to die. The differences of opinions have resulted in several court challenges to the right to die. Bioethicists must make the dilemmas clear, and we must make ourselves aware of the issues. What is at stake is a matter of life and death. What do you think?

 Search Online with InfoTrac College Edition For more information on these controversies, explore InfoTrac College Edition, your online library. Go to http://www.infotrac-college.com/wadsworth and use the passcode that came on the card with your book. Try these search terms: assisted suicide, right to die, death with dignity.

---

of 1990, which requires health care facilities receiving Medicare funds to inform patients about their right to prepare advance directives stating their preferences for terminal care (Markson, 1995). Although there is widespread belief that such directives, either through a living will or a durable power of attorney, are a good idea, relatively few people have actually prepared documents indicating their preferences for life-sustaining treatment (Markson et al., 1995). Moreover, most physicians do not explain the success rates of various types of medical interventions; for example, only 15% of people under 70 and nearly none of those older who suffer cardiac arrest survive even if cardiopulmonary resuscitation (CPR) is used (Nuland, 1993). Clearly, the decision to use such interventions may be affected by the knowledge family members have about the effectiveness of the intervention.

Bioethicists must make the different sides of the dilemmas clear, and we must make ourselves aware of the issues. Given that the last days of life often are complicated by the lack of advance directives concerning the types of care they really want, helping older adults prepare a living will or durable power of attorney is very important (Foley et al., 1995). What is at stake is a matter of life and death. Take a minute to reflect on these issues in the Current Controversies feature.

The Price of Life-Sustaining Care

A growing debate in Western society concerns the financial, personal, and moral costs of keeping people alive on life-support machines. For example, many people argue that treating secondary

Dying and Bereavement

diseases in terminally ill older adults or keeping them alive on life support makes little sense. They argue that such treatment is extremely expensive, that these people will soon die anyway, and that needlessly prolonging their lives is a burden on society. In these cases, it is argued, both the person and society would be better off if the person is allowed to die.

In contrast, many people—including many physicians—go to extraordinary lengths to keep very premature infants alive, despite high risks of permanent brain damage or physical disability from the intervention. Some people point out that not only is the medical care at the time often more expensive for infants (an average of several thousand dollars per day for neonatal intensive care), but the potential cost to families and society if the person needs constant care could be enormous. Additionally, the emotional costs can be devastating to many families. But many such children are not affected negatively by the intervention and grow up to be normal in all respects.

There are no easy solutions to these dilemmas. At present, there is no way to predict which premature infant will develop normally or which seriously ill older person will recover.

_____

CONCEPT CHECKS

1. What are the 10 ways in which death can be viewed socioculturally?
2. What are the criteria for determining brain death and clinical death?
3. What is the difference between active and passive euthanasia?
4. What are the costs of life-sustaining interventions?

THINKING ABOUT DEATH: PERSONAL ASPECTS

_____

LEARNING OBJECTIVES

• How do feelings about death change over adulthood?
• How do people deal with their own death?
• What is death anxiety, and how do people show and cope with it?

Ricardo recently learned that he has amyotrophic lateral sclerosis, better known as Lou Gehrig's disease. He knows that the disease is fatal, and he is afraid of dying. He cannot understand why this has happened to him, and he is very angry at God for "doing this to him." Formerly a very religions person, he now refuses to go to church or to talk with his friend, a parish priest.

Being afraid to die is considered normal by most people. Certainly, Ricardo could relate to this. As one research participant put it, "You are nuts if you aren't afraid of death" (Kalish & Reynolds, 1976). Still, death is a paradox, as we noted at the beginning of the chapter. That is, we are afraid of or anxious about death, but we are drawn to it, sometimes in very public ways. We examine this paradox at the personal level in this section. Specifically, we focus on two questions: How do people's feelings about death differ with age? What is it about death that we fear or that makes us anxious?

Before proceeding, however, take a few minutes to complete the exercise in the Discovering Development feature. Although it may be daunting and difficult at first, writing your own obituary is a way to gain insight into what you think are your most important accomplishments and relationships. In a way, it serves as a process for conducting a life review.

A Life Course Approach to Dying

How do you feel about dying? Do you think people of different ages feel the same way? It probably doesn't surprise you to learn that feelings about dying vary across adulthood.

Because young adults are just beginning to pursue the family, career, and personal goals they have set, they tend to be more intense in their feelings toward death. When asked how they feel about death, young adults report a strong sense that those who die at this point in their lives would be cheated out of their future (Attig, 1996).

Understanding how young adults deal with death is best understood from the perspective of attachment theory (Balk, 1996; Jacobs, 1993). In this view, a person's reactions are a natural consequence of

If you have ever looked carefully at a newspaper, you know that everyone who dies has a brief summary of his or her life published in an obituary. Obituaries serve several purposes, including telling the world the important aspects of one's life and listing one's surviving family members. If you have ever read an obituary, you also realize that they tend to be fairly short, usually less than 200 words in most cases.

Imagine that unlike most people, you have the opportunity to write your own obituary. Imagine further that you can create the obituary based on the life you hope to have. Take a moment to reflect on this, and then compose a 150- to 200-word obituary that includes your age at the time of your death, the cause of death, your major life accomplishments, and your family survivors. When finished, read it over carefully. You may want to keep it for future reference to see how closely your life turns out in relation to your dreams.

forming attachments and then losing them. We consider adult grief a bit later in the chapter.

Although not specifically addressed in research, the shift from formal operational to postformal thinking could be important in young adults' contemplation of death. Presumably, this shift in cognitive development is accompanied by a lessening of the feeling of immortality as young adults begin to integrate personal feelings and emotions with their thinking.

Midlife is the time when most people confront the death of their parents. Up until that point, people tend not to think much about their own death; the fact that their parents are still alive buffers them from reality. After all, in the normal course of events, our parents are supposed to die before we do.

Once their parents have died, people realize that they are now the oldest generation of their family—the next in line to die. Reading the obituary pages, they are reminded of this, as the ages of many of the people who have died get closer and closer to their own.

Probably as a result of this growing realization of their own mortality, middle-aged adults' sense of time undergoes a subtle yet profound change. It changes from an emphasis on how long they have already lived to how long they have left to live (Attig, 1996; Neugarten, 1969). This may lead to occupational change or other redirection such as improving relationships that had deteriorated over the years.

In general, older adults are less anxious about death and more accepting of it than any other age group (Kastenbaum, 1999; Keller et al., 1984). In part, this results from the achievement of ego integrity, as described in Chapter 10. For many older adults, the joy of living is diminishing (Kalish, 1987). More than any other group, they have experienced loss of family and friends and have come to terms with their own mortality. Older adults have more chronic diseases, which are not likely to go away. They may feel that their most important life tasks have been completed (Kastenbaum, 1999).

Dealing with One's Own Death

Thinking about death from an observer's perspective is one thing. Thinking about one's own is quite another. The reactions people have to their own impending death, long thought to be the purview of religion and philosophy, were not researched until well into the 20th century.

KÜBLER-ROSS'S THEORY. Elisabeth Kübler-Ross became interested in the experience of dying as an instructor in psychiatry at the University of Chicago in the early 1960s. When she began her investigations into the dying process, such research was controversial; her physician colleagues initially were outraged, and some even denied that their patients were terminally ill. Still, she persisted. More than 200 interviews with terminally ill people convinced her that most people experienced several emotional reactions. Using her experiences, she described five that represented the ways in which people dealt with death: denial, anger, bargaining, depression, and acceptance (Kübler-Ross, 1969). Although they were first presented as a sequence, it was subsequently realized that the emotions can overlap and can be experienced in different orders.

When people are told that they have a terminal illness, their first reaction is likely to be shock and disbelief. Denial is a normal part of getting ready to die. Some want to shop around for a more favorable diagnosis, and most feel that a mistake has been made. Others try to find assurance in religion. Eventually, though, reality sets in for most people.

At some point, people express anger as hostility, resentment, and envy toward health care workers, family, and friends. Ricardo, whom we met in the vignette, is feeling this way. People ask, "Why me?" and express a great deal of frustration. The fact that they are going to die when so many others will live seems so unfair. With time and work, most people confront their anger and resolve it.

In the bargaining phase, people look for a way out. Maybe a deal can be struck with someone, perhaps God, that would allow survival. For example, a woman might promise to be a better mother if only she could live. Or a person sets a timetable: "Just let me live until my daughter graduates from college." Eventually, the person becomes aware that these deals will not work.

When one can no longer deny the illness, perhaps because of surgery or pain, feelings of depression are very common. People report feeling deep loss, sorrow, guilt, and shame over their illness and its consequences. Kübler-Ross believes that allowing people to discuss their feelings with others helps move them to an acceptance of death.

In the acceptance stage, the person accepts the inevitability of death and often seems detached from the world and at peace. "It is as if the pain is gone, the struggle is over, and there comes a time for the 'final rest before the journey' as one patient phrased it" (Kübler-Ross, 1969, p. 100).

Although she believes that these five stages represent the typical range of emotional development in the dying, Kübler-Ross (1974) cautions that not everyone experiences all of them or progresses through them at the same rate or in the same order. Research supports the view that her "stages" should not be viewed as a sequence (Neimeyer, 1997). In fact, we could actually harm dying people by considering these stages as fixed and universal. Individual differences are great, as Kübler-Ross points out. Emotional responses may vary in intensity throughout the dying process. Thus, the goal in applying Kübler-Ross's theory to real-world settings would be to help people achieve an appropriate death. An appropriate death is one that meets the needs of the dying person, allowing him or her to work out each problem as it comes.

A CONTEXTUAL THEORY OF DYING. One of the difficulties with most theories of dying is a general lack of research evaluating them in a wide variety of contexts (Kastenbaum & Thuell, 1995). By their very nature, stages or sequences imply a particular directionality. Stage theories, in particular, emphasize qualitative differences between the various stages. However, the duration of a particular stage, or a specific phase, varies widely from person to person. Such theories assume some sort of underlying process for moving through the stages or phases but do not clearly state what causes a person to move from one to another.

One reason for these problems is the realization that there is no one right way to die, although there may be better or worse ways of coping (Corr, 1991–1992). A perspective that recognizes this realization would approach the issue from the perspective of the dying person and the issues or tasks he or she must face. Corr (1991–1992) identified four dimensions of such tasks: bodily needs, psychological security, interpersonal attachments, and spiritual energy and hope. This holistic approach acknowledges individual differences and rejects broad generalizations. Corr's task work approach also recognizes the importance of the coping efforts of family members, friends, and caregivers as well as those of the dying person.

Kastenbaum and Thuell (1995) argue that what is needed is an even broader, contextual approach that takes a more inclusive view of the dying process. They point out that theories must be able to handle people who have a wide variety of terminal illnesses and be sensitive to dying people's own perspectives and values related to death. The socioenvironmental context within which dying occurs, which often changes over time, must be recognized. For example, a person may begin the dying process living independently but end up in a long-term care facility. Such moves may have profound implications for how the person copes with dying. A contextual approach would also provide guidance for health care professionals, families, and others in terms of how to protect the quality of life, provide better care, prepare caregivers, and provide research questions.

We do not yet have such a comprehensive theory of dying. But as Kastenbaum and Thuell point out, we can move in that direction by rejecting a reductionistic approach for a truly holistic one. One way to accomplish this is to examine people's experiences as a narrative that can be written from many points of view (e.g., the patient, family members, caregivers). What would emerge would be a rich description of a dynamically changing process.

Death Anxiety

We have seen that how people view death varies with age. In the process, we encountered the notion of feeling anxious about death. Death anxiety is tough to pin down; indeed, it is the ethereal nature of death, rather than something about it in particular, that usually makes us feel so uncomfortable. We cannot put our finger on something specific about death that is causing us to feel uneasy. Because of this, we must look for indirect behavioral evidence to document death anxiety. Research findings suggest that death anxiety is a complex, multidimensional construct.

In the late 1990s, researchers began using terror management theory (Pyszczynski et al., 1997, 1999) as a framework to study death anxiety. Terror management theory addresses the issue of why people engage in certain behaviors to achieve particular psychological states. The theory proposes that ensuring that one's life continues is the primary motive underlying behavior; all other motives can be traced to this basic one. Thus, death anxiety is a reflection of one's concern over dying, an outcome that would violate the prime motive.

On the basis of several diverse studies using many different measures, researchers conclude that death anxiety consists of several components. Each of these components is most easily described with terms that resemble examples of fear but cannot be tied to anything specific. Early research indicated that components of death anxiety included pain, body malfunction, humiliation, rejection, nonbeing, punishment, interruption of goals, and negative impact on survivors (Fortner & Neimeyer, 1999). To complicate matters further, any of these components can be assessed at any of three levels: public, private, and nonconscious. That is, what we admit feeling about death in public may differ greatly from what we feel when we are alone with our own thoughts. In short, the measurement of death anxiety is complex, and researchers need to specify which aspects they are assessing.

Much research has been conducted to learn what demographic and personality variables are related to death anxiety. Although the results often are ambiguous, some patterns have emerged. For example, lower ego integrity, more physical problems, and more psychological problems are predictive of higher levels of death anxiety in older adults (Fortner & Neimeyer, 1999).

Strange as it may seem, death anxiety may have a beneficial side. For one thing, being afraid to die means that we often go to great lengths to make sure we stay alive, as argued by terror management theory (Pyszczynski et al, 1997, 1999). Because staying alive helps to ensure the continuation and socialization of the species, fear of death serves as a motivation to have children and raise them properly.

Clearly, death anxiety is complex. We are uncertain about many of its aspects. Yet we can see death anxiety and fear in action all the time in the many behaviors we show.

HOW DO WE SHOW DEATH ANXIETY? When we are afraid or anxious, our behavior changes in some way. One of the most common ways in which this occurs in relation to death is through avoidance (Kastenbaum, 1985, 1999). Avoiding situations that remind us of death occurs at both the unconscious and conscious levels. People who refuse to go to funerals because they find them depressing or who will not visit dying friends or relatives may be consciously avoiding death. Unconscious avoidance may take the form of being too busy to help out a dying person. Society provides several safeguards to help us avoid the reality of death, from isolating dying people in institutions to providing euphemisms for referring to death, such as saying that a person has "passed away."

Some people who engage in very dangerous activities do so as a way of challenging death.

A second way of showing fear or anxiety is the opposite of the first; rather than avoiding death, we challenge it (Kalish, 1984). In this case people deliberately and repeatedly put themselves in dangerous, life-threatening situations such as skydiving, auto racing, rock climbing, and war. These people have not been studied sufficiently to know whether they feel a need to assert their superiority over death. But interestingly enough, a study of pedestrian behavior at a busy intersection in Detroit revealed that people who took chances in crossing the street (for example, not looking before crossing, walking against the light, and jaywalking) were more likely to have thought about suicide and expected to live a significantly shorter time than more cautious pedestrians (Kastenbaum & Briscoe, 1975).

Death anxiety can be exhibited in numerous other ways. Some of the more common include changing lifestyles, dreaming and fantasizing, using humor, displacing fear or anxiety onto something else such as work, and becoming a professional who deals with death (Kalish, 1984). Such behaviors are indicative of large individual variations in how we handle our feelings about death. Still, each of us must come to grips with death and learn how to deal with it on our own terms.

LEARNING TO DEAL WITH DEATH ANXIETY. Although some degree of death anxiety may be appropriate, we must guard against letting it become powerful enough to interfere with our normal daily routines. Several ways exist to help us in this endeavor. Perhaps the one most often used is to live life to the fullest. Kalish (1984, 1987) argues that people who do this enjoy what they have; although they may still fear death and feel cheated, they have few regrets. In a sense they "realize that [they] might die any moment, and yet live as though [they] were never going to die" (Lepp, 1968, p. 77).

Koestenbaum (1976) proposes several exercises and questions to increase one's death awareness. Some of these are to write your own obituary and plan your own death and funeral services, as you did in the Discovering Development feature. You can also ask yourself, "What circumstances would help make my death acceptable?" "Is death the sort of thing that could happen to me right now?"

These questions serve as a basis for an increasingly popular way to reduce anxiety: death education. Most death education programs combine factual information about death with issues aimed at reducing anxiety and fear to increase sensitivity to others' feelings. These programs vary widely in orientation; they can include such topics as philosophy, ethics, psychology, drama, religion, medicine, art, and many others. Additionally, they can focus on death, the process of dying, grief and bereavement, or any combination of them. In general, death education programs help primarily by increasing our awareness of the complex emotions felt and expressed by dying people and their families. Research shows that participating in experiential workshops about death significantly lowers death anxiety in younger, middle-aged, and older adults (Abengozar et al., 1999).

CONCEPT CHECKS

1. How do people of different ages deal with the thought of dying?
2. How do people conceptualize their own death?
3. What is death anxiety, and how is it shown and confronted?

END-OF-LIFE ISSUES

LEARNING OBJECTIVES

- What is a personal final scenario?
- What are hospices, and what options do they provide?

Jean is a 72-year-old woman who was diagnosed with advanced colon cancer recently. She has vivid memories of her father dying a long, protracted death in great pain. Jean is very afraid that she will suffer the same fate. She has heard that the hospice in town emphasizes pain management and provides a lot of support for families. Jean wonders whether that is something she should explore in the time she has left.

Where and how do most of us want to die? Ideally, most people would not like to die alone; indeed, this is one aspect of death anxiety (Kastenbaum, 1999). Whether death occurs in a hospital, hospice, or at home seems less important than having friends and family around. However, most of us do not get our wish. We are most likely to die surrounded by health care workers rather than family. The increasing institutionalization of death has two major consequences (Kastenbaum, 1999). First, health care professionals are playing a more important role in dying people's lives. This means that the medical staff is being forced to provide emotional support in situations largely antithetical to their main mission of healing and curing. This dilemma presents health care workers with problems that we consider later.

A second important result of the institutionalization of death is that dying is being removed from our everyday experience. Not long ago, each of us would have known what it was like to interact with a dying person and to be present when someone died. Institutions isolate us from death, and some argue that the institutions are largely to blame for our increasing avoidance of death and dying people. Unfortunately, we cannot evaluate this opinion because we cannot randomly have some people die at home and others die at hospitals to compare the effects of each in an experiment.

What we can do, though, is consider how we may be able to create a final scenario about our own deaths and explore options for end-of-life care. Let's see what is involved in each.

Creating a Final Scenario

When given the chance, many older adults would like to discuss a variety of issues, collectively called **end-of-life issues:** *management of the final phase of life, after-death disposition of their body and memorial services, and distribution of assets* (Kastenbaum, 1999). People want to manage the final part of their lives by thinking through the choices between traditional care (e.g., provided by hospitals and nursing homes) and alternatives (such as hospices), completing advance directives (e.g., durable power of attorney, living will), resolving key personal relationships, and perhaps choosing the alternative of ending one's life prematurely.

What happens to one's body and how one is memorialized is very important to most people. Is a traditional burial preferred over cremation? A traditional funeral over a memorial service? Such choices often are based in people's religious beliefs and their desire for privacy for their families after they have died.

Making sure that one's estate and personal effects are passed on appropriately often is overlooked. Making a will is especially important in ensuring that one's wishes are carried out. Providing for the informal distribution of personal effects also helps prevent disputes between family members.

Whether people choose to address these issues formally or informally, it is important that they be given the opportunity to do so. In many cases, family members are reluctant to discuss these matters with the dying relative because of their own anxiety about death. *Making such choices known about how they do and do not want their lives to end constitutes a* **final scenario.**

One of the most crucial parts of a final scenario for most people is the process of separation from family and friends (Kastenbaum, 1999). The final days, weeks, and months of life provide opportunities to affirm love, resolve conflicts, and provide peace to dying people. The failure to complete this process often leaves survivors feeling that they did not achieve closure in the relationship, which can result in bitterness toward the deceased.

Health care workers realize the importance of giving dying patients the chance to create a final scenario and recognize the uniqueness of each person's final passage. Any given final scenario reflects the person's personal past, which is the unique combination of the development forces the person experienced. Primary attention is paid to how people's total life experiences have prepared them to face end-of-life issues (Neimeyer, 1997).

One's final scenario helps family and friends interpret one's death, especially when the scenario is constructed jointly (Byock, 1997; Kastenbaum, 1992). The different perspectives of everyone involved are unlikely to converge without clear communication and discussion. Respecting each person's perspective is key and greatly helps in creating a good final scenario. As discussed in the Forces in Action feature, developing a final scenario involves considering all the developmental forces.

The Hospice Option

As we have seen, most people would like to die at home among family and friends. An important barrier to this choice is the availability of support systems when the person has a terminal disease. In this case most people believe that they have no choice but to go to a hospital or nursing home. However, an-

other alternative exists. *A* **hospice** *is an approach to assisting dying people that emphasizes pain management, or palliative care, and death with dignity* (Saunders, 1997). The emphasis in a hospice is on the quality of life. This approach grows out of an important distinction between the prolongation of life and the prolongation of death, a distinction that is important to Jean, the woman we met in the vignette. In a hospice the concern is to make the person as peaceful and comfortable as possible, not to delay an inevitable death. Although medical care is available at a hospice, it is aimed primarily at controlling pain and restoring normal functioning. This orientation places hospices between hospitals and homes in terms of contexts for dying.

Modern hospices are modeled after St. Christopher's Hospice in England, founded in 1967 by Dr. Cicely Saunders. Hospice services are requested only after the person or physician believes that no treatment or cure is possible, making the hospice program markedly different from hospital or home care. The differences are evident in the principles that underlie hospice care: Clients and their families are viewed as a unit, clients should be kept free of pain, emotional and social impoverishment must be minimal, clients must be encouraged to maintain competencies, conflict resolution and fulfillment of realistic desires must be assisted, clients must be free to begin or end relationships, and staff members must seek to alleviate pain and fear (Saunders, 1997).

Two types of hospices exist: inpatient and outpatient. Inpatient hospices provide all care for clients; outpatient hospices provide services to clients who remain in their own homes. The outpatient variation is becoming increasingly popular, largely because more clients can be served at a lower cost. Having hospice services available to people at home is a viable option for many more people (Appleton & Henschell, 1995).

Hospices do not follow a hospital model of care. The role of the staff in a hospice is not so much to treat the client as it is just to be with the client. A client's dignity is always maintained; often more attention is paid to appearance and personal grooming than to medical tests. Hospice staff members also

As discussed in the text, creating a final scenario is something most people desire but many people are unable to accomplish. When you think about it, developing a good final scenario entails considering all the developmental forces.

Biological forces are apparent because one usually has a terminal disease when one begins creating a final scenario. If the condition is genetic, one may feel concern about one's children or other relatives and think about the chances that they may end up with the same disorder. Biological forces may also come into play in various treatment options,

such as chemotherapy or medication for pain management.

Psychological forces also are apparent. The anxiety one feels about dying and the feelings one has toward various family members and friends remind us that psychological ties are very strong. Our cognitive abilities may allow us to understand fully the situation we are in and the fact that we are terminally ill. How we decide to cope with these issues influences the decisions we make about our course of treatment and the options we want to exercise at the end of our life.

Sociocultural forces influence our choices as well. What our ethnic group or culture teaches us about death

influences how we conceptualize what happens to us when we die, what type of funeral (if any) we have, and how our survivors express their grief.

Finally, life-cycle forces color how we feel about dying. The younger we are, the more likely we are to feel cheated and concerned about our survivors. Also, the younger we are the more likely it is that health care professionals will exert more effort in trying to find an appropriate treatment. Our age at death also affects how our survivors grieve.

Taken together, the developmental forces influence us throughout our lives, even at the time of death.

---

provide a great deal of support to the client's family. At inpatient hospices visiting hours are unrestricted, and families are strongly encouraged to take part in the client's care (VandenBos et al., 1982).

Researchers have documented important differences between inpatient hospices and hospitals (Kastenbaum, 1999). Hospice clients are more mobile, less anxious, and less depressed; spouses visit hospice clients more often and participate more in their care; and hospice staff members are perceived as more accessible. In addition, Walsh and Cavanaugh (1984) showed that most hospice clients who were in hospitals before coming to a hospice strongly preferred the care at the hospice.

Although the hospice is a valuable alternative for many people, it may not be appropriate for everyone. Most people who select hospice are suffering from cancer, AIDS, or a progressive neurological condition (most often amyotrophic lateral sclerosis, also known as Lou Gehrig's disease; Kastenbaum, 1999). Other disorders may necessitate treatments or equipment not available at hospices, and some people may find that a hospice does not meet their needs or fit with

their personal beliefs. Walsh and Cavanaugh (1984) found that the perceived needs of hospice clients, their families, and the staff did not always coincide. In particular, the staff and family members emphasized pain management, whereas many clients wanted more attention paid to personal issues. The important point from this study is that the staff and family members may need to ask clients what they need more often rather than making assumptions about what they need.

How do people decide to explore the hospice option? Kastenbaum (1999) lists six key considerations:

Is the person completely informed about the nature and prognosis of his or her condition? Full knowledge and the ability to communicate with health care personnel is essential to understand what hospice has to offer.

What options are available at this point in the progress of the person's disease? Knowing about all available treatment options is essential. Exploring treatment options also requires health care professionals to be aware of the latest approaches and willing to disclose them.

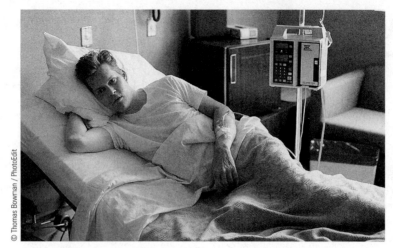

Hospice is an end-of-life care option that focuses mainly on relieving pain and helping the person die a good death.

What are the person's expectations, fears, and hopes? Some older adults, like Jean, remember or have heard stories about people who suffered greatly at the end of their lives. This can produce anxiety about one's own death. Similarly, fears of becoming dependent play an important role in a person's decision making. Discovering and discussing these anxieties helps clarify options.

How well do the people in the person's social network communicate with each other? Talking about death in many families is still taboo (Book, 1996). In others, intergenerational communication is difficult or impossible. Even in families with good communication, the pending death of a loved relative is difficult. As a result, the dying person may have difficulty expressing his or her wishes. The decision to explore the hospice option is best made when it is discussed openly.

Are family members available to participate actively in terminal care? Hospice relies on family members to provide much of the care, which is supplemented by professionals and volunteers. We saw in Chapter 11 that being a primary caregiver can be highly stressful. Having a family member who is willing to accept this responsibility is essential for the hospice option to work.

Is a high-quality hospice care program available? Hospice programs are not uniformly good.

As with any health care provider, patients and family members must investigate the quality of local hospice programs before making a choice. The Hospice Foundation of America provides excellent material for evaluating a hospice program; its home page is listed at the end of the chapter.

Hospice provides an important end-of-life option for many terminally ill people and their families. Moreover, the supportive follow-up services they provide are used by many surviving family and friends. Most important, the success of the hospice option has had important influences on traditional health care. For example, much discussion occurred in the American Medical Association in 1999 about putting more emphasis on pain management.

Despite the importance of the hospice option for end-of-life decisions, terminally ill older adults cannot benefit from it unless two barriers are overcome (Kastenbaum, 1999): family reluctance to face the reality of terminal illness and participate in the decision-making process; and physician reluctance to approve hospice care for patients until very late in the terminal process, thereby depriving them of the supportive benefits they may have otherwise received.

As the end of life approaches, the most important thing to keep in mind is that the dying person has the right to state-of-the-art approaches to treatment and pain management. Irrespective of the choice of traditional health care or hospice, the wishes of the dying person should be honored, and family members must participate.

CONCEPT CHECKS

1. What is a final scenario?
2. What are the primary characteristics of a hospice?

SURVIVORS: THE GRIEVING PROCESS

LEARNING OBJECTIVES

- How are deaths at different ages viewed?
- What are the characteristics and developmental patterns of normal grief?
- What are the characteristics of abnormal grief?
- What effects do different types of loss have on grief?

After 67 years of marriage, Bertha lost her husband recently. At age 90, Bertha knew that neither she nor her husband was likely to live much longer, but the death was a shock just the same. Bertha thinks about him much of the time and often finds herself making decisions on the basis of "what John would have done" in the same situation.

Each of us suffers many losses over a lifetime. Whenever we lose someone close to us through death or other separation, like Bertha we experience bereavement, grief, and mourning. **Bereavement** *is the state or condition caused by loss through death.* **Grief** *is the sorrow, hurt, anger, guilt, confusion, and other feelings that arise after a loss.* **Mourning** *concerns the ways in which we express our grief.* For example, in some ethnic groups you can tell that a woman is bereaved and in mourning because she wears a black dress and a veil. Mourning is highly influenced by culture. For some, mourning may involve wearing black, attending funerals, and observing an official period of grief;

for others, it means drinking, wearing white, and marrying the deceased spouse's sibling. Grief corresponds to the emotional reactions after loss, whereas mourning is the culturally approved behavioral manifestations of those feelings. Even though mourning rituals may be fairly standard within a culture, how people grieve varies, as we will see next. We will also see how Bertha's reactions are fairly typical of most people.

In this section we examine how people deal with loss. Because the grieving process is affected by the circumstances surrounding the death, we must first differentiate between expected and unexpected loss. Next, because grief can be expressed in many ways, the differences between normal and abnormal reactions are explored. Finally, how well we cope with the death of a loved one is related to the kind of relationship that existed. Thus, we compare grieving after different kinds of loss.

A Life-Span View of Loss through Death

The feelings associated with death and dying are personal and powerful. Yet we know from Chapter 1 that life-cycle forces are important ingredients in understanding the richness of any developmental issue. So it is with feelings associated with dying.

Think for a minute how you would react to the news that each of the following people had died in a plane crash: a young girl, a recent college graduate, a middle-aged electrical worker, and an old man. How would you feel? Would your feelings be different for the different people? Let's consider how the age of a dying person changes the way death is viewed and experienced.

Intellectually, we realize that dying is not something that happens only to one age group. But most of us tend not to think about it because we are used to associating dying with old age. Death knows no age limits, yet one person's death often seems more acceptable than another's (Kastenbaum, 1985, 1999). The death of a 95-year-old woman is considered natural; she has lived a long, full life. But the death of an infant is considered a tragedy. Whether or not such feelings are justified, they point to the fact that death is viewed and experienced differently depending on age.

Children die from acute diseases and accidents, young adults die mainly from accidents, and the old die mainly from chronic diseases such as heart disease and cancer (National Center for Health Statistics, 1999). Because people of different ages die in different ways, their dying processes differ (Kalish, 1984), a point not usually made by theorists. Most notably, older adults' dying trajectory is longer, and they are more likely to die in isolation than any other age group (Kastenbaum, 1999). From the perspective of Corr's theory, older adults have a more difficult time successfully completing the tasks of dying.

Many of the concerns of dying people have to do with their age (Kalish, 1987). The most obvious difference comes in the extent to which people feel cheated, or possibly angry in Kübler-Ross's approach. Younger people feel cheated in that they are losing what they might attain; older adults feel cheated in that they are losing what they have. Beyond these general differences, not much is known about how people of various ages differ in how they face death.

One important factor that affects dying older adults is that their deaths are viewed by the community as less tragic than the deaths of younger people (Kalish & Reynolds, 1976; Kastenbaum, 1985). Consequently, older adults receive less intense life-saving treatment and are perceived as less valuable and not as worthy of a large investment of time, money, or energy. "The terminally ill aged may be as helpless as a child, but they seldom arouse tenderness" (Weisman, 1972, p. 144). Many dying older adults reside in long-term care facilities, where contacts with family and friends are fewer. Older adults, especially the ill and the frail, offer less to their communities. Consequently, when their death occurs, the emotional pain is not as great because the resulting losses are viewed as less significant and meaningful (Kalish, 1987; Kastenbaum, 1999).

This does not mean that the deaths of older adults are not felt deeply by family and friends. On the contrary, the loss is felt throughout the generations (Anderson, 1997). It is simply that society at large puts less emotional value on the death of older people than on children and young adults. Let's examine how people deal with the loss.

When we consider the different meanings of loss, we are in a better position to understand and explain how grief and bereavement occur. Bonanno and Kaltman (1999) provide an innovative approach in which they view bereavement from several perspectives: the context of the loss, the subjective meaning of the loss, changing representations of the lost relationship, and coping and emotional regulation.

The impact of a particular loss depends critically on its context. We have already seen that the age of the person who died is important. But other factors also matter, including gender, income level, expectedness of the loss, previous experience with loss, perceived social support, and ethnicity. How people construe meaning from the loss matters as well. Is the loss viewed as a blessing? A challenge from God? A devastating punishment? How people appraise the situation strongly influences the meaning people place on the loss. As time goes on, people often change their descriptions of the relationship they had with the deceased person. A common finding is that people tend to view a relationship much more positively after the loss than before, which provides the basis in some cultures for ancestor worship. Finally, how people select coping strategies to deal with their emotions is a very important aspect of grief, as we will see next. In sum, how people experience bereavement is a complex process that is shaped by many influences.

Experiencing Grief

How do people grieve? What do they experience? Perhaps you already have a good idea about the answers to these questions from your own experience. If so, you already know that the process of grieving is complicated and personal. Just as there is no right way to die, there is no right way to grieve. Recognizing that there are plenty of individual differences, we consider these patterns in this section.

The grieving process often is described as reflecting many themes and issues that people confront (Attig, 1996; Stroebe et al., 1996, 2001). Like the process of dying, grieving does not have clearly de-marcated stages through which one passes in a neat sequence. When someone close to us dies, we must reorganize our lives, establish new patterns of behavior, and redefine relationships with family and friends. Indeed, Attig (1996) considers grief to be the process by which we relearn the world.

Unlike bereavement, over which we have no control, grief involves choices in coping (Attig, 1996). From this perspective, grief is an active process in which a person must do several things (Worden, 1991):

Acknowledge the reality of the loss. We must overcome the temptation to deny the reality of our loss, fully and openly acknowledge it, and realize that it affects every aspect of our lives.

Work through the emotional turmoil. We must find effective ways to confront and express the complete range of emotions we feel after the loss and must not avoid or repress them.

Adjust to the environment where the deceased is absent. We must define new patterns of living that adjust appropriately and meaningfully to the fact that the deceased is not present.

Loosen ties to the deceased. We must free ourselves from the bonds of the deceased to reengage with our social network. This means finding effective ways to say goodbye.

The notion that grief is an active coping process emphasizes that survivors must come to terms with the physical world of things, places, and events as well as our spiritual place in the world; the interpersonal world of interactions with family and friends, the dead, and, in some cases, God; and aspects of inner selves and our personal experiences (Attig, 1996). Bertha, the woman in the vignette, is in the middle of this process. Even the matter of deciding what to do with the deceased's personal effects can be part of this active coping process (Attig, 1996).

In considering grief, we must avoid making several mistakes. First, grieving is a highly individual experience. The process that works well for one person may not be the best for someone else. Second, we must not underestimate the amount of time people need to deal with the various issues. To a casual ob-

When a loved one dies unexpectedly, the grief associated with that death can be especially difficult.

server, it may appear that a survivor is "back to normal" after a few weeks. Actually, it takes much longer to resolve the complex emotional issues that are faced during bereavement (Attig, 1996; Stroebe et al., 1996). Researchers and therapists alike agree that a person needs at least 1 year after the loss to begin recovery, and 2 years is not uncommon.

Finally, *recovery* may be a misleading term. It is probably more accurate to say that we learn to live with our loss rather than that we recover from it (Attig, 1996). The impact of the loss of a loved one lasts a very long time, perhaps for the rest of one's life. Recognizing these aspects of grief makes it easier to know what to say and do for bereaved people. Among the most useful things are to simply let the person know that you are sorry for his or her loss, are there for support, and mean what you say.

EXPECTED VERSUS UNEXPECTED DEATH. When the death of a loved one is expected, people respond differently than when the death is unexpected. When death is anticipated, people go through a period of anticipatory grief before the death (Attig, 1996). This supposedly buffers the impact of the loss when it does come and facilitates recovery. The opportunity for anticipatory grieving results in a lower likelihood of psychological problems such as depression 1 year after the death of a spouse (Ball, 1976–1977), greater acceptance by parents after the death of a child

(Binger et al., 1969), and more rapid recovery of effective functioning and subsequent happiness (Glick et al., 1974). However, anticipating the death of someone close produces great stress in itself (Attig, 1996; Norris & Murrell, 1987). Caregivers of patients with Alzheimer's disease, for example, show a decline in feelings of anticipatory grief during the middle stages of caregiving, only to have these feelings increase in intensity later (Ponder & Pomeroy, 1996).

The reasons why recovery from anticipated deaths is sometimes quicker and sometimes not are not yet fully understood. We know that the long-term effects of stressful events generally are less problematic if they are expected, so the same principle probably holds for death. Perhaps it is helpful that there is an opportunity to envision life without the dying person and a chance to make appropriate arrangements. In practicing, we may realize that we need support, may feel lonely and scared, and may take steps to get ourselves ready. Moreover, if we recognize that we are likely to have certain feelings, they may be easier to understand and deal with when they come.

Also, an anticipated death often is less mysterious (Attig, 1996). Most of the time, we understand why (e.g., from what disease) the person died. An unexpected death leaves us with many questions: Why *my* loved one? Why now? Survivors may feel vulnerable; what happened to their loved one could just as easily happen to them. Understanding the real reason why someone dies makes adjustment easier.

These findings do not mean that people who experience the anticipated death of a loved one do not grieve. Indeed, one study revealed that widows whose husbands had been ill for at least 1 month before their deaths grieved just as intensely as did widows whose husbands died unexpectedly, as Figure 13-2 shows (Hill et al., 1988). In fact, widows who anticipated the deaths of their husbands had greater levels of grief 6 months after the death than did widows whose husbands died unexpectedly. Similarly, African American and European American widows whose husbands died of natural causes showed more distress than widows whose husbands died due to violence (Kitson, 2000). The knowledge that one's spouse will die soon does not necessarily make the feelings of loss any easier to handle in the long run. It

FIGURE 13.2 Comparison of grief intensity in widows whose husbands' death was expected and unexpected.

may be that the key to understanding anticipatory grief is that the advance warning of a loss per se is not as important as reconstructing meaning in one's life after the loss occurs (Fulton et al., 1996).

NORMAL GRIEF REACTIONS. The feelings experienced during grieving are intense, which not only makes it difficult to cope but also can make a person question her or his own reactions. The feelings involved usually include sadness, denial, anger, loneliness, and guilt. These feelings are summarized in the following list (Vickio et al., 1990). Take a minute to read through them to see whether they agree with what you might expect.

Disbelief

Sadness

Guilt

Confusion

Loneliness

Happiness

Denial

Anger

Fear

Helplessness

CHAPTER 13

Acceptance

Lack of enthusiasm

Shock

Hatred

Anxiety

Emptiness

Relief

Absence of emotion

Many authors call the psychological side of coming to terms with bereavement **grief work.** This notion fits well with the earlier discussion of grief as active coping (Attig, 1996). Even without personal experience of the death of close family members, people recognize the need to give survivors time to deal with their many feelings. One study asked college students to describe the feelings they thought were typically experienced by a person who had lost particular loved ones (such as a parent, child, sibling, friend). The students were well aware of the need for grief work, recognized the need for at least a year to do it, and were very sensitive to the range of emotions and behaviors demonstrated by the bereaved (Vickio et al., 1990).

Although the concept of grief work has dominated the literature on bereavement for several decades, research support for it is weak (Bonanno & Kaltman, 1999). A better approach is to view grief from the multidimensional approach presented earlier, in which the context, meaning, representation, and coping perspectives are considered.

After the death of a loved one, dates that have personal significance may reintroduce feelings of grief. For example, holidays such as Thanksgiving or birthdays that were spent with the deceased person may be difficult times. The actual anniversary of the death can be especially troublesome. *An* **anniversary reaction** *is the changes in behavior related to feelings of sadness on this date.* Personal experience and research show that recurring feelings of sadness or other examples of the anniversary reaction are very common in normal grief (Attig, 1996; Rosenblatt, 1996).

GRIEF OVER TIME. Most research on how people react to the death of a loved one is cross-sectional. However, some work has been done to examine how people continue grieving many years after the loss. Rosenblatt (1996) reports that people still felt the effects of the deaths of family members 50 years after the event. The depth of the emotions over the loss of loved ones never totally went away; people still cried and felt sad when discussing the loss despite the length of time that had passed.

Norris and Murrell (1987) conducted a longitudinal study of older adults' grief work; three interviews were conducted before the death and one after. The fascinating results of their research are described in more detail in the How Do We Know? feature. The results of this study fit nicely with the earlier discussion of expected and unexpected death. They also have important implications for interventions. That is, interventions aimed at reducing stress or promoting health may be more effective if performed before the death. Additionally, because health problems increased only among those in the bereaved group who felt no stress before the death, it may be that the stress felt before the death is a product of anticipating it. Lundin (1984) also found that health problems increased only for those experiencing sudden death.

EFFECTS OF NORMAL GRIEF ON ADULTS' HEALTH. Many people have assumed that losing a close loved one must have obvious negative effects on the health of the survivor, especially if the survivor is an older adult. As the Norris and Murrell study showed, however, such health effects are not inevitable.

Additional research supports this point (Perkins & Harris, 1990). Middle-aged adults are most likely to report physical health problems after bereavement; younger and older adults report few health problems. Younger adults may be able to deal with their losses because they are better equipped overall to handle stress. Older adults have more experience with such losses and anticipate them, and they may draw on their background to cope physically. In contrast, middle-aged adults have less experience, and they are also in the midst of dealing with their own mortality. As a result, the loss of a close family member is an emotionally unsettling reminder of their own fate (Perkins & Harris, 1990).

Who were the investigators, and what was the aim of the study? What happens to a family that experiences the death of a loved one? Norris and Murrell (1987) sought to answer this question by tracking families before and after bereavement.

How did the investigators measure the topic of interest? As part of a very large normative longitudinal study, they conducted detailed interviews approximately every 6 months. The researchers used a variety of instruments to obtain extensive information on physical health, including functional abilities and specific ailments, psychological

distress, and family stress. The psychological distress measure tapped symptoms of depression. The family stress measure assessed such things as new serious illness of a family member, having a family member move in, additional family responsibilities, new family conflict, and new marital conflict.

Who were the participants in the study? Sixty-three older adults in families experiencing the death of an immediate family member were compared with 387 older adults in families who had not experienced such a death to document the extra stress people feel as a result of grief.

What was the design of the study? Norris and Murrell used a longitudinal design and assessed people every 6 months, from 18 months before bereavement to 12 months after bereavement.

Were there ethical concerns in the study? Like all researchers who study bereavement, Norris and Murrell needed to be sensitive to people's feelings and monitor their participants for signs of abnormal reactions.

What were the results? Among bereaved families, overall family stress increased before the death and then decreased. The level of stress

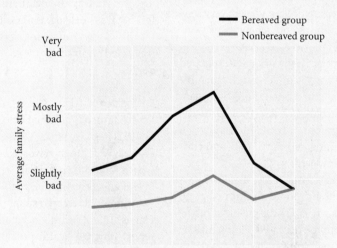

North & Murrell, 1987.

FIGURE 13.3   Average level of family stress of bereaved and nonbereaved older adults.

Source: Norris, F. N., & Murrell, S. A. (1987). Older adult family stress and adaptation before and after bereavement. *Journal of Gerontology, 42,* 609.

experienced by these families was highest in the period right around the death. Moreover, bereavement was the only significant predictor of family stress, meaning that the anticipation and experience of bereavement caused stress.

Even more interesting were the findings concerning the relationship between health and stress. As shown in Figure 13-3, bereaved people reported significantly higher levels of family stress than nonbereaved people. However, as shown in Figure 13-4, bereaved people reporting prior stress showed a significant drop in physical symptoms 6 months after the death; bereaved people reporting no prior stress reported a slight increase. The net result was that both groups ended up with about the same level of physical symptoms 6 months after bereavement.

What did the investigators conclude? Norris and Murrell described two major implications. First, bereavement does not appear to cause poor health; the bereaved groups were not very different from the group of nonbereaved people in nonstressful families. Second, bereavement appears to increase psychological distress substantially. In sum, marked changes in psychological distress after bereavement are normal, but marked changes in physical health are not.

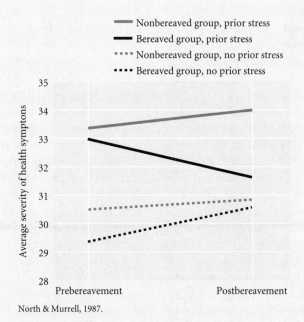

North & Murrell, 1987.

FIGURE 13.4   **Number of health symptoms reported 6 months after a loss as a function of stress level before the loss.**

Source: Norris, F. N., & Murrell, S. A. (1987). Older adult family stress and adaptation before and after bereavement. *Journal of Gerontology, 42,* 610.

Abnormal Grief Reactions

Not everyone is able to cope with grief well and begin rebuilding a life. Sometimes the feelings of hurt, loneliness, and guilt are so overwhelming that they become the focus of the survivor's life to such an extent that there is never any closure and the grief continues to interfere indefinitely with one's ability to function. Thus, what distinguishes normal from abnormal grief is not the kind of reaction but rather its intensity and duration (Schulz, 1985).

Overall, the most common manifestation of abnormal grief is excessive guilt and self-blame (Anderson, 1996). In some people, guilt results in a disruption of everyday routines and a diminished ability to function. People begin to make judgment errors, may reach a state of agitated depression, may experience problems sleeping or eating, and may have intense recurring thoughts about the deceased person. Many of these people seek professional help voluntarily or are referred by concerned family members or friends. Unfortunately, the long-term prognosis for people suffering abnormal grief responses is not good unless they obtain professional help (Schulz, 1985). The most common problem is depression, which can become severe and chronic. Other problems include social withdrawal, with a resulting loss of the person's social network.

How long intense grief must continue before it is considered abnormal is a matter of subjective judgment. As we have seen, several research studies indicate that it takes at least 1 year for survivors to begin to move forward with their lives, and in many cases it may take longer. There are cultural variations in the process of grief that must be respected (Anderson, 1996). Consequently, clinicians tend to suspect that the person's grief is interfering with his or her daily life if intense grief reactions are still present more than 2 years after the loss. However, such judgments must be made on a case-by-case basis; no set period of time is used as a firm criterion.

Types of Loss and Grief

Consider the following deaths from cancer: an adolescent, a middle-aged mother, and an older man. Our reaction to each of them is different, even though all of them died of the same disease. The way we feel when someone dies is partially determined by the age of that person. Our society tends to view some deaths as more tragic or as easier to accept than others. Even though we know that this approach has no research support, people nevertheless act as if it did. For example, people typically consider the death of a child as extremely traumatic unless it occurred at birth. If one's parent dies when one is young, the loss is considered greater than if one is middle-aged and the parent is old.

The point is that our society makes judgments about how much grief one should have after different types of loss. We have noted that death is always a traumatic event for survivors. But unfortunately the survivors are not always allowed to express their grief over a period of time or even to talk about their feelings. These judgments that society makes impose arbitrary time limits on the grieving process, despite the fact that almost all the evidence we have indicates that we should not do that.

We must also recognize that the customs and traditions we observe in American society do not reflect the views of cultures earlier in history or other cultures around the world (Jecker & Schneiderman, 1994). For example, some cultures throughout history have practiced infanticide when they have been unable to support their children. Keeping these cultural differences in mind, let's consider three types of loss and see how these judgments occur.

DEATH OF ONE'S PARENT. Most parents die after their children have grown. But whenever it occurs, parental death hurts. We lose not only a key relationship but also an important psychological buffer between us and death. We, the children, are next in line. Indeed, when one's parent dies, it often leads the surviving children to redefine the meaning of parenthood and the importance of time together (Malinak et al., 1979).

For most people, the death of a parent deprives them of many important things: a source of guidance and advice, a source of love, and a model for their own parenting style. It may also deny them the opportunity to improve aspects of their relationship with a parent. The loss of a parent is perceived as very significant; society allows us to grieve for a reasonable length of time.

In the context of our earlier discussion of anticipated and unanticipated deaths, how do people grieve when their parents die after a stay in a long-term care facility? In a study of 84 adults whose parents had died during a stay in a nursing home, Pruchno and colleagues (1995) found that the majority of the people were upset about the death, even though it was anticipated. Even though all participants experienced partial grief during their parents' stay in the nursing home, these researchers found that the greater the stress experienced by the adult before his or her parent's death, the more difficult the bereavement process. This is especially true for participants who viewed the nursing home placement as negative; these people are sadder and take less comfort in memories of their deceased parent than people who view the nursing home placement as the right thing to do. Not surprisingly, the greater the mental impairment of the parent before death, the more relief the adult children felt after the death. Thus, even for adult children for whom the death of a parent is anticipated, the breaking of the tie between parent and child inevitably results in emotional sadness and upset, as well as feelings of separation, relief, and a loss of a buffer against death. Nevertheless, after one's parent has died, the memories of the relationship serve as a comfort for many people.

DEATH OF ONE'S CHILD. The death of a child generally is perceived as a great tragedy because children are not supposed to die before their parents. It is as if the natural order of things has been violated. The loss is es-

The death of one's child is extremely traumatic for most parents.

pecially traumatic if it occurs suddenly, as in sudden infant death syndrome or an automobile accident. But parents of terminally ill children still suffer a great deal, even with the benefit of anticipatory grieving. Mourning is always intense, and some parents never recover or attempt to reconcile the death of their child. Even many years after the loss, time does not seem to diminish parents' grief or their willingness to relinquish their attachment to the deceased child (Malkinson & Bar-Tur, 1999).

One of the most overlooked losses is the loss of a child through stillbirth, miscarriage, abortion, or neonatal death (Borg & Lasker, 1981). Attachment to one's child begins prenatally. His or her death hurts deeply, so to contend that the loss of a child before or at birth is not as tragic as the loss of an older child makes little sense. Yet parents who experience this type of loss are expected to recover very quickly and often are subjected to unfeeling comments if these societal expectations are not met. However, research indicates that parents experience much grief. For example, Thomas and Striegel (1994–1995) found that because both mothers and fathers bond with the fetus or baby during the early stages of pregnancy, they both grieve for their loss, but in different ways. Mothers grieve most for their lost child, whereas fathers grieve more for their wives. The most important factor in coping with the loss was the couple's support and reliance on each other.

Finally, grandparents' feelings can be overlooked. They, too, feel the loss when their grandchild dies. Moreover, they grieve not only for the grandchild but also for their own child's loss (Hamilton, 1978). Grandparents must also be included in whatever rituals or support groups the family chooses.

DEATH OF ONE'S SPOUSE. More has been written about the death of a spouse than about any other type of loss. It clearly represents a deep personal loss, especially when the couple had a very long and close relationship. In a very real way, when one's spouse dies, a part of oneself dies, too. Bertha, whom we met in the vignette, provides a good example of these feelings; her reaction is typical of bereaved partners in long-term relationships.

The death of a spouse is different from other losses. There is pressure from society to mourn for a period of time. Typically, this pressure is manifested if the survivor begins to show interest in finding another mate before an acceptable period of mourning has passed. Although Americans no longer define the length of such periods, many feel that about a year is appropriate. That such pressure and negative commentary usually do not accompany other losses is another indication of the seriousness with which most people take the death of a spouse.

Another important point concerning the loss of one's spouse involves the age of the survivor. Young adult spouses tend to show more intense grief reactions immediately after the death than do older spouses. However, the situation 18 months later is reversed. At that time, older spouses report more grief than do younger spouses (Sanders, 1980–1981). Indeed, older bereaved spouses may grieve for at least 30 months (Thompson et al., 1991). The differences seem to be related to four factors: The death of a young spouse is more unexpected, there are fewer same-aged role models for young widows or widowers, the dimensions of grief vary with age, and the opportunities for remarriage are greater for younger survivors. Older widows anticipate fewer years of life and prefer to cherish the memory of their deceased spouse rather than attempt a new marriage (Raphael, 1983).

Gender also matters (Lee et al., 2001). Widowhood is more depressing for widowers than for widows. Specifically, prior to bereavement, married men are much less depressed than married women. After bereavement, widowers and widows are comparably depressed.

Some longitudinal studies have examined the grief process in reaction to the death of a spouse. Dimond and colleagues (1987) found that social support played a significant role in the outcome of the grieving process during the first 2 years after the death of a spouse. In particular, it is the quality of the support system, rather than the number of friends, that is particularly important.

Other longitudinal research shows that the degree to which the surviving spouse was highly dependent on the deceased spouse predicts adjustment following bereavement (Carr et al., 2000). Widowed spouses who were highly dependent show higher anxiety and yearned for their deceased spouses more than nondependent widowed spouses.

One interesting aspect of spousal bereavement concerns how the surviving spouse rates the marriage. Futterman and colleagues (1990) had bereaved older adults rate their relationships at 2, 12, and 30 months after the death of their spouses. Nonbereaved older adults were also studied as a comparison group. Bereaved widows and widowers rated their marriage more positively than nonbereaved older adults, indicating a positive bias in remembering a marriage lost through death. However, bereaved spouses' ratings were related to depression in an interesting way. The more depressed the bereaved spouse, the more positively the marriage was rated. In contrast, depressed nonbereaved spouses rated their marriage negatively. This result suggests that the loss of a positive relationship through death, as well as its consequences (for instance, loss of other social contacts), is viewed as a negative outcome.

COMPARING TYPES OF LOSS. Little research has been done comparing people's grief reactions to different types of loss. In general, bereaved parents are the most depressed and have more grief reactions in general than either bereaved spouses or adult children (Owen et al., 1982). Other research shows that the intensity of depression in a bereaved person after loss is related to the perceived importance of the relationship with the deceased person (Murphy, 1988). Survivors are more often and more seriously depressed after the death of someone particularly important to them.

One study compared the grief reactions of 255 middle-aged women who had experienced the loss of a spouse, a parent, or a child within the preceding 2 years. Bereaved mothers reported significantly higher levels of depression than widows, who in turn reported significantly greater depression than adult children. In fact, more than 60% of the bereaved mothers had depression scores in the moderate to severe depression range (Leahy, 1993).

Care must be exercised in interpreting these data. As noted earlier, there are many aspects of grief other than depression. Until researchers study these other aspects, it is premature to conclude that some types of loss always result in greater grief than others. All we can say in the meantime is that after some types of loss, some people report more symptoms of depression at more serious levels.

CONCEPT CHECKS

1. What are the major components of a life-span view of loss through death?

2. What are grief and bereavement, and how do people experience them?

3. What is abnormal grief?

4. How do people cope with different types of loss?

PUTTING IT ALL TOGETHER

In this chapter we considered the last chapter of life: death. We saw that people like Ernesto and Paulina struggle with ethical and moral decisions about ending the life of someone in severe pain. Like Ricardo, people experience many different feelings when they learn they are going to die. Jean is like many people who want to die with dignity and seek out appropriate alternatives to traditional health care. After people who were very close to us die, we may find that we are like Bertha and think about the advice they would have given to us. Of all the topics we considered in this text, none is more personal than death. Writing the final chapter can be up to us, if we have the desire to do so.

Summary

DEFINITIONS AND ETHICAL ISSUES

Sociocultural Definitions of Death

Different cultures have different meanings for death. Some of the meanings in Western culture include images, statistics, events, a state of being, an analogy, a mystery, a boundary, a thief of meaning, a basis for fear and anxiety, and a reward or punishment.

Legal and Medical Definitions

Three legal criteria of death have been proposed: clinical death, brain death, and cortical death. Brain death, which includes eight specific criteria, is the definition used most often in the United States and other industrialized societies. If brainstem functioning continues after cortical function stops, the person is said to be in a persistent vegetative state.

Ethical Issues

Bioethics examines the interface between values and technological advances. Two types of euthanasia are distinguished. Active euthanasia is deliberately ending someone's life through some sort of intervention or action. Passive euthanasia is ending someone's life by withholding treatment.

Personal preferences for medical intervention can be communicated through a living will or a durable power of attorney.

Thinking about Death: Personal Aspects

A Life Course Approach to Dying

Young adults report a sense of being cheated by death. Cognitive developmental level is important for understanding how young adults view death.

Middle-aged adults begin to confront their own mortality and undergo a change in their sense of time lived and time until death.

Older adults are more accepting of death.

Dealing with One's Own Death

Kübler-Ross's theory includes five stages: denial, anger, bargaining, depression, and acceptance. Some people do not progress through all these stages, and some people move through them at different rates. People may be in more than one stage at a time and do not necessarily go through them in order.

A contextual theory of dying emphasizes the tasks a dying person must face. Four dimensions of these tasks have been identified: bodily needs, psychological security, interpersonal attachments, and spiritual energy and hope. A contextual theory would be able to incorporate differences in reasons people die and the places people die.

Death Anxiety

Most people exhibit some degree of anxiety about death, even though it is difficult to define and measure. Individual difference variables include gender, religiosity, age, ethnicity, and occupation. Death anxiety may have some benefits.

The main ways death anxiety is shown are by avoiding death (e.g., refusing to go to funerals) and deliberately challenging it (e.g., engaging in dangerous sports). Other ways of showing it include changing lifestyles, dreaming and fantasizing, using humor, displacing fears, and becoming a death professional.

Several ways to deal with anxiety exist: living life to the fullest, personal reflection, and education. Death education has been shown to be extremely effective.

End-of-Life Issues

Creating a Final Scenario

Managing the final aspects of life, after-death disposition of the body and memorial services, and distribution of assets are important end-of-life issues. Making choices about what people do and do not want done constitutes making a final scenario.

The Hospice Option

The goal of a hospice is to maintain the quality of life and to manage the pain of terminally ill patients. Hospice clients typically have cancer, AIDS, or a progressive neurological disorder. Family members tend to stay involved in the care of hospice clients.

Survivors: The Grieving Process

Bereavement is the state or condition caused by loss through death. Grief is the sorrow, hurt, anger, guilt, confusion, or other feelings that arise after a loss. Mourning concerns the way in which we express our grief.

A Life-Span View of Loss through Death

Society assigns different values on the death of people of different ages. The older the person is at death, the less tragic it is perceived to be.

Experiencing Grief

Grief is an active process in which a person must acknowledge the reality of the loss, work through the emotional turmoil, adjust to the environment where the deceased is absent, and loosen ties to the deceased. How these are accomplished is an individual matter.

Grief is equally intense in both expected and unexpected death but may begin before the actual death when the patient has a terminal illness. Unexpected death often is called high-anxiety death; expected death often is called low-anxiety death. Expected deaths usually are less mysterious than unexpected deaths.

Normal grief reactions include sorrow, sadness, denial, guilt, and religious beliefs. Grief often returns around the anniversary of the death. Longitudinal findings indicate that interventions to reduce stress relating to loss and promote health would be more effective if done before the death.

In general, experiencing the death of a loved one does not directly influence physical health. Middle-aged adults have the most difficult time dealing with grief. Poor copers tend to have low self-esteem before losing a loved one.

Abnormal Grief Reactions

Excessive guilt and self-blame are common signs of abnormal grief. Abnormal grief reactions typically are assessed in terms of how long feelings of grief last.

Types of Loss and Grief

The death of a parent reminds people of their own mortality and deprives them of a very important person in their lives.

The death of a child (including miscarriage and perinatal death) is thought to be the most traumatic type of loss.

Loss of a spouse is a great loss of a lover and companion. Bereaved spouses tend to have a positive bias about their marriage.

Review Questions

DEFINITIONS AND ETHICAL ISSUES

- What are the various sociocultural meanings of death?
- What are the three legal criteria for death?
- What are the criteria necessary for brain death?
- What is bioethics, and what kinds of issues does it deal with?

- What are the two types of euthanasia? How do they differ?

THINKING ABOUT DEATH: PERSONAL ASPECTS

- What is a life-span view of dying?
- How do cognitive development and issues at midlife influence feelings about death?
- Describe Kübler-Ross's theory of dying. How do people progress through the different feelings?
- What is necessary for creating a contextual theory of dying?
- What is death anxiety? What factors influence death anxiety?
- How do people demonstrate death anxiety?
- How do people learn to deal with death anxiety?

END-OF-LIFE ISSUES

- What are end-of-life issues?
- How do people create a final scenario?
- What is a hospice? How does hospice care differ from hospital care?

SURVIVORS: THE GRIEVING PROCESS

- What influences how people of different ages view death?
- What effects do expected and unexpected deaths have on the grieving process?
- What are the stages of grief? How long does grief usually last?
- What are the differences between normal and abnormal grief reactions? What age differences are there in grief reactions?
- How does the type of loss affect grief?

Integrating Concepts in Development

1. What effect do you think being at different levels of cognitive development has on people's thinking about death?

2. What parallels are there between the stages of dying and the experience of grief? Why do you think they may be similar?

3. How can we use the study of death, dying, bereavement, and grief to provide insights into the psychological development of people across adulthood?

Key Terms

active euthanasia Deliberately ending a person's life through an intervention or action.

anniversary reaction Feelings of sadness and loneliness on holidays, birthdays, and the anniversary of a loved one's death.

bereavement The state or condition caused by loss through death.

bioethics The study of the interaction between human values and technological advances in the health and life sciences.

brain death Definition of death based on eight criteria, including lack of brain function.

clinical death Definition of death based on lack of heartbeat and respiration.

end-of-life issues Management of the final phase of life, after-death disposition of the body and memorial services, and distribution of assets.

euthanasia Meaning "good death," the practice of allowing people who have a terminal illness to die.

final scenario Making one's choices about end-of-life issues known to others.

grief The feelings that arise after one suffers a loss.

grief work The psychological side of coming to terms with bereavement.

hospice An approach to assisting dying people that emphasizes pain management and death with dignity.

mourning The ways in which we express grief.

passive euthanasia Allowing a person to die by withholding an available treatment.

persistent vegetative state A state in which a person's brainstem is the only part of the brain that is functioning, a state from which the person does not recover.

Resources

Readings

Albom, M. (1997). *Tuesdays with Morrie.* New York: Doubleday. A moving account of the reconnection between a middle-aged man and his former teacher that includes both an excellent example of a final scenario and intergenerational transmission of wisdom. Easy reading.

Fulton, R., & Bendiksen, R. (Eds.). (1994). *Death and identity* (3rd ed.). Philadelphia: Charles Press. A collection of classic and original articles that take a life-span perspective. Easy to moderately difficult depending on the article.

Jaffe, C. (1997). *All kinds of love: Experiencing hospice.* Amityville, NY: Baywood. An excellent source of information about the philosophy and role of hospice. Easy reading.

Kushner, H. S. (1981). *When bad things happen to good people.* New York: Schocken. A classic book that is very thought provoking. This book was written by a rabbi after the death of his son. Easy reading, but take it slowly.

Nuland, S. B. (1994). *How we die: Reflections on life's final chapter.* New York: Knopf. A very important and informative book that provides an excellent discussion of what happens when people die. Great for dispelling myths about dying. Easy reading.

Taylor, N. (1993). *A necessary end.* New York: Nan A. Talese. A personal story of the author's coping with the death of his parents and his search for meaning. Easy reading.

Web Sites

The Hospice Foundation of America provides leadership in the development of hospices and the hospice philosophy. Its Web site has a variety of information about hospices and related resources. The home page can be found at http://www.hospicefoundation.org.

Choice in Dying is an organization that led the development of living wills in the late 1960s. Today it provides information and advocacy about complex end-of-life issues. The site contains information and resources on a variety of topics. Its home page can be found at http://www.choices/org.

The Compassionate Friends is a national organization dedicated to helping parents deal with the loss of a child. In addition to providing information and resources, the home page has a link to help you find a chapter in your area. The home page can be found at http://www.compassionatefriends.org.

Search Online with

InfoTrac College Edition

For more information on the topics in this chapter, explore InfoTrac College Edition, your online library. Go to http://www.infotrac-college.com/wadsworth and use the passcode that came on the card with your book. Try these search terms: bereavement, hospice care, grief, death, euthanasia.

REFERENCES

AARP. (1999a). *AARP/Modern Maturity sexuality survey: Summary of findings.* Online document available at the Web site http://www.aarp.org/mmaturity/sept_oct99/greatsex.html.

AARP. (1999b). *Surfing in cyberspace.* Online document available at the Web site http://www.aarp.org/ampie/res0799.html.

Abengozar, M. C., Bueno, B., & Vega, J. L. (1999). Intervention on attitudes toward death along the life span. *Educational Gerontology, 25,* 435–447.

Adams, C., Labouvie-Vief, G., Hakim-Larson, J., DeVoe, M., & Hayden, M. (1988). *Modes of thinking and problem solving: Developmental transitions from pre-adolescence to middle-adulthood.* Unpublished manuscript.

Adams, C., Labouvie-Vief, G., Hobart, C. J., & Dorosz, M. (1990). Adult age group differences in story recall style. *Journal of Gerontology: Psychological Sciences, 45,* P17–P27.

Adams, C., Smith, M. C., Gaden, C. P., & Perlmutter. (1994). *Memory in a storytelling context: A story recalled by young and old adults.* Unpublished manuscript.

Adams, C., Smith, M. C., Pasupathi, M., & Vitolo, L. (in press). Story recall and ageing: Does the listener make the difference? *Journal of Gerontology: Psychological Sciences.*

Adams, R. D. (1980). Morphological aspects of aging in the human nervous system. In J. E. Birren & R. B. Sloane (Eds.), *Handbook of mental health and aging* (pp. 149–160). Englewood Cliffs, NJ: Prentice Hall.

Adams, V. H., & Hummert, M. L. (in preparation). *African American stereotypes of older adults.*

Adelman, C. (1991). *Women at thirtysomething: Paradoxes of attainment.* Washington, DC: U.S. Department of Education, Office of Educational Research, Office of Research.

Adler, S., & Aranya, N. (1984). A comparison of the work needs, attitudes, and preferences of professional accounts at different career stages. *Journal of Vocational Behavior, 25,* 574–580.

Adler, W. H., & Nagel, J. E. (1994). Clinical immunology and aging. In W. R. Hazzard, E. L. Bierman, J. P. Blass, W. H. Ettinger, & J. B. Halter (Eds.), *Principles of geriatric medicine and gerontology* (3rd ed., pp. 67–75). New York: McGraw-Hill.

Adlersberg, M., & Thorne, S. (1990). Emerging from the chrysalis: Older women in transition. *Journal of Gerontological Social Work, 16,* 4–8.

Administration on Aging. (1999a). *A profile of older Americans: 1998.* Online document available at the Web site http://www.aoa.dhhs.gov/aoa/stats/profile/default.htm.

Administration on Aging. (1999b). *Number and percent of persons reporting problems with two or more activities of daily living (ADLs), by age, race, gender, poverty, living arrangements, region, and area of residence, 1994–1995.* Online document available at the Web site http://www.aoa.dhhs.gov/aoa/stats/Disabilities/2plusadls.html.

Albert, S. M. (1997). Assessing health-related quality of life in chronic care populations. *Journal of Mental Health and Aging, 3,* 101–118.

Albert, S. M. (1999). Assessing health-related quality of life in chronic care populations. *Journal of Mental Health and Aging, 5,* 101–118.

Aldersberg, M., & Thorne, S. (1990). Emerging from the chrysalis: Older women in transition. *Journal of Gerontological Social Work, 16,* 4–8.

Aldwin, C. M., & Gilmer, D. F. (1999). Immunity, disease processes, and optimal aging. In J. C. Cavanaugh & S. K. Whitbourne (Eds.), *Gerontology: Interdisciplinary perspectives* (pp. 123–154). New York: Oxford University Press.

Aldwin, C. M., Sutton, K. J., Chiara, G., & Spiro, A., III. (1996). Age differences in stress, coping, and appraisal: Findings from the Normative Aging Study. *Journal of Gerontology: Psychological Sciences, 51B,* P179–P188.

Aldwin, C. M., Sutton, K. J., & Lachman, M. (1996). The development of coping resources in adulthood. *Journal of Personality, 64,* 837–871.

Allaire, J. C., & Marsiske, M. (1999). Everyday cognition: Age and intellectual ability correlates. *Psychology and Aging, 14,* 627–644.

Allen, K. R., & Chin-Sang, V. (1990). A lifetime of work: The context and meanings of leisure for aging black women. *The Gerontologist, 30,* 734–740.

Allen, P. A., Madden, D. J., Groth, K. E., & Crozier, L. C. (1992). Impact of age, redundancy, and perpetual noise on visual search. *Journal of Gerontology, 47,* P69–P74.

Allen, P. A., Madden, D. J., & Slane, S. (1995). Visual world encoding and the effect of adult age and word frequency. In P. A. Allen & T. R. Bashore (Eds.), *Age differences in word and language processes* (pp. 30–71). Amsterdam: North-Holland.

Allen, P. A., Webber, T. A., & Madden, D. J. (1994). Adult age differences in attention: Filtering or selection? *Journal of Gerontology, 49,* P213–P222.

Allen-Burge, R., & Haley, W. E. (1997). Individual differences and surrogate medical decisions: Differing preferences for life-sustaining treatments. *Aging and Mental Health, 1,* 121–131.

Allen-Burge, R., Storandt, M., Kinscherf, D. A., & Rubin, E. H. (1994). Sex differences in the sensitivity of two self-report depression scales in older depressed inpatients. *Psychology and Aging, 9,* 443–445.

Alspaugh, M. E. L., Stephens, M. A. P., Townsend, A. L., Zarit, S. H., & Greene, R. (1999). Longitudinal patterns of risk for depression in dementia caregivers: Objective and subjective primary stress as predictors. *Psychology and Aging, 14,* 34–43.

Alwin, D. F. (1994). Aging, personality, and social change: The stability of individual differences over the adult life span. In D. L. Featherman, R. M. Lerner, & M. Perlmutter (Eds.), *Lifespan development and behavior* (Vol. 12, pp. 135–185). Hillsdale, NJ: Erlbaum.

Alzheimer's Association. (1999). *Statistics/prevalence.* Online document available at the Web site http://www.alz.org/facts/rstats.htm.

American Cancer Society. (1999a). *1999 Cancer facts and figures.* Online document available at the Web site http://www.cancer.org/media/fact99.html.

American Cancer Society. (1999b). *The prostate cancer resource center.* Online document available at the Web site http://www3.cancer.org/cancerinfo/res_home.asp?ct36.

American Cancer Society & National Comprehensive Cancer Network. (1999). *Prostate cancer: Treatment guidelines for patients* (Version 1, 1999). Online document available at the Web site http://www.cancer.org.

American Council on Education. (1997). Many college graduates participate in training courses to improve their job skills. *Higher Education and National Affairs, 46*(19), 3.

American Geriatrics Society Ethics Committee. (1996). Making treatment decisions for incapacitated older adults without advance directives. *Journal of the American Geriatrics Society, 44,* 986–987.

American Heart Association. (1998). *1999 Heart and stroke statistical update.* Dallas: Author.

American Heart Association. (1999). *Heart and stroke A–Z guide.* Online document available at the Web site http://www.americanheart.org.

American Lung Association. (1998). *Trends in chronic bronchitis and emphysema: Morbidity and mortality.* Online document available at the Web site http://www.lungusa.org/data/index.html.

American Psychiatric Association. (1994). *Diagnostic and statistical manual of mental disorders* (4th ed.). Washington, DC: Author.

Anderson, N. D., Craik, F. I. M., & Naveh-Benjamin, M. (1998). The attentional demands of encoding and retrieval in younger and older adults: I. Evidence from divided attention costs. *Psychology and Aging, 13,* 405–423.

Anderson, W. T. (1997). Dying and death in aging intergenerational families. In T. D. Hargrave & S. M. Hanna (Eds.), *The aging family* (pp. 270–291). New York: Brunner/Mazel.

Aneshensel, C. S., Pearlin, L. I., Mullan, J. T., Zarit, S. H., & Whitlach, C. J. (1995). *Profiles in caregiving: The unexpected career.* San Diego: Academic Press.

Anschutz, L., Camp, C. J., Markley, R. P., & Kramer, J. J. (1985). Maintenance and generalization of mnemonics for grocery shopping by older adults. *Experimental Aging Research, 11,* 157–160.

Anschutz, L., Camp, C. J., Markley, R. P., & Kramer, J. J. (1987). Remembering mnemonics: A three-year follow-up on the effects of mnemonic training in elderly adults. *Experimental Aging Research, 13,* 141–143.

Antonovsky, A., & Sagy, S. (1990). Confronting developmental tasks in the retirement transition. *The Gerontologist, 30,* 362–368.

Antonucci, T. C. (1985). Personal characteristics, social support, and social behavior. In R. H. Binstock & E. Shanas (Eds.), *Handbook of aging and the social sciences* (2nd ed., pp. 94–128). New York: Van Nostrand Reinhold.

Antonucci, T. C., Akiyama, H., & Lansford, J. E. (1998). Negative effects of close social relations. *Family Relations, 47,* 379–384.

Appleton, M., & Henschell, T. (1995). *At home with terminal illness: A family guide to hospice in the home.* Englewood Cliffs, NJ: Prentice-Hall.

Arbona, C. (1990). Career counseling research and Hispanics: A review of the literature. *Counseling Psychologist, 18,* 300–323.

Arbuckle, T. Y., Maag, U., Pushkar, D., & Chaikleson, J. S. (1998). Individual differences in trajectory of intellect development over 45 years of adulthood. *Psychology and Aging, 13,* 663–675.

Aryee, S. (1993). Dual-earner couples in Singapore: An examination of work and nonwork sources of their experienced burnout. *Human Relations, 46,* 1441–1468.

Aryee, S., & Luk, V. (1996). Work and nonwork influences on the career satisfaction of dual-earner couples. *Journal of Vocational Behavior, 49,* 38–52.

Ashman, R. D., Bishu, R. R., Foster, B. G., & McCoy, P. T. (1994). Counter measures to improve the driving performance of older drivers. *Educational Gerontology, 20,* 567–577.

Atchley, R. C. (1982). Retirement as a social institution. *American Review of Sociology, 8,* 263–287.

Atchley, R. C. (1996). Retirement. In J. E. Birren (Ed.), *Encyclopedia of gerontology: Age, aging, and the aged* (Vol. 2, pp. 437–449). San Diego: Academic Press.

Attig, T. (1996). *How we grieve: Relearning the world.* New York: Oxford University Press.

Avis, N. E. (1999). Women's health at midlife. In S. L. Willis & J. D. Reid

(Eds.), *Life in the middle: Psychological and social development in middle age* (pp. 105–146). San Diego: Academic Press.

Avolio B. J., & Sosik J. J. (1999). A life-span memory framework for assessing the impact of work on white collar workers. In S. L. Willis & J. D. Reid (Eds.), *Life in the middle: Psychological and social development in middle age* (pp. 249–274). San Diego: Academic Press.

Ayers, M. S., & Reder, L. M. (1988). A theoretical review of the misinformation effect: Predictions from an activation-based memory model. *Psychonomic Bulletin & Review, 5,* 1–21.

Bäckman, L. (1985). Further evidence for the lack of adult age differences on free recall of subject performed tasks: The importance of motor action. *Human Learning, 4,* 79–87.

Bäckman, L., & Forsell, Y. (1994). Episodic memory functioning in a common-based sample of older adults with major depression: Utilization of cognitive support. *Journal of Abnormal Psychology, 103,* 361–370.

Bäckman, L., Hassing, L., Forsell, Y., & Vittanen, M. (1996). Episodic remembering in a population-based sample of nonagenarians: Does major depression exacerbate the memory deficiencies seen in Alzheimer's disease. *Psychology and Aging, 11,* 649–657.

Bäckman, L., & Larrson, M. (1992). Recall of organizable words and objects in adulthood: influence of instructions, retention, interval, and retrieval cues. *Journal of Gerontology, 47,* P237–P278.

Bäckman, L., & Nilsson, L.-G. (1984). Aging effects in free recall: An exception to the rule. *Human Learning, 3,* 53–69.

Bäckman, L., & Nilsson, L.-G. (1985). Prerequisites for the lack of age differences in memory performance. *Experimental Aging Research, 11,* 67–73.

Bäckman, L., Small, B. J., & Wahlin, A., & Larsson, M. (2000). Cognitive functioning in very old age. In F. I.

M. Craik & T. A. Salthouse (Eds.), *The handbook of aging and cognition* (2nd ed., pp. 449–558). Mahwah, NJ: Erlbaum.

Baddeley, A. D. (1990). The development of the concept of working memory: Implications and contributions of neuropsychology. In A. Vallar, T. Shallice, et al. (Eds.), *Neuropsychological impairments of short-term memory* (pp. 54–73). New York: Cambridge University Press.

Bahrick, H. P., Bahrick, P. P., & Wittlinger, R. P. (1975). Fifty years of memory for names and faces: A cross-sectional approach. *Journal of Experimental Psychology, 104,* 54–75.

Balk, D. E. (1996). Attachment and the reactions of bereaved college students: A longitudinal study. In D. Klass, P. R. Silverman, & S. L. Nickman (Eds.), *Continuing bonds: New understandings of grief* (pp. 311–328). Washington, DC: Taylor & Francis.

Ball, K., Beard, B. L., Roenker, D. L., Miller, R. L., & Griggs, (1998). Age and visual search: Expanding the useful field of view. *Journal of the Optical Society of America, A, 5,* 2210–2219.

Ball, J. F. (1976–1977). Widow's grief: The impact of age and mode of death. *Omega: Journal of Death and Dying, 7,* 307–333.

Ball, K., & Owsley, C. (1991). Identifying correlates of accident involvement for the older driver. *Human Factors, 33,* 583–595.

Ball, K., Owsley, C., Sloane, Roenker, & Bruni, (1993). Visual attention problems as a predictor of vehicle accidents among older drivers. *Investigative Ophthalmology and Visual Science, 34*(11), 3110–3123.

Ball, K., & Rebok, G. W. (1994). Evaluating the driving ability of older adults. *Journal of Applied Gerontology, 13,* 20–38.

Baltes, M. M. (1994). Aging well and institutional living: A paradox? In R. P. Abeles, H. C. Gift, & M. G. Ory (Eds.), *Aging and quality of life* (pp. 185–201). New York: Springer.

Baltes, M. M., Maas, I., Wihms, H. U., Borchett, M., & Little, T. D. (1999).

Everyday competence in old and very old age: Theoretical considerations and empirical findings. In P. B. Baltes, K. U. Mayer, et al. (Eds.), *The Berlin Aging Study* (pp. 384–402). New York: Cambridge University Press.

Baltes, P. B. (1987). Theoretical propositions of life-span developmental psychology: On the dynamics between growth and decline. *Developmental Psychology, 23,* 611–626.

Baltes, P. B. (1993). The aging mind: Potential and limits. *The Gerontologist, 33,* 580–594.

Baltes, P. B., & Baltes, M. M. (1990). Psychological perspectives on successful aging: The model of selective optimization with compensation. In P. B. Baltes & M. M. Baltes (Eds.), *Successful aging: Perspectives from the behavioral sciences* (pp. 1–27). New York: Cambridge University Press.

Baltes, P. B., & Kliegl, R. (1992). Further testing of limits of cognitive plasticity: Negative age differences in mnemonic skill are robust. *Developmental Psychology, 28,* 121–125.

Baltes, P. B., & Lindenberger, U. (1997). Emergence of a powerful connection between sensory and cognitive function across the adult life span: A new window to the study. *Psychology and Aging, 12,* 12–21.

Baltes, P. B., & Lindenberger, U. (1998). On the range of cognitive plasticity in old age as a function of experience: 15 years of intervention research. *Behavior Therapy, 19,* 283–300.

Baltes, P. B., Lindenberger, U., & Staudinger, U. M. (1998). Life-span theory in developmental psychology. In R. M. Lerner (Ed.), *Handbook of child psychology, Vol. 1. Theoretical models of human development* (5th ed., pp. 1029–1143). New York: Wiley.

Baltes, P. B., Reese, H. W., & Nesselroade, J. R. (1977). *Life-span developmental psychology: Introduction to research methods.* Pacific Grove, CA: Brooks/Cole.

Baltes, P. B., & Schaie, K. W. (1974). Aging and IQ: The myth of the twilight years. *Psychology Today, 7,* 35–40.

Baltes, P. B., & Smith, J. (1990). The psychology of wisdom and its ontogenesis. In R. J. Sternberg (Ed.), *Wisdom: Its nature, origins, and development* (pp. 87–120). New York: Cambridge University Press.

Baltes, P. B., & Staudinger, U. M. (1996). *Interactive minds: Life-span perspectives on the social foundations of cognition.* New York: Cambridge University Press.

Baltes, P. B., & Staudinger, U. M. (2000). Wisdom: A metaheuristic (pragmatic) to orchestrate mind and virtue toward excellence. *American Psychologist, 55,* 122–126.

Baltes, P. B., Staudinger, U. M., & Lindenberger, U. (1999). Lifespan psychology: Theory and application to intellectual functioning. *Annual Review of Psychology, 50,* 471–507.

Baltes, P. B., Staudinger, U. M., Maercker, A., & Smith, J. (1995). People nominated as wise: A comparative study of wisdom-related knowledge. *Psychology and Aging, 10,* 155–166.

Baltes, P. B., & Willis, S. L. (1982). Enhancement (plasticity) of intellectual functioning: Penn State's Adult Development and Enrichment Project (ADEPT). In F. I. M. Craik & S. Trehub (Eds.), *Aging and cognitive processes* (pp. 353–389). New York: Plenum.

Barfield, R. E., & Morgan, J. N. (1978). Trends in satisfaction with retirement. *The Gerontologist, 18,* 19–23.

Bargh, J. A. (1997). The automaticity of everyday life. In R. S. Wyer, Jr. (Ed.), *Advances in social cognition* (Vol. 10, pp. 1–61). Mahwah, NJ: Erlbaum.

Bargh, J. A., Chaiken, S., Raymond, P., and Hymes, C. (1996). The automatic evaluation effect: Unconditional automatic attitude activation with a pronunciation task. *Journal of Experimental Psychology, 32,* 104–128.

Baron, J. N., & Bielby, W. T. (1985). Organizational barriers to gender equality: Sex segregation of jobs and opportunities. In A. S. Rossi (Ed.), *Gender and the life course* (pp. 233–251). New York: Aldine.

Baruch, G. K. (1994). The psychological well-being of women in the middle years. In G. K. Baruch & J.

Brooks-Gunn (Eds.), *Women in midlife* (pp. 161–180). New York: Plenum.

Bashore, T. R., Ridderinkhof, K. R., & Van Der Molen, M. W. (1997). The decline of cognitive processing in old age. *Current Directions in Psychological Science, 6,* 163–169.

Basseches, M. (1984). *Dialectical thinking and adult development.* Norwood, NJ: Ablex.

Bastida, E., & Gonzalez, G. (1995). Mental health status and needs of the Hispanic elderly: A cross-cultural analysis. In D. K. Padgett (Ed.), *Handbook on ethnicity, aging, and mental health* (pp. 99–112). Westport, CT: Greenwood.

Baugh, S. G., Lankau, M. J., & Scandura, T. A. (1996). An investment of the effects of protégé gender on responses to mentoring. *Journal of Vocational Behavior, 49,* 309–323.

Baumgartner, R. N., Heymsfield, S. B., & Roche, A. F. (1995). Human body composition and the epidemiology of chronic disease. *Obesity Research, 3,* 73–95.

Bayen, U. J., & Murnane, K. (1996). Aging and the use of perceptual and temporal information in source memory tasks. *Psychology and Aging, 11,* 293–303.

Baylor, & Spirduso, (1988). Systemic aerobic exercise and components of reaction time in older women. *Journal of Gerontology, 43,* P121–P126.

Bean, F., & Tienda, M. (1987). *The Hispanic population in the United States.* New York: Russell Sage Foundation.

Beck, A. T. (1967). *Depression: Clinical, experimental, and theoretical aspects.* New York: Harper & Row.

Beck, A. T., Rush, J., Shaw, B., & Emery, G. (1979). *Cognitive therapy of depression.* New York: Guilford.

Belenky, M. F., Clinchy, B. M., Goldberger, N. R., & Tarule, J. M. (1986). *Women's ways of knowing: The development of self, voice, and mind.* New York: Basic Books.

Bendiksen, M. S., & Bendiksen, I. (1996). Multimodal memory rehabilitation for the toxic solvent injured person. In D. Herman, C. McEvoy, C. Hertzog, P. Herter, &

M. K. Johnson (Eds.), *Basic and applied memory research* (Vol. 2, pp. 469–480). Hillsdale, NJ: Erlbaum.

Bengtson, V. L. (1985). Diversity and symbolism in grandparental roles. In V. L. Bengtson & J. F. Robertson (Eds.), *Grandparenthood* (pp. 11–25). Beverly Hills, CA: Sage.

Bengtson, V. L., Rosenthal, C., & Burton, L. (1995). Paradoxes of families and aging. In R. H. Binstock & L. K. George (Eds.), *Handbook of aging and the social sciences* (4th ed., pp. 253-282). San Diego: Academic Press).

Benin, M. H., & Agostinelli, J. (1988). Husbands' and wives' satisfaction with the division of labor. *Journal of Marriage and the Family, 50,* 349–361.

Berdahl, J. L., Magley, V. J., & Waldo, C. R. (1996). The sexual harassment of men? *Psychology of Women Quarterly, 20,* 527–547.

Berg, C. A., & Klaczynski, P. A. (1996). Practical intelligence and problem-solving: Searching for perspectives. In F. Blanchard-Fields & T. M. Hess (Eds.), *Perspectives on cognitive change in adulthood and aging* (pp. 323–357). New York: McGraw-Hill.

Berg, C. A., & Sternberg, R. J. (1992). Adults' conceptions of intelligence across the adult life span. *Psychology and Aging, 7,* 221–231.

Berg, C. A., Strough, J., Calerone, K. S., Sansone, C., & Weir, C. (1998). The role of problem definitions in understanding age and context effects on strategies for solving every day problems. *Psychology and Aging, 13,* 29–44.

Bergeman, C. S. (1997). *Aging: Genetic and environmental influences.* Thousand Oaks, CA: Sage.

Bernal, D., Snyder, D., & McDaniel, M. (1998). The age and job satisfaction relationship: Do its shape and strength still evade us? *Journal of Gerontology: Psychological Sciences and Social Sciences, 53B,* P287–P293.

Berry, J. M., West, R. L., & Dennehey, D. M. (1989). Reliability and validity of the Memory Self-Efficacy Questionnaire. *Developmental Psychology, 25,* 701–713.

Berry, M. E. (1999). The development and constructive validation of the revised supervisor work and family support scale. *Dissertation Abstracts International: The Sciences and Engineering, 60,* 1335.

Besdine, R. W. (1995). Hyperthermia and accidental hypothermia. In W. B. Abrams, M. H. Beers, & R. Berkow (Eds.), *The Merck manual of geriatrics* (2nd ed., pp. 47–57). Whitehouse Station, NJ: Merck Research Laboratories.

Best, D. L., & Williams, J. E. (1993). A cross-cultural viewpoint. In A. E. Beall & R. J. Sternberg (Eds.), *The psychology of gender* (pp. 215–250). New York: Guilford.

Betz, E. L. (1984). A study of career patterns of women college graduates. *Journal of Vocational Behavior, 24,* 249–263.

Betz, E. L., Harmon, L. W., & Borgen, F. H. (1996). The relationships of self-efficacy for the Holland themes to gender, occupational group membership, and vocational interests. *Journal of Counseling Psychology, 43,* 90–98.

Betz, N. E., Heesacker, R. S., & Shuttleworth, C. (1990). Moderators of the congruence and realism of major and occupational plans in college students: A replication and extension. *Journal of Counseling Psychology, 37,* 269–276.

Bieman-Copland, S., & Charness, N. (1994). Memory knowledge and memory monitoring in adulthood. *Psychology and Aging, 9,* 287–302.

Bieman-Copland, S., Ryan, E. B., & Cassano, J. (1998). Responding to the challenges of late life. In D. Pushkar, W. M. Bukowski, A. E. Schwartzman, D. M. Stack, & D. R. White (Eds.), *Improving competence across the lifespan: Building interventions based on theory and research* (pp. 141–157). New York: Plenum.

Binet, H. (1903). *L'etude experimentale de l'intelligence.* Paris: Schleicher.

Binger, C. M., Ablin, A. R., Feuerstein, R. C., Kushner, J. H., Zoger, S., & Mikkelson, C. (1969). Childhood leukemia—Emotional impact on patient and family. *New England Journal of Medicine, 280,* 414.

Binstock, R. H. (1999). Public policy issues. In J. C. Cavanaugh & S. K.

Whitbourne (Eds.), *Gerontology: An interdisciplinary perspective* (pp. 414–447). New York: Oxford University Press.

Birren, J. E., & Cunningham, W. (1985). Research on the psychology of aging: Principles, concepts, and theory. In J. E. Birren & K. W. Schaie (Eds.), *Handbook of the psychology of aging* (2nd ed., pp. 3–34). New York: Van Nostrand Reinhold.

Birren, J. E., Lubben, J. E., Rowe, J. C., & Deutchman, D. E. (Eds.), *The concept and measurement of quality of life in the frail elderly.* San Diego: Academic Press.

Birren, J. E., & Renner, V. J. (1980). Concepts and issues of mental health and aging. In J. E. Birren & R. B. Sloane (Eds.), *Handbook of mental health and aging* (pp. 3–33). Englewood Cliffs, NJ: Prentice Hall.

Birren, J. E., Woods, A. M., & Williams, M. V. (1980). Behavioral slowing with age: Causes, organization, & consequences. In L. W. Poon (Ed.), *Aging in the 1980s: Psychological issues* (pp. 293–308). Washington, DC: American Psychological Association.

Black, P., Markowitz, R. S., & Cianci, S. (1975). Recovery of motor function after lesions in motor cortex of a monkey. In R. Porter & D. W. Fitzsimmons (Eds.), *Outcome of severe damage to the central nervous system* (pp. 65–70). Amsterdam: Elsevier.

Blackburn, J. A., & Papilia, D. E. (1992). The study of adult cognition from a Piagetian perspective. In R. J. Sternberg, C. A. Berg, et al. (Eds.), *Intellectual development* (pp. 141–160). New York: Cambridge University Press.

Blanchard-Fields, F. (1986). Reasoning on social dilemmas varying in emotional saliency: An adult developmental study. *Psychology and Aging, 1,* 325–333.

Blanchard-Fields, F. (1994). Age differences in causal attributions from an adult developmental perspective. *Journal of Gerontology: Psychological Sciences, 49,* P43–P51.

Blanchard-Fields, F. (1996). Causal attributions across the adult life span: The influence of social schemas, life

context, and domain specificity. *Applied Cognitive Psychology, 10* (Spec. Issue) 5137–5146.

Blanchard-Fields, F. (1999). Social schematicity and causal attributions. In T. M. Hess & F. Blanchard-Fields (Eds.), *Social cognition and aging* (pp. 219–236). San Diego: Academic Press.

Blanchard-Fields, F., & Abeles, R. P. (1996). Social cognition and aging. In J. Birren & K. W. Schaie (Eds.), *Handbook of the psychology of aging* (4th ed., pp. 150–161). New York: Van Nostrand Reinhold.

Blanchard-Fields, F., Baldi, R. A., & Constantin, L. P. (in preparation). *Interrole conflict across the adult lifespan: The role of parenting stage. Career stages and quality of experiences.*

Blanchard-Fields, F., Baldi, R. A., & Stein, R. (1999). Age relevance and context effects on attributions across the adult life span. *International Journal of Behavioral Development, 23,* 665–683.

Blanchard-Fields, F., & Camp, C. J. (1990). Affect, individual differences, and real world problem solving across the adult life span. In T. Hess (Ed.), *Aging and cognition: Knowledge organization and utilization* (pp. 461–497). Amsterdam: North-Holland.

Blanchard-Fields, F., Chen, Y., Herbert, C. E. (1997). Interrole conflict as a function of life stage gender and gender-related personality attributes. *Sex Roles, 37,* 155–174.

Blanchard-Fields, F., Chen, Y., Schrocke, M., & Hertzog, C. (1998). Evidence for content-specificity of causal attributions across the adult life-span. *Aging, Neuropsychology, & Cognition, 5*(4), 241–263.

Blanchard-Fields, F., & Hertzog, C. (2000). Age differences in schematicity. In U. von Hecker, S. Dutke, & G. Sedek (Eds.), *Processes of generative mental representation and psychological adaptation.* Dordrecht, The Netherlands: Kluwer.

Blanchard-Fields, F., & Irion, J. C. (1988). The relation between locus of control and coping in two contexts: Age as a moderator variable. *Psychology and Aging, 3,* 197–203.

Blanchard-Fields, F., Jahnke, H. C., & Camp, C. (1995). Age differences in problem-solving style: The role of emotional salience. *Psychology and Aging, 10,* 173–180.

Blanchard-Fields, F., & Norris, L. (1994). Casual attributions from adolescence through adulthood: Age differences, ego level, and generalized response style. *Aging and Cognition, 1,* 67–86.

Blazer, D., George, L. K., & Hughes, D. C. (1988). Schizophrenic symptoms in an elderly community population. In J. A. Brody & G. L. Maddox (Eds.), *Epidemiology and aging: An international perspective* (pp. 134–149). New York: Springer.

Blessed, G., Tomlinson, B. E., & Roth, M. (1968). The association between quantitative measures of dementia and of senile changes in the cerebral gray matter of elderly subjects. *British Journal of Psychiatry, 114,* 797–811.

Block, J. (1995). A contrarian view of the five-factor approach to personality description. *Psychological Bulletin, 117,* 187–215.

Block, R., DeVoe, M., Stanley, B., Stanley, M., & Pomara, N. (1985). Memory performance in individuals with primary degenerative dementia: Its similarity to diazepam-induced impairments. *Experimental Aging Research, 11,* 151–155.

Blumenthal, J. A., & Madden, D. J. (1988). Effects of aerobic exercise training, age, and physical fitness on memory-search performance. *Psychology and Aging, 3,* 280–285.

Bobrow, D. G., & Collins, A. (1971). *Representation and understanding: Studies in cognitive science.* New York: Academic Press.

Boise, L., Camicioli, R., Morgan, D. L., Rose, J. H., & Congleton, L. (1999). Diagnosing dementia: Perspectives of primary care physicians. *The Gerontologist, 39,* 457–464.

Bonanno, G. A., & Kaltman, S. (1999). Toward an integrative perspective on bereavement. *Psychological Bulletin, 125,* 760–776.

Bondareff, W. (1983). Age and Alzheimer's disease. *Lancet, 1,* 1447.

Book, P. L. (1996). How does the family narrative influence the individual's ability to communicate about death? *Omega, Journal of Death and Dying, 33,* 323–342.

Booth, F. W., Weeden, S. H., & Tseng, B. S. (1994). Effect of aging on human skeletal muscle and motor function. *Medicine and Science in Sports and Exercise, 26,* 556–560.

Borg, S., & Lasker, J. (1981). *When pregnancy fails.* Boston: Beacon.

Bosman, E. A., & Charness, N. (1996). Age-related differences in skilled performance and skill acquisition. In F. Blanchard-Fields & T. M. Hess (Eds.), *Perspectives on cognitive change in adulthood and aging* (pp. 428–453). New York: McGraw-Hill.

Bossé, R., Aldwin, C. M., Levenson, M. R., Spiro, A., & Mroczek, D. K. (1993). Change in social support after retirement: Longitudinal findings from the Normative Aging Study. *Journal of Gerontology: Psychological Sciences, 48,* P210–P217.

Bossé, R., & Ekerdt, D. J. (1981). Change in self-perception of leisure activities with retirement: Longitudinal findings from the Normative Aging Study. *Journal of Gerontology: Psychological Sciences, 48,* P210–P217.

Botwinick, J. (1977). Intellectual abilities. In J. E. Birren & K. W. Schaie (Eds.), *Handbook of the psychology of aging* (pp. 580–605). New York: Van Nostrand Reinhold.

Bouchard, T. J., Jr. (1997). The genetics of personality. In K. Blum & E. P. Noble (Eds.), *Handbook of psychiatric genetics* (pp. 273–296). Boca Raton, FL: CRC Press.

Boult, C., Kane, R. L., Louis, T. A., Boult, L., & McCaffrey, D. (1994). Chronic conditions that lead to functional limitations in the elderly. *Journal of Gerontology: Medical Sciences, 49,* M28–M36.

Bozett, F. W. (1988). Gay fatherhood. In P. Bronstein & C. P. Cowan (Eds.), *Fatherhood today: Men's changing role in the family* (pp. 214–235). New York: Wiley.

Brabeck, M. M., & Weisgerber, K. (1989). College students' perception of men and women choosing teaching and management: The effects of gender and sex role egalitarianism. *Sex Roles, 21,* 841.

Brainerd, C. J. (1995). Interference processes in memory development: The case of cognitive triage. In F. N. Dempster & C. J. Brainerd (Eds.), *Interference and inhibition on cognition* (pp. 108–139). San Diego: Academic Press.

Brandtstädter, J. (1997). Action culture and development: Points of convergence. *Culture and Psychology, 3,* 335–352.

Brandtstädter, J. (1999). Sources of resilience in the aging self. In T. M. Hess & F. Blanchard-Fields (Eds.), *Social cognition and aging* (pp. 123–141). San Diego: Academic Press.

Brandtstädter, J., & Rothermund, K. (1994). Self-percepts of control in middle and later adulthood: Buffering losses by rescaling goals. *Psychology and Aging, 9,* 265–273.

Brandt, J., & Rich, J. B. (1995). Memory disorders in the dementias. In A. D. Baddeley, B. A. Wilson, & F. N. Watts (Eds.), *Handbook of memory disorders* (pp. 243–270). Chichester, England: Wiley.

Brant, L. J., & Fozard, J. L. (1990). Age changes in pure-tone hearing thresholds in a longitudinal study of normal human aging. *Journal of the Acoustical Society of America, 88,* 813–820.

Bray, D. W., & Howard, A. (1983). The AT&T longitudinal study of managers. In K. W. Schaie (Ed.), *Longitudinal studies on adult psychological development* (pp. 266–312). New York: Guilford.

Breitner, J. C. S. (1988). Alzheimer's disease: Possible evidence for genetic causes. In M. K. Aronson (Ed.), *Understanding Alzheimer's disease* (pp. 34–49). New York: Scribner.

Brewer, M. B., & Lui, L. (1984). Categorization of the elderly by the elderly. *Personality and Social Psychology Bulletin, 10,* 585–595.

Bridges, C. R. (1990). The characteristics of career achievement perceived by African American college administrators. *Journal of Black Studies, 26,* 748–767.

Bridges, C. R. (1996). The characteristics of career achievement perceived by African American college administrators. *Journal of Black Studies, 26,* 748–767.

Brod, M., Stewart, A. L., Sands, L., & Walton, P. (1999). Conceptualization and measurement of quality of life in dementia: The Dementia Quality of Life Instrument (DQoL). *The Gerontologist, 39,* 25–35.

Brody, E. M. (1981). Women in the middle and family help to older people. *The Gerontologist, 21,* 471–480.

Broman, C. L. (1988). Household work and family life satisfaction of blacks. *Journal of Marriage and the Family, 50,* 743–748.

Brooks, L., & Betz, N. E. (1990). Utility of expectancy theory in predicting occupational choices in college students. *Journal of Counseling Psychology, 37,* 57–64.

Brown, N. M. (1990). Age and children in the Kalahari. *Health and Human Development Research, 1,* 26–30.

Brown, S. A., Hutchinson, R., Morrisett, J., Boerwinkle, E., Davis, C. E., & Gotto, A. M. (1993). Plasma lipid, lipoprotein cholesterol and apoprotein distributions in selected US communities. *Arteriosclerosis and Thrombosis, 13,* 1139–1158.

Bruce, P. R., Coyne, A. C., & Botwinick, J. (1982). Adult age differences in metamemory. *Journal of Gerontology, 37,* 354–357.

Brush, J. A., & Camp, C. J. (1998). *A therapy technique for improving memory: Spaced retrieval.* Beachwood, OH: Menorah Park Center for Senior Living.

Buckle, L., Gallup, C. G., Jr., & Rodd, Z. A. (1996). Marriage as a reproductive contract: Patterns of marriage, divorce, and remarriage. *Ethnology and Sociobiology, 17,* 363–377.

Buffum, M. D., & Buffum, J. C. (1998). Psychotropic drug management. In P. Ebersole & P. Hess, *Toward healthy aging: Human needs and nursing response* (5th ed.). St. Louis: Mosby.

Bunce, D. J., Barrowclough, A., & Morris, I. (1996). The moderating influence of physical fitness on age gradients in vigilance and serial choice

response tasks. *Psychology and Aging, 11,* 671–682.

Bunce, D. J., Warr, P. B., & Cochrane, T. (1993). Blocks in choice responding as a function of age and physical fitness. *Psychology and Aging, 8,* 26–33.

Burdz, M. P., Eaton, W. D., & Bond, J. B. (1988). Effect of respite care on dementia and nondementia patients and their caregivers. *Psychology and Aging, 3,* 38–42.

Burgess, D., & Borgida, E. (1997). Sexual harassment: An experimental test of sex-role spillover theory. *Personality and Social Psychology and Bulletin, 23,* 63–75.

Burgio, K. L., Locher, J. L., Roth, D. L., & Goode, P. S. (2001). Psychological improvements associated with behavioral and drug treatment of urge incontinence in older women. *Journal of Gerontology: Psychological Sciences, 56B,* P46–P51.

Burgio, L. D. (1996). Interventions for the behavioral complications of Alzheimer's disease: Behavioral approaches. *International Psychogeriatrics, 8*(Suppl. 1), 45–52.

Burgio, L. D., Hardin, M., Sinnott, J., Janosky, J., & Hohman, M. J. (1995). Acceptability of behavioral treatments and pharmacotherapy for behaviorally disturbed older adults: Ratings of caregivers and relatives. *Journal of Clinical Geropsychology, 1,* 19–32.

Burgio, L. D., McCormick, K. A., Scheve, A. S., Engel, B. T., Hawkins, A., & Leahy, E. (1994). The effects of changing prompted voiding schedules in the treatment of incontinence in nursing home residents. *Journal of the American Geriatrics Society, 42,* 315–320.

Burke, D. M. (1997). Language, aging, and inhibitory deficits: Evaluation of a theory. *Journal of Gerontology: Psychological Sciences, 52B,* P254–P264.

Burke, D. M., & Harold, R. M. (1988). Automatic and effortful semantic processes in old age: Experimental and naturalistic approaches. In L. L. Light & D. M. Burke (Eds.), *Language, memory, and aging* (pp. 100–116). New York: University Press.

Burke, R. J. (1991a). Organizational treatment of minority managers and professionals: Costs to the majority? *Psychological Reports, 68,* 439–449.

Burke, R. J. (1991b). Work experiences of minority managers and professionals: Individual and organizational costs of perceived bias. *Psychological Reports, 69,* 1011–1023.

Burnette, D. (1999). Social relationships of Latino grandparent caregivers: A role theory perspective. *The Gerontologist, 39,* 49–58.

Burns, A. (1992). Mother-headed families: An international perspective and the case of Australia. *Society for Research in Child Development: Social Policy Report, 6,* 1–22.

Burr, D. C., Morrone, M. C., & Frorentini, A. (1996). Spatial and temporal properties of infant color vision. In F. Vital-Dwand & J. Atkinson (Eds.), *Infant vision* (pp. 63–77). Oxford, England: Oxford University Press.

Burr, J. A. (1990). Race/sex comparisons of elderly living arrangements. *Research on Aging, 12,* 507–530.

Burrus-Bammel, L. L., & Bammel, G. (1985). Leisure and recreation. In J. E. Birren & K. W. Schaie (Eds.), *Handbook of the psychology of aging* (2nd ed., pp. 848–889). New York: Van Nostrand Reinhold.

Burt, D. B., Zembar, M. J., & Niedereche, G. (1995). Depression and memory impairment. A meta-analysis of the association, its pattern, and specificity. *Psychological Bulletin, 117,* 285–305.

Busch, J. W. (1985). Mentoring in graduate schools of education: Mentors' perceptions. *American Educational Research Journal, 22,* 257–265.

Buschmann, M. T., & Hollinger, L. M. (1994). Influence of social support and control on depression in the elderly. *Clinical Gerontologist, 14,* 13–28.

Buss, D. M., Abbott, M., Angeleitner, A., Asherian, A., Biaggio, A., Blanco Villasenor, A., Bruchon-Schweitzer, M., Chu'u, H.-Y., Czapinski, J., Deraad, B., Ekehammar, B., El Lohamy, N., Fioravanti, M., Georgas, J., Gjerde, P., Guttman, R., Hazan, F., Iwawaki, S., Janakiramaiah, N., Khosroshani, F., Kreitler, S., Lachenicht, L., Lee, M., Liik, K.,

Little, B., Mika, S., Moadel-Shahid, M., Moane, G., Montero, M., Mundy-Castle, A. C., Niit, T., Nsenduluka, E., Pienkowski, R., Pirttila-Backman, A.-M., Pone de Leon, J., Rousseau, J., Runco, M. A., Safir, M. P., Samuels, C., Sanitioso, R., Serpell, R., Smid, N., Spencer, C., Tadinac, M., Todoreva, E. N., Troland, K., Van Den Brande, L., Van Heck, G., Van Langenhove, Yang, K.-S. (1990). International preferences in selecting mates: A study of 37 cultures. *Journal of Cross-Cultural Psychology, 21,* 5–47.

Byock, I. (1997). *Dying well.* New York: Riverhead.

Calasanti, T. M. (1996). Gender and life satisfaction in retirement: An assessment of the male model. *Journal of Gerontology: Social Sciences, 51B,* S18–S29.

Calciano, R., Chodak, G. W., Garnick, M. B., Kuban, D. A., & Resnick, M. I. (1995, April 15). The prostate cancer conundrum. *Patient Care, 29,* 84–88, 91–95, 99–102, 104.

Camp, C. J. (1998). Memory interventions and pathological older adults. In R. Schulz, G. Maddox, & M. P. Lawton (Eds.), *Annotated review of gerontology and geriatrics* (Vol. 18, pp. 155–189). New York: Springer.

Camp, C. J. (Ed.). (1999). *Montessori-based activities for persons with dementia* (Vol. 1). Beachwood, OH: Menorah Park Center for Senior Living.

Camp, C. J., Foss, J. W., Stevens, A. B., Reichard, C. C., McKitrick, L. A., & O'Hanlon, A. M. (1993). Memory training in normal and demented elderly populations: The E-I-E-I-O model. *Experimental Aging Research, 19,* 277–290.

Camp, C. J., Judge, K. S., Bye, C. A., Fox, K. M., Bowden, J., Bell, M., Valencic, K., & Mattern, J. M. (1997). An intergenerational program for persons with dementia using Montessori methods. *The Gerontologist, 37,* 688–692.

Camp, C. J., & McKitrick, L. A. (1991). Memory interventions in Alzheimer-type dementia populations: Methodological and theoretical issues. In R. L. West & J. D. Sinnott (Eds.), *Everyday memory and aging: Current research and methodology* (pp. 155–172). New York: Springer-Verlag.

Cannon, C. (1996). *Marital stress and coping in alpha 1-antitrypsin deficiency emphysema.* Unpublished dissertation, University of Delaware.

Cantor, N. (1990). From thought to behavior: "Having" and "doing" in the study of personality and cognition. *American Psychologist, 45,* 735–750.

Cantor, N., & Harlow, R. E. (1994). Personality, strategic behavior, and daily-life problem solving. *Current Directions in Psychological Science, 3,* 169–172.

Caplan, L. J., & Lipman, P. D. (1995). Age and gender differences in the effectiveness of map-like learning aids in memory for routes. *Journal of Gerontology: Psychological Sciences, 50B,* P126–P133.

Capowski, G. (1994). Ageism and the new diversity issue. *Management Review, 83*(10), 1–15.

Carlson, M. C., Hasher, L., Connelly, S. L., & Zacks, R. T. (1995). Aging distraction and benefits of predictable location. *Psychology and Aging, 10,* 427–436.

Carr, D., House, J. S., Kessler, R. C., Nesse, R. M., Sonnega, J., & Wortman, C. (2000). Marital quality and psychological adjustment to widowhood among older adults: A longitudinal analysis. *Journal of Gerontology: Social Sciences, 55B,* S197–S207.

Carr, D., & Rebok, G. W. (2000). The older driver. In J. J. Gallo, T. Fulmer, G. J. Paveza, & W. Reichel (Eds.), *Handbook of geriatric assessment* (3rd ed., pp. 149–157). Rockland, MD: Aspen.

Carstensen, L. L. (1993). Motivation for social contact across the lifespan: A theory of socioemotional selectivity. In J. Jacobs (Ed.), *Nebraska Symposium on Motivation* (Vol. 40, pp. 209–254). Lincoln: University of Nebraska Press.

Carstensen, L. L. (1995). Evidence for a life-span theory of socioemotional selectivity. *Current Directions in Psychological Science, 4,* 151–156.

Carstensen, L. L., & Freund, A. M. (1994). The resilience of the aging self. *Developmental Review, 14,* 81–92.

Carstensen, L. L., Gottman, J. M., & Levenson, R. W. (1995). Emotional behavior in long-term marriage. *Psychology and Aging, 10,* 140–149.

Carstensen, L. L., & Turk-Charles, S. (1994). The salience of emotion across the adult life span. *Psychology and Aging, 9,* 259–264.

Caserta, M. S., & Gillett, P. A. (1998). Older women's feelings about exercise and their adherence to an aerobic regimen over time. *The Gerontologist, 38,* 602–609.

Caserta, M. S., Lund, D. A., Wright, S. D., & Redburn, D. E. (1987). Caregivers to dementia patients: The utilization of community services. *The Gerontologist, 27,* 209–214.

Cascio, W. F. (1995). Whither industrial and organizational psychology in a changing world of work? *American Psychologist, 50,* 928–939.

Casten, R. J., Rovner, B. W., Edmonds, S. E., DeAngelis, D., & Basford, C. (1999, August). *Personality traits as predictors of vision-specific function among older people experiencing vision loss.* Paper presented at the meeting of the American Psychological Association, Boston.

Castro, I. L. (1997). Worth more than we earn: Fair pay as a step toward gender equity. *National Forum, 77*(2), 17–21.

Cavanaugh, J. C. (1987). Age differences in adults' self-reports of memory ability: It depends on how and what you ask. *International Journal of Aging and Human Development, 24,* 241–277.

Cavanaugh, J. C. (1996). Memory self-efficacy as a key to understanding memory change. In F. Blanchard-Fields & T. M. Hess (Eds.), *Perspectives on cognitive changes in adulthood and aging* (pp. 488–507). New York: McGraw-Hill.

Cavanaugh, J. C. (1999a). Caregiving to adults: A life event challenge. In I. H. Nordhus, G. R. VandenBos, S. Berg, & P. Fromholt (Eds.), *Clinical geropsychology* (pp. 131–135). Washington, DC: American Psychological Association.

Cavanaugh, J. C. (1999b). Friendships and social networks among older people. In I. H. Nordhus, G. R. VandenBos, S. Berg, & P. Fromholt (Eds.), *Clinical geropsychology* (pp. 137–140). Washington, DC: American Psychological Association.

Cavanaugh, J. C. (1999c). Theories of aging in the biological, behavioral, and social sciences. In J. C. Cavanaugh & S. K. Whitbourne (Eds.), *Gerontology: Interdisciplinary perspectives* (pp. 1–32). New York: Oxford University Press.

Cavanaugh, J. C., & Baskind, D. (1996). Relations among basic processes, beliefs, and performance: A lifespan perspective. In D. Herrmann, M. Johnson, C. McEvoy, C. Hertzog, & P. Hertel (Eds.), *Basic and applied memory: Research on practical aspects of memory.* Hillsdale, NJ: Erlbaum.

Cavanaugh, J. C., Feldman, J., & Hertzog, C. (1998). Memory beliefs as social cognition: A reconceptualization of what memory questionnaires assess. *Review of General Psychology, 2,* 48–65.

Cavanaugh, J. C., Grady, J. G., & Perlmutter, M. (1983). Forgetting and use of memory aids in 20 to 70 year olds' everyday life. *International Journal of Aging and Human Development, 17,* 113–122.

Cavanaugh, J. C., & Green, E. E. (1990). I believe, therefore I can: Self-efficacy beliefs in memory aging. In E. A. Lovelace (Ed.), *Aging and cognition: Mental processes, self-awareness, and interventions* (pp. 189–230). Amsterdam: North-Holland.

Cavanaugh, J. C., Kinney, J. M. (1994, July). *Marital satisfaction as an important contextual factor in spousal caregiving.* Paper presented at the 7th International Conference on Personal Relationships, Groningen, The Netherlands.

Cavanaugh, J. C., Kramer, D. A., Sinnott, J. D., Camp, C. J., & Markley, R. J. (1985). On missing links and such: Interfaces between cognitive research and everyday problem solving. *Human Development, 28,* 146–168.

Cavanaugh, J. C., Morton, K. R., & Tilse, C. R. (1989). A self-evaluation framework for understanding everyday memory aging. In J. D. Sinnott

(Ed.), *Everyday problem solving: Theory and application* (pp. 266–284). New York: Praeger.

Cavanaugh, J. C., & Nocera, R. (1994). Cognitive aspects and interventions in Alzheimer's disease. In J. D. Sinnott (Ed.), *Interdisciplinary handbook of adult lifespan learning* (pp. 389–407). New York: Greenwood.

Cavanaugh, J. C., & Stafford, H. (1989). Being aware of issues and biases: Directions for research on post-formal thought. In M. L. Commons, J. D. Sinnott, F. A. Richards, & C. Armon (Eds.), *Adult development: Vol. 1. Comparisons and applications of adolescent and adult development models* (pp. 272–292). New York: Praeger.

Cavanaugh, J. C., & Whitbourne, S. K. (1999). Research methods. In J. C. Cavanaugh & S. K. Whitbourne (Eds.), *Gerontology: An interdisciplinary perspective* (pp. 33–64). New York: Oxford University Press.

Centers for Disease Control and Prevention. (1999). *HIV/AIDS surveillance supplemental report: Characteristics of persons living with AIDS at the end of 1997* (Vol. 5, No. 1). Online document available at the Web site http://www.cdc.gov/nchstp/hiv_aids/stats/hasrsupp51.pdf.

Centers for Disease Control and Prevention. (2000). *Deaths: Final data for 1998. (National Vital Statistics Reports, Vol. 48 No. 11).* Available at the Web site http://www.cdc.gov/nchs/data/nvs48_11.pdf.

Cerella, J. (1990). Aging and information-processing rate. In J. E. Birren & K. W. Schaie (Eds.), *Handbook of the psychology of aging* (3rd ed., pp. 201–221). San Diego: Academic Press.

Cerella, J., & Hale, S. (1994). The rise and fall of information processing rates over the life span. *Acta Psychologica, 86,* 109–197.

Chambless, D. L., Sanderson, W. C., Shoham, V., Bennett Johnson, S., Pope, K. S., Crits-Christoph, P., Baker, M., Johnson, B., Woody, S. R., Sue, S., Beutler, L., Williams, D. A., & McCurry, S. (1996). An update on empirically validated therapies. *Clinical Psychologist, 49,* 5–18.

Chambré, S. M. (1993). Voluntarism by elders: Past trends and future prospects. *The Gerontologist, 33,* 221–228.

Chance, J., Overcast, T., & Dollinger, S. J. (1978). Aging and cognitive regression: Contrary findings. *Journal of Psychology, 98,* 177–183.

Chandler, M. J. (1980). Life-span intervention as a symptom of conversion hysteria. In R. R. Turner & H. W. Reese (Eds.), *Life-span developmental psychology: Intervention* (pp. 79–91). New York: Academic Press.

Chao, P. (1997). *Chinese kinship.* London: Kegan Paul.

Charles, S. T. (1998). Genetic and environmental influences on osteoarthritis. *Dissertation Abstracts International: Section B: The Sciences and Engineering, 58(11B),* 6272.

Charness, N. (1981). Aging and skilled problem solving. *Journal of Experimental Psychology, 110,* 21–38.

Charness, N., & Bosman, E. A. (1990). Expertise and aging: Life in the lab. In T. M. Hess (Ed.), *Aging and cognition: Knowledge organization and utilization* (pp. 343–385). Amsterdam: North-Holland.

Chasseigne, G., Mullett, E., & Stewart, T. R. (1997). Aging and multiple cue probability learning: The case of inverse relationships. *Acta Psychologica, 97,* 235–252.

Chasteen, A. L. (1994). "The world around me": The environment and single women. *Sex Roles, 31,* 309–328.

Chen, Y., & Blanchard-Fields, F. (1997). Age differences in stages of attributional processing. *Psychology and Aging, 12,* 694–703.

Cherkin, A. (1984). Effects of nutritional status on memory function. In H. J. Armbrecht, J. M. Prendergast, & R. M. Coe (Eds.), *Nutritional intervention in the aging process* (pp. 229–249). New York: Springer-Verlag.

Cherlin, A. J. (1992). *Marriage, divorce, remarriage* (rev. ed.). Cambridge, MA: Harvard University Press.

Cherlin, A. J. & Furstenberg, F. F., Jr. (1986). *The new American grandparent: A place in the family, a life apart.* New York: Basic Books.

Cherlin, A. J., & Furstenberg, F. F., Jr. (1994). Stepfamilies in the United States: A reconsideration. *Annual Review of Sociology, 20,* 359–381.

Cherry, K. E., & Park, D. C. (1993). Individual difference and contextual variables influence spatial memory in younger and older adults. *Psychology and Aging, 8,* 517–526.

Cherry, K. E., Park, D. C., & Donaldson, H. (1993). Adult age differences in spatial memory: Effects of structural context and practice. *Experimental Aging Research, 19,* 333–350.

Childs, H. W., Hayslip, B., Jr., Radika, L. M., & Reinberg, J. A. (2000). Young and middle-aged adults' perceptions of elder abuse. *The Gerontologist, 40,* 75–85.

Chinen, A. B. (1989). *In the ever after.* Willmette, IL: Chiron.

Christiansen, H., Mackinnon, A. J., Korten, A. E., Jorm, A. F., Henderson, A. S., Jacomb, P., & Rogers, B. (1999). An analysis of diversity in the cognitive performance of elderly community dwellers: Individual differences in change scores as a function of age. *Psychology and Aging, 14,* 365–379.

Cicirelli, V. G., Coward, R. T., & Dwyer, J. W. (1992). Siblings as caregivers for impaired elders. *Research on Aging, 14,* 331–350.

Clancy, S. M., & Hoyer, W. J. (1993). Skill and hemispheric specialization in detecting disparity in visual images. *Brain and Cognition, 21,* 192–202.

Clausen, J. A. (1981). Men's occupational careers in the middle years. In D. H. Eichorn, N. Haan, J. Clausen, M. Honzik, & P. Mussen (Eds.), *Present and past in middle life* (pp. 321–351). New York: Academic Press.

Clayton, V. P., & Overton, W. F. (1973, November). *The role of formal operational thought in the aging process.* Paper presented at the meeting of the Gerontological Society of America, Miami.

Clemons, A. W., & Axelson, L. J. (1985). The not-so-empty nest: The return of the fledgling adult. *Family Relations, 34,* 259–264.

Cohen, G. (1993). Memory and aging. In G. M. Davies, & R. H. Logic

(Eds.), *Memory in everyday life* (pp. 419–459). Amsterdam: North-Holland.

Cohen, G. D., Conway, M. A., & Maylor, E. A. (1994). Flashbulb memories in older adults. *Psychology and Aging, 9,* 454–463.

Cohen, R. M., Weingartner, H., Smallberg, S. A., Pickar, D., & Murphy, D. L. (1982). Effort and cognition in depression. *Archives of General Psychiatry, 39,* 593–597.

Cohen, S., & Herbert, T. B. (1996). Health psychology: Psychological factors and physical disease from the perspective of human psychoneuroimmunology. *Annual Review of Psychology, 47,* 113–142.

Cohen, S., Kessler, R. C., & Gordon, L. U. (1995). Strategies for measuring stress in studies of psychiatric and physical disorders. In S. Cohen & L. U. Gordon (Eds.), *Measuring stress* (pp. 3–26). New York: Oxford University Press.

Cohler, B. J. (1993). Aging, morale, and meaning: The nexus of narrative. In T. R. Cole, W. A. Achenbaum, P. L. Jakobi, & R. Kastenbaum (Eds.), *Voices and visions of aging: Toward a critical gerontology* (pp. 107–133). New York: Springer.

Coke, M. M. (1992). Correlates of life satisfaction among elderly African Americans. *Journal of Gerontology: Psychological Sciences, 47,* 316–320.

Colditz, G. A., Hankinson, S. E., Hunter, D. J., Willett, W. C., Manson, J. E., Stampfer, M. J., Hennekens, C., Rosner, B., & Speitzer, F. E. (1995). The use of estrogens and progestins and the risk of breast cancer in postmenopausal women. *New England Journal of Medicine, 332,* 1589–1593.

Cole, T. R., & Holstein, M. (1996). Ethics and aging. In R. H. Binstock & L. K. George (Eds.), *Handbook of aging and the social sciences* (4th ed., pp. 480–497). San Diego: Academic Press.

Coleman, K. A., Casey, V. A., & Dwyer, J. T. (1991, June). *Stability of autobiographical memories over four decades.* Paper presented at the meeting of the American Psychological Society, Washington.

Coleman, M., & Ganong, L. H. (1990). Remarriage and stepfamily research in the 1980s: Increased interest in an old family form. *Journal of Marriage and the Family, 52,* 925–940.

Collopy, B. J. (1988). Autonomy in long term care: Some crucial distinctions. *The Gerontologist, 28*(Suppl.), 10–17.

Colonia-Willner, R. (1998). Practical intelligence at work: Relationships between aging and cognitive efficiency among managers in a bank environment. *Psychology and Aging, 13,* 45–47.

Commons, M. L., Richards, F. A., & Armon, C. (Eds.). (1984). *Beyond formal operations: Late adolescent and adult cognitive development.* New York: Praeger.

Commons, M. L., Richards, F. A., & Kuhn, D. (1982). Systematic and metasystematic reasoning: A case for levels of reasoning beyond Piaget's stage of formal operations. *Child Development, 53,* 1058–1069.

Commons, M. L., Sinnott, J. D., Richards, F. A., & Armon, C. (Eds.). (1989). *Adult development: Vol. 1. Comparisons and applications of adolescent and adult developmental models.* New York: Praeger.

Connelly, S. L., & Hasher, L. (1993). Aging and the inhibition of spatial location. *Journal of Experimental Psychology: Human Perception and Performance, 19,* 1238–1250.

Connelly, S. L., Hasher, L., & Zacks, R. T. (1991). Age and reading: The impact of distraction. *Psychology and Aging, 6,* 533–541.

Connidis, I. (1988, November). *Sibling ties and aging.* Paper presented at the Gerontological Society of America, San Francisco.

Connidis, I. (1994). Sibling support in older age. *Journal of Gerontology: Social Sciences, 49,* S309–S317.

Connor, L. T., Dunlowsky, J., & Hertzog, C. (1997). Age-related differences in absolute but not relative meta-memory accuracy. *Psychology and Aging, 12,* 50–71.

Cook-Greuter, S. (1989). Maps for living: Ego development theory from symbiosis to conscious universal embeddedness. In M. L. Commons,

J. D. Sinnott, F. A. Richards, & C. Armon (Eds.), *Adult development: Vol. 2. Comparisons and application of adolescent and adult developmental models* (pp. 79–104). New York: Praeger.

Cooney, T. M., Pedersen, F. A., Indelicato, S., & Palkovitz, R. (1993). Timing of fatherhood: Is "on-time" optimal? *Journal of Marriage and the Family, 55,* 205–215.

Cooper, R. S., Rotimi, C. N., & Ward, R. (1999). The puzzle of hypertension in African-Americans. *Scientific American.* Online document available at the Web site http://www.sciam.com/1999/0299issue/0299cooper.html.

Cordes, C. L., & Dougherty, T. W. (1993). A review and integration of research on job burnout. *Academy of Management Review, 18,* 621–656.

Corkin, S., Growdon J. H., Sullivan, E. V., Nissen, M. J., & Huff, F. J. (1986). Assessing treatment effects: A neuropsychological battery. In L. W. Poon (Ed.), *Handbook for clinical memory assessment of older adults* (pp. 156–167). Washington, DC: American Psychological Association.

Cornelius, S. W. (1990). Aging and everyday cognitive abilities. In T. M. Hess (Ed.), *Aging and cognition: Knowledge organization and utilization* (pp. 411–459). Amsterdam: North-Holland.

Cornelius, S. W., & Caspi, A. (1987). Everyday problem solving in adulthood and old age. *Psychology and Aging, 2,* 144–153.

Cornish, N. (1994). Over the hill? *News Journal* (Wilmington, DE), D10–D11.

Cornman, J. M., & Kingston, E. R. (1996). Trends, issues, perspectives, and values for the aging of the baby boom cohorts. *The Gerontologist, 36,* 15–26.

Corr, C. A. (1991-92). A task-based approach to coping with dying. *Omega, 24,* 81–94.

Corrigan, P. W., et al. (1994). Staff burnout in a psychiatric hospital: A cross-lagged panel design. *Journal of Organizational Behavior, 15,* 65–74.

Cosby, A. (1974). Occupational expectations and the hypothesis of increasing realism of choice. *Journal of Vocational Behavior, 5,* 53–65.

Costa, P. T., Jr., & McCrae, R. R. (1978). Objective personality assessment. In M. Storandt, I. C. Siegler, & M. F. Elias (Eds.), *The clinical psychology of aging* (pp. 119–143). New York: Plenum.

Costa, P. T., Jr., & McCrae, R. R. (1980). Somatic complaints in males as a function of age and neuroticism: A longitudinal analysis. *Journal of Behavioral Medicine, 3,* 245–258.

Costa, P. T., Jr., & McCrae, R. R. (1988). Personality in adulthood: A six-year longitudinal study of self-reports and spouse ratings on the NEO Personality Inventory. *Journal of Personality and Social Psychology, 54,* 853–863.

Costa, P. T., & McCrae, R. R. (1994). Set like plaster? Evidence for the stability of adult personality. In T. F. Heatherton & J. L. Weinberger (Eds.), *Can personality change?* (pp. 21–40). Washington, DC: Academic Psychological Association.

Costa, P. T., Jr., & McCrae, R. R. (1995). Solid ground in the wetlands of personality: A reply to block. *Psychological Bulletin, 117,* 216–220.

Costa, P. T., & McCrae, R. R. (1997). Longitudinal stability of adult personality. In R. Hogan, J. Johnson, & S. Briggs (Eds.), *Handbook of personality psychology* (pp. 269–292). San Diego: Academic Press.

Costa, P. T., & McCrae, R. R. (1998). Six approaches to the explication of facet-level traits examples from conscientiousness. *European Journal of Personality, 12,* 117–134.

Costa, P. T., McCrae, R. R., & Holland, J. L. (1984). Personality and vocational interests in an adult sample. *Journal of Applied Psychology, 42,* 390–400.

Costa, P. T., McCrae, R. R., & Holland, J. L. (1996). Personality and vocational interests in adult males. *Journal of Personality and Social Psychology, 38,* 793–800.

Cotton, S., Anthill, J. K., & Cunningham, J. D. (1989). The work motivations of mothers with preschool children. *Journal of Family Issues, 10,* 189–210.

Counts, D. A., & Counts, D. R. (1985). I'm not dead yet! Aging and death: Processes and experiences in Kalia. In D. A. Counts & D. R. Counts (Eds.), *Aging and its transformations* (pp. 131–156). Langham, MD: University of America Press.

Cournoyer, R. J., & Mahalik, J. R. (1995). Cross-sectional study of gender role conflict examining college-aged and mid-aged men. *Journal of Counseling Psychology, 42,* 11–19.

Cousins, S. O. (2000). "My heart couldn't take it": Older women's beliefs about exercise benefits and risks. *Journal of Gerontology: Psychological Sciences, 55B,* P283–P294.

Craik, F. I. M. (1977). Age differences in human memory. In J. E. Birren & K. W. Schaie (Eds.), *Handbook of the psychology of aging* (pp. 384–420). New York: Van Nostrand Reinhold.

Craik, F. I. M., Anderson, N. D., Kerr, S. A., & Li, K. Z. H. (1995). Memory changes in normal aging. In A. D. Baddely & B. A. Wilson et al. (Eds.), *Handbook of memory disorders* (pp. 211–241). Chichester, England: Wiley.

Craik, F. I. M., & Byrd, M. (1982). Aging and cognitive deficits: The role of attentional sources. In F. I. M. Craik & S. Trehub (Eds.), *Aging and cognitive processes* (pp. 191–211). New York: Plenum.

Crimmins, E. M., Saito, Y., & Reynolds, S. L. (1997). Further evidence on recent trends in the prevalence and incidence of disability among older Americans from two sources: The LSOA and the NHIS. *Journal of Gerontology: Social Sciences, 52B,* S59–S71.

Cristofalo, V. J., Tresini, M., Francis, M. K., & Volker, C. (1999). Biological theories of senescence. In V. L. Bengtson & K. W. Schaie (Eds.), *Handbook of theories of aging* (pp. 98–112). New York: Springer.

Crook, T. H., & Larrabee, G. J. (1992). Normative data on a self-rating scale for evaluating memory in everyday life. *Archives of Clinical Neuropsychology, 7,* 41–51.

Crook, T. H., West, R. L., & Larrabee, G. J. (1993). The driving–reaction time test: Assessing age declines in dual-task performance. *Developmental Neuropsychology, 9,* 31–39.

Cross, S., & Markus, H. (1991). Possible selves across the lifespan. *Human Development, 34,* 230–255.

Cunningham, W. R. (1987). Intellectual abilities and age. In K. W. Schaie (Ed.), *Annual review of gerontology and geriatrics* (Vol. 7, pp. 117–134). New York: Springer.

Currey, J. D., Brear, K., & Zioupos, P. (1996). The effects of ageing and changes in mineral content in degrading the toughness of human femora. *Journal of Biomechanics, 29,* 257–260.

Cusack, B. J. (1995). Clinical pharmacology. In W. B. Abrams, M. H. Beers, & R. Berkow (Eds.), *The Merck manual of geriatrics* (2nd ed., pp. 255–276). Whitehouse Station, NJ: Merck.

Cutler, S. J., & Hendricks, J. (1990). Leisure and time use across the life course. In R. H. Binstock & L. K. George (Eds.), *Handbook of aging and the social sciences* (3rd ed., pp. 169–185). San Diego: Academic Press.

Cutrona, C. E. (1996). *Social support in couples.* Thousand Oaks, CA: Sage.

Cutter, M. A. G. (1991). Euthanasia: Reassessing the boundaries. *Journal of NIH Research, 3(5),* 59–61.

Dalton, S. T. (1992). Lived experience of never-married women. *Issues in Mental Health Nursing, 13,* 69–80.

Davies, D. R., et al. (1991). Aging and work. In C. L. Cooper & I. T. Robertson (Eds.), *International review of industrial and organizational psychology* (Vol. 6, pp. 175–199). Chichester: Wiley.

Davis, M., McKay, M., & Eshelman, E. R. (2000). *The relaxation and stress reduction workbook.* Oakland, CA: New Harbinger.

Dawson Hughes, B. (1996). Calcium and vitamin D nutritional needs of elderly women. *Journal of Nutrition, 126,* 1165s–1167s.

Day, D. V., & Bedeian, A. G. (1995). Personality similarity and work-related outcomes among African-American nursing personnel: A test of the supplementary model of person–

environment congruence. *Journal of Vocational Behavior, 46,* 55–70.

Day, S. X., Rounds, J., & Swaney, K. (1998). The structure of vocational interests for diverse racial–ethnic groups. *Psychological Science, 9,* 40–44.

de Groot, C. P., Perdigao, A. L., & Deurenberg, P. (1996). Longitudinal changes in anthropometric characteristics of elderly Europeans. SENECA Investigators. *European Journal of Clinical Nutrition, 50,* 2954–3007.

de St. Aubin, E., & McAdams, D. P. (1995). The relations of generative concern and generative action to personality traits, satisfaction/happiness with life, and ego development. *Journal of Adult Development, 2,* 99–112.

de Vries, B. (1996). The understanding of friendship: An adult life course perspective. In C. Magai & S. H. McFadden (Eds.), *Handbook of emotion, adult development, and aging.* (San Diego: Academic Press.)

Deeg, D. J. H., Kardaun, J. W. P. F., & Fozard, J. L. (1996). Health, behavior, and aging. In K. W. Schaie & J. E. Birren (Eds.), *Handbook of the psychology of aging* (4th ed., pp. 129–149). San Diego: Academic Press.

Denney, N. W. (1984). A model of cognitive development across the life span. *Developmental Review, 4,* 171–191.

Denney, N. W. (1990). Adult age differences in traditional and practical problem solving. In E. A. Lovelace (Ed.), *Aging and cognition: Mental processes, self-awareness, and interventions* (pp. 329–349). Amsterdam: North-Holland.

Denney, N. W., & Cornelius, S. W. (1975). Class inclusion and multiple classification in middle and old age. *Developmental Psychology, 11,* 521–522.

Denney, N. W., Dew, J. R., & Kihlstrom, J. F. (1992). An adult developmental study of the encoding of spatial location. *Experimental Aging Research, 18,* 25–32.

Denney, N. W., Dew, J. R., & Kroupa, S. L. (1995). Perceptions of wisdom: What is it and who has it? *Journal of Adult Development, 2,* 37–47.

Denney, N. W., & Pearce, K. A. (1989). A developmental study of practical problem solving in adults. *Psychology and Aging, 4,* 438–442.

Denney, N. W., Pearce, K. A., & Palmer, A. M. (1982). A developmental study of adults' performance on traditional and practical problem-solving tasks. *Experimental Aging Research, 8,* 115–118.

Devine, P. G. (1989). Stereotypes and prejudice: Their automatic and controlled components. *Journal of Personality and Social Psychology, 56,* 5–18.

Devolder, P. A., Brigham, M. C., & Pressley, M. (1990). Memory performance awareness in younger and older adults. *Psychology and Aging, 5,* 291–303.

Diamond, J. (1986). I want a girl just like the girl. . . . *Discover, 7(11),* 65–68.

Diehl, M. (1998). Everyday competence in later life: Current status and future directions. *The Gerontologist, 4,* 422–433.

Diehl, M., Coyle, N., & Labouvie-Vief, G. (1996). Age and sex differences in strategies of coping and defense across the life span. *Psychology and Aging, 11,* 127–139.

Diehl, M., Willis, S. L., & Schaie, K. W. (1995). Everyday problem solving in older adults: Observational assessment and cognitive correlates. *Psychology and Aging, 10,* 478–491.

Dimond, M., Lund, D. A., & Caserta, M. S. (1987). The role of social support in the first two years of bereavement in an elderly sample. *The Gerontologist, 27,* 599–604.

Diprete, T. A., & Soule, W. T. (1988). Gender and promotion in segmented job ladder systems. *American Sociological Review, 53,* 26–40.

Ditre, C. M., Griffin, T. D., Murphy, G. F., Sueki, H., Telegan, B., Johnson, W. C., Yu, R. J., & Van Scott, E. J. (1996). Effects of alpha-hydroxy acids on photoaged skin: A pilot clinical, histologic, and ultrastructural study. *Journal of the American Academy of Dermatology, 34,* 187–195.

Dixon, R. A. (1989). Questionnaire research on metamemory and aging: Issues of structure and function. In L. W. Poon, D. C. Rubin, & B., A,. Wilson (Eds.), *Everyday cognition in adulthood and late life* (pp. 394–415). New York: Cambridge University Press.

Dixon, R. A. (1999). Exploring cognition in interactive situations: Aging of N +1 minds. In T. A. Hess & F. Blanchard-Fields (Eds.), *Social cognition and aging* (pp. 267–290). San Diego: Academic Press.

Dixon, R. A., & Bäckman, L. (Eds.). (1995). *Compensating for psychological deficiencies and declines: Managing less and promoting gains.* Mahwah, NJ: Erlbaum.

Dixon, R. A., & Gould, O. N. (1998). Younger and older adults collaborating on retelling everyday stories. *Applied Development Science, 2,* 160–171.

Dixon, R. A., Hultsch, D. F., & Hertzog, C. (1989). The Metamemory in Adulthood questionnaire. *Psychopharmacology Bulletin, 24,* 671–688.

Dobson, S. H., Kirasic, K. C., & Allen, G. L. (1995). Age-related differences in adults' spatial task performance: Influences of task complexity and perceptual speed. *Aging and Cognition, 2,* 19–38.

Dorgan, J. F., Stanczyk, F. A., Longcope, C., Stephenson, H. E., Jr., Chang, L., Miller, R., Franz, C., Falk, R. T., & Kahle, L. (1997). Relationship of serum dehydroepiandrosterone (DHEA), DHEA sulfate, and 5-androstene-3 beta, 17 beta-diol to risk of breast cancer in post-menopausal women. *Cancer Epidemiology, Biomarkers and Prevention, 6,* 177–181.

Doka, K. J., & Mertz, M. E. (1988). The meaning and significance of great-grandparenthood. *The Gerontologist, 28,* 192–197.

Doyle, K. O., Jr. (1974). Theory and practice of ability testing in ancient Greece. *Journal of the History of the Behavioral Sciences, 10,* 202–212.

Drew, L. M., & Smith, P. (1999, November). *The mental health of grandparents in Britain: Regular contact compared to those who have lost contact due to parental separation/divorce.* Paper presented at the annual meeting of the Gerontological Society, San Francisco.

DuBois, P. H. (1968). A test dominated society: China 1115 B.C.–1905 A.D. In J. L. Barnette (Ed.), *Readings in psychological tests and measurements* (pp. 249–255). Homewood, IL: Dorsey Press.

Dunlosky, J., & Hertzog, C. (1998). Training programs to improve learning in later adulthood: Helping older adults educate themselves. In D. J. Hacker, J. Dunlosky, & A. C. Graessen (Eds.), *Metacognition in educational theory and practice* (pp. 249–275). Hillsdale, NJ: Erlbaum.

Dunn, T. R., & Merriam, S. B. (1995). Levinson's age thirty transition: Does it exist? *Journal of Adult Development, 2,* 113–124.

Dupree, L. W., & Schonfeld, L. (1996). Substance abuse. In M. Hersen & V. B. Van Hasselt (Eds.), *Psychological treatment of older adults* (pp. 281–297). New York: Plenum.

Duvall, E. M. (1977). *Marriage and family development* (5th ed.). Philadelphia: Lippincott.

Dwyer, J. W., & Coward, R. T. (1991). A multivariate comparison of the involvement of adult sons versus daughters in the care of impaired parents. *Journal of Gerontology: Social Sciences, 46,* S259–S269.

Dywan, J., & Jacoby, L. L. (1990). Effects of aging on source monitoring: Differences in susceptibility to false fame. *Psychology and Aging, 5,* 379–387.

Earles, J. L., Connor, L. T., Frieske, D., Park, D. C., et al. (1997). Age differences in inhibition: Possible causes and consequences. *Aging, Neuropsychology, and Cognition, 4,* 45–57.

Earles, J. L., & Coon, V. E. (1994). Adult age differences in long-term memory for performed activities. *Journal of Gerontology: Psychological Sciences, 49,* P32–P34.

Ebersole, P., & Hess, P. (1998). *Toward healthy aging: Human needs and nursing response* (5th ed.). St. Louis: Mosby.

Edelstein, B., & Kalish, K. (1999). Clinical assessment of older adults. In J. C. Cavanaugh & S. K. Whitbourne (Eds.), *Gerontology: An interdisciplinary perspective* (pp. 269–304). New York: Oxford University Press.

Edelstein, B., & Semenchuck, E. M. (1996). Interviewing older adults. In L. L. Carstensen, B. A. Edelstein, & L. Dornbrand (Eds.), *The practical handbook of clinical gerontology* (pp. 153–173). Thousand Oaks, CA: Sage.

Einstein, G. O., & McDaniel, M. A. (1990). Normal aging and prospective memory. *Journal of Experimental Psychology: Learning, Memory, and Cognition, 16,* 717–726.

Einstein, G. O., & McDaniel, M. A. (1997). Aging and mind wandering: Reduced inhibition in older adults. *Experimental Aging Research, 23,* 343–354.

Einstein, G. O., McDaniel, M. A., Richardson, S. L., Guyhn, M. J., & Cunfer, (1995). Aging and prospective memory: Examining the influences of self initiated retrieval processes. *Journal of Experimental Psychology: Learning, Memory, and Cognition, 21,* 996–1107.

Eisner, D. A. (1973). *The effect of chronic brain syndrome upon concrete and formal operations in elderly men.* Unpublished manuscript cited in Papalia & Bielby (1974).

Ekerdt, D. J. (1987). Why the notion persists that retirement harms health. *The Gerontologist, 27,* 454–457.

Ekstrom, R. K., French, J. W., & Harman, H. H. (1979). Cognitive factors: Their identification and replication. *Multivariate Behavioral Research Monographs, 79,* 2.

Elias, M. F., Elias, P. K., Cobb, J., D'Agostino, R., White, L. R., & Wolf, P. A. (1995). Blood pressure affects cognitive functioning: The

Framingham Studies revisited. In J. E. Dimsdale & A. Braum (Eds.), *Quality of life in behavioral medicine research* (pp. 121–143). Hillsdale, NJ: Erlbaum.

Ellison, C. G. (1990). Family ties, friendships, and subjective well-being among black Americans. *Journal of Marriage and the Family, 52,* 298–310.

Emick, M. A., & Hayslip, B., Jr. (1999). Custodial grandparenting: Stresses, coping skills, and relationships with grandchildren. *International Journal of Aging and Human Development, 48,* 35–61.

Emlet, C. A. (1997). HIV/AIDS in the elderly: A hidden population. *Home Care Provider, 2,* 22–28.

Engle, E., Miguel, R., Steelman, L., & McDaniel, M. A. (1994, April). *The relationship between age and work needs: A comprehensive research integration.* Paper presented at the National Meetings of the Society for Industrial and Organizational Psychology, Nashville, TN.

Epstein, S., Lipson, A., Holstein, C., & Huh, E. (1992). Irrational reactions to negative outcomes: Evidence for two conceptual systems. *Journal of Personality and Social Psychology, 62,* 328–339.

Erber, J. T., & Prager, I. G. (1997). Age and forgetfulness: Absolute versus comparative decisions about capability. *Experimental Aging Research, 23,* 355–367.

Erber, J. T., & Prager, I. G. (1999). Perceptions of forgetful young and older adults. In T. M. Hess & F. Blanchard-Fields (Eds.), *Social cognition and aging* (pp. 197–217). San Diego: Academic Press.

Erber, J. T., Prager, I. G., Williams, M., & Cainola, M. A. (1996). Age and forgetfulness: Confidence in ability and attribution for memory failures. *Psychology and Aging, 11,* 310–315.

Erber, J. T., Szuchman, L. T., & Etheart, M. E. (1993). Age and forgetfulness: Young perceivers' impressions of young and older neighbors. *International Journal of Aging and Human Development, 37,* 91–103.

Erber, J. T., Szuchman, L. T., & Rothberg, S. T. (1990). Everyday memory failure: Age differences in appraisal and attribution. *Psychology and Aging, 5,* 236–241.

Ericsson, K. A., & Charness, N. (1994). Expert performance: Its structure and acquisition. *American Psychology, 49,* 725–747.

Erikson, E. H. (1968). *Identity: Youth and crisis.* New York: Norton.

Erikson, E. H. (1982). *The life cycle completed: Review.* New York: Norton.

Espino, D. V., & Maldonado, D. (1990). Hypertension and acculturation in elderly Mexican Americans: Results from 1982–84 Hispanic HANES. *Journal of Gerontology: Medical Sciences, 45,* M209–M213.

Ettinger, W. H. (1995). Bone, joint, and rheumatic disorders. In W. B. Abrams, M. H. Beers, & R. Berkow (Eds.), *The Merck manual of geriatrics* (2nd ed., pp. 925–945). Whitehouse Station, NJ: Merck Research Laboratories.

Etzion, D., & Bailyn, L. (1994). Patterns of adjustment to the career/family conflict of technically trained women in U.S. and Israel. *Journal of Applied Social Psychology, 24,* 1520–1549.

Evans, G. W., Brennan, P. L., Skorpanich, M. A., & Held, D. (1984). Cognitive mapping and elderly adults: Verbal and location memory for urban landmarks. *Journal of Gerontology, 39,* 452–457.

Farrell, M. P., Rosenberg, S., & Rosenberg, H. T. (1993). Changing texts of identity from early to late middle age: On the emergent prominence of fatherhood. In J. Demick, K. Bursik, et al. (Eds.), *Parental development* (pp. 203–224). Hillsdale, NJ: Erlbaum.

Fehr, B. (1996). *Friendship processes.* Thousand Oaks, CA: Sage.

Feldman, D. C. (1994). The decision to retire early: A review and conceptualization. *Academy of Management Review, 19,* 285–311.

Felton, B. J., & Revenson, T. A. (1987). Age differences in coping with chronic illness. *Psychology and Aging, 2,* 164–170.

Femia, E. E., Zarit, S. H., & Johansson, B. (2001). The disablement process in very late life: A study of the oldest-old in Sweden. *Journal of Gerontology: Psychological Sciences, 56B,* P12–P23.

Feminist Majority Foundation. (1991). *Empowering women in business.* Washington, DC: Author.

Ferraro, K. F., & Su, Y. (1999). Financial strain, social relations, and psychological distinctiveness among older people: A cross-cultural analysis. *Journal of Gerontology: Psychological Sciences and Social Sciences, 54B,* S3–S15.

Ferris, S. H., & Crook, T. H. (1983). Cognitive assessment in mild to moderately severe dementia. In T. H. Crook, S. Ferris, & R. Bartus (Eds.), *Assessment in geriatric psychopharmacology.* New Canaan, CT: Mark Powley Associates.

Fiatarone, M. A., Marks, E. C., Ryan, N. D., Meredith, C. N., Lipsitz, L. A., & Evans, W. J. (1990). High-intensity strength training in nonagenarians: Effects on skeletal muscle. *Journal of the American Medical Association, 263,* 3029–3034.

Field, D., & Millsap, R. E. (1991). Personality in advanced old age: Continuity or change? *Journal of Gerontology: Psychological Sciences, 46,* 299–308.

Field, D., & Minkler, M. (1988). Continuity and change in social support between young-old and old-old or very-old age. *Journal of Gerontology: Psychological Sciences, 43,* P100–P106.

Fields, T. M., & Widmayer, S. M. (1982). Motherhood. In B. B. Wolman (Ed.), *Handbook of developmental psychology* (pp. 681–701). Englewood Cliffs, NJ: Prentice Hall.

Fillenbaum, G. G. (1985). Screening the elderly: A brief instrumental activities of daily living measure. *Journal of the American Geriatrics Society, 33,* 698–706.

Finch, C. E., & Seeman, T. E. (1999). Stress theories of aging. In V. L. Bengtson & K. W. Schaie (Eds.), *Handbook of theories of aging* (pp. 81–97). New York: Springer.

Fisher, D. L., Fisk, A. D., & Duffy, S. A. (1995). Why latent models are needed to test hypothesis about slowing of word and language processes in older adults. In P. A. Allen & T. R. Bashore (Eds.), *Age differences in word and language processing* (pp. 1–29). Amsterdam: North–Holland.

Fisk, A. D., Cooper, B. P., Hertzog, C., & Anderson-Garlach, M. M. (1995). Age-related retention of skilled memory search: Examination of associative learning, interference, and task-specific skills. *Journal of Gerontology: Psychological Sciences, 50B,* P150–P161.

Fisk, A. D., Cooper, B. P., Hertzog, C., Anderson-Garlach, M. M., & Lee, M. D. (1995). Understanding performance and learning in consistent memory search: An age-related perspective. *Psychology and Aging, 10,* 255–268.

Fisk, A. D., & Rogers, W. A. (1991). Toward an understanding of age-related memory and visual search effects. *Journal of Experimental Psychology: General, 120,* 131–149.

Fiske, S. (1993). Social cognition and social perception. *Annual Review of Psychology, 50,* 229–238.

Fitzgerald, J. M. (1999). Autobiographical memory and social cognition: Development of the remembered self in adulthood. In T. M. Hess & F. Blanchard-Fields, *Social cognition in aging* (pp. 147–171). San Diego: Academic Press.

Fitzgerald, J. M., & Lawrence, R. (1984). Autobiographical memory across the life span. *Journal of Gerontology, 39,* 692–698.

Fitzgerald, L. F., & Ormerod, A. J. (1991). Perceptions of sexual harassment: The influence of gender and academic context. *Psychology of Women Quarterly, 15,* 281–294.

Fitzgerald, L. F., & Shullman, S. L. (1993). Sexual harassment: A research analysis and agenda for the 1990s. *Journal of Vocational Behavior, 32,* 5–27.

Fitzgerald, L. F., Shullman, S. L., Bailey, N., Richards, M., Swecker, J., Gold, Y., Ormerod, M., & Weitzman, L. (1988). The incidences and dimensions of sexual harassment in academia and the workplace. *Journal of Vocational Behavior, 32*(2), 152–175.

Flaks, D. K., Ficher, I., Masterpasqua, F., & Joseph, G. (1995). Lesbians choosing motherhood: A comparative study of lesbian and heterosexual parents and their children. *Developmental Psychology, 31,* 105–114.

Fleischman, D. A., & Gabrieli, J. D. E. (1998). Repetition priming in normal aging and Alzheimer's disease: A review of findings and theories. *Psychology and Aging, 13,* 88–119.

Flynn, T. M., & Storandt, M. (1990). Supplemental group discussions in memory training for older adults. *Psychology and Aging, 5,* 178–181.

Foley, D. J., Miles, T. P., Brock, D. B., & Phillips, C. (1995). Recounts of elderly deaths: Endorsements for the Patient Self-Determination Act. *The Gerontologist, 35,* 119–121.

Folkman, S., Lazarus, R. S., Pimley, S., & Novacek, J. (1987). Age differences in stress and coping processes. *Psychology and Aging, 2,* 171–184.

Folstein, M. F., Folstein, S. E., & McHugh, P. R. (1975). Mini-mental state: A practical method for grading the cognitive state of patients for the clinician. *Journal of Psychiatric Research, 12,* 189–198.

Foos, P. W. (1995). Working memory resource allocation by young, middle-aged, and old adults. *Experimental Aging Research, 21,* 239–250.

Fortner, B. V., & Neimeyer, R. A. (1999). Death anxiety in older adults: A quantitative review. *Death Studies, 23,* 387–411.

Fox, A. (1979, January). Earnings replacement rates of retired couples: Findings from the Retirement History Study. *Social Security Bulletin, 42,* 17–39.

Fozard, J. L. (1981). Speed of mental performance and aging: Costs of age and benefits of wisdom. In F. J. Piorzzolo & G. J. Maletta (Eds.), *Behavioral assessment and psychopharmacology* (pp. 59–94). New York: Praeger.

Fozard, J. L., Vercruyssen, M., Reynolds, S. L., Hancock, P. A., & Quilter, R. E. (1994). Age differences and changes in reaction time: The Baltimore longitudinal study of aging. *Journal of Gerontology: Psychological Sciences, 49,* 179–189.

Frank, L., Smyer, M. A., Grisso, T., & Appelbaum, P. (1999). Measurement of advance directive and medical treatment decision-making capacity of older adults. *Journal of Mental Health and Aging, 5,* 257–274.

Frerichs, F., & Naegele, G. (1997). Discrimination of older workers in Germany: Obstacles and options for the integration into employment. *Journal of Aging and Social Policy, 9,* 89–101.

Freund, A. M., & Baltes, P. B. (1998). Selection, optimization, and compensation as strategies of life management: Correlations with subjective indicators of successful aging. *Psychology and Aging, 13,* 531–543.

Friedhoff, A. J. (1994). Consensus development conference statement: Diagnosis and treatment of depression in late life. In L. S. Schneider, C. F. Reynolds, B. D. Lebowitz, & A. J. Friedhoff (Eds.), *Diagnosis and treatment of depression in late life: Results of the NIH Consensus Development Conference* (pp. 493–511). Washington, DC: American Psychiatric Press.

Froman, L. (1994). Adult learning in the workplace. In J. D. Sinnott (Ed.), *Interdisciplinary handbook of adult lifespan learning* (pp. 203–217). Westport, CT: Greenwood.

Fromholt, P., & Bruhn, P. (1999). Cognitive dysfunction and dementia. In I. H. Nordhus, G. R. VandenBos, S. Berg, & P. Fromholt (Eds.), *Clinical geropsychology* (pp. 183–188). Washington, DC: American Psychological Association.

Frone, M. R., & Yardley, J. K. (1996). Workplace family-supportive programs: Predictors of employed parents' importance ratings. *Journal of Occupational and Organizational Psychology, 69,* 351–366.

Fuller-Thompson, E., Minkler, M., & Driver, D. (1997). A profile of grandparents raising grandchildren in the United States. *The Gerontologist, 37,* 406–411.

Fulton, G., Madden, C., & Minichiello, V. (1996). The social construction of anticipatory grief. *Social Science and Medicine, 43,* 1349–1358.

Furstenberg, F. F., Jr. (1982). Conjugal succession: Reentering marriage after divorce. In P. B. Baltes & O. G. Brim, Jr. (Eds.), *Life-span development and behavior* (Vol. 5, pp. 108–146). New York: Academic Press.

Futterman, A., Gallagher, D., Thompson, L. W., Lovett, S., & Gilewski, M. (1990). Retrospective assessment of marital adjustment and depression during the first two years of spousal bereavement. *Psychology and Aging, 5,* 277–283.

Gabrieli, J. D. E. (1998). Cognitive neuroscience in human memory. *Annual Review of Psychology, 49,* 87–115.

Gabrieli, J. D. E., Brewer, J. B., Desmond, J. E., & Glover, G. H. (1997). Separate neural bases of two fundamental memory processes in the human medial temporal lobe. *Science, 276,* 264–266.

Gaerta, T. J., Lapolla, C., & Melendez, E. (1996). AIDS in the elderly. *Journal of Emergency Medicine, 14,* 19–23.

Gailey, C. W. (1987). Evolutionary perspectives in gender hierarchy. In B. B. Hess & M. M. Feree (Eds.), *Analyzing gender: A handbook of social science research* (pp. 32–67). Thousand Oaks, CA: Sage.

Galinsky, E., Bond, J. T., & Friedman, D. E. (1996). The role of employers in addressing the needs of employed parents. *Journal of Social Issues, 52,* 111–136.

Gall, T. L., Evans, D. R., & Howard, J. (1997). The retirement adjustment process: Changes in the well-being of male retirees across time. *Journal of Gerontology: Psychological Sciences, 52B,* 110–117.

Gallagher, M. (1996). Re-creating marriage. In D. Popenoe, J. B. Elshtain, & D. Blankenhorn (Eds.), *Promises to keep: Decline and renewal of marriage in America* (pp. 233–246). Lanham, MD: Rowman & Littlefield.

Gallo, J. J., Anthony, J. C., & Muthen, B. O. (1994). Age differences in the symptoms of depression: A latent trait analysis. *Journal of Gerontology:*

Psychological Sciences, 49, P251–P264.

Gallo, J. J., Rebok, G. W., & Lesikar, S. E. (1999). The driving habits of adults aged 60 years and older. *Journal of the American Geriatric Society, 47,* 335–341.

Gatz, M. (2000). Variations on depression in later life. In S. H. Qualls & N. Abeles (Eds.), *Psychology and the aging revolution* (pp. 239–254). Washington, DC: American Psychological Association.

Gatz, M., Fiske, A., Fox, L. S., Kaskie, B., Kasl-Godley, J. E., McCallum, T. J., & Loebach Wetherell, J. (1998). Empirically validated psychological treatments for older adults. *Journal of Mental Health and Aging, 4,* 9–46.

Gatz, M., Kasl-Godley, J. E., & Karel, M. (1996). Aging and mental disorders. In J. E. Birren & K. W. Schaie (Eds.), *Handbook of the psychology of aging* (4th ed., pp. 365–382). San Diego: Academic Press.

Gatz, M., Pedersen, N. L., Berg, S., Johansson, B., Johansson, K., Mortimer, J. A., Posner, S. F., Viitanen, M., Winblad, B., & Ahlbom, A. (1997). Heritability for Alzheimer's disease: The study of dementia in Swedish twins. *Journal of Gerontology: Medical Sciences, 52A,* M117–M125.

Gatz, M., Pedersen, N. L., Plomin, R., & Nesselroade, J. R. (1992). Importance of shared genes and shared environments for symptoms of depression in older adults. *Journal of Abnormal Psychology, 101,* 701–708.

Gatz, M., & Zarit, S. H. (1999). A good old age: Paradox or possibility. In V. L. Bengtson & K. W. Schaie (Eds.), *Handbook of theories of aging* (pp. 396–416). New York: Springer.

Gaylord, S. A., & Zung, W. W. K. (1987). Affective disorders among the aging. In L. L. Carstensen & B. A. Edelstein (Eds.), *Handbook of clinical gerontology* (pp. 76–95). New York: Pergamon.

Gazzaniga, M. S. (1995). *The cognitive neurosciences.* Cambridge, MA: MIT Press.

Gentry, M., & Schulman, A. D. (1988). Remarriage as a coping response for

widowhood. *Psychology and Aging, 3,* 191–196.

George, L. K., & Gwyther, L. P. (1986). Caregiver well-being: A multidimensional examination of family caregivers of demented adults. *The Gerontologist, 26,* 253–259.

Gerhart, T. N. (1995). Fractures. In W. B. Abrams, M. H. Beers, & R. Berkow (Eds.), *The Merck manual of geriatrics* (2nd ed., pp. 79–98). Whitehouse Station, NJ: Merck Research Laboratories.

German, P. S. (1995). Prevention and chronic disease in older individuals. In L. A. Bond, S. J. Cutler, & A. Grams (Eds.), *Promoting successful and productive aging* (pp. 95–108). Thousand Oaks, CA: Sage.

Giambra, L. M. (1993). Sustained attention in older adults: Performance and processes. In J. Cerella, J. Rybash, W. Hoyer, & M. L. Commons (Eds.), *Adult information processing: Limits on loss* (pp. 259–272). San Diego: Academic Press.

Gibran, K. (1923). *The prophet.* New York: Knopf.

Gibson, R. C. (1986). *Blacks in an aging society.* New York: Carnegie.

Gibson, R. C. (1987). Reconceptualizing retirement for black Americans. *The Gerontologist, 27,* 691–698.

Gibson, R. C. (1991). The subjective retirement of black Americans. *Journal of Gerontology: Social Sciences, 46,* S204–S209.

Gignac, M. A. M., Cott, C., & Badley, . M. (2000). Adaptation to chronic illness and disability and its relationship to perceptions of independence and dependence. *Journal of Gerontology: Psychological Sciences, 55B,* P362–P372.

Gignac, M. A. M., Kelloway, E. K., & Gottlieb, B. H. (1996). The impact of caregiving on employment: A mediational model of work-family conflict. *Canadian Journal on Aging, 15,* 525–542.

Gilbert, D. T., & Malone, P. S. (1995). The correspondence bias. *Psychological Bulletin, 117,* 21–38.

Gilchrest, B. A. (1995). Skin changes and disorders. In W. B. Abrams, M. H. Beers, & R. Berkow (Eds.), *The*

Merck manual of geriatrics (2nd ed., pp. 1255–1286). Whitehouse Station, NJ: Merck Research Laboratories.

Gilewski, M. J., & Zelinski, E. M. (1986). Questionnaire assessments of memory complaints. In L. W. Poon (Ed.), *Handbook for clinical memory assessment of older adults* (pp. 93–107). Washington, DC: American Psychological Association.

Gilewski, M. J., Zelinski, E. M., & Schaie, K. W. (1990). The Memory Functioning Questionnaire for assessment of memory complaints in adulthood and old age. *Psychology and Aging, 5,* 482–490.

Ginn, J., & Arber, S. (1996). Gender, age, and attitudes toward retirement in midlife. *Aging and Society, 16,* 27–55.

Glamser, F., & Hayslip, B., Jr. (1985). The impact of retirement on participation in leisure activities. *Therapeutic Recreation Journal, 19,* 28–38.

Glass, T. A. (1998). Conjugating the "tenses" of function: Discordance among hypothetical, experimental, and enacted function in older adults. *The Gerontologist, 38,* 101–112.

Glick, I. O., Weiss, R. S., & Parkes, C. M. (1974). *The first year of bereavement.* New York: Wiley.

Go, C. G., Brustrom, J. E., Lynch, M. F., & Aldwin, C. M. (1995). Ethnic trends in survival curves and mortality. *The Gerontologist, 35,* 318–326.

Goff, S. J., Fick, D. S., & Opplinger, R. A. (1997). The moderating effect of spouse support on the relation between serious leisure and spouses' perceived leisure–family conflict. *Journal of Leisure Research, 29,* 47–60.

Goff, S. J., Mount, M. K., & Jamison, R. L. (1990). Employer supported child care, work–family conflict, and absenteeism: A field study. *Personnel Psychology, 43,* 793–809.

Gold, D. T. (1990). Late-life sibling relationships: Does race affect typological distribution? *The Gerontologist, 30,* 741–748.

Gold, D. T., Woodbury, M. A., & George, L. K. (1990). Relationship classification using grade of membership analysis: A typology of sibling relationships in later life. *Journal of Gerontology: Social Sciences, 45,* S43–S51.

Goldberg, L. R., & Saucier, G. (1995). So what do you propose we use instead? A reply to Block. *Psychological Bulletin, 117,* 221–225.

Goldfried, M. R., & Wolfe, B. E. (1998). Toward a more clinically valid approach to therapy research. *Journal of Consulting and Clinical Psychology, 66,* 143–150.

Goldstein, E. (1979). Effect of same-sex and cross-sex role models on the subsequent academic productivity of scholars. *American Psychologist, 34,* 407–410.

Goode, K. T., Haley, W. E., Roth, D. L., & Ford, G. R. (1998). Predicting longitudinal changes in caregiver physical and mental health: A stress process model. *Health Psychology, 17,* 190–198.

Gordon, C., Gaitz, C. M., & Scott, J. (1986). Leisure and lives: Personal expressivity across the life span. In R. H. Binstock & E. Shanas (Eds.), *Handbook of aging and the social sciences* (2nd ed., pp. 310–341). New York: Van Nostrand Reinhold.

Gordon-Salant, S., & Fitzgibbons, P .J. (1997). Selected cognitive factors and speech recognition performance among young and elderly listeners. *Journal of Speech, Language, and Hearing Resources, 40,* 423–431.

Gorelick, P. B., Shanmugam, V., & Pajeau, A. K. (1996). Stroke. In J. E. Birren (Ed.), *Encyclopedia of gerontology* (Vol. 2). San Diego: Academic Press.

Gotlib, I. H., Roberts, J. E., & Gilboa, E. (1996). Cognitive interference in depression. In I. G. Sarason, G. R. Pierce, & B. R. Sarason (Eds.), *Cognitive interference: Theories, methods, and findings* (pp. 347–377). Mahwah, NJ: Erlbaum.

Gotthardt, U., Schweiger, U., Fahrenburg, J., Lauer, C. J., Holsboer, F., & Heuser, I. (1995). Cortisol, ACTH, and cardiovascular response to a cognitive challenge paradigm in aging and depression. *American Journal of Physiology, 268,* 865–873.

Gould, O. N. (1999). Cognition and affect in medication adherence. In D. C. Park & R. W. Morrell (Eds.), *Processing of medical information in aging patients: Cognitive and human factors perspectives* (pp. 167–183). Hillsdale, NJ: Erlbaum.

Gould, O. N., Kurzman, D., & Dixon, R. A. (1994). Communication during prose recall conversations by young and old dyads. *Discourse Processes, 17,* 149–165.

Gould, S. J. (1999). A critique of Heckhausen and Schulz's (1995) life-span theory of control from a cross-cultural perspective. *Psychological Review, 106,* 597–604.

Grady, C. L., McIntosh, A. R., Horwitz, B., Maisong, J. M., Ungerleider, L. G., Mentis, M. J., Pietrini, P., Schapiro, M. B., & Haxby, J. V. (1995). Age-related reductions in human recognition memory due to impaired encoding. *Science, 269,* 218–221.

Graf, P., & Mandler, G. (1984). Activation makes words more accessible but not necessarily more retrievable. *Journal of Verbal Learning and Verbal Behavior, 23,* 553–568.

Gratzinger, P., Sheikh, J. I., Friedman, L., & Yesavage, J. A. (1990). Cognitive interventions to improve face–name recall: The role of personality trait differences. *Developmental Psychology, 26,* 889–893.

Green, C. R. (1999). *Total memory workout: 8 steps to maximum memory fitness.* New York: Bantam.

Greenglass, E. R. (1991). Burnout and gender: Theoretical and organizational implications. *Canadian Psychology, 32*(4), 562–574.

Greenglass, E. R., Burke, R. J., & Konarski, R. (1998). Components of burnout, resources, and gender-related differences. *Journal of Applied Social Psychology, 28,* 1088–1106.

Greenhaus, J. H., Parasuraman, S., & Wormely, W. M. (1990). Effects of race on organizational experiences, job performance evaluations, and career outcomes. *Academy of Management Journal, 33,* 64–86.

Greenwald, A. G., & Banji, M. R. (1995). Implicit social cognition: Attitudes, self-esteem, and stereotypes. *Psychological Review, 102,* 4–27.

Greenwald, A. G., McGhee, D. E., & Schwaartz, J. L. K. (1998). Measuring individual differences in implicit cognition: The implicit association test. *Journal of Personality and Social Psychology, 74,* 1464–1480.

Greer, J. (1992). *Adult sibling rivalries.* New York: Crown.

Greller, M., & Stroh, L. (1995). Careers in midlife and beyond: A fallow field in need of sustenance. *Journal of Vocational Behavior, 47,* 232–247.

Gresham, G. E., Duncan, P. W., & Stason, W. B. (1995). *Post-stroke rehabilitation: Assessment, referral, and patient management.* Rockville, MD: USDHHS, Agency for Health Care Policy and Research.

Grey, R. (1756). *Memoria technica* (4th ed.). London: Hinton.

Grinker, J. A., Tucker, K., Vokonas, P. S., & Rush, D. (1995). Body habitus changes among adult males from the normative aging study: Relations to aging, smoking history and alcohol intake. *Obesity Research, 3,* 435–446.

Grob, A., Little, T. D., & Wanner, B. (1999). Control judgements across the lifespan. *International Journal of Behavioral Decisions, 23,* 833–854.

Groger, L. (1995). A nursing home can be a home. *Journal of Aging Studies, 9,* 137–153.

Grossman, A. H., D'Augelli, A. R., & Hershberger, S. L. (2000). Social support networks of lesbian, gay, and bisexual adults 60 years of age and older. *Journal of Gerontology: Psychological Sciences, 55B,* P171–P179.

Grover, D. R., & Hertzog, C. (1991). Relationships between intellectual control beliefs and psychometric intelligence in adulthood. *Journal of Gerontology: Psychological Sciences, 46,* 109–115.

Guelzow, M. G., Bird, G. W., & Koball, E. H. (1991). An exploratory path analysis of the stress process for dual-career men and women. *Journal of Marriage and the Family, 53,* 151–164.

Guilford, J. P. (1959). *Personality.* New York: McGraw-Hill.

Guinn, B. (1999). Leisure behavior motivation and the life satisfaction of retired persons. *Activities, Adapting, and Aging, 23,* 13–20.

Gulya, A. J. (1995). Ear disorders. In W. B. Abrams, M. H. Beers, & R. Berkow (Eds.), *The Merck manual of geriatrics* (2nd ed., pp. 1315–1342). Whitehouse Station, NJ: Merck Research Laboratories.

Gunter, N. C., & Gunter, B. G. (1990). Domestic division of labor among working couples: Does androgyny make a difference? *Psychology of Women Quarterly, 14,* 355–370.

Guralnick, J. M., & Simonsick, E. M. (1993). Physical disability in older Americans. *Journal of Gerontology, 48*(Special Issue), 3–10.

Gutmann, D. (1987). *Reclaimed powers: Toward a new psychology of men and women in later life.* New York: Basic Books.

Gutmann, D. (1994). *Reclaimed powers: Men and women in later life.* Evanston, IL: Northwestern University Press.

Haan, N. (1985). Common personality dimensions or common organization across the life span. In J. M. Munnichs, P. Mussen, E. Olbrich, & P. G. Coleman (Eds.), *Life-span and change in gerontological perspective* (pp. 17–44). New York: Academic Press.

Haan, N., Millsap, R., & Hartka, E. (1986). As time goes by: Change and stability in personality over fifty years. *Psychology and Aging, 1,* 220–232.

Haas, L. (1990). Gender equality and social policy: Implications of a study of parental leave in Sweden. *Journal of Family Issues, 11,* 401–423.

Hale, S., Myerson, J., Rhee, S. H., Weiss, C. S., & Abrams, R. A. (1996). Selective interference with the maintenance of location information in working memory. *Neuropsychology, 10,* 228–240.

Haley, W. E., Han, B., & Henderson, J. N. (1998). Aging and ethnicity: Issues for clinical practice. *Journal of Clinical Psychology in Medical Settings, 5,* 393–409.

Hall, D. T., & Mirvis, P. H. (1995). The new career contract: Developing the whole person at mid-life and beyond. *Journal of Vocational Behavior, 47,* 269–289.

Hamachek, D. (1990). Evaluating self-concept and ego status in Erikson's last three psychosocial stages. *Journal of Counseling and Development, 68,* 677–683.

Hamilton, J. (1978). Grandparents as grievers. In J. O. Sahler (Ed.), *The child and death.* St. Louis: C. V. Mosby.

Hamon, R. R., & Blieszner, R. (1990). Filial responsibility expectations among adult child-older parent pairs. *Journal of Gerontology: Psychological Sciences, 45,* P110–P112.

Hancock, H. E., Rogers, W. A., & Fisk, A. D. (1998). *Product usage and warning symbol comprehension for older adults.* Paper presented at the Human Factors and Ergonomics Society 42nd Annual Meeting, Chicago.

Hannon, D. J., & Hoyer, W. J. (1994). Mechanisms of visual–cognitive aging: A neural network account. *Aging and Cognition, 1,* 105–119.

Hansson, R. O., DeKoekkoek, P. D., Neese, W. M., & Patterson, D. W. (1997). Successful aging at work: Annual review, 1992-1996: The older worker and transitions to retirement. *Journal of Vocational Behavior, 51,* 202–233.

Hareven, T. K., & Adams, K. J. (1996). The generation in the middle: Cohort comparisons in assistance to aging parents in an American community. In T. K. Hareven (Ed.), *Aging and generational relations: Life-course and cross-cultural perspectives* (pp. 3–29). New York: Aldine De Gruyter.

Harkins, S. W., & Kwentus, J. (1990). Pain, discomfort, and suffering in the elderly. In J. J. Bonica (Ed.), *Clinical management of pain.* Philadelphia: Lea & Febinger.

Harris, J. E. (1984). Methods of improving memory. In B. Wilson & N. Moffat (Eds.), *Clinical management of memory problems* (pp. 46–62). Rockville, MD: Aspen.

Harris, J. E., & Sunderland, A. (1981). A brief survey of the management of memory disorders in rehabilitation units in Britain. *International Rehabilitation Medicine 3,* 206–209.

Harris, R. L., Ellicott, A. M., & Holmes, D. S. (1986). The timing of psychosocial transitions and changes in women's lives: An examination of women aged 45 to 60. *Journal of Personality and Social Psychology, 51,* 409–416.

Hartley, A. A. (1992). Attention. In F. I. M. Craik & T. A. Salthouse (Eds.), *The handbook of aging and cognition* (pp. 3–50). Hillsdale, NJ: Erlbaum.

Hartley, A. A., & McKenzie, C. R. M. (1991). Attentional and perceptual contributions to the identification of extrafoveal stimuli: Adult age comparisons. *Journal of Gerontology: Psychological Sciences, 46,* P202–P206.

Hartley, J. T. (1993). Reader and text variables as determinants of discourse memory in adulthood. *Psychology and Aging, 1,* 150–158.

Hartley, J. T., Stojack, C. C., Mushaney, T. J., Annon, T. A. K., & Lee, D. W. (1994). Reading speed and prose memory in older and younger adults. *Psychology and Aging, 9,* 216–223.

Harwood, J., Ryan, E. B., Giles, H., & Tysoski, S. (1997). Evaluations of patronizing speech and three response styles in a non-service-providing context. *Journal of Applied Communication Research, 25,* 170–195.

Hasher, L., & Zacks, R. T. (1988). Working memory, comprehension, and aging: A review and new view. In G. T. Bower (Ed.), *The psychology of learning and motivation* (Vol. 22, pp. 193–225). New York: Academic Press.

Hasher, L., Zacks, R. T., & May, C. P. (1999). Inhibitory control, circadian arousal, and age. In D. Gopher & A. Koriat (Eds.), *Attention and performance: XVII. Cognitive regulation of performance: Interaction of theory and application.* Cambridge, MA: MIT Press.

Hashtroudi, S., Johnson, M. K., Vnek, N., & Ferguson, (1994). Aging and the effects of affective and factual focus on source monitoring and re-

call. *Psychology and Aging, 9,* 160–170.

Hastie, R. (1999). Decision making and cognitive aging. In D. Park & N. Schwartz (Eds.), *Cognitive aging: A primer.* Philadelphia: Psychology Press.

Havighurst, R. J. (1982). The world of work. In B. B. Wolman (Ed.), *Handbook of developmental psychology* (pp. 771–787). Englewood Cliffs, NJ: Prentice Hall.

Hawkins, H. L., Kramer, A. F., & Capaldi, D. (1992). Aging, exercise, and attention. *Psychology and Aging, 7,* 643–653.

Hay, J. F., & Jacoby, L. L. (1999). Separation habits in young and older adults: Effects of elaborative processing and distinctiveness. *Psychology and Aging, 14,* 122–124.

Hayflick, L. (1996). *How and why we age* (2nd ed.). New York: Ballantine.

Hayflick, L. (1998). How and why we age. *Experimental Gerontology, 33,* 639–653.

Hayslip, B., Jr. (1988). Personality–ability relationships in aged adults. *Journal of Gerontology, 43,* P79–P84.

Hayslip, B., Jr. (1989). Alternative mechanisms for improvements in fluid ability performance among older adults. *Psychology and Aging, 4,* 122–124.

Hayslip, B., Jr., Maloy, R. M., & Kohl, R. (1995). Long-term efficacy of fluid ability interventions with older adults. *Journal of Gerontology: Psychological Sciences, 50B,* P141–P149.

Hayslip, B., Jr., Shore, R. J., Henderson, C. E., & Lambert, P. L. (1998). Custodial Grandparenting and the impact of grandchildren with problems on role satisfaction and role meaning. *Journal of Gerontology: Social Sciences, 53B,* S164–S173.

Hayward, M. D., Friedman, S., & Chen, H. (1998). Career trajectories and older men's retirement. *Journal of Gerontology: Social Sciences, 53B,* S91–S103.

Heckhausen, J., Dixon, R. A., & Baltes, P. B. (1989). Gains and losses in development throughout adulthood as perceived by different adult age

groups. *Developmental Psychology, 25,* 109–121.

Heckhausen, J., & Lang, F. R. (1996). Social construction and old age: Normative conceptions and interpersonal processes. In G. R. Semin & K. Fiedler (Eds.), *Applied social psychology* (pp. 374–399). London: Sage.

Heckhausen, J., & Schulz, R. (1995). A life-span theory of control. *Psychological Review, 102,* 284–304.

Heckhausen, J., & Schulz, R. (1998). Developmental regulation in adulthood: Selection and compensation via primary and secondary control. In J. Heckhausen & C. Dweck (Eds.), *Motivation and self-regulation across the lifespan* (pp. 50–77). New York: Cambridge University Press.

Heckhausen, J., & Schulz, R. (1999). Selectivity in lifespan development: Biological and societal canalizations and individuals developmental goals. In J. Brandtstädter, B. M. Lerner, et al. (Eds.), *Action and self development: Theory and research through the lifespan* (pp. 67–130). Thousand Oaks, CA: Sage.

Heidrich, S. M., & Denney, N. W. (1994). Does social problem solving differ from other types of problem solving during the adult years? *Experimental Aging Research, 20,* 105–126.

Heimann, B., & Pittinger, K. K. S. (1996). The impact of formal mentorship on socialization and commitment of newcomers. *Journal of Managerial Issues, 8,* 108–117.

Helmer, C., Barberger-Gateau, P., Letenneur, L., & Dartigues, J.-F. (1999). Subjective health and mortality in French elderly women and men. *Journal of Gerontology: Social Sciences, 54B,* S84–S92.

Helson, R., Mitchell, V., & Moane, G. (1984).Personality and patterns of adherence and nonadherence to the social clock. *Journal of Personality and Social Psychology, 46,* 1079–1096.

Helson, R., & Moane, G. (1987). Personality change in women from college to midlife. *Journal of Personality and Social Psychology, 53,* 176–186.

Helson, R., Stewart, A. J., & Ostrove, J. (1995). Identity in the cohorts of midlife women. *Journal of Personality and Social Psychology, 69,* 544–557.

Henderson, K. A. (1990). The meaning of leisure for women: An integrative review of the research. *Journal of Leisure Research, 22,* 228–243.

Henkel, J. (1998). Parkinson's disease: New treatments slow onslaught of symptoms. *FDA Consumer, 32*(4), 13–18. Online document available at the Web site http://www.fda.gov/fdac/features/1998/498_pd.html.

Henkens, K. (1999). Retirement intentions and spousal support: A multiactor approach. *Journal of Gerontology: Social Sciences, 54B*(2), S63–S73.

Hennessy, C. H., & John, R. (1995). The interpretation of burden among Pueblo Indian caregivers. *Journal of Aging Studies, 9,* 215–229.

Hennon, C. B. (1983). Divorce and the elderly: A neglected area of research. In T. H. Brubaker (Ed.), *Family relationships in later life* (pp. 149–172). Thousand Oaks, CA: Sage.

Henretta, J. C. (1997). Changing perspectives on retirement. *Journal of Gerontology: Social Sciences, 52B,* S1–S3.

Henretta, J. C., Chan, C. G., & O'Rand, A. M. (1992). Retirement reason versus retirement process: Examining the reasons for retirement typology. *Journal of Gerontology: Social Sciences, 47,* S1–S7.

Herrera, C. O. (1995). Sleep disorders. In W. B. Abrams, M. H. Beers, & R. Berkow (Eds.), *The Merck manual of geriatrics* (2nd ed., pp. 110–125). Whitehouse Station, NJ: Merck Research Laboratories.

Herrmann, D. J. (1993). *Basic research contributions to the improvement of rehabilitation of memory.* Paper presented at the annual meeting of the American Psychological Association, Washington, DC.

Hertz, R. (1997). A typology of approaches to child care: The centerpiece of organizing family life for dual-earner couples. *Journal of Family Issues, 18,* 355–385.

Hertzog, C., & Dixon, R. (1996). Methodological issues in research on cognition and aging. In F. Blanchard-Fields & T. Hess (Eds.), *Perspectives on cognitive change in adulthood and aging* (pp. 66–121). New York: McGraw-Hill.

Hertzog, C., Dixon, R. A., & Hultsch, D. F. (1990). Relationships between metamemory, memory predictions, and memory task performances. *Psychology and Aging, 5,* 215–223.

Hertzog, C., & Dunlosky, J. (1996). The aging of practical memory: An overview. In D. Hermann, C. McEvoy, C. Hertzog, P. Hertel, & M. J. Johnsons (Eds.), *Basic and applied memory research* (vol. 1, pp. 337–358). Mahwah, NJ: Erlbaum.

Hertzog, C., & Hultsch, D. F. (2000). Metacognition in adulthood and old age. In F. I. M. Craik & T. A. Salthouse (Eds.), *The handbook of aging and cognition* (2nd ed., pp. 417–466). Mahwah, NJ: Erlbaum.

Hertzog, C., Hultsch, D. F., & Dixon, R. A. (1989). Evidence for the convergent validity of two self-report metamemory questionnaires. *Developmental Psychology, 25,* 687–700.

Hertzog, C., Hultsch, D. F., & Dixon, R. A. (1999). On the problem of detecting effects of lifestyle on cognitive change in adulthood: Reply to Pushkar et al. (1999). *Psychology and Aging, 14,* 528–534.

Hertzog, C., McGuire, C. L., & Lineweaver, T. T. (1998). Aging attributions, perceived control, and strategy use in a free recall task. *Aging, Neuropsychology, and Cognition, 5,* 85–106.

Hertzog, C., Park, D. C., Morrell, R. W., & Martin, M. (2000). Ask and ye shall receive: Behavioral specificity in the accuracy of subjective memory complaints. *Applied Cognitive Psychology, 14,* 257–275.

Hertzog, C., Saylor, L. L., Fleece, A. M., & Dixon, R. A. (1994). Metamemory and aging: Relations between predicted, actual, and perceived memory task performance. *Aging and Cognition, 1,* 203–237.

Hertzog, C., Vernon, M. C., & Rympa, B. (1993). Age differences in mental rotation task performance: The influence of speed/accuracy trade off.

Journal of Gerontology, 48, P150–P156.

Herzog, A. R., Kahn, R. L., Morgan, J. N., Jackson, J. S., & Antonucci, T. C. (1989). Age differences in productive activities. *Journal of Gerontology: Social Sciences, 44,* S129–S138.

Hess, P., & Lee, S. (1998). Pharmacology and drug use. In P. Ebersole & P. Hess, *Toward healthy aging* (5th ed., pp. 352–380). St. Louis: Mosby.

Hess, T. M. (1999). Cognitive and knowledge-based influences on social representations. In T. M. Hess & F. Blanchard-Fields (Eds.), *Social cognition and aging* (pp. 237–263). San Diego: Academic Press.

Hess, T., Follet, K., & McGee, K. A. (1998). Aging and impression information: The impact of processing skills and goals. *Journal of Gerontology: Psychological Sciences, 53B,* P175–188.

Hess, T. M., & Pullen, S. M. (1994). Adult age differences in informational biases during impression formation. *Psychology and Aging, 9,* 237–250.

Hess, T. M., & Pullen, S. M. (1996). Memory in context. In F. Blanchard-Fields & T. M. Hess (Eds.), *Perspectives on cognitive change in adulthood and aging* (pp. 387–427). New York: McGraw-Hill.

Hess, T. M., & Slaughter, S. J. (1990). Schematic knowledge influences on memory for scene information in young and older adults. *Developmental Psychology, 26,* 855–865.

Hestad, K., Ellersten, J., & Kløve, H. (1999). Neuropsychological assessment in old age. In I. H. Nordhus, G. R. VandenBos, S. Berg, & P. Fromholt (Eds.), *Clinical geropsychology* (pp. 259–288). Washington, DC: American Psychological Association.

Higgins, E. T., Rholes, W. S., & Jones, C. R. (1977). Category accessibility and impression formation. *Journal of Experimental Social Psychology, 13,* 141–154.

Hill, C. D., Thompson, L. W., & Gallagher, D. (1988). The role of anticipatory bereavement in older women's adjustment to widowhood. *The Gerontologist, 28,* 792–796.

Hilton, J. L., von Hippel, W. (1996). Stereotypes. *Annual Review of Psychology, 47,* 237–271.

Himsel, A. J., Hart, H., Diamond, A., & McAdams, D. P. (1997). Personality characteristics of highly generative adults as assessed in Q-sort ratings of life stories. *Journal of Adult Development, 4,* 149–161.

Hobart, C. (1988). The family system in remarriage: An exploratory study. *Journal of Marriage and the Family, 50,* 649–661.

Hofland, B. F. (1988). Autonomy in long term care: Background issues and a programmatic response. *The Gerontologist, 28*(Suppl.), 3–9.

Holland, C. A., & Rabbitt, P. M. A. (1994). The problems of being an older driver: Comparing the perceptions of an expert group and older drivers. *Applied Ergonomics, 25,* 17–27.

Holland, J. L. (1985). *Self-directed search professional manual.* Lutz, FL: Psychological Assessment Resources.

Holland, J. L. (1987). Current status of Holland's theory of careers: Another perspective. *Career Development Quarterly, 36,* 24–30.

Holland, J. L. (1996). Exploring careers with a typology: What we have learned and some new directions. *American Psychologist, 51,* 397–406.

Hooker, K. (1991). Change and stability in self during the transition to retirement: An individual study using P-technique factor analysis. *International Journal of Behavioral Development, 14,* 209–233.

Hooker, K. (1992). Possible selves and perceived health in older adults and college students. *Journal of Gerontology, 47,* P85–P95.

Hooker, K., Fiese, B. H., Jenkins, L., Morfei, M. Z., et al. (1996). Possible selves among parents of infants and pre-schoolers. *Developmental Psychology, 32,* 542–550.

Hooker, K., & Kaus, C. R. (1994). Health-related possible selves in young and mid-adulthood. *Psychology and Aging, 9,* 126–133.

Hooyman, N., & Kiyak, H. A. (1999). *Social gerontology: A multidisciplinary perspective* (5th ed.). Boston: Allyn & Bacon.

Horn, J. L. (1982). The aging of human abilities. In B. B. Wolman (Ed.), *Handbook of developmental psychology* (pp. 847–870). Englewood Cliffs, NJ: Prentice Hall.

Horn, J. L., & Hofer, S. M. (1992). Major abilities and development in the adult period. In R. J. Sternberg & C. A. Berg (Eds.), *Intellectual development* (pp. 44–99). Cambridge, UK: Cambridge University Press.

Hornblum, J. N., & Overton, W. F. (1976). Area and volume conservation among the elderly: Assessment and training. *Developmental Psychology, 12,* 68–74.

Houghston, G. A., & Protinsky, H. O. (1978). Conservation ability of elderly men and women: A comparative investigation. *Journal of Psychology, 98,* 23–26.

Howard, A., & Bray, D. W. (1980, August). *Career motivation in mid-life managers.* Paper presented at the meeting of the American Psychological Association, Montreal.

Hoyer, W. J., & Rybash, J. M. (1994). Characterizing adult cognitive development. *Journal of Adult Development, 1,* 7–12.

Hu, M.-H., & Woollacott, M. H. (1994a). Multisensory training of standing balance in older adults: I. Postural stability and one-leg stance balance. *Journal of Gerontology: Medical Sciences, 49,* M52–M61.

Hu, M.-H., & Woollacott, M. H. (1994b). Multisensory training of standing balance in older adults: II. Kinetic and electromyographic postural responses. *Journal of Gerontology: Medical Sciences, 49,* M62–M71.

Hudson, R. B. (1996). Social protection and services. In R. H. Binstock & L. K. George (Eds.), *Handbook of aging and the social sciences* (4th ed., pp. 446–466). San Diego: Academic Press.

Hughston, G. A., & Protinsky, H. W. (1978). Conservation abilities of elderly men and women: A comparative investigation. *Journal of Psychology, 98,* 23–26.

Hultsch, D. F., & Dixon, R. A. (1990). Learning and memory in aging. In J. E. Birren & K. W. Schaie (Eds.), *Handbook of the psychology of aging* (3rd ed., pp. 258–274). San Diego: Academic Press.

Hummert, M. L. (1999). A social cognitive perspective on age stereotypes. In T. M. Hess & F. Blanchard-Fields (Eds.), *Social cognition and aging* (pp. 175–196). San Diego: Academic Press.

Hummert, M. L., & Garstka, T. A. (1998). *Target age and activation cues for stereotypes of older adults.* Unpublished manuscript, University of Kansas, Lawrence.

Hummert, M. L., Garstka, T. A., & Shaner, J. L. (1995). Beliefs about language performance: Adults' perceptions about self and elderly targets. *Journal of Language and Social Psychology, 14,* 235–259.

Hummert, M. L., Garstka, T. A., Shaner, J. L., & Strahm, S. (1994). Stereotypes of the elderly held by young, middle-aged, and elderly adults. *Journal of Gerontology: Psychological Sciences, 49,* P240–249.

Hummert, M. L., Shaner, J. L., Garstka, T. A., & Henry, C. (1998). Communication with older adults: The influence of age stereotypes, context, and communicator age. *Human Communication Research, 25,* 124–151.

Humphrey, D. G., & Kramer, A. F. (1997). Age differences in visual search for feature conjunction and triple-conjunction targets. *Psychology and Aging, 12,* 704–717.

Huyck, M. H. (1990). Gender differences in aging. In J. E. Birren & K. W. Schaie (Eds.), *Handbook of the psychology of aging* (3rd ed., pp. 124–132). San Diego: Academic Press.

Huyck, M. H. (1996). Continuities and discontinuities in gender roles and gender identity. In V. Bengston (Ed.), *Continuities and discontinuities in the adult life course and aging.* New York: Springer.

Huyck, M. H. (1999). Gender roles and gender identity in midlife. In S. Willis & J. D. Reid (Eds.), *Life in the middle* (pp. 209–233). San Diego: Academic Press.

Hyde, J. S., Krajnik, M., & Skuldt-Niederberger, K. (1991). Androgyny across the life span: A replication and longitudinal follow-up. *Developmental Psychology, 27,* 516–519.

Idler, E. L., & Benyamini, Y. (1997). Self-rated health and mortality: A review of twenty-seven community studies. *Journal of Health and Social Behavior, 38,* 21–37.

Iida, I., & Noro, K. (1995). An analysis of the reduction of elasticity on the ageing of human skin and the recovering effect of a facial massage. *Ergonomics, 38,* 1921–1931.

Isaacowitz, D. M., Turk-Charles, S., & Carstensen, L. (2000). Emotion and cognition. In F. I. M. Craik & T. A. Salthouse (Eds.), *Handbook of aging and cognition* (2nd ed.). New York: Academic Press.

Ishler, A. L., Johnson, R. T., & Johnson, D. W. (1998). Long term effectiveness of a statewide staff development program on cooperative learning. *Teaching and Teacher Education, 14,* 273–281.

Ishler, K., Pargament, K. I., Kinney, J. M., & Cavanaugh, J. C. (1995, November). *Religious coping, general coping, and controllability: Testing the hypothesis of fit.* Paper presented at the meeting of the Gerontological Society, Los Angeles.

Iskra, G., Folkard, S., Marek, T., & Noworol, C. (1996). Health, well-being and burnout of ICU nurses on 12- and 8-h shifts. *Work and Stress, 10,* 251–256.

Ivy, D. K., & Hamlet, S. (1996). College students and sexual dynamics: Two studies of peer sexual harassment. *Communication Education, 45,* 149–166.

Izraeli, D. N. (1993). Work/family conflict among women and men managers in dual career couples in Israel. *Journal of Social Behavior and Personality, 8,* 371–385.

Jackson, B., Taylor, J., & Pyngolil, M. (1991). How age conditions the relationship between climacteric status and health symptoms in African American women. *Research in Nursing and Health, 14,* 1–9.

Jackson, J. S. (1993). Racial influences on adult development and aging. In R. Kastenbaum (Ed.), *The encyclopedia of adult development* (pp. 18–26). Phoenix, AZ: Oryx.

Jackson, J. S., Antonucci, T. C., & Gibson, R. C. (1995). Ethnic and cultural factors in research on aging and mental health: A life-course perspective. In D. K. Padgett (Ed.), *Handbook on ethnicity, aging, and mental health* (pp. 22–46). Westport, CT: Greenwood.

Jackson, J. S., & Gibson, R. C. (1985). Work and retirement among the black elderly. In Z. Blau (Ed.), *Current perspectives on aging and the life cycle* (pp. 193–222). Greenwich, CT: JAI.

Jackson, J. S., Jayakody, R., & Antonucci, T. C. (1996). Exchanges within black American three-generation families. In T. K. Hareven (Ed.), *Aging and generational relations: Life-course and cross-cultural perspectives* (pp. 83–114). New York: Aldine De Gruyter.

Jacobs, S. (1993). *Pathologic grief: Maladaptation to loss.* Washington, DC: American Psychological Association.

Jacoby, L. L. (1991). A process dissociation framework: Separating automatic from intentional uses of memory. *Journal of Memory and Language, 30,* 513–541.

Jacoby, L. L. (1999). Ironic effects of repetition: Measuring age-related differences in memory. *Journal of Experimental Psychology: Learning, Memory, and Cognition, 25,* 3–22.

Jacoby, L. L., Yonelinas, A. P., & Jennings, J. M. (1997). The relation between conscious and unconscious (automatic) influences: A declaration of independence. In J. D. Cohen & J. W. Schooler, et al. (Eds.), *Scientific approaches to consciousness* (pp. 13–47). Mahwah, NJ: Erlbaum.

James, J. W., & Haley, W. E. (1995). Age and health bias in practicing clinical psychologists. *Psychology and Aging, 10,* 610–616.

James, W. (1890). *The principles of psychology.* New York: Holt.

Jecker, N. S., & Schneiderman, L. J. (1994). Is dying young worse than dying old? *The Gerontologist, 34,* 66–72.

Jeffko, W. G. (1979, July 6). Redefining death. *Commonweal,* 394–397.

Jelicic, M., Craik, F. I. M., & Moscovich, M. (1996). Effects of ageing on different explicit and implicit memory

tasks. *European Journal of Cognitive Psychology, 8,* 225–334.

Jenkins, C. L. (1997). Women, work, and caregiving: How do these roles affect women's well-being? *Journal of Women and Aging, 9,* 27–45.

Jennings, J. M., & Jacoby, L. L. (1993). Automatic vs. intentional uses of memory: Ageing, attention and control. *Psychology and Aging, 8,* 283–293.

Jeste, D. V., Naimark, D., Halpain, M. C., & Lindamer, L. A. (1995). Strengths and limitations of research on late-life psychoses. In M. Gatz (Ed.), *Emerging issues in mental health and aging* (pp. 72–96). Washington, DC: American Psychological Association.

Johannes, C. B., Crawford, S. L., Posner, J. G., & McKinlay, S. M. (1994). Longitudinal patterns and correlates of HRT use in middle-aged women. *American Journal of Epidemiology, 140,* 439–452.

Johansson, B., Whitfield, K., Pedersen, N. L., Hofer, S. M., Ahern, F., & McClearn, G. E. (1999). Origins of individual differences in episodic memory in the oldest-old: A population-based study of identical and same-sex fraternal twins aged 80 and older. *Journal of Gerontology: Psychological Sciences, 54B,* P173–P179.

Johnson, C. L., & Troll, L. E. (1994). Constraints and facilitators to friendships in late late life. *The Gerontologist, 34,* 79–87.

Johnson, M. K., Hashtroundi, S., & Lindsay, D. S. (1993). Source monitoring. *Psychological Bulletin, 114,* 3–28.

Johnson, M. M. S. (1990). Age differences in decision making: A process methodology for examining strategic information processing. *Journal of Gerontology: Psychological Sciences, 45,* P75–P78.

Johnson, R. J., & Wolinsky, F. D. (1994). Gender, race, and health: The structure of health status among older adults. *The Gerontologist, 34,* 24–35.

Jones, C. J., & Meredith, W. (1996). Patterns of personality change across the life span. *Psychology and Aging, 11,* 57–65.

Jones, F. L. (1996). Convergence and divergence in ethnic divorce patterns:

A research note. *Journal of Marriage and the Family, 58,* 213–218.

Jones, L. Y. (1980). *Great expectations: America and the baby boom generation.* New York: Coward, McCann, & Geoghegan.

Jorm, A. F. (1996). Assessment of cognitive impairment and dementia using informant reports. *Clinical Psychological Review, 16,* 51–73.

Joshi, A., & Sastry, N. (1995). Work and family: Conflict and its resolution. *Indian Journal of Gender Studies, 2,* 227–241.

Joynt, R. J. (1995). Normal aging and patterns of neurologic disease. In W. B. Abrams, M. H. Beers, & R. Berkow (Eds.), *The Merck manual of geriatrics* (2nd ed., pp. 1129–1133). Whitehouse Station, NJ: Merck Research Laboratories.

Jung, C. (1933). *Modern man in search of a soul* (W. S. Dell & C. F. Baynes, Trans.). New York: Harcourt, Brace, & World.

Jylhä, M., Guralnik, J. M., Ferrucci, L., Jokela, J., & Heikkinen, E. (1998). Is self-rated health comparable across cultures and genders? *Journal of Gerontology: Social Sciences, 53B,* S144–S152.

Kahana, E. (1982). A congruence model of person–environment interaction. In M. P. Lawton, P. G. Windley, & T. O. Byerts (Eds.), *Aging and the environment: Theoretical approaches* (pp. 97–121). New York: Springer.

Kahana, E., & Kahana, B. (1983). Environmental continuity, futurity, and adaptation of the aged. In G. D. Rowles & R. J. Ohta (Eds.), *Aging and milieu: Environmental perspectives on growing old* (pp. 205–230). New York: Academic Press.

Kail, R., & Salthouse, T. A. (1994). Processing speed as a mental capacity. *Acta Psychologica, 86,* 199–225.

Kalish, R. A. (1984). *Death, grief, and caring relationships* (2nd ed.). Pacific Grove, CA: Brooks/Cole.

Kalish, R. A. (1987). Death and dying. In P. Silverman (Ed.), *The elderly as modern pioneers* (pp. 320–334). Bloomington: Indiana University Press.

Kalish, R. A., & Reynolds, D. (1976). *Death and ethnicity: A psychocultural study.* Los Angeles: University of Southern California Press.

Kallman, D. A., Plato, C. C., & Tobin, J. D. (1990). The role of muscle loss in the age-related decline of grip strength: Cross-sectional and longitudinal perspectives. *Journal of Gerontology: Medical Sciences, 45,* M82–M88.

Kane, M. J., Hasher, L., Stoltzfus, E. R., Zacks, R. T., & Connelly, S. L. (1994). Inhibitory attentional mechanisms and aging. *Psychology and Aging, 9,* 103–112.

Kane, R. A., & Wilson, K. B. (1993). *Assisted living in the United States: A new paradigm for residential care for frail older persons?* Washington, DC: AARP.

Kanekar, S., Koswalla, M. B., & Nazareth, T. (1989). Occupational prestige as a function of occupant's gender. *Journal of Applied Social Psychology, 19,* 681–688.

Kanter, R. M. (1976, May). Why bosses turn bitchy. *Psychology Today,* pp. 56–59.

Karney, B. R., & Bradbury, T. N. (1995). The longitudinal course of marital quality and stability: A review of theory, method, and research. *Psychological Bulletin, 118,* 3–34.

Karon, B. P., & VandenBos, G. R. (1999). Schizophrenia and psychosis in elderly populations. In I. H. Nordhus, G. R. VandenBos, S. Berg, & P. Fromholt (Eds.), *Clinical geropsychology* (pp. 219–227). Washington, DC: American Psychological Association.

Kasl-Godley, J. E., Gatz, M., & Fiske, A. (1999). Depression and depressive symptoms in old age. In I. H. Nordhus, G. R. VandenBos, S. Berg, & P. Fromholt (Eds.), *Clinical geropsychology* (pp. 211–217). Washington, DC: American Psychological Association.

Kastenbaum, R. (1985). Dying and death: A life-span approach. In J. E. Birren & K. W. Schaie (Eds.), *Handbook of the psychology of aging* (2nd ed., pp. 619–643). New York: Van Nostrand Reinhold.

Kastenbaum, R. (1992). *The psychology of death* (rev. ed.). New York: Springer.

Kastenbaum, R. (1999). Dying and bereavement. In J. C. Cavanaugh & S. K. Whitbourne (Eds.), *Gerontology: An interdisciplinary perspective* (pp. 155–185). New York: Oxford University Press.

Kastenbaum, R., & Briscoe, L. (1975). The street corner: Laboratory for the study of life-threatening behavior. *Omega: Journal of Death and Dying, 6,* 33–44.

Kastenbaum, R., & Thuell, S. (1995). Cookies baking, coffee brewing: Toward a contextual theory of dying. *Omega, 31,* 175–187.

Kausler, D. H. (1982). *Experimental psychology and human aging.* New York: Wiley.

Kausler, D. H. (1985). Episodic memory: Memorizing performance. In N. Charness (Ed.), *Aging and human performance* (pp. 101–141). Chichester, England: Wiley.

Kausler, D. H. (1994). *Learning and memory in normal aging.* San Diego: Academic Press.

Kausler, D. H., & Lichty, W. (1988). Memory for activities: Rehearsal independence and aging. In M. L. Howe & C. J. Brainerd (Eds.), *Cognitive development in adulthood: Progress in cognitive development research* (pp. 93–131). New York: Springer-Verlag.

Kausler, D. H., Lichty, W., & Davis, R. T. (1985). Temporal memory for performed activities intentionally and adult age differences. *Developmental Psychology, 21,* 1132–1138.

Kausler, D. H., Lichty, W., Hakami, M. K., & Freund, J. S. (1986). Activity duration and adult age differences in memory for activity performance. *Psychology and Aging, 1,* 80–81.

Kawas, C. Resnick, S., Morrison, A., Brookmeyer, R., Corrada, M., Zonderman, A., Bacal, C., Lingle, D. C., & Metter, E. (1997). A prospective study of estrogen replacement therapy and the risk of developing Alzheimer's disease: The Baltimore Longitudinal Study of Aging. *Neurology, 48,* 1517–1521.

Kegan, R. (1982). *The evolving self.* Cambridge, MA: Harvard University Press.

Keith, J. (1990). Age in social and cultural context: Anthropological perspectives. In R. H. Binstock & L. K. George (Eds.), *Handbook of aging and the social sciences* (3rd ed., pp. 91–111). San Diego: Academic Press.

Keller, J. W., Sherry, D., & Piotrowski, C. (1984). Perspectives on death: A developmental study. *Journal of Psychology, 116,* 137–142.

Kelley, C. M. (1986). Depressive mood effects on memory and attention. In L. W. Poon (Ed.), *Handbook for the clinical memory assessment of older adults* (pp. 238–243). Washington, DC: American Psychological Association.

Kelley, H. H. (1967). Attribution theory in social psychology. *Nebraska Symposium on Motivation, 15,* 192–241.

Kelly, J. B. (1982). Divorce: The adult perspective. In B. B. Wolman (Ed.), *Handbook of developmental psychology* (pp. 734–750). Englewood Cliffs, NJ: Prentice Hall.

Kelly, J. R. (1996). Activities. In J. E. Birren (Ed.), *Encyclopedia of gerontology: Age, aging, and the aged* (Vol. 1, pp. 37–49). San Diego: Academic Press.

Kemper, S., Ferrell, P., Harden, T., Finter-Urczyk, A., & Billington, C. (1998). The use of elders-peak by young and older adults to impaired and unimpaired listeners. *Aging, Neuropsychology, and Cognition, 5,* 43–55.

Kemtes, K. A., & Kemper, S. (1997). Younger and older adults on-line processing of syntactic ambiguities. *Psychology and Aging, 12,* 362–371.

Keyes, C. M., & Ryff, C. D. (1999). Psychological well-being in midlife. In S. Willis & J. D. Reid (Eds.), *Life in the middle* (pp. 161–181). San Diego: Academic Press.

Kiernan, R. J., Mueller, J., Langston, J. W., & Vandyke, C. (1987). The neurobehavioral cognitive status examination: A brief but differentiated approach to cognitive assessment. *Annals of Internal Medicine, 107*(4), 481–485.

Kimmel, D. C. (1995). Lesbians and gay men grow old. In L. A. Bond, S. J. Cutler, & A. Grams (Eds.), *Promoting successful and productive aging.* Thousand Oaks, CA: Sage.

Kimmel, D. C., & Sang, B. E. (1995). Lesbians and gay men in midlife. In A. R. D'Augelli & C. J. Patterson (Eds.), *Lesbian, gay, and bisexual identities over the lifespan* (pp. 190–214). New York: Oxford University Press.

Kinderman, S. S., & Brown, G. G. (1997). Depression and memory in the elderly: A meta-analysis. *Journal of Clinical and Experimental Neuropsychology, 19,* 625–642.

King, P. M., & Kitchener, K. S. (1994). *Developing reflective judgment: Understanding and promoting intellectual growth and critical thinking in adolescents and adults.* San Francisco: Jossey-Bass.

King, P. M., Kitchener, K. S., Wood, P. K., & Davison, M. L. (1989). Relationships across developmental domains: A longitudinal study of intellectual, moral, and ego development. In M. L. Commons, J. D. Sinnott, F. A. Richards, & C. Armon (Eds.), *Adult development: Vol. 1. Comparisons and applications of adolescent and adult developmental models* (pp. 57–72). New York: Praeger.

Kingston, P. W., & Nock, S. L. (1987). Time together among dual-earner couples. *American Sociological Review, 52,* 391–400.

Kinney, J. M., & Cavanaugh, J. C. (1993, November). *Until death do us part: Striving to find meaning while caring for a spouse with dementia.* Paper presented at the meeting of the Gerontological Society of America, New Orleans.

Kinney, J. M., & Stephens, M. A. P. (1989). Hassles and uplifts of giving care to a family member with dementia. *Psychology and Aging, 4,* 402–408.

Kirasic, K. C. (1991). Spatial cognition and behavior in young and elderly adults: Implications for learning new environments. *Psychology and Aging, 6,* 10–18.

Kirasic, K. C., & Allen, G. L. (1985). Aging, spatial performance, and spatial competence. In N. Charness (Ed.), *Aging and human performance* (pp. 191–223). Chichester, UK: Wiley.

Kirasic, K. C., Allen, G. L., & Haggerty, D. (1992). Age-related differences in adults' macrospatial cognitive processes. *Experimental Aging Research, 18,* 33–39.

Kitchener, K. S., & Fischer, K. W. (1990). A skill approach to the development of reflective thinking. In D. Kuhn (Ed.), *Contributions to human development: Developmental perspectives on teaching and learning* (Vol. 21, pp. 48–62). Basel, Switzerland: Karger.

Kitson, G. C. (2000). Adjustment to violent and natural deaths in later and earlier life for black and white widows. *Journal of Gerontology: Social Sciences, 55B,* S341–S351.

Kitson, G. L., & Sussman, M. B. (1982). Marital complaints, demographic characteristics, and symptoms of mental distress in divorce. *Journal of Marriage and the Family, 44,* 87–101.

Kittrell, D. (1998). A comparison of the evolution of men's and women's dreams in Daniel Levinson's theory of adult development. *Journal of Adult Development, 5,* 105–115.

Kivett, V. R. (1991). Centrality of the grandfather role among older rural black and white men. *Journal of Gerontology: Social Sciences, 46,* S250–S258.

Kivnick, H. Q. (1982). *The meaning of grandparenthood.* Ann Arbor, MI: UMI Research.

Klass, D. (1996). Grief in Eastern culture: Japanese ancestor worship. In D. Klass, P. R. Silverman, & S. L. Nickman (Eds.), *Continuing bonds: New understandings of grief* (pp. 59–70). Washington, DC: Taylor & Francis.

Kliegl, R., Smith, J., & Baltes, P. B. (1990). On the focus and process of magnification of age differences during mnemonic training. *Developmental Psychology, 26,* 894–904.

Kline, D. W. (1994). Optimizing the visibility of displays for older observers. *Experimental Aging Research, 20,* 11–23.

Kline, D. W., & Schieber, F. (1985). Vision and aging. In J. E. Birren &

K. W. Schaie (Eds.), *Handbook of the psychology of aging* (2nd ed., pp. 296–331). New York: Van Nostrand Reinhold.

Kline, T. J., Ghali, L. A., Kline, D. W., & Brown, S. (1990). Visibility distance of highway signs among young, middle-aged, and older observers; Icons are better than text. *Human Factors, 32,* 609–619.

Knight, R. G., & Godfrey, H. P. D. (1995). Behavioural and self-report methods. In A. D. Baddeley, B. A. Wilson, & F. N. Watts (Eds.), *Handbook of memory disorders* (pp. 393–410). Chichester, England: Wiley.

Knodel, J., Chayovan, N., & Siriboon, S. (1996). Familial support and the life course of Thai elderly and their children. In T. K. Hareven (Ed.), *Aging and generational relations: Life-course and cross-cultural perspectives* (pp. 217–240). New York: Aldine De Gruyter.

Koenig, H. G., George, L. K., & Siegler, I. C. (1988). The use of religion and other emotion-regulating coping strategies among older adults. *The Gerontologist, 28,* 303–310.

Koestenbaum, P. (1976). *Is there an answer to death?* Englewood Cliffs, NJ: Prentice-Hall.

Kogan, N. (1990). Personality and aging. In J. E. Birren & K. W. Schaie (Eds.), *The handbook of psychology and aging* (3rd ed., pp. 330–346). New York: Academic Press.

Kornhaber, A. (1985). Grandparenthood and the "new social contract." In V. L. Bengtson & J. F. Robertson (Eds.), *Grandparenthood* (pp. 159–172). Beverly Hills: Sage Publications.

Kosik, K. S. (1992). Alzheimer's disease: A cell biological perspective. *Science, 256,* 780–783.

Kosnik, W., Winslow, L., Kline, D. W., Rasinski, & Sekular, R. (1988). Visual changes in everyday life throughout adulthood. *Journal of Gerontology, 43,* P63–P70.

Kotary, V., & Hoyer, W. J. (1995). Age and the ability to inhibit distracter information in visual selective attention. *Experimental Aging Research, 21,* 159–171.

Kotre, J. N. (1984). *Outliving the self: How we live on in future generations.* New York: Norton.

Kram, K. E. (1980). *Mentoring processes at work: Developmental relationships in managerial careers.* Unpublished doctoral dissertation, Yale University, New Haven, CT.

Kram, K. E. (1985). *Mentoring at work: Developmental relationships in organizational life.* Glenview, IL: Scott, Foresman.

Kramer, A. F., & Larish, J. F. (1996). Aging and dual-task performance. In W. R. Rogers, A. D. Fisk, & N. Walker (Eds.), *Aging and skilled performance* (pp. 83–112). Hillsdale, NJ: Lawrence Erlbaum Associates.

Kramer, A. F., Larish, J. F., & Strayer, D. L. (1995). Training for attentional control in dual task settings: A comparison of young and old adults. *Journal of Experimental Psychology: Applied, 1,* 50–76.

Kramer, A. F., Larish, J. F., Weber, T. A., & Bardell, L. (in press). Training for executive control: Task coordination strategies and aging. In D. Gopher & A. Koriat (Eds.), *Attention and performance: XVIII.* San Diego: Academic Press.

Kramer, D. A. (1989). A developmental framework for understanding conflict resolution processes. In J. D. Sinnott (Ed.), *Everyday problem solving: Theory and applications* (pp. 138–152). New York: Praeger.

Kramer, D. A. (1990). Conceptualizing wisdom: The primacy of affect–cognition relations. In R. J. Sternberg (Ed.), *Wisdom: Its nature, origins, and development* (pp. 279–313). New York: Cambridge University Press.

Kramer, D. A., & Kahlbaugh, P. E. (1994). Memory for a dialectical and a nondialectical prose passage in young and older adults. *Journal of Adult Development, 1,* 13–26.

Kramer, D. A., Kahlbaugh, P. E., & Goldston, R. B. (1992). A measure of paradigm beliefs about the social world. *Journal of Gerontology, 47,* 180–189.

Kramer, D. A., & Woodruff, D. S. (1986). Relativistic and dialectical thought in three adult age-groups. *Human Development, 29,* 280–290.

Krause, N. (1995). Religiosity and self-esteem among older adults. *Journal of Gerontology: Psychological Sciences, 50B,* 236–246.

Krause, N. (1999). Stress and devaluation of highly salient roles in late life. *Journal of Gerontology: Social Sciences, 54B,* S99–S108.

Kriseman, N. L. & Claes, J. A. (1997). Gender issues and elder care. In T. D. Hargrave & S. M. Hanna (Eds.), *The aging family: New visions in theory, practice, and reality* (pp. 199–208). New York: Brunner/Mazel.

Kruglanski, A. W., Atash, M. N., DeGrada, E., Mannetti, L., Pierro, A., & Webster, D. M. (1997). Psychological theory testing vs. psychometric nay-saying: Comment on Neuberg et al.'s (1997) critique of the Need for Closure Scale. *Journal of Personality and Social Psychology, 76,* 1005–1016.

Kruglanski, A. W., & Webster, D. W. (1996). Motivated closing of the mind, "seizing" and "freezing." *Psychological Review, 103,* 263–283.

Kübler-Ross, E. (1969). *On death and dying.* New York: Macmillan.

Kübler-Ross, E. (1974). *Questions and answers on death and dying.* New York: Macmillan.

Kuhn, D. (1992). Cognitive development. In M. Bornstein & M. Lamb (Eds.), *Developmental psychology: An advanced textbook* (pp. 211–272). Hillsdale, NJ: Erlbaum.

Kupfer, C. (1995). Ophthalmologic disorders. In W. B. Abrams, M. H. Beers, & R. Berkow (Eds.), *The Merck manual of geriatrics* (2nd ed., pp. 1289–1314). Whitehouse Station, NJ: Merck Research Laboratories.

Kurdek, L. A. (1995a). Developmental changes in relationship quality in gay male and lesbian cohabiting couples. *Developmental Psychology, 31,* 86–94.

Kurdek, L. A. (1995b). Lesbian and gay couples. In A. R. D'Augelli & C. J. Patterson (Eds.), *Lesbian, gay, and bisexual identities over the lifespan* (pp. 243–261). New York: Oxford University Press.

Kurz, D. (1995). *For richer, for poorer: Mothers confront divorce.* Philadelphia: Women's Studies Program, University of Pennsylvania.

Kutza, J., Kaye, D., & Murasko, D. M. (1995). Basal natural killer cell activity of young versus elderly humans. *Journal of Gerontology: Biological Sciences, 50A,* B110–B116.

Labouvie-Vief, G. (1980). Beyond formal operations: Uses and limits of pure logic in life-span development. *Human Development, 23,* 141–161.

Labouvie-Vief, G. (1981). Proactive and reactive aspects of constructivism: Growth and aging in life-span perspective. In R. M. Lerner & N. A. Busch-Rossnagel (Eds.), *Individuals as producers of their development* (pp. 197–230). New York: Academic Press.

Labouvie-Vief, G. (1984). Logic and self-regulation from youth to maturity: A model. In M. L. Commons, F. A. Richards, & C. Armon (Eds.), *Beyond formal operations: Late adolescent and adult cognitive development* (pp. 158–179). New York: Praeger.

Labouvie-Vief, G. (1985). Intelligence and cognition. In J. E. Birren & K. W. Schaie (Eds.), *Handbook of the psychology of aging* (2nd ed., pp. 500–530). New York: Van Nostrand Reinhold.

Labouvie-Vief, G. (1990). Modes of knowledge and the organization of development. In M. L. Commons & C. Armon (Eds.), *Adult development volume 2: Models and methods in the study of adolescent and adult thought* (pp. 43–62). New York: Praeger.

Labouvie-Vief, G. (1992). Neo-Piagetian perspective on adult cognitive development. In R. J. Sternberg & C. A. Berg (Eds.), *Intellectual development* (pp. 197–229). New York: Cambridge University Press.

Labouvie-Vief, G. (1997). Cognitive–emotional integration in adulthood. In K. W. Schaie & M. P. Lawton (Eds.), *Annual review of gerontology and geriatrics* (Vol. 17, pp. 206–237). New York: Springer.

Labouvie-Vief, G., Chiodo, L. M., Goguen, L. A., Diehl, M., & Orwoll, L. (1995). Representations of self across the life span. *Psychology and Aging, 10,* 404–415.

Labouvie-Vief, G., & Diehl, M. (1999). Self and personality development. In J. C. Cavanaugh & S. K. Whitbourne (Eds.), *Gerontology: An interdisciplinary perspective* (pp. 238–268). New York: Oxford University Press.

Labouvie-Vief, G., Hakim-Larson, J., & Hobart, C. J. (1987). Age, ego level, and the life-span development of coping and defense processes. *Psychology and Aging, 2,* 286–293.

Lachman, M. E. (1983). Perceptions of intellectual aging: Antecedent or consequence of intellectual functioning? *Developmental Psychology, 19,* 482–498.

Lachman, M. E. (1986). Locus of control in aging research: A case for multidimensional and domain-specific assessment. *Psychology and Aging, 1,* 34–40.

Lachman, M. E., Bandura, M., Weaver, S. L., & Elliott, E. (1995). Assessing memory control beliefs: The Memory Controllability Inventory. *Aging and Cognition, 2,* 67–84.

Lachman, M. E., & Leff, R. (1989). Perceived control and intellectual functioning in the elderly: A 5-year longitudinal study. *Developmental Psychology, 25,* 722–728.

Lachman, M. E., Lewkowicz, C., Marcus, A., & Peng, Y. (1994). Images of midlife development among young, middle-aged, and older adults. *Journal of Adult Development, 1,* 201–211.

Lachs, M. S., Williams, C., O'Brien, S., Hurst, L., & Horwotz, R. (1997). Risk factors for reported elder abuse and neglect: A nine-year observational cohort study. *The Gerontologist, 37,* 469–474.

Lai, G. (1995). Work and family roles and psychological well-being in urban China. *Journal of Health and Social Behavior, 36,* 11–37.

Lakatta, E. G. (1995). Normal changes of aging. In W. B. Abrams, M. H. Beers, & R. Berkow (Eds.), *The Merck manual of geriatrics* (2nd ed., pp. 425–441). Whitehouse Station, NJ: Merck Research Laboratories.

Lam, R. E., Pacala, J. T., & Smith, S. L. (1997). Factors related to depressive symptoms in an elderly Chinese American sample. *Clinical Gerontologist, 17,* 57–70.

Lambert, L. D., & Fleury, M. (1994). Age, cognitive style, and traffic signs. *Perceptual and Motor Skills, 78,* 611–624.

Lampman, C., & Dowling-Guyer, S. (1995). Attitudes toward voluntary and involuntary childlessness. *Basic and Applied Social Psychology, 17,* 213–222.

Landi, F., Zuccalà, G., Gambassi, G., Incalzi, R. A., Manigrasso, L., Pagano, F., Carbonin, P., & Bernabei, R. (1999). Body mass index and mortality among older people living in the community. *Journal of the American Geriatrics Society, 47,* 1072–1076.

Langer, E. J. (1985). Playing the middle against both ends: The usefulness of older adult cognitive activity as a model for cognitive activity in childhood and old age. In S. Yussen (Ed.), *The growth of reflection in children* (pp. 267–285). New York: Academic Press.

Langer, E. J. (1989). *Mindfulness.* Reading, MA: Addison-Weasley.

Langer, E. J., & Rodin, J. (1976). The effects of choice and enhanced personal responsibility for the aged: A field experiment in an institutional setting. *Journal of Personality and Social Psychology, 34,* 191–198.

Larson, R. W., Gillman, S. A., & Richards, M. H. (1997). Divergent experiences of family leisure: Fathers, mothers, and young adolescents. *Journal of Leisure Research, 29,* 78–97.

LaRue, A., Swan, G. E., & Carmelli, D. (1995). Cognition and depression in a cohort of aging men: Results from the Western Collaborative Group Study. *Psychology and Aging, 10,* 30–33.

Latack, J. C. (1984). Career transitions within organizations: An exploratory study of work, nonwork, and coping. *Organizational Behavior & Human Decision Processes, 34*(3), 296–322.

Laver, G. D., & Burke, D. M. (1993). Why do semantic priming effects increase with age? A meta-analysis. *Psychology and Aging, 8,* 34–43.

LaVoie, D., & Light, L. L. (1994). Adult age differences in repetition priming: A meta-analysis. *Psychology and Aging, 9,* 539–555.

Lawton, M. P. (1980). *Environment and aging.* Pacific Grove, CA: Brooks/Cole.

Lawton, M. P. (1982). Competence, environmental press, and the adaptation of old people. In M. P. Lawton, P. G. Windley, & T. O. Byerts (Eds.), *Aging and the environment: Theoretical approaches* (pp. 33–59). New York: Springer.

Lawton, M. P. (1996). *Assessing quality of life.* Unpublished manuscript, Philadelphia Geriatric Center.

Lawton, M. P. (1999). Environmental design features and the well-being of older persons. In M. Duffy (Ed.), *Handbook of counseling and psychotherapy with older adults* (pp. 350–363). New York: Wiley.

Lawton, M. P., Moss, M. S., & Fulcomer, M. (1986–1987). Objective and subjective uses of time by older people. *International Journal of Aging and Human Development, 24,* 171–188.

Lawton, M. P., Moss, M., Hoffman, C., Grant, R., Have, T. T., & Kleban, M. H. (1999). Health, valuation of life, and the wish to live. *The Gerontologist, 39,* 406–416.

Lawton, M. P., Moss, M., Hoffman, C., & Perkinson, M. (2000). Two transitions in daughters' caregiving careers. *The Gerontologist, 40,* 437–448.

Lawton, M. P., & Nahemow, L. (1973). Ecology of the aging process. In C. Eisdorfer & M. P. Lawton (Eds.), *The psychology of adult development and aging* (pp. 619–674). Washington, DC: American Psychological Association.

Lazarus, R. S. (1984). Puzzles in the study of daily hassles. *Journal of Behavioral Medicine, 7,* 375–389.

Lazarus, R. S., DeLongis, A., Folkman, S., & Gruen, R. (1985). Stress and adaptational outcomes. *American Psychologist, 40,* 770–779.

Lazarus, R. S., & Folkman, S. (1984). *Stress, appraisal, and coping.* New York: Springer.

Leahy, J. M. (1993). A comparison of depression in women bereaved of a spouse, a child, or a parent. *Omega, 26,* 207–217.

Leana, C. R., & Feldman, D. C. (1992). *Coping with job loss.* New York: Lexington.

Lee, G. R., DeMaris, A., Bavin, S., & Sullivan, R. (2001). Gender differences in the depressive effect of widowhood in later life. *Journal of Gerontology: Social Sciences, 56B,* S56–S61.

Lee, T. R., Mancini, J. A., & Maxwell, J. W. (1990). Sibling relationships in adulthood: Contact patterns and motivation. *Journal of Marriage and the Family, 52,* 431–440.

Leirer, V. O., Morrow, D. G., Sheikh, J. I., & Pariante, G. M. (1990). Memory skills elders want to improve. *Experimental Aging Research, 16,* 155–158.

Leirer, V. O., Tanke, E. D., & Morrow, D. G. (1994). Time of day and naturalistic prospective memory. *Experimental Aging Research, 20,* 127–134.

Lentzner, H. R., Pamuk, E. R., Rhodenhiser, R. R., & Powell-Griner, E. (1992). The quality of life in the year before death. *American Journal of Public Health, 82,* 1093–1098.

Leon, G. R., Gillum, B., Gillum, R., & Gouze, M. (1979). Personality stability and change over a 30-year period: Middle to old age. *Journal of Consulting and Clinical Psychology, 47,* 517–524.

Lepp, I. (1968). *Death and its mysteries.* New York: Macmillan.

Lerner, R. M. (1986). *Concepts and theories of human development* (2nd ed.). New York: Random House.

Lerner, W. (1994). Giving the older driver enough perception-reaction time. *Experimental Aging Research, 20,* 25–33.

Lester, D. (1996). Trends in divorce and marriage around the world. *Journal of Divorce and Remarriage, 25,* 169–171.

Levenson, R. W., Carstensen, L. L., & Gottman, J. M. (1993). Long-term marriage: Age, gender, and satisfaction. *Psychology and Aging, 8,* 301–313.

Levin, J. S., Taylor, R. J., & Chatters, L. M. (1994). Race and gender differences in religiosity among older adults: Findings from four national surveys. *Journal of Gerontology: Social Sciences, 49,* 137–145.

Levinson, D. J., Darrow, C., Kline, E., Levinson, M., & McKee, B. (1978). *The seasons of a man's life.* New York: Knopf.

Levinson, D., & Levinson, J. D. (1996). *The seasons of a woman's life.* New York: Knopf.

Levenson, R. W., Carstensen, L. L., & Gottman, J. M. (1994). The influence of age and gender on affect, physiology, and their interrelations: A study of long-term marriages. *Journal of Personality and Social Psychology, 67,* 56–68.

Levy, B. (1996). Improving memory in old age through implicit stereotyping. *Journal of Personality and Social Psychology, 71,* 1092–1107.

Levy, B., & Langer, E. (1994). Aging free from negative stereotypes: Successful memory in China and among the American deaf. *Journal of Personality and Social Psychology, 66,* 989–997.

Lewin, K. (1936). *Principles of topological psychology.* New York: McGraw-Hill.

Lewinsohn, P. M. (1975). The behavioral study and treatment of depression. In M. Hersen, R. M. Eisler, & P. M. Miller (Eds.), *Progress in behavior modification* (Vol. 1, pp. 19–64). New York: Academic Press.

Lewis, K. G., & Moon, S. (1997). Always single and single again women: A qualitative study. *Journal of Marital and Family Therapy, 23,* 115–134.

Lewis, M. I. (1995). Sexuality. In W. B. Abrams, M. H. Beers, & R. Berkow (Eds.), *The Merck manual of geriatrics* (2nd ed., pp. 827–838). Whitehouse Station, NJ: Merck Research Laboratories.

Lewis, R. A., & Lin, L.-W. (1996). Adults and their midlife parents. In N. Vanzetti & S. Duck (Eds.), *A lifetime of relationships* (pp. 364–382). Pacific Grove, CA: Brooks/Cole.

Lezak, M. D. (1995). *Neuropsychological assessment* (3rd ed.). New York: Oxford University Press.

Lichtenberg, P. A., MacNeill, S. E., & Mast, B. T. (2000). Environmental press and adaptation to disability in hospitalized live-alone older adults. *The Gerontologist, 40,* 549–556.

Lidz, C. W., Appelbaum, P. S., & Meisel, A. (1988). Two models of implementing informed consent. *Archives of Internal Medicine, 148,* 1385–1389.

Lieberman, A. (1974). Parkinson's disease: A clinical review. *American Journal of Medical Science, 267*, 66–80.

Light, L. L. (1990). Interactions between memory and language in old age. In J. E. Birren & K. W. Schaie (Eds.), *Handbook of the psychology of aging* (3rd ed., pp. 275–290). San Diego: Academic Press.

Light, L. L. (1996). Memory and aging. In E. C. Carterette & M. P. Friedman (Eds.), *Handbook of perception and cognition* (2nd cd, pp. 443–490). San Diego: Academic Press.

Light, L. L., Capps, J. L., Singh, A., & Albertson-Owens, S. A. (1994). Comprehension of metaphors by young and older adults. In J. Cerella, J. Rybash, W. Hoyer, & M. L. Commons (Eds.), *Adult information processing: Limits on loss* (pp. 459–488). San Diego: Academic Press.

Lindenberger, U., & Baltes, P. B. (1994). Sensory functioning and intelligence in old age. *Psychology and Aging, 9*, 339–355.

Lindenberger, U., & Baltes, P. B. (1995). Testing-the-limits and experimental simulation: Two methods to explicate the role of learning development. *Human Development, 38*, 349–360.

Lindenberger, U., & Baltes, P. B. (1997). Intellectual functioning in old and very old age: Cross sectional results from the Berlin Aging Study. *Psychology and Aging, 12*, 410–432.

Lindenberger, U., & Reischies, F. M. (1999). Limits and potentials of intellectual functioning in old age. In P. B. Baltes & K. U. Mayer (Eds.), *The Berlin ageing study: Ageing from 70 to 100*. New York: Cambridge University Press.

Lindsay, D. S., & Johnson, M. K. (1989). The eyewitness suggestibility effect and memory for source. *Memory & Cognition, 17*, 349–358.

Lineweaver, T. T., & Hertzog, C. (1998). Adults' efficacy and control beliefs regarding memory and ageing: Separating general from personal beliefs. *Aging, Neuropsychology, and Cognition, 5*, 264–296.

Lipman, P. D. (1991). Age and exposure differences in acquisition of route information. *Psychology and Aging, 6*, 128–133.

Lisansky Gomberg, E. S., & Zucker, R. A. (1999). Substance use and abuse in old age. In I. H. Nordhus, G. R. VandenBos, S. Berg, & P. Fromholt (Eds.), *Clinical geropsychology* (pp. 189–204). Washington, DC: American Psychological Association.

Livingston, M. M., & Burley, K. A. (1991). Surprising initial findings regarding sex, sex roles, and anticipated work/family conflict. *Psychological Reports, 68*, 735–738.

Livson, F. B. (1981). Paths to psychological health in the middle years: Sex differences. In D. Eichorn, N. Haan, J. Clausen, M. Honzik, & P. Mussen (Eds.), *Past and present in middle life* (pp. 183–194). New York: Academic Press.

Lo, R., & Brown, R. (1999). Stress and adaptation: Preparation for successful retirement. *Australian and New Zealand Journal of Mental Health Nursing, 8*, 30–38.

Lock, M. (1991). Contested meanings of the menopause. *The Lancet, 337*, 1270–1272.

Loevinger, J. (1976). *Ego development*. San Francisco: Jossey-Bass.

Loevinger, J. (1997). Stages of personality development. In R. Hogan & J. A. Johnson, et al. (Eds.), *Handbook of personality psychology*. St Louis: Washington University Department of Psychology.

Loftus, E. F. (1975). Spreading activation with in semantic categories: Commenting on Rosch's "Cognitive representation of semantic categories." *Journal of Experimental Psychology: General, 104*, 234–240.

Logan, R. D. (1986). A reconceptualization of Erikson's theory: The repetition of existential and instrumental themes. *Human Development, 29*, 125–136.

Logie, R. H. (1995). *Visuo-spatial working memory*. Hove, England: Erlbaum.

Lombardi, W. J., & Weingartner, H. (1995). Pharmacological treatment of impaired memory function. In A.

D. Baddeley, B. A. Wilson, & F. N. Watts (Eds.), *Handbook of memory disorders* (pp. 577–601). Chichester, England: Wiley.

Lomranz, J., Bergman, S., Eyal, N., & Shmotkin, D. (1988). Indoor and outdoor activities of aged women and men as related to depression and well-being. *International Journal of Aging and Human Development, 26*, 303–314.

Lopata, H. Z. (1993). The interweave of public and private: Women's challenge to American society. *Journal of Marriage and the Family, 55*, 176–190.

Lorayne, H., & Lucas, J. (1996). *The memory book*. New York: Ballantine.

Lorist, M. M., Snell, J., Mulder, G., & Kok, A. (1995). Aging, caffeine, and information processing: An event-related potential analysis. *Electroencephalography & Clinical Neuropsychology: Evoked Potential, 96*, 453–467.

Luborsky, M. R., & McMullen, C. K. (1999). Culture and aging. In J. C. Cavanaugh & S. K. Whitbourne (Eds.), *Gerontology: An interdisciplinary perspective* (pp. 65–90). New York: Oxford University Press.

Luborsky, M. R., & Rubinstein, R. (1997). The dynamics of ethnic identity in elderly widowers' reactions to bereavement. In J. Sokolovsky (Ed.), *The cultural context of aging: Worldwide perspectives* (pp. 304–315). New York: Bergin & Garvey.

Lundin, T. (1984). Morbidity following sudden and unexpected bereavement. British *Journal of Psychiatry, 144*, 84–88.

Luo, T. Y. (1996). Sexual harassment in the Chinese workplace: Attitudes toward and experiences of sexual harassment among workers in Taiwan. *Violence Against Women, 2*, 284–301.

Lyness, K. S., & Thompson, D. E. (1997). Above the glass ceiling? A comparison of matched samples of female and male executives. *Journal of Applied Psychology, 82*, 359–375.

Maas, H. S. (1985). The development of adult development: Recollections and reflections. In J. M. A.

Munnichs, P. Mussen, E. Olbrich, & P. G. Coleman (Eds.), *Life-span and change in a gerontological perspective* (pp. 161–175). New York: Academic Press.

Maas, H. S., & Kuypers, J. A. (1974). *From thirty to seventy.* San Francisco: Jossey-Bass.

Maccoby, E. E., Depner, C. E., & Mnookin, R. H. (1990). Coparenting in the second year after divorce. *Journal of Marriage and the Family, 52,* 141–155.

MacDermid, S. M., De Haan, L. G., & Heilburn, G. (1996). Generativity in multiple roles. *Journal of Adult Development, 3,* 145–158.

MacKay, D. G., & Abrams, L. (1996). Language, memory, and aging. Distributed deficiencies and the structure of new-vs-old connect. In J. E. Birren & K. W. Schaie (Eds.), *Handbook of the psychology of aging* (4th ed., pp. 251–265). San Diego: Academic Press.

Madden, D. J. (1990). Adult age differences in the time course of visual attention. *Journal of Gerontology: Psychological Sciences, 45,* P9–P16.

Madden, D. J., & Gottlob, L. R. (1997). Adult age differences in strategic and dynamic components of focusing visual attention. *Aging, Neuropsychology, and Cognition, 4,* 185–210.

Madden, D. J., & Plude, D. J. (1993). Selective preservation of selective attention. In J. Cerella, J. Rybash, W. Hoyer, & M. L. Commons (Eds.), *Adult information processing: Limits on loss* (pp. 273–300). San Diego: Academic Press.

Malinak, D. P., Hoyt, M. F., & Patterson, V. (1979). Adults' reaction to the death of a parent: A preliminary study. *American Journal of Psychiatry, 136,* 1152–1156.

Malkinson, R., & Bar-Tur, L. (1999). The aging of grief in Israel: A perspective of bereaved parents. *Death Studies, 23,* 413–431.

Mancil, G. L., & Owsley, C. (1988). "Vision through my aging eyes" revisited. *Journal of the American Optometric Association, 59,* 288–294.

Manson, J. E., Hu, F. B., Rich-Edwards, J. W., Colditz, G. A., Stampfer, M. J., Willett, W. C., Speizer, F. E., & Hennekens, C. H. (1999). A prospective study of walking as compared with vigorous exercise in the prevention of coronary heart disease in women. *New England Journal of Medicine, 341,* 650–658.

Manton, K. G., & Vaupel, J. (1995). Survival after age 80 in the United States, Sweden, France, England, and Japan. *New England Journal of Medicine, 333,* 1232–1235.

Manton, K. G., Wrigley, J. M., Cohen, H. J., & Woodbury, M. A. (1991). Cancer mortality, aging, and patterns of comorbidity in the United States: 1968–1986. *Journal of Gerontology: Social Sciences, 46,* S225–S234.

Mäntylä, T. (1994). Remembering to remember: Adult age differences in prospective memory. *Journal of Gerontology: Psychological Sciences, 49,* P276–P282.

Markson, L. J., Fanale, J., Steel, K., Kern, D., & Annas, G. (1995). Implementing advance directives in the primary care setting. *Archives of Internal Medicine, 154,* 2321–2327.

Markus, H., & Nurius, P. (1986). Possible selves. *American Psychologist, 41,* 954–969.

Marquis, K. S., & Detweiler, R. A. (1985). Does adopted mean different? An attributional analysis. *Journal of Personality and Social Psychology, 48,* 1054–1066.

Marshall, V., Matthews, S., & Rosenthal, C. (1993). Elusiveness of family life: A challenge for the sociology of aging. In G. Maddox & M. P. Lawton (Eds.), *Annual review of gerontology and geriatrics, Vol. 13: Kinship, aging, and social change* (pp. 39–72). New York: Springer.

Marsiske, M., Lang, F. R., Baltes, P. B., & Baltes, M. M. (1996). Selective optimization with compensation: Life-span perspectives on successful human development. In R. A. Dixon & L. Bäckman (Eds.), *Compensating for psychological deficits and declines: Managing losses and promoting gains* (pp. 35–79). Mahwah, NJ: Erlbaum.

Marsiske, M., & Willis, S. L. (1995). Dimensionality of everyday problem solving in older adults. *Psychology and Aging, 10,* 269–283.

Marson, D. C., Chatterjee, A., Ingram, K. K., & Harrell, L. E. (1996). Towards a neurologic model of competency: Cognitive predictors of capacity to consent in Alzheimer's disease using three different legal standards. *Neurology, 46,* 666–672.

Martin, G. M. (1998). Toward a genetic analysis of unusually successful neural aging. In E. Wang & D. Snyder (Eds.), *Handbook of the aging brain* (pp. 125–142). San Diego: Academic Press.

Masheter, C. (1991). Postdivorce relationships between ex-spouses: The roles of attachment and interpersonal conflict. *Journal of Marriage and the Family, 53,* 103–110.

Masheter, C. (1997). Healthy and unhealthy friendship and hostility between ex-spouses. *Journal of Marriage and the Family, 59,* 463–475.

Maslow, A. H. (1968). *Toward a psychology of being* (2nd ed.). New York: Van Nostrand Reinhold.

Mason, S. E. (1986). Age and gender as factors in facial recognition. *Experimental Aging Research, 12,* 151–154.

Matsui, T., Ikeda, H., & Ohnisha, R. (1989). Relation of sex-typed socializations to career self-efficacy expectations of college students. *Journal of Vocational Behavior, 35,* 1–16.

Matthews, A. M., & Brown, K. H. (1987). Retirement as a critical life event: The differential experiences of men and women. *Research on Aging, 9,* 548–571.

Matthews, S. H. (1996). Friendships in old age. In N. Vanzetti & S. Duck (Eds.), *A lifetime of relationships* (pp. 406–430). Pacific Grove: Brooks/Cole.

Mattis, S. (1976). Mental status examination for organic mental syndrome in the elderly patient. In L. Bellak & T. B. Karasu (Eds.), *Geriatric psychiatry: A handbook for psychiatrists and primary health care physicians* (pp. 79–121). New York: Grune & Stratton.

Mattis, S. (1988). *Dementia rating scale.* Odessa, FL: Psychological Assessment Resources.

Maurer, T. J. (in press). Career-relevant learning and development, worker age, and beliefs about self-efficacy for development. *Journal of Management.*

Maurer, T., & Tarulli, B. (1994). Acceptance of peer/upward performance appraisal systems: Role of work context factors and beliefs about managers' development capability. *Human Resource Management Journal, 35,* 217–241.

Mayes, A. R. (1995). The assessment of memory disorders. In A. D. Baddeley, B. A. Wilson, & F. N. Watts (Eds.), *Handbook of memory disorders* (pp. 367–391). Chichester, England: Wiley.

Maylor, E. A. (1990). Recognizing and naming faces: Ageing memory and retrieval and the tip of the tongue state. *Journal of Gerontology: Psychological Sciences, 45,* P215–P226.

Mayr, U., Kliegl, R., & Kampe, R. J. (1996). Sequential and coordinative processing dynamics in figural transformations across the lifespan. *Cognition, 59,* 61–90.

McAdams, D. P. (1992). The five-factor model in personality: A critical appraisal. *Journal of Personality, 60,* 329–361.

McAdams, D. P. (1993). *The stories we live by: Personal myths and the making of the self.* New York: William Morrow.

McAdams, D. P. (1994). Can personality change? Levels of stability and growth in personality across the life span. In T. F. Heatherton & J. L. Weinberger (Eds.), *Can personality change?* (pp. 299–313). Washington, DC: American Psychological Association.

McAdams, D. P. (1995). What do we know when we know a person? *Journal of Personality, 63,* 365–396.

McAdams, D. P., de St. Aubin, E., & Logan, R. (1993). Generativity in young, midlife, and older adults. *Psychology and Aging, 8,* 221–230.

McAdams, D. P., Hart, H. M., & Maruna, S. (1998). The anatomy of generativity. In D. P. McAdams & E. de St. Aubin (Eds.), *Generativity and adult development: How and why*

we care for the next generation. Washington, DC: American Psychological Association.

McAllister, T. W. (1981). Cognitive functioning in the affective disorders. *Comprehensive Psychiatry, 22,* 572–586.

McAuley, E., Katula, J., Mihalko, S. L., Blissmer, B., Duncan, T. E., Pena, M., & Dunn, E. (1999). Mode of physical activity and self-efficacy in older adults: A latent growth curve analysis. *Journal of Gerontology: Psychological Sciences, 54B,* P283–P292.

McAvay, G. J., Seeman, T. E., & Rodin, J. (1996). A longitudinal study of change in domain-specific self-efficacy among older adults. *Journal of Gerontology: Psychological Sciences, 51B,* P243–P253.

McClelland, J. L., Rumelhart, D. E., & the PDP Research Group. (1986). *Parallel distributed processing: Explorations in the microstructure of cognition.* Cambridge, MA: MIT Press.

McCrae, R. R., & Costa, P. T., Jr. (1990). *Personality in adulthood.* New York: Guilford.

McCrae, R. R., & Costa, P. T. (1994). The stability of personality: Observation and evaluations. *Current Directions in Psychological Sciences, 3,* 173–175.

McDonald, R. S. (1986). Asessing treatment effects: Behavior rating scales. In L. W. Poon (Ed.), *Handbook for the clinical memory assessment of older adults* (pp. 129–138). Washington, DC: American Psychological Association.

McDonald-Miszczak, L., Hertzog, C., & Hultsch, D. F. (1995). Stability and accuracy of metamemory in adulthood and aging: A longitudinal analysis. *Psychology and Aging, 10,* 553–564.

McDowd, J. M. (1997). Inhibition in attention and aging. *Journal of Gerontology, 52B,* P265–273.

McDowd, J. M., & Birren, J. E. (1990). Aging and attentional processes. In J. E. Birren & K. W. Schaie (Eds.), *Handbook of the psychology of aging* (3rd ed., pp. 222–233). San Diego: Academic Press.

McDowd, J. M., Filion, D. L., & Oseas-Kreger, D. M. (1991, June). *Inhibitory*

deficits in selective attention and aging. Paper presented at the annual meeting of the American Psychological Society, Washington, DC.

McDowd, J. M., & Shaw, R. J. (2000). Attention and aging. In F. I. M. Craik & T. A. Salthouse (Eds.), *The handbook of aging and cognition* (2nd ed., pp. 221–292). Mahwah, NJ: Erlbaum.

McEvoy, C. L., & Moon, J. R. (1988). Assessment and treatment of everyday memory problems in the elderly. In M. M. Gruneberg, P. E. Morris, & R. N. Sykes (Eds.), *Practical aspects of memory: Current research and issues* (Vol. 2, pp. 155–160). Chichester, England: Wiley.

McFadden, J. (1996). A transcultural perspective and reaction to C. A. Patterson's "Multi-cultural counseling: From diversity to universality." *Journal of Counseling and Development, 74,* 232–235.

McGuire, F. A., Boyd, R. K., & Tedrick, R. K. (1996). *Leisure and aging: Ulyssean living in later life.* Champaign, IL: Sagamore.

McGuire, L. C., & Codding, R. (1998, August). *Improving older adults' memory for medical information: The efficacy of note taking and elder speak.* Paper presented at the annual meeting of the American Psychological Association, San Francisco.

McLeod, J. D. (1996). Life events. In J. E. Birren (Ed.), *Encyclopedia of gerontology* (Vol. 2, pp. 41–51). San Diego: Academic Press.

McMahon, P., & Koch, W. (1999). Assisted suicide: A right or a surrender? *USA Today, November 22,* 21A–22A.

Mehta, K. K. (1997). The impact of religious beliefs and practices on ageing: A cross-cultural comprehension. *Journal of Aging Studies, 11,* 101–114.

Meisami, E. (1994). Aging of the sensory systems. In P. Timiras (Ed.), *Physiological basis of aging and geriatrics* (2nd ed., pp. 115–131). Boca Raton, FL: CRC Press.

Mendes de Leon, C. F., Seeman, T. E., Baker, D. I., Richardson, E. D., & Tinetti, M. E. (1996). Self-efficacy, physical decline, and change in functioning in community-living elders: A prospective study. *Journal of*

Gerontology: Social Sciences, 51B, S183–S190.

Mera, S. L. (1998). The role of telomeres in ageing and cancer. *British Journal of Biomedical Science, 55*, 221–225.

Metropolitan Area Agency on Aging. (1998). *Checklist on adult day care.* Available at the Web site http://www.tcaging.org/com_adck.htm.

Meyer, B. J. F. (1999). Importance of text structure in everyday reading. In A. Ram & K. Moorman (Eds.), *Understanding language understanding: Computational models of reading* (pp. 227–253). Cambridge, MA: MIT Press.

Meyer, B. J. F., Russo, C., & Talbot, A. (1994). Discourse comprehension and problem solving: Decisions about the treatment of breast cancer by women across the lifespan. *Psychology and Aging, 10*, 84–103.

Milford, M. (1997, November 9). Making a tough transition. *Sunday News Journal* (Wilmington, DE), pp. G1, G6.

Miller, G. A. (1956). The magical seven plus or minus two. Some limits on our capacity for processing information. *Psychological Review, 63*, 81–97.

Miller, R. A. (1996a). Aging and the immune response. In E. L. Schneider & J. W. Rowe (Eds.), *Handbook of the biology of aging* (4th ed., pp. 355–392). San Diego: Academic Press.

Miller, R. A. (1996b). The aging immune system: Primer and prospectus. *Science, 273*, 70–74.

Miller, R. B., Hemesath, K., & Nelson, B. (1997). Marriage in middle and later life. In T. D. Hargrave & S. M. Hanna (Eds.), *The aging family: New visions in theory, practice, and reality* (pp. 178–198). New York: Brunner/Mazel.

Miller, S. S., & Cavanaugh, J. C. (1990). The meaning of grandparenthood and its relationship to demographic, relationship, and social participation variables. *Journal of Gerontology: Psychological Sciences, 45*, P244–P246.

Mischel, W., & Shoda, Y. (1995). A cognitive–affective system theory of personality: Reconceptualizing situations, dispositions, dynamics, and

invariance in personality structure. *Psychological Review, 102*, 246–268.

Mobily, K. E., Lemke, J. H., & Gisin, G. J. (1991). The idea of leisure repertoire. *Journal of Applied Gerontology, 10*, 208–223.

Moen, P., & Wethington, E. (1999). Midlife development in a life course context. In S. L. Willis & J. D. Reid (Eds.), *Life in the middle: Psychological and social development in middle age* (pp. 2–23). San Diego: Academic Press.

Mohs, R. C., Kim, Y., Johns, C. A., Dunn, D. D., & Davis, K. I. (1986). Assessing changes in Alzheimer's disease: Memory and language. In L. W. Poon (Ed.), *Handbook for the clinical memory assessment of older adults* (pp. 149–155). Washington, DC: American Psychological Association.

Monane, M., Gurwitz, J. H., & Avorn, J. (1993). Pharmacotherapy with psychoactive medications in the long-term care setting: Challenges, management, and future directions. *Generations, 17*, 57–60.

Monczunski, J. (1991). That incurable disease. *Notre Dame Magazine, 20*(1), 37.

Moon, A., & Williams, O. (1993). Perceptoins of elder abuse and help-seeking patterns among African-American, Caucasian American, and Korean-American elderly women. *The Gerontologist, 33*, 386–395.

Moos, R. H., & Lemke, S. (1984). *Multiphasic environmental assessment procedure: Manual.* Palo Alto, CA: Social Ecology Laboratory, Stanford University Press.

Moos, R. H., & Lemke, S. (1985). Specialized living environments for older people. In J. E. Birren & K. W. Schaie (Eds.), *Handbook of the psychology of aging* (2nd ed., pp. 864–889). New York: Van Nostrand Reinhold.

Morganti, C. M., Nelson, M. E., Fiatarone, M. A., Dallal, G. E., Economos, C. D., Crawford, B. M., & Evans, W. J. (1995). Strength improvements with 1 yr of progressive resistance training in older women. *Medicine and Science in Sports and Exercise, 27*, 906–912.

Morioka, K. (1996). Generational relations and their changes as they affect the status of older people in Japan. In T. K. Hareven (Ed.), *Aging and generational relations: Life-course and cross-cultural perspectives* (pp. 263–280). New York: Aldine De Gruyter.

Morrison, A. M., White, R. P., Van Vesor, E., & the Center for Creative Leadership. (1992). *Breaking the glass ceiling: Can women reach the top of America's largest corporations?* (Updated ed.). Reading, MA: Addison-Wesley.

Morrow, D. G., Hier, C. M., Menard, W. E., & Von Leirer, O. (1998). Icons improve older and younger adults' comprehension of medication information. *Journal of Gerontology: Psychological Sciences, 53B*, P240–P254.

Morrow, D. G., Von Leirer, O., & Altieri, P. A. (1992). Aging, expertise and narrative processing. *Psychology and Aging, 7*, 376–388.

Morrow, D. G., Von Leirer, O., Altieri, P. A., & Fitzsimmons, C. (1994). When expertise reduces age differences in performance. *Psychology and Aging, 9*, 134–148.

Morrow, D. G., Von Leirer, O., Andrassy, J. M., Tanke, E. D., & Stine-Morrow, L. A. L. (1996). Medication instruction design: Younger and older adult schemas for taking medication. *Human Factors, 38*, 556–573.

Morrow, D. G., Von Leirer, O., Carver, L. M., Tanke, E. D., & McNally, A. D. (1999). Effects of aging, message repetition, and note-taking on memory for health information. *Journal of Gerontology: Psychological Sciences, 54B*, P369–P379.

Morrow, D. G., Stine-Morrow, E. A. L., Von Leirer, O., Andrassy, J. M., & Kahn, J. (1997). The role of reader age and focus of attention in creating situation models from narratives. *Journal of Gerontology, 52B*, 73–80.

Morrow, P. C., & McElroy, J. C. (1987). Work commitment and job satisfaction over three career stages. *Journal of Vocational Behavior, 30*, 330–346.

Morrow-Howell, N., & Mui, A. (1989). Elderly volunteers: Reasons for initiating and terminating service. *Journal of Gerontological Social Work, 13*, 21–34.

Morse, C., & Wisocki, P. (1991). Residential factors in programming for elderly. In P. A. Wisocki (Ed.), *Handbook of clinical behavior therapy with the elderly client* (pp. 97–120). New York: Plenum.

Mortimer, J. T., Finch, M. D., & Kumka, D. (1982). Persistence and change in development: The multidimensional self-concept. In P. B. Baltes & O. G. Brim, Jr. (Eds.), *Life-span development and behavior* (Vol. 4, pp. 263–313). New York: Academic Press.

Moscovitch, M. C. (1982). A neuropsychological approach to perception and memory in normal and pathological aging. In F. I. M. Craik & S. Trehub (Eds.), *Aging and cognitive processes* (pp. 55–78). New York: Plenum.

Mouloua, M., & Parasuraman, R. (1995). Aging and cognitive vigilance: Effects of spatial uncertainty and event rate. *Experimental Aging Research, 21,* 17–32.

Mouton, C. P. (1997). Special health considerations in African-American elders. *American Family Physicians, 55,* 1243–1253.

Mroczek, D. K., & Spiro, A. III. (in press). *Modeling intraindividual change in personality traits: Findings from the normative aging study.*

Mui, A. C. (1995). Caring for frail elderly parents: A comparison of adult sons and daughters. *The Gerontologist, 35,* 86–93.

Multhaup, K. S., Hersher, L., & Zacks, R. T. (1998). *Age and memory for distracting information: A double dissociation.* Manuscript submitted for publication.

Murphy, S. (1988). Mental distress and recovery in a high-risk bereavement sample three years after untimely death. *Nursing Research, 37,* 30–35.

Murray, B. (1998). Workplace harassment hurts everyone on the job. *APA Monitor, 29,* 36.

Murray, H. A. (1938). *Explorations in personality.* New York: Oxford University Press.

Murrell, A. J., Freize, I. H., & Frost, J. L. (1991). Aspiring to careers in male- and female-dominated professions: A study of black and white college women. *Psychology of Women Quarterly, 15,* 103–126.

Mussen, P. (1985). Early adult antecedents of life satisfaction at age 70. In J. M. A. Munnichs, P. Mussen, E. Olbrich, & P. G. Coleman (Eds.), *Life-span and change in a gerontological perspective* (pp. 45–61). New York: Academic Press.

Mutchler, J. E., Burr, J. A., Massagli, M. P., & Pienta, A. (1999). Work transitions and health in later life. *Journal of Gerontology, 54B,* 252–261.

Mutchler, J. E., Burr, J. A., Pienta, A. M., & Massagli, M. P. (1997). Pathways to labor force exit: Work transitions and work instability. *Journal of Gerontology: Social Sciences, 52B,* S4–S12.

Mutter, S. A., & Pliske, R. M. (1994). Judging event covariation: Effects of age and memory demand. *Journal of Gerontology, 51B,* P70–P80.

Myerson, J., Hale, S., Rhee, S. H., & Jenkins, L. (1999). Selective interference with verbal and spatial working memory in young and older adults. *Journal of Gerontology: Psychological Sciences, 54B,* P161–P164.

Myerson, J., Hale, S., Wagstaff, D., Poon, L. W., & Smith, G. A. (1990). The information-loss model: A mathematical theory of age-related cognitive slowing. *Psychological Review, 97,* 475–487.

Nachbar, F., & Korting, H. C. (1995). The role of vitamin E in normal and damaged skin. *Journal of Molecular Medicine, 73,* 7–17.

Nagi, S. Z. (1965). Some conceptual issues in disability and rehabilitation. In M. B. Sussman (Ed.), *Sociology and rehabilitation* (pp. 100–113). Washington, DC: American Sociological Association.

Nagi, S. Z. (1991). Disability concepts revisited: Implications for prevention. In A. M. Pope & A. R. Tarlov (Eds.), *Disability in America: Toward a national agenda for prevention* (pp. 309–327). Washington, DC: National Academy Press.

Napholz, L. (1995). Mental health and American Indians women's multiple roles. *American Indian and Alaska Native Mental Health Resource, 6,* 57–75.

National Academy on an Aging Society. (2000a). *Diabetes: A drain on U.S. resources.* Washington, DC: Author.

National Academy on an Aging Society. (2000b). *Caregiving: Helping the elderly with activity limitations.* Washington, DC: Author.

National Academy on an Aging Society. (2000c). *Depression: A treatable disease.* Washington, DC: Author.

National Center on Elder Abuse. (1998). *The national elder abuse incidence study: Final report September 1998.* Online document available at the Web site http://www.aoa.gov/abuse/report/default.htm.

National Center on Elder Abuse. (1999). *The basics: What is elder abuse?* Online document available at the Web site http://www.gwjapan.com/NCEA/basic/index.html.

National Center for Health Statistics. (1999a). *Deaths: Final data for 1997.* Vol. 47, No. 19. Available at the Web site http://www.cdc.gov/nchswww/releases/99facts/99sheets/97mortal.htm.

National Center for Health Statistics. (1999b). *Health, United States, 1998, with socioeconomic status and chartbook.* Online document available at the Web site http://www.cdc.gov/nchswww/data/hus98ncb.pdf.

National Highway Traffic Safety Administration. (1988). *Traffic safety plan for older drivers.* Washington, DC: U.S. Department of Transportation.

National Institute on Alcohol Abuse and Alcoholism. (1995). *Prevalence and population estimates of DSM–IV alcohol abuse and dependence by age, sex, and ethnicity, United States, 1992.* Online document available at the Web site http://www.niaaa.nih.gov.

Neely, A. S., & Bäckman, L. (1993). Long-term maintenance of gains from memory training in older adults: Two 3-year follow-up studies. *Journal of Gerontology, 48,* 233–237.

Neimark, E. D. (1975). Longitudinal development of formal operational thought. *Genetic Psychology Monographs, 91,* 171–225.

Neisser, U. (1976). *Cognition and reality.* San Francisco: W.H. Freeman.

Neimeyer, R. (1997). Knowledge at the margins. *The Forum Newsletter* (Association for Death Education and Counseling), *23(2),* 2, 10.

Neugarten, B. L. (1977). Personality and aging. In J. E. Birren & K. W. Schaie (Eds.), *Handbook of the psychology of aging* (pp. 626–649). New York: Van Nostrand Reinhold.

Neumann, O. (1996). Theories of attention. In O. Neumann, A. F. Sanders, et al. (Eds.), *Handbook of perception and action, Volume 3: Attention.* London: Academic Press.

Neuberg, A. B., Newberg, S. K., & d'Aquili, E. G. (1997). The philosophy and psychology of consciousness. *American Psychologist, 52,* 177–178.

Neugarten, B. L. (1969). Continuities and discontinuities of psychological issues into adult life. *Human Development, 12,* 121–130.

Neugarten, B. L., & Weinstein, K. K. (1964). The changing American grandparent. *Journal of Marriage and the Family, 26,* 299–304.

Newhouse, P. A. (1996). Use of serotonin selective reuptake inhibitors in geriatric depression. *Journal of Clinical Psychiatry, 57*(suppl. 5), 12–22.

Newmann, J. P., Engel, R. J., & Jensen, J. E. (1990). Depressive symptom patterns among older women. *Psychology and Aging, 5,* 101–118.

Newmann, J. P., Engel, R. J., & Jensen, J. E. (1991). Changes in depressive-symptom experiences among older women. *Psychology and Aging, 6,* 212–222.

Newsom, J. T. (1999). Another side to caregiving: Negative reactions to being helped. *Current Directions in Psychological Science, 8,* 183–187.

Nicolson, N., Storms, C., Ponds, R., & Sulon, J. (1997). Salivary cortisol levels and stress reactivity in human aging. *Journal of Gerontology: Medical Sciences, 53A,* M68–M75.

Niederehe, G., & Schneider, L. S. (1998). Treatment of depression and anxiety in the aged. In P. E. Nathan & J. M. Gorman (Eds.), *Treatments that work.* New York: Oxford University Press.

Niederehe, G., & Yoder, C. (1989). Metamemory perceptions in depression in younger and older adults. *Journal of Nervous and Mental Disease, 177,* 4–14.

Noe, R. A. (1987). *An exploratory investigation of the antecedents and consequences of mentoring.* Unpublished manuscript, University of Minnesota, Minneapolis.

Norman, K. A., & Schacter, D. L. (1997). False recognition in younger and older adults: Exploring characteristics of illusionary memories. *Memory & Cognition, 25,* 838–848.

Norris, F. N., & Murrell, S. A. (1987). Older adult family stress and adaptation before and after bereavement. *Journal of Gerontology, 42,* 606–612.

Nuland, S. B. (1994). *How we die: Reflections on life's final chapter.* New York: Knopf.

Nyberg, L., Lars-Goeran, N., Olofsson, U., & Backman, L. (1997). Effects of division of attention during encoding and retrieval on age differences in episodic memory. *Experimental Aging Research, 23,* 137–143.

Nydegger, C. N. (1986). Asymmetrical kin and the problematic son-in-law. In N. Datan, A. L. Greene, & H. W. Reese (Eds.), *Life-span developmental psychology: Intergenerational relations* (pp. 99–124). Hillsdale, NJ: Erlbaum.

O'Connor, M., Verfaellie, M., & Cermak, L. S. (1995). Clinical differentiation of amnesic subtypes. In A. D. Baddeley, B. A. Wilson, & F. N. Watts (Eds.), *Handbook of memory disorders* (pp. 53–80). Chichester, England: Wiley.

Offerman, L. R., & Growing, M. K. (1990). Organizations of the future: Changes and challenges. *American Psychologist, 45,* 95–108.

O'Hanlon, A. M. (1993). *Inter-individual patterns of intellectual change: The influence of environmental factors.* Unpublished doctoral dissertation, Pennsylvania State University.

O'Leary, K. D. (1993). Through a psychological lens: Personality traits, personality disorders, and levels of violence. In R. J. Gelles & D. R. Loseke (Eds.), *Current controversies on family violence* (pp. 7–30). Newbury Park, CA: Sage Publications.

Olian, J. D., Carroll, S. J., Giannantonia, C. M., & Feren, D. B. (1988). What do protégés look for in a mentor? Results from three experimental studies. *Journal of Vocational Behavior, 33,* 15–37.

Orr, R., & Luszcz, M. (1994). Rethinking women's ways of knowing: Gender commonalities and intersections with postformal thought. *Journal of Adult Development, 1,* 225–233.

Orwoll, L., & Perlmutter, M. (1990). The study of wise persons: Integrating a personality perspective. In R. J. Sternberg (Ed.), *Wisdom: Its nature, origins, and development* (pp. 160–177). Cambridge, UK: Cambridge University Press.

Osgood, N. J. (1992). *Suicide in later life.* Lexington, MA: Lexington Books.

Owen, G., Fulton, R., & Markusen, E. (1982). Death at a distance: A study of family survivors. *Omega, 13,* 191–225.

Panek, P. E., & Reardon, J. R. (1986). *Age and gender effects on accident types for rural drivers.* Paper presented at the meeting of the Gerontological Society of America, Chicago.

Papalia, D. E. (1972). The status of several conservation abilities across the life-span. *Human Development, 15,* 229–243.

Papalia, D. E., & Bielby, D. (1974). Cognitive functioning in middle and old age adults: A review of research based on Piaget's theory. *Human Development, 17,* 424–443.

Papalia, D. E., Salverson, S. M., & True, M. (1973). An evaluation of quantity conservation performance during old age. *International Journal of Aging and Human Development, 4,* 103–109.

Papalia-Finlay, D. E., Blackburn, J., Davis, E., Dellmann, M., & Roberts, P. (1980). Training cognitive functioning in the elderly: Inability to replicate previous findings. *International Journal of Aging and Human Development, 12,* 111–117.

Parasuraman, R., & Giambra, L. (1991). Skill development in vigilance: Effects of event rate and age. *Psychology and Aging, 6,* 155–169.

Pargament, K. I., Sullivan, M. S., Balzer, W. K., VanHatsma, K. S., et al. (1995). The many meanings of religiousness: A policy-capturing approach. *Journal of Personality, 63,* 953–983.

Park, D. C., Cherry, K. E., Smith, A. D., & Lafronza, V. N. (1990). Effects of distinctive context on memory for objects and their locations in young and elderly adults. *Psychology and Aging, 5,* 250–255.

Park, D., Hertzog, C., Leventhal, H., Morrell, R. W., Leventhal, E., Birchmore, D., Martin, M., & Bennett, J. (1999). Medication adherence in rheumatoid arthritis patients: Older is wiser. *Journal of the American Geriatric Society, 47,* 172–183.

Park, D. C., Hertzog, C., Kidder, D. P., Morrell, M. W., et al. (1997). Effects of age on event-based and time-based prospective memory. *Psychology and Aging, 12,* 314–327.

Park, D. C., Morrell, R. W., Frieske, D. A., Blackburn, A. B., & Birchmore, D. (1991). Cognitive factors and the use of over-the-counter medication organizers by arthritis patients. *Human Factors, 33,* 57–67.

Park, D. C., Morrell, R. W., Frieske, D., & Kincaid, D. (1992). Medication adherence behaviors in older adults: Effects of external cognitive supports. *Psychology and Aging, 7,* 252–256.

Park, D. C., Morrell, R. W., & Shifrin, K. (Eds.). (1999). *Processing of medical information in aging patients: Cognitive and human factors perspectives.* Mahwah, NJ: Erlbaum.

Park, D. C., Puglisi, J. T., & Smith, A. D. (1986). Memory for pictures: Does an age-related decline exist? *Psychology and Aging, 1,* 11–17.

Park, D. C., Puglisi, J. T., & Sovacool, M. (1983). Memory for pictures, words, and spatial location in older adults: Evidence for pictorial superiority. *Journal of Gerontology, 38,* 582–588.

Park, D. C., Puglisi, J. T., & Sovacool, M. (1984). Picture memory in older adults: Effects of contextual detail at encoding and retrieval. *Journal of Gerontology, 39,* 213–215.

Park, D. C., Royal, D., Dudley, W., & Morrell, R. (1988). Forgetting of pictures over a long retention interval in young and older adults. *Psychology and Aging, 3,* 94–95.

Park, D. C., Smith, A. D., Lautenschlager, G., Earles, J., Frieske, D., Zwahr, M., & Gaines, C. (1994, April). *Mediation of long-term memory performance across the life span.* Paper presented at the Cognitive Aging Conference, Atlanta.

Park, D. C., Smith, A. D., Lautenschlager, G., Earls, J. L., et al. (1996). Mediators of long-term memory performance over the life-span. *Psychology and Aging, 11,* 621–237.

Parker, R. A., & Aldwin, C. M. (1997). Do aspects of gender identity change from early to middle adulthood? Disentangling agem cohort, and period effects. In M. E. Lachman & J. B. James (Eds.), *Multiple paths of midlife development* (pp. 67–107). Chicago: University of Chicago Press.

Pascual-Leone, J. (1990). Essay on wisdom: Toward organismic processes that make it possible. In R. J. Sternberg (Ed.), *Wisdom: Its nature, origins, and development* (pp. 244–278). New York: Cambridge University Press.

Pasley, K., & Ihinger-Tallman, M. (1987). *Remarriage and stepparenting.* New York: Guilford.

Pastalan, L. A. (1982). Research in environment and aging: An alternative to theory. In M. P. Lawton, P. G. Windley, & T. O. Byerts (Eds.), *Aging and the environment: Theoretical approaches* (pp. 122–131). New York: Springer.

Patel, V. L., & Groen, G. J. (1986). Knowledge-based solution strategies in medical reasoning. *Cognitive Science, 10*(1), 91–116.

Patterson, C. J. (1995). Lesbian mothers, gay fathers, and their children. In A. R. D'Augelli & C. J. Patterson (Eds.), *Lesbian, gay, and bisexual identities over the lifespan* (pp. 262–290). New York: Oxford University Press.

Patton, G. W., & Meit, M. (1993). Effect of aging on prospective and incidental memory. *Experimental Aging Research, 19,* 165–176.

Pauls, J. (1985). Review of stair safety research with an emphasis on Canadian studies. *Ergonomics, 28,* 999–1010.

Pearson, J. C. (1996). Forty-forever years? Primary relationships and senior citizens. In N. Vanzetti & S. Duck (Eds.), *A lifetime of relationships* (pp. 383–405). Pacific Grove, CA: Brooks/Cole.

Pender, N. (1996). *Health promotion in nursing practice* (3rd ed.). Stamford, CT: Appleton & Lange.

Peplau, L. A. (1991). Lesbian and gay relationships. In J. C. Gonsiorek & J. D. Weinrich (Eds.), *Homosexuality: Research implications for public policy* (pp. 177–196). Thousand Oaks, CA: Sage.

Perdue, C. W., & Gurtman, M. B. (1990). Evidence for the automaticity of ageism. *Journal of Experimental Social Psychology, 26,* 199–216.

Perkins, H. W., & Harris, L. B. (1990). Familial bereavement and health in adult life course perspective. *Journal of Marriage and the Family, 52,* 233–241.

Perlmutter, M., Adams, C., Berry, J., Kaplan, M., Person, D., & Verdonik, F., (1987). Aging and memory. In K. W. Schaie (Ed.), *Annual review of gerontology and geriatrics* (Vol. 7, pp. 57–92). New York: Springer.

Perls, T. T. (1995). The oldest old. *Scientific American,* 70-75.

Perry, W. I. (1970). *Forms of intellectual and ethical development in the college years.* New York: Holt, Rinehart & Winston.

Peterson, B. E., & Klohnen, E. C. (1995). Realization of generativity in two samples of women at midlife. *Psychology and Aging, 10,* 20–29.

Pfost, K. S., & Fiore, M. (1990). Pursuit of nontraditional occupations: Fear of success or fear of not being chosen? *Sex Roles, 23,* 15–24.

Phillips, P. A., Bretherton, M., Johnston, C. I., & Gray, L. (1991). Reduced osmotic thirst in healthy elderly men. *American Journal of Physiology, 261,* R166–R171.

Piaget, J. (1970). Piaget's theory. In P. H. Mussen (Ed.), *Carmichael's manual of child psychology: Vol. 1* (3rd ed., pp. 703–732). New York: Wiley.

Piaget, J. (1980). *Les formes et les mentaires de la dialectique.* Paris: Gallimard.

Pichora-Fuller, M. K., Schneider, B. A., & Daneman, M. (1995). How young and old adults listen to and remember speech in noise. *Journal of the Acoustical Society of America, 89,* 382–398.

Picot, S. J., Debanne, S. M., Namazi, K. H., & Wykle, M. L. (1997). Religiosity and perceived rewards of black and white caregivers. *Gerontologist, 37,* 89–101.

Pierce, C. A., & Aguinis, H. (1997). Bridging the gap between romantic relationships and sexual harassment in organizations. *Journal of Organizational Behavior, 18,* 197–200.

Pillemer, K. (1993). The abused offspring are dependent. In R. J. Gelles & D. R. Loseke (Eds.), *Current controversies on family violence* (pp. 237–249). Newbury Park, CA: Sage Publications.

Piotrkowski, C. (1998). Gender harassment, job satisfaction, and distress among employed white and minority women. *Journal of Occupational Health Psychology, 3,* 33–43.

Planned Parenthood. (1998). *Menopause: Another change in life.* Online document available at the Web site http://www.plannedparenthood.org/WOMENSHEALTH/menopause.htm.

Plosker, G. L., & McTavish, D. (1996). Intranasal salcatonin (salmon calcitonin). A review of its pharmacological properties and role in the management of postmenopausal osteoporosis. *Drugs and Aging, 8,* 378–400.

Plude, D. J., & Doussard-Roosevelt, J. A. (1989). Aging, selective attention, and feature integration. *Psychology and Aging, 4,* 98–105.

Plude, D. J., & Doussard-Roosevelt, J. A. (1990). Aging and attention: Selectivity, capacity, and arousal. In E. A. Lovelace (Ed.), *Aging and cognition: Mental processes, self-awareness, and interventions* (pp. 97–133). Amsterdam: North-Holland.

Plude, D. J., & Hoyer, W. J. (1985). Attention and performance: Identifying and localizing age deficits. In N. Charness (Ed.), *Aging and human performance* (pp. 47–99). Chichester, England: Wiley.

Plude, D. J., Schwartz, L. K., & Murphy, L. J. (1996). Active selection and in-hibition in the aging of attention. In F. Blanchard-Fields & T. M. Hess (Eds.), *Perspectives on cognitive change in adulthood and aging* (pp. 165–189). New York: McGraw-Hill.

Pollack, R. D., Overton, W. F., Rosenfeld, A., & Rosenfeld, R. (1995). Formal reasoning in late adulthood: The role of semantic content and metacognitive strategy. *Journal of Adult Development, 2,* 1–14.

Ponder, R. J., & Pomeroy, E. C. (1996). The grief of caregivers: How pervasive is it? *Journal of Gerontological Social Work, 27,* 3–21.

Poon, L. W. (1985). Differences in human memory with aging: Nature, causes, and clinical implications. In J. E. Birren & K. W. Schaie (Eds.), *Handbook of the psychology of aging* (2nd ed., pp. 427–462). New York: Academic Press.

Poon, L. W., & Fozard, J. L. (1980). Age and word frequency effects in continuous recognition memory. *Journal of Gerontology, 35,* 77–86.

Pope, A. M., & Tarlov, A. R. (Eds.). (1991). *Disability in America: Toward a national agenda for prevention.* Washington, DC: National Academy Press.

Portenoy, R. K. (1995). Pain. In W. B. Abrams, M. H. Beers, & R. Berkow (Eds.), *The Merck manual of geriatrics* (2nd ed., pp. 125–152). Whitehouse Station, NJ: Merck Research Laboratories.

Protinsky, H., & Hughston, G. (1978). Conservation in elderly males: An empirical investigation. *Developmental Psychology, 14,* 114.

Pruchno, R. (1999). Raising grandchildren: The experiences of black and white grandmothers. *The Gerontologist, 39,* 209–221.

Pruchno, R. A., Smyer, M. A., Rose, M. S., Hartman-Stein, P. E., & Henderson-Laribee, D. L. (1995). Competence of long-term care residents to participate in decisions about their medical care: A brief, objective assessment. *The Gerontologist, 35,* 622–629.

Prull, M. W., Gabrielli, J. D. E., & Bunge, S. A. (2000). Age-related changes in memory: A cognitive, neuroscience perspective. In F. I. M. Craik, T. A. Salthouse, et al. (Eds.), *The handbook of aging and cognition* (2nd ed., pp. 91–153). Mahwah, NJ: Erlbaum.

Pryor, J. B., Desouza, E. R., Fitness, J., & Hutz, C. (1997). Gender differences in the interpretation of social–sexual behavior: A cross-cultural perspective on sexual harassment. *Journal of Cross-Cultural Psychology, 28,* 509–534.

Puglisi, J. T., & Park, D. C. (1987). Perceptual elaboration and memory in older adults. *Journal of Gerontology, 42,* 160–162.

Pushkar, D., Andres, D., Etezadi, J., Arbuckle, T., Schwartzman, A., & Chaikelson, J. (1995). Structural equation model of intellectual change and continuity and predictors of intelligence in older men. *Psychology and Aging, 10*(2), 294–303.

Pushkar, D., Etezadi, J., Andres, D., Arbuckle, T., Schwartzman, A. E., & Chaikelson, J. (1999). Models of intelligence in late life: Comment on Hultsch et al. (1999). *Psychology and Aging, 14,* 520–527.

Pyszczynski, T., Greenberg, J., & Solomon, S. (1997). Why do we need what we need? A terror management perspective on the roots of human social motivation. *Psychological Inquiry, 8,* 1–20.

Pyszczynski, T., Greenberg, J., & Solomon, S. (1999). A dual-process model of defense against conscious and unconscious death-related thoughts: An extension of terror management theory. *Psychological Review, 106,* 835–845.

Qualls, S. H. (1999). Mental health and mental disorders in older adults. In J. C. Cavanaugh & S. K. Whitbourne (Eds.), *Gerontology: An interdisciplinary perspective* (pp. 305–328). New York: Oxford University Press.

Quayhagen, M. P., & Quayhagen, M. (1988). Alzheimer's stress: Coping with the caregiving role. *The Gerontologist, 28,* 391–396.

Query, J. L., Jr., & Flint, L. J. (1996). The caregiving relationship. In N. Vanzetti & S. Duck (Eds.), *A lifetime of relationships* (pp. 455–483). Pacific Grove, CA: Brooks/Cole.

Quigley, M. W. (1979, June 19). Executive corps: Free advice pays off for both sides. *Newsday,* p. 9.

Rabinowitz, J. C., Craik, F. I. M., & Ackerman, B. P. (1982). A processing resource account of age differences in recall. *Canadian Journal of Psychology, 36,* 325–344.

Rabins, P. V. (1992). Schizophrenia and psychotic states. In J. E. Birren, R. B. Sloane, & G. D. Cohen (Eds.), *Handbook of mental health and aging* (2nd ed., pp. 463–475). San Diego: Academic Press.

Rabins, P. V., Kasper, J. D., Kleinman, L., Black, B. S., & Patrick, D. L. (1999). Concepts and methods in the development of the ADRQL: An instrument for assessing health-related quality of life in persons with Alzheimer's disease. *Journal of Mental Health and Aging, 5,* 33–48.

Raeburn, P. (1995, November 7). Genetic trait may delay Alzheimer's. *News Journal* (Wilmington, DE), p. A3.

Ragozin, A. S., Basham, R. B., Crnic, K. A., Greenberg, M. T., & Robinson, N. M. (1982). Effects of maternal age on parenting role. *Developmental Psychology, 18,* 627–634.

Rahman, O., Strauss, J., Gertler, P., Ashley, D., & Fox, K. (1994). Gender differences in adult health: An international comparison. *The Gerontologist, 34,* 463–469.

Raphael, B. (1983). *The anatomy of bereavement.* New York: Basic Books.

Rapoport, J. L., & Rapoport, R. N. (1975). *Leisure and the family life cycle.* London, UK: Routledge & Kegan Paul.

Raskind, M. A., & Peskind, E. R. (1992). Alzheimer's disease and other dementing disorders. In J. E. Birren, R. B. Sloane, & G. D. Cohen (Eds.), *Handbook of mental health and aging* (2nd ed., pp. 477–513). San Diego: Academic Press.

Ratcliff, R., Spieler, D., & McKoon, G. (2000). Explicitly modeling the effects of aging on response time. *Psychonomic Bulletin & Review, 7,* 1–25.

Rawlins, W. K. (1992). *Friendship matters.* Hawthorne, NY: Aldine de Gruyter.

Raz, N. (2000). Aging of the brain and its impact on cognitive performance: Integration of structural and functional findings. In F. I. M. Craik, T. A. Salthouse, et al. (Eds.), *The handbook of aging and cognition* (2nd ed., pp. 1–90). Mahwah, NJ: Erlbaum.

Reder, L. M., Wible, C., & Martin, J. (1986). Differential memory changes with age: Exact retrieval vs. plausible interference. *Journal of Experimental Psychology: Learning, Memory, and Cognition, 12,* 72–81.

Redmore, C. D., & Loevinger, J. (1979). Ego development in adolescence: Longitudinal studies. *Journal of Youth and Adolescence, 8,* 129–134.

Reed, D., Satariano, W. A., Gildengorin, G., McMahon, K., Fleshman, R., & Schneider, E. (1995). Health and functioning among the elderly of Marin County, California: A glimpse of the future. *Journal of Gerontology: Medical Sciences, 50A,* M61–M69.

Reese, H. W., & Rodeheaver, D. (1985). Problem solving and complex decision making. In J. E. Birren & K. W. Schaie (Eds.), *Handbook of the psychology of aging* (2nd ed., pp. 474–499). New York: Van Nostrand Reinhold.

Regnier, V. (1983). Urban neighborhood cognition: Relationships between functional and symbolic community elements. In G. D. Rowles & R. J. Ohta (Eds.), *Aging and milieu: Environmental perspectives on growing old* (pp. 63–82). New York: Academic Press.

Reid, J., & Hardy, M. (1999). Multiple roles and well being among midlife women: Testing role strain and role enhancement theories. *Journal of Gerontology: Social Sciences, 54B,* S329–S338.

Reifler, B. V. (1994). Depression: Diagnosis and comorbidity. In L. S. Schneider, C. F. Reynolds III, B. D. Lebowitz, & A. J. Friedhoff (Eds.), *Diagnosis and treatment of depression in late life* (pp. 55–59). Washington, DC: American Psychiatric Press.

Reigel, K. F. (1973). Dialectic operations: The final period of cognitive development. *Human Development, 16,* 371–381.

Reigel, K. F. (1976). The dialectic of human development. *American Psychologist, 31,* 689–700.

Reinke, B. J., Holmes, D. S., & Harris, R. L. (1985). The timing of psychosocial change in women's lives: The years 25 to 45. *Journal of Personality and Social Psychology, 48,* 1353–1364.

Reisberg, B., Ferris, S. H., Anand, R., de Leon, M. J., Schneck, M. K., & Crook, T. H. (1985). Clinical assessment of cognitive decline in normal aging and primary degenerative dementia: Concordant ordinal measures. In P. Pinchot, P. Berner, R. Wolf, & K. Thau (Eds.), *Psychiatry* (Vol. 5, pp. 333–338). New York: Plenum.

Reisberg, B., Ferris, S. H., Borenstein, J., Sinaiko, E., de Leon, M. J., & Buttinger, C. (1986). Assessment of presenting symptoms. In L. W. Poon (Ed.), *Handbook for clinical memory assessment of older adults* (pp. 108–128). Washington, DC: American Psychological Association.

Reisberg, B., Ferris, S. H., de Leon, M. J., & Crook, T. H. (1982). The global deterioration scale for assessment of primary degenerative dementia. *American Journal of Psychiatry, 139,* 1136–1139.

Reker, G. T., Peacock, E. J., & Wong, P. T. (1987). Meaning and the purpose in life and well-being: A life-span perspective. *Journal of Gerontology, 42,* 44–49.

Reynolds, S. L., Crimmins, E. M., & Saito, Y. (1998). Cohort differences in disability and disease presence. *The Gerontologist, 38,* 578–590.

Rice, E. H., Sombrotto, L. B., Markowitz, J. C., & Leon, A. C. (1994). Cardiovascular morbidity in high-risk patients during ECT. *American Journal of Psychiatry, 151,* 1637–1641.

Rice, G. E., & Okun, M. A. (1994). Older readers' processing of medical information that contradicts their beliefs. *Journal of Gerontology: Psychological Sciences, 49,* P119–P128.

Richardson, V. E. (1993). *Retirement counseling.* New York: Springer.

Rico, H., Revilla, M., Hernandez, E. R., Gonzalez-Riola, J. M., & Villa, L. F. (1993). Four-compartment model of body composition of normal elderly women. *Age and Ageing, 22,* 265–268.

Riggs, D. S., & O'Leary, K. D. (1992). *Violence between dating partners: Background and situational correlates of courtship aggression.* Unpublished manuscript, State University of New York, Stony Brook.

Rikli, R., & Busch, S. (1986). Motor performance of women as a function of age and physical activity level. *Journal of Gerontology, 41,* 645–649.

Riley, K. P., Snowden, D. A., Saunders, A. M., Roses, A. D., Mortimer, J. A., & Nanayakkara, N. (2000). Cognitive function and apolipoprotein E in very old adults: Findings from the nun study. *Journal of Gerontology: Social Sciences, 55B,* S69–S75.

Riley, M. W., & Riley, J. W., Jr. (1996). Generational relations: A future perspective. In T. K. Hareven (Ed.), *Aging and generational relations: Life-course and cross-cultural perspectives* (pp. 283–291). New York: Aldine de Gruyter.

Roberto, K. A., & Scott, J. P. (1986). Equity considerations in the friendships of older adults. *Journal of Gerontology, 41,* 241–247.

Roberts, B. W., & Del Vecchio, W. F. (2000). The rank-order consistency of personality traits from childhood to old age: A qualitative review of longitudinal studies. *Psychological Bulletin, 126,* 3–25.

Roberts, G. (1999). Age effects and health appraisal: A meta-analysis. *Journal of Gerontology: Social Sciences, 54B,* S24–S30.

Roberts, J. D. (1980). *Roots of a black future: Family and church.* Philadelphia: Westminster.

Roberts, P., & Newton, P. M. (1987). Levinsonian studies of women's adult development. *Psychology and Aging, 2,* 154–163.

Robin, D. W. (1995). Falls and gait disorders. In W. B. Abrams, M. H. Beers, & R. Berkow (Eds.), *The Merck manual of geriatrics* (2nd ed., pp. 65–78). Whitehouse Station, NJ: Merck Research Laboratories.

Rodin, J., & Langer, E. J. (1977). Long-term effects of a control-relevant intervention with the institutionalized aged. *Journal of Personality and Social Psychology, 35,* 897–902.

Rodin, J., McAvay, G., & Timko, C. (1988). A longitudinal study of depressed mood and sleep disturbances in elderly adults. *Journal of Gerontology, 43,* P45–P53.

Roediger, H. L., II, & McDermott, K. B. (1993). Implicit memory in normal human subjects. In F. Boller & J. Grafman (Eds.), *Handbook of neuropsychology* (Vol. 8, pp. 63–131). New York: Elsevier.

Roediger, H. L., II, & McDermott, K. B. (1995). Creating false memories: Remembering words not presented on lists. *Journal of Experimental Psychology: Learning, Memory, and Cognition, 21,* 803–814.

Rogers, S. J., & Amato, P. R. (1997). Is marital quality declining? The evidence from two generations. *Social Forces, 75,* 1089–1100.

Rogers, W. A., Bertus, E. L., & Gilbert, D. K. (1994). Dual-task assessment of age differences in automatic process development. *Psychology and Aging, 9,* 398–413.

Rogers, W. A., & Fisk, A. D. (1997, January). ATM design and training issues. *Ergonomics in Design,* 4–9.

Rogers, W. A., & Fisk, A. D. (2000). Human factors applied cognition and aging. In F. I. M. Craik, T. A. Salthouse, et al. (Eds.), *The handbook of aging and cognition* (2nd ed, pp. 559–591). Mahwah, NJ: Erlbaum.

Rogers, W. A., Fisk, A. D., Mead, S. E., Walker, N., & Cabrera, E. F. (1996). Training older adults to use automatic teller machines. *Human Factors, 38,* 425–433.

Rogers, W. A., Gilbert, D. K., & Cabrera, E. F. (1997). An analysis of automatic teller machine usage by older adults: A structured interview approach. *Applied Ergonomics, 28,* 173–180.

Rogers, W. A., Hertzog, C., & Fisk, A. D. (2000). An individual differences analysis of ability and strategy influences: Age-related differences in associated learning. *Journal of Experimental Psychology: Learning, Memory, and Cognition, 26,* 359–394.

Rook, K. S. (1994). Assessing the health-related dimensions of older adults' social relationships. In M. P. Lawton & J. A. Teresi (Eds.), *Annual review of gerontology and geriatrics: Focus on assessment techniques* (Vol. 14, pp. 142–181). New York: Springer.

Rook, K. S. (2000). The evolution of social relationships in later adulthood. In S. H. Qualls & N. Abeles (Eds.), *Psychology and the aging revolution* (pp. 173–191). Washington, DC: American Psychological Association.

Rosenberg, E. B. (1992). *The adoption life cycle.* Lexington, MA: Lexington Books.

Rosenberg, R. N. (Ed.). (1991). *Comprehensive neurology.* New York: Raven.

Rosenberg, S. D., Rosenberg, H. J., & Farrell, M. P. (1999). Midlife crisis revisited. In S. L. Willis & J. D. Reid (Eds.), *Life in the middle: Psychological and social development in middle age* (pp. 47–70). San Diego: Academic Press.

Rosenblatt, P. C. (1996). Grief that does not end. In D. Klass, P. R. Silverman, & S. L. Nickman (Eds.), *Continuing bonds: New understandings of grief* (pp. 45–58). Washington, DC: Taylor & Francis.

Rosenthal, M. J., & Goodwin, J. S. (1985). Cognitive effects of nutritional deficiency. In H. H. Draper (Ed.), *Advances in nutritional research* (vol. 7, pp. 71–100). New York: Plenum.

Rosin, H. M., & Korabik, K. (1990). Marital and family correlates of women managers' attrition from organizations. *Journal of Vocational Behavior, 37,* 104–120.

Rosin, H. M., & Korabik, K. (1991). Workplace variables, affective responses, and intention to leave among women managers. *Journal of Occupational Psychology, 64,* 317–330.

Roskies, E., & Louis-Guerin, C. (1990). Job insecurity in managers: Antecedents and consequences. *Journal of Organizational Behavior, 11,* 345–359.

Roth, G. S., Ingram, D. K., & Lane, M. A. (1995). Slowing ageing by caloric restriction. *Nature Medicine, 1,* 414–415.

Roth, W. F. (1991). *Work and rewards: Redefining our work-life reality.* New York: Praeger.

Rouleau, N., & Belleville, S. (1996). Irrelevant speech effects in aging: An assessment of inhibitory processes in working memory. *Journal of Gerontology, 51B,* 356–363.

Rousseau, G. K., Lamson, N., & Rogers, W. A. (1998). Designing warnings to compensate for age-related changes in perceptual and cognitive abilities. *Psychology and Marketing, 15,* 643–662.

Rousseau, G. K., & Rogers, W. A. (1998). Computer usage patterns of university faculty members across the life span. *Computers in Human Behavior, 14,* 417–428.

Rowe, J. W., & Kahn, R. L. (1997). Successful aging. *The Gerontologist, 37,* 433–440.

Rowe, J. W., & Kahn, R. L. (1998). *Successful aging.* New York: Pantheon.

Rowles, G. D., & Ohta, R. J. (1983). Emergent themes and new directions: Reflections on aging and milieu research. In G. D. Rowles & R. J. Ohta (Eds.), *Aging and milieu: Environmental perspectives on growing old* (pp. 231–240). New York: Academic Press.

Roxburgh, S. (1997). The effect of children on the mental health of women in the paid labor force. *Journal of Family Issues, 18,* 270–289.

Rubenfeld, M. I., & Gilroy, F. D. (1991). Relationship between college women's occupational interests and a single-sex environment. *Career Development Quarterly, 40,* 64–70.

Rubin, D. C., & Kozin, M. (1984). Vivid memories. *Cognition, 16,* 81–95.

Rubin, D. C., Rahhal, T. A., & Poon, L. W. (1998). Things learned in early adulthood are remembered best. *Memory & Cognition, 26,* 3–19.

Rubin, D. C., & Schulkind, M. D. (1997). Distribution of important and word-cued auto-biographical memories in 20-, 35-, and 70-year old adults. *Psychology and Aging, 12,* 524–535.

Ruhm, C. J. (1990). Career jobs, bridge employment, and retirement. In P. Doeringer (Ed.), *Bridges to retirement: Older workers in a changing labor market* (pp. 92–107). Ithaca, NY: ILR Press.

Rush–Presbyterian St. Luke's Medical Center. (1998). Chronic illness. In *The World Book Rush–Presbyterian St. Luke's Medical Center medical encyclopedia.* Online document available at the Web site http://my. webmd.com/encyclopedia_article/ DMK_ARTICLE_1457076.

Ryan, E. B., Giles, H., Bartolucci, G., & Henwood, K. (1986). Psycholinguistic and social psychological components of communication by and with the elderly. *Language and Communication, 6,* 1–24.

Ryan, E. B., Hamilton, J. M., & Kwong See, S. (1993). Patronizing the old: How do younger and older adults respond to baby talk in the nursing home? *International Journal of Aging and Human Development, 41,* 89–107.

Ryan, E. B., Kennaley, D. E., Pratt, M. W., & Shumovich, M. A. (2000). Evaluations by staff, residents, and community seniors of patronizing speech in the nursing home: Impact of passive, assertive, or humorous responses. *Psychology and Aging, 15,* 272–285.

Ryan, E. B., & Kwong See, S. (1993). Age-based beliefs about memory changes for self and others across adulthood. *Journal of Gerontology: Psychological Sciences, 48,* P199–P201.

Ryan, E. B., Meredith, S. D., MacLean, M. J., & Orange, J. B. (1995). Changing the way we talk with elders: Promoting health using the communication enhancement model. *International Journal of Aging and Human Development, 41,* 89–107.

Ryan, E. B., Meredith, S. D., & Schantz, G. B. (1994). Evaluative perceptions of patronizing speech addressed to institutionalized elders in contrasting conversational contexts. *Canadian Journal on Aging, 13,* 236–248.

Rybash, J. M. (1996). Implicit memory and aging: A cognitive neuropsychological perspective. *Developmental Neuropsychology, 12,* 127–179.

Rybash, J. M., Hoyer, W. J., & Roodin, P. A. (1986). *Adult cognition and aging.* New York: Pergamon.

Ryff, C. D. (1989). Happiness is everything, or is it? Explorations on the meaning of psychological well-being. *Journal of Personality and Social Psychology, 57,* 1069–1081.

Ryff, C. D. (1991). Possible selves in adulthood and old age: A tale of shifting horizons. *Psychology and Aging, 6,* 286–295.

Ryff, C. D., Lee, Y. H., Essex, M. J., & Schmutte, P. S. (1994). My children and me: Mid-life evaluations of grown children and of self. *Psychology and Aging, 9,* 195–205.

Sackeim, H. A. (1994). Use of electroconvulsive therapy in late-life depression. In L. S. Schneider, C. F. Reynolds, B. D. Lebowitz, & A. J. Friedhoff (Eds.), *Diagnosis and treatment of depression in late life: Results of the NIH Consensus Development Conference* (pp. 259–273). Washington, DC: American Psychiatric Press.

Salomone, P. R. (1996). Tracing Super's theory of vocational development: A 40-year retrospective. *Journal of Career Development, 22,* 167–184.

Salthouse, T. A. (1984). Effects of age and skill in typing. *Journal of Experimental Psychology: General, 113,* 345–371.

Salthouse, T. A. (1988). The role of processing resources in cognitive aging. In M. L. Howe & C. J. Brainerd (Eds.), *Cognitive development in adulthood* (pp. 185–239). New York: Springer-Verlag.

Salthouse, T. A. (1991). *Theoretical perspectives on cognitive aging.* Hillsdale, NJ: Erlbaum.

Salthouse, T. A. (1992). Influences of processing speed on adult age differences in working memory. *Acta Psychologica, 79,* 155–170.

Salthouse, T. A. (1994). The aging of working memory. *Neuropsychology, 8,* 535–543.

Salthouse, T. A. (1996). The processing speed theory of adult age differences in cognition. *Psychological Review, 103,* 403–428.

Salthouse, T. A., & Babcock, R. L. (1991). Decomposing adult age differences in working memory. *Developmental Psychology, 27,* 763–776.

Salthouse, T. A., Babcock, R. L., & Shaw, R. J. (1991). Effects of adult age on structural and operational capacities in working memory. *Psychology an Aging, 6,* 118–127.

Salthouse, T. A., Fristoe, N. M., Lineweaver, T. T., & Coon, V. E.

(1995). Aging of attention: Does the ability to decide decline? *Memory & Cognition, 23,* 59–71.

Salthouse, T. A., Fristoe, N., McGuthry, K. E., & Hambrick, D. Z. (1998). Relation of task switching to speed, age, and fluid intelligence. *Psychology and Aging, 13,* 445–461.

Salthouse, T. A., Kausler, D. H., & Saults, J. S. (1988). Utilization of path analytic procedures to investigate the role of processing resources in cognitive aging. *Psychology and Aging, 3,* 158–166.

Salthouse, T. A., & Mienz, E. J. (1995). Aging inhibition working memory and speed. *Journal of Gerontology, 50B,* 297–306.

Salthouse, T. A., Toth, J. P., Hancock, H. E., & Woodard, J. L. (1997). Controlled and automatic forms of memory and attention: Process purity and the uniqueness of age-related influences. *Journal of Gerontology, 52B,* 216–228.

Sanders, C. M. (1980-81). Comparison of younger and older spouses in bereavement outcome. *Omega: Journal of Death and Dying, 11,* 217–232.

Sands, L. P., & Meredith, W. (1992). Blood pressure and intellectual functioning in late midlife. *Journal of Gerontology: Psychological Sciences, 47,* P81–P84.

Sarvis, C. M. (1995). *Pain management in the elderly.* Sacramento, CA: CMW Resources.

Saunders, S. (1997). Hospices worldwide: A mission statement. In C. Saunders & R. Kastenbaum (Eds.), *Hospice care on the international scene* (pp. 3–12). New York: Springer.

Saxon, S. V., & Etten, M. J. (1994). *Physical changes and aging* (3rd ed.). New York: Tiresias.

Schacter, D. L., Koustaal, W., Johnson, M. K., Gross, M. S., & Angell, K. E. (1997). False recollection induced by photograph: A comprehension of older and younger adults. *Psychology and Aging, 12,* 203–215.

Schacter, D. L., Verifaelie, M., Anes, M. D., & Rancine, C. (1998). When true recognition: Evidence from amnesic patients. *Journal of Cognitive Neuroscience, 10,* 668–679.

Schaie, K. W. (1977–1978). Toward a stage theory of adult cognitive development. *International Journal of Aging and Human Development, 8,* 129–138.

Schaie, K. W. (1983). The Seattle longitudinal study: A twenty-one year exploration of psychometric intelligence in adulthood. In K. W. Schaie (Ed.), *Longitudinal studies of adult psychological development* (pp. 64–155). New York: Guilford.

Schaie, K. W. (1984). Historical time and cohort effects. In K. A. McCluskey & H. W. Reese (Eds.), *Life-span developmental psychology: Historical and generational effects* (pp. 1–45). New York: Academic Press.

Schaie, K. W. (1990). Intellectual development in adulthood. In J. E. Birren & K. W. Schaie (Eds.), *Handbook of the psychology of aging* (3rd ed., pp. 291–309). San Diego: Academic Press.

Schaie, K. W. (1994). The course of adult intellectual development. *American Psychologist, 49,* 304–313.

Schaie, K. W. (1995). *Intellectual development in adulthood: The Seattle longitudinal study.* New York: Cambridge University Press.

Schaie, K. W. (1996). Intellectual functioning in adulthood. In J. E. Birren & K. W. Schaie (Eds.), *Handbook of the psychology of aging* (4th ed., pp. 266–286). San Diego: Academic Press.

Schaie, K. W., & Hertzog, C. (1985). Measurement in the psychology of adulthood and aging. In J. E. Birren & K. W Schaie (Eds.), *Handbook of the psychology of aging* (2nd ed., pp. 61–92). New York: Van Nostrand Reinhold.

Schaie, K. W., Plomin, R., Willis, S. L., Gruber-Baldini, A., & Dutta, R. (1992). Natural cohorts: Family similarity in adult cognition. In T. Sonderegger (Ed.), *Psychology and aging: Nebraska symposium on motivation, 1991* (pp. 205–243). Lincoln: University of Nebraska Press.

Schaie, K. W., & Willis, S. L. (1986). Can decline in adult intellectual functioning be reversed? *Developmental Psychology, 22,* 223–232.

Schaie, K. W., & Willis, S. L. (1995). Perceived family environment across generations. In V. L. Bengston & K. W. Schaie (Eds.), *Adult intergenerational relations: Effects of societal change* (pp. 174–226). New York: Springer.

Schaie, K. W., & Willis, S. L. (1999). Theories of everyday competence and aging. In V. L. Bengston & K. W. Schaie (Eds.), *Handbook of theories of aging* (pp. 174–195). New York: Springer.

Schaie, K. W., Willis, S. L., & O'Hanlon, A. M. (1994). Perceived intellectual performance change over seven years. *Journal of Gerontology: Psychological Sciences, 49,* P108–P118.

Schaller, M., Boyd, C., Yohannes, J., & O'Brien, M. (1995). The prejudiced personality revisited: Personal need for structure and formation of erroneous group settings. *Journal of Experimental and Social Psychology, 68,* 544–555.

Scheibel, A. B. (1996). Structural and functional changes in the aging brain. In J. E. Birren & K. W. Schaie (Eds.), *Handbook of the psychology of aging* (4th ed., pp. 105–128). San Diego: Academic Press.

Schick, F. L., & Schick, R. (1994). *Statistical handbook on aging Americans.* Phoenix: Oryx Press.

Schmeeckle, M., Giarusso, R., & Wang, Q. (1998, November). *When being a brother or sister is important to one's identity: Life stage and gender differences.* Paper presented at the annual meeting of the Gerontological Society, Philadelphia.

Schmidt, D. F., & Boland, S. M. (1986). The structure of impressions of older adults: Evidence for multiple stereotypes. *Psychology and Aging, 1,* 255–260.

Schmitz-Scherzer, R., & Thomae, H. (1983). Constancy and change of behavior in old age: Findings from the Bonn Longitudinal Study on Aging. In K. W. Schaie (Ed.), *Longitudinal studies of adult psychological development* (pp. 191–221). New York: Guilford.

Schneider, E. (1996). *Demographics update: Blind persons who use guide dogs.* New York: American Foundation for the Blind.

Schneider, K. T., Swan, S., & Fitzgerald, L. F. (1997). Job-related and psychological effects on sexual harassment in the workplace: Empirical evidence from two organizations. *Journal of Applied Psychology, 82,* 401–415.

Schneider, L. S. (1995). Efficacy of clinical treatment for mental disorders among older persons. In M. Gatz (Ed.), *Emerging issues in mental health and aging* (pp. 19–71). Washington, DC: American Psychological Association.

Schneider, B. A., & Pichora-Fuller, M. R. (2000). Implications of perceptual deterioration of cognitive aging research. In F. I. M. Craik & T. A. Salthouse (Eds.), *The handbook of aging and cognition* (2nd ed., pp.). Mahwah, NJ: Erlbaum.

Schone, B. S., & Weinick, R. M. (1998). Health-related behaviors and the benefits of marriage for elderly persons. *The Gerontologist, 38,* 618–627.

Schooler, C. (1990). Psychosocial factors and effective cognitive functioning in adulthood. In J. E. Birrens & K. W. Schaie (Eds.), *Handbook of the psychology of aging* (3rd ed., pp. 347–358). San Diego: Academic Press.

Schooler, C., Mulatu, M. S., & Oats, G. (1999). The continuing effects of substantively complex workers. *Psychology and Aging, 14,* 483–506.

Schooler, K. K. (1982). Response of the elderly to environment: A stress-theoretical perspective. In M. P. Lawton, P. G. Windley, & T. O. Byerts (Eds.), *Aging and the environment: Theoretical approaches* (pp. 80–96). New York: Springer.

Schulz, R. (1985). Emotion and affect. In J. E. Birren & K. W. Schaie (Eds.), *Handbook of the psychology of aging* (2nd ed., pp. 531–543). New York: Van Nostrand Reinhold.

Schulz, R., Bookwala, J., Knapp, J. E., Scheier, M., & Williamson, G. M. (1996). Pessimism, age, and cancer mortality. *Psychology and Aging, 11,* 304–309.

Schulz, R., & Hanusa, B. H. (1979). Environmental influences on the effectiveness of control- and competence-enhancing interventions. In L. C. Perlmuter & R. A. Monty (Eds.), *Choice and perceived control* (pp. 315–337). Hillsdale, NJ: Erlbaum.

Schulz, R., Tompkins, C. A., & Rau, M. T. (1988). A longitudinal study of the psychosocial impact of stroke on primary support persons. *Psychology and Aging, 3,* 131–141.

Schwartz, F., & Zimmerman, J. (1992). *Breaking with tradition: Women and work, the new facts of life.* New York: Warner.

Schwarz, N., Park, D., Knauper, B., Davidson, N., & Smith, P. (1998, April). Aging, cognition, and self-reports: Age-dependent context effects and misleading conclusions about age differences in attitudes and behavior. Paper presented at the Bi-Annual Cognitive Aging Conference, Atlanta.

Schwarz, N., Park, D., Knauper, B., & Sudman, S. (1999). *Aging, cognition, and self-reports.* Philadelphia: Psychology Press.

Scialfa, C. T., Guzy, L. T., Leibowitz, H. W., Garvey, P. M., & Tyrrell, R. A. (1991). Age differences in estimating vehicle velocity. *Psychology and Aging, 6,* 60–66.

Scogin, F. R. (1999). Anxiety in old age. In I. H. Nordhus, G. R. VandenBos, S. Berg, & P. Fromholt (Eds.), *Clinical geropsychology* (pp. 205–209). Washington, DC: American Psychological Association.

Scogin, F. R., & McElreath, L. (1994). Efficacy of psychosocial treatments for geriatric depression. *Journal of Consulting and Clinical Psychology, 62,* 69–74.

Scozzaro, P. P., & Subich, L. M. (1990). Gender and occupational sex-type differences in job outcome factor perceptions. *Journal of Vocational Behavior, 36,* 109–119.

Sears, P. S., & Barbee, A. H. (1978). Career and life satisfaction among Terman's gifted women. In J. C. Stanley, W. C. George, & C. H. Solano (Eds.), *The gifted and the creative: Fifty-year perspective* (pp. 28–66). Baltimore: Johns Hopkins University Press.

Segal, D. L., Coolidge, F. L., & Hersen, M. (1999). Psychological testing of older people. In I. H. Nordhus, G. R. VandenBos, S. Berg, & P. Fromholt (Eds.), *Clinical geropsychology* (pp. 231–257). Washington, DC: American Psychological Association.

Seginer, R., Trommsdorf, G., & Essau, C. (1993). Adolescent control beliefs: Cross-cultural. *Journal of Behavioral Development, 16,* 243–260.

Seibert, S. (1999). The effectiveness of facilitated mentoring: A longitudinal quasi-experiment. *Journal of Vocational Behavior, 54,* 483–502.

Shaiko, R. G. (1996). Female participation in public interest nonprofit governance: Yet another glass ceiling? *Nonprofit and Voluntary Sector Quarterly, 25,* 302–320.

Shainess, N. (1984). *Sweet suffering: Woman as victim.* Indianapolis: Bobbs-Merril.

Shaw, E., & Burns, A. (1993). Guilt and the working parent. *Australian Journal of Marriage and Family, 14,* 30–43.

Sheehy, G. (1976). *Passages.* New York: Dutton.

Sheehy, G. (1981). *Pathfinders.* New York: Morrow.

Sheehy, G. (1995). *New passages: Mapping your life across time.* New York: Random House.

Shelton, B. A., & John, D. (1993). Ethnicity, race, and difference: A comparison of white, black, and Hispanic men's household labor time. In J. C. Hood (Ed.), *Men, work, and family* (pp. 131–150). Thousand Oaks, CA: Sage.

Shephard, R. J. (1997). *Aging, physical activity, and health.* Champaign, IL: Human Kinetics.

Sher, T. G. (1996). Courtship and marriage: Choosing a primary relationship. In N. Vanzetti & S. Duck (Eds.), *A lifetime of relationships* (pp. 243–264). Pacific Grove, CA: Brooks/Cole.

Sherrington, R., Rogaev, E. I., Liang, Y., Rogaeva, E. A., Levesque, G., Ikeda, M., Chi, H., Lin, C., Li, G., Holman, K., Tsuda, T., Mar, L., Foncin, J.-F., Bruni, A. C., Montesi, M. P., Sorbi, S., Rainero, I., Pinessi, L., Nee, L., Chumakov, I., Pollen, D., Brookes, A., Sanseau, P., Polinsky, R. J., Wasco, W., Da Silva, H. A. R., Haines, J. L., Pericak-Vance, M. A., Tanzi, R. E.,

Roses, A. D., Fraser, P. E., Rommens, J. M., & St. George-Hyslop, P. H. (1995). Cloning of a gene bearing missense mutations in early-onset familial Alzheimer's disease. *Nature, 375,* 754–760.

Sherwin, B. B. (1997). Estrogen effects on cognition in menopausal women. *Neurology, 48*(5 Suppl. 7), S21–S26.

Shield, R. R. (1988). *Uneasy endings: Daily life in an American nursing home.* Ithaca, NY: Cornell University Press.

Shimamura, A. P. (1986). Priming effects in amnesia: Evidence for a dissociable memory function. *Quarterly Journal of Experimental Psychology, 38A,* 619–644.

Shimamura, A. P., Berry, J. M., Mangels, J. A., Rusting, C. L., & Jurica, P. J. (1995). Memory and cognitive abilities in university professors: Evidence for successful aging. *Psychological Science, 6,* 271–277.

Shirom, A., & Mazeh, T. (1988). Periodicity in seniority–job satisfaction relationship. *Journal of Vocational Behavior, 33,* 38–49.

Siegler, I. C., George, L. K., & Okun, M. A. (1979). A cross-sequential analysis of adult personality. *Developmental Psychology, 15,* 350–351.

Siegler, I. C., Kaplan, B. H., Von Dras, D. D., & Mark, D. B. (1999). Cardiovascular health: A challenge for midlife. In S. L. Willis & J. D. Reid (Eds.), *Life in the middle: Psychological and social development in middle age* (pp. 147–157). San Diego: Academic Press.

Silverman, P. (1987). Community settings. In P. Silverman (Ed.), *The elderly as modern pioneers* (pp. 185–210). Bloomington: Indiana University Press.

Simmons, L. W. (1945). *Role of the aged in primitive society.* New Haven, CT: Yale University Press.

Simon, R. (1996). Too damn old. *Money, 25*(7), 118–126.

Simons, L. A., McCallum, J., Friedlander, Y., & Simons, J. (1996). Predictors of mortality in the prospective Dubbo study of Australian elderly. *Australian and New Zealand Journal of Medicine, 26,* 40–48.

Simonton, D. K. (1990). Creativity and wisdom in aging. In J. E. Birren & K. W. Schaie (Eds.), *Handbook of the psychology of aging* (3rd ed., pp. 320–329). San Diego: Academic Press.

Sinaki, M. (1996). Effect of physical activity on bone mass. *Current Opinions in Rheumatology, 8,* 376–383.

Sinnott, J. D. (1984a). *Everyday memory and solution of everyday problems.* Paper presented at the annual meeting of the American Psychological Association, Toronto.

Sinnott, J. D. (1984b). Postformal reasoning: The relativistic stage. In M. L. Commons, F. A. Richards, & C. Armon (Eds.), *Beyond formal operations: Late adolescent and adult cognitive development* (pp. 298–325). New York: Praeger.

Sinnott, J. D. (1986). Sex roles and aging: Theory and research from a systems perspective. *Contributions to human development* (Vol. 15). New York: Karger.

Sinnott, J. (1992). The developmental approach: Post-formal thought as adaptive intelligence. In F. Blanchard-Fields & T. H. Hess (Eds.), *Perspectives on cognitive change in adulthood and aging* (pp. 358–383). New York: McGraw-Hill.

Sinnott, J. D. (1994a). New science models for teaching adults: Teaching as a dialogue with reality. In J. D. Sinnott (Ed.), *Interdisciplinary handbook of adult lifespan learning* (pp. 90–104). Westport, CT: Greenwood.

Sinnott, J. D. (1994b). The relationship of postformal thought, adult learning, and lifespan development. In J. D. Sinnott (Ed.), *Interdisciplinary handbook of adult lifespan learning* (pp. 105–119). Westport, CT: Greenwood.

Sinnott, J. D. (1994c). *Interdisciplinary handbook of adult lifespan learning.* Westport, CT: Greenwood.

Sinnott, J. D. (1996). The developmental approach: Postformal thought as adaptive intelligence. In F. Blanchard-Fields & T. M. Hess (Eds.), *Perspectives on cognitive change in adulthood and aging* (pp. 358–383). New York: McGraw-Hill.

Skelton, D. A., Greig, C. A., Davies, J. M., & Young, A. (1994). Strength, power, and related functional ability of healthy people aged 65–89 years. *Age and Ageing, 23,* 371–377.

Skinner, E. A. (1995). *Perceived control, motivation, and coping.* Thousand Oaks, CA: Sage.

Skowronski, J. J., & Carlston, D. E. (1989). Negativity and extremity bias in impression formation: A review of explanations. *Psychological Bulletin, 105,* 131–142.

Skultety, K. M., Whitbourne, S. K., & Collins, K. (1999, August). *Relationship between identity and exercise in middle-aged men and women.* Paper presented at the annual meeting of the American Psychological Association, Boston.

Slivinske, L. R., & Fitch, V. L. (1987). The effect of control enhancing intervention on the well-being of elderly individuals living in retirement communities. *The Gerontologist, 27,* 176–181.

Small, B. J., Hultsch, D. F., & Masson, M. E. J. (1995). Adult age differences in perceptually based, but not conceptually based implicit tests of memory. *Journal of Gerontology: Psychological Sciences, 50B,* P162–P170.

Smith, A. D. (1975). Aging and interference with memory. *Journal of Gerontology, 30,* 319–325.

Smith, A. D. (1996). Memory. In J. E. Birren & K. W. Schaie (Eds.), *Handbook of the psychology of aging* (4th ed., pp. 236–250). San Diego: Academic Press.

Smith, A. D., & Park, D. C. (1990). Adult age differences in memory for pictures and images. In E. A. Lovelace (Ed.), *Aging and cognition: Mental processes, self-awareness, and interventions* (pp. 69–96). Amsterdam: North-Holland.

Smith, D. B. D. (1990). Human factors and aging: An overview of research needs and application opportunities. *Human Factors, 32,* 509–526.

Smith, J., & Baltes, P. B. (1990). Wisdom-related knowledge: Age/cohort differences in responses to life-planning problems. *Developmental Psychology, 26,* 494–505.

Smith, J., & Earles, J. L. (1996). Memory. In J. E. Birren & K. W. Schaie (Eds.), *Handbook of the psychology of aging* (4th ed., pp. 236–250). San Diego: Academic Press.

Smith, J., Staudinger, U. M., & Baltes, P. B. (1994). Occupational settings of wisdom-related knowledge: The sample case of clinical psychologists. *Journal of Consulting and Clinical Psychology, 62,* 989–1000.

Smith, K. R., & Zick, C. D. (1996). Risk of mortality following widowhood: Age and sex differences by mode of death. *Social Biology, 43,* 59–71.

Smyer, M. A., & Allen-Burge, R. (1999). Older adults' decision-making capacity: Institutional settings and individual choices. In J. C. Cavanaugh & S. K. Whitbourne (Eds.), *Gerontology: An interdisciplinary perspective* (pp. 391–413). New York: Oxford University Press.

Smyer, M. A., Gatz, M., Simi, N. L., & Pedersen, N. L. (1998). Childhood adoption: Long-term effects in adulthood. *Psychiatry, 61,* 191–205.

Smyer, M. A., & Qualls, S. H. (1999). *Aging and mental health.* Malden, MA: Blackwell.

Snyder, C. J., & Barrett, G. V. (1988). The Age Discrimination in Employment Act: A review of court decisions. *Experimental Aging Research, 14,* 3–47.

Soederberg Miller, L. M., & Lachman, M. (1999, August). *Stress reactivity and cognitive performance in adulthood.* Paper presented at the annual meeting of the American Psychological Association, Boston.

Somary, K., & Stricker, G. (1998). Becoming a grandparent: A longitudinal study of expectations and early experiences as a function of sex and lineage. *The Gerontologist, 38,* 53–61.

Somberg, B. L., & Salthouse, T. A. (1982). Divided attention abilities in young and old adults. *Journal of Experimental Psychology: Human Perception and Performance, 8,* 651–663.

Soulsman, G. (1999, March 15). Understanding hearing loss. *The News Journal* (Wilmington, DE), E1–2.

Spencer, W. D., & Raz, N. (1995). Differential effects of aging on memory for content and context: A meta-

analysis. *Psychology and Aging, 10,* 527–539.

Spencer, W. D., Steele, C. M., & Quinn, D. M. (1999). Stereotype threat and women's math performance. *Journal of Experimental Social Psychology, 35,* 4–28.

Spirduso, W. W. (1980). Physical fitness, aging, and psychomotor speed: A review. *Journal of Gerontology, 35,* 850–865.

Spirduso, W. W., & MacRae, P. G. (1990). Motor performance and aging. In J. E. Birren & K. W. Schaie (Eds.), *Handbook of the psychology of aging* (3rd ed., pp. 183–200). San Diego: Academic Press.

Stajkovic, A., & Luthans, F. (1998). Self-efficacy and work-related performance: A meta-analysis. *Psychological Bulletin, 124,* 240–261.

Stanford, E. P., & DuBois, B. C. (1992). Gender and ethnicity patterns. In J. E. Birren, R. B. Sloane, & G. D. Cohen (Eds.), *Handbook of mental health and aging* (2nd ed., pp. 99–117). San Diego: Academic Press.

Stanford, E. P., Happersett, C. J., Morton, D. J., Molgaard, C. A., & Peddecord, K. M. (1991). Early retirement and functional impairment from a multi-ethnic perspective. *Research on Aging, 15,* 5–38.

Stankov, L., & Dunn, S. (1993). Physical substrata of mental energy: Brain capacity and efficiency of cerebral metabolism. *Learning and Individual Differences, 5,* 241–257.

Stanton-Rich, H. M., Iso-Ahola, S. E., & Seppo, E. (1998). Burnout and leisure. *Journal of Applied Social Psychology, 28,* 1931–1950.

Starck, P. A., Looft, W. R., & Hooper, F. H. (1972). Interrelationships among Piagetian tasks and traditional measures of cognitive abilities in mature and aged adults. *Journal of Gerontology, 27,* 461–465.

Stark, E. (1992, May). *From dependency to empowerment: Framing and reframing the battered woman.* Paper presented at the Second Annual Conference: Domestic Violence: The Family/Community Connection, State University of New York, Division of Nursing, Stony Brook.

Staudinger, U. M. (1999). Social cognition and a psychological approach to the act of life. In T. M. Hess, F. Blanchard-Fields, et al. (Eds.), *Social cognition and aging* (pp. 343–375). San Diego: Academic Press.

Staudinger, U. M., & Baltes, P. B. (1994). The psychology of wisdom. In R. J. Sternberg (Ed.), *Encyclopedia of intelligence* (pp. 1143–1152). New York: Macmillan.

Staudinger, U. M., & Baltes, P. B. (1996). Interactive minds: A facilitative setting for wisdom-related performance. *Journal of Personality and Social Psychology, 71,* 746–762.

Staudinger, U. M., Lopez, D. F., & Baltes, P. B. (1997). The psychometric location of wisdom related performance: Intelligence, personality, and, more? *Personality and Social Psychology Bulletin, 23,* 1200–1214.

Staudinger, U. M., Smith, J., & Baltes, P. B. (1992). Wisdom-related knowledge in a life review task: Age differences in the role of professional specialization. *Psychology and Aging, 7,* 271–281.

Steele, C. M. (1997). A threat in the air: How stereotypes shape intellectual identity and performance. *American Psychologist, 52,* 613–629.

Steele, C. M., & Aronson, J. (1995). Stereotype threat and the intellectual test performance of African Americans. *Journal of Personality and Social Psychology, 69,* 797–811.

Steen, T. A., & Peterson, C. (2000, August). *Predicting young adults' return to the next.* Paper presented at the annual meeting of the American Psychological Association, Washington, DC.

Stein, R. (1999). *The effects of age stereotype priming on the memory performance of older adults.* Master's thesis, Georgia Institute of Technology.

Steinmetz, S. K. (1993). The abused elderly are dependent. In R. J. Gelles & D. R. Loseke (Eds.), *Current controversies on family violence* (pp. 222–236). Newbury Park, CA: Sage Publications.

Stephens, M. A. P., & Clark, S. L. (1997). Reciprocity in the expression of emotional support among later-life couples coping with stroke. In B. H. Gottlieb (Ed.), *Coping with chronic stress* (pp. 221–242). New York: Plenum.

Stephens, M. A. P., & Franks, M. M. (1999). Intergenerational relationships in later-life families: Adult daughters and sons as caregivers to aging parents. In J. C. Cavanaugh & S. K. Whitbourne (Eds.), *Gerontology: An interdisciplinary perspective* (pp. 329–354). New York: Oxford University Press.

Stephens, M. A. P., Franks, M. M., & Atienza, A. A. (1997). Where two roles intersect: Spillover between parent care and employment. *Psychology and Aging, 12,* 30–37.

Stephens, M. A. P., Townsend, A. L., Martire, L. M., & Druley, J. A. (2001). Balancing parent care with other roles: Interrole conflict of adult daughter caregivers. *Journal of Gerontology: Psychological Sciences, 56B,* P24–P34.

Sternberg, R. J. (1981). The effectiveness of pimozide on CSF norepinephrine in schizophrenia. *American Journal of Psychiatry, 138,* 1045–1051.

Sternberg, R. J. (1985). *Beyond IQ: A triarchic theory of human intelligence.* New York: Cambridge University Press.

Sternberg, R. J. (1986). A triangular theory of love. *Psychological Review, 93,* 119–135.

Sternberg, R. J. (1998). Metacognition, abilities, and developing expertise: What makes an expert student? *Instructional Science, 26,* 127–140.

Sternberg, R. J., Conway, B. E., Ketron, J. L., & Bernstein, M. (1981). People's conceptions of intelligence. *Journal of Personality and Social Psychology, 41,* 37–55.

Sterns, A. A., Marsh, B. A., & McDaniel, M. A. (1994). *Age and job satisfaction; A comprehensive review and meta-analysis.* Unpublished manuscript, University of Akron.

Sterns, H. L., & Gray, J. H. (1999). Work, leisure, and retirement. In J. C. Cavanaugh & S. K. Whitbourne (Eds.), *Gerontology: Interdisciplinary perspectives.* New York: Oxford University Press.

Sterns, H. L., Laier, M. P., & Dorsett, J. G. (1994). Work and retirement. In B. R. Bonder & M. B. Wagner (Eds.), *Functional performance in older adults* (pp. 148–164). Philadelphia: F.A. Davis.

Sterns, H. L., & Sanders, R. E. (1980). Training and education of the elderly. In R. R. Turner & H. W. Reese (Eds.), *Life-span developmental psychology: Intervention* (pp. 307–330). New York: Academic Press.

Stevens, J. C. (1992). Aging and spatial acuity of touch. *Journal of Gerontology: Psychological Sciences, 47,* P35–P40.

Stevens, J. C., Cruz, L. A., Hoffman, J. M., & Patterson, M. Q. (1995). Taste sensitivity and aging: High incidence of decline revealed by repeated threshold measures. *Chemical Senses, 20,* 451–459.

Steward, R. J., & Krieshok, T. S. (1991). A cross-cultural study of vocational identity: Does a college education mean the same for all persisters? *Journal of College Student Development, 32,* 562–563.

Stewart, A. J. (1996). *Personality in middle age: Gender, history, and mid-course corrections.* Murray Award Lecture presented at the American Psychological Association, Toronto, Canada.

Stewart, A. J., & Ostrove, J. M. (1998). Women's personality in middle age: Gender, history, and mid-course corrections. *American Psychologist, 53,* 1185–1194.

Stigsdotter Neely, A., & Bäckman, L. (1993a). Maintenance of gains following multifactorial and unifactorial memory training in late adulthood. *Educational Gerontology, 19,* 105–117.

Stigsdotter Neely, A., & Bäckman, L. (1993b). Long-term maintenance of gains from memory training in older adults: Two 3-year follow-up studies. *Journal of Gerontology: Psychological Sciences, 48,* P233–P237.

Stigsdotter Neely, A., & Bäckman, L. (1995). Effects of multifactorial memory training in old age: Generalizability across tasks and individuals. *Journal of Gerontology: Psychological Sciences, 50B,* P134–P140.

Stine, E. L. (1990). The way reading and listening work: A tutorial review of discourse processing and aging. In E. A. Lovelace (Ed.), *Aging and cognition: Mental processes, self-awareness, and interventions* (pp. 301–327). Amsterdam: North-Holland.

Stine, E. L., & Wingfield, A. (1994). Older adults can inhibit high-probability competitors in speech recognition. *Aging and Cognition, 1,* 152–157.

Stine, E. L., Wingfield, A., & Poon, L. W. (1986). How much and how fast: Rapid processing of spoken language in later adulthood. *Psychology and Aging, 1,* 303–311.

Stoltzfus, E. R., Hasher, L., & Zacks, R. T. (in press). Working memory and aging: Current status of the inhibitory view. In T. J. E. Richardson (Ed.), *Working memory and human cognition.* New York: Oxford University Press.

Storck, P. A., Looft, R., & Hooper, F. H. (1972). Interrelationships among Piagetian tasks and traditional measures of cognitive abilities in mature and aged adults. *Journal of Gerontology, 27,* 461–465.

Strawbridge, W. J., Shema, S. J., Balfour, J. L., Higby, H. R., & Kaplan, G. A. (1998). Antecedents of frailty over three decades in an older cohort. *Journal of Gerontology: Social Sciences, 53B,* S9–S16.

Strayer, D. L., & Kramer, A. F. (1994). Aging and skill acquisition: Learning–performance distinctions. *Psychology and Aging, 9,* 589–605.

Stroebe, M. S., Gergen, M., Gergen, K., & Stroebe, W. (1996). Broken hearts or broken bonds? In D. Klass, P. R. Silverman, & S. L. Nickman (Eds.), *Continuing bonds: New understandings of grief* (pp. 31–44). Washington, DC: Taylor & Francis.

Stroebe, M. S., & Stroebe, W. (1983). Who suffers more? Sex differences in health risks of the widowed. *Psychological Bulletin, 93,* 279–301.

Stroebe, M. S., Stroebe, W., Hansson, R. O., & Schut, H. (2001). *Handbook of bereavement research: consequences, coping, and care.* Washington, DC: American Psychological Association.

Strough, J., Berg, C. A., & Sansone, C. (1996). Goals for solving everyday problems across the interpersonal concerns. *Developmental Psychology, 32,* 1106–1115.

Sullivan, S. E. (1999). The changing nature of careers: A review and research agenda. *Journal of Management, 25,* 457–484.

Suls, J., & Wills, T. A. (1991). *Social comparison: Contemporary theory and research.* Hillsdale, NJ: Erlbaum.

Super, D. E. (1957). *The psychology of careers.* New York: Harper & Row.

Super, D. E. (1980). A life span, life space approach to career development. *Journal of Vocational Behavior, 16,* 282–298.

Surgeon General. (1996). *Physical activity and health: A report of the Surgeon General.* Washington, DC: Public Health Service.

Swanson, J. L. (1992). Vocational behavior, 1989–1991: Life-span career development and reciprocal interaction of work and non-work. *Journal of Vocational Behavior, 41,* 101–161.

Szinovacz, M. (1992). Social activities and retirement adaptation: Gender and family variations. In M. Szinovacz & D. J. Ekerdt (Eds.), *Families and retirement* (pp. 236–253). Thousand Oaks, CA: Sage.

Szinovacz, M. (1996). Couples' employment/retirement patterns and perceptions of marital quality. *Research on Aging, 18,* 243–268.

Szinovacz, M. E. (1998). Grandparents today: A demographic profile. *The Gerontologist, 38,* 37–52.

Szinovacz, M. E., & DeViney, S. (1999). The retiree identity: Gender and race differences. *Journals of Gerontology: Psychological Sciences & Social Sciences, 54B,* S207–S218.

Taaffe, D. R., Jin, I. H., Vu, T. H., Hoffman, A. R., & Marcus, R. (1996). Lack of effect of recombinant human growth hormone (GH) on muscle morphology and GH–insulin–like growth factor expression in resistance-trained elderly men. *Journal of Clinical Endocrinology and Metabolism, 81,* 421–425.

Takema, Y., Yorimoto, Y., Kawai, M., & Imokawa, G. (1994). Age-related changes in the elastic properties and thickness of human facial skin. *British Journal of Dermatology, 131,* 641–648.

Talaga, J. A., & Beehr, T. A. (1995). Are there gender differences in predicting retirement decisions? *Journal of Applied Psychology, 80,* 16–28.

Tang, T. L. P., & McCollum, S. L. (1996). Sexual harassment in the workplace. *Public Personnel Management, 25,* 53–58.

Tannen, D. (1990). *You just don't understand.* New York: Morrow.

Taylor, Allsopp, N. K., & Parkes, D. G. (1995). Preferred room temperature of young vs aged males: The influence of thermal sensation, thermal comfort, and affect. *Journal of Gerontology: Medical Sciences, 50,* M216–221.

Teachman, J. (1986). First and second marital dissolution: A decomposition exercise for whites and blacks. *Sociological Quarterly, 27,* 571–590.

Tennstedt, S. L., Crawford, S., & McKinley, J. (1993). Determining the pattern of community care: Is coresidence more important than caregiver relationship? *Journal of Gerontology: Social Sciences, 48,* S74–S83.

Teri, L., Truax, P., Logsdon, R., Uomoto, J., Zarit, S., & Vitaliano, P. P. (1992). Assessment of behavioral problems in dementia: The Revised Memory and Behavior Problems Checklist. *Psychology and Aging, 7,* 622–631.

Terkel, S. (1974). *Working.* New York: Pantheon.

Thomas, D. A. (1990). The impact of race on managers' experiences of developmental relationships (mentoring and sponsorship): An intra-organizational study. *Journal of Organizational Behavior, 11,* 479–492.

Thomas, J. L. (1986). Age and sex differences in perceptions of grandparenthood. *Journal of Gerontology, 41,* 417–423.

Thomas, J. L., Bence, S. L., & Meyer, S. M. (1988, August). *Grandparenting satisfaction: The roles of relationship meaning and perceived responsibility.* Paper presented at the annual meeting of the American Psychological Association, Atlanta.

Thomas, V., & Striegel, P. (1994-95). Stress and grief of a perinatal loss: Integrating qualitative and quantitative methods. *Omega, 30,* 299–311.

Thompson, L.W., Gallagher-Thompson, D., Futterman, A., Gilewski, M.J., & Peterson, J. (1991). The effects of late-life spousal bereavement over a 30-month interval. *Psychology and Aging, 6,* 434–441.

Thompson, M. M., Naccarato, M. E., & Parker, K. (1992). *Measuring cognitive needs: The development and validation of the Personal Need for Structure and Personal Fear of Invalidity Scales.* Unpublished manuscript.

Thorne, A. (1989). Conditional patterns, transference, and the coherence of personality over time. In D. M. Buss & N. Cantor (Eds.), *Personality psychology: Recent trends and emerging directions* (pp. 149–159). New York: Springer-Verlag.

Thorne, A., & Klohnen, E. (1993). Interpersonal memories as maps for personality consistency. In D. Funder, R. Parke, C. Tomlinson-Keasey, & K. Widaman (Eds.), *Studying lives through time: Personality and development* (pp. 223–253). Washington, DC: American Psychological Association.

Thurstone, L. L. (1938). *Primary mental abilities.* Chicago: University of Chicago Press.

Tice, C. J., & Perkins, K. (1996). *Mental health issues and aging.* Pacific Grove, CA: Brooks/Cole.

Titus, P. A., & Everett, P. B. (1996). Consumer wayfinding tasks, strategies, and errors: An exploratory field study. *Psychology and Marketing, 13,* 265–290.

Tomlinson, B. E., Blessed, G., & Roth, M. (1970). Observations on the brains of demented old people. *Journal of the Neurological Sciences, 11,* 205–242.

Tomlinson-Keasey, C. (1972). Formal operations in females from eleven to fifty-four years of age. *Developmental Psychology, 6,* 364.

Tomporowski, P. D., & Ellis, N. R. (1986). Effects of exercise on cognitive processes: A review. *Psychological Bulletin, 99,* 338–346.

Trappe, S. W., Costill, D. L., Vukovich, M. D., Jones, J., & Melham, T. (1996). Aging among elite distance runners: A 22-year longitudinal study. *Journal of Applied Physiology, 80,* 285–290.

Troll, L. E. (1971). The family of later life: A decade review. *Journal of Marriage and the Family, 33,* 263–290.

Troll, L. E., & Bengtson, V. (1982). Intergenerational relations throughout the life span. In B. B. Wolman (Ed.), *Handbook of developmental psychology* (pp. 890–911). Englewood Cliffs, NJ: Prentice Hall.

Troll, L. E., & Fingerman, K. L. (1996). Connections between parents and their adult children. In C. Magai & S. H. McFadden (Eds.), *Handbook of emotion, adult development, and aging* (pp. 185–205). San Diego: Academic Press.

Tsang, P. S., & Shaner, T. L. (1998). Age, attention, expertise, and time-sharing performance. *Psychology and Aging, 13,* 323–347.

Tulving, E., Markowitsch, H. J., Kabur, S., Habib, R., et al. (1994). Novelty encoding networks in the human brain: Position emission tomography data. *An International Journal for the Rapid Communication of Research in Neuropsychology, 5,* 2525–2528.

Tulving, F., & Schacter, D. L. (1990). Priming and human memory systems. *Science, 247,* 301–306.

Tun, P. A., & Wingfield, A. (1993). Is speech special? Perception and recall of spoken language in complex environments. In J. Cerella, W. Hoyer, J. Rybash, & M. L. Commons (Eds.), *Adult information processing: Limits on loss* (pp. 425–457). New York: Academic Press.

Tun, P. A., & Wingfield, A. (1995). Does dividing attention become harder with age? Findings from the Divided Attention Questionnaire. *Aging and Cognition, 2,* 39–66.

Tun, P. A., Wingfield, A., Rosen, M. J., & Blanchard, L. (1998). Response latencies for false memories: Gist based processes in normal aging. *Psychology and Aging, 13,* 230–241.

Tuokko, H., Gaillie, K. A., & Crockett, D. J. (1990). Patterns of memory deterioration in normal and memory impaired elderly. *Developmental Neuropsychology, 6,* 291–300.

Turner, B. F. (1982). Sex-related differences in aging. In B. B. Wolma (Ed.), *Handbook of developmental psychology* (pp. 912–936). Englewood Cliffs, NJ: Prentice Hall.

Uhlenberg, P., Cooney, T. M., & Boyd, R. (1990). Divorce for women after midlife. *Journal of Gerontology: Social Sciences, 45,* S3–S11.

United Nations. (1999). *Indicators on youth and elderly populations.* Online document available at the Web site http://www.un.org?Depts/unsd/social/youth.htm#pop.

U.S. Bureau of the Census. (1993). *Statistical abstracts of the United States* (113th ed.). Washington, DC: U.S. Government Printing Office.

U.S. Bureau of the Census. (1997). *Statistical abstract of the United States.* Washington, DC: U.S. Government Printing Office.

U.S. Bureau of the Census. (1999). *Statistical abstract of the United States.* Washington, DC: U.S. Government Printing Office.

U.S. Department of Health and Human Services. (1991). *Healthy people 2000: National health promotion and disease prevention* (Publication No. PHS 91-50212). Washington, DC: U.S. Government Printing Office.

U.S. Department of Labor. (1991). *A report on the glass ceiling initiative.* Washington, DC: Author.

U.S. Department of Labor. (1996). *Current population survey.* Washington, DC: Author.

U.S. Department of Labor. (1997). *Current population survey.* Washington, DC: Author.

U.S. Department of Transportation. (1994). *Traffic safety facts.* Washington, DC: National Center for Statistics and Analysis.

Vaillant, G. E. (1977). *Adaptation to life.* Boston: Little, Brown.

Vaillant, G. E., & Vaillant, C. O. (1990). Natural history of male psychological health: 12. A 45-year study of predictors of successful aging. *American Journal of Psychiatry, 147,* 31–37.

Van der Linden, M. H., Feyereisen, P., Schelstraete, M. Bestgen, Y., Bruyer, R., Lories, G., El Ahmadi, A., & Seron, X. (1999). Cognitive mediators of age-related differences in language comprehension and verbal memory performance. *Aging, Neuropsychology, and Cognition, 6,* 32–55.

Van Geert, P. (1987). The structure of Erikson's model of eight stages: A generative approach. *Human Development, 30,* 236–254.

Van Maanen, J., & Schein, E. H. (1977). Career development. In R. J. Hackman & J. L. Suttle (Eds.), *Improving life at work* (pp. 30–95). New York: Goodyear.

Van Manen, K., & Whitbourne, S. K. (1997). Psychosocial development and life experience. *Psychology and Aging, 12,* 239–246.

Vandell, D. L., Pierce, K., & Stright, A. (1997). Childcare. In G. Bear, K. Minke, & A. Thomas (Eds.), *Children's needs II: Development, problems, and alternatives* (pp. 575–584). Washington, DC: National Association of School Psychologists.

VandenBos, G. (1999). Life-span developmental perspectives on aging: An introductory overview. In I. H. Nordhus, G. R. VandenBos, S. Berg, & P. Fromholt (Eds.), *Clinical geropsychology* (pp. 3–14). Washington, DC: American Psychological Association.

Verbrugge, L. M. (1994). Disability in late life. In R. P. Abeles, H. C. Gift, & M. G. Ory (Eds.), *Aging and quality of life* (pp. 79–98). New York: Springer.

Verbrugge, L. M., & Jette, A. M. (1994). The disablement process. *Social Science and Medicine, 38,* 1–14.

Verhaeghen, P., & Marcoen, A. (1994). Production deficiency hypothesis revisited: Adult age differences in strategy use as a function of processing resources. *Aging and Cognition, 1,* 323–338.

Verhaeghen, P., Marcoen, A., & Goossens, L. (1993). Facts and fiction about memory aging: A quantitative integration of research findings. *Journal of Gerontology: Psychological Sciences, 48,* P157–P171.

Verhaeghen, P., & Salthouse, T. A. (1997). Meta-analysis of age–cognition relations in adulthood: Establishment of linear and non-linear age effects and structural models. *Psychological Bulletin, 122,* 231–249.

Verwoerdt, A. (1980). Anxiety, dissociative and personality disorders in the elderly. In E. W. Busse & D. G. Blazer (Eds.), *Handbook of geriatric psychiatry* (pp. 368–380). New York: Van Nostrand Reinhold.

Verwoerdt, A. (1981). *Clinical geropsychiatry* (2nd ed.). Baltimore: Williams & Wilkins.

Vickio, C. J., Cavanaugh, J.C., & Attig, T. (1990). Perceptions of grief among university students. *Death Studies, 14,* 231–240.

Villa, R. F., & Jaime, A. (1993). La fe de la gente. In M. Sontomayor & A. Garcia (Eds.), *Elderly Latinos: Issues and solutions for the 21st century.* Washington, DC: National Hispanic Council on Aging.

Viney, L. L. (1987). A sociophenomenological approach to life span development complementing Erikson's sociodynamic approach. *Human Development, 30,* 125–136.

Vinovskis, M. A. (1988). The historian and the life course: Reflections on recent approaches to the study of American family life in the past. In P. B. Baltes, D. L. Featherman, & R. M. Lerner (Eds.), *Life-span development and behavior*(Vol. 8, pp. 33–59). Hillsdale, NJ: Erlbaum.

Vitiello, M. V. (1996). Sleep disorders and aging. *Current Opinions in Psychiatry, 9,* 284–289.

Waddell, K. J., & Rogoff, B. (1981). Effect of contextual organization on spatial memory of middle-aged and older women. *Developmental Psychology, 17,* 878–885.

Wagenaar, W. A., & Groeneweg, J. (1990). The memory of concentration camp survivors. *Applied Cognitive Psychology, 4,* 77–87.

Wahl, H. W. (1991). Dependence in the elderly from an interactional point of view: Verbal and observational data. *Adult Residential Care Journal, 5,* 113–129.

Waite, L. M., Broe, G. A., Casey, B., Bennett, H. P., Jorm, A. F., Creasey, H., Cullen, J., & Grayson, D. A. (1998). Screening for dementia using an informant interview. *Aging, Neuropsychology and Cognition, 5*(3), 194–202.

Walker, L. E. A. (1984). *The battered woman syndrome.* New York: Springer.

Walker, N., Fain, W. B., Fisk, A. D., & McGuire, C. L. (1997). Aging and decision making: Driving-related problem solving. *Human Factors, 39,* 439–444.

Wall, P. D. (1975). Signs of plasticity and reconnection in spinal cord damage. In R. Porter & D. W. Fitzsimons (Eds.), *Outcome of severe damage to the central nervous system* (pp. 35–54). Amsterdam: Elsevier.

Wall, S., & Arden, H. (1990). *Wisdomkeepers: Meetings with Native American spiritual elders.* Hillsboro, OR: Beyond Words Publishing.

Wallace, J. I., Buchner, D. M., Grothaus, L., Leveille, S., Tyll, L., LaCroix, A. Z., & Wagner, E. H. (1998). Implementation and effectiveness of a community-based health promotion program for older adults. *Journals of Gerontology: Medical Sciences, 53A,* M301–M306.

Walsh, B. W., Kuller, L. H., Wild, R. A., Paul, S., Farmer, M., Lawrence, J. B., Shah, A. S., & Anderson, P. W. (1998). Effects of raloxifene on serum lipids and coagulation factors in healthy postmenopausal women. *Journal of the American Medical Association, 279,* 1445–1451.

Walsh, D. A., & Hershey, D. A. (1993). Mental models and the maintenance of complex problem-solving skills in old age. In J. Cerella, W. Hoyer, J. Rybash, & M. L. Commons (Eds.), *Adult information processing: Limits on loss* (pp. 553–584). San Diego: Academic Press.

Walsh, E. K., & Cavanaugh, J. C. (1984, November). *Does hospice meet the needs of dying clients?* Paper presented at the annual meeting of the Gerontological Society of America, San Antonio.

Wanberg, C. R. (1995). A longitudinal study of the effects of unemployment and quality of reemployment. *Journal of Vocational Behavior, 46,* 40–54.

Wanberg, C. R., & Marchese, M. C. (1994). Heterogeneity in the unemployment experience: A cluster analytic investigation. *Journal of Applied Social Psychology, 24,* 473–488.

Ward, R., Logan, J., & Spitze, G. (1992). The influence of parent and child needs on coresidence in middle and later life. *Journal of Marriage and the Family, 54,* 209–221.

Ward-Griffin, C., & Ploeg, J. (1997). A feminist approach to health promotion for older women. *Canadian Journal on Aging, 16,* 279–296.

Watts, F. N. (1995). Depression and anxiety. In A. D Baddeley, B. A. Wilson, & F. N. Watts (Eds.), *Handbook of memory disorders* (pp. 293–317). Chichester, England: Wiley.

Webster, D. M., & Kruglanski, A. W. (1994). Individual differences in need for cognitive closure. *Journal of Personality and Social Psychology, 67,* 1049–1062.

Wechsler, D. (1958). *The measurement and appraisal of adult intelligence* (4th ed.). Baltimore: Williams & Wilkins.

Weibel-Orlando, J. (1990). Grandparenting styles: Native American perspectives. In J. Sokolovsky (Ed.), *The cultural context of aging* (pp. 109–125). New York: Bergin & Garvey.

Weingartner, H., Cohen, R. M., & Bunney, W. E. (1982). Memory-learning impairments in progressive dementia and depression. *American Journal of Psychiatry, 139,* 135–136.

Weishaus, S., & Field, D. (1988). A half century of marriage: Continuity or change? *Journal of Marriage and the Family, 50,* 763–774.

Weisman, A. D. (1972). *On dying and denying.* New York: Behavioral Publications.

Welch, D. C., & West, R. L. (1995). Self-efficacy and mastery: Its application to issues of environmental control, cognition, and aging. *Developmental Review, 15,* 150–171.

Welle, S., Thornton, C., Statt, M., & McHenry, B. (1996). Growth hormone increases muscle mass and strength but does not rejuvenate myofibrillar protein synthesis in healthy subjects over 60 years old. *Journal of Clinical Endocrinology and Metabolism, 81,* 3239–3243.

Wentkowski, G. (1985). Older women's perceptions of great-grandparenthood: A research note. *The Gerontologist, 25,* 593–596.

West, R. L. (1992). Everyday memory and aging: A diversity of tests, tasks, and paradigms. In R. L. West & J. D. Sinnott (Eds.), *Everyday memory and aging: Current research and methodology* (pp. 3–21). New York: Springer-Verlag.

West, R. L. (1995). Compensatory strategies for age-associated memory impairment. In A. D. Baddeley, B. A. Wilson, & F. Watts (Eds.), *Handbook of memory disorders* (pp. 481–500). London: Wiley.

Whitbourne, S. K. (1986). The psychological construction of the life span. In J. E. Birren & K. W. Schaie (Eds.), *Handbook of the psychology of aging* (pp. 594–618). New York: Van Nostrand Reinhold.

Whitbourne, S. K. (1987). Personality development in adulthood and old age: Relationships among identity style, health, and well being. In K. W. Schaie (Ed.), *Annual review of gerontology and geriatrics* (Vol. 7, pp. 189–216). New York: Springer.

Whitbourne, S. K. (1996a). *The aging individual: Physical and psychological perspectives.* New York: Springer.

Whitbourne, S. K. (1996b). *Development of a scale to measure identity processes in adults.* Unpublished manuscript, University of Massachusetts.

Whitbourne, S. K. (1996c). *Identity and adaptation to the aging process.* Unpublished paper, University of Massachusetts.

Whitbourne, S. K. (1999). Physical changes. In J. C. Cavanaugh & S. K. Whitbourne (Eds.), *Gerontology: Interdisciplinary perspectives* (pp. 91–122). New York: Oxford University Press.

Whitbourne, S. K., & Connolly, L. A. (1999). The developing self in midlife. In S. L. Willis & J. D. Reid (Eds.), *Life in the middle* (pp. 25–45). San Diego: Academic Press.

Whitbourne, S. K., Culgin, S., & Cassidy, E. (1995). Evaluation of infantilizing intonation and content of speech directed at the aged. *International Journal of Aging and Human Development, 41,* 109–116.

White, A. T., & Spector, P. E. (1987). An investigation of age-related factors in the age–job satisfaction relationship. *Psychology and Aging, 2,* 261–265.

Whiting, W. L., IV, & Smith, A. D. (1997). Differential age-related processing limitations in recall and recognition tasks. *Psychology and Aging, 12,* 216–224.

Wickens, C. D., Braune, R., & Stokes, A. (1987). Age differences in the speed and capacity of information processing. 1: A dual task approach. *Psychology and Aging, 2,* 70–78.

Wiener, R. L., Hurt, L., Russell, B., Mannen, K., & Gasper, C. (1997). Perceptions of sexual harassment: The effects of gender, legal standard, and ambivalent sexism. *Law and Human Behavior, 21,* 71–93.

Wilk, C. (1986). *Career, women, and childbearing: A psychological analysis of the decision process.* New York: Van Nostrand Reinhold.

Wilkniss, S. M., Jones, M. G., Korol, D. L., Gold, P. E., et al. (1997). Age-related differences in an ecologically based study of route learning. *Psychology and Aging, 12,* 372–375.

Williams, A. F., & Carsten, O. (1989). Driver age and crash involvement. *American Journal of Public Health, 79,* 326–327.

Williams, A., Giles, H., Ota, H., Pierson, H. D., Gallois, C., Ng, S. H., Lim, T.-S., Ryan, E. B., Somera, L., Maher, J., & Harwood, J. (1997). Young people's beliefs about intergenerational communication: An initial cross-cultural comparison. *Communication Research, 24,* 370–393.

Williams, J. E., & Best, D. L. (1990). *Measuring sex stereotypes: A multination study* (Rev. ed.). Thousand Oaks, CA: Sage.

Williamson, G. M., & Schulz, R. (1990). Relationship orientation, quality of prior relationship, and distress among caregivers of Alzheimer's patients. *Psychology and Aging, 5,* 502–509.

Willis, S. L. (1990). Current issues in cognitive training research. In E. A. Lovelace (Ed.), *Aging and cognition: Mental processes, self-awareness, and interventions* (pp. 263–280). Amsterdam: North-Holland.

Willis, S. L. (1991). Cognition and everyday competence. In K. W. Schaie (Ed.), *Annual review of gerontology and geriatrics* (Vol. 11, pp. 80–109). New York: Springer.

Willis, S. L. (1996a). Everyday competence in elderly persons: Conceptual issues and empirical findings. *The Gerontologist, 36,* 595–601.

Willis, S. L. (1996b). Everyday problem solving. In J. E. Birren & K. W. Schaie (Eds.), *Handbook of the psychology of aging* (4th ed., pp. 287–307). San Diego: Academic Press.

Willis, S. L., Jay, G. M., Diehl, M., & Marsiske, M. (1992). Longitudinal change and prediction of everyday task competence in the elderly. *Research on Aging, 14,* 68–91.

Willis, S. L., & Nesselroade, C. S. (1990). Long-term effects of fluid ability training in old-old age. *Developmental Psychology, 26,* 905–910.

Willis, S. L., & Schaie, K. W. (1992, November). *Maintaining and sustaining cognitive training effects in old age.* Paper presented at the annual meeting of the Gerontological Society of America, Washington, DC.

Willis, S. L., & Schaie, K. W. (1993). Everyday cognition: Taxonomic and methodological considerations. In J. M. Puckett & H. W. Reese (Eds.), *Mechanisms of everyday cognition* (pp. 33–53). Hillsdale, NJ: Erlbaum.

Willis, S. L., & Schaie, K. W. (1994). Cognitive training in the normal elderly. In F. Forette, U. Christen, & F. Boller (Eds.), *Cerebral plasticity and cognitive stimulation* (pp. 91–113). Paris Fondation Nationale de Gerontoliogie.

Willis, S. L., & Schaie, K. W. (1999). Intellectual functioning in midlife. In S. L. Willis & J. D. Reid (Eds.), *Life in the middle: Psychological and social development in middle age* (pp. 233–247). San Diego: Academic Press.

Wilson, R. S., Gilley, D. W., Bennett, D. A., Beckett, L. A., & Evans, D. A. (2000). Person-specific paths of cognitive decline in Alzheimer's disease and their relation to age. *Psychology and Aging, 15,* 18–28.

Wingfield, A., & Lindfield, K. C. (1995). Multiple memory systems in the processing of speech: Evidence from aging. *Experimental Aging Research, 21,* 101–121.

Wingfield, A., & Stine, E. L. (1986). Organizational strategies in immediate recall of rapid speeds by young and elderly adults. *Experimental Aging Research, 12,* 79–83.

Wingfield, A., & Stine-Morrow, E. A. L. (2000). Language and speech. In F. I. M. Craik & T. A. Salthouse (Eds.), *The handbook of aging and cognition* (2nd ed., pp. 359–416). Mahwah, NJ: Erlbaum.

Wingfield, A., Tun, P. A., & Rosen, M. J. (1995). Age differences in veridical and reconstructive recall of syntactically and randomly segmented speech. *Journal of Gerontology, 50B,* P257–P266.

Wingfield, R. P. (1996). Factors motivating black male students to pass the VA Literacy Passport Test after failing several administrations and being labeled "ungraded." *Dissertation Abstracts International Section A: Humanities and Social Sciences, 56,* 4332.

Wolf, R. S., Godkin, M. A., & Pillemer, K. A. (1986). Treatment of the elderly: A comparative analysis. *Journal of Long Term Home Health Care, 5(4),* 10–17.

Wolf, S. L., Barnhart, H. X., Kutner, N. G., McNeely, E., Coogler, C., Xu, T., & the Atlanta FICSIT Group. (1996). Balance and strength training in older adults: Intervention gains of tai chi and computerized balance training. *Journal of the American Geriatrics Society, 44,* 489–497.

Wolfson, L., Whipple, R., Derby, C., Judge, J., King, M., Amerman, P., Schmidt, J., & Smyers, D. (1996). Balance and strength training in older adults: Intervention gains and tai chi maintenance. *Journal of the American Geriatrics Society, 44,* 498–506.

Wolinsky, F. D., & Tierney, W. M. (1998). Self-rated health and adverse health outcomes: An exploration and refinement of the trajectory hypothesis. *Journal of Gerontology: Social Sciences, 53B,* S336–S340.

Woodruff-Pak, D. S. (1988). *Psychology and aging.* Englewood Cliffs, NJ: Prentice Hall.

Woodruff-Pak, D., & Papka, M. (1999). Theories of neuropsychology and aging. In V. L. Bengtson & K. W. Schaie (Eds.), *Handbook of theories of aging* (pp. 113–132). New York: Springer.

World Health Organization. (1980). *International classification of impairments, disabilities, and handicaps.* Geneva: Author.

Worden, W. (1991). *Grief counseling and grief therapy: A handbook for the mental health practitioner* (2nd ed.). New York: Springer.

Wright, L. K. (1991). The impact of Alzheimer's disease on the marital relationship. *The Gerontologist, 31,* 224–237.

WuDunn, S. (1997, September 2). The face of the future in Japan. *New York Times,* D1, D14.

Yamagata, H., Yeh, K. S., Stewman, S., & Dodge, H. (1997, August). *Sex segregation and glass ceilings: A comparative statics model of women's career opportunities in the federal government over a quarter of a century.* Paper presented at the annual meeting of the American Sociological Association, Toronto.

Yang, J. H., Lee, H. C., & Wei, Y. H. (1995). Photoaging-associated mitochondrial DNA length mutations in human skin. *Archives of Dermatological Research, 287,* 641–648.

Yanik, A. J. (1994). Barriers to the design of vehicles for mature adults. *Experimental Aging Research, 20,* 5–10.

Yanklovich, D. (1981). *New rules: Searching for self-fulfillment in a world turned upside down.* New York: Random House.

Yates, F. (1966). Developing therapeutic computer programs with a particular reference to a program to teach coping strategies to problem drinkers. *Journal of Mental Health, 5,* 57–63.

Yesavage, J. A. (1983). Imagery pre-training and memory training in the elderly. *Gerontology, 29,* 271–275.

Yesavage, J. A., Brink, T. L., Rose, T. L., Lum, O., Huang, V., Adey, M., & Leirer, V. O. (1983). Development and validation of a geriatric depression screening scale: A preliminary report. *Journal of Psychiatric Research, 17,* 37–49.

Yesavage, J. A., Lapp, D., & Sheikh, J. I. (1989). Mnemonics as modified for use by the elderly. In L. W. Poon, D. C. Rubin, & B. A. Wilson (Eds.), *Everyday cognition in adulthood and later life* (pp. 598–611). New York: Cambridge University Press.

Yesavage, J. A., Sheikh, J., Tanke, E. D., & Hill, R. (1988). Response to memory training and individual differences in verbal intelligence and state anxiety. *American Journal of Psychiatry, 145,* 636–639.

Zacks, R. T., Hasher, L., & Li, K. Z. H. (2000). Human memory. In F. I. M. Craik & T. A. Salthouse (Eds.), *Handbook of aging and cognition* (2nd ed.). Mahwah, NJ: Erlbaum.

Zappert, L. T. (1996). Psychological aspects of sexual harassment in the academic workplace: Considerations for forensic psychologists. *American Journal of Forensic Psychology, 14,* 5–17.

Zarit, S. H., Dolan, M. M., & Leitsch, S. A. (1999). Interventions in nursing homes and other alternative living settings. In I. H. Nordhus, G. R. VandenBos, S. Berg, & P. Fromholt (Eds.), *Clinical geropsychology* (pp. 329–343). Washington, DC: American Psychological Association.

Zarit, S. H., & Knight, B. G. (Eds.). (1996). *A guide to psychotherapy and aging: Effective clinical interventions in a life-stage context.* Washington, DC: American Psychological Association.

Zarit, S. H., Stephens, M. A. P., Townsend, A., & Greene, R. (1998). Stress reduction for family caregivers: Effects of adult day care use. *Journal of Gerontology: Social Sciences, 53B,* S267–S277.

Zelinski, E. M., Gilewski, M. J., & Anthony-Bergstone, C. R. (1990). Memory Functioning Questionnaire: Concurrent validity with memory performance and self-reported memory failures. *Psychology and Aging, 5,* 388–399.

Zelinski, E. M., & Light, L. L. (1988). Younger and older adults' use of context in spatial memory. *Psychology and Aging, 3,* 99–101.

Zick, C. D., & McCullough, J. L. (1991). Trends in married couples' time use: Evidence from 1977/78 and 1987/88. *Sex Roles, 24,* 459–488.

Zisook, S., & Schucter, S. R. (1994). Diagnostic and treatment considerations in depression associated with late life bereavement. In L. S. Schneider, C. F. Reynolds, B. D. Lebowitz, & A. J. Friedhoff (Eds.), *Diagnosis and treatment of depression in late life: Results of the NIH Consensus Development Conference.* Washington, DC: American Psychiatric Press.

Zsembik, B. A., & Singer, A. (1990). The problem of defining retirement among minorities: The Mexican Americans. *The Gerontologist, 30,* 749–757.

Zwaan, R. A., & Radvansky, G. A. (1998). Situation models in language comprehension and memory. *Psychological Bulletin, 123,* 162–185.

Name Index

Glossary/Subject Index

Attention
divided type, 185–186
selective type, 182–185
sustained type or vigilance, 186–187
types of, 180–182
Attentional capacity Amount of information that can be processed at a time. 185–186
Attentional processes, 180
Attentional resources, 187–189
Attention switching,
183–184
Attribution
of control, 317–318
stereotype and, 306–307
types of, 312–314
Auditory organization, 264
Autobiographical memory Remembering information and events from one's life. 215–217
Autoimmunity Process by which the immune system begins attacking the body. 77
Automatic attention response Processing of a specific and well-trained stimulus, such as a target letter, that automatically captures attention. 188–189
Automatic processes Processes that are fast, reliable, and insensitive to increased cognitive demands. 188–189
Automatic processing Processing that places minimal demands on attentional capacity. 181–182
Automatic retrieval, 221–222
Autonomic nervous system, 60–61
Autosomal dominant pattern A type of genetic transmission in which only one gene from one parent is necessary for a person to acquire a trait or a disease. 126, 129
Average longevity Length of time it takes for half of all people born in a certain year to die. 70–74
Avoidance and death anxiety, 458
Axon, 57, 58

Balance, 46, 47
Battered woman syndrome A situation in which a woman believes that she cannot leave an abusive relationship and may even go so far as to kill her abuser. 371
Behavior therapy A type of psychotherapy that focuses on and attempts to

alter current behavior. Underlying causes of the problem may not be addressed. 120, 122, 132
Bereavement State or condition caused by loss through death. 463, 465
Bias
in assessment, 112–113
negativity type, 301, 303
in workplace, 419–420
Bioethics Study of the interaction between human values and technological advances in the health and life sciences. 451
Biological age, 13
Biological forces One of four basic forces of development that includes all genetic and health-related factors. 7, 109
Biological theories of aging, 32–34
Bipolar disorder, 121–122
Body build, changes in, 36
Body mass index (BMI) A ratio of body weight and height that is related to total body fat. 170–171
Body temperature, 60
Bones, changes in, 37–38
Brain death Definition of death based on eight criteria, including lack of brain function. 450
Brain imaging techniques, 59–60, 237
Burnout Feeling that results when the pace and pressure of one's occupation becomes more than one can bear, depleting a person's energy and motivation. 414–415

Cancer, 86–89, 90–91
Cardiovascular disease, 85–86
Cardiovascular system, 49–52
Career plateauing Lack of promotional opportunity from the organization or the person's decision not to seek advancement. 424
Caregiving
dual-earner couples, 426–431
elder abuse and neglect, 372–374
by family, 130–132, 133, 135, 395–398
by spouse, 379–380
Case study An intensive investigation of individual people. 17
Causal attributions Explanations people construct to explain their behavior, which can be situational, dispositional, or interactive. 312–314
Cell body, 57, 58
Cellular theories, 32–33

Central nervous system, 57–60
Cerebrovascular accident (CVA) An interruption of the blood flow in the brain. 50, 135
Cerebrovascular disease, 85–86
Choice reaction time The time it takes to make separate responses to separate stimuli. 190
Chronic diseases Conditions that last a longer period of time (at least 3 months) and may be accompanied by residual functional impairment that necessitates long-term management. 78–79, 84–92
Chronic obstructive pulmonary disease (COPD) A family of age-related lung diseases that block the passage of air and cause abnormalities inside the lungs. 52
Chronological age, 13
Climacteric Transition during which a woman's reproductive capacity ends and ovulation stops. 53
Clinical death Definition of death based on lack of heartbeat and respiration. 450
Cognition (*See also* Intelligence; Memory; Social cognition)
attention, 180–189
driving and accident prevention, 194–200
information-processing model, 178–180
language processing, 200–203
sequence of, 177–178
speed of processing, 189–194
Cognitive structural approach An approach to intelligence that emphasizes the ways in which people conceptualize problems and focuses on modes or styles of thinking. 257–258
Piaget's theory, 274–277
postformal thought, 277–283
Cognitive style A pattern of behavior one uses when solving a problem. 316–317
Cognitive therapy A type of psychotherapy aimed at altering the way people think as a cure for some forms of psychopathology, especially depression. 120, 122
Cognitive training, 271–273
Cohort effects One of three basic influences examined in developmental research that reflects differences

caused by experiences and circumstances unique to the historical time in which one lives. 17, 18
intellectual performance and, 266, 267

Collaborative cognition Cognitive performance that results from the interaction of two or more people. 320–321, 322

Communication with nursing home residents, 153, 160–162

Community ties, 439

Comparable worth Notion that people should be paid equally for similar work regardless of gender. 420

Competence Theoretical upper limit of a person's ability to function. 148–150, 153, 164–166

Complex reaction time The time it takes to make separate responses to separate stimuli as quickly as possible. 190

Computers, older adults and, 178

Concrete operational period (Piaget), 275, 277

Confounding Any situation in which one cannot determine which of two or more effects is responsible for the behaviors being observed. 18

Congestive heart failure A condition occurring when cardiac output and the ability of the heart to contract severely decline, making the heart enlarge, increasing pressure to the veins, and making the body swell. 49

Congruence model Notion that people need to find the environment in which they fit and that best meets their needs. 150–151, 158

Conscientiousness, 333

Conservation task, 277

Constructed knowing, 283

Context (*See also* Personal concerns; Social cognition)
importance of, 12
memory performance, 227
speech, understanding, 201–202

Contextual theory, 456–457, 464

Continuity—discontinuity controversy Debate over whether a particular developmental phenomenon represents smooth progression over time (continuity) or a series of abrupt shifts (discontinuity). 10–11

Contracture, 85

Control strategies Behavior patterns used to obtain a sense of control over how an outcome or goal will be achieved. 318–320

Coping In the stress and coping paradigm, any attempt to deal with stress. 81

Correlational study An investigation in which the strength of association between variables is examined. 16–17

Correspondence bias Relying more on dispositional information in explaining behavior and ignoring compelling situational information such as extenuating circumstances. 312

Cross-linking Random interaction between proteins that produce molecules that make the body stiffer. 33

Cross-sectional study A developmental research design in which people of different ages and cohorts are observed at one time of measurement to obtain information about age differences. 18–19, 22–23, 266

Crystallized intelligence Knowledge that is acquired through life experience and education in a particular culture. 263–265, 270–271, 285

Culture, 9, 320 (*See also* Ethnicity)

Death (*See also* Grieving process)
anxiety about, 455, 457–459
of child, 471–472, 473
definitions of, 448–450
education programs, 458–459
ethical issues, 450–454
expected vs. unexpected, 465–466
institutionalization of, 459
life course approach to, 454–455
paradoxical relationship with, 447–448, 454
of parents, 455, 470–471, 473
price of life-sustaining care, 453–454
of self, 455–457
of spouse, 472–473
theories of process of, 455–457

Decision making, 284–285

Delirium A disorder characterized by a disturbance of consciousness and a change in cognition that develop over a short period of time. 123, 124

Dementia A family of diseases characterized by cognitive decline.

Alzheimer's disease is the most common form. 123–125 (*See also* Alzheimer's disease)
forms of, 135–136
memory and, 237–238

Demographics of aging, 4–5

Dendrites, 57, 58

Dependent care, 426–428

Dependent life expectancy Age to which one can expect to live. 72

Dependent variable Behaviors or outcomes measured in an experiment. 16

Depletion syndrome of the elderly, 118

Depression
assessment scales, 118–119
causes of, 119–120
gender and, 118
memory and, 238
prevalence of, 116–117
symptoms of, 117–118, 124
treatment of, 120–123

Designs for research, 17–21

Developmental perspective
controversies in, 9–12
forces in, 6–9
Piagetian thought and, 276–277
research designs, 17–21
theories of aging and, 34
therapy, 115–116

Diabetes mellitus A disease that occurs when the pancreas produces insufficient insulin. 86

Dialectical thinking, 281

Diet, 170–171, 240–241

Disability Effects of chronic conditions on the ability to engage in activities that are necessary, expected, and personally desired in society. 95–97, 98–101

Discourse memory
situation model, 224–226
text-based levels, 225
text memory and episodic memory, 228
text variables, 226–228

Discrimination, 419–420, 422–423

Dispositional attribution An explanation for someone's behavior that resides within the actor. 312–313

Dispositional trait A stable, enduring aspect of personality. 330–331, 336–337
five-factor model, 331–334
longitudinal studies of, 334–336

Distraction (*See* Selective attention)

Distribution of medication, 93

Diversity (*See* Ethnicity)

Divided attention Ability to pay attention and successfully perform more than one task at a time. 181, 185–186, 219

Divorce, 380–381, 392

Do Not Resuscitate (DNR) medical order, 452

Down syndrome, 126, 129

Driving, 194–199

Drugs (*See* Medication; Substance abuse)

Dual-component model of intellectual functioning, 256

Dual-earner couples, 426–431

Durable power of attorney, 451–452, 453

Dysphoria Feeling down or blue, marked by extreme sadness; the major symptom of depression. 117

Effortful processing Processing that uses all available attentional capacity. 181–182

Ego development Fundamental changes in the ways in which our thoughts, values, morals, and goals are organized. Transitions from one stage to another depend on both internal biological changes and external social changes to which the person must adapt. 344–346

Ego development perspective and intelligence, 268–269

Ego integrity, 455

E-I-E-I-O framework (Camp et al.), 241–242

Elder abuse and neglect, 372–374

Electroconvulsive therapy (ECT), 122

Emotionality and problem solving, 287

Emotion-focused coping, 81

Emphysema Severe lung disease that greatly reduces the ability to exchange carbon dioxide for oxygen. 52–53

Encapsulation Idea that the processes of thinking become connected to the products of thinking. 289

Encoding Process of getting information into the memory system. 202–203, 210, 219–221

End-of-life issues Management of the final phase of life, after-death disposition of the body and memorial services, and distribution of assets. 459–463

Environmental factors
Alzheimer's disease and, 10
average longevity and, 73

Environmental press Demands put on a person by the environment. 149–150

Epigenetic principle Notion that development is guided by an underlying plan in which certain issues have their own particular times of importance. 339

Episodic memory General class of memory having to do with the conscious recollection of information from a specific event or time. 213–214, 228

Erikson, Erik, stages of psychosocial development, 339–343

Ethical issues
death and dying, 450–454
research, 21–24

Ethnicity
of aging population, 5, 6, 9
average longevity and, 73–74
cancer and, 88, 90–91
division of household labor and, 429
divorce and, 380–381
grandparent role and, 392–393
health, disability, and, 99–101
mental health and, 110–111
occupational development and, 418–419
religiosity, spiritual support, and, 357–360
remarriage and, 382
retirement and, 435–436

Euthanasia Meaning "good death," the practice of allowing people who have a terminal illness to die. 451–452

Everyday competence A person's potential ability to perform a wide range of activities considered essential for independent living. 153

Exacerbator, 97

Exchange theory A theory of relationships based on the idea that each partner contributes something to the relationship that the other would be hard pressed to provide. 377

Excretion of medication, 94

Exercise and attention, 183–184

Exercising memory, 244

Expectations, occupational, 411–412

Experiment A study in which participants are randomly assigned to experimental and control groups and in which an independent variable is manipulated to observe its effects on a dependent variable so that cause-and-effect relations can be established. 16

Experimental design, 15–16

Expertise, 288–289

Explicit memory Conscious and intentional recollection of information. 213, 241

Extended family A family consisting of parents, children, grandparents, and other relatives all living together. 385

External aids Memory aids that rely on environmental resources. 241–242

External locus of control, 317

Extreme age groups design, 21

Extroversion, 332, 338–339

Eye, changes in, 40–42

Factor Relations between performances on similar tests of psychometric intelligence. 259

Falls, 199–200

False fame effect, 221–222

False memory Memory of items or events that did not occur. 222–224

Family issues (*See* Caregiving)

Family life cycle A series of predictable changes that most families experience. 384–385

Femininity, 339, 360–361, 417

Filial obligation Feeling that, as an adult child, one must care for one's parents. 395–396

Final scenario Making one's choices about end-of-life issues known to others. 459–460, 461

Five-factor model A model of dispositional traits with the dimensions of neuroticism, extroversion, openness to experience, agreeableness, and conscientiousness. 331–334

Flashbulb memories, 217

Fluid intelligence Abilities that make one a flexible and adaptive thinker, allow one to draw inferences, and allow one to understand the relations between concepts independent of acquired knowledge and experience. 263–265, 270–271, 285

Formal operational period (Piaget), 275–279

Frail older adults Older adults who have physical disabilities, are very ill, and may have cognitive or psychological disorders and who need assistance with everyday tasks. 97–98

Framing effect Influence of information just processed on subsequent social judgments. 304

Free radicals Deleterious and short-lived chemicals that cause changes in cells that are thought to result in aging. 33

Friendship, 368–370, 438–439

Functional health, 97–101

Gay male and lesbian couples, 375–376, 387

Gender
    aging and, 13
    average longevity and, 74
    bias, glass ceiling, and, 419–420
    cancer and, 86–87, 88, 90–91
    caregiving and, 395
    depression and, 118
    divorce and, 381
    friendship and, 369–370
    health, disability, and, 99–101
    mentor-protégé relationship and, 413
    occupational choice and, 416–417
    postformal thought and, 282–283
    retirement and, 435

Gender role identity, 360–361

Generativity, 340, 342–344, 412–413

Genetic factors and average longevity, 72

Genetic testing, 131

Gerontology, 2

Glass ceiling An invisible but real barrier to the occupational development of women and minorities that allows them to advance to a certain level in an organization and no higher. 419–420

Glass elevator The means by which men in traditionally female occupations rise at a quicker rate than their female counterparts. 420

Grandparenting style Various ways in which grandparents interact with their grandchildren. 390–394

Grief Feelings that arise after one suffers a loss. 463 (*See also* Grieving process)

Grief work Psychological side of coming to terms with bereavement. 467

Grieving process
    abnormal grief reactions, 470
    coping and, 464–465
    expected vs. unexpected death, 465–466
    health and, 467
    life-span view of, 463–464
    normal grief reactions, 466–467
    over time, 467, 468–469
    types of loss and, 470–473

Hair, changes in, 36

Health Absence of acute and chronic physical or mental disease and impairments. 75
    grieving process and, 383, 467
    intelligence and, 269–270
    retirement and, 435

Healthy People 2000, 79, 166, 167

Hearing, changes in, 42–43, 45

Highway accidents, 197–199

Holland's occupational choice theory, 408–410

Homogamy Notion that similar interests and values are important in forming strong, lasting interpersonal relationships. 377

Hormone replacement therapy, 55

Hospice An approach to assisting dying people that emphasizes pain management and death with dignity. 460–463

Household chores, dividing, 428–429, 430

Housing options, 154–155 (*See also* Long-term care facilities)

Human factors Study of how people interact with machines and other objects in their environment. 195

Huntington's disease, 126, 131, 135–136

Hypertension A disease in which one's blood pressure is too high. 51

Hypotension, 85

Hypotheticodeductive thought, 275–276

Identity
    gender role and, 360–361
    life-story model, 350–351
    loss perspective, 358–359
    possible selves, 354–357
    religiosity and spiritual support, 357–360
    self-concept, 353–354
    Whitbourne's theory of, 351–353

Illness Presence of a physical or mental disease or impairment. 75

Immune system, 76–78

Implicit memory Effortless and unconscious recollection of information. 217–218, 241

Implicit social beliefs, 309–311

Implicit stereotyping Stereotype beliefs that affect one's judgments of others without one's knowledge. 307–308

Impression formation Way in which people combine the components of another person's personality and come up with an integrated perception of the person. 301–303

Incontinence Loss of the ability to control the elimination of urine and feces on an occasional or consistent basis. 89–91

Independent variable Variable manipulated in an experiment. 16

Infantilization A type of speech that involves the unwarranted use of a person's first name, terms of endearment, simplified expressions, short imperatives, an assumption that the recipient has no memory, and cajoling as a means of demanding compliance. 160–162

Information loss model, 192–193

Information-processing approach Study of how people take in stimuli from their environment and transform them into memories; the approach is based on a computer metaphor. 178–179, 180
    attentional processes, 180
    driving and highway safety, 195–199
    intelligence, 257–258, 260, 266–267
    language processing, 200–203
    memory and, 210–218
    sensory memory, 179
    social cognition, 300–301

Inhibition of processing of irrelevant information, 184–185

Instrumental activities of daily living (IADLs) Actions that entail some intellectual competence and planning. 98

Intelligence
    cognitive structural approaches, 274–283
    decision making, 284–285
    dual-component model of, 256
    in everyday life, 254–255, 283–284
    expertise, 288–289

Intelligence *(continued)*
    fluid and crystallized, 263–265, 270–271, 285
    life-span approach, 255–256
    measuring, 258–260, 270–271
    mechanics and pragmatics of, 257, 261
    moderators of change, 265–271
    primary abilities, 260–261, 262, 271–273
    problem solving, 285–288
    research approach to, 256–258
    secondary abilities, 261, 263–265
    wisdom, age, and, 253–254, 289–292
Interindividual variability An acknowledgment that adults differ in the direction of their intellectual development. 256
Internal aids Memory aids that rely on mental processes. 241–244
Internal locus of control, 317
Interrole conflict A clash between competing or incompatible sets of roles, most often seen in work and family setting. 427
Intimacy, 340
Intraindividual change, 334, 335
Introversion, 338–339
Irrelevant information and selective attention, 184–185

Job satisfaction How happy one is with one's job. 413–415
Joints, changes in, 38–39
Jung, Carl, theory of, 338–339

Knowledge accessibility, 303–304
Kübler-Ross's theory of dying process, 455–456, 464

Language processing, 200–203
Legal definitions of death, 450
Leisure, 431–433
Life-cycle forces One of four basic forces of development that reflects differences in how the same event or combination of biological, psychological, and sociocultural forces affects people at different points in their lives. 7, 110
Life narrative Aspects of personality that pull everything together, the integrative aspects that give a person an identity or sense of self. 330
Life-span construct Way in which people build a view of who they are. 351–353

Life-span perspective A view of the human life span that divides it into two phases: childhood/adolescence and young/middle/late adulthood. 2–4
    intelligence, 255–256
    loss through death, 463–464
    optimal aging, 165–166
    psychopathology, 109–110
Life-story model, 350–351
Lifestyle variables
    aging and, 169–171
    intelligence and, 267–268, 269
Life transition theories, 346–349
Living will, 451–452, 453
Locus of control, 317
Loevinger, Jane, theory of, 344–346
Longevity, 70–74
Longitudinal sequential design, 20
Longitudinal study A developmental research design that measures one cohort over two or more times of measurement to examine age changes. 19–20, 22–23
Long-term care facilities
    characteristics of, 153–154, 157–159
    communication in, 160–162, 163
    decision-making, choice, and, 162, 164
    financing of, 156
    perception of as home, 159–160
    residents of, 155–157
    types of, 154–155
Long-term memory Aspects of memory involved in remembering extensive amounts of information over long periods of time. 213–215
Long-term storage and retrieval, 264
Loss continuum Theory of person-environment interactions based on the notion that social participation declines as personal losses increase. 152
Love relationships, 370–371

Marriage, 376–380, 438
Masculinity, 339, 360–361
Maximum longevity Maximum length of time an organism can live, roughly 120 years for humans. 72
McAdams's life-story model, 350–351
Measurement in research, 14–15
Medical definitions of death, 450
Medication
    adherence to regimes, 94–95
    Alzheimer's disease, 130
    anxiety disorders, 137–138
    depression, 120–122

    effectiveness of, 93–94
    memory and, 240–241, 244–245
    patterns of use, 92–93
    schizophrenia, 139
    side effects and interactions, 94
Memory
    of activities, 230–231
    automatic retrieval, 221–222
    behavioral assessment of, 239–240
    clinical tests, 238–240
    discourse type, 224–228
    encoding and retrieval, 219–221
    episodic type, 213–214, 228
    explicit type, 213, 241
    flashbulb type, 217
    implicit type, 217–218, 241
    information processing and, 210–218
    long-term type, 213–215
    mental health and, 238
    metamemory, 233–234
    misinformation and, 222–224
    monitoring of, 233, 235–236
    neuropsychological tests, 238–239
    normal vs. abnormal, 236–238
    nutrition, drugs, and, 240–241
    of pictures, 232–233
    prospective type, 231–232
    rating scales, 240
    remote or autobiographical type, 215–217
    self-efficacy and, 234–235
    self-evaluations, 233–236
    self-reports, 239–240
    semantic type, 213–214, 215
    sensory type, 179
    social context and, 321–322
    sources of age differences in, 218–224
    spatial type, 228–230
    strategies, 220–221, 241–245
    text type, 228
    training skills in, 241–246
    uses of, 209–210
    working type, 211–213
Memory monitoring Awareness of what we are doing in memory right now. 233, 235–236
Memory self-efficacy Belief in one's ability to perform a specific memory task. 234–235
Menopause Cessation of the release of eggs by the ovaries. 53
Mental health (*See also* Psychopathology)
    assessment, 111–115
    ethnicity and, 110–111
    memory and, 238
    nature of, 108

Mental illness (*See* Psychopathology)

Mental status exam A screening test that assesses mental competence, usually used as a brief indicator of dementia or other serious cognitive impairment. 112, 113

Mentor A person who teaches a newer employee the informal rules of an organization. 412–413

Metabolism, 94

Metamemory Memory about how memory works and what one believes to be true about it. 233–234

Midlife correction Reevaluating one's roles and dreams and making the necessary corrections. 349

Midlife crisis, 347–349

Mobility, changes in, 36–39

Mourning Ways in which we express grief. 463

Multidimensional Notion that intelligence consists of many dimensions. 255–256

Multidimensional approach to assessment, 112

Multidirectionality Distinct patterns of change in abilities over the life span, with these patterns being different for different abilities. 3, 256

Muscles, changes in, 37

Myocardial infarction A heart attack. 50

Narratives, 350–351, 361

Naturalistic observation, 14, 114–115

Nature–nurture controversy Debate over the relative influence of genetics and the environment on development. 10

Negativity bias Bias that occurs when negative information is weighed more heavily in a social judgment than positive information. 301, 303

Nervous system, 57–61

Neural network model, 192, 193

Neuritic plaques A normative change in the brain involving amyloid protein collecting on dying or dead neurons. 58

Neurofibrillary tangles A normative age-related change in the brain involving the production of new fibers in the neuron. 58

Neurons Basic cells in the brain. 57, 58–59

Neuropsychological memory tests, 238–239

Neuroticism, 332

Neurotransmitters, 57, 58

Nonnormative influences Random events that are important to an individual but do not happen to most people. 8–9

Normative age-graded influences Experiences caused by biological, psychological, and sociocultural forces that are closely related to a person's age. 8

Normative history-graded influences Events experienced by most people in a culture at the same time. 8

Nuclear family A family consisting of parents and children. 385

Nursing homes (*See* Long-term care facilities)

Nutrition (*See* Diet)

Observed Tasks of Daily Living (OTDL) measure, 286

Occupational choice, 408–410, 416–417

Occupational development, 410–413, 417–419

Occupational priorities The reasons one works and how the worker views them. 406

Openness to experience, 332–333

Optimal aging
competence and, 164–166
health promotion, disease prevention, and, 166–169
lifestyle factors, 169–171

Optimal level In the reflective judgment framework, the highest level of information-processing capacity that a person is capable of doing. 279, 281

Optimally exercised ability The ability a normal, healthy adult would demonstrate under the best conditions of training or practice. 285

Osteoarthritis A form of arthritis marked by gradual onset and progression of pain and swelling, caused primarily by overuse of a joint. 38

Osteoporosis A degenerative bone disease more common in women in which bone tissue deteriorates severely to produce honeycomblike bone tissue. 37, 38, 39, 85

Pain management, 91–92

Parental role
alternative forms of parenting, 386–387
description of, 385–386

dual-earner couples, 426–431
grandparent role, 390–394
launching children, 387–390
in middle age, 394–395

Parkinson's disease A brain disease caused by an extreme drop in the neurotransmitter dopamine, marked by tremor and difficulty walking. 59, 135

Participant dropout, 19–20

Passive euthanasia Allowing a person to die by withholding an available treatment. 451

Patient Self-Determination Act, 162, 164

Patronizing speech Inappropriate speech to older adults that is based on stereotypes of incompetence and dependence. 160–162, 163, 308

Perceived age, 13

Persistent vegetative state A state in which a person's brainstem is the only part of the brain that is functioning and from which the person does not recover. 450

Personal concerns Things that are important to people, their goals, and their major concerns in life. 330, 337–338, 349

Personal control Belief that what one does influences the outcome of an event. 317–320

Personality
dispositional traits, 330–337
Erikson's theory, 339–343
gender role identity, 360–361
identity theory, 351–353
intelligence and, 268–269
Jung's theory, 338–339
levels of structure and function, 330
life-story model, 350–351
life transition theory, 346–349
Loevinger's theory, 344–346
occupational choice and, 408–410
personal concerns, 337–338, 349
possible selves, 354–357
religiosity and spiritual support, 357–360
self-concept, 353–354
stability of, 11, 329–330

Person–environment interactions Interface between people and the world in which they live that forms the basis for development, meaning that behavior is a function of both the person and the environment. 148
competence and environmental press, 148–150

Person-environment interactions
(continued)
congruence model, 150–151
everyday competence, 152–153
loss continuum concept, 152
stress and coping framework,
151–152

Piaget, Jean, 274–277

Plasticity The range of functioning within a person and the conditions under which a person's abilities can be modified within a specific age range. 3, 256, 273

Polypharmacy Use of multiple medications. 94

Population, 15

Possible selves Aspects of the self-concept involving oneself in the future in both positive and negative ways. 354–357

Postformal thought Thinking characterized by a recognition that truth varies across situations, that solutions must be realistic to be reasonable, that ambiguity and contradiction are the rule rather than the exception, and that emotion and subjective factors play a role in thinking.
absolutist, relativistic, and dialectical thinking, 281
developmental progressions, 278–279
gender and, 282–283
integrating emotion and logic, 281–282
as modification of Piaget's theory, 277–279
reflective judgment, 279–281

Practice effects, 19

Preoperational period (Piaget), 275

Preretirement education program A program aimed at educating workers about the broad range of issues they will face in retirement, including health, adjustment, and finances. 436

Presbycusis A normative age-related loss of the ability to hear high-pitched tones. 43

Presbyopia Normative age-related loss of the ability to focus on nearby objects, resulting in the need for glasses. 41

Prevention of disease, 166–169

Primary aging Normal, disease-free development during adulthood. 12

Primary appraisal First step in the stress and coping paradigm in which events are categorized into three groups based on the significance they have for our well-being: irrelevant, benign or positive, and stressful. 80

Primary mental abilities Independent abilities within psychometric intelligence based on different combinations of standardized intelligence tests. 259–261, 262, 271–273

Primary prevention Any intervention that prevents a disease or condition from occurring. 168, 169

Problem-focused coping, 81

Problem solving, 285–288

Procedural knowing, 282–283

Process dissociation paradigm, 221–222

Processing capacity Degree to which processing resources are available to a person during a cognitive task. 304

Processing goal
cognitive style as, 316–317
emotion as, 315–316

Processing resources Amount or attention one has to apply to a particular situation. 184–185

Processing resources hypothesis, 187–188

Processing speed (*See* Speed of processing)

Programmed cell death theories, 34

Prospective memory Process involving remembering to remember something in the future. 231–232

Prostate cancer, 90

Psychological age, 13

Psychological forces One of four basic forces of development that includes all internal perceptual, cognitive, emotional, and personality factors. 7, 109–110

Psychometric approach An approach in which intelligence is defined as performance on standardized tests. 256–257, 258–260

Psychoneuroimmunology Study of the relations between psychological, neurological, and immunological systems that raise or lower our susceptibility to and ability to recover from disease. 77–78

Psychopathology
anxiety disorders, 137–138
delirium, 123

dementia, 123–136
depression, 116–123
mental health compared to, 108
multidimensional life-span approach to, 109–110
psychotic disorders, 138–139
substance abuse, 138–139, 140

Psychophysiological assessment, 114

Psychosocial development, stages of, 339–343

Psychotic disorders, 137–138

Quality of life, 76

Quaternary prevention Efforts specifically aimed at improving the functional capacities of people who have chronic conditions. 168, 169

Rate-of-living theories, 32

Rating scales Instruments designed to assess memory from the viewpoint of an observer, usually a mental health professional. 240

Reaction time Speed with which one makes a response. 183
measurement of, 189–190
slowing of, 11, 191–194

Reality shock Realization of the complexities and difficulties of the real world. 412

Reappraisal In the stress and coping paradigm, this step involves making a new primary or secondary appraisal resulting from changes in the situation. 81

Reasonable woman standard Appropriate basis for defining sexual harassment; the standard by which a reasonable woman would consider a behavior offensive. 421

Recall Process of remembering information without the help of hints or cues. 214

Received knowing, 282

Recognition Process of remembering information by selecting previously learned information from among several items. 214

Reflective judgment Thinking that involves how people reason through problems involving current affairs, religion, science, and the like. 279–281

Rehearsal Process by which information is held in working memory, either by repeating items over and over or by making meaningful connections between the information in working memory and information already known. 219

Relationships
    divorce, 380–381, 392
    friendship, 368–370
    gay male and lesbian couples, 375–376
    intergenerational, 384–385
    love type, 370–371
    marriage, 376–380, 438
    mentor-protégé, 412–413
    remarriage, 381–382
    retirement and, 438–439
    sibling type, 370
    violence in, 371–374
Relativism, 279
Relativistic thinking, 281, 283
Reliability Ability of a measure to produce the same value when used repeatedly to measure the identical phenomenon over time. 14
Religiosity and spiritual support, 357–360
Remarriage, 381–382
Remote memory Aspect of memory involved with information kept over very long periods of time. 215–217
Representative sampling, 15
Reproductive system, 53–56
Research methods
    designs, 15–21
    ethical issues, 21, 24
    intelligence, 256–258
    measurement, 14–15
Respiratory system, 52–53
Respite care, 133, 135
Retinal changes, 41–42
Retirement
    adjusting to, 437–438
    changing nature of, 434
    decision making, 434–436
    definition of, 433–434
    interpersonal ties and, 438–439
    planning for, 436–437
Retraining workers, 424–425
Retrieval Process of getting information back out of memory. 210, 219–221
Rheumatoid arthritis A destructive form of arthritis involving more swelling and more joints than osteoarthritis. 38–39
Route learning, 229–230

Sample, 15
Sampling behavior with tasks, 15

Schizophrenia, 138–139
Secondary aging Developmental changes that are related to disease, lifestyle, and other environmental changes that are not inevitable. 12
Secondary appraisal In the stress and coping paradigm, an assessment of our perceived ability to cope with harm, threat, or challenge. 80–81
Secondary mental abilities Broad-ranging skills composed of several primary mental abilities. 259, 261, 263–265
Secondary prevention Program instituted early after a condition has begun and before significant impairments have occurred. 168, 169
Selective attention Process by which information is chosen for further processing in attention. 181, 182–185
Self-concept Organized, coherent, integrated pattern of self-perceptions. 353–354
Self-efficacy, 158–159
Self-evaluations of memory, 233–236
Self-reports One's answers to questions about a topic of interest. 15, 114, 239–240
Semantic memory Learning and remembering the meaning of words and concepts that are not tied to specific occurrences of events in time. 213–214, 215
Senility, 61
Sensorimotor period (Piaget), 275
Sensory memory Earliest step in information processing in which new, incoming information is first registered. 179
Sensory systems, changes in, 40–48
Sentence Completion Test (Loevinger), 346
Sequential designs Types of developmental research involving combinations of cross-sectional and longitudinal designs. 20–21
Sex discrimination Denying a person a position or a promotion solely on the basis of gender. 419–420
Sexual harassment, 420–422
Short-term acquisition and retrieval, 264
Sibling relationships, 370
Silent knowing, 282
Simple reaction time The time it takes to respond to a stimulus. 190
Singlehood, 375

Situational attribution An explanation for someone's behavior that is external to the actor. 312–313
Situation model A level at which people use world knowledge to construct a more global understanding of what a text is about. 224–226
Skepticism, 279
Skill acquisition In the reflective judgment framework, the gradual, somewhat haphazard process by which people learn new abilities. 281
Skin, changes in, 35–36
Sleep, changes in, 60–61
Smell, changes in, 48
Social cognition
    causal attributions, 312–314
    collaborative cognition, 320–321, 322
    impression formation, 301–303
    knowledge accessibility, 303–304
    memory and, 321–322
    motivation and social processing goals, 314–317
    overview of, 299–300
    personal control, 317–320
    processing capacity, 300–301
Social knowledge A cognitive structure that represents one's general knowledge about a given social concept or domain. 303
Social knowledge structures and social beliefs
    definition of, 304–305
    implicit social beliefs, 309–311
    stereotypes, 305–309
Social variables in intelligence, 267–268
Sociocultural age, 13
Sociocultural definitions of death, 448–450
Sociocultural forces One of four basic forces of development that includes interpersonal, societal, cultural, and ethnic factors. 7, 110
Socioeconomic factors in health and disability, 99
Socioemotional selectivity A theory of relationships that argues that social contact is motivated by a variety of goals, including information seeking, self-concept, and emotional regulation. 315, 369
Sociophenomenological approach, 342
Somesthesia, 43–46

Wage gap, 420, 421
Warning signs and labels, 197, 199
Whitbourne's identity theory, 351–353
Widowhood, 382–383
Wisdom, 253–254, 289–292, 321
Women
    occupational development and, 417–418
    personality development in, 336
    thinking in, 282–283
Work (*See also* Retirement)
    age discrimination, 422–423
    alienation and burnout, 414–415

bias and sex discrimination, 419–420
changing nature of, 407–408
dual-earner couples, 426–431
job satisfaction, 413–415
meaning of, 406–407
occupational choice, 408–410, 416–417
occupational development, 410–413, 417–419
occupational insecurity and job loss, 425–426
retraining, 424–425

sexual harassment, 420–422
wage gap, 420, 421
Work-family conflict Competing demands between work and family. 429–431
Working memory Processes and structures involved in holding information in mind and simultaneously using that information, sometimes in conjunction with incoming information, to solve a problem, make a decision, or learn new information. 211–213

CREDITS

This page constitutes an extension of the copyright page. We have made every effort to trace the ownership of all copyrighted material and to secure permission from copyright holders. In the event of any question arising as to the use of any material, we will be pleased to make the necessary corrections in future printings. Thanks are due to the following authors, publishers, and agents for permission to use the material indicated.

Figure Credits

CHAPTER 1

4: Figure 1.1 Baltes, P. B., Lindenberger, U., & Staudinger, U. M. (1998). Lifespan theory in developmental psychology. In R. M. Lerner (Ed.), *Handbook of child psychology: Vol. 1. Theoretical models of human development.* Copyright © 1998. Reprinted by permission of John Wiley & Sons, Inc. **6:** Figure 1.2 Data from the U.S. Census Bureau. **22:** Figure 1.4 Schaie, K. W. (1994). The course of adult intellectual development. *American Psychologist, 49,* 304–313. Copyright © 1994 by the American Psychological Association. Reprinted with permission. **23:** Figure 1.5 Schaie, K. W. (1994). The course of adult intellectual development. *American Psychologist, 49,* 304–313. Copyright © by the American Psychological Association. Reprinted with permission.

CHAPTER 2

39: Figure 2.2 Ebersole, P., & Hess, P. (1998). *Toward healthy aging* (5th ed., p. 395). St. Louis: Mosby. **44:** Figure 2.3 Ordy, J. M., Brizzee, K. R., Beavers, T., & Medart, P. (1979). Age differences in the functional and structural organization of the auditory system in man. In J. M. Ordy and K. R. Brizzee (Eds.), *Sensory systems and communication in the elderly.* Copyright © Lippincott, Williams & Wilkins, 1979. **50:** Figure 2.4 American Heart Association (1999). *2000 Heart and stroke statistical update* (p. 5).

CHAPTER 3

71: Figure 3.1 National Center for Health Statistics, 1999. **78:** Figure 3.2 Ebersole, P., & Hess, P. (1998). *Toward healthy aging: Human needs and nursing response* (5th ed., p. 41). St. Louis: Mosby. **80:** Figure 3.3 From *Measuring stress: A guide for health and social scientists,* edited by Sheldon Cohen, Kessler, and Gordon, copyright © 1995 by Oxford University Press, Inc. Used by permission of Oxford University Press, Inc. **87:** Figure 3.4 National Cancer Institute; National Center for Health Statistics, 1999. **88:** Table 3.1 Incidence Rates Mortality Rates–Vital Statistics of the United States, 1998.—NCI Surveillance, Epidemiology, and End Results Program, 1998. **96:** Figure 3.5 Verbrugge, L. M., & Jette, A. M. (1994). The disablement process. *Social Science and Medicine, 38,* 4. **98:** Figure 3.6 National Center for Health Statistics, 1999.

CHAPTER 4

109: Figure 4.1 Rabins, P. V. (1992). Prevention of mental disorder in the elderly: Current perspectives and future prospects. *Journal of the American Geriatrics Society, 40,* 728. **113:** Table 4.1 Folstein, M. F., Folstein, S., & McHugh, P. R. (1975). Mini-mental state: A practical method for grading the cognitive state of patients for the clinician. *Journal of Psychiatric Research, 12,* 189–198. **117:** Figure 4.2 Adapted with the permission of The Free Press, a division of Simon & Schuster, Inc., from *Psychiatric Disorders in America: The Epidemiologic Catchment Area Study* by Lee N. Robins and Darrel A. Regier. Copyright © 1991 by Lee Robins and Darrel A. Regier. **118:** Table 4.2 Sunderland, T., Lawlor, B. A., Molchan, S. E., & Martinez, R. A. (1988). Depressive syndromes in the elderly: Special concerns. *Psychopharmacology Bulletin, 24,* 567–576. **121:** Table 4.3 U.S. Public Health Service (1993). **124:** Table 4.4 Foreman, M. D., Fletcher, K., Mion, L. C., et al. (1996). Assessing cognitive function. *Geriatric Nursing, 17,* 228. **127:** Figure 4.3 Alzheimer's Association online document. Developed and endorsed by the TriAD Advisory Board. Copyright 1996 Pfizer Inc. and Esai Inc. with special thanks to J. L. Cummings. Algorithm reprinted from TriAD, *Three for the Management of Alzheimer's Disease,* with permission. **129:** Table 4.5 National Institute on Aging (1995). **140:** Figure 4.4 National Institute on Alcohol Abuse and Alcoholism, 2000.

CHAPTER 5

150: Figure 5.1 Lawton, M. P. & L. Nahemow, "Ecology of the Aging Process" in C. Eisdorfer & M. P. Lawton (Eds.) *The Psychology of Adult Development and Aging,* p. 661. Copyright © 1973 by the American Psychological Association. Reprinted with permission. **155:** Table 5.1 Freedman, V. A. (1996). Family structure and the risk of nursing home admission. *Journal of Gerontology: Social Sciences, 51B,* S61–S69. **157:** Figure 5.2 National Center for Health Statistics, 1997. **161:** Figure 5.3 Ryan E. B., Meredith, S. D., MacLean, M. J., & Orange, J. B. (1995). Changing the way we talk with elders: Promoting health using the communication enhancement model. *International Journal of Aging and Human Development, 41,* 96. **166:** Figure 5.4 From *Successful Aging* by John Wallis Rowe and Robert L. Kahn, copyright © 1998 by John Wallis Rowe, M. D., and Robert L. Kahn, Ph.D. Used by permission of Pantheon Books, a division of Random House, Inc. **171:** Figure 5.5 National Institute of Health, 1999.

CHAPTER 6

193: Figure 6.1 Cerella, J. (1990). Aging and information-processing rate. In J. E. Birren & K. W. Schaie (Eds.), Handbook of the psychology of aging (3rd ed., p. 203). San Diego: Academic Press. With permission from the *Annual Review of Psychology,* volume 50 © 1999 by Annual Reviews. www.AnnualReviews.org. **194:** Figure 6.2 Salthouse, T. A. (1984). Effects of age and skill in typing.

Journal of Experimental Psychology: General, 113, 345–371. Copyright © 1984 by the American Psychological Association. Reprinted with permission of the author. **197:** Figure 6.3 Ball, K., & Rebok, G. W. (1994). Evaluating the driving ability of older adults. *Journal of Applied Gerontology, 13*, p. 29. **198:** Figure 6.4 Ball, K., & Rebok, G. W. (1994). Evaluating the driving ability of older adults. *Journal of Applied Gerontology, 13*, p. 32. **202:** Figure 6.5 Bergman, M. (1971). Hearing and aging: Implications of recent research findings. *Audiology, 10*, 164–171. Copyright © 1971 S. Karger AG. Reprinted with permission.

CHAPTER 7

217: Figure 7.1 Fitzgerald, J. (1999). Autobiographical memory and social cognition. In T. M. Hess & F. Blanchard-Fields (Eds.), *Social cognition and aging* (p. 161). San Diego: Academic Press. **220:** Figure 7.2 From Herzog, C. et al. (1998), *Aging, Neuropsychology, and Cognition*, pp. 85–106, © Swets & Zeitlinger. Used with permission. **227:** Figure 7.3 Adams, C., Smith, M. C., Pasupathi, M., & Vitolo, L. (in press). Story recall and aging: Does the listener make a difference? *Journal of Gerontology: Psychological Sciences.* **243:** Figure 7.4 Yesavage, J. A. (1983). Imagery pretraining and memory training in the elderly. *Gerontology, 29*, 273. Copyright 1983 by S. Karger. Reprinted with permission.

CHAPTER 8

257: Figure 8.1 Baltes, P. B., Staudinger, U. M., & Lindenberger, U. (1999). Lifespan psychology: Theory and application to intellectual functioning. *Annual Review of Psychology, 50,* 471–507. With permission from the *Annual Review of Psychology,* volume 50 © 1999 by Annual Reviews. www.AnnualReviews.org. **262:** Figure 8.2 Schaie, K. W. (1994). The course of adult intellectual development. *American Psychologist, 49,* 304–313. Copyright © 1994, American Psychological Association. Reprinted with permission. Figure 8.3 Schaie, K. W. (1989). The hazards of cognitive aging. *The Gerontologist, 29,* 490. **264:** Table 8.1 Horn, J. L. (1982). The aging of human abilities. In B. B. Wolman (Ed.), *Handbook developmental psychology* (pp. 847–870). Englewood Cliffs, NJ: Prentice Hall. **265:** Figure 8.4 Horn, J. L. (1970). Organization of data on life-span development of human abilities. In L. R. Goulet & P. B. Baltes (Eds.), *Life-span developmental psychology: Research and theory* (p. 463). Copyright © 1970 by Academic Press, reproduced by permission of the publisher. **267:** Figure 8.5 Schaie, K. W. (1994). The course of adult intellectual development. *American Psychologist, 49,* 304–313. Copyright © 1994, American Psychological Society. Reprinted with permission. **280:** Table 8.2 Adapted from King P. M., & Kitchener, K. S. (1994). *Developing reflective judgement: Understanding and promoting intellectual growth and critical thinking in adolescents and adults.* Copyright © 1994. Reprinted by permission of Jossey-Bass, Inc., a subsidiary of John Wiley & Sons, Inc. **282:** Figure 8.6 Blanchard-Fields, F. (1986). Reasoning on social dilemmas varying in emotional saliency: An adult developmental study. *Psychology and Aging, 1,* 325–333. Copyright © 1986 by the American Psychological Association. Reprinted with permission. **291:** Table 8.3 Copyright 1999 from "Older and wiser? Integrating results on the relationship between age and wisdom-related performance" by U. M. Staudinger, *International Journal of Behavioral Development,* 23. Reproduced by permission of Taylor & Francis, Inc., http://www.routledge-ny.com. Table 8.4 Baltes, P. B., & Staudinger, U. M. (2000). Wisdom: A metaheuristic (pragmatic) to orchestrate mind and virtue toward excellence. *American Psychologist, 55,* 136.

CHAPTER 9

302: Figure 9.1 Hess, T. M., & Pullen, S. M. (1994). Adult age differences in informational biases during impression formation. *Psychology and Aging, 9,* 239. **306:** Table 9.1 Hummert, M. L. (1999). A social cognitive perspective on age stereotypes. In T. M. Hess & F. Blanchard-Fields (Eds.), *Social cognition and aging.* Copyright © 1999 by Academic Press, reproduced by permission of the publisher. **315:** Figure 9.4 Chen, Y., & Blanchard-Fields, F. (1997). Age differences in stages of attributional processing. *Psychology and Aging, 12,* 698. **316:** Figure 9.5 Carstensen, L. L., & Turk-Charles, S. (1994). The salience of emotion across the adult life span. *Psychology and Aging, 9,* 262. Copyright © 1994 by the American Psychological Association. Adapted with permission. **319:** Figure 9.6 Grob, A., Little, T. D., & Wanner, B. (1999). Control judgements across the lifespan. *International Journal of Behavioral Decisions, 23,* 844.

CHAPTER 10

340: Table 10.1 From *The life cycle completed: A review* by Erik H. Erikson. Copyright © 1982 by Rikan Enterprises, Ltd. Used by permission of W. W. Norton & Company, Inc. **344:** Figure 10.1 McAdams, D. P., H. M. Hart, & S. Mzrnna, "The Anatomy of Generativity," 1998, p. 7. In D. P. McAdams & E. de St. Aubin (eds.), *Generativity & adult development: How and why we care for the next generation.* Copyright © 1998 by the American Psychological Association. Adapted by permission. **353:** Figure 10.2 Whitbourne, S. K. (1986). The psychological construction of the life span. In J. E. Birren & K. W. Schaie (Eds.), *Handbook of the psychology of aging* (pp.594–618). New York: Van Nostrand Reinhold. **359:** Figure 10.3 Ryff, C. D. (1991). Possible selves in adulthood and old age: A tale of shifting horizons. *Psychology and Aging, 6,* 286–295.

CHAPTER 11

370: Figure 11.1 Schmeeckle, M., Giarusso, R., & Wang, Q. (1998, November). *When being a brother or sister is important to one's identity: Life stage and gender differences.* Paper presented at the annual meeting of the Gerontological Society, Philadelphia. **373:** Figure 11.2 From K. D. O'Leary, Through a psychological lens: Personality traits, personality disorders, and levels of violence, R. J. Gelles & D. R. Loseke (eds.), *Current Controversies on Family Violence,* pp. 7–30, copyright © 1993 by Sage Publications, Inc. Reprinted by permission of the publisher. **377:** Figure 11.3 U.S. Bureau of the Census, 1999. Online document at http://www.cdc.gov/nchs/fastats/marriage.htm. **379:** Table 11.1 Levenson, R. W., Carstenson, L. L., & Gottman, J. M. (1993). Long-term marriage: Age, gender, and satisfaction. *Psychology and Aging, 8,* 307. **381:** Figure 11.4 U.S. Bureau of the Census, 1999. **389:** Figure 11.5 Ryff, C. D., Lee, Y. H., Essex, M. J., & Schmutte, P. S. (1994). My children and me: Mid-life evaluations of grown children and self. *Psychology and Aging, 9,* 197. **394:** Table 11.2 Pruchno, R. (1999). Raising grandchildren: The experiences of black and white grandmothers. *The Gerontologist, 39,* 214. **397:** Table 11.3 Stephens, M. A. P., & Franks, M. M. (1999). Intergenerational relationships in later-life families: Adult daughters and sons as caregivers to aging parents. In J. C. Cavanaugh & S. K. Whitbourne (Eds.), *Gerontology: An interdisciplinary perspective* (pp. 329–354). New York: Oxford University Press. **398:** Figure 11.6 Newsom, J. T. (1999). Another side to caregiving: Negative reactions to being helped. *Current Directions in Psychological Science, 8,* 185.

CHAPTER 12
407: Figure 12.1 Howard, A., & Bray, D. W. (1980, August). *Career motivation in mid-life managers.* Paper presented at the meeting of the American Psychological Association, Montreal. **421:** Figure 12.2 Castro, I. L. (1997). Worth more than we earn: Fair pay as a step toward gender equity. *National Forum, 77*(2), 17–21. **427:** Figure 12.3 U.S. Department of Labor. (1997). *Current population survey.* Washington, DC: Author.

CHAPTER 13
468: Figure 13.3 Norris, F. N., & Murrell, S. A. (1987). Older adult family stress and adaptation before and after bereavement. *Journal of Gerontology, 42,* 609. **469:** Figure 13.4 Norris, F. N., & Murrell, S. A. (1987). Older adult family stress and adaptation before and after bereavement. *Journal of Gerontology, 42,* 610.

Photo Credits

TO THE OWNER OF THIS BOOK:

I hope that you have found *Adult Development and Aging,* Fourth Edition, useful. So that this book can be improved in a future edition, would you take the time to complete this sheet and return it? Thank you.

School and address: _____

_____

Department: _____

Instructor's name: _____

1. What I like most about this book is: _____

_____

_____

2. What I like least about this book is: _____

_____

_____

3. My general reaction to this book is: _____

_____

_____

4. The name of the course in which I used this book is: _____

_____

5. Were all of the chapters of the book assigned for you to read? _____

   If not, which ones weren't? _____

6. In the space below, or on a separate sheet of paper, please write specific suggestions for improving this book and anything else you'd care to share about your experience in using this book.

_____

_____

OPTIONAL:

Your name: _____ Date: _____

May we quote you, either in promotion for *Adult Development and Aging,* Fourth Edition, or in future publishing ventures?

Yes: _____ No: _____

Sincerely yours,

John C. Cavanaugh and Fredda Blanchard-Fields

FOLD HERE

FOLD HERE